D0141801

Handbook of New Product Development Management

Handbook
of New Product
Development
Management

Christoph H. Loch
and
Stylianos Kavadias

AMSTERDAM • BOSTON • HEIDELBERG • LONDON • NEW YORK • OXFORD
PARIS • SAN DIEGO • SAN FRANCISCO • SINGAPORE • SYDNEY • TOKYO
Butterworth-Heinemann is an imprint of Elsevier

Butterworth-Heinemann is an imprint of Elsevier
Linacre House, Jordan Hill, Oxford OX2 8DP, UK
30 Corporate Drive, Suite 400, Burlington, MA 01803, USA

First edition 2008

Copyright © 2008, Elsevier Ltd. All rights reserved

No part of this publication may be reproduced, stored in a retrieval system
or transmitted in any form or by any means electronic, mechanical, photocopying,
recording or otherwise, without the prior written permission of the publisher

Permissions may be sought directly from Elsevier's Science & Technology Rights
Department in Oxford, UK: phone (+44) (0) 1865 843830; fax (+44) (0) 1865 853333;
email: permissions@elsevier.com. Alternatively you can submit your request online by
visiting the Elsevier web site at http://elsevier.com/locate/permissions, and selecting
Obtaining permission to use Elsevier material

Notice
No responsibility is assumed by the publisher for any injury and/or damage to persons
or property as a matter of products liability, negligence or otherwise, or from any use
or operation of any methods, products, instructions or ideas contained in the material
herein.

British Library Cataloguing in Publication Data
A catalogue record for this book is available from the British Library

Library of Congress Cataloging-in-Publication Data
A catalog record for this book is available from the Library of Congress

ISBN: 978-0-7506-8552-8

HF 541 5.15
.H36S
2008x
0180465535

For information on all Butterworth-Heinemann publications
visit our web site at books.elsevier.com

Printed and bound in Hungary
08 09 10   10 9 8 7 6 5 4 3 2 1

Working together to grow
libraries in developing countries

www.elsevier.com | www.bookaid.org | www.sabre.org

ELSEVIER   BOOK AID
              International   Sabre Foundation

Contents

List of contributors

Edward G. Anderson Jr.
Associate Professor of Information, Risk, and Operations Management
McCombs School of Business
University of Texas at Austin
1 University Station B6500, CBA 5.202
Austin, Texas 78712
Phone 512-471-6394
Edward.anderson@mccombs.utexas.edu

Shantanu Bhattacharya
Associate Professor of Technology and Operations Management
INSEAD
1 Ayer Rajah Avenue, 138676 Singapore
Phone +65 6799 5266
shantanu.bhattacharya@insead,edu

Raul O. Chao
PhD Candidate, Operations Management
GeorgiaTech College of Management
800 West Peachtree Street NW
Atlanta, Georgia 30308-0520
Phone: 404.395.1391
raul.chao@mgt.gatech.edu

Alison Davis-Blake
Dean
Investors in Leadership Distinguished Chair in Organizational Behavior
Carlson School of Management
University of Minnesota

321 Nineteenth Avenue South
Suite 4-300
Minneapolis, MN 55455-9940
Phone 612/624-7876
adavis-blake@csom.umn.edu

Arnoud De Meyer
Director of the Judge Business School
Professor of Management Studies
Judge Business School
University of Cambridge
Trumpington Street, Cambridge, CB2 1AG, UK
Phone +44 (0)1223 339700
a.demeyer@jbs.cam.ac.uk

S. Sinan Erzurumlu
PhD Candidate, Operations Manaagement
McCombs School of Business
University of Texas at Austin
1 University Station B6500, CBA 5.202
Austin, TX 78712
sinan@mail.utexas.edu

Sebastian K. Fixson
Assistant Professor of Industrial & Operations Engineering
University of Michigan
1205 Beal Avenue, IOE 2793
Ann Arbor, MI, USA
Phone 734 615 7259
fixson@umich.edu

Lee Fleming
Assistant Professor of Business Administration
Harvard Business School
Soldiers Field
Boston, Massachusetts 02163
Phone 617-495-6613
lfleming@hbs.edu

Keith Goffin
Professor of Innovation and New Product Development
Cranfield School of Management
Cranfield

Bedfordshire
MK43 0AL
Phone +44 (0) 1234 754871
k.goffin@cranfield.ac.uk

Nitin R. Joglekar
Associate professor of Operations and Technology Management
School of Management
Boston University
595 Commonwealth Avenue
Boston, MA 02215
Phone (617) 353-4290
Joglekar@bu.edu

Stylianos Kavadias
Assistant Professor of Operations Management
GeorgiaTech College of Management
800 West Peachtree Street NW
Atlanta, Georgia 30308-0520
Phone: 404-894-4370
stylianos.kavadias@mgt.gatech.edu

Vish V. Krishnan
Sheryl and Harvey White Endowed Chair in Management Leadership
Rady School of Management
Pepper Canyon Hall, Room 316
9500 Gilman Dr., MC 0093
La Jolla, CA 92093-0093
Phone: (858) 822-1991
vkrishnan@ucsd.edu

Nalin Kulatilaka
Wing Tat Lee Family Professor in Management
Professor of Finance and Economics
Boston University School of Management
595 Commonwealth Ave.
Boston, MA 02215
Phone 617-353-4603
nalink@bu.edu

Jeffrey K. Liker
Director, Japan Technology Management Program
Professor, Department of Industrial and Operations Engineering

College of Engineering
The University of Michigan
1205 Beal Ave., 2863 IOE Bldg.
Ann Arbor, MI 48109-2117.
Phone (734) 763-0166
liker@umich.edu

Christoph H. Loch
The GlaxoSmithKline Professor of Corporate Innovation
Professor of Technology and Operations Management
Dean of the PhD Program
INSEAD
Boulevard de Constance, 77305 Fontainebleau, France
Phone +33 1 6072 4326
christoph.loch@insead.edu

Michael Meyer
Product Strategy Consultant
Batten Research Fellow
Darden Graduate School of Business
University of Virginia
Charlottesville, VA 22906

Jürgen Mihm
Assistant Professor of Technology and Operations Management
INSEAD
Boulevard de Constance, 77305 Fontainebleau, France
Phone +33 1 6072 4442
Jurgen.mihm@insead.edu

Santiago Mingo
Doctor of Business Administration Candidate
Wyss House 302 B
Harvard Business School
24 Harvard Way
Boston, MA 02163
Phone 617 496 5034 (voice mail only)
smingo@hbs.edu

Elie Ofek
Associate Professor of Marketing
Harvard Business School
Soldiers Field

Boston, Massachusetts 02163
Phone (617)495-6301
eofek@hbs.edu

Geoffrey G. Parker
Director – Entergy Tulane Energy Institute
Associate Professor – Economic Sciences
A. B. Freeman School of Business
Tulane University
New Orleans, LA 70118
Phone 504-865-5472
gparker@tulane.edu

Michael T. Pich
Affiliate Professor of Technology and Operations Management
INSEAD
1 Ayer Rajah Avenue, 138676 Singapore
Phone +65 6799 5336
michael.pich@insead,edu

Karthik Ramachandran
PhD Candidate, Operations Management
McCombs School of Business
University of Texas at Austin
1 University Station B6500, CBA 5.202
Austin, TX 78712
karthikr@mail.utexas.edu

Kamalini Ramdas
Associate Professor of Business Administration
The Darden School
University of Virginia
P.O. Box 6550
Charlottesville, VA 22906-6500
Phone 434-243-7685
ramdask@darden.virginia.edu

Taylor Randall
Associate Professor of Accounting
David Eccles School of Business
University of Utah
1654 E. Central Campus Drive

Salt Lake City, Utah 84112
Phone (801) 581-3074
acttr@business.utah.edu

Young Ro
Assistant Professor of Management Studies
School of Management
University of Michigan at Dearborn
Fairlane Center South
19000 Hubbard Drive
Dearborn, Michigan 48126
Phone 313-593-4078
yro@umich.edu

Glen Schmidt
Associate Professor of Management
David Eccles School of Business
University of Utah
1645 East Campus Center Dr.
Salt Lake City, UT 84112-9304
Phone 801 585 3160
glen.schmidt@business.utah.edu

Svenja C. Sommer
Assistant Professor of Management
Krannert School of Business
Purdue University
403 W. State Street
West Lafayette, IN 47907-2056
Phone (756) 496 1342
ssommer@krannert.purdue.edu

Manuel E. Sosa
Assistant Professor of Technology and Operations Management
INSEAD
Boulevard de Constance, 77305 Fontainebleau, France
Phone +33 1 6072 4536
manuel.sosa@insead.edu

Mohan V. Tatikonda
Associate Professor of Operations and Technology Management
The Kelley School of Business
Indiana University

801 W. Michigan St.
Indianapolis, IN 46202-5151
Phone 317 274 2751
tatikond@iu.edu

Christian Terwiesch
Associate Professor of Operations and Information Management
The Wharton School
University of Pennsylvania
500 Jon M. Huntsman Hall
3730 Walnut Street
Philadelphia, PA 19104-6340
Phone 215.898.8541
terwiesch@wharton.upenn.edu

Stefan Thomke
William Barclay Harding Professor of Business Administration;
Chair, MBA Required Curriculum
Harvard Business School
Soldiers Field, Morgan Hall 489
Boston, MA 02163
Phone (617) 495-6569
sthomke@hbs.edu

Weiyu Tsai
Assistant Professor of Management
David Eccles School of Business
University of Utah
1645 E. Campus Center Dr. #106
Salt Lake City, Utah 84112-9304
Phone 801-585-9073
mgtwt@business.utah.edu

Karl T. Ulrich
CIBC Professor; Professor of Operations and Information Management
Chairperson, Operations and Information Management Department
The Wharton School
University of Pennsylvania
500 Jon M. Huntsman Hall
3730 Walnut Street
Philadelphia, PA 19104-6340
Phone 215.898.6727
ulrich@wharton.upenn.edu

Rohit Verma
Associate Professor of Hospitality Facilities and Operations
Cornell University School of Hotel Administration
338 Statler Hall
Ithaca, NY 14853-6902
Phone: 607-255-2688
rv54@cornell.edu

Foreword and introduction

The idea for writing this book was triggered by a panel discussion on research in New Product Development (NPD) at the 2004 INFORMS National Meeting in San Francisco. The question was raised, "What is the theory of NPD?" One of the panelists responded with the opinion that there is no "body of theory" of NPD: the problems associated with NPD are so different (short- and long-term, individual and group, deterministic and uncertain, technology dependent, etc.) that we need different theories for different decision challenges related to NPD rather than a "theory of NPD".

Hmmm! Interesting observations raise interesting questions. Management practitioners clearly recognize a field of expertise in NPD. If there is no theory, does that mean that those practicing experts have simply accumulated a junkyard of unrelated experiences and observations that are vaguely connected to NPD, unconnected by a red thread of logical patterns? Or is the red thread, the 'pattern', too vague to be captured by scientific theories? Or is there a set of common patterns that academics have not yet paid enough attention to? The question also has implications for the academic NPD research community: If there is no theory of NPD, does an academic field of NPD even exist?

Creativity results from the combination of seemingly unrelated events. Well, this event of the panel discussion somehow turned our attention to the observation that there has not been a lot of activity in book-length overviews of NPD in recent years, in a period when NPD has made significant progress in insights. Thus the idea of this book came about: let's collect overviews of leading experts and see whether anything emerges that might look like a common theory, something like an overarching framework of causal explanations.

Which leading experts? NPD is such a large body of knowledge it is necessary to choose a focus – a handbook of *all* research in NPD would require many volumes. We chose to center this book in Operations Management (OM). This choice certainly reflects our background. We are both academics in "Operations" and "Technology and Operations" departments, and moreover, we are both interested in NPD more than adjacent areas (such as general technology management, or new process development, or organizational development and change management). Still, other reasons make OM a useful starting point: as OM is about processes (repeated sequences of tasks to get from opportunity to the market), it is "in the middle" of several disciplines across which the processes cut. The OM view of NPD overlaps with all other disciplines that have been interested in the topic. In addition, NPD research within OM has been carried forward by an identifiable group of scholars and has produced a sufficiently relevant and consistent body of work to merit summary in a book. While this book does not focus on the other disciplines, important theories relevant to NPD originated there, and several chapters of this book are centered in neighboring disciplines or at least address a number of interdisciplinary issues. As a result, we have a disciplinary 'anchor,' but the topics discussed reach beyond the classical boundaries of OM.

Collecting the chapters with insights from different angles brought us back to the starting point: "Is there an NPD theory?" The first chapter takes a stand on this question. We propose that there is a rigorous theoretical structure at least visible at the horizon that could possibly encompass NPD as a whole – multi-level evolutionary theory. Only a few of the chapters explicitly work with evolutionary theories because our field has not yet looked for an overarching framework. And yet, one can argue that the chapters collectively are actually compatible with a common evolutionary view. This is speculative and certainly not widely accepted. However, proposing a speculative framework because one believes that it might prove useful is a nice outcome of such a book.

We have had a privilege to work with a terrific group of scholars. When we began to ask around, we met great interest in the idea for this book. We ended up with a team of well-known researchers in the field who were willing to engage in the painful process of writing and rewriting to deadlines (which, of course, inevitably slipped). We can only thank them for the quality of their thinking, the originality of their contributions, and their good attitude in tolerating our reminders and admonitions. The resulting chapters are not only overviews of current knowledge, not only lists of previous work, but also reflections on the strengths and weaknesses of what we know, and directions of where promising new areas might lie.

We hope that readers both from the academic research community and from NPD practice find useful insights and ideas in the chapters individually as well as in the collection. We also hope that this work becomes a starting point of ideas for future colleagues, inquisitive Ph.D. students. We have enjoyed participating in the knowledge of our colleagues while putting together this book.

We also want to thank Maggie Smith and Julie Walker from Butterworth Heinemann Elsevier. They understood the value of this overview book and were flexible in their marketing approach to allow wide availability of the chapters.

Fontainebleau and Atlanta, February 2007,
Christoph Loch and Stelios Kavadias

1 Managing new product development: An evolutionary framework[1]

*Christoph H. Loch and
Stylianos Kavadias*

1. Introduction

The purpose of this chapter is to introduce a theoretical framework that integrates research from various disciplines on different areas of New Product Development (NPD) in a common context. NPD encompasses a large number of topics and challenges in a firm, such as strategy formulation, deployment, resource allocation, and coordinated collaboration among people of different professions and nationalities, and systematic planning, monitoring, and control. In that light, NPD has long been an important topic for several business research disciplines, certainly economics, marketing, organizational theory, operations management, and strategy.

Each of these very different topics represents a field of inquiry, and each has developed its own 'micro-theories' that focused on explaining and predicting phenomena pertinent to this field. To our knowledge, no 'theory of NPD' exists, and there is no consensus on whether one can and should exist. For example, a project-scheduling researcher and a researcher on alliances in technology strategy will find very little commonality between their core research questions, limiting the possibility of a fruitful exchange.

However, parallel work in strategy, organization theory, operations and economics (search theory), psychology, and anthropology suggests that a theory exists with the potential to describe a large part of NPD phenomena in a comprehensive causal framework. We propose *multi-level evolutionary theory* as a candidate for such a theory. It considers the evolutionary dynamics at multiple nested levels of aggregation (Sober and Wilson 1999, 101). In this chapter, we argue that an evolutionary process is present at the level of an industry (with a population of firms), at the level of a firm (with a population

[1] This chapter has benefited from comments and suggestions by Manuel Sosa and Raul Chao.

of procedures, rules, and processes), and at the level of the NPD process (with a population of innovation ideas). The evolutionary framework allows characterizing commonalities across the different levels of aggregation, and at the same time provides enough flexibility to accommodate the differences between the aggregation levels in the units of the population and the laws of their evolutionary dynamics.

For example, in an *industry*, firms are born by partially serendipitous ideas (such as Bill Gates starting a software company or Michael Dell assembling computers in a college room), they are selected by market success, and they may (through imitation and competition) cause changes in the structure of their industries. Eventually, they may 'die' (go bankrupt or be acquired), and they leave inherited traces in the companies into whom they have merged or into which groups of their employees have migrated (Hannan and Freeman 1977). Within a *firm*, processes and structures arise partially randomly (e.g., because new employees are hired, or because individual employees invent new rules to improve their daily reality), compete, and are selected based on efficiency and success (but success may be socially defined rather than 'objective'), and inherit traces in future process generations (Nelson and Winter 1982). Within a given *process*, such as the NPD process, innovative ideas arise, sometimes randomly through unforeseeable recombinations of existing but separate knowledge. The innovations compete for resources and are selected (based on 'success potential'); the successful ones enter the market and inherit improved competencies and know how in trajectories of product generations (Basalla 1988, Mokyr 1990, Fleming 2001).

Thus, at all three levels of aggregation – the industry, the firm, and the (NPD) process – all three characteristics of evolution are present: (partially random) generation of a variety of organisms, selection according to some criteria that are stable for a while, and elaboration and inheritance (Dawkins 1996). Evolutionary theory, therefore, offers a set of causal explanations, which allow the identification of robust, recurring patterns at all three levels of aggregation. At the same time, evolutionary theory allows for the acknowledgment that the replicating entities, the rules of generation, selection and inheritance, and the dynamics differ across the three levels of aggregation. Moreover, evolutionary theory accommodates a description of the dynamics not only of Darwinian evolution (in which the inheritance of successful traces happens only across generations) but also of cultural evolution (in which changes propagate horizontally also within the same generation through social learning, Boyd and Richerson 1985 and 2005).

To establish the evolutionary framework, we need to use a common vocabulary. Therefore, we first define 'new product development', and then present evolutionary theory and apply it to the three levels of aggregation of NPD (industry, firm, and NPD process). Finally, we outline a 'map' of the chapters, to illustrate how they fit within the framework.

2. What is new product development?

Ulrich and Eppinger (2004:2) define NPD as 'the set of activities beginning with the perception of a market opportunity and ending in the production, sale, and delivery of a product.' With a small modification, this definition includes also new service development (NSD): in contrast to a manufactured product, a service is co-produced with the customer, and therefore, NSD must include a customer interface mechanism. Still, this definition focuses on individual new products, while the NPD activities within a larger firm must consider a stream of multiple ideas and products, selection among them and their evolution over generations.

Addressing this larger context, Wheelwright and Clark (1992: Chapter 1) defined NPD as 'the effective organization and management [of activities] that enable an organization to bring successful products to market, with short development times and low development costs.' Clark and Fujimoto (1991: 7) add that 'performance results from consistency in total organization and management.'

We build on these definitions, while making the evolutionary perspective more explicit:

> New product development (NPD) consists of the activities of the firm that lead to a stream of new or changed product market offerings over time. This includes the generation of opportunities, their selection and transformation into artifacts (manufactured products) and activities (services) offered to customers, and the institutionalization of improvements in the NPD activities themselves.

The definition emphasizes the offering of either products or services, and it distinguishes NPD from pure (or scientific) research, which, in contrast to NPD, may neglect commercialization of the output.

The definition implies that an NPD system has three fundamental elements: generation of variants, selection, and elaboration with inheritance. We add one element that does not follow from the definition of evolution but is an outcome of evolution among higher animals that solve the most complex adaptive problems: NPD activities are distributed always (except in very small companies) over multiple parties. In parallel to higher animals (such as social insects, large sea mammals, and primates), the problems solved by NPD are too complex to be done by a small group. Therefore, we add an element of NPD that ensures co-ordination and exchange among those parties. This is summarized in Table 1.1.

While the elements of the NPD system follow a fundamental evolutionary logic, they occur in myriad different forms and shapes in different organizations. Thus, NPD research has also been performed with many different theoretical lenses and study approaches. In the remainder of this Chapter, we try to argue that evolutionary theory can represent the fundamental functions

Table 1.1
Fundamental elements of new product development

- A *variant generation process,* which identifies new combinations of technologies, processes, and market opportunities with the potential to create economic value. Variants are generated by directed search and 'blind' combination of unrelated elements (creativity).
- A *selection process,* which chooses the most promising among the new combinations for further investment (of financial, managerial, physical, and/or human resources) according to consistent criteria.
- A *transformation process,* which converts ('develops') opportunities into economic goods and codified knowledge (embodied in a design) – products or services to be offered to customers.
- A *coordination process,* which ensures the information flow, collaboration, and cooperation among multiple parties, involved in the NPD activities.

of NPD elements, while encompassing a large variety of variant generation mechanisms, selection criteria (e.g., driven by market conditions as well as stakeholder collations), and transformation and inheritance rules (e.g., reflecting technical constraints).

3. Viewing NPD in an evolutionary framework

It must not be forgotten that although a high standard of morality gives but a slight or no advantage to each individual man and his children over the other men of the same tribe, yet that an increase in the number of well-endowed men and an advancement in the standard of morality will certainly give an immense advantage to one tribe over another. (. . .) This would be natural selection. (Darwin 1871, 166)

Evolution can be characterized as the 'slow, cumulative, one-step-at-a-time, non-random (because driven by natural selection) survival of random variants' (Dawkins 1996, 79). Darwinian evolution involves three steps: first, the generation of *variation* produces a potential for improvements. The variants do not have to be directed, they may be (partially) random or 'blind'. Second, the *selection* according to a set of criteria that remains stable over some period, which introduces a direction. Third, *retention* (inheritance) maintains the selected features into the next generation of artifacts and enables the cumulative capability of the system (Dawkins 1996). Evolutionary theory describes how the *population level frequencies of variants change over time*, driven by how variants are created, selected, and what they inherit (Boyd and Richerson 1985, 6).

Natural selection operates at more than one level of the biological hierarchy (Sober and Wilson 1999), as the citation of Darwin's discussion at the beginning of this section suggests. Individual organisms are derived from genes that interact with one another and with the environment; and populations are subdivided into competing social groups with limited exchange of members. Thus, Darwinian evolutionary theory can be applied (at least) at the level of genes, individuals, and groups (Boyd and Richerson 2005, 256).[2] In addition, Darwinian evolutionary theory can be broadened to include the creation of variants not only between generations (through, e.g., chromosome crossovers, sexual mixing, and mutations) but also culturally, through the exchange of ideas, knowledge, and decision rules horizontally among members of one generation (Boyd and Richerson 1985 and 2005).

It has long been known that evolutionary theory applies to innovation systems, and thus to NPD which produces product innovations. A common definition of an innovation is something novel that is (economically) useful and actually implemented in processes or artifacts (Campbell 1960, Simonton 1999). Innovations are therefore like adaptations in an evolutionary system, in which artifacts that are more complex are produced over time via 'cumulative finding' (Dawkins 1986, see also Fleming and Ming in this volume). For example, Mokyr (1990) showed that in the history of technology, the generation of variants was undirected and random. A selection of innovations was constantly at work, and the resulting artifacts exhibited a strong continuity across generations. Indeed, 'technology trajectories' have been observed regularly in the technology management literature, referring to the continuity of many product innovations (Utterback 1994).

Once we accept an evolutionary view of innovation, we can adopt a hierarchically nested set of theories, as in biology and anthropology. Indeed, the evolution of innovations can be analyzed with existing theories of cultural evolution. We start with identifying three distinct levels, analogous to Boyd and Richerson's (2005) levels of gene, individual, and group. A *process*, consisting of procedures, rules, and norms, i.e., 'the way things get done,' and it corresponds to an 'individual': in the context of building a framework of NPD. We anchor our view at this level, where an NPD process is one of a population of processes that together make up the firm. At the ('gene') level below, individual *innovations* are generated, selected, and evolve, and a population of innovations lives and evolves within an NPD process. At the aggregated level above the process, a *firm* corresponds to the group (the firm is made up by a population of processes together with the people), and the population of firms forms an industry that evolves over time. The three levels of evolution are described in more detail in Fig. 1.1.

---

[2] Certain body cells also develop in a Darwinian fashion during the body's growth, e.g., brain cells and immune system cells (Edelman and Tononi 2000).

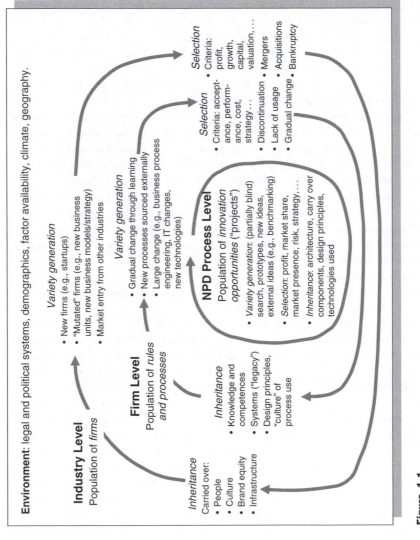

Environment: legal and political systems, demographics, factor availability, climate, geography.

Industry Level
Population of *firms*

Variety generation
• New firms (e.g., startups)
• "Mutated" firms (e.g., new business units, new business models/strategy)
• Market entry from other industries

Firm Level
Population of *rules and processes*

Variety generation
• Gradual change through learning
• New processes sourced externally
• Large change (e.g., business process engineering, IT changes, new technologies)

NPD Process Level
Population of *innovation opportunities* ("projects")

• *Variety generation:* (partially blind) search, prototypes, new ideas, external ideas (e.g., benchmarking)
• *Selection:* profit, market share, market presence, risk, strategy,....
• *Inheritance:* architecture, carry over components, design principles, technologies used

Selection
• Criteria: acceptance, perform-ance, cost, strategy....
• Discontinuation
• Lack of usage
• Gradual change

Selection
• Criteria: profit, growth, capital, valuation,....
• Mergers
• Acquisitions
• Bankruptcy

Inheritance
Carried over:
• People
• Culture
• Brand equity
• Infrastructure

Inheritance
• Knowledge and competences
• Systems ("legacy")
• Design principles, "culture" of process use

Figure 1.1
Three-level evolutionary view of NPD.

For the sake of this discussion, we take the industry's environment as given; a discussion of how innovations change the environment over time (e.g., innovation makes some natural resources more valuable or allows market entry) is beyond the scope of this book. The three levels of evolution interact: the lower level 'makes up' the next higher level (e.g., the industry is the population of firms), and in turn, the structure of the higher level influences the creation, selection criteria, and inheritance of the lower level. The levels may contradict one another: what is adaptive at one level may not be adaptive for the higher level (Sober and Wilson 1999, 27). In anthropology, selfish behavior by individuals may reduce the survival chance of the group. In the NPD context, short-term profit maximization by firms may depress the growth of the industry because of the focus on 'cash-cow' projects. Safe innovation projects may also reduce the selective fitness of the NPD process because it has become too incremental.

At the most aggregate evolutionary cycle in Fig. 1.1, an industry, a *population* of interacting firms evolves as firms are created, grown, and developed or are selected out. In the context of NPD, this is relevant in two ways. First, both the environment and the structure of the industry influence the firms. The creation of new firms and the type of innovations they pursue is influenced by the regulatory and legal environment, and by the availability of capital and qualified labor. For example, the Bayh-Dole Act provided a major boost of new firm creation by allowing the commercialization of federal funded university research. The selection criteria for firm survival depend on the life cycle stage of the industry (architecture driven in the beginning, and moving toward process efficiency as the industry matures). Work in industrial organization has examined how the environment and the population itself influence the strategies and the number of firms that can survive.

Second, the individual firm chooses a strategic position and behaves in response to the industry selection criteria imposed by the industry. The firm strategy refers to the 'battle plan' that aims to outperform competition on the selection criteria and to endure the threatening environmental shifts.

At the intermediate level, the processes and routines that make up a firm arise and are chosen in the company in a way that is not fully conscious and 'strategic' (Nelson and Winter 1982). Processes are imposed by change projects or arise from the imitation of outside benchmarking examples (sometimes without a full understanding of the implications). Thus, creation is partially random. Processes are selected by their performance, which is often difficult to measure (success is stochastic, causally ambiguous, and can be assessed only in the long term), thus selection is noisy. Processes that are 'selected out' may be officially discontinued or fall in disuse. Processes have strong inheritance that persist over a long time – recall the example of the two men that 'hold the horses' next to World War I cannons long after horses had been abandoned (Morison 1966).

The lowest-level evolutionary cycle operates *within the NPD process of a firm*. A population of new products and process opportunities (ideas) are created through (at least partially) random idea combinations from differing areas of expertise and knowledge. The structure of the NPD process (the higher-level evolutionary system) constrains and biases the idea creation. Ideas are then selected for more resource access by explicit strategic decision-making (such as formal portfolio analysis) or by (possibly implicit) value judgments in the organization. Funded innovations are developed and elaborated in a sequence of experimental cycles, and design styles and technologies are inherited across product generations. The transformation of ideas into products, e.g. in the process of design companies such as IDEO, visibly exhibits the evolutionary steps of creativity to produce many ideas, selection (by voting), and inheritance in artifacts and through a technology database (Thomke 2003).

The multi-level evolutionary theory framework sets the stage for grouping and comparing the different theories that have studied NPD phenomena. Section 4 briefly summarizes these theories and argues that they are at least compatible with the evolutionary framework, if not explicitly consistent with it. Thus, evolutionary theory could indeed serve as an organizing logic for understanding NPD in its entirety.

4. Theories relevant to NPD research

4.1. Past overviews of NPD research

It is not surprising that a field of study as important as NPD has seen efforts to organize research into frameworks. Among the many overviews, we mention three influential framework papers: Deshmukh and Chikte (1980), Brown and Eisenhardt (1995), and Krishnan and Ulrich (2001).

Deshmukh and Chikte (1980) considered the R&D management decisions within the firm, viewing them primarily from a normative (decision theory-based) standpoint. While leaving out organizational issues, this framework was one of the first to attempt a comprehensive classification of NPD research. Figure 1.2 summarizes the ideas of the framework, which center on resource management in the product development process. Resources influence all relevant tasks and activities in R&D; therefore, two main decisions require special attention: investment in resources that specialize in different tasks, and allocation of resources across the various activities. This approach allows examining questions about the necessary capabilities that a firm should build as well as the methods and tools that enhance resource efficiency.

Brown and Eisenhardt (1995) classify NPD research depending on its methodological approach. They aggregate previous empirical results of NPD project success drivers into a framework that emphasizes a strategic management angle. This framework does not focus on normative approaches (see Fig. 1.3).

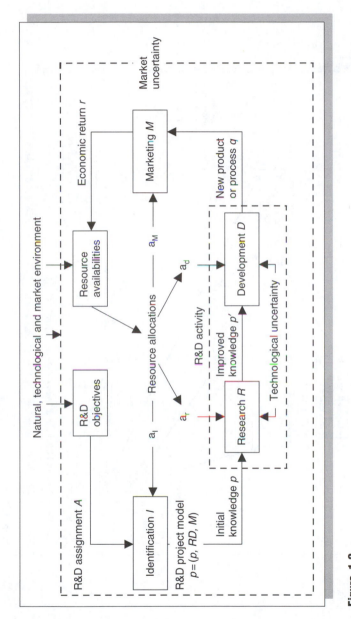

Figure 1.2
The Deshmukh and Chikte (1980) process model.

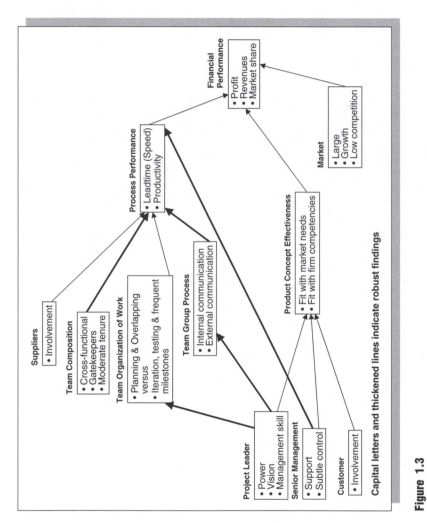

Figure 1.3
The Brown and Eisenhardt (1995) framework.

The main results of Brown and Eisenhardt emphasize the organizational drivers of success and revolve around the top management characteristics and the communication capabilities of the firm. Management control systems and executive power are shown to robustly impact the project success both through planning and through efficiently communicating policies, decisions, and project-specific information. At the same time, this work highlights the features of the organizational structure (e.g., gatekeepers, cross-functional project teams) that facilitate the flow of information and contribute as fundamental enablers to product development success. In this sense, Brown and Eisenhardt complement the Deshmukh and Chikte (1980) framework.

Krishnan and Ulrich (2001) combine views from different disciplines and divide the literature in two broad categories: decisions within a development project (encompassing the major steps in the development process), and decisions in setting up a development project (including strategic and organization related decisions). They recognize two large groups of success drivers and methods in the growing body of NPD literature. The two groups are distinguished by the duration of their influence – short-term within a project versus long-term across multiple projects. Within those two categories, the authors classify research in clusters to minimize interdependencies. The clustering analysis identifies three fundamental enablers in NPD decisions: product features (market and design), architecture-related issues (also encompassing organizational issues), and portfolio-selection decisions that address the strategic aspects of development. Figure 1.4 summarizes the main finding.

In summary, each of these frameworks have emphasized certain theories and phenomena within NPD but not targeted an overall view. In particular, the three frameworks identify success drivers and normatively attractive structures of NPD decision rules and processes, focusing on the innermost evolutionary cycle in Fig. 1.1. In addition, none of the three frameworks uses the fundamental steps of variety generation–selection–elaboration and inheritance to structure the many activities and phenomena. We now turn to theories from various fields, viewed in the context of evolutionary theory.

4.2. An overview of NPD theories in the evolutionary theory framework

The three levels of evolutionary dynamics represent differing levels of aggregation and address different timeframes and questions. Thus, several disciplines have examined the various questions with a wide set of theories. Few theories to date have explicitly considered the dynamic evolutionary theory of variety generation and natural selection acting upon population frequencies, mostly in the strategy field: At the industry level, Schumpeter (1942) emphasized the selection and creation of firms in an emerging process of 'creative destruction.' Population ecologists (Hannan and Freeman 1977) have treated

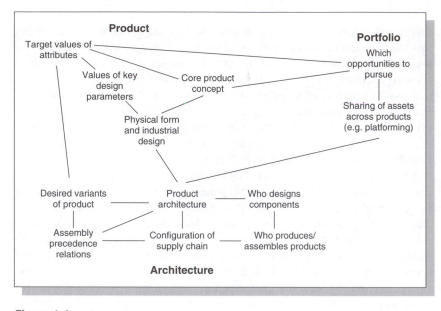

Figure 1.4
The Krishnan and Ulrich (2001) classification.

firms as organisms that evolve through Darwinian selection, and Tushman and Rosenkopf (1992) have considered an industry life cycle of random variety creation followed by incremental elaboration (consistent with a 'punctuated equilibrium' model of evolution). At the firm level, Nelson and Winter (1982) adopted an explicitly evolutionary approach to the way processes and routines form in organizations. At the process level, work on search and creativity has emphasized the Darwinian nature of idea creation, selection, and elaboration (Fleming 2001).

While most work has not considered evolutionary theory, many of the theories and findings are consistent with an overall evolutionary view. Figure 1.5 summarizes some key theories, which we discuss in some more detail below.

The external environment level

Research in political science, political economy, sociology, and economics has examined the effects of the environment at large on innovation. The extent and sophistication of innovative activities in a country are influenced by culture, climate, and geography, and by the institutional system (the governing bodies that the society has put in place, such as laws, courts, e.g., Porter 1990, O'Sullivan 2000). In particular, the protection of intellectual property rights has an influence on innovative activity, as the current debate on innovation piracy in China attests (French 2005, Zhao 2006). Policy makers also need to

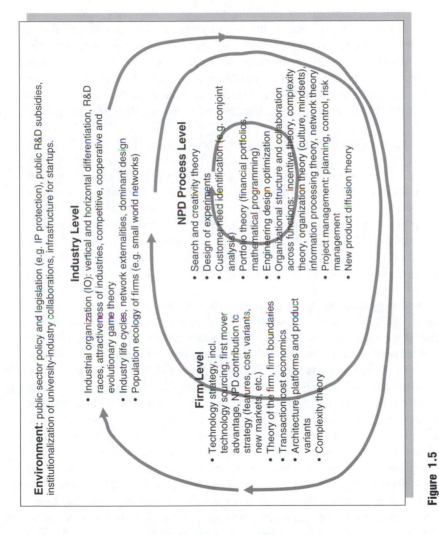

Environment: public sector policy and legislation (e.g. IP protection), public R&D subsidies, institutionalization of university–industry collaborations, infrastructure for startups.

Industry Level

- Industrial organization (IO): vertical and horizontal differentiation, R&D races, attractiveness of industries, competitive, cooperative and evolutionary game theory
- Industry life cycles, network externalities, dominant design
- Population ecology of firms (e.g. small world networks)

Firm Level

- Technology strategy, incl. technology sourcing, first mover advantage, NPD contribution to strategy (features, cost, variants, new markets, etc.)
- Theory of the firm, firm boundaries
- Transaction cost economics
- Architecture platforms and product variants
- Complexity theory

NPD Process Level

- Search and creativity theory
- Design of experiments
- Customer need identification (e.g. conjoint analysis)
- Portfolio theory (financial portfolios, mathematical programming)
- Engineering design optimization
- Organizational structure and collaboration across functions: incentive theory, complexity theory, organization theory (culture, mindsets), information processing theory, network theory
- Project management: planning, control, risk management
- New product diffusion theory

Figure 1.5
NPD-related theories in the multi-level evolutionary framework.

support the production of public (non-excludable) goods, such as fundamental research, which would be undersupplied by commercial entities (Gibbons and Johnston 1975; Cohen et al. 2002).

The industry level (I): Industry evolution and populations of firms

Some strategy research has explicitly used an evolutionary framework to examine populations of firms as the unit of analysis. For example, population ecology approaches have explained a substantial amount of observed phenomena with the simplifying assumption of purely Darwinian selection: firms are born with certain gene-like endowments, go through their lives without much learning (change of this endowment), and die when the endowment no longer fits the environment (e.g., Hannan and Freeman 1977, Silverberg et al. 1988).

A large amount of work has examined the industry life cycle, the emergence, growth, maturity, and decline of product categories (Henderson 1979, Porter 1980). Abernathy and Utterback (1978) introduced the concept of dominant designs and pointed out the changing nature of innovation over the life cycle. Tushman and Anderson (1986) characterized the phases of the life cycle as a stochastic search phase, an 'era of ferment' (consistent with Schumpeter's (1942) 'creative destruction'), followed by a more predictable period of incremental fine-tuning; Tushman and Rosenkopf (1992) linked the life cycle to evolutionary theory. For overviews, see also Adler (1989), and Burgelman et al. (1995).

The theory of Industrial Organization (IO) has heavily influenced the academic fields of Strategic Management, Operations, and R&D Management. The IO is concerned with 'the study of market functioning [. . .] the structure and behavior of the firms (market strategy and internal organization)' (Tirole 1988, 3): it focuses on explaining firm boundaries and firm performance in the industry context. The IO has not taken an explicit evolutionary view, focusing rather on an understanding of industry equilibria. It has identified two key contributions of NPD to industry structure as well as the individual firm's strategic position: (i) The amount of differentiation that the NPD offering introduces, which can be vertical or horizontal and (ii) the strong association between the resource expenditure and the competitive advantage from innovations (either this is a timing advantage, see R&D races and product diffusion, or a quality-offering advantage in the event of vertically differentiated products). The relative importance of these two drivers depends on IP protection regimes, externalities, and complementary assets. In addition to IO and strategy, the marketing field has heavily contributed to these theories (Bass 1969, Mussa and Rosen 1978, Moorthy 1984).

In the terminology of our evolutionary framework, this area of work examines the structure of the entire firm population (in the industry), and the emerging selection criteria that this structure implies for the individual firms in the population.

The industry level (II): Technology strategy and the firm as an industry actor

A second area of work still fits the industry level of Fig. 1.1 but has focus on individual firms as the unit of analysis. At this level, the question is how the firm can maximize, through its behavior, its survival *given* the industry population and the selection criteria. This is the classical scope of strategy and competitive advantage.

A few works have looked at the firm's life cycle from an evolutionary angle. Different literatures have examined different stages of the firm's life: work in entrepreneurship has examined how firms are created and how innovativeness influences their initial success chances (Bhide 2000, Shane 2000, Gompers et al. 2005). Work in technology strategy has examined what competitive position allows larger firms to remain successful, and how the competitive position can be adjusted over time through innovation (e.g., Porter 1985, Markides 1999).

The NPD strategy literature has identified four outcomes of NPD activities that are relevant for the competitive position of the firm: product features, product variety, time to market, and first mover status, and cost position (including the cost of NPD as well as the manufacturing or delivery cost as driven by design). All these outcomes are treated as different functions of the amount and type of resources (financial, human capital, and competencies) that goes into the activities as well as the effectiveness of them realizing the output (uncertainty resolution, design architecture).

The firm level

A firm is made by the sum of its competences. They are embodied in the *routines* (organizational processes) that perform every function within the firm. Following Nelson and Winter (1982), a routine is the combination of rules, competencies, and resources that perform a function (e.g., the engineers, the know-how, the NPD plan and its execution stages would describe the NPD routine of a firm). Routines describe 'how things are getting done in this organization.'

Nelson and Winter examined the evolutionary character of how the organization's competences evolve: through (at least partially) random generation of variants, and (noisy) elaboration and selection of those variants. Strategy work in general has examined routines but has emphasized how firms should consciously, in the spirit of 'optimization', manage those routines over time. Leonard-Barton (1992, 1995) agrees with Nelson and Winter: she defines the organizational competence as the sum of the skills, physical systems, management systems, and values – the cultural rules of the organization.

Then she examines how a firm can evolve those competences, but her work acknowledges that this process is noisy.

Other strategy scholars have taken a more normative view of internal competences, examining how they should evolve to support a competitive position (Teece et al. 1997, Zott 2002). A stream of work has argued that architectural knowledge is a core competence of the firm, and architectural innovation (that is, innovation not in the product components but in the way they fit together) can produce a sustainable competitive advantage (e.g., Clark 1985, Henderson and Clark 1990). An extreme position claims that the quality of the employees comes first and drives the choice of strategy, as excellent employees will be able to appropriately adjust the firm's position to the environment and competition (Collins 2001). Economists have also focused on the 'job design' elements that drive certain employee behaviors, such as allowing exploration and risk taking (Zwiebel 1995, Roberts 2004).

The NPD process level

The process level has been the focus of most NPD literature in Operations Management. An 'optimization' view has been typical; an evolutionary view of how products are developed is quite recent (see Chapter 5 of this book).

The first stage is the emergence of innovation ideas. Organizational search and creativity involve the organizational structures and processes that lead to project initiation, through technology search and benchmarking and creative combinations of ideas. Here, creativity theories in psychology and engineering (e.g., Simonton 1999, Pahl and Beitz 1988, Sutton 2001) combine with theories of organizational creativity from strategy and sociology (e.g., Van de Ven et al. 1989), as well as technological search in complex systems (e.g., Fleming 2001, Fleming and Sorenson 2004).

The next stage is the selection of ideas. Most approaches have tried to identify 'optimal' choice criteria for the firm's success. Portfolio theories exist in Finance (emphasizing the balance between risk and return), Operations Research (mathematical programming models have emphasized the highest return use of a limited resource budget) and Strategy (emphasizing the balance of different strategic priorities in the business and product mix). For a literature overview, see Kavadias and Loch (2003) and Chapter 6 in this book.

Development of innovation ideas into products happens through projects. Project management has been early on defined as a stand-alone field of study. A well-developed theory exists in Operations Research on project planning, coordination, and scheduling (a recent overview is offered in Demeulemeester and Herroelen 2002). There is a body of work on risk management, both model-based and empirical (Chapman and Ward 2003, Loch et al. 2006). Also, novel projects fundamentally involve search and iteration, which has, again, be researched empirically as well as with decision-theory models (see an overview in Thomke 2003 and Chapter 17 of this book). Related work has examined different configurations of processes (or PM methods), depending on the uncertainty of the project's mission (MacCormack et al. 2001, Pich et al. 2002, Sommer and Loch 2004). Relationships of project teams with their stakeholders have been explained by network theory (e.g., Burt 2000), group identity (see, e.g., Levy et al. 2001), and their boundary spanning role (Ancona and Caldwell 1992), and empirical work on socially driven escalation of commitment (e.g., Boulding et al. 1997). In addition, work in sociology and psychology has examined team management and leadership.

Another large area of work is related to the difficulty of coordinating multiple actors in the NPD process (see Chapter 12 of this book). Starting with coordination theory (Thompson 1967, Galbraith 1973), coordination has been examined through different lenses: incentive theory (Kerr 1975, Holmström and Milgrom 1991, Feltham and Xie 1994, Gibbons 2005), complexity theory in the case of many interdependencies among actors (Terwiesch et al. 2002, Mihm et al. 2003), and the study of cultural barriers to communication (Lawrence and Lorsch 1967, Weick 1993, Dougherty 1992).

Coordination is even more difficult when it must occur across firms. Two large bodies of work can be identified. (i) Some work has identified the advantage of long standing buyer–supplier relationships in overcoming transaction costs and opportunism (e.g., Dyer and Ouchi 1993, Dyer 1996, Liker et al. 1996; Baker et al. 2002). (ii) R&D alliances or formally established R&D networks allow firms to share risks and gain access to knowledge or to markets (Doz and Hamel 1997, Goyal and Moranga 2001, Bloch 2002). Recent empirical research suggests that R&D alliances increase NPD performance (Rothaermel and Deeds 2004, Hoang and Rothaermel 2005). We refer the reader to Chapters 9 and 10 of this book.

5. What can we learn from an overview of theories in NPD?

We have outlined an evolutionary view of the NPD process, including three levels of the 'vary – select – elaborate and inherit' cycle, and we have identified academic theories that aim to explain the dynamics and success factors of this process. In Section 4, we have tried to demonstrate that these theories, which come from many fields, can reasonably fit into an overarching framework of multi-level evolutionary dynamics. The question arises, of course, what value the evolutionary framework brings to NPD research. Below, we list just a few questions that one may be able to ask based on the multi-level evolutionary framework.

- Biologists and anthropologists have been able to understand evolutionary dynamics at multiple levels, e.g., individuals and groups, and to learn from characterizing the nature of the evolutionary forces at each level. For example, the 'fitness'(performance as compared to the selection criteria in force) of groups rests on resource control as well as cultural knowledge and cooperation of its members (in resource acquisition and in mobilization against other groups). Individual fitness, in contrast, depends on capabilities (genes), learning of cultural rules and collaboration with allies. Therefore, selection has differing characteristics for individuals. Can similar characterizations of selection and competition help to better understand NPD processes and innovations?

- If not parallel model analysis, can the characterization of variant creation-selection-inheritance in different NPD levels at least identify similar problem structures and spur comparative work? For example, complexity theory, network theory, and group identity appear in multiple sub-areas of NPD at the within-firm level. Can we explore commonalities of problem structures that have not yet been exploited to gain insight?

- Multi-level evolutionary theory may help us to better understand how the levels of aggregation interact. How do decisions at a higher level become constraints at a lower level? Looking upward, how do new variants at the lower level influence the choices at the higher level? For example, how does the variant generation of opportunities upwards influence the shape of the NPD process? How do process changes influence the firm's selection survival? Chapter 11 overviews hierarchical planning approaches, a research tradition that has been guided by an 'optimization' approach and is limited by exploding complexity. Does the aggregation (upward) and constraining by selection criteria (downward) view from evolutionary theory offer new ways of understanding the interactions? For example, imagine a firm level decision to temporarily emphasize short-term projects, which leads to selection criteria implemented at the project level that, in turn, make it later impossible for the organization to return to longer-term projects. Can we characterize when multi-level interactions might lead to such spirals?

- Multi-level evolutionary theory identifies across-level tradeoffs. For example, the individual wants to be selfish to maximize its own fitness, but if everyone is selfish, the group suffers, and everyone is worse off. This is parallel to team production and public good problems in economics. However, economics assumes that rational decision makers make choices, whereas evolutionary theory allows behaviors to be selected (without the individuals necessarily making choices or understanding the emerging behavior). This view may be applicable to partnerships and supplier collaborations, where interest conflicts and tradeoffs among players are fundamental. Is there anything to be gained by asking whether certain observed behaviors in alliances are not decided but emerge through selection of practices that constitute equilibria? For example, could allowing selection alongside optimal choice in models of NPD bridge the gap between traditional OM thinking ('optimization') and OB thinking ('following norms, possibly without awareness')?

Perhaps there is indeed no 'theory of NPD'. However, multi-level evolutionary theory can identify patterns across a wider set of phenomena, which offers the potential of additional insights. This potential has been explored only in a few research areas, and there is much work to do. The chapters of this book show how rudimentary the identification of evolutionary dynamics is in research to date. Yet, a few of them prepare the ground for evolutionary perspectives and emphasize the need for an overarching view that bridges isolated theories.

6. Outline of the book

We have already observed that the evolutionary view has influenced only a few areas of work to date. This is reflected in the chapters – most do not use the framework because it has not been used in the respective field. The evolutionary framework is explicitly represented in Chapters 2, 5 and 15, and it is reflected in the structure of the book (Fig. 1.6). We hope that the ensemble of the chapters invites researchers to identify opportunities where an application of the evolutionary framework can generate additional insights on NPD.

The focus of the book on operations issues implies that the three evolutionary levels are not equally represented. NPD from the operations viewpoint has focused on the execution of innovation, and therefore on the firm and process levels. The external environment and industry levels have been virtually absent from operations-related NPD literature. This is reflected in the structure of the book.

Chapter 2 gives a view of Technology Strategy. It touches upon literature that looks at population of firms and the evolution of an entire industry. The focus of the chapter lies on industry life cycles and on the contribution of NPD to the firm's strategy (reflecting the focus of past research). Two related chapters summarize important aspects of technology strategy that have seen a lot of attention in NPD literature: the contribution of NPD to the firm's competitive positioning (Chapter 3, a view from the Industrial Organization and the Marketing discipline), and the strategic structuring of product families (Chapter 4).

The rest of the book focuses on the firm level, reflecting the emphasis in the existing work. First, the firm level view encompasses the firm's decision rules and processes. Existing work has largely taken the approach of 'optimizing' process structure given the strategy. Thus, the chapters themselves do not elaborate on an evolutionary framework (except Chapter 5). We see the evolutionary framework reflected in the chapter structure: idea generation (Chapter 5), (portfolio) selection (Chapter 6), and elaboration and execution, the latter seen in the aggregate through the organizational structure (Chapter 7). Selection appears again in the Chapter 8 in the context of performance measurement: what are the criteria according to which the NPD function as a whole is evaluated (and thus investments in NPD are justified)? Finally, two chapters explore coordination across multiple organizations at the institutionalized process level, with suppliers (Chapter 9) and partners (Chapter 10).

The aggregate firm level is linked to the process level, the execution of individual projects, through hierarchical planning, the reconciliation between operational short-term plans and longer-term goals (Chapter 11). The remaining chapters turn to the process level, or the execution of individual projects to transform an opportunity into a new product or service.

Throughout execution, or the transformation of an opportunity into a product, multiple players are involved who must coordinate and communicate to be effective (Chapter 12). Product opportunities are created (at least in products of moderate novelty) by systematic customer input (Chapter 13); a

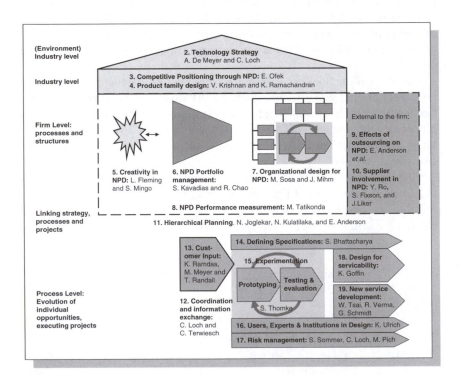

Figure 1.6
Structure of the book.

perceived opportunity is translated into a set of activities by product specifications (Chapter 14), which determine the link between the design and
the performance targets (that come from the aggregate strategy and process
levels). Appropriate and stable product specifications are very important for
achieving a fast time to market and capacity utilization.

At the heart of execution, the evolutionary cycle appears again in
Chapter 15, which discusses design iterations. The design and development
of products evolves in *iterative loops*. A recent version of design iterations
and testing is collaborative testing with customers (Chapter 16). Using customer insight increases the information gained from tests and is becoming
widely used. In addition, project execution means risk reduction, from a
poorly defined task at the outset to well defined tasks at the beginning of
manufacturing or service delivery. Chapter 17 summarizes methods of risk
reduction.

Chapter 18 on downstream design for serviceability is concerned with the
effect of NPD on the operations of product delivery. A separate chapter
describes the similarities and differences of service design as compared to the
design of manufactured products (Chapter 19).

This overview shows that the evolutionary framework repeatedly appears
in the structure of the book; at the same time, evolutionary dynamics are mentioned in several chapters but are not yet widely used as a common theoretical
guide to understand and structure observed phenomena. We believe that this
represents unused potential and a major opportunity for future improvements
of our understanding of NPD. Each chapter offers some future research opportunities at a 'micro' level. We encourage the reader to keep in mind this
overarching opportunity to discover patterns of success drivers.

References

Abernathy W., and Utterback J. (1978). "Patterns of Industrial Innovation,"
Technology Review, 80 (7), 40–47.

Adler P. S. (1989). "Technology Strategy: A Guide to the Literatures",
In: *Research in Technological Innovation Management, and Policy*,
(Eds) R. S. Rosenbloom and R. A. Burgelman, 4, 25–151, JAI Press,
Greenwich, CT.

Ancona D. G., and Caldwell D. F. (1992). "Bridging the Boundary: External
Activity and Performance in Organizational Teams," *Administrative Science
Quarterly*, 37 (4), 634–665.

Baker G., Gibbons R., and Murphy K. (2002). "Relational Contracts and The
Theory of the Firm," *Quarterly Journal of Economics*, 117 (1), 37–84.

Basalla G. (1988). *The Evolution of Technology*. Cambridge: Cambridge
University Press.

Bass F. M. (1969). "A New Product Growth Model for Consumer Durables," *Management Science*, 15, 215–227.

Bhide A. V. (2000). *The Origin and Evolution of New Businesses.* Oxford, UK: Oxford University Press.

Bloch F. D. (2002). "Coalitions and Networks in Industrial Organization," *The Manchester School*, 70 (1), 36–55.

Boyd R., and Richerson P. J. (1985). *Culture and the Evolutionary Process.* Chicago: Chicago University Press.

Boyd R., and Richerson P. J. (2005). *The Origin and Evolution of Cultures.* NY: Oxford University Press.

Brown S. L., and Eisenhardt K. M. (1995). "Product Development: Past Research, Present Findings, and Future Directions," *Academy of Management Review*, 20 (2), 343–378.

Boulding W., Rusking M., and Staelin R. (1997). "Pulling the Plug to Stop the New Product Drain," *Journal of Marketing Research*, 34 (1), 164–176.

Burgelman R. A., Maidique M. A., and Wheelwright S. C. (1995). *Strategic Management of Technology and Innovation.* Chicago, IL: Irwin.

Burt R. S. "The Network Structure of Social Capital," 2000, in R. I. Sutton and B. M. Staw (eds.) Research in Organizational Behavior, JAI Press, Greenwich, CT.

Campbell D. T. (1960). "Blind Variation and Selective Retention in Creative Thought as in Other Knowledge Processes," *Psychological Review,* 67, 380–400.

Chapman C. B., and Ward S. C. (2003). *Project Risk Management: Processes, Techniques, and Insights,* 2nd edition, Chichester, UK: John Wiley and Sons.

Clark K. B. (1985). "The Interaction of Design Hierarchies and Market Concepts in Technological Evolution," *Research Policy*, 14, 235–251.

Clark K. B., and Fujimoto T. (1991), *Product Development Performance*, Boston, MA: Harvard Business School Press.

Collins J. (2001).*Good to Great.* NY: Harper Collins.

Cohen W. M., Nelson R. R., and Walsh J. P. (2002). "Links and Impacts: The Role of Public Research on Industrial R&D," *Management Science*, 48 (1), 1–23.

Darwin C. (1871). *The Descent of Man and Selection in Relation to Sex.* NY: Murray.

Dawkins R. (1986). *The Blind Watchmaker.* NY: Penguin.

Dawkins R. (1996). *Climbing Mount Improbable.* W.W. Norton, New York, NY.

Demeulemeester E. L., and Herroelen W. S. (2002). *Project Scheduling: A Research Handbook.* Kluwer Academic Publishers, Amsterdam, Netherlands.

Deshmukh S. D., and Chikte S. D. (1980). "A Unified approach for Modeling and Analyzing New Product R&D Decisions," *TIMS Studies in the Management Sciences*, 15, 163–182.

Dougherty D. (1992). "Interpretive Barriers to Successful Product Innovation in Large Firms," *Organization Science*, 3 (2), 179–202.

Doz Y. Z., and Hamel G. (1997). *Winning Alliances.* Boston, MA: Harvard Business School Press.

Dyer J. H., and Ouchi W. G. (1993). "Japanese Style Partnerships: Giving Companies a Competitive Edge," *Sloan Management Review*, 35 (1).

Dyer J. H. (1996). "Specialized Supplier Networks as a Source of Competitive Advantage: Evidence from the Auto Industry," *Strategic Management Journal*, 17 (4), 271–292.

Edelman G. M., and Tononi G. A. (2000). "Universe of Consciousness: How Matter Becomes Imagination," Basic Books, New York, NY.

Feltham G. A., and Xie J. (1994). "Performance Measure Congruity and Diversity in Multitask Principal Agent Relations," *Accounting Review*, 69 (3), 429–453.

Fleming L. (2001). "Recombinant uncertainty in technological search," *Management Science,* 47 (1), 117–132.

Fleming L., and Sorenson O. (2004). "Science as a map in technological search," *Strategic Management Journal*, 25, 8, 909–928.

French H. (2005). "Whose Patent is it Anyway?" *New York Times*.

Galbraith J. (1973). *Designing Complex Organizations.* Cambridge, MA: Addison Wesley.

Gibbons M., and Johnston R. (1975). "The Roles of Science in Technological Innovation," *Research Policy*, 3, 220–242.

Gibbons R. (2005). "Incentives Between Firms (and Within)," *Management Science*, 51 (1), 2–17.

Gompers P., Lerner J., and Scharfstein D. (2005). "Entrepreneurial Spawning: Public Corporations and the Formation of New Ventures 1986–1999," *Journal of Finance*, 60 (2), 577–614.

Goyal S., and Moranga J. L. (2001). "R&D Networks," *Rand Journal of Economics*, 32 (4), 686–707.

Hannan M. T., and Freeman J. H. (1977). "The Population Ecology of Organizations", *American Journal of Sociology*, 82 (2), 929–964.

Henderson B. D. (1979). *Henderson on Corporate Strategy.* Cambridge: Abt Books.

Henderson R. M., and Clark K. B. (1990). "Architectural Innovation: The Reconfiguration of Existing Product Technologies and the Failure of Established Firms," *Administrative Science Quarterly*, 35, 9–30.

Hoang H., and Rothaermel F. T. (2005). "The Effect of General and Partner-Specific Alliance on Joint R&D Project Performance," *Academy of Management Journal*, 48 (2), 332–345.

Holmström B., and Milgrom P. (1991). "Multitask Principal-Agent Analyses: Incentive Contracts, Asset Ownership, and Job Design," *Journal of Law, Economics and Organization*, 9 (1), 25–52.

Kavadias S., and Loch C. H. (2003). *Dynamic Portfolio Selection Under Uncertainty*. Kluwer Academic Publishers, Boston, MA.

Kerr S. (1975). "On the Folly of Rewarding A While Hoping for B," *Academy of Management Journal*, 18, 769–783.

Krishnan V., and Ulrich K. T. (2001). "Product Development Decisions: A Review of the Literature," *Management Science*, 47 (1), 1–21.

Lawrence P., and Lorsch J. (1967). "Differentiation and Integration in Complex Organizations," *Administrative Science Quarterly*, 12 (1), 1–30.

Leonard-Barton D. (1992). "Core capabilities and core rigidities," *Strategic Management Journal*, 13, 111–125.

Leonard-Barton D. (1995). *Wellsprings of Knowledge*. Boston: Harvard Business School Press.

Levy S. R., Plaks J., Hong Y., Chin C., and Dweck C. S. (2001). "Static vs. Dynamic Theories of Groups: Different Routes to Different Destinations," *Personality and Social Psychology Review*, 5, 155–167.

Liker J. K., Kamath R. R., Wasti S. N., and Nagamachi M. (1996). "Supplier Involvement in Automotive Component Design: Are there Really Large US Japan Differences?" *Research Policy*, 25 (1), 59–89.

Loch C. H., De Meyer A., Pich M. T. (2006). *Managing the Unknown*. Hoboken, NJ: Wiley.

MacCormack A., Verganti R., and Iansiti M. (2001). Developing Products on "Internet Time: The Anatomy of A flexible Development Process," *Management Science*, 47 (1), 133–150.

Markides C. (1999). "Dynamic View of Strategy," *Sloan Management Review*, 40(3), 55–63.

Mihm J., Loch C. H., and Huchzermeier A. (2003). "Problem Solving Oscillations in Complex Projects," *Management Science*, 49 (6), 733–750.

Mokyr J. (1990). *The Lever of Riches*. New York: Oxford University Press.

Moorthy K. S. (1984). "Market Segmentation, Self-Selection, and Product Line Design," *Marketing Science*, 3 (4), 288–307.

Morison E. (1966). "Gunfire at Sea". In: *Men, Machines and Modern Times*. Cambridge: MT Press, 17–44.

Mussa M., and Rosen S. (1978). "Monopoly and Product Quality," *Economic Theory*, 18, 301–317.

Nelson R. R., and Winter S. G. (1982). "An Evolutionary Theory of Economic Change," Harvard Business School Press, Cambridge, MA.

O'Sullivan M. A. (2000). *Contests for Corporate Control: Corporate Governance and Economic Performance in the United States and Germany*. Oxford: Oxford University Press.

Pahl G., and Beitz W. (1988). *Engineering Design: A Systematic Approach*, NY: Springer-Verlag.

Pich M. T., Loch C. H., and De Meyer A. (2002). "On Uncertainty, Ambiguity, and Complexity in Project Management," *Management Science*, 48 (8), 1008–1023.

Porter M. E. (1980). *Competitive Advantage*, NY: Free Press, 164–200.

Porter M. E. (1985). *Competitive Advantage: Creating and Sustaining Superior Performance.* NY: Free Press.

Porter M. E. (1990). *The Competitive Advantage of Nations*. New York: The Free Press.

Roberts J. D. (2004). *The Modern Firm: Organizational Design for Performance and Growth*. Oxford, UK: Oxford University Press.

Rothaermel F. T., and Deeds D. L. (2004). "Exploration and Exploitation Alliances in Biotechnology: A System of New Product Development," *Strategic Management Journal*, 25 (3), 201–221.

Schumpeter J. (1942). *Capitalism, Socialism, and Democracy.* NY: Harper Brothers.

Shane S. (2000). "Prior Knowledge and the Discovery of Entrepreneurial Opportunities," *Organization Science*, 11 (4), 448–469.

Simonton D. K. (1999). *Origins of Genius.* Oxford: Oxford University Press.

Silverberg G., Dosi G., and Orsenigo L. (1988). "Innovation, Diversity and Diffusion: A Self-organisation Model," *Economic Journal*, 98 (393), 1032–1054. Royal Economic Society.

Sober E., and Wilson D. S. (1999). *Unto Others: The Evolution and Psychology of Unselfish Behavior.* Boston: Harvard University Press.

Sommer S., and Loch C. H. (2004). "Selectionism and Learning in Projects with Complexity and Ambiguity," *Management Science,* 50 (10), 1334–1347.

Sutton R. I. (2001). "The Weird Rules of Creativity," *Harvard Business Review*, 79 (8), 94–103.

Teece D. J., Pisano G., and Shuen A. (1997). "Dynamic Capabilities and Strategic Management," *Strategic Management Journal*, 18 (7), 509–533.

Terwiesch C., Loch C. H., and De Meyer A. (2002). "Exchanging Preliminary Information in Concurrent Engineering: Alternative Coordination Strategies," *Organization Science*, 13 (4), 402–419.

Thomke S. H. (2003). *Experimentation Matters.* Massachusetts: Harvard Business School Press.

Thompson J. D. (1967). *Organizations in Action*, New York: McGraw Hill.

Tirole J. (1988). *Theory of Industrial Organization*, MIT Press, Cambridge, MA.

Tushman M., and Anderson P. (1986). "Technological Discontinuities and Organizational Environments," *Administrative Science Quarterly*, 31, 439–465.

Tushman M. L., and Rosenkopf L. (1992). "Organizational determinants of technological change: Towards a sociology of technological evolution." In: *Research in Organizational Behavior*, (Eds.) B. M. Staw and L. L. Cummings, Greenwich: JAI Press, 311–347.

Ulrich K. T., and Eppinger S. D. (2004). *Product Design and Development* 3rd edition, NY: McGraw Hill.

Utterback J. M. (1994). *Mastering the Dynamics of Innovation*. Cambridge MA: HBS Press.

Van de Ven A. H., Angle H., and Pole M. S. (1989). *Research on the Management of Innovation: The Minnesota Studies*. New York: Harper and Row.

Weick K. E. (1993). "Collapse of Sensemaking in Organizations: The Mann Gulch Disaster," *Administrative Science Quarterly*, 38, 628–652.

Wheelwright S. C., and Clark K. B. (1992). "Revolutionizing Product Development," Maxwell-Macmillan, New York, NY.

Zhao M. (2006). "Conducting R&D in countries with weak intellectual property rights protection," *Management Science,* 52 (8), 1185–1199.

Zott C. (2002). "Dynamic Capabilities and the Emergence of Intraindustry Differential Firm Performance: Insights from a Simulations Study," *Strategic Management Journal*, 24 (2), 97–125.

Zwiebel J. (1995). "Corporate Conservativism and Relative Compensation," *Journal of Political Economy*, 103 (1), 1–25.

2 Technology strategy

Arnoud De Meyer and
Christoph H. Loch

1. Introduction

Technology strategy, like any functional strategy, has the purpose of linking the activities of technical functions of the organization to the business strategy of the organization. This encompasses, on the one hand, the translation of the competitive strategy into coherent goals and programs for the organization responsible for technology development (top down). On the other hand, it also includes the development of technology-based opportunities or options for future competitive advantage (bottom up). Since this entire book looks at new product development (NPD) from an operations and execution perspective more than other angles, a general characterization of competitive strategy is beyond the scope of this chapter. We will focus on the alignment of technology with strategy.

Let us begin with a metaphor: Competitive strategy is like a battle plan in a war for market territory, waging battles alongside alliance partners against competitors (where a partner in one area may be a competitor on another area!) and conquering customer terrain (market segments) with tools (products, services, and solutions) appropriate for succeeding on that terrain.

The competitive strategy outlines what terrain to target with what products, and what position to defend against competitors (using Porter's (1980) generic strategies terminology, differentiation through more targeted features, focus on terrain niches, or lower cost). This must include decisions about configuration and development of internal resources to be able to build and defend the desired position.

What role does technological innovation play in this battle plan? It allows *changing* the position to make it more attractive to customers, more damaging to competitors, or to respond to changes in the landscape, in other words, to modify the position for enhanced competitive advantage: targeting new terrain, new customer value or functionalities, or lower cost (Markides, 1999).

This metaphor has several implications. First, modification of position is an *unpredictable search*. Seeking a new position is a creative process, in an infinitely complex environment that, moreover, incessantly changes. The question for the 'best' innovation will never be settled. Second, battles with competitors happen in a context of *strategic interaction* – what is best for you depends on the actions of the other side. Therefore, what went out of style yesterday (because it was foreclosed by competitive action) may be successful again tomorrow (because the foreclosing actions have disappeared).

Therefore, Schumpeter's (1942) observation of markets evolving through 'creative destruction' is as valid today as it was 60 years ago. Research on (technology) strategy will never produce the definitive recipe for success. Therefore, strategy research has moved from content prescriptions to process recommendations on how to learn and change capabilities. The question is not 'what to optimally do,' but 'how to learn to do something reasonable in the future, when the environment has changed?'

In this Chapter, we will first give a brief and selective overview of some important ideas in technology management over the last 25 years (each study cited is but a representative of a whole literature – doing justice to all research in this vast area is beyond the scope of the space available). We will then discuss challenges of implementing and executing technology strategy.

2. Technology strategy at the industry level

2.1. Technology and the ecology of an industry

As innovation results from searching a complex and uncertain search space, it has many characteristics of an evolutionary process (see Chapter 1 of this book): ideas are 'genotypes' that express themselves in an environmental context and spread based on their socially judged 'fitness' (Mokyr, 1990; p. 275). Although this evolution is not purely Darwinian, but cultural (involving not only vertical spreading from one generation to the next, but also horizontal spreading, see Boyd and Richerson, 1985), many conclusions can be drawn from this insight. Innovation is stochastic in its direction, driven as much by (social or market) selection as by the production of ideas, and its dynamics may cycle between gradual 'micro-innovations' and large sudden 'macro-inventions' ('punctuated equilibria' in evolutionary biology). The dynamics of the switching regimes are driven by a combination of exhausting the potential of local search, society's degree of conservatism, by the embeddedness and compatibility needs of the invention, and by the non-localness of its potential (Mokyr, 1990; p. 295–300).

This cyclic dynamics has been observed by innovation scholars, e.g., Tushman and Anderson (1986) observed that industries, driven by key technologies, evolve through periods of incremental change punctuated by technological breakthroughs, which produce higher uncertainty as well as opportunities in the industry. Tushman and Rosenkopf (1992) emphasized the sociological compatibility needs among multiple stakeholders as a major force of stability in incremental phases. This view is related to the field of Industrial Organization (see Chapter 3); Industrial Organization has emphasized competitive equilibria more than the transient dynamics of innovative disruption.

Hannan and Freeman (1977) and Nelson and Winter (1982) pioneered an application of evolutionary theory to firms. Nelson and Winter observed that firms produce ideas at least partially blindly and get selected by markets or society (through institutions). Hannan and Freeman proposed that changes in an industry might happen less by firms learning and changing, but predominantly by some firms being selected (and others die). This sparked a literature in which the evolutionary unit is not the technological innovation, but actually the entire firms – the organization possesses certain routines and capabilities that are relatively fixed (or at least slow to change). Organizations, to some degree, grow and die with those capabilities (Silverberg et al., 1990).

2.2. Technology and the product life cycle

The evolutionary cycles described in Section 2.1 were widely observed in the form of the 'product life cycle' and associated with growth S-curves. While consistent with an evolutionary perspective, the explicit connection to evolutionary dynamics has rarely been drawn (with some exceptions, such as Tushman and Anderson, 1986).

After the Second World War, it was observed that products and product categories go through 'life cycles' (Foster, 1986). A new category starts out as risky and fragile idea, which might likely be dead; a few of many ideas start conquering the market and rapidly grow. For example, televisions achieved 90 per cent market penetration within three decades starting in the 1950s, and PCs did so within two decades starting in 1980. When the market is saturated, growth slows down, and at some point, the product is replaced by something new (black and white TVs by color TVs and now by flat screens, pocket calculators by PCs, etc.).

In the 1970s, the 'Boston Consulting Matrix' (Henderson, 1979; MacMillan et al., 1982) combined this insight with the concept of the experience curve and its associated economies of scale, to arrive at explicit technology investment rules: invest technical innovation resources in growing markets to gain market share (and thus economies and a cost advantage), use 'cash cows' with high-market share and slowing growth to produce the cash that is invested in the growing markets, and divest from products with low growth, in which market share has deteriorated or a high-market share has never been achieved. A similar view of plannable strategy, rooted on Operations Research, was given by Ansoff (1984), who devised optimal strategies of allocating resources between new or current products and new or current markets (the still cited 'Ansoff matrix').

At the end of the 1970s, however, this view of technology strategy was criticized because it became a self-fulfilling prophecy when applied by many firms, and it did not seem to allow for creative redefinition of competitive advantage (e.g., Hayes and Abernathy, 1980). Abernathy and Utterback (1978) introduced a broader view of the strategic role of R&D, identifying the changing contribution of R&D over the product lifecycle. Some of their ideas are summarized in Fig. 2.1. Products do indeed go through lifecycle phases characterized by market penetration. Over these phases, the character of innovation shifts from true product innovation to process innovation.

The early life of a new technology is fluid because the technology is not yet fully mastered, and market requirements and needs are not yet defined. Then, a dominant design (or market paradigm) for the product category emerges (Utterback and Abernathy, 1975). This is a sort of milestone or quasi-standard in an industry. The product that becomes a dominant design embodies the requirements of many classes of users, even though it may not perfectly match the requirements of one particular group of users. The emergence of the dominant design changes the nature of competition. From competition based on the functionality of the product, one moves to a competition based on cost

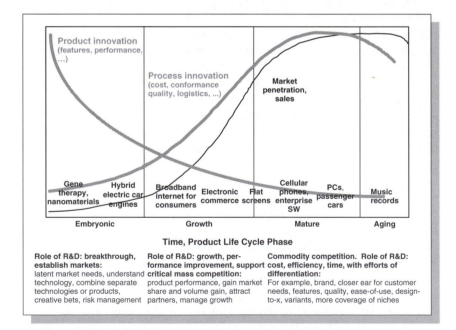

Figure 2.1
The role of R&D and technology over the product life cycle.

and quality. The challenge is no longer to define your product, but to offer a product similar to the competition at a lower price. That requires usually heavy investments in automation, business re-engineering, and a much leaner organization. This is a period of intensive process innovation. Finally, there is a fourth phase in the technological life cycle, when innovation, both in process and product, becomes less relevant to competitive survival, rather, amenities and services associated with the product become an essential element of the competition. Now, innovation serves more as a source of efficiency and cost reduction, while also differentiating products ever closely to segmented customer needs and offering the means to increase product variety (e.g., through platforms) to open up more opportunities for differentiation.

Typically, market entry happens in the growth phase of a product category or industry, and when a dominant design has been reached, market exit dominates (mainly through acquisitions and mergers); for example, 80 firms entered the television industry between 1948 and 1955, and the number shrunk to 40 in 1962, 8 in 1982 and 0 today. Although period durations differ, similar patterns have been observed in many industries (Utterback and Suarez, 1993; Utterback, 1994).

This view is compatible with the evolutionary view described in Section 2.1, and it is less deterministic than the BCG matrix view: there is always room for creativity. While the shift from the growth phase to the mature phase is inevitable (there is an upper limit to market size; although each consumer may have more than one television, PC or mobile phone, saturation is sooner or later reached), the shift to decline is not. For example, the car industry is still fiercely innovating (on cost and differentiation) and still dynamic after 40 years in the mature phase. Moreover, dying product categories can be renewed through major enhancements or new uses. For example, mainframe computers were predicted to die (as a victim of PCs) at the end of the 1980s, but found a major new use as network severs in the internet age and have experienced, through R&D, order-of-magnitude performance enhancements through new architectures (such as massively parallel low-cost processors). Thus, mainframes simply have refused to enter the decline stage until today (as does the car industry). Another example is that of turntables, which were doomed to disappear when vinyl records became obsolete. However, they came back as a tool for DJ's producing house music in clubs (a smaller specialized market).

3. Technology strategy at the company level

While industry dynamics are an important context, much technology strategy literature has focused at the individual company. While the industry level emphasizes the question what compositions of firm populations might arise,

31

the battle plan of the firm takes the other players as given and focuses on the question, 'how can I win.'

3.1. Porter's technology strategy

An important and still useful conceptualization of technology strategy was developed by Michael Porter (1985). He started by observing that technological change is not important for its own sake, but it is important if it affects competitive advantage and industry structure (p. 165). Technology, however, pervades a firm's value chain and extends beyond those technologies associated directly with the product; it therefore encompasses areas well outside the boundaries traditionally for R&D and inherently involves suppliers and buyers (p. 169). Since technology is embodied in every value activity, it can have powerful effects on both cost and differentiation. Favorable effects of a technological change are that it lowers the firm's cost or enhances its differentiation directly, or that it shifts cost or uniqueness drivers to the firm's advantage. The technology translates into other first mover advantages, or it improves the overall industry structure (in terms of diminished buyer or supplier power or the threat from substitutes and more favorable competition, p. 172).

Technology strategy then, in Porter's view, includes three fundamental decisions: what technologies to develop (decided not by scientific merit but by its effect on competitive advantage alone), whether or not to seek technology leadership in those technologies (balancing first mover advantages with benefits from learning from others), and whether or not to exploit technologies that the firm has developed through licensing. The formulation of a technology strategy consists of the following steps (p. 198):

1. Identify relevant technologies in the value chain as well as potentially relevant technologies in other industries;
2. Determine the likely path of change in these technologies;
3. Determine which ones are the most relevant for competitive advantage;
4. Assess the firm's relative capabilities in important technologies and the costs of making improvements;
5. Select a strategy, a portfolio of important technologies (developed internally or obtained from the outside) that reinforces the firm's competitive strategy.

Although Porter's technology strategy, viewed from today's perspective, may perhaps seem too 'static' and not complete, it still provides some insight. Moreover, it foreshadows two important concepts that were more fully developed later: the notion of capabilities driving the technology choice, and the notion that the strategy is embodied and executed via a portfolio of technology undertakings, or projects.

3.2. Technology strategy and IP protection

An influential strategic framework of innovation in the context of the industry life cycle has been proposed by Teece (1986). This framework prioritizes innovation investments in terms of the industry conditions with respect to dominant design (has the industry already settled on a dominant design or not), timing (is the a first mover or not), the availability of intellectual property (IP) protection, and the importance of complementary assets (products that make the technology in question more attractive, e.g., the availability of video movies makes the video recorder as a product more attractive).

Teece's framework can be organized in a decision tree (Fig. 2.2) (De Meyer, 1999). It summarizes the framework in five questions that are represented as binary (yes or no; weak or strong). The framework seems deterministic at first glance, but it is not because the answers to the questions are uncertain, and the very choice by the firm may influence the situation in the industry and, thus, the answers. The five questions in the decision tree are as follows:

1. **IP protection**. How easily can the organization protect the know-how developed and thus, appropriate its benefits in the form of rents? The source of protection may lie in patents, but it may also take other forms, such as brands, trade secrets, copyrights, a monopoly on critical resources, speed in development, or market dominance.
2. **Pre- or post-dominant design**. Has a dominant design already emerged or not? Before the dominant design, one needs to be in close contacts with customers and/or users to be able to observe the sometimes quite dramatic changes in customer preferences. After the breakthrough of the dominant design, standard techniques of market research will be sufficient to measure (the usually smaller) changes in customer preferences.
3. **Cost and speed of prototyping**. The faster the firm can experiment, the higher is its chance of staying ahead of the copying competition (if the firm is a first mover) or can be a fast follower and capture a large part of the market. For example, Iansiti (1995) showed that the performance of technology development and the competitive position of the firm are significantly influenced by the speed at which prototypes can be turned around (see also Thomke, 2004 and 2006).
4. **Importance of complementary assets** in the realization of the benefits provided by the project. The importance of overcoming network externalities in the success of a project have been widely documented, and partners can play an important role in building up the network of products and processes that enable market penetration. The success of a project thus often depends on the balance of power with these partners.

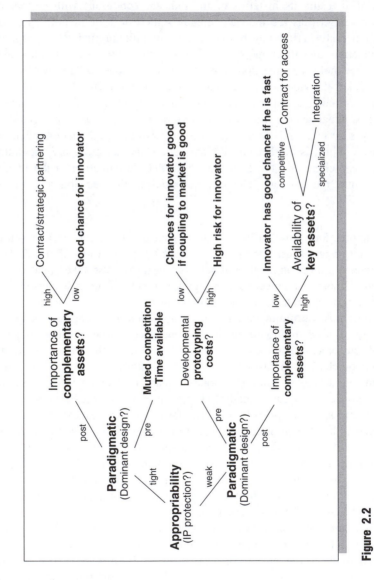

Figure 2.2
Decision tree to strategically evaluate a technology project.

5. **Accessibility of the complementary assets**. Are these complementary assets available on a competitive basis, and can the organization put the suppliers of these assets in competition with each other? Alternatively, are the providers specialized and in a monopoly-like position? In the latter case, it is more difficult to secure access (e.g., the supplier may have to be bought).

3.3. Technology strategy in operations management

Around 1990, work in the field of operations management (prominently, Clark and Fujimoto, 1991; Wheelwright and Clark, 1992) built on Porter's technology strategy concept and married it with execution, arguing that execution and strategy cannot be separated. Thus, Wheelwright and Clark (1992) see as the purpose of a technology strategy to (note the order going from execution to strategic context):

- Define a set of NPD or technology projects,
- Integrate and coordinate functional tasks, technical tasks, and organizational units involved in NPD,
- Make NPD converge to achieve overarching business purposes, and
- Create and improve capabilities to make NPD a competitive advantage.

The strategy then consists of three fundamental steps. First, identify technologies critical for competitive advantage, and focus on a few in which the organization intends to create truly superior capabilities. Second, decide where to source these technologies, internally through own development, or externally (from universities, joint ventures, licenses, acquisitions, etc.). Third, implement the strategy in an aggregate *plan*, a product and technology roadmap that identifies platforms and derivatives, and a set of performance measures against which to track progress, including target fractions of revenue sources and project targets. The implementation plan should obey certain principles, such as the separation of invention and application (e.g., include only proven technologies in market-targeted NPD projects), and the integration of product and process technologies in the overall portfolio.

3.4. Dynamic and emerging strategy

Over the last 15 years, research in Strategy has increasingly recognized that (static) strategic planning is insufficient to respond to complex and fast moving environment; strategy must emerge in response to the moving environment. Of course, this insight mirrors the evolutionary view at the industry level: 'I cannot take the other players as static in my battle plan, and to think through all possible scenarios is too difficult.'

For example, Burgelman and Rosenbloom (1989) observe that technology strategy is not fully decided but also partially follows the trajectories of industry and internal past decisions capabilities, partially dictated by the environment, and partially 'selected out' by the environment, and thus, an evolutionary perspective is instructive. Nelson and Winter (1982: 257) had already described this as technology trajectories. Hamel and Prahalad (1994) emphasize that technology decisions today refer to markets in the future, the competitive rules and customer preferences of which not only are not fully known, but also actually do not yet exist and are shaped by the very actions the firms take. Teece et al. (1997) viewed identifying new opportunities and organizing oneself to embrace them as more important than strategic planning of a competitive positioning – in other words, emerging strategy is required. Pisano (1997) showed in the pharmaceutical industry that learning about technologies (through process development and feeding back the learning to product development) is an important basis for developing flexible strategies.

Strategy literature has taken two approaches to the problem of lacking foreseeability and emergence. First, Kester (1984) introduced the concept of 'real options,' or the creation of opportunities (but not obligations) of taking some course of actions. The term coined in parallel to financial options, has been adopted in strategy, technology strategy in particular, because technological knowledge represents assets with exactly this feature of an opportunity of taking some course of action. The idea is that firms no longer can commit to investments associated with single scenarios but must maintain the flexibility of pursuing alternatives (Bowman and Hurry, 1993; Kogut and Kulatilaka, 1994; Williamson, 1999). A portfolio of 'experiments' represents options that are not optimal in a static sense but, rather, offer robustness: they can become relevant under different market or technology scenarios (Beinhocker, 1999). The more ambiguous and less describable the environment becomes, though, the less explicitly and quantitatively real options can be used in decision making (Adner and Levinthal, 2004).

A second response to emergence in strategy literature is that of learning and capability building.[1] As a prominent example, Leonard-Barton (1992) observed that every innovation project represents an opportunity for the organization to learn something that can be added to its core capabilities. An organization's capability are embedded in its technical systems (such as procedures and processes), managerial systems (such as incentives and promotion criteria), skills and knowledge (tacit as well as explicit knowledge in manuals),

---

[1] Of course, learning and capabilities could be seen as 'options' as well. However, they are different in a fundamental way because a capability allows a broad set of 'actions' that are not specific to any particular scenario; because of this generality and 'fuzziness' they cannot be quantified in their value as real options can (indeed, quantitative treatment is at the heart of options theory).

and values (such as aesthetic judgments of what a good opportunity is). These capabilities are not fully conscious or articulated and not easy to change.

Therefore, core capabilities can become 'core rigidities,' or barriers of change and innovation (Leonard-Barton, 1992). They subtly and possibly unconsciously limit the breadth of problem solving (e.g., because things are taken for granted), prevent an organization from adopting certain novel tools, tempt an organization to screen out certain external knowledge (e.g., because it seems inappropriate or is immediately judged irrelevant, remember the classic 'not invented here' syndrome), and limit experimentation. Indeed, any technological change happens in the context of a sociological system of technical externalities (such as the need for associated change in complementary products, see Cusumano et al., 1992) and social externalities (such as the need for related actors to change their beliefs or attitudes, see Tushman and Rosenkopf, 1992), which often makes the environment of the innovation conservative and resisting.

A particular prominent example of core rigidities is Christensen's 'Innovator's Dilemma' (Christensen, 1992a,b, 1997). Large companies are driven by large opportunities and, in eternal need to focus, are pushed by their sense of relevance and incentives, or by their locked-in investment in a certain product architecture (Henderson and Clark, 1990), to overlook or dismiss niche opportunities served by new technologies that, in the short run, are not competitive in the main market. However, technical progress in the niche may be faster than in the main market, and the time may come when the niche technology (while possibly still inferior to the old technology on the traditional performance measure) is 'good enough' for the main market and even superior on some new dimension, and so the niche technology takes over the main market. Moreover, the incumbent is caught unaware by the small startup that had enough incentive to pursue the niche. This is by no means inevitable, but the danger exists.

Leonard-Barton (1995) develops a set of practices that can help large organizations to recognize and act upon technological opportunities: distributed experimentation and creativity throughout the organization, following shared criteria of funding and evaluation and disseminated results ('shared problem solving'), ongoing efforts to keep introducing new tools and processes, ongoing experimentation and prototyping, and openness of the organization to information and learning from the outside, both from customers and partners. Eric von Hippel (von Hippel, 2001; Thomke and von Hippel, 2002) popularized the idea that in many cases, the source of innovative ideas lies outside the organization, often with users. They have deep knowledge about the use environment, and they have a stake in the development of the innovation because they can reap the benefits of it.

In the face of high uncertainty and the emergence of unforeseeable events and circumstances, adaptation rather than planning is fundamental. Two fundamental ways exist of accomplishing adaptation (Pich et al., 2002): experimentation, or trial-and-error learning (Leonard-Barton, 1995 refers to it as 'product morphing'), and 'selectionism,' or parallel trials, choosing the best-performing ex post (Leonard Barton calls this 'vicarious selection'). Both approaches are widely used and have been observed in literature (for example, Chew et al., 1991, or McGrath, 2001). Theory and empirical evidence suggest that trial-and-error learning offers a higher potential when uncertainty is high, while selectionism offers higher potential when the complexity of the situation (many interacting influence factors and variables) is high (Sommer and Loch, 2004, Sommer and Loch, 2006, Loch et al., 2006). An important application of selectionism is given in Christensen and Raynor (2003). They offer examples how companies can develop emerging capabilities and strategic positions by flexibly experimenting with small entrepreneurial organizational units that are dynamically created and eliminated.

A different approach in the emergence of strategy is the proposal to attempt deliberately to broaden innovation based on new dimensions of competition. A concept that has been influential in practice is value innovation (Kim and Mauborgne, 1997, 2005), a structured method to discover hidden and under emphasized performance parameters for a product or a service. Once such additional dimensions of product performance have been identified, one might be able redefine the rules of the competitive game by reducing the performance offer on obsolete parameters and investing ahead of the competition in the yet undiscovered performance parameters. This is, on the one hand, a creativity technique to derive new product feature dimensions, but it is also a strategic orientation of seeking new territory rather than competing for established territory. Of course, developing products with new dimensions is risky, requires experimentation (as discussed above), and may fail. Value innovation is related to Hamel's (2000) idea of Business Concept Innovation, where he makes a related point of widening the set of dimensions.

3.5. Partnerships and global networks

As innovation results from a search process, it becomes more productive the more sources of information and ideas are applied and shared across the parties involved. This is a robust result from search theory, creativity theory (see Chapter 5 in this book) and from economic growth models that incorporate endogenously developed knowledge as a production factor (Romer, 1990). The associated question for the individual company is how to increase competitiveness from collaboration with others.

Openness to the outside, prominently partners and a network of global outposts, is part of the organization's ability to learn (De Meyer, 1999). However, we discuss these two topics in a separate section because the demands of globalization are becoming particularly prominent (Eisenhardt, 2002).

First, the learning benefits of partnerships have been observed. For example, Doz and Hamel (1998) describe that long-lasting partnerships between companies usually are not only concerned with short-term benefits (such as cost reduction, or access to a specific technology or market), but have at their core learning and a mutual and mutually beneficial 'journey' of co-development, which is not defined at the outset. The learning and co-development cannot be governed by purely contractual agreements but must be supported by relationships. Particularly, four 'initial conditions' influence the chances of the partners achieving a constructive working relationship: the common understanding of the task definition, the partner's organizational routines, the interface structure, and mutual expectations of performance, behavior, and motives. They shape mutual experiences, attitudes, and in the long run, success (Doz, 1996; in the context of projects, see Loch et al., 2006 Chapter 10).

Networks matter not only with partners but also in the global structure of the company. Doz et al. (2001) have developed the concept of the metanational organization, or an international organization that is able to take advantage of its global presence to combine information and knowledge from different parts of the world to create innovation. Let us take a stylized example to illustrate this. Assume that you need to develop a new mobile phone that combines the sophisticated use of SMS as one finds it in the Philippines (which is one of the most sophisticated market for mobile messaging), the patents of Qualcom in the US, the fashion trend for electronic gadgets as it is prevalent in Los Angeles, the technology of miniaturization developed in Japan or Korea, and the competitive benchmarking with Nokia in Finland. You need antennae in different parts of the world to capture the knowledge, and you need the ability to combine this knowledge and roll it out. Doz et al. (2001) call these three activities sensing, melding, and deploying. Sensing refers to gathering knowledge about user needs all over the world. 'Melding' (a combination of welding and melting) requires the entrepreneurial insight of identifying an opportunity to create an innovative product, service, or process. Deployment in one or several markets also requires the cumulated wisdom of the organization. To roll out the innovation and get global leverage as quickly as possible, one needs to be flexible about building the most efficient and rapidly scalable global supply chain.

4. Executing technology strategy

The first part of this chapter has outlined different views and aspects of technology strategy, including the link to competitive strategy, emergence, and learning, and the link to operations. In particular, the operations view has emphasized that technology strategy is not separable from execution and ultimately, is expressed in a set of research and development projects to be implemented. Implementation may happen in one organization, or be distributed over a set of laboratories spread out over different locations and organizational subdivisions. In many cases, they entail the cooperation of representatives from different functional departments or organizational roles. However, whatever the organization, the focus of a technology strategy remains on the definition and the development of the portfolio of projects. The key decisions in technology strategy are thus choosing the individual 'attractive' projects, but also determining the shape of the portfolio of projects that will support the organization's strategy.

A simple framework of technology strategy execution is summarized in Fig. 2.3. Implementation of the technology strategy is embedded in a clearly articulated and communicated strategic context. This clear context may create the conditions where creativity can blossom and where market and user information may meet the technological capabilities developed within the organization, leading to the generation of various ideas. Normally, such an organization will have an overload of ideas, and one of the essential tasks in the implementation of the technology strategy is to evaluate project on their own merits as well with respect to their contribution within the portfolio. Projects thus selected are prime candidates for investment, and for them to succeed, those investment opportunities need to be fit in the available capacity of the technology organization. The final project program is the result of these

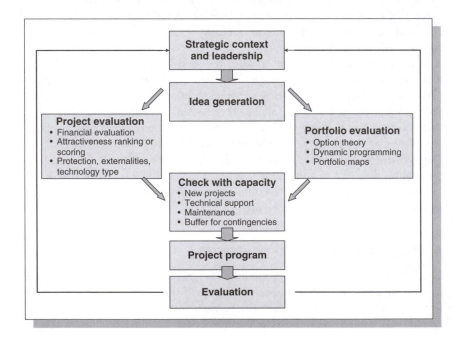

Figure 2.3
A simple framework of technology strategy execution.

three evaluations: individual attractiveness, strategic portfolio contribution, and capacity availability. Finally, the execution of this program needs to be evaluated for its contribution to the overall competitive strategy.

Strategic context and leadership. We have already discussed the connection of the 'technology vision' to competitive strategy. In addition, a good vision in technology strategy should fulfill two conditions: combine a long-term view with concrete short-term goals, and not be too constraining. The organization should not feel too comfortable because the challenges are defined too far in the future. Technology strategy needs to stretch the organization beyond its comfort zone. Too constraining and too focused a vision is not helpful either. A narrow tunnel vision, which constrains technology development to a very narrow path inhibits creativity and creates a false sense of security because the organization knows too well what it needs to do.

A provision of that clear vision is not sufficient. Real leadership also ensures that the organization takes ownership of the goals, understands them and acts according to them. Innovative leadership requires a lot of communication, convincing and cajoling until the vision has been absorbed throughout the organization. This includes both clarity of what it is (e.g., through 'mapping' of strategy down to operational goals, see Kaplan and Norton, 1996, 2000) and giving the technical employees the possibility of speaking up and a feeling of involvement, leading to buy-in (Loch and Tapper, 2002).

This combination of defining and communicating the vision is what is called *the strategic context* in Fig. 2.3. Organizations rely on it to harness their creativity. Without a clear strategic context, creativity may be discouraged due to the lack of direction, or be disjointed. Strategic context gives purpose and direction, benchmarks and role models, and it allows measuring progress.

Generation of ideas. Producing a promising technology portfolio requires the raw materials of innovation ideas. Increasing the stock of good project ideas requires two things: having access to stimulating information and an environment that stimulates creativity to transform this information into project ideas. Discussing the rich literature on creativity here is beyond our scope; we refer to Chapter 5 that addresses idea generation in the organization.

Creativity is not produced by methods alone but is resident in the personal knowledge, rather than personally researched knowledge, of people in the organization. Only 8 per cent of innovative information came from experimentation and calculation, and 7 per cent from printed materials (Myers and Marquis, 1969). Moreover, many ideas are generated by informal interactions across organizational units, mediated by people who have relationships across several units (Allen, 1977). Such empirical findings, repeatedly replicated, suggest that 'innovation is more a matter of flexible, productive and focused employee relations in the workplace than it is the result of technological resources or the impact of science . . .' (Carnegie and Butlin, 1993). This seems to suggest that the interactions among the employees of different parts of the firm, and between the employees of the firm and external parties, are important sources of project ideas.

Project and portfolio evaluation. In Fig. 2.3, project evaluation and portfolio evaluation are shown in parallel rather than sequentially. This reflects the interactive nature of these evaluation procedures: on the one hand, individual projects need to be evaluated within the context of the portfolio, because of direct spillover effects, because they compete for the same scarce resources, and because only *together* do they constitute strategy. On the other hand, projects need to contribute returns, or capabilities, or something else needed, to the organization. Thus, projects must be evaluated individually also to verify that each 'stands on its own feet.' Cooper et al. (1998) refer to this parallel evaluation as 'value balance' versus the 'strategic balance.' Established processes and methods, qualitative and quantitative, of project evaluation are discussed in Chapter 6 in this book.

Evaluation and performance measurement. The 'loop needs to be closed': A technology strategy will be effective only when it is regularly reviewed. This includes checking whether the projects have fulfilled their objectives, and searching what learning and new opportunities relevant for the strategy of the organization have emerged.

While this seems conceptually straightforward, it is difficult in practice because of uncertainty and long time frames involved in innovation (Feltham and Xie, 1994). In addition, a comprehensive tracking and performance measurement system of technology strategy not only allows verification, but also has effects on motivation and innovation activities of the technical employees (Loch and Tapper, 2002). Anecdotal observations from our work with companies suggest that companies may often struggle with performance measurement of technology strategy. Yet, there is a dearth of conceptual and empirical studies on this subject. Chapter 8 in this book gives an overview of this topic.

5. Future directions

As stated in the introduction of this chapter, technology strategy is inherently about modifying an existing strategic position, and therefore, about novel opportunities and the search for them, while maintaining some stability and cohesiveness of the overall set of activities: because of the stickiness and inertia of existing capabilities, the strategy of an organization cannot be changed at a moment's notice.

The 'right' balance between novelty and stability, between incremental and radical innovation efforts, is an open question. A well-known conceptual paper on 'exploration and exploitation' (March, 1991) has outlined the trade-offs between the two directions: effectiveness versus unlocking new potential. However, how can this balance be executed? A recent working paper explores the portfolio balance between incremental and radical efforts in a model; the study finds that this balance depends on the complexity and the frequency of shifts in the technological and competitive environment (Chao and Kavadias, 2006). Related work empirically shows how the complexity of the technology environment can be empirically operationalized and demonstrates that technical innovation is indeed well represented by the model of search on a complex landscape (Fleming, 2001; Fleming and Sorenson, 2001). Moreover, this work shows how scientific knowledge can serve as a rough 'map' of that landscape, a map that can help the organization decide when the safe bet of incremental innovation is preferable, and when 'large jumps' of risky radical innovations is worth a try (Fleming and Sorenson, 2004). The structure of search is particularly relevant since some studies conclude that sustainable competitive advantage can only be achieved by innovation that is complex, embedded in specialized knowledge, and thus uncertain (Miller and Lessard, 2000). Much work needs to be done to offer corporations good decision rules on this balance.

A second open area of work is the cascading down of technology strategy, or in other words, the operationalization of priorities and performance targets at the department level, from the overarching strategy, and in turn, the feeding back up of discoveries at the operative level to modify strategy, as well as performance measurement in the context of the strategy. As we observed at the end of the previous section, it is our anecdotal observation that firms struggle with this, and no good guidelines from academia seem to be available. The effect of cascading seems to be large, as it not only aligns the organization but also motivates employees and helps to channel, and thus energize, the creation of new ideas.

A third area that needs much more work is the creation of technology competence – what does it look like, 'on the ground,' when new capabilities are created? Is it simply the succession of experimentation cycles, over the course of which experience is accumulated? How do the organization of problem solving and the organizational memory (be it informally in people networks or in formal documents) impact the accumulation of knowledge? How are Leonard Barton's physical and managerial systems, skills, and values constructively changed? Work exists in organizational behavior: for example, Hargadon and Sutton (1997) document how the design IDEA stores knowledge, and Dragonetti (2007) documents in an ethnographic study of three startup organizations how their teams developed new knowledge. However, much more room exists to develop operational guides for structuring the capability building process.

A fourth area for further research is associated with the consequence of the increased efforts to outsource R&D and to develop new technologies in networks of partners. Most of the work carried out until recently was about technology strategies over which an organization had full control.

Subcontractors might help in the implementation of the technology strategy but would have no significant impact on it. In today's world of outsourcing and partnering, the technology strategy becomes a shared strategy, competencies and rigidities become shared competencies, etc. While there is a rich body of work on managing partners and suppliers (see Chapters 9 and 10 in this book), we need models and empirical work that help us to understand how to develop and implement technology *strategies* through networks of more or less independent partners.

Coming back to our opening metaphor, technology strategy is a battle plan that is stable enough for the various players involved to coordinate around it, and flexible enough to be modified in response to events, as well as proactively. The potential for innovations and modifications is infinite – there will never be the 'definitive strategy statement.' However, academic research must do more to help corporations understand the structure of the search for modifications, and the principles of incorporating changes into the battle plan.

References

Abernathy, W. J., J. M. Utterback. 1978. Patterns of industrial innovation. *Technology Review* June/July, 41–47.

Adner, R., D. Levinthal. 2004. What is not a Real Option: Considering boundaries for the application of real option to business strategy. *Academy of Management Review* 29(1), 74–85.

Allen, T. J. 1977. *Managing the Flow of Technology*. Cambridge: MIT Press.

Ansoff, I. 1984. *Implanting Strategic Management*. London: Prentice Hall.

Beinhocker, E. D. 1999. Robust adaptive strategies. *Sloan Management Review*, Spring, 95–106.

Bowman, E. H., D. Hurry. 1993. Strategy through the option lens: An integrated view of resource investments and the incremental-choice process. *Academy of Management Review* 18, 760–782.

Boyd, R., P. J. Richerson. 1985. *Culture and the Evolutionary Process*. Chicago: Chicago University Press.

Burgelman, R. A., R. S. Rosenbloom. 1989. Technology strategy: An evolutionary process perspective. *Research on Technological Innovation, Management and Policy*, Vol. 4, Greenwich, CT: JAI Press.

Carnegie, R., M. Butlin. 1993. *Managing the Innovating Enterprise*. Melbourne: The Business library.

Chao, R. O., S. Kavadias. 2006. *Strategic Portfolio Management in Highly Complex and Uncertain Environments*. Georgia Tech Working paper.

Chew, W.B., D. Leonard-Barton, R. E. Bohn. 1991. Beating Murphy's law. *Sloan Management Review* Spring, 5–16.

Christensen, C. M. 1992a. Exploring the limits of the technology s-curve. Part i: Component technologies. *Production and Operations Management* 1(4), 334–357.

Christensen, C. M. 1992b. Exploring the limits of the technology s-curve. Part ii: Architectural technologies. *Production and Operations Management* 1(4), 358–366.

Christensen, C. M. 1997. *The Innovator's Dilemma*. Boston: Harvard Business School Press.

Christensen, C. M., M. E. Raynor. 2003. *The Innovator's Solution: Creating and Sustaining Successful Growth.* Boston: Harvard Business School Press.

Clark, K. B., T. Fujimoto. 1991. *Product Development Performance*. Boston: Harvard Business School Press.

Cooper, R., S. J. Edgett, E. J. Kleinschmidt. 1998. *Portfolio Management for New Products*. Cambridge: Perseus.

Cusumano, M. A., Y. Mylonadis, R. S. Rosenbloom. 1992. Strategic maneuvering and mass market dynamics: The triumph of VHS over Beta. *Business History Review* 66, Spring, 51–94.

De Meyer, A. 1999. Using Strategic partnerships to create a sustainable competitive position for hi-tech start-up firms. *R&D Management* 29(4), 323–328.

Doz, Y. 1996. The evolution of cooperation in strategic alliances: Initial conditions or learning processes? *Strategic Management Journal* 17, 55–83.

Doz, Y., G. Hamel. 1998. *Alliance Advantage: The Art of Creating Value through Partnering*. Boston: Harvard Business School Press.

Doz, Y., J. Santos, P. Williamson. 2001. *From Global to Metanational: How Companies win in the Knowledge Economy*. Boston: Harvard Business School Press.

Dragonetti, N. 2007. How do Teams Create Knowledge? An Ethnographic Study of the Emergence of Firm-specific Resources. PhD Dissertation, INSEAD.

Eisenhardt, K. 2002. Has strategy changed? *Sloan Management Review*, Winter, 88–91.

Feltham, G. A., J. Xie. 1994. Performance measure congruity and diversity in multitask principal-agent relations. *The Accounting Review* 69(3), 429–453.

Fleming, L. 2001. Recombinant Uncertainty in Technological Search. *Management Science* 47(1).

Fleming, L., O. Sorenson. 2001. Technology as a Complex Adaptive System: Evidence from Patent Data. *Research Policy* 30(7).

Fleming, L., O. Sorenson. 2004. Science as a Map in Technological Search. *Strategic Management Journal* 25(8–9), 909–928.

Foster, R. 1986. The S-curve: A New Forecasting Tool. Chapter 4 In: *Innovation, The Attacker's Advantage*, NY: Simon and Schuster, 88–111.

Hamel, G., C. K. Prahalad. 1994. *Competing for the Future*. Boston: Harvard Business School Press.

Hamel, Gary. 2000. Leading the Revolution. Harvard Business School Press.

Hannan, M. T., J. Freeman. 1977. The population ecology of organizations. *American Journal of Sociology* 82, 929–964.

Hargadon, A. B., R. I. Sutton. 1997. Technology Brokering and Innovation in a Product Development Firm. *Administrative Science Quarterly* 42, 716–749.

Hayes R. H., W. J. Abernathy. 1980. Managing Our Way to Economic Decline. *Harvard Business Review* 58, July-August, 67–77.

Henderson, B. D. 1979. *Henderson on Corporate Strategy*. Cambridge: Abt Books.

Henderson, R. M., K. B. Clark. 1990. Architectural innovation: The reconfiguration of existing product technologies and the failure of established firms. *Administrative Science Quarterly* 35, 9–30.

Iansiti M. 1995. Technology integration: Managing technological evolution in a complex environment. *Research Policy* 24, 521–542.

Kaplan, R. S., D. P. Norton. 1996. *The Balanced Score Card*. Boston: Harvard Business School Press.

Kaplan, R. S., D. P. Norton. 2000. Having trouble with your strategy, then map it. *Harvard Business Review*, September-October, 167–176.

Kester, W. C. 1984. Today's options for tomorrow's growth. *Harvard Business Review*, March-April, 153–160.

Kim, W. C., R. Mauborgne. 1997. Value Innovation, the Strategic Logic of High Growth. *Harvard Business Review*, January-February, 103–112.

Kim, W. C., R. Mauborgne. 2005. *Blue Ocean Strategy*. Boston: Harvard Business School Press.

Kogut, B., N. Kulatilaka. 1994. Options Thinking and Platform Investments: Investing in Opportunity. *California Management Review*, Winter, 52–71.

Leonard-Barton. D. 1992. Core capabilities and core rigidities. *Strategic Management Journal* 13, 111–125.

Leonard-Barton. D. 1995. *Wellsprings of Knowledge*. Boston: Harvard Business School Press.

Loch, C. H., U. A. S. Tapper. 2002. Implementing a strategy-driven performance measurement system for an applied research group. *The Journal of Product Innovation Management* 19, 185–198.

Loch, C. H., A. De Meyer, M. T. Pich. 2006. *Managing the Unknown: A Novel Approach to Managing Projects Under High Uncertainty and Risk*. Hoboken, NJ: Wiley.

MacMillan, I. C., D. C. Hambrick, D. L. Day. 1982. The Product Portfolio and Profitability - A PIMS-Based Analysis of Industrial-Product Businesses. *Academy of Management Journal* 25(4), 733–755.

Markides, C. C. 1999. A dynamic view of strategy. *Sloan Management Review*, Spring, 55–63.

McGrath, R.G. 2001. Exploratory learning, innovative capacity, and managerial oversight. *Academy of Management Journal* 44(1), 118–131.

Mokyr, J. 1990. *The Lever of Riches.* Oxford: Oxford University Press.

Myers, S., D.G. Marquis. 1969. *Successful Industrial Innovations: A Study of Factors Underlying Innovation in Selected Firms.* National Science Foundation.

Miller, R., D. L. Lessard. 2000. *The Strategic Management of Large Engineering Projects.* Boston: MIT Press.

Nelson, Richard R., and Sidney G. Winter. 1982. An Evolutionary Theory of Economic Change. Cambridge, Mass: Belknap.

Pich, M. T., C. H. Loch, A. De Meyer. 2002. On uncertainty, ambiguity and complexity in project management. *Management Science* 48(8), 1008–1023.

Pisano, G. P. 1997. *The Development Factory.* Boston: Harvard Business School Press.

Porter, M. E. 1980. *Competitive Strategy.* NY: The Free Press.

Porter, M. E. 1985. *Competitive Advantage.* NY: The Free Press.

Romer, P. M. 1990. Endogenous technological change. *Journal of Political Economy* 98(5), S71-S102.

Schumpeter, J. A. 1942. *Capitalism, Socialism and Democracy.* NY: Harper.

Silverberg, G., G. Dosi, L. Orsenigo. 1990. Innovation, diversity and diffusion: A self organizing model. In: *The Economics of Innovation*, (Ed.) C. Freeman, UK: Elgar, 68–104.

Sommer, S. C., C. H. Loch. 2004. Selectionism and learning in complex and ambiguous projects. *Management Science* 50(10), 1334–1347.

Sommer, S. C., C. H. Loch. 2006. Mastering Unforeseeable Uncertainty in Startup Companies: An Empirical Study. Krannert School/INSEAD Working Paper.

Teece D. J. 1986. Profiting from Technological Innovation. *Research Policy* 15(6), 639–656.

Teece, D. J., G. P. Pisano, A. Shuen. 1997. Dynamic capabilities and strategic management. *Strategic Management Journal* 18(7), 509–533.

Thomke, S. 2004. *Experimentation Matters: Unlocking the Potential of New Technologies for Innovation.* Boston: Harvard Business School Press.

Thomke, S. 2006. Capturing the Real value of Innovation Tools. *Sloan Management Review* 47(2), 24–32.

Thomke, S., E. von Hippel. 2002. Customers as Innovators: A New Way to Create Value. *Harvard Business Review*, April, 74–81.

Tushman, M. L., P. Anderson. 1986. Technological discontinuities and organizational environments. *Administrative Science Quarterly* 31(3), 439–465.

Tushman, M. L., L. Rosenkopf. 1992. Organizational determinants of technological change: Towards a sociology of technological evolution. In: *Research in Organizational Behavior*, (Eds.) B. M. Staw and L. L. Cummings, Greenwich: JAI Press, 311–347.

Wheelwright, S. C., K. B. Clark. 1992. *Revolutionizing Product Development*. NY: The Free Press.

Utterback, J. M. 1994. *Mastering the Dynamics of Innovation*. Boston: Harvard Business School Press,

Utterback, J. M., W. Abernathy. 1975. A Dynamic model of Product and Process Innovation. *Omega* 3(6), 639–656.

Utterback, J. M., F. F. Suarez. 1993. Innovation, competition and industry structure. *Research Policy* 22, 1–21.

Von Hippel, E. 2001. User toolkits for innovation. *Journal of Product Innovation Management* 18(4), 247–257.

Williamson, P. J. 1999. Strategy as options on the future. *Sloan Management Review*, Spring, 117–126.

3 Competitive positioning through new product development

Elie Ofek[1]

Launching new products is perhaps the most prevalent way for start-up firms to establish themselves in a market and is a common strategy for incumbent firms to retain their industry position and grow top line profits. To reap the rewards from new product introductions, the characteristics of the new product must first be conceived, developed, and ultimately sold in the marketplace. While new products hold the promise of greater profitability, the process from start to finish is costly, time-consuming, and fraught with uncertainties. According to the National Science Foundation, in the US alone industrial R&D expenditure reached a level of $291 Billion annually in 2004, with that number expected to grow in the years to come (NSF, 2006). At the same time, R&D expenditure alone does not guarantee commercial success as new product failure rates are estimated to be as high as 80 per cent in a host of industries (Berggren and Nacher, 2000; Tait, 2002).

How do firms determine where to direct their R&D resources to ensure a healthy commercial return on their investment? What considerations go into formulating new product strategy while managing the associated risks? Once a new product has been developed, how does the firm price it to achieve maximal return?

Addressing these kinds of questions requires the firm to balance three primary considerations. First, the firm needs to have an understanding of what market opportunities exist in terms of which end users can be targeted and with what specific benefits. Second, the firm needs to have a handle on the development feasibility of any proposed new product aimed at addressing a given market opportunity. These two aspects of new product strategy introduce market and technical uncertainty, respectively, into NPD decision-making. Market uncertainty reflects the fact that before a new product is actually

---

[1] Elie Ofek is Associate Professor of Business Administration at the Harvard Business School. Address: Harvard Business School, Morgan 195, Soldiers Field, Boston MA 02163. E-mail: eofek@hbs.edu

launched, there will exist some degree of doubt as to whether consumers perceive the benefits that the new product can provide to be large enough to offset any adoption obstacles – such as switching costs and risks of product failure.[2] Technical uncertainty reflects the fact that development challenges may be difficult to overcome – resulting in more R&D investment than initially expected or a delay in the timing of introduction. Technical uncertainty may also be associated with having to forecast the variable manufacturing costs the new product will entail. Across a number of studies, it has been shown that approximately 46 per cent of new products fail in the technical phase, i.e., do not result in a result in a working product, while 35 per cent of new products that were technically completed failed post launch due to lack of market acceptance (see Cooper and Kleinschmidt (1987) for a review).

However, as a firm navigates through these sources of uncertainty, yet a third factor must be reckoned with – namely, competition. In the context of developing new products, the presence, or in some case the potential threat of, rivals can have considerable implications for which opportunities a firm ultimately chooses to pursue. On the one hand, new product development is a way for firms to pro-actively improve their standing relative to competition but, on the other hand, anticipating competitors' actions and plans may critically affect how a firm sets its own new product strategy.

The goal of this chapter is to provide an understanding of how firms make new product decisions taking into account the existing positions, moves, and counter-attacks of rivals. To provide a complete picture, we examine how the confluence of market uncertainty, technical uncertainty and competitive pressures affects optimal NPD strategy. A firm will be assumed to seek development of those products that, given the uncertainties and competition, will maximize its expected profits. Therefore, this chapter bears on the R&D Assignment aspect of NPD and attempts to couch that within the firm's desire to secure Economic Returns (see Fig. 1.2 in this book). More specifically, the presentation is organized as follows: In the next section, we consider how firms determine what product features to include in a new product given the existing market structure. We describe how a firm would map consumers' perceptions of the current product offerings and the positions competitors occupy in the attribute/benefit space – thus revealing desirable new product opportunities the firm could pursue. This analysis is at a 'micro' level in the sense that it generates specific new product profiles (attribute level combinations, particular new dimensions or features to include). However, it does so at the expense of limited analysis of competitor reactions (only

---

[2] One organizing framework for classifying the benefits vis-à-vis barriers to adoption of an innovation was proposed by Rogers (2003). According to Rogers, the uncertainty around the rate and scale of the adoption of any new product or service can be understood along five factors – relative advantage, complexity, compatibility, trialability, and observability.

short run adjustments, like pricing, are considered), limited indication of the cost a firm should incur on its chosen new product profile (i.e., the strategic incentives to invest in R&D), and is in some sense static (gives a limited sense of how firms evolve in terms of their relative industry standing). The second section of the chapter complements the first section, and gets more directly at strategic and dynamic issues. Specifically, a firm's performance in terms of securing economic rents from NPD is analyzed in greater depth within the context of competitors executing NPD plans of their own. To gain insights, new product opportunities are treated in a reduced form fashion – the various opportunities are characterized by their risk-reward profile without a full characterization of the specific combination of product attributes. The approach presented models each new market-offering opportunity in a way that captures the essence of how it can generate economic rents, and then looks at how competition unfolds in terms of which opportunities are pursued more aggressively (in terms of R&D costs) and by which firm. This more 'macro' view of NPD allows for flexibility in handling the nature of competition with new products (introduction timing, patent races, winner take all scenarios, etc.), and in examining dynamic issues related to industry evolution (do current leaders that possess the most lucrative product stay leaders with the next generation of products?). The chapter ends with a section that describes a number of prominent limitations to extant theories on competitive positioning through NPD, and offers direction for how future research could fill the gaps in our understanding.

1. Competitive market structure and new product opportunities

Understanding the set of benefits that customers seek in a given category and determining how current offerings by different firms deliver on those benefits, is often used to identify new product positioning opportunities. Many times the benefits to end users are obvious from the physical attributes or the features of the product (e.g., greater speed of a computer processor saves time and increases productivity, greater memory capacity of a hard drive offers storage convenience). Other times this mapping is not as straightforward and engineering creativity may be needed to translate the derived benefits into physical attributes or features (e.g., a desire for a software to be 'more user friendly,' for a car to be 'safer,' for a laptop to be more 'aesthetically appealing').[3] Then by figuring out how end users are distributed in terms of their preference for current and potential offerings, it is possible to identify

---

[3] Several studies (e.g., Hauser and Simmie, 1981; Narasimhan and Sen, 1989) have been able to demonstrate how the perceptual consumer space can be translated into physical product attributes.

new locations that would be most profitable to occupy. An extensive literature has emerged, particularly in marketing, to describe the processes by which a firm might go about identifying new product opportunities given the market structure. In this section, we review recent developments in this area. We concentrate on the case whereby a focal firm is either considering entry with a new product or repositioning its existing brand. (Issues of product line are discussed in chapter 4 of this book).

The following steps describe a general approach that leads to the selection of an optimal new product position. The approach is grounded in economic theory and allows quantitative predictions of the type desired with a competitive new product launch (see also Ofek and Srinivasan, 2002, and Schmalensee and Thisse, 1988).

Step 1: Determine attributes or dimensions most relevant for consumer choice in the category.

Step 2: Define and estimate a preference model on a sample of consumers or segments. This gives the distribution of consumer preference parameters.

Step 3: Define the competitive landscape, i.e., which brands (and their product profiles) are in the evoked consideration set of consumers.

Step 4: Apply the preference model to the competitive set. This enables computing market shares under current conditions for each alternative in the competitive set.

Step 5: Determine the performance of any proposed new product; select the optimal location of a new product or the direction in which to reposition an existing product.

Though it is possible to position the new product to maximize sales revenue or market share, it is preferable to maximize profits as the objective. In addition, one must have a clear sense of what is being assumed about competitors' reaction to a new brand positioning. The two extremes are: not allowing existing products to react in any way, or allowing them to change all marketing activity as well as their own product profiles. In between, one could allow adjusting some short run marketing mix variables. With a desire to specify the characteristics of the new market offering (levels for each attribute, specific features to include), usually only short run competitive reactions are examined, with price being the most common variable allowed to change. Next, we describe in more detail a framework for achieving these five steps.

1.1. A framework for maximizing profits through new product positioning

When products can be considered as a bundle of well-defined attributes, each product concept under consideration can be represented by a vector (or profile) of attribute levels $(x_a, x_b, x_c, \ldots x_K)$, where x_k is the level of attribute k and

K is the set of relevant attributes (K includes price as an attribute).[4] The typical first task (Step 1) is to conduct qualitative research (e.g., externally with lead users, industry experts, and retailers; and internally with engineers, marketing personnel, and salespeople) to figure out which attributes are most relevant in a given category. Some quantitative testing can be done to limit consideration to the key attributes, e.g. through Factor Analysis of survey responses (see Horsky and Nelson (1992) for an application in the automotive industry to reduce the number of attributes from 19 to 5).

For Step 2, one needs to specify a preference model. The model describes the researcher's belief of how each attribute contributes to an individual's overall utility, and how consumers trade-off the various attributes and price. The utility individual i derives from product profile j is typically written as:

$$U_j^i = \sum_{k=1}^{K} g_k^i(x_{jk}) + \varepsilon_j^i, \text{ where} \tag{1}$$

g_k^i is the function relating level of attribute k into units of utility for individual i, and ε_j^i is a random component.

Consumers are assumed to choose the brand that provides them with the highest utility. If choice is assumed deterministic, one sets the random component to zero. However, deterministic choice is typically a very strong assumption, given the approximations of actual behavior made in any preference model, the issue of omitted variables, and the inherent variability of consumer behavior. Moreover, as will be discussed later, the error term allows moving naturally from individual utilities to choice probabilities, which is convenient for subsequent analysis.

Many applications assume that the g functions are linear (also called the vector model; Green and Srinivasan, 1978), in which case there is a simple monotonic relationship between attribute levels and resulting utility (more of an attribute is either better or worse). Other applications assume a quadratic form, in which case ideal points may arise depending on the range of allowed attribute levels. If only a finite number of levels for each attribute are relevant (or tested for), then it is common to use a partworth model for the g functions (i.e., for each level of an attribute a specific utility equivalent is estimated; interpolation can be used for levels in between those estimated). When income effects are not a critical issue, it is common to treat price as one of the product attributes (Schmalensee and Thisse, 1988).

Once the preference model has been specified, one needs to map out the demand structure for the category. The goal is to find a representative sample

---

[4] A product feature that is either absent or present (such as a 'side air bag') can be represented with two levels ('1' for presence and '0' for absence).

upon which a preference elicitation study, prominently conjoint analysis (Green and Srinivasan, 1978, 1990), can be conducted.

In some markets, it is fairly straightforward to construct the current competitive set (Step 3) in other cases the boundaries may be less distinct (e.g., mid-sized cars and sporty sedans) and one can conduct surveys or personal interviews to determine consumers evoked set of competing alternatives (Horsky and Nelson, 1992). It is also realistic to include an outside good as one of the options. This allows any new product considered not only to build share at the expense of existing brands but also to increase overall demand. Moreover, invariably some consumers will not purchase a particular brand in the category.

One can then use a number of techniques to link consumer preferences to market shares for any set of alternative product profiles (Step 4). For example, in the deterministic case, one can use a max-choice rule, i.e., each individual would choose the alternative that maximizes her utility. Each firm's share is then the total number of consumers in the sample that would choose it divided by the total sample.[5] When a random component affecting choice is included, a distribution for the error term has to be specified. Using this distribution, one can compute for each individual the probability that a given option yields the maximal utility (and hence the probability of it being chosen). If the error term is assumed to be distributed double exponential,[6] an individual's probability of choosing any option conforms to the multinomial logit model of choice. This model has been extensively used in marketing and econometrics, primarily because it yields a closed form solution for the choice probabilities as a function of product attribute levels (and any other marketing actions incorporated), and serves as a good approximation of observed behavior.[7] By summing up all individuals' probability of choosing a given alternative (and dividing by the sample size) one obtains the market share for that alternative. In both the deterministic and probabilistic cases, the fact that data is gathered at the individual level ensures that heterogeneity has been captured, and avoids having to assume some a priori stylized distribution of tastes.

The above analysis and market representation then sets the stage for making new product decisions (Step 5). In particular, a focal firm would use the preference structure of consumers, along with the positions of current competitors,

---

[5] One can also use an 'alpha-rule' (Green and Krieger, 1992), in which each individual has a probability for choosing each alternative according to: $(U_j^i)^\alpha / \sum_{j'=1}^{n} (U_{j'}^i)^\alpha$, where the parameter α is either specified by the researcher or estimated.

[6] The double exponential distribution is also called the Gumbel or extreme value distribution. Ben-Akiva and Lerman (1985) pg. 104–105, discuss the basic properties of this distribution.

[7] The multinomial logit choice model has other desirable features that have contributed to its wide use. See Train (2003) for an excellent review of the properties of the multinomial logit model as well as examples of its use.

to consider new profiles. The profile selected should maximize profits. More formally, if there are $n+1$ competing alternatives (including the new product to be developed) the profits that will accrue to the focal firm in each period for a given new product profile it introduces are:

$$\pi_f = (p_f - c_f(\vec{x}_f))D_f(\vec{x}_1, \vec{x}_2, \ldots, \vec{x}_f, \ldots, \vec{x}_{n+1}; p_1, p_2, \ldots, p_f, \ldots p_{n+1}), \tag{2}$$

where π_f are the profits of the focal firm,
     p_f the price set by the focal firm,
     c_f the variable cost of producing the new product,
     D_f is the demand generated for the focal firm's new product, given the product profiles of each competing alternative $\vec{x}_j = (x_{ja}, x_{jb}, x_{jc}, \ldots, x_{jK})$, and the prices charged by each firm p_j.

The variable cost of manufacturing each product profile c_f is generally taken to be a function of the attribute levels (typically additive or multiplicative formulations are used to determine total variable costs). Several methods have been proposed for estimating these variable costs.[8] Each new profile is expected to be priced to maximize profits in Eq. (2). Summing profits across multiple periods (for a relevant time horizon of T periods) and comparing to the development costs, allows determining which new profile yields the highest return on investment:

$$\Pi_f = \sum_{t=1}^{T} \delta^t \pi_f - C_f(\vec{x}_f), \tag{3}$$

where Π_f are the discounted profits of the focal firm,
     δ is the discount factor,
     C_f the R & D cost of developing the new product profile.

1.2. Competitive considerations

In many cases, the introduction (or repositioning) of a product will make the existing brands worse off. Hence, in selecting the optimal new product location, a firm would be advised to anticipate competitive reactions. Not doing so will likely result in a suboptimal product position. In the short-run, it is reasonable to assume that price is the primary strategic variable firms can

---

[8] If the variable costs of production for each alternative currently in the market are known, one can use a regression analysis to obtain the cost function parameters for each attribute (Ofek and Srinivasan, 2002). If not readily available, the variable costs of production can also be obtained by reverse engineering existing alternatives (Srinivasan et al., 1997), or by applying an equilibrium framework to past market share data (Horsky and Nelson, 1992).

readily change (Horsky and Nelson, 1992; Choi and DeSarbo, 1994; Ofek and Srinivasan, 2002; the next section explicitly considers rival actions in NPD effort and direction). The most realistic assumption to make is that, given the product profiles of existing brands, the market had been in a Nash pricing equilibrium prior to the introduction of the new product by the focal firm and that it will be in a new Nash pricing equilibrium post introduction. As such, all firms will simultaneously be maximizing (2) with respect to price. Provided the equilibrium exists, one can either search for it analytically or computationally.[9] The profit achievable from each new product profile is now based on its price equilibrium performance. Aside from adjusting price, rivals may seek to react through other marketing variables, such as advertising spend or distribution intensity (Shankar, 1997). The reaction may depend on how 'close' the new product profile is to the rival's existing product (Hauser and Shugan, 1983). Ultimately, existing firms may seek product changes of their own. The full implication of this would require the market to be in a product and price equilibrium.

1.3. New product locations and the degree of market and technical uncertainty

The process described above will most likely lead to new products that fall into one of three types: (*i*) those that do not push the performance frontier beyond currently achievable attribute levels but find unoccupied space, (*ii*) those that offer higher levels of a given dimension than currently offered by any of the alternatives, and (*iii*) those that identify entirely new dimensions or product features to include. These new product opportunities are depicted in Fig. 3.1. For simplicity, the figure only depicts two attributes (labeled 'a' and 'b') and two pre-existing firms (labeled '1' and '2'). Dashed lines indicate new market offering opportunities.

i. *Locating in Unoccupied Space*: Given the alternatives currently in the marketplace, a firm may find it optimal to develop and launch a product that lies within the bounds set by the maximal level of each of the non-price attributes (see the *Unoccupied Space* in Fig. 3.1). More formally, define the maximal level on a given non-price attribute k offered by any of the n currently available alternatives as:

$$x_k^{\max} = Max\{x_{jk}\}_{j=1}^n \tag{4}$$

---

[9] See Choi et al. (1990), Choi and DeSarbo (1993), and Anderson et al. (1989) for existence conditions.

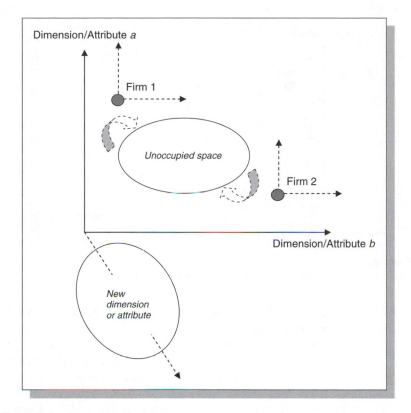

Figure 3.1
Competitive market structure and new product opportunities.

A new product profile in this case will lie in the interior of the region defined by the intersection of lines originating from the maximum level on any attribute (see Fig. 3.2). Note that there can be two possibilities here. A new product concept may be placed in a region that is entirely dominated by at least one of the alternatives (as the shaded area in Fig. 3.2) or in an area that is not dominated by any of the existing alternatives.

If there are acute dis-economies of scope in R&D or production, firms may find it more suitable to look for new product or re-positioning opportunities on a restricted curve connecting the existing alternatives (see the dotted line connecting the current offerings of firms 1 and 2 in Fig. 3.2). Said differently, when offering more of one attribute makes it increasingly difficult to offer the existing levels on other attributes, this cost-to-improvement trade-off may limit the feasible positions to consider to an 'effective frontier.' The effective frontier defines a subset of the

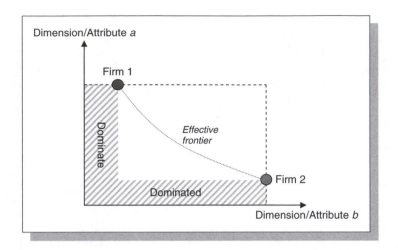

Figure 3.2
Dominated and non-dominated options when preference for each attribute is monotonic.

full range determined by the maximal level on each attribute of currently offered alternatives. New R&D capabilities or increased efficiency in production may shift the curve out and increase the possibilities.[10]

There are several reasons why a firm might end up choosing an interior position in the unoccupied space region. First, from a cost standpoint, both the variable costs and the R&D costs should be well understood in this region and involve relatively known manufacturing and development skills. As long as a firm positions on or to the left of the effective frontier, the production and development costs involved should be manageable. Moreover, positioning strictly in the interior of the effective frontier is likely to result in lower costs. If enough consumers exist that are relatively price sensitive, then the savings on the variable costs c_f and C_f in Eqs (2) and (3), respectively, may merit such a new product positioning. In such a case, the focal firm may be able to price low enough (yet still earn enough margin due to the lower costs) to differentiate itself. For this positioning therefore, it is imperative to have a realistic assumption regarding how rivals will react through price changes.

---

[10] The curve need not be strictly convex as in Fig. 3.2; but the point is that it will originate from alternatives with maximal attribute levels and be interior to the dashed lines connecting them (the intersection of the dashed lines offers maximal level on both dimensions within a single product). The discussion here on an effective frontier bears a connection to work in manufacturing dealing with trade-offs in the nature of the technology and operations strategies available and how complementary actions of the firm may move the frontier outward or change its shape (see Clark, 1996).

Second, in the unoccupied space consumers will have strong familiarity with the range of attribute levels being considered. Hence, the measurement of consumer preferences from a representative sample is likely to be reliable (Step 2 described earlier). Market uncertainty will thus be low. Depending on the distribution of demand, there may exist profitable interior locations because they are more favorable to a big enough set of consumers.

Another related reason to position a new product in the unoccupied space has to do with the nature of heterogeneity in consumer preferences. If there are enough consumers whose preferences are not monotonically increasing or decreasing in all attributes (i.e., more of an attribute is not always better or worse), there may exist profitable areas in the product and price space in which enough consumers find the new product closer to their ideal point.

ii. *Pushing the Envelope through Attribute Improvement*: Another opportunity that can arise from the process is for a new product to locate (or reposition) so that one or more of the attributes are improved beyond the maximal level in the existing offerings. Said differently, there is at least one attribute k' along which the new product by the focal firm (indexed f) will satisfy:

$$x_{fk'} > Max\{x_{jk'}\}_{j=1}^n.$$

The realm of such new product locations is depicted in Fig. 3.1 by the directions of the dashed arrows emanating from each of the offerings by firms 1 and 2. This product development direction typically requires undertaking more market and technical uncertainty than with a positioning into unoccupied space (as outlined previously in option (*i*)). From a demand perspective, in conducting Step 2 of the framework for identifying the optimal location (i.e., defining and estimating a preference model), it is advisable to include levels that are well outside the range of existing offerings (e.g., in the conjoint study). Otherwise, merely extrapolating using demand parameters estimated based on existing offerings may result in misleading predictions. That said, since consumers have never encountered the new levels being tested, their responses may be prone to error (both over-reaction and under-reaction can be observed in practice), resulting in a non-negligible degree of market uncertainty.

From a cost perspective, it is important to have a handle on how an improvement along a certain attribute level increases variable and R&D costs. In some cases the increase will be roughly linear, in other cases it may be convex (i.e., a unit improvement in the attribute level becomes increasingly costly). Moreover, there may be negative interaction effects. Specifically, to maintain a given level on other attributes, a huge cost will have to be incurred to improve certain attributes (e.g., a unit improvement in the processing speed of a microprocessor may require other components to be addressed to keep heat level constant). Hence, a firm would most likely consider only a small set of attributes to improve upon at any one time. In this context, Ofek and Srinivasan (2002) develop a cost-benefit metric that takes into account the competitive landscape and rank orders the relevant attributes according to the profits they would generate if improved (one at a time). The approach transforms individual-level data, as from a standard conjoint study, into an aggregate market measure and yields insights into which consumers are most sensitive to an improvement.[11]

iii. *Pre-empting a New Attribute/Dimension*: Early in the process of deciding where to position a new product, a firm determines the attributes or dimensions relevant for consumer choice (Step 1, described earlier). Beyond mapping the set of attributes and features that are present in current offerings, a firm may also scout for new dimensions or features that have been ignored. These new dimensions may have become relevant due to new available technologies, developments in related categories, or shifts in consumer tastes. The need to look for new dimensions (or dimensions that were previously thought to be unimportant) may be more acute as more firms compete in the market. In such cases, there are no profitable locations in the unoccupied space and attribute improvement would need to be very substantial to result in healthy profits. In Fig. 3.1, this is depicted as a new dimension in the product space.

To identify such dimensions, a firm would need to approach the market with an eye toward unarticulated or latent needs (Narver et al., 2000) or towards the needs of emerging segments (Govindarajan and Kopalle, 2004). Moreover, a firm may want to track the behaviors of lead users (Von Hippel, 1986) or individuals that are at the forefront of new cultural, social, or technological trends to see whether they are seeking new benefits relative to mainstream customers using currently available products.[12] In terms of then trying to gauge the demand for a product profile that includes such a new feature or attribute, one needs to exercise care. For example, if still using conjoint analysis so that trade-offs with existing attributes can be ascertained, the new dimension may

---

[11] When the analysis is conducted for an existing brand seeking to reposition by improving one of its attributes, it turns out that the most responsive consumers are not the ones currently very inclined to buy the brand; but rather those that are indifferent between buying the focal firm's current product and all the remaining alternatives in the competitive set.

[12] The use of such approaches is becoming more and more prevalent, as evidenced by a number of recently established third-party providers that offer such services. For example, Tremor is a marketing service firm that '. . . is made up of over a quarter of a million influential teens from across the U.S. Our members help develop product ideas and marketing programs that teens want to talk about' (www.tremor.com).

require the researcher to present prototypes, pictorials or demos that illustrate the manner by which the new dimension is part of the product and how it can be used (Green and Srinivasan, 1990). This also poses a challenge in identifying a representative sample that is most appropriate. Contemplating new dimensions, therefore, involves considerable market uncertainty. Several new consumer research techniques have recently emerged in marketing for attempting to reduce such uncertainty (e.g., Hoeffler, 2003).

With respect to technical uncertainty, the answer is qualified. In some cases, incorporating a new feature or capability into an existing device is fairly straightforward (e.g., if it is already offered in products from a different category), while in other cases it can be difficult and challenging (because it is entirely new to the world). Often there is no obvious or single way to translate the newly identified need into an actionable engineering product specification.

Indeed, because of the market uncertainty and difficulty in gauging demand for a new benefit on the one hand, and the difficulty in selecting or evaluating the technical approach to use in development on the other, firms may find it useful to iteratively involve customers in the development cycle. In a 'probe and learn' approach (Lynn et al., 1996), the firm sequentially experiments with various, often immature, versions of an innovation that offers a new benefit. The key is to learn from each probing what exact form the new benefit should take in the final product, how to trade-it off with other attributes, and which customers are most relevant. Though the process can be expensive and time consuming, the more discontinuous the benefit and the more potential it has for creating a new category, or completely taking over an existing category, the more advantageous this approach becomes. At the very extreme, due to the inherent problems of getting consumers to articulate new benefits they desire, a form of using 'customers as innovators' (Thomke, 2002) may be applicable. In such cases, the firm supplies end users with a flexible toolkit and lets them experiment to create new products.

Despite the greater uncertainties involved (at least from the consumer adoption standpoint), there can be huge advantages to positioning along a new dimension. The firm can brand itself in relation to the new dimension; thereby creating a first mover advantage around being the initial firm to significantly offer the benefit (Lieberman and Montgomery, 1988). Such a strategy may be particularly attractive for new entrants to a market. Existing firms have likely built equities around the ability to deliver reliable performance on the established attributes (which can be accommodated in the formulation of (1) by assuming that each alternative also has a utility component related to brand equity).[13] Hence, providing a new dimension may help overcome a disadvantage with respect to existing equities along the established product dimensions.

---

[13] See, for example, Park and Srinivasan (1994) and references therein.

1.4. Additional considerations and comments

In concluding this section, a number of issues are worth highlighting in connection with the analysis and themes presented thus far.

Horizontal or Vertical Differentiation? The topic of competitive positioning is obviously linked to firms' ability to differentiate in the marketplace. Differentiation is only possible in as much as consumers are heterogeneous; in the context presented here that would mean the part-worth functions of (1) are generally different for each individual (or at least segment). The Industrial Organization literature in Economics has emphasized two distinct types of differentiation: horizontal and vertical (see also Tirole, 1988). Differentiation is purely horizontal if consumers would choose different brands despite prices being equal for all brands. Said differently, the various locations in the product space (excluding price) are valued differently by different consumers. The classic horizontal differentiation model was introduced by Hotelling (1929), in which case each producer (or some characteristic of the product they offer) lies at the extremes of a line of unit length and consumers are distributed along this line.[14] The closer an individual is to one of the products, the more utility derived from that product and the less utility derived from the other product. Each consumer's place on the line reflects his/her ideal point. More recent work has extended the single dimension analysis to multiple dimensions (e.g., Irmen and Thisse, 1998) and shows that firms will tend to maximally differentiate on one attribute but minimally differentiate on other attributes.

In the multi-attribute setting presented in this chapter, horizontal differentiation can be captured in the formulation (1) by assuming that the g_k^i functions take as an argument the 'distance' between the level of each attribute and consumers' preference location or ideal point (see also Schmalensee and Thisse, 1988). Through new product positioning, a firm seeks to identify that profile of attribute levels which minimizes the distance from the ideal point of enough consumers so that they prefer the new product to existing alternatives.

On the other hand, the pure vertical differentiation case is one where all non-price attributes of a product can be lumped into one measure of 'quality.' All consumers agree on the ranking of each product profile in terms of quality. Now, heterogeneity exists in consumers' willingness to pay for greater levels of quality. In other words, with vertical differentiation ideal points are homogeneous and firms can differentiate along the quality dimension (and charge different prices). If a firm offers the same quality location as a rival, intense price competition is likely to ensue. In analytic models of vertical differentiation, where quality location is chosen in a first stage and price in a

---

[14] d'Aspermont et al. (1979) show that when firms are allowed to endogenously choose positions along the line and then compete in price, the equilibrium results in firms maximally differentiated at the extremes of the line.

second stage, two forces operate: each firm would like to choose the quality and price location that a monopolist would choose, but at the same time seeks to avoid locating too close to a rival. In addition, results may depend on the cost assumption. If the marginal cost of production is the same regardless of quality, Shaked and Sutton (1982) show that being the high quality firm yields the higher profits. By contrast, Moorthy (1988) shows that if the marginal cost of production is convex (quadratic) in quality then the lower quality firm will earn higher profits.[15] In the formulation presented in (1), a preference model consistent with pure vertical differentiation would aggregate all non-price attributes and allow only one weight on the aggregate measure to differ by consumers (the weight for price can be normalized to one).

In its general form, expression (1) can capture both types of differentiation. In particular, a mixture will arise even if all consumers agree on the monotonicity of the part-worths g_k^i but have different importance weightings. Only few theoretical models have analyzed firm behavior when both types of differentiation are part of the strategy space. When each firm positions one product, Neven and Thisse (1987) show in a duopoly context that the firms will tend to maximally differentiate on quality (vertical location) and choose the same feature (horizontal location) if the range of the former is relatively higher than the latter, and vice versa. Qu et al. (2005) look at this product-positioning problem from the standpoint of a single firm designing multiple products and show that pure vertical differentiation across the products is never optimal. In fact, under some plausible conditions – such as symmetric design costs, uniform distribution of preferences, and symmetric feature deviation losses to consumers from their ideal point – the firm will find it optimal to design products that have the same quality level, i.e., no vertical differentiation, but that are differentiated on the horizontal dimension. As is evident, the prominent models that have dealt with vertical and horizontal positioning do not incorporate market and technical uncertainties.

New product entry or a new product in the line? Many times a firm already has a product offering in the category. The critical question is then whether the firm plans on phasing out its current offering and introducing a new product or whether it seeks to have multiple products in the category. In the former case, the considerations are similar to those of a new entrant – with the caveat that the prevailing market conditions, such as the pricing and marketing actions of rivals, take into account the firm's current product. In the latter case of multiple products, a firm must understand the cannibalization implications of the new product and perform a joint maximization; as the firm optimizes (2) it will have to take into account that some of the existing offerings are its

---

[15] This is true when firms choose their qualities simultaneously in the first stage. When qualities are chosen sequentially, once again the higher quality firm earns higher profits.

own. In particular, in the case that firms are allowed to re-price, the focal firm will be setting the price of its existing and new products simultaneously so that joint profits are optimized.

Optimal attribute location or optimal concept selection? The framework presented thus far has assumed that each product in the space has a profile that can be described and formalized. Product dimensions, expressed as physical product attributes or perceived consumer benefits, were well-defined. For all practical purposes, this meant that attribute levels were quantifiable (numerical degree or absence/presence) and could be incorporated into conjoint studies. However, in some cases there are product aspects that do not fall squarely into this paradigm. This happens when there is no reliable and generally accepted measure that can order the set of products based on these aspects. Srinivasan et al. (1997) describe *aesthetics, emotional appeal,* and *usability* as three prominent such dimensions and offer a way to present consumers with product concepts for gauging future demand and selecting an optimal concept to introduce. The marketplace is replete with examples of firms that have competitively positioned around such non-quantifiable dimensions (e.g., Apple's desktop designs and color schemes compared to designs for most IBM PCs).

Product Positioning or Perceptual Mapping? As depicted in Fig. 3.1, the multi-attribute framework can be used to construct a map of the locations of existing products. Though product attributes form the least ambiguous way of describing the market structure, many scholars have emphasized that due to the manner by which consumers process information, there may exist intermediate constructs, referred to as perceptions, by which consumers interpret the physical attributes (Hauser and Simmie, 1981). Of course, to influence choice, firms would need to take such perceptions into account. This is also the reason why representations of products in a space for purposes of identifying new product positioning opportunities is sometimes referred to as perceptual mapping.

Once a perceptual map is constructed, there is a managerial belief that new products should be introduced to 'fill the holes' in this map (Moorthy, 1988; Dolan, 1990). While there might be some validity to thinking that a location that is furthest away from a set of existing brands is a recipe for success, without the full consideration of the underlying distribution of preferences, the incorporation of competitive response (at least in pricing), and a sound criterion for optimizing actions – this will likely lead to suboptimal positioning. Because the approach of filling the holes is based on 'distance' from other alternatives, a common way to construct a perceptual map is based on similarity judgments (Dolan, 1990), i.e., respondents are asked to provide a measure of how each of the existing alternatives is similar to the others (with n existing alternatives this would result in $(n)*(n-1)/2$ pairs to evaluate, and multidimensional scaling can be used to analyze the data). The approach can also be expanded to include a new product concept and check where it falls in the perceptual map vis-à-vis existing options. Such approaches are generally limited in their ability to yield quantitative predictions of demand and to allow competitive reactions.

Process Innovation: Though this chapter focuses on product innovation as a way to succeed in the face of competitive offerings, firms may engage in R&D strategies aimed at creating new processes that reduce the variable costs of producing existing products. This allows lowering price. Process innovation can be particularly powerful when enough consumers are very price sensitive and don't require very high product performance or complex benefits.

2. Industry position, market evolution, and NPD strategy

In the previous section, we described a process for competitive product positioning that was based on delineating the market structure (how consumers base their purchase decisions on a set of attribute bundles, and which market offerings are in their evoked set). This enables finding optimal new interior locations, improvement directions, or new dimensions along which to innovate. The advantages of the approach presented thus far are its micro-level characterization of the features included in the product and consumer preference for them, and the ability to characterize how different new market offerings would fare relative to the positioning of competitors' existing products. The analysis also allowed understanding the implications of uncertainty (market, technical, and production) on the future profitability of a proposed new product.

But to better understand the incentives to incur development costs on a given new product opportunity, and to more precisely characterizes how firms compete with each other in NPD strategies, it is often useful to abstract from detailed product profiles. This is fruitful if one can meaningfully capture the essence of a proposed new product opportunity, in terms of its reward potential and associated ex-ante risk, in a parsimonious way (i.e., without getting explicitly into full product specs). Though sacrificing on the specific details of new product offerings, and their exact relation to what rivals have been offering, such an approach can often better represent the outcome of NPD competition in terms of the future relative performance in securing economic rents. Firms can be modeled as occupying distinct industry positions based on the relative success of their new products. The identity of the firm in a given position could change depending on who competes more effectively or aggressively in the next round of NPD, thus allowing for a more dynamic view. This makes it possible to examine the strategic interaction among firms at a much more detailed level. In particular, one can study all firms' considerations for NPD – compared to the previous section where actions of rivals were restricted to pricing.

As explained, the level of abstraction in market offering performance often takes a discrete form – that is, there are a number of distinct industry positions a firm can occupy. In many industries there tend to emerge a very small number of firms, typically even a single firm, that hold the lion's share of profits, while other firms lag behind and either make normal profits or lose money. The reasons for being in an advantageous industry position can be rooted in having introduced a product that: embodies superior performance or quality on a certain dimension (vertical advantage), that pre-empted the most favorable market space in terms of consumer tastes (horizontal advantage), or that is produced at lower cost. In some cases, patents can be secured that are difficult to circumvent and provide a source of monopoly rents. If the sales dynamics are such that increasing returns to scale arise, either on the demand-side through network externalities or on the supply-side through learning by doing, then subsequent to new product introductions one dominant industry leader will likely emerge through winner-take-all eventualities. In other markets, alongside superior versus inferior positions there may also exist equal level positions; particularly if product market competition is not very intense (as in a Cournot or multinomial logit set-up). In such instances, firms can earn roughly the same profits.

Being in a certain industry position need not always be directly linked to new product success. However, the desire to dislodge an industry incumbent, and at the same time the manner by which industry leaders seek to stay on top, is primarily achieved through NPD. Therefore, the extant literature has devoted much attention to how firms' relative position in an industry evolves through actions that clearly apply to the new product development setting. Significant emphasis has been given to decisions regarding: how much and where to direct R&D effort, the timing of new product introduction, whether to acquire market information upfront, and whether to pre-announce. Given the focus on strategic interaction, many of the models constructed to understand and offer guidance on firm behavior employ game-theory. The common terminology refers to the firm occupying the most favorable position as the 'leader' or incumbent and refers to all other firms as 'followers' or entrants. A central question that has been asked in this context is whether to expect continued incumbent dominance, that is, whether the firm currently in the lead industry position will tend to stay in the lead with the next generation of new products. The distinct industry positions are often described as linked directly to the technology, quality, or performance level embodied in the firms' products (with the leader having the most advanced level).

2.1. The nature of competition with new products and industry evolution

Most models allow for a discrete number of industry positions and differ in the manner in which a follower can advance: Leapfrogging or Step-By-Step. Many treatments here assume one indistinguishable direction that R&D takes and are only concerned with the final outcome – which firm moves into which position. More recent models have explicitly considered the issue of endogenous path selection. We elaborate on such models and the implications for new product planning decisions later.

Leapfrogging – in these models the only way for a follower to advance is by superseding the erstwhile incumbent. R&D is typically stochastic and success is restricted to only one firm. Common scenarios (see also Reinganum, 1989) include patent races – in which the firm that introduces the innovation first is awarded monopoly rents for the duration of the patent, and tournaments – where firms compete as in a contest-like fashion with only one winner.[16] One can also construct deterministic bidding models to capture leapfrogging (the firm that bids the most is the one to introduce the new product and hence become the leader). Leapfrogging models are much in the spirit of Schumpeter's (1942) description of markets evolving through 'creative destruction.' In discrete analyses, two industry positions are necessary: at any given moment there is a leader and a follower but the identity of the firms in each position can change over time (see Fig. 3.3).

Step-by-Step – in such models a laggard firm cannot overtake the leadership position in one R&D round. Instead it must first catch-up and draw level with the current leader and only then can it advance further. This gives rise to at least three industry positions (and two states of the industry, see Fig. 3.3).

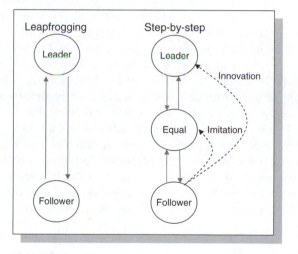

Figure 3.3
Industry progress paths.

[16] With leapfrogging, when R&D follows a success/failure pattern then if more than one firm succeeds it is typically assumed that with an arbitrary probability one firm advances (or wins the patent) while the others lose.

With the simple three-position scenario, when the entrant succeeds in its R&D efforts while the incumbent fails, the two firms evolve into an equal state. From there, in the next round one firm can become the leader while the other the follower (or if more than one firm succeeds in the equal state then the firms can stay level). Of course, if the leader succeeds then the firms stay in their respective positions. If products are indexed along a quality ladder, then one can allow an infinite number of ordered positions, with the firms progressing along the this ladder in increments of one step every time R&D efforts are successful (Aghion et al., 2001).

2.2. Incentives to undertake R&D and industry position

In both leapfrogging and step-by-step models, one can identify several general effects that influence firms' incentives to invest in R&D, and hence impact the evolution of industry structure. It is common to assume that firms are risk-neutral and maximize expected payoffs.

The Efficiency Effect – relates to the sum of firms' profits following the introduction of an innovation. If joint profits are higher when a particular firm innovates rather than a rival, this results in higher incentives for that firm to invest in R&D. For example, if the incumbent retains monopoly profits when it innovates and those profits are higher than the sum of entrant and incumbent profits if the entrant succeeds, we can expect greater incumbent R&D level and prolonged dominance as the industry pattern.[17] The nature of how firms compete in a market given their product offerings obviously impacts joint duopoly profits and hence bears on the efficiency effect. Vickers (1986) shows that under Cournot competition an alternating pattern of leadership tends to emerge where firms take turns being in the lead position, whereas under Bertrand competition incumbent dominance tends to be sustained.

The efficiency effect is also related to what has been termed a 'preemptive incentive.' This incentive is linked to the difference in a firm's (competitive) profits if it innovates as opposed to its rival. A firm will have a greater desire to invest in R&D than its rival if its preemptive incentive is higher.[18]

The Replacement Effect – relates to fact that the incumbent is currently earning profits and thus has less of an incentive to shorten the duration till a new product is introduced than rivals do. When the replacement effect is

---

[17] This is related to whether an innovation is 'drastic' or 'incremental' in the economic sense (Arrow 1962), i.e., whether the new technology obsoletes the old one or not.

[18] The relationship is easy to show mathematically. Consider a duopoly where the efficiency effect would compare $\pi_E(S) + \pi_I(F)$ to $\pi_E(F) + \pi_I(S)$, where subscripts are for entrant and incumbent, respectively, and (S,F) denote success and failure in NPD, respectively. The preemptive effect would be linked to $\pi_E(S) - \pi_E(F)$ vs. $\pi_I(S) - \pi_I(F)$. Clearly setting up an inequality expression and re-arranging terms one can show the equivalence of these two comparisons.

prevalent, followers typically have a greater incentive to invest in R&D and leadership tends to change hands from generation to generation.

The replacement effect is also related to what has been termed a 'stand-alone' incentive (Katz and Shapiro, 1987), whereby a firm compares its increase in profits from innovating assuming its rival fails (or decides not to develop). If a next-generation merely obsoletes the current technology, then an incumbent's stand alone incentive is zero whereas a challenging entrant has the full extent of monopoly rewards as an incentive. If, on the other hand, an incumbent can reap higher rewards from the innovation (due say to marketing advantages, reputation, or consumer loyalty), then the incumbent may have a higher stand-alone incentive than a rival for a given innovation.

2.3. Capability differences related to industry position and R&D incentives

The effects outlined above on firms' incentives to invest in R&D had to do directly with the profit structure and nature of product market competition. That said, one might expect that being in a certain industry position affects capabilities that bear on the success or failure of new product efforts. This can have two implications: First, firms' marginal productivity of R&D can be different. Second, firms might have an incentive to attain a certain position due to the advantages conferred for next-generation product success. Conceptual work in strategy and marketing (Wernerfelt, 1984; Day, 1994) has emphasizing firm-specific capabilities and assets as impacting performance in an industry. When this is taken a step further, one would like to understand how the existence of and opportunity to obtain capability differences plays out in the NPD context. The notion of dynamic capabilities (Teece et al., 1997) can be seen as highlighting the need for such an understanding. We focus first on advantages that have been identified as accruing to industry leaders. In as much as these advantages are semi-permanent, i.e., cannot be imitated or do not dissipate too quickly, they bear on how firms strategically approach NPD competition and their incentives to invest in R&D.

Innovative Advantage – if a firm has attained the lead industry position because its current offering embodies the most advanced state-of-the-art technology or design, it is plausible that it has accumulated a certain degree of R&D know-how that may be relevant for future product generations; this can be in the actual skills of the engineers, the way R&D is managed, or the way information relevant for innovation flows in the organization. Prominent examples of this include Intel's ability in the mid-1990s to 'double-up-on-design,' whereby engineers from the current version being developed would already be re-assigned to design the next generation microprocessor, and evidence from the pharmaceutical industry on the effectiveness of current R&D

based on past success in discovery (Henderson and Cockburn, 1994). When this is the case, at any given level of investment an additional dollar spent on R&D by the leader yields a higher marginal increase in success probability than by followers. In the context of a tournament model, Ofek and Sarvary (2003) show that with innovative advantage leaders will tend to invest more than followers and retain their lead position over time. At the extreme, one could assume that only the incumbent has innovative capability and the only role for rivals is to put pressure on the incumbent by being able to introduce clones (Purohit, 1994).

Reputation Advantage – In some cases, being in the lead position engenders certain intangible advantages that become relevant for the next-generation of products. For example, consumers may place more weight on new product claims from an established firm than from an unknown entrant; having current relations with channel members can form the basis for more easily pushing a new product in the future (see also Chandy and Tellis (2000) for sources of reputation advantage). All these can result in greater chances for the success of a new product by the current leader relative to followers. Here, Ofek and Sarvary (2003) show that the incumbent firm will be induced to invest less in R&D (indirectly, its R&D productivity is reduced) while rivals are motivated strongly by the prospect of attaining reputation advantage in the future. Hence, leadership shifts will be relatively frequent.[19]

Disadvantages to Incumbency – Though there have been several empirical accounts of ways in which current leaders leverage their position for future new product success; there are also several arguments and pieces of evidence to the contrary. It has been claimed that current leadership fosters organizational structures that can filter out important information, resulting in less effective new product skills (Henderson and Clark, 1990). If the leader keeps honing the skills necessary to have developed the current successful product, this may result in core rigidities (Leonard-Barton, 1992) on the technology side with respect to the ability to develop an alternative next-generation winning design. When this is the case, one can expect the leader to under-invest in R&D in the direction for which it is disadvantaged. Furthermore, having an installed base of customers that incur a cost when switching to an entrant's product (seemingly an advantage to incumbency), yields investment inertia on the part of the incumbent due to cannibalization fears (Ghemawat, 1991).[20]

---

[19] Ofek and Sarvary (2003) show that the R&D level of the incumbent has an inverted-U pattern when innovative advantage increases, while follower R&D level has an inverted-U pattern when reputation advantage increases.

[20] In his model, the incumbent can sell its old generation product even when an entrant introduces a new generation product. Hence, the incumbent's incentives to invest in the next-generation product are lower (this is related to the replacement effect described earlier).

2.4. Competition and innovation path selection

While the 'one-dimensional' view of next-generation product development (as in the quality ladder representation of NPD) yields excellent insights into the incentives to invest in R&D effort and into the evolution of market structure, it does not capture one of the most important dilemmas confronting firms in the new product planning phase – where should these efforts be directed? As one sifts through recent management articles and the trade press regarding innovation, one observes that the choice of which new product path to focus on is at the heart of what has been documented to separate winners from losers. For example, in the late 1980s firms in the disk drive industry, such as Seagate and Conner, were contemplating improving memory capacity versus reducing the size of drives (Christensen, 1997); recently firms in the cell phone handset market (Nokia and Motorola) faced a decision on whether to invest in the 'candy-bar' style of phones versus the 'clam-shell' design (Economist, 2004).

The decision regarding which new product opportunity to pursue is governed by (a) how uncertain a firm is about the rewards to a given innovation path, (b) how uncertain the project is from the standpoint of developing the technology, (c) which path the rival will be taking, (d) what is the initial industry position of the firm. Each of these considerations impacts the risk-reward structure that the firm needs to consider. There is also the possibility of differences in firms' assessment of the market potential or the technical difficulties of each new product opportunity. Furthermore, the need to incorporate strategic interactions gives rise to other issues, such as whether to pre-announce the path pursued and whether to take more time upfront in market research or rush to develop. We discuss these issues as they relate to specific types of innovation path decisions firms face.

Risky or Safe Path? Different R&D projects can entail different levels of ex-ante perceived risk (as measured by the variance of the random reward). The substantive question is, given two projects with equal expected return, when would a firm select the high risk–high reward project over the low risk–low reward project? Cabral (2003) studies this problem within the leader-follower paradigm by fixing the R&D budget. The safe path can advance a firm one step forward with certainty while the risky path can advance a firm two steps with some probability less than one; the second path is a mean preserving spread of the first but with greater reward variance. He establishes the conditions for the follower to prefer the risky path (an attitude of 'having nothing to lose') while the incumbent chooses the safe path.

Correlated or Uncorrelated Paths? The asymmetry in firm positions, leader-follower, also has implications for the degree of correlation in NPD paths that firms prefer. In a quality-ladder setup (each R&D success moves a firm one step up the ladder), if payoffs are concave as a function of the gap between firms (in terms of the number of steps that separate them), then the leader has more to lose from being caught up by the follower than from extending its lead (an attitude of 'things can only get worse'). The leader prefers to choose a path that is correlated with the follower so that the current gap between them remains constant (since if both succeed they move concomitantly one step up). The follower, on the other hand, typically has a convex payoff in improving its state from lagging to being level. Hence, it prefers a path that is uncorrelated with the leader's so that if it succeeds (and the leader fails), it can indeed catch-up (an attitude of 'things can only get better'). If one path is more promising ex-ante, i.e., is more probable to succeed and hence yields greater expected payoffs, then Cabral (2002) shows that the leader will choose the more promising path while the follower the less promising but uncorrelated path. This will result in increasing dominance on average.

Innovation or Imitation? When considering market entry, a firm faces a decision between developing a product that embodies the same technical sophistication and features as in products currently offered by an incumbent in the market, vis-à-vis attempting to drastically improve on the current state-of-the-art. The innovation-imitation dilemma in some sense endogenizes the question of whether industry structure progresses in a leapfrogging or step-by-step fashion (see Fig. 3.3). Ofek and Turut (2007) examine how an entrant would decide between these paths while allowing the incumbent firm to innovate. They show that the likelihood of incumbent dominance follows an inverse-U shape pattern in the profit levels (duopoly and monopoly) and in the R&D cost factor – this pattern can only arise if the decision between innovation and imitation is endogenous.[21] Another interesting feature is that if the entrant conducts upfront market research (to resolve market uncertainty) – then the entry NPD strategy it pursues may reveal fully, partially, or not at all the information that it has obtained from the market research to the incumbent.

In terms of linking back to the previous section: imitative effort can be regarded as developing a product that is close to an existing alternative in the attribute space or that offers a different combination of attribute levels that results in roughly equal profits from (2) (*locating in Unoccupied Space*). Drastic innovative effort can be regarded as significantly improving on an existing attribute(s) or offering a completely new dimension (*Attribute Improvement* or *Pre-empting a New Attribute/Dimension*).

Radical or Incremental? A radical product innovation has been classified as that which 'incorporates a substantially different core technology and provides substantially higher customer benefits relative to previous products in the industry' (Chandy and Tellis, 2000). By contrast, incremental innovations

---

[21] Interestingly, it is shown that in terms of R&D responsiveness, the incumbent has a reactive approach to R&D-increasing its level whenever it senses the entrant is inclined to choose a higher R&D level- while the opposite is true for the entrant.

typically build on existing technology and offer only limited additional benefits. In the field of innovation, a question that has received much attention is whether to expect incumbents to undertake a radical versus incremental path. Many accounts have depicted incumbents as being sluggish with respect to radical but aggressive with respect to incremental (Christensen, 1997; Henderson, 1993). Common reasons forwarded are: a desire to avoid cannibalizing existing development or marketing assets relevant only for the incremental path, too much focus on existing customers and their inability to articulate future needs as opposed to focusing on emerging segments, and internal information processing barriers that create a bias towards incremental NPD. The point made is that these firms may still invest heavily into R&D but that they direct their efforts towards the incremental rather than radical path. More recent literature, however, has shown that this view may have been based on only selective evidence. A more rigorous sampling of new product data reveals that incumbents are responsible for roughly the same proportion of radical innovations as non-incumbents (Chandy and Tellis, 2000).

Turut and Ofek (2006) have examined this topic from a novel perspective. Assuming that firms are roughly equally competent in terms of development skills, they examine the implications of differences in market potential assessment. This is quite realistic; given the huge difficulty in predicting market acceptance for radical innovations, each firm will possibly receive a different private signal for market potential. Moreover, the reliability of such signals can differ across industry position; capturing the asymmetries described in the literature regarding the advantages or disadvantages to leadership in this respect (Jovanovic and Rob, 1987 versus Christensen 1997). Two prominent results in Turut and Ofek (2006) show that an incumbent firm might act counter to the private signal it receives regarding the market potential for radical innovation: (1) if the entrant's signal is relatively unreliable, then despite receiving a high signal the incumbent might still optimally decide to pursue incremental innovation – the reason is to avoid validating the high market potential to the entrant. (2) Conversely, if the incumbent's signal is relatively unreliable, then despite receiving a low signal the incumbent might still pursue radical innovation – the reason is to be preemptive and avoid letting the entrant think that it is the only firm developing the radical innovation. In both cases, the end result is a less aggressive entrant. When the signal reliabilities of the firms are roughly equal, the incumbent acts on its signal (radical if signal is high, incremental if signal is low).

Linking back to the previous section: incremental innovation can be regarded as improving on an attribute(s) only to certain degree, and radical innovation as significantly improving on an attribute (that consumers place considerable weight on) or offering a completely new dimension (i.e., significant *Attribute Improvement* or *Pre-empting a New Attribute/Dimension*).

Ex-ante firms might be uncertain about whether the new feature or dimension would be valued or whether consumers care enough about a huge improvement in a given attribute.

Which attribute to innovate upon? Study the market or speed to market? In many NPD contexts, firms are aware of the possible features or attributes end-users might care about but are not sure which is more important ex ante. Due to dis-economies of scope in R&D, it is often not economically viable to pursue multiple NPD paths and firms will have to choose a single path.[22] Hence, firms need to decide upfront which attribute will be the focus of their innovative efforts. Moreover, firms may have an incentive to conduct upfront market research to resolve market uncertainty prior to making R&D decisions (direction and amount). This would correspond to the strategic desire to conduct Step 2 in the framework of the previous section. Lauga and Ofek (2006) examine these issues by looking at identical firms, thus eliminating any asymmetries in capabilities or industry position. They find that asymmetric equilibria in firm actions can arise, either in the decision to conduct upfront market research, the decision on which attribute to innovate upon, or both decisions. When market research costs are low, both firms conduct market research. Because they both discover which attribute is preferred by consumers, they choose the same NPD path. When at the other extreme market research costs are high, neither firm conducts such research. Here, an interplay between market uncertainty and technical uncertainty emerges: under high development costs both firms choose the same NPD path, while under low development costs and high market uncertainty each firm chooses a different attribute to innovate upon.[23] When the cost of market research is in a mid-range, an asymmetric equilibrium emerges whereby only one firm conducts market research; reflecting the fact that the value of information on consumer tastes goes down when your rival possesses it as well (so at a mid cost level one firm forgoes market research). In this case, the firm that conducts market research selects a higher R&D level than its rival – this is because market research increases the marginal productivity of R&D effort by directing the effort to the higher reward. This asymmetric equilibrium can also hold if market research significantly delays launch. In this case, the firm that forgoes market research and speeds to market may invest more in R&D

---

[22] Consider the decision between improving the passenger capacity or speed of airplanes. Boeing and Airbus made distinct decisions in this regard; Airbus went for capacity and Boeing for speed and fuel efficiency (*Economist,* 2002).

[23] The intuition is that when development is expensive firms can only afford low R&D levels; hence the likelihood that both firms succeed in their R&D efforts is low and each firm worries more about market uncertainty (which is common). When development costs are low the reverse occurs and firms worry more about launching identical products that compete fiercely and hence they differentiate.

than its rival that takes the time to study the market. These results help understand under what conditions a firm that is more market oriented (by spending resources on learning about consumers; Narver et al. (2000)), is then more or less technology oriented (by spending more or less on R&D; Gatignon and Xuereb (1997)).

3. Limits to existing theory, directions for future research, and concluding remarks

A new product is ultimately deemed a success from the firm's standpoint if enough end consumers choose to buy it over what competitors offer. The resulting profits (after accounting for production costs) should be sustainable for enough time to at least recoup the costs of upfront development. Research in the domain of competitive new product positioning has therefore attempted to shed light on (1) how to conceptualize and estimate consumer demand for new market offerings and (2) how to incorporate competitive considerations. In closing this chapter, it is useful to briefly summarize our current understanding of these two areas and to reflect on where there seem to be gaps or inadequacies that future research could hopefully address.

3.1. Consumer demand for new products and the reference to existing products

At the heart of characterizing profitable locations to position new products is measuring and anticipating consumers' desire for the proposed benefits. We have discussed in this chapter three primary areas that serve as potential avenues (see also Fig. 3.1). (*i*) Locating within the effective frontier – that is, finding a feasible new combination of existing attributes that is not dominated by any of the current offerings, (*ii*) Improving on the maximal levels of attributes currently offered so that new offerings dominate (at least some of) the existing ones, (*iii*) Establishing a new benefit or dimension which consumers care about. Though we have discussed common ways in which firms can attempt to quantify consumer acceptance for each of these new product opportunities, recent evidence in the technology management and strategy domains suggest gaps in current approaches that can lead to suboptimal decisions. At the core of these limitations is a sense that consumer information, gathered in advance of development, may be misleading. We list several of the prominent situations and conjecture on sources of the problem.

a) Difficulties When More of One Attribute but Less of Another are Offered – As noted, most product development efforts entail dis-economies of scope. In the context of the themes presented in this chapter, this means that when a firm tries to significantly improve on one dimension it may be difficult to keep offering high levels on other dimensions (at least in the short run), or that less of existing features can be offered when trying to accommodate a new feature into the product. For instance, increasing the speed of a processor may lead to higher heat emission, or building a faster aircraft may make it difficult to keep its passenger capacity high. This may create serious problems when trying to estimate demand for new products that embody such trade-offs. It would further seem that disruptive technologies (Christensen, 1997) are sometimes ignored as viable opportunities because many potential customers that are polled respond negatively to a new product that offers improvement on one attribute (e.g., a reduction in the size of the disk drive) while worsening another attribute (e.g., getting much lower disk drive memory capacity).[24] The problem seems to be that in market research to guide development, consumers tend to overweigh the downside of being offered less on some dimensions (having been used to getting high levels), to underweigh the upside of being offered more on other dimensions, or both. This issue may be related to prospect theory (Kahneman and Tversky, 1979), which suggests that 'losses loom larger than gains' in decision-making. The problem may also be related to which decision rules consumers use to evaluate potential new products (e.g., a lexicographic rule may lead to dismissing the new product merely because it is slightly inferior on a certain dimension relative to current offerings). Alternatively, given past experience, consumers may have an easier time understanding what it would mean to have less on an existing attribute but are quite unsure about how much utility they will derive from more of a different attribute – leading them to base their response on the aspects that they are more confident about. Of course, ex-post and over time it may turn out that improvement on a secondary attribute is of significant value to consumers and that lower levels of attributes currently perceived as primary are less detrimental to utility than consumers originally thought. Future research could provide better ways for firms to deal with this issue. Models may be constructed that correct for these biases so that a firm receives a more accurate picture. On the other hand, perhaps new ways to engage consumers in the market research task can be devised. At a minimum, more work is needed to identify in which contexts customers that use existing offerings exhibit such biases.

---

[24] Particularly if this latter attribute is currently perceived as primary. Part of the account in the emergence of disruptive technologies is related to the issue of whom the innovation is initially targeted to and the dynamics of demand – this is picked up in the next item discussed in this section.

b) Aggregation Issues and the Relevance of Serving New Segments – Step 4 in the procedure described for selecting a new product location calls for aggregating the respondents' preferences in the sample (either their deterministic choice or probability of adopting) to produce a market share metric. Though this procedure allows getting a single metric for revenue and profitability, which may be particularly useful when quick decision-making is required, there are several dangers involved in aggregation. If only a small portion of respondents exhibits a strong demand for improvement on a specific dimension or new feature, while the majority is pulling in a different direction, the former will likely be ignored in the aggregation process. Even if the new product planning team observes that demand is non-uniform, the question is when to ignore smaller segments as being insignificant and when to pay more attention to them because they may be indicative of where demand is evolving. In part, the examples given in Blue Ocean Strategy (Kim and Mauborgne, 2004) reveal that offering new dimensions while divesting others may appeal to different segments than those that comprise the bulk of demand for current offerings (for instance, the concept behind Cirque de Soleil appeals to adults and corporate clients and not children or parents looking for entertainment for kids) – and that over time these new segments turn out to be quite big. Several issues may hinder firms' ability to identify these new segments and hence pursue the development of products that cater to them. First, because firms typically frame their effort as finding a new product that will compete 'in the category,' they seek input from subjects that are currently heavy users of existing products – in which case the aggregation problem will be very acute because very few consumers that belong to other segments will be included to begin with. Second, the market research itself may frame consumers to think they are being asked to respond about existing benefits; thus, even if there are sufficient individuals in the sample that may be part of the new segment, their responses will tend to conform to the way the research has been framed. The challenge for future research is to provide better means for conducting the relevant research to pick up on new segments that may value new dimensions. Even if new segments are acknowledged, they may be too small at first and only grow over time. In this case, the firm is left with the problem of separating 'noise from signal' – for many new dimensions tested there will seem to be some consumer segments that exhibit a desire for them. What may be lacking is an approach to correctly extrapolate from the responses of small emerging segments, and determine which of them will grow to be representative of the bulk of future demand.

c) Managing the Leap from Early Adopters to Early Switchers – It has been recognized in a number of studies (e.g., Rogers, 2003) that new products typically get adopted in phases – starting with the early market (innovators and early adopters) to the main market (early majority and late majority). When trying to identify novel opportunities, firms often seek the input of potential innovators and early adopters, who are presumed to be at the forefront of the curve and can even help in co-design and innovation (as lead users). When products are initially launched, they are often targeted to the early market to start the adoption process and serve a reference for later segments. However, more often than not, foreseeing adoption by the main market proves to be challenging. The problem is that while a number of opportunities present themselves from the standpoint of the early market, the firm needs to decide which one to bet on with respect to later success with the main market. A firm would be advised to anticipate this issue in advance of actually developing the product to avoid ultimate product failure due to the inability to conquer enough mainstream customers. The theory of the 'chasm' (Moore, 1995) is consistent with the above characterization, and proposes strategies to assist in moving from the early market to the main market post-launch. Three issues are potentially relevant for future research. First, Moore's theory has mainly dealt with business to business type products (e.g., enterprise software) and the link to consumer products is not well established. Second, if indeed ultimate success hinges on getting several main market adopters to switch from their current products to new ones, this may have implications for the new product-planning phase of development. More often than not firms have a number of options on where to position new products but need to decide which one(s) to actually develop. If firms could ascertain which of these options has a higher chance of actually getting main market customers to switch – this would increase the odds of commercial success.[25] What is lacking is a process to analyze upfront the existence of main market customers prone to switch (in analogy to the way lead users can be identified); these 'lead switchers' would be indicators of how a product will continue to diffuse after initial success in the early market.

3.2. Competitive new-product reaction and anticipation

The reality is that new products typically have to compete for consumer demand. Indeed, most new products are developed in order to improve a firm's standing relative to rivals. Positioning in marketing terms embodies the notion of a unique selling proposition relative to what rivals offer.[26] In this chapter,

---

[25] It is highly unlikely that all innovations can cross the chasm, even if the appropriate steps in Moore (1995) are taken post launch. In this case, having a way to screen out opportunities upfront based on a better understanding of what it would take, in a given market, to cross to the main market would be useful.

[26] See, e.g., Deshpande (2000).

an attempt has been made to explain how translating consumer preferences for various benefits can help a firm competitively position a new product. Abstracting away from specific product features, we have also been able to examine the interaction among firms with respect to their NPD strategies. This afforded a more dynamic analysis of the competitive landscape, with firms seeking to evolve into positions that generated greater economic rents. Though existing research provides many useful models and frameworks to incorporate rival actions, there are several areas where a greater understanding could help firms formulate more effective NPD strategy.

a) Level of Analysis of Competitors' Actions and the Relevance to Actual Management Practice – It is obvious from the treatment in this chapter that the more micro-level one gets in terms of actual product characteristics (i.e., on which specific attributes development will take place) the more difficult it gets to incorporate reactions by rivals. This is particularly true if one wishes to anticipate the characteristics that rivals will potentially innovate upon and at the same time include the full mix of strategic factors related to new product success – such as pricing, advertising, trade deals and slotting allowances, and partnerships with complementary product suppliers. Moreover, most models that employ game-theory to incorporate rival actions need to make numerous abstractions to remain tractable. Two issues arise here. First, there is the question of how representative is game-theoretic analysis of how managers actually treat NPD. It would be useful to try and understand better what assumptions firms make about their rivals, how much they invest in competitive intelligence, and in what way they make NPD decisions that incorporate rival activity. This can be done through interviews or surveys. Second, there is room for more work on how to construct models that are good approximations of how real NPD projects unfold competitively, provide sufficient guidance to firms on how to make decisions, and yet at the same time are not overly complex. More empirical tests of existing theory would be useful in shedding light on how to refine existing models and confirm or disconfirm the assumptions in the literature.

b) 'Co-location' of New Products and Positive Reinforcement Oligopoly Profits – it is generally assumed that differentiation is what the firm seeks to achieve with a new product – either vertically by offering much greater performance on a key attribute or horizontally by mapping better to the taste or ideal point of some consumers. Differentiation is generally considered desirable as it softens competition on price or quantity and hence leads to higher profits. However, there seems to be a sense that in some instances, particularly when new dimensions or categories are being created, that it may be beneficial for multiple firms to offer similar products. There could be several reasons: more firms embracing a certain feature or attribute reduces uncertainty for consumers or retail partners with respect to the need for the feature and its reliability; multiple firms will create more awareness than a single firm (through advertising and other communications); only when multiple firms offer similar new products will indirect network externalities emerge to induce switching away from existing products. Such benefits to the co-location of new products may introduce incentives for 'co-opetition' (Brandenburger and Nalebuff, 1996) or collaboration among firms in NPD, which have not been fully explored in the extant literature. It also means there is a need to better understand when similar positioning in the attribute space of new products is beneficial to firms due to the above forces (even if for a limited time), versus when anticipation of rival positioning should drive the firm to select a very distinct positioning. It would also be useful to understand better the implications of firms introducing similar versus very distinct new products on how consumers perceive or learn about market offerings in the category.

c) The Broader Business Context and Alternatives to New Product Development – Though NPD represents a major avenue for firms to compete effectively, in reality firms weigh developing new products with other strategies they could employ: A firm could decide to not make any changes to the physical product but change the image or the way its product is perceived (e.g., from a safe and reliable car to a more fun and active car). A firm could decide to change the way it captures value with an existing product from customers (e.g., whether it charges separately for certain features that have up to now been included in the main price). A firm could decide to not develop a new core product but rather offer additional add-on benefits or services (e.g., expansion packs for video games, ability to use the product/service in additional formats or contexts such as the internet to listen to satellite radio). A host of other strategies may be possible. Though some of these alternative strategies may be partially translated back into the framework on competitive positioning of new products presented in Section 1 (by reframing them in terms of benefits they provide), more work is needed to understand when developing an entirely new product is the path to take and when other business strategies are better suited.

4. Concluding remarks

New product development has become a strategic agenda item for firms in many industries. The decision regarding which product concepts to develop and launch is no longer driven by technological feasibility concerns alone. Increasingly, firms must consider how to position new products to maximize commercial viability in the face of competition. As this chapter has tried to convey, the product profiles of competitors and their ability to react to a new product at least through pricing, place a significant constraint on the attractiveness of certain locations in the attribute/benefit space, and on which improvement directions are most profitable. At the same time, understanding the incentives of rivals to undertake R&D activity depending on industry position – both direction and level – is critical for a firm as it makes its own R&D decisions.

Ultimately, those firms that are able to anticipate and manage the confluence of Market, Technical, and Competitive pressures on a systematic basis – conducting the analysis with fresh eyes upon each successive generation by using input on consumer tastes, technology advances, and rivals' expected actions – will be the ones most likely to repeatedly succeed in positioning new products.

References

Aghion, P., C. Harris, P. Howitt, and J. Vickers 2001. "Competition, Imitation, and Growth with Step-by-Step Innovation," *Review of Economic Studies*, 68, 467–492.

Arrow, K. J. 1962. "Economic Welfare and the Allocation of Resources for Inventions," In: R. Nelson, (Ed.) *The Rate and Direction of Inventive Activity: Economic and Social Factors*. Princeton, NJ: Princeton University Press.

Anderson, Simon P., Andre De Palma, and Jacque-Francois Thisse 1989. "Demand for Differentiated Products, Discrete Choice Models, and the Characteristics Approach," *The Review of Economic Studies*, 56, 21–35.

Ben-Akiva, Moshe and Steven R. Lerman 1985. *Discrete Choice Analysis: Theory and Applications to Travel Demand*. Cambridge, MA: MIT Press.

Berggren, Eric and Thomas Nacher 2000. "Why Good Ideas Go Bust," *Management Review*, February 1, 32.

Brandenburger, Adam M. and Barry J. Nalebuff 1996. *Co-opetition*. New York: Currency/Doubleday.

Cabral, Luis M. B. 2002. "Increasing Dominance with No Efficiency Effect," *Journal of Economic Theory,* 102, 471–479.

Cabral, Luis M. B. 2003. "R&D Competition When Firms Choose Variance," *Journal of Economics and Management Strategy,* 12 (1), 139–150.

Chandy, Rajesh K. and Gerard J. Tellis 2000. "The Incumbent's Curse? Incumbency, Size, and Radical Product Innovation," *Journal of Marketing*, 64 (3), 1–17.

Choi, S. Chan, Wayne S. DeSarbo, and Patrick T. Harker 1990. "Product Positioning Under Price Competition," *Management Science*, 36 (2), 175–199.

Choi, S. Chan and Wayne S. DeSarbo 1993. "Game Theoretic Derivations of Competitive Strategies in Conjoint Analysis," *Marketing Letters*, 4 (October), 337–348.

Choi, S. Chan and Wayne S. DeSarbo 1994. "A Conjoint-based Product Designing Procedure Incorporating Price Competition," *Journal of Product Innovation Management*, 11, 451–459.

Christensen, Clayton M. 1997. *The Innovators Dilemma: When New Technologies Cause Great Firms to Fail.* Boston MA: Harvard Business School Press.

Clark, Kim B. 1996. "Competing Through Manufacturing and the New Manufacturing Paradigm: Is Manufacturing Strategy Passé?" *Production and Operations Management,* 5 (1), 42–58.

Cooper, R. G. and E. J. Kleinschmidt 1987. "New Products: What Separates Winners from Losers?" *Journal of Product Innovation Management,* 4, 169–184.

d'Aspermont, C., J. Gabszewics, and J. Thisse 1979. "On Hotelling's 'Stability in Competition'," *Econometrica*, 47, 1145–1150.

Day, George S. 1994. "The Capabilities of Market-Driven Organizations," *Journal of Marketing,* 58 (October), 37–52.

Deshpande, Rohit 2000. "Creating Value," Harvard Business School Note, 9-501-039.

Dolan, Robert J. 1990. "Perceptual Mapping: A Manager's Guide," Harvard Business School Note, 9-590-121.

Economist 2002. "Towards the Wild Blue Yonder," New York: The Economist Newspapers Ltd., April 25.

Economist 2004. "Too Many Candy Bars?" New York: The Economist Newspapers Ltd., June 19.

Gatignon, Hubert, Xuereb, Jean-Marc 1997. "Strategic orientation of the firm new product performance," *Journal of Marketing Research*, 34 (1), 77–90.

Ghemawat, Pankaj 1991. "Market Incumbency and Technological Inertia," *Marketing Science*, 10 (2), 161–171.

Govindarajan, Vijay and Praveen K. Kopalle 2004. "Can Incumbents Introduce Radical and Disruptive Innovations?" MSI Report No. 04-100.

Green, Paul E. and V. Srinivasan 1978. "Conjoint Analysis in Consumer Research: Issues and Outlook," *Journal of Consumer Research*, 5 (September), 103–123.

Green, Paul E. and V. Srinivasan 1990. "Conjoint Analysis in Marketing: New Developments With Implications for Research and Practice," *Journal of Marketing*, 54 (October), 3–19.

Green, Paul and Abba Krieger 1992. "An Application of a Product Positioning Model to Pharmaceutical Products," *Marketing Science,* 11, 117–132.

Hauser, John R. and Patricia Simmie 1981. "Profit Maximizing Perceptual Positions: An Integrated Theory for the Selection of Product Features and Price," *Management Science*, 27, 33–56.

Hauser, John R. and Steven M. Shugan 1983. "Defensive Marketing Strategies," *Marketing Science*, 2 (4), 319–359.

Henderson, Rebecca M. and Kim B. Clark. 1990. "Architectural Innovation: The Reconfiguration of Existing Product Technologies and the Failure of Established Firms," *Administrative Science Quarterly*, 35, 9–30.

Henderson, Rebecca 1993. "Underinvestment and Incompetence as Responses to Radical Innovation: Evidence from the Photolithographic Alignment Equipment Industry," *Rand Journal of Economics*, 24 (Summer), 248–271.

Henderson, Rebecca and Ian Cockburn 1994. "Measuring Competence? Exploring Firm Effects in Pharmaceutical Research," *Strategic Management Journal,* 15, 63–84.

Hoeffler, Steve 2003. "Measuring Preferences for Really New Products," *Journal of Marketing Research*, Vol XL (November), 406–420.

Horsky, Dan and Paul Nelson 1992. "New Brand Positioning and Pricing in an Oligopolistic Market," *Marketing Science,* 11 (2), 133–153.

Hotelling, H. 1929. "Stability in Competition," *Economic Journal*, 39, 41–57.

Irmen, Andreas and Jacque-Francois Thisse 1998. "Competition in Multi-Characteristics Spaces: Hotelling Was Almost Right," *Journal of Economic Theory,* 78, 76–102.

Jovanovic, B. and R. Rob 1987. "Demand Driven Innovation and Spatial Competition Over Time," *Review of Economic Studies*, 54, 63–72.

Kahneman, Daniel and Amos Tversky 1979. "Prospect Theory: An Analysis of Decision Under Risk," *Econometrica*, 47 (2), 263–292.

Katz, Michael L. and Carl Shapiro. 1987. "R&D Rivalry with Licensing or Imitation," *The American Economic Review*, 77, 3 (June), 402–420.

Kim, W. Chan and Renee Mauborgne. 2004. "Blue Ocean Strategy," *Harvard Business Review*, October.

Lauga, Dominique and Elie Ofek 2006. "Market Research and Innovation Strategy," HBS Working paper.

Leonard-Barton, D. A. 1992. "Core Capabilities and Core Rigidities: A Paradox in Managing New Product Development," *Strategic Management Journal,* 13, 111–125.

Lieberman, Marvin B. and David B. Montgomery 1988. "First-Mover Advantages," *Strategic Management Journal*, 9 (Summer), 41–58.

Lynn, Gary, Joseph Morone, Albert Paulson 1996. "Marketing and discontinuous innovation: The probe and learn process," *California Management Review*, 38 (3), 8–29.

Moorthy, Sridhar K. 1988. "Product and Price Competition in a Duopoly," *Marketing Science*, 7 (2), 141–168.

Moore, Geoffrey A. 1995. *Inside the Tornado: Marketing Strategies from Silicon Valley's Cutting Edge*. New York: HarperCollins.

National Science Foundation (NSF) 2006. Division of Science Resources Statistics, *National Patterns of Research and Development Resources: 2006*, NSF 05–308, Brandon Shackelford (Arlington, VA 2005).

Narasimhan, Chakravarthi and Subrata K. Sen 1989. "Linking Engineering Attributes to Perceptual Characteristics," Working Paper, New Haven, CT: Yale University.

Narver, John C., Stanley F. Slater, and Douglas F. MacLachlan 2000. "Total Market Orientation, Business Performance, and Innovation," MSI Report No. 00-116.

Neven. D. and J. Thisse 1987. "On Quality and Feature Competition. Economic Decision-Making: Games," *Econometrics and Optimisation*, 7, 175–199.

Ofek, Elie and V. Srinivasan 2002. "How Much Does the Market Value an Improvement in a Product Attribute?" *Marketing Science*, 21 (4), 398–411.

Ofek, Elie and Miklos Sarvary 2003. "R&D, Marketing, and the Success of Next-Generation Products," *Marketing Science*, 22 (3), 355–370.

Ofek, Elie and Ozge Turut 2007. "To Innovate or Imitate? Entry Strategy and the Role of Market Research" HBS Working Paper.

Park, Chan Su and V. Srinivasan 1994. "A Survey Based Method for Measuring and Understanding Brand Equity" *Journal of Marketing Research*, 31 (2), 271–288.

Purohit, Devavrat 1994. "What Should You Do When Your Competitors Send In the Clones?" *Marketing Science*, 13 (Fall), 392–411.

Qu, Chengxin, Stylianos Kavadias, and Christoph Loch 2005. "Product Positioning in a Two-Dimensional Market Space," INSEAD working paper.

Reinganum, Jeniffer 1989. "The Timing of Innovation: Research, Development, and Diffusion," In: *Handbook of Industrial Organization*, Vol. I, Chapter 14.

Rogers, Everett M. 2003. *Diffusion of Innovations*. 5th edition, New York: Free Press.

Schmalensee, Richard and Jacque-Francois Thisse 1988. "Perceptual Maps and the Optimal Location of New Products: An Integrative Essay," *International Journal of Research in Marketing*, 5, 225–259.

Schumpeter, Joseph A. 1942. *Capitalism, Socialism and Democracy*. New York: Harper and Brothers.

Shaked, A. and J. Sutton 1982. "Relaxing Price Competition Through Product Differentiation," *Review of Economic Studies*, 49, 3–13.

Shankar, Venkatesh 1997. "Pioneer's Marketing Mix Reactions to Entry in Different Competitive Game Structures: Theoretical Analysis and Empirical Illustration". *Marketing Science*, 16 (3), 271–293.

Srinivasan V., William S. Lovejoy, and David Beach 1997. "Integrated Product Design for Marketability and Manufacturing," *Journal of Marketing Research,* 34 (February), 154–163.

Tait, Bruce 2002. "Top of Mind," *Brandweek*, April 8.

Teece, David J., Gary Pisano and Amy Shuen. 1997. "Dynamic Capabilities and Strategic Management," *Strategic Management Journal*, 18 (7), 509–533.

Thomke, Stefan E. and Eric von Hippel 2002. "Customers As Innovators: A New Way to Create Value," *Harvard Business Review*, 80, no. 4.

Tirole, Jean 1988. *The Theory of Industrial Organization.* Cambridge MA: MIT press.

Train, Kenneth E. 2003. *Discrete Choice Methods with Simulation.* Cambridge, UK: Cambridge University Press.

Turut, Ozge and Elie Ofek 2006. "When Should a Firm Go Radical? Signaling Market Potential Through Innovation Strategy," HBS working paper.

Vickers, John 1986. "The Evolution of Market Structure When There is a sequence of Innovations," *Journal of Industrial Economics*, 35 (September), 1–12.

Von Hippel, Eric 1986. "Lead Users: A Source of Novel Product Concepts," *Management Science,* 32 (July), 791–805.

Wernerfelt, Birger 1984. "A Resource Based View of the Firm," *Strategic Management Journal*, 5 (2), 171–180.

4 Economic models of product family design and development

Vish V. Krishnan and Karthik Ramachandran

1. Introduction: Product family-based design and development

Firms in many industries are experiencing the need to offer increasing levels of product variety. While the length of the product lifecycle during which profits can be earned is becoming shorter due to intense competition and rapid technological advances, the cost of developing and offering products has been rising sharply due to the increasing technological complexity of products. As a consequence of these trends, the ability to share design elements and development resources across products has become important for such firms to reduce costs and to benefit from product variety (Macduffie et al., 1996; Fisher, Ramdas, and Ulrich, 1999).

In their quest to manage the complexity and costs of product variety while ensuring high levels of product performance, some firms have begun exploring the use of a *product family-based approach to development* (Sanderson and Uzumeri, 1996). In this approach, a firm meets the market need for variety through a family of externally differentiated but internally closely related products. Figure 4.1, from Gupta and Krishnan (1999), illustrates how such an approach differs from a 'conventional' product development process in which individual product variants are developed independently (Pahl and Beitz, 1988). Two key factors differentiate product family development from the conventional individual product-based approach. First, the optimal product line offerings, or number of products and their locations on an attribute space, are decided by integrating marketing, design, manufacturing, and distribution considerations (Dobson and Kalish, 1988; Krishnan, Singh and Tirupati, 1999; Moore et al., 1999). We call this *product family-based design*. Second, the products in a family are *developed* in an integrated manner as much as possible before detailed differences necessitate a more dedicated effort (Gupta and Krishnan, 1999). Integrated product family-based development involves joint decision-making about components and suppliers of a product family, leading

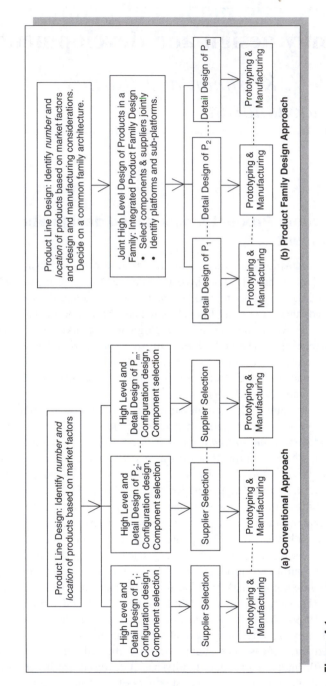

Figure 4.1
Two approaches to product development (from Gupta and Krishnan, 1999).

The following text appears within the figure:

(a) Conventional Approach

Product Line Design: Identify *number and location* of products based on market factors

- High Level and Detail Design of P_1: Configuration design, Component selection
- High Level and Detail Design of P_2: Configuration design, Component selection
- High Level and Detail Design of P_m: Configuration design, Component selection

Supplier Selection

Prototyping & Manufacturing

(b) Product Family Design Approach

Product Line Design: Identify *number* and *location* of products based on market factors and design and manufacturing considerations. Decide on a common family architecture.

Joint High Level Design of Products in a Family: Integrated Product Family Design
- Select components & suppliers jointly
- Identify platforms and sub-platforms.

Detail Design of P_1

Detail Design of P_2

Detail Design of P_m

Prototyping & Manufacturing

to the development of subsystems and vendors common to all the products in the family, thereby maximizing the profits from the product family.

When a firm faces a market of heterogeneous customers, it is useful to offer a *Product Line* that meets individual preferences and functional requirements of different customers. To maximize its profits (especially minimize cost of development, production, and distribution), the set of offerings in the line must be limited in the number and the degree to which they are different from each other. A major source of complexity faced by firms offering product lines is the *proliferation of components and component suppliers*, which leads to higher product development costs and overhead burden. General Motors Corporation, for instance, carried 131 different rear-axle components in its pickup truck division, while the variety of pickup trucks that reached the consumer was much lower (Fonte, 1994).

The classical economic models of product line design do not model the costs of products or the inter-relationships among the products in a line adequately. These inter-relationships are often operationally manifested in the sharing of component subsystems resulting in economies of scale and scope that different products in a firm's line might enjoy. The automotive industry popularized the notion of *product platforms*, which are component and subsystem assets shared across different products. Robertson and Ulrich (1998) define platforms in general as intellectual and material assets shared across a family of product. Figure 4.2 provides a schematic conceptualization of such a platform-based product family. Product family-based development helps address these component and supplier proliferation driven complexity and costs resulting from product line design occasionally by common platforms.

Platform-based approach offers a number of benefits. First, their *'design-once-deploy-throughout the product family'* effect can potentially reduce the fixed cost of developing individual product variants. Second, the platform's greater degree of reuse often encourages firms to invest more time and effort in their design and development, which results in better architecture, tighter integration of components, and lower unit variable cost. Because a platform is common to many products in a line, the shared subsystems may enjoy lower variable costs due to higher volume usage. Platforms may also enhance responsiveness of firms, as the product variants can be developed quickly once time has been invested in architecting and developing the platform.

Though the idea of platform-based design and development is alluring from the perspective of minimizing costs and time, managers typically face challenges in this approach. First, the fixed cost and time of developing platforms can be enormous. Second, sharing a platform across a family with both high- and low-end products may make the products appear similar or lead to the usage of higher functionality and priced components in low-end products.

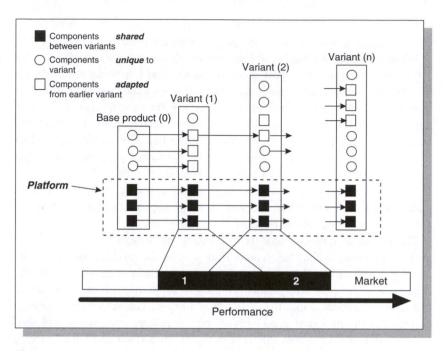

Figure 4.2
Schematic view of a product family (from Krishnan et al., 1999).

Managers face several questions regarding the development of platforms and platform-based product families that will help them meet the conflicting demands placed on design and development activities placed by changing market needs, shrinking budgets, and increasing competitive pressures. In this chapter, we review economic models that have been developed to provide managerial insights on (a) the design of platform-based product lines in achieving profitable product differentiation, (b) balancing trade-offs in making product family-design decisions, and (c) the selection of components and suppliers for a product family.

2. Product family-based development approach: An illustration

While offering a single black Model-T no longer works in today's market environment, designing and developing each offering to a customer's order is still not economically viable despite advances in information technology and development productivity. The set of products that a firm offers clearly depends on the nature of market heterogeneity: specifically whether the market is *vertically differentiated* market (in which customers can be sorted on their willingness to pay for product quality) or *horizontally differentiated* (in which customers differ in their taste and cannot be sorted on their willingness to pay but can be distributed on an attribute space). In this section, we consider an example from a high-technology firm (adapted from Krishnan and Gupta, 2001) to illustrate the benefits of product family-based design in developing a product line for vertically and horizontally differentiated markets.

Accu-Data, a market leader in electronic instrumentation, offers data-acquisition (DAQ) products capable of acquiring data (in the form of electrical signals) at rates of several thousand samples per second. (The company name is disguised.) Data thus acquired from the physical world is pre-processed and converted into digital signals that can be processed by a personal computer without specialized instrumentation. These products are used in a variety of industries (industrial automation, telecom, etc.) in conjunction with personal computers and often as a substitute for traditional dedicated measurement equipment. The company pioneered this class of software-driven instrumentation products and enjoys strong market share and market power in the segments it competes.

Figure 4.3 shows a block diagram that describes the various components of a DAQ product. A typical DAQ product works as follows. An analog signal destined for the PC is read through an input channel, amplified to an appropriate level, and converted into a digital signal before being processed by the PC. The processed signal is converted back into an analog form, and transferred to the user through the output channel. All the products in the family share the same architecture, in which functional elements such as the amplifier, A/D converter, and resistors are connected together in a specific fashion. These products deliver different levels of performance, such as number of input/output channels, speed, and resolution, through the choice of components selected to implement the different functions such as amplification, and A/D conversion. For a given family, product-development hinges on offering products with different performance characteristics using the design of components MU, A, ADC, and TC (Fig. 4.3).

Requirements for Accu-data's customers vary widely in terms of the sampling-rate performance required to accurately represent an analog signal in digital form. Market research indicated that their base of customers for DAQ products could be categorized into multiple 'horizontally differentiated' market segments, with different *ideal points* for attributes such as sampling rate (the rate at which a board can sample data reliably). For example, while the more traditional industrial customer segments preferred slower sampling rates and more channels for data sampling, the emergence of a new class of

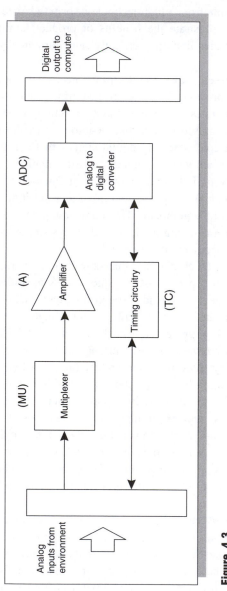

Figure 4.3

Architecture of a data acquisition product (Krishnan and Gupta, 2001).

applications (based on the Peripheral Computer Interconnect (PCI[1]) architecture) created the rapid growth of a segment with the need for faster sampling rates.

Further, Accu-data's market research suggested that within each of these market segments, customers were vertically differentiated. For instance, although customers in a specific segment preferred more channels for data sampling (for their ideal products), they differed significantly in their willingness to pay for more input/output channels. In this environment with customer heterogeneity at multiple levels, Accu-Data embarked on an initiative to develop a set of products that meet the range of attributes desired by customers. Two main questions regarding design for product positioning and product development arose.

- How many products should be offered, and at what performance levels?
- How should these products be related to each other in terms of commonality of component sub-systems? How should components and suppliers be selected?
- What is the sequence in which these products should be introduced?

Considering the huge costs involved in the development of this line of new products, Accu-data explored the option of investing in the designing a product family instead of the conventional approach of independently designing offerings in the product line. Many questions needed to be answered before they could proceed:

- Does product family-based design and development approach offer a greater profit than other alternative options available in the product-planning phase?
- What is the effect of platforms on product positioning? How does creating a reusable platform influence the composition of the product family?
- How will pursuing the product family approach influence the order of new product introduction in a market where customers are time-conscious?
- Which components should be used in which products, and where should they be procured from?

These questions are intricately interrelated and a single simple model to tackle all these questions becomes too complex that is devoid of insights.

---

[1] PCI stands for Peripheral Component Interconnect, an emerging computer bus architecture that provides a high-speed data path between a computer's CPU and peripheral devices (video, disk, network, etc.), and thereby greatly increases data throughput rates over the alternative AT bus architecture.

However, the main issues related to product family-based design and development can be isolated and answered using appropriately designed models of representation. Economic models that address three different facets of this problem generally fall into three categories. The first two models are concerned with designing a product family for vertically and horizontally differentiated markets. The problem of selecting components and suppliers for a product family requires a more detailed set of models with component and supplier costs.

Products designed by Accu-data are also typical of other industries in a very important sense that has received limited attention in product line design research. These belong to a set of products that we refer to as *Development Intensive Products* (DIPs) with their development costs dominating the fixed production costs. It has been observed that managerial insights could be significantly different for production intensive products and DIPs for similar market conditions (Krishnan and Zhu, 2006).

2.1. Literature review

The rationale for developing a family of products – customer demand for product variety and its associated complexity and costs (such as loss of scale economies) – has been studied by researchers in the economics literature (Baumol, Panzar, and Willig, 1988). Managerial decisions in product design and development have been important research topics in the operations management community. Krishnan and Ulrich (2001) offer a review of recent research in product development. Early work in product line design can be traced to the seminal work of Mussa and Rosen (1978), who studied a monopolist's product quality decision. Moorthy (1984) and Moorthy and Png (1992) pioneered the discrete market segment model in the management literature, which has been further developed by Kim and Chhajed (2002), Krishnan and Gupta (2001), and others. Several researchers have also extended these works to multiple dimensions of product quality (Chen, 2001; Kim and Chhajed, 2002) While we present models of product families for horizontal or vertical differentiation of customers, Weber (2002) considers the case of joint vertical and horizontal differentiation, and finds that with linear utility, linear development cost and uniformly distributed consumers, either a pure vertical or a pure horizontal differentiation dominates 'mixed differentiation' if all products are launched at the same time.

Based on their empirical study, Kekre and Srinivasan (1990) found that broader product lines were more profitable, despite the increase in production costs. Quelch and Kenny (1993), however, argue that more products may not always mean greater profitability. It is important that firms carefully consider huge upfront investments entailed by designing a line of products with sufficient variety to meet the requirements and tastes of differentiated customers.

Further, a large fraction of life cycle costs for products is determined at the product design stage itself (Whitney, 1988). These costs arise not only from the development effort but also from design choices that impact manufacturing costs associated with producing a variety of components. Variety also impacts logistical and procurement related costs by forcing the firm to interface with a number of suppliers (Gupta and Krishnan, 1999). By developing products as a family, the firm can reduce the cost of developing individual product variants due to the reuse of a common *product platform*. Such a platform, designed in an aggregate-planning phase that precedes the development of individual product variants, is itself expensive to develop. Hence, its costs must be weighed against the benefits of its reuse in a family.

Identifying common subsystems or platforms in a product family has attracted much interest on the parts of both researchers and practitioners (Meyer and Lehnerd, 1997, Fisher, Ramdas and Ulrich 1999). Several ideas fundamentally based in optimization theory are readily applicable to product development practice. In the context of family-based product development, results regarding the substitutability of lower functionality components with high-performance components are particularly useful (Goldberg and Zhu, 1989; Rutenberg, 1969). Fisher, Ramdas, and Ulrich (1999), who develop parts commonization strategies for automobile braking systems, note that such component sharing between products has the potential to increase as well as decrease production costs. While it is clear that additional costs are incurred by this substitution, commonality also affects the inventory management and service costs over the product life cycle (Bagchi and Gutierrez, 1992; Baker, Magazine and Nuttle, 1986; Gerchak, Magazine and Gamble 1988). More recent optimization models in the Operations Management literature have taken the marketing requirements of variety into consideration, which specifically model the various costs involved in developing shared platforms instead of individual variants. Apart from serving as good models for managerial decision-making, these models have the additional advantage of identifying structural properties of the design problems and *optimal designs*, which are useful in solving design problems efficiently and verifying the appropriateness of product line designs quickly.

2.2. A decision-making framework

The literature surveyed above has considered different aspects of product family-based development separately, but a generalized framework emerges when these decisions are considered together. This framework, presented here, captures the challenge for program managers in product family-based development, namely, balancing the need for product variety with the cost of component proliferation. Any platform-based product family is characterized by the functionalities of the platform itself, $\mathbf{P}$, the number of variants offered n, and also the vector of variant qualities $\mathbf{q}$. The demands of the different variants d_i depend on the cost of manufacturing each variant, c_i, the development cost C_D, the production cost of the platform C_P, prices $\mathbf{p}$, and C_S, the transaction cost of procuring components for the products from the supply base $\mathbf{v}$. The firm's profit maximization for the design and pricing of the product family can be represented as follows.

$$\max_{q,p,P,v} \left\{ \sum_{i=1}^{n} d_i(q, p, P)(p_i - c_i) - C_P(P) - C_D(q, P) - C_S(v, q, P) \right\} \quad (1)$$

Naturally, the demand itself depends on the characteristics of the variants and also on market variables, which we simply represent by Θ.

$$d_i(q, p, P) = f_i(q_i, p_i; q, p, P, \Theta) \quad (2)$$

While this formulation is general in that it encompasses a wide variety of circumstances, we present three broad economic models that arise in different settings in the rest of this chapter. In Sections 3 and 4, we consider models of product family-based design for markets that are vertically and horizontally differentiated. In doing these, we will assume that the firm designs or manufactures all the components required for the products in the family. However, procuring common outside components is an important aspect of managing product families. We consider the problem of selecting components and suppliers for the product family in Section 5.

3. Product family design under vertical differentiation

Many markets consist of heterogeneous, vertically differentiated customers who can typically be ordered based on their willingness to pay for products of higher quality. As a means of price discrimination, firms develop a line of products that cater to different segments of the market. While a firm in this marketplace may face competition from products made by other firms, market leaders with monopoly power (like Accu-Data discussed above) should also consider a common variety of competition between its own products namely, *Cannibalization*. Cannibalization refers to the fact that a low-end product in a firm's product line has the potential to detract high-value customers who might have otherwise been interested in the firm's high-end product. In offering the product line, one of the important challenges for a firm is to carefully position and price its products so that low-end products will be suitable for low-end customers without being attractive to high-end customers.

The earliest economic models that were developed to analyze vertical differentiation generally assumed that a firm could clearly identify the particular characteristics of individual customers (dating back to Pigou (1920)). While this might have been an appropriate model for a more local economy in which salespeople knew their customers intimately, it requires a stretch of imagination to assume that a firm can identify its customers in a world of conspicuous consumption where keeping up with the Joneses is easy for customers and real valuations can be kept discreet. In these impersonal markets where products are often sold through the internet, most goods have to be offered on a take-it-or-leave-it basis and identifying customer-types before the point of sale is not a feasible option for firms.

Models of price-discrimination under *Self-Selection* are used to design product lines for indistinguishable, yet heterogeneous customers (Mussa and Rosen, 1978; Moorthy and Png, 1992). Self-selection based models do require firms to have a general idea of the distribution of customer types and their propensities to spend on quality attributes. The fundamental idea in these models involves the relative positioning of products in the quality-price space such that customers in different segments automatically select a product that is tailored to their segment. As Mussa and Rosen (1978) put it, (product line design . . .) '*smokes out customer preferences . . . and assigns different customers to different varieties of good.*' Smoking customers out of their screens of anonymity requires careful positioning and design of the products.

The self-selection model for vertical differentiation

In this section, we develop a simple model of a vertically differentiated market that allows us to derive the demands d_i for the two versions (Eq. 2). Consider a firm that caters to the needs of a high-end and a low-end segment in a vertically differentiated market (Moorthy and Png, 1992). Both segments agree on the relative qualities of the product, and would like a product of higher quality, which is for simplicity represented in a single dimension (e.g. speed of sampling). Let v_h and v_l denote the willingness to pay (also called valuation) per unit of performance of the high-end and the low-end consumer segments, where $v_h > v_l > 0$ to reflect a vertically differentiated market. Suppose the sizes of the two segments are n_h and n_l, respectively. The high- and low-end segments value a product with performance level q at $v_h q$ and $v_l q$, respectively. Let q_h and q_l ($q_l \leq q_h$) denote the performance levels of products catering to the high-end and the low-end segments. Let the cost of producing a unit of a product of quality q is given by $c(q)$, which is increasing and convex in q.

Note that the demands d_i can be either n_h, n_l or $n_h + n_l$ depending on the firm's pricing strategy. The firm has several options in designing the product line[2]: (a) introduce two separate products, one for each customer segment; (b) offer one product that serves both segments; or (c) introduce one product catering to only to the high-end segment. The model below shows the firm's *Product Line Design* problem in standard form when the firm offers two separate product, one targeted towards each segment. Here, the firm tries to achieve $d_l = n_l$ and $d_h = n_h$ by setting prices p_h and p_l.

$$\max_{q,p} \Pi = \{ n_l \left(p_l - c(q_l) \right) + n_h \left(p_h - c(q_h) \right) \}$$

subject to \hspace{5cm} (3)

$$v_l q_l - p_l \geq v_l q_h - p_h$$
$$v_h q_h - p_h \geq v_h q_l - p_l$$
$$v_l q_l - p_l \geq 0$$
$$v_h q_h - p_h \geq 0$$

In this optimization problem, the natural objective is to maximize the combined profits from sales to the two segments in the market. The last two constraints reflect the basic requirement that the products are not overpriced such that customers are not interested in them. The first two constraints are the *self-selection* constraints, which are not placed on the firm if it can isolate its customers and address each segment specifically. Consider the first constraint as an example: It states that the low-end customer is attracted to the product that is designed for him, but not to the other product in the line. Note that this places a higher limit on the price of the low-end product. More importantly, the second constraint ensures that the low-end product *does not cannibalize* its superior sibling. The inclusion of this constraint in product-line design alters the firm's problem significantly.

Based on the structure of this constraint, we can see that the firm may avoid cannibalization in two ways: (i) Decrease the price p_h such that high-end customers find the product with quality q_h more attractive, (ii) Lower the quality of the low-end product q_l to a level that makes it undesirable to high-value customers. An obvious drawback of the first approach is the way it negatively impacts the profitability of the product line. This makes the second approach superior from a profit maximization perspective. The effect of this quality reduction is two-fold: (a) limit the low-end product's quality such that the low-end product is a lesser version/subset of the high-end product and (b) offer a level of quality to the low-end customer that is even below the level which would be offered to the low-end customer if the high-end market were to not exist. This is referred to as the *subsumed*

---

[2] Issues related to commitment or timing of new product introductions can be accommodated in this model.

product line approach, in which the low-end product is a subsumed and limited version of the high-end product (Krishnan and Zhu, 2006). Deneckere and McAfee (1996) offer several examples of how companies take extreme steps to mitigate cannibalization and have even damaged their high-end good to obtain a crimped and subsumed low-end variant. This is done by turning off features in the low-end product that would otherwise make it attractive to high-value customers. While these insights are useful, research on product positioning and market segmentation has largely ignored the relationships among a firm's products.

The product family approach to vertical differentiation

As mentioned earlier, product family-based approach aims to model the inter-relationships among the products in a line. Here, we discuss one specific approach to modeling the cost of platform-based product family development. Consider the earlier model with two segments and two products. In addition to the production cost $c(q)$, let the cost of designing and developing a product of performance q from a base product of performance q_0 is given by the function $A(q^\beta - q_0^\beta)$. Suppose that the firm opts to develop the products based on a common platform that delivers q_p units of performance (a designer decision variable $q_p \leq q_l$). Let the fixed cost of developing a platform from scratch be modeled by the polynomial function Pq_p^β. Complexity and the cost-intensive nature of platform design imply that $P \geq A$.

Scale economies are realized when multiple units of same product are produced, which can be separated into platform and non-platform components. The maximum number of units that the firm can produce is n_t, where $n_t = n_h + n_l$ (total size of the market). The variable cost of product equals $\alpha c(q)$ ($0 < \alpha < 1$) when n_t units are manufactured. Here α is the parameter depicting the *coefficient of scale economy* of non-platform units. The platform is procured or produced in large volumes (for the whole market of size n_t). In addition, effort spent in designing the platform results in a more cost-efficient design. These are referred to as the *integration benefits of platforms* and are captured by the parameter g (the *coefficient of integration*, $0 < g < 1$), applied as a multiplier to the unit variable cost.

In general, platforms may lead to a loss of perceived differentiation among products. For functional, technological products (such as I the case of Accu-Data), the effect of platforms is an over-design of low-end prod-ucts or under-design of high-end products. The over-design cost due to plat-forms applied to the low-end product only is denoted by the *over-design coefficient e* ($e \geq 1$). High e means greater over-design costs due to platforms.

A similar approach may be used to capture the underdesign of high-end products. The model formulation for the platform-based product design is shown below:

$$\max_{q,p} \Pi = \left\{ \begin{array}{l} n_l\{p_l - egc(q_l)[1 - \frac{(1-\alpha)}{n_t}n_l]\} + n_h\{p_h - gc(q_h)[1 - \frac{(1-\alpha)}{n_t}n_h]\} \\ -Aq_h^{\beta} - Aq_l^{\beta} - (P - 2A)q_p^{\beta} \end{array} \right\}$$

subject to

$$
\begin{aligned}
v_l q_l - p_l &\geq v_l q_h - p_h \\
v_h q_h - p_h &\geq v_h q_l - p_l \\
v_l q_l - p_l &\geq 0 \\
v_h q_h - p_h &\geq 0
\end{aligned}
$$

(4)

The model combines operational and strategic aspects of designing product families based on platforms with marketing considerations such as cannibalization and self-selection. Analysis of this model shows that using product family-based approaches can lead to overdesign of low-end products and under-design of high-end products. It is also useful in identifying some important determinants of a firm's product design and positioning strategies. Krishnan and Gupta's (2001) main insights for the model (without introduction timing) are represented in Table 4.1, which shows the optimal design strategy for a firm for various levels of market and design characteristics.

This model may be easily modified to study questions of optimal timing in this setting. One of the main differences between Krishnan and Gupta (2001) and Moorthy and Png (1992) is the inclusion of fixed costs of development. With firms investing more than ever before in R&D efforts, and with the advances in production technologies, more and more products belong to the class of *Development Intensive Products* (DIPs).

Table 4.1
Appropriateness of different product positioning options (Single period)

		Market Diversity (R)		
		Low	Medium	High
Non-platform.	*Low*	Standardized product	Product family with or without a platform	Niche product
Economies.	*Medium*	Standardized product	Platform-based product family	Niche product
of Scale.	*High*	Standardized product	Standardized product	Standardized product

Designing and developing DIPs for vertical differentiation

In a recent paper, Krishnan and Zhu (2006) have developed a similar model for product positioning to obtain insights regarding Development Intensive Products for a vertically differentiated market. They also extend the model to include multiple dimensions of performance qualities that were not considered in the literature before. They suggest some generalizations and changes to the models discussed above to enable analysis of DIPs. Let the utility functions of customers in the high- and low-end segments be $U_H(q_{A1}, q_{A2})$ and $U_L(q_{A1}, q_{A2})$, respectively for a product A which may two-dimensions of quality, namely, q_{A1} and q_{A2}. Developing product A costs the firm $c_1 q_{A1}^2 + c_2 q_{A2}^2 + 2d q_{A1} q_{A2}$, where d represents the degree of coupling or super modularity between improvements in the two dimensions. This parameter captures the extent to which improvements in one dimensions complement or substitute improvements in the other. Unit production costs, like in previous models, are represented by the convex function $c_v q_{Ai}^2$ for quality dimension i for product A. Several insights that are valid for production intensive product lines are shown to be inapplicable in the case of DIPs by analyzing the model below:

$$\max_{q,p} \Pi = \left\{ \begin{array}{l} n_H(p_H - c_{v1}q_{H1}^2 - c_{v2}q_{H2}^2) - c_1 q_{H1}^2 - c_2 q_{H2}^2 - 2d q_{H1} q_{H2} \\ + n_L(p_L - c_{v1}q_{L1}^2 - c_{v2}q_{L2}^2) - c_1 q_{L1}^2 - c_2 q_{L2}^2 - 2d q_{L1} q_{L2} \end{array} \right\}$$

subject to (5)

$$U_H(q_{h1}, q_{h2}) - p_h \geq U_H(q_{l1}, q_{l2}) - p_l$$
$$U_L(q_{l1}, q_{l2}) - p_l \geq U_L(q_{h1}, q_{h2}) - p_h$$
$$U_H(q_{h1}, q_{h2}) - p_h \geq 0$$
$$U_L(q_{l1}, q_{l2}) - p_l \geq 0$$

Krishnan and Zhu (2006) find that it is not necessary to subsume (or damage) low-end products to avoid cannibalization. Quite interestingly, they find that even offering a product line may be far from optimal for DIPs with single quality dimensions. Further, when the firm innovates along multiple vertical quality dimensions, it can benefit from the trade-off among the two dimensions in the cost function and the difference in relative willingness to pay along the two quality dimensions. In juxtaposition with previous models of vertical differentiation, this demonstrates the importance of using the appropriate economic model that behooves the design and development related costs in making product line related decisions.

4. Product family design under horizontal differentiation

Designing new products to meet the requirements of a 'horizontally differentiated market' presents a different set of challenges for a firm. In such a market, customers vary in the extent to which they value different attributes of a product. However, horizontally differentiated customers can neither be rank-ordered according to their willingness to pay for quality improvements, nor are they unanimous in ordering different products based on their performances. The main objective for firms when facing such variety is to provide a line of products that meets demands of different customer segments sufficiently, yet economically. Economic models are useful in understanding the trade-offs between the cost of variety and benefit of providing customers their *ideal products*.

A traditional approach to modeling horizontally differentiated markets is to consider different segments as being separated in space. This can be traced to Hotelling (1929) who assumed that customers are distributed in a line of varying preferences with customers on either end of the line representing those with completely different preferences with respect to product characteristics. Naturally, meeting the specific needs of an infinite number of customers is impossible. A more realistic approach is to identify the exact preferences of different clusters of customers that exist in the market. An effective approach to identifying these segments is to infer the weights different customers place on various attributes by performing a *conjoint analysis* (Green and Krieger, 1989). While the marketing models are useful in understanding the need for product variety itself, models that are more sophisticated are needed to understand the costs of providing this variety and to explore alternatives in design & development of the product line. Krishnan, Singh, and Tirupati (1999) present the following model that integrates customer-demand information with the design cost information to make platform and product family-planning decisions in a horizontal differentiation context.

Firms target a performance interval Q in which to introduce products, which is generally aimed to cover the customers at the ends of the preference spectrum. Suppose the firm considers n variants in the product family with respective performance levels $q_1, q_2, .., q_n (q_i \,\varepsilon\, Q, i = 1..n)$ such that $q_1 < q_2 < ... < q_n$. The maximum performance q_T in the product family that the firm can offer (such that $q_T \leq q_T$) is determined by the technology T that the firm develops at a cost $C_D(q_T, P)$, where P is due to the level of technology already possessed by the firm, or in other words, the quality of the platform.

As with vertically differentiated markets, the price p_i a consumer will pay for the product will depend on the product's characteristics q_i as well as on other products that he has the option of purchasing. The life-cycle demand for variant i, $\mathbf{d}_i$ (Eq. 2), can be obtained from a general distribution of consumer tastes (or preference for performance levels). For instance, if $f(z)$ denotes the distribution of consumer attributes z, and π_{zi} represents the proportion of consumers with performance levels z that purchase variant i, the demand for this variant can be calculated as follows.

$$d_i = \int_0^\infty \pi_{z,i}\, f(z)\, dz \qquad (6)$$

Such a model also permits the incorporation of demand uncertainty by allowing the distribution $f(z)$ to be a random variable at performance level z. When π_{zi} is independent of $f(z)$, the expected demand $E[d_i]$ is given by:

$$E[d_i] = \int_0^\infty \pi_{z,i} E[f(z)]\, dz \qquad (7)$$

The demand model described above is similar to a consumer choice model in which consumers choose products 'closest' to their ideal points (Carpenter and Nakamoto, 1990). The ideal-point model of demand is based on the premise that (i) consumers have different preferences for each price-performance combination; and (ii) each consumer prefers one price-performance combination over any other, where product performance defines the ideal product for the consumer.

While this model is adequate to calculate demands for different variants in a product line, it is also useful to understand how consumers seek the best fit before deciding the variants that should be offered in the product family. A consumer with an ideal performance level z associates a utility value $u_z(q_i, p_i)$ with variant I (for convenience, we will henceforth simply use the term $u_{z,i}$ for this utility function). Consumers are performance-sensitive, and do not consider a product for purchase if a product with a performance closer to their ideal point is already available. Thus, the only products considered by the consumer are the two neighboring products i and $i+1$ such that $q_i \leq z \leq q_{i+1}$. Using a share of utility-based choice rule (see Green and Kreiger, 1989) to describe the probability of purchase of a product by any consumer in the market, the purchase probabilities (when the choice is limited to the two products q_i and q_{i+1}) can be described by.

$$\begin{pmatrix} \pi_{z,i} \\ \pi_{z,i+1} \end{pmatrix} = \begin{pmatrix} \dfrac{u_{z,i}}{u_{z,i} + u_{z,i+1} + u_{z0}} \\ \dfrac{u_{z,i+1}}{u_{z,i} + u_{z,i+1} + u_{z0}} \end{pmatrix} \qquad (8)$$

where u_{z0} is the consumer's utility if neither i nor $i+1$ is chosen ('balking'). With the above model to determine $\pi_{z,i}$, the expected life-cycle demand can be written as follows:

$$E[d_i] = \int_{q_{i-1}}^{q_{i+1}} \pi_{z,i}\, E[f(z)]\, dz \text{ for } i = 1, 2, \ldots n-1$$

$$E[d_0] = \int_0^{q_1} \pi_{z,i}\, E[f(z)]\, dz; \; E[d_n] = \int_{q_{n-1}}^{\infty} \pi_{z,i}\, E[f(z)]\, dz$$

(9)

On the cost side, a platform comprising of reusable components is assumed to be architected in the planning phase and reused in all product variants. Each variant consists of components that are either unique to the variant, are a part of the platform, or are adapted from existing variants (see Fig. 4.2). Development cost $F_{agg}(\gamma)$ in the aggregate-planning phase involves the development of the platform and depends on the scope γ of the platform P (the number and complexity of functional elements that are reused throughout the family). Creating a platform that allows for greater reusability (larger γ) may require more effort in the specification of task structures and components, which in the individual development phase would pay off in the simplification of development tasks (Clark and Baldwin, 1993).

Development costs for an individual variant are incurred in the phase following aggregate development, and consist of (i) creative design cost $I(\eta, \gamma, q_j)$ that involves creation of functional elements which are unique for each variant, and (ii) adaptation costs $g(\eta, q_i, q_j)$ that involve the reuse and adaptation of components designed for earlier variants. Effort invested in creating a platform γ can contribute to the decrease of both the creative design and the adaptation costs. The cost of creating components unique to variant j is $g(\eta, q_i, q_j)$, where η is an efficiency parameter that is dependent upon the process of design creation: all else being equal, a firm with a more efficient design process, or greater η (perhaps as a result of investments in systems and processes such as CAD/CAM and rapid prototyping), will incur smaller costs in the development of the platform and individual variants.

This comprehensive consideration of development costs can be succinctly summarized as the total development cost function below, where $S = \{1, 2, \ldots, n\}$ is the set of products in the family.

$$G(\gamma, S) = F_{agg}(\gamma) + \sum_{i=1}^{n} [I(\eta, \gamma, q_i) + g(\gamma, q_{i-1}, q_i)]$$

(10)

Production costs are affected not only by both the specific configuration of the variant, but also by the design of the platform: $\nu(\gamma, q_i)$. Now the total cost function for the output (volume) vector $d_S = \{d_1, d_2, \ldots, d_n\}$ can be written as.

$$C_D(\gamma, d_S) = G(\gamma, S) + \sum_{i \in S} d_i \nu(\gamma, q_i) \tag{11}$$

Such cost models, as shown in this instance, can be developed without interfering with the model of demand. A simplified model of the market may capture the price offered for any variant as $p(q_i)$. The optimization problem for the firm may be written as.

$$\Pi(\gamma, q_1, q_2, \ldots, q_n, n) = \sum_{i=0}^{n} [p(q_i) - \nu(\gamma, q_i)]d_i - F_{agg}(\gamma)$$
$$- \left[\sum_{i=1}^{n} I(\eta, \gamma, q_i) + g(\gamma, q_{i-1}, q_i) \right] - C_T(q_n, q_P) \tag{12}$$

s.t.
$$q_0 \leq q_1 \leq q_2 \leq \cdots \leq q_n$$
$$\gamma \in \{\gamma_1, \gamma_2, \ldots\}$$

Interpreting the optimal design formulation

Interestingly, despite its complex structure, the entire problem of selecting the optimal product family from any platform can be reduced (with a few assumptions) to a well-known and readily solvable network optimization problem called the Shortest Path problem (Fig. 4.4). The optimal solution to the problem selects the least cost path to meeting customer needs with the platform's derivatives. The nodes through which the shortest path flows represent the variants that are actually offered in the optimal product line.

There are many benefits to reducing the formulation to a simple form. This formulation is now easily extendable for a firm that is considering extensions to or deletions from an existing product family. The solution gives ready and intuitive insights about the width and spacing of the product line, and even allows managers to identify the platform. This is an important function of modeling these decisions because a big challenge for many managers who are interested in developing platform-based product families is identifying the basic platform. These explicit models also allow managers to explicitly calculate the benefits of using a platform. The model is amenable to incorporating competitive forces into the decision-making process. Firms can use these models to evaluate even dynamic, strategic benefits of platforms. Further, these models and the structure of the product line are robust to extensions such as consideration of multiple dimensions of performance.

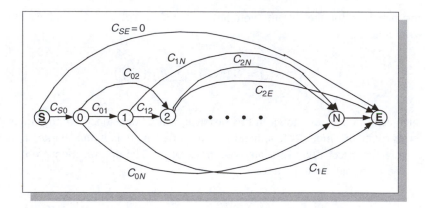

Figure 4.4
Network representation of the product family design problem.

5. Product family-based component selection

Poor design decisions made in the early stages of product development can greatly increase the costs of complexity and rapidly offset the effort invested in developing new products. Using the product family-based approach to respond to new market conditions modifies the design decision-making process so that the choices made in the process ensure not only the performance of products but also the reduction in complexity of a product family. In the conventional approach, suppliers are selected after the conceptual and detailed design of a product is completed, resulting in the usage of several unique suppliers. Integrating supplier capabilities and costs in design decision-making results in the reduction in the number of unique suppliers. While supply chain management has generated substantial interest in the context of manufacturing operations, there exists little work, which focuses on supply chain issues related to product development. The problem of selecting components and suppliers in an integrated fashion during the design stage has received minimal attention (Gupta and Krishnan, 1999).

In the conventional approach for supplier selection, component selection, and sourcing, decisions are made independently for each product to maximize its performance. Unfortunately, that is hardly optimal considering the economics of consolidated procurement from a smaller set of suppliers. Indeed, such individual component optimization may have the effect of undoing any gains that may have been achieved by using a product family-based design approach. Gupta and Krishnan (1999) model the *Integrated Component and Supplier Selection* (ICSS) problem with one-way substitutability of functionalities, which is equivalent to allowing overdesign in lower-end products in the family. They present the following example to motivate their model.

Consider two data acquisition (DAQ) products, P1 and P2, the first of which is higher along the resolution and speed dimensions. These product-level requirements translate into performance and quality requirements for the components. Consider, for instance, one of the components, a resistance network (or 'resnet'), custom designed by the firm. P1, being a higher resolution product, requires a resnet of higher quality than P2. Let R1 and R2 be the resnets that satisfy the quality requirements of P1 and P2, respectively. Supplier data sheets indicate that while several suppliers supply each of the components, none of them supply both components. In the individual product-oriented approach, whereby components are selected to individually minimize cost of each product, R1 will be chosen for P1 and R2 for P2. Due to the above-mentioned supply constraints, an individual product-oriented approach will result in two resnets from two different suppliers. Under ICSS, components would be chosen to minimize the total cost of designing, procuring, and using components for the entire family. In this case, the higher quality component R1 can be used in place of the lower quality R2 but not otherwise. Since the higher quality resnets are more expensive, substitution increases the unit variable cost of components in product P2. However, replacing R2 with R1 creates scale economies in component design, testing, and supplier selection.

This stylized example shows the value of modeling the ICSS problem as an aggregate optimization problem with all components used in the product family included as decisions. However, in industrial settings, the ICSS problem is often complicated with scores of components and dozens of suppliers. Gupta and Krishnan (1999) provide the following model for this problem.

6. Model

Similar to models in Sections 3 and 4, the ICSS model is a special instance of Problem 2.1. To focus on the role of transaction costs with suppliers in configuring the product platform, Gupta and Krishnan (1999) consider a more detailed model of procurement, while simplifying the market specifications. (The joint component and supplier selection is already a complex problem, so to keep the model tractable, the demand side must be abstracted away to set the objective function to the total cost of design and procurement.)

As a first step in ICSS, components offering different levels of the same functionality are grouped together and sorted in decreasing order of functionality in the Replaceable Component Set (RCS). Let the RCS be indexed from $1, 2, .., i, .., I$ and N_i be the number of elements in RCS i. Let L be a set comprising all RCSs. A component that is the jth element in the ith RCS is denoted as $L(i, j)$ where $(i = 1, 2, \ldots, I)$ and $(j = 1, 2, \ldots N_i)$. The number of components, N_i, in an RCS is bounded by the total number (M) of products in the family. The firm's estimate of the lifecycle demand for each product in the family be $<\iota> \lambda_k$ (k=1, . . . , M)$</\iota>$. Let d_{ij} denote the demand for component $L(i, j)$.

Let V represent the set of available suppliers that are capable of meeting the firm's expected quality levels and lead time requirements. For each supplier $v \in V$, let the set P_v contain the Ω_v components (belonging to set L) that supplier v is capable of supplying at full demand. If the firm chooses to contract with supplier v, it incurs a fixed cost G_v. In choosing to use a component $L(i, j)$ in its product family, a firm incurs two different costs: the fixed cost (F_{ij}) of designing, prototyping, and testing the component, and its unit variable cost (A_{ij}). Using these elements, the total cost C_{ij}, of using a component $L(i, j)$ may be written as $C_{ij}(x_{ij}) = \begin{cases} F_{ij} + A_{ij}x_{ij} \ if \ x_{ij} > 0 \\ 0 \ otherwise \end{cases}$, where x_{ij} is the usage of the component $L(i, j)$. The ICSS problem may now be simply represented as a (linear) integer program with components and their suppliers as the decisions. The interaction cost $C_S(\mathbf{v}, \mathbf{q}, \mathbf{P})$ can be represented as the sum of supplier selection costs and component procurement costs. The ICSS problem may then be stated as follows.

$$[ICSS(a)] \quad \underset{\delta_v, x_{ij}}{Min} \sum_{v \in V} G_v \delta_v + \sum_{i=1}^{I} \sum_{j=1}^{N_i} C_{ij}(x_{ij})$$

$$subject \ to \ \sum_{k=1}^{j} x_{ik} \geq \sum_{k=1}^{j} d_{ik}, \forall i = 1, 2, \ldots, I; \ j = 1, 2, \ldots, N_i \quad (13)$$

$$t_{vij} = 0 \forall L(i, j) \notin P_v, \forall v \in V$$

$$\sum_{v \in V} t_{vij} = z_{ij}, \forall L(i, j)$$

$$\sum_{L(i,j) \in P_v} t_{vij} - \Omega_v \delta_v \leq 0, \forall v \in V$$

$$x_{ij} \geq 0 \ and \ integer, \forall L(i, j)$$

$$z_{ij}, t_{vij}, \delta_v = \{0, 1\}$$

It is shown easily that if a component is replaced, it is replaced fully. Firms that do not implement ICSS or implement ICSS only partially will never be able to come to this simple conclusion. In reality, these mistakes occur in part due to the incentive systems in practice and in part to the performance orientation of individual product design methodologies used by firms.

The formulation above can rewritten in terms of additional costs incurred by overdesigning a component, i.e., selecting a replacement that provides superior performance. This may be optimal if the resultant consolidation of suppliers offsets the additional cost of the component. The revised formulation (see Gupta and Krishnan, 1999) maps to the classical *Set Covering problem* in graph theory after some simplifying assumptions about costs are made. Since the set covering problem, and consequently the ICSS problem, is very hard when the size of the problem is large, the authors develop heuristic procedures to solve it.

In summary, product family-based component selection helps balance the design, procurement, and component variable costs. One outcome is the identification of the *limits on the level of commonality* placed by an increase in variable costs due to the excess functionality of components. Trivially over-designing many components to minimize the number of supply sources would result in increased variable component costs and cannibalization among products in a family. On the contrary, picking the ideal component in all cases would increase the fixed procurement costs. The optimal solution finds a happy middle ground between these extremes.

7. Conclusions, managerial implications, and research directions

Product family-based design and development is a useful approach for firms to adapt to an age of shortening product lifecycles, increasing development costs, and demanding customers. In this chapter, we have presented an integrated view of product family-based design and development in which the optimal product family-based design (decisions about the number of products and their locations on attribute space) precedes their detailed development (architecture, configuration design, and component/supplier selection).

Models of product family development explicitly allow firms to represent the relationships between products. These models differ significantly based on whether the markets for these products are vertically or horizontally differentiated. Implicitly, the models serve as a decision support system for managers who want to identify ideal platforms for their family, or sharpen the definition of their platform with cost minimization as an objective. An important current limitation of these models is that they are largely restricted to a monopolistic environment and do not capture the competitive dynamics involved in product-family design. A second area of further research is the incorporation of technological uncertainty and channel interactions in distributing product families.

While the models presented above are all driven by problems faced in realistic situations, they also suffer from the simplistic assumptions required to develop insights. These models have been found to be useful in directing managers, but require further calibration and modification to become decision support models.

One of the primary obstacles to more realistic decision-support modeling is the limited availability of data that would drive such a model. We believe that future research in this area should also focus on gathering data to validate these models and refine them for real-life applications. Collecting an exhaustive table of required data for such models may seem daunting at first, but two factors come to the manager's aid. First, firms can draw from engineers' experiences and design cookbooks to calculate design costs. Second, the most challenging part of data collection for using this model is marketing related, estimates of which are generally available in most firms.

In conclusion, product family approach can help managers balance the benefits and costs of variety and manage the complexity associated with product variety. Such an approach can be particularly suited for incumbent firms with a wide product line and the associated proliferation of components and suppliers.

References

Bagchi, U., and G. Gutierrez (1992), "Effect of Increasing Component Commonality on Service Level and Holding Cost," *Naval Research Logistics*, 39, 6, 815–832.

Baker, K. R., M. J. Magazine, and H. L. W. Nuttle (1986), "The Effect of Commonality on Safety Stock in a Simple Inventory Model," *Management Science*, 32, 8, 982–988.

Baumol, William J., John C. Panzar, and Robert D. Willig (1988), *Contestable Markets and the Theory of Industry Structure*, New York: Harcourt Brace Jovanovich.

Carpenter, G. and K. Nakamoto (1990), "Competitive Strategies for Late Entry into a Market with a Dominant Brand," *Management Science,* 16, 10, 1268–1278.

Chen, C. (2001), "Design for the environment: A quality-based model for green product development," *Management Science*, 47, 2, 250–264.

Clark, Kim B., and Y. Clariss Baldwin (1993), "Modularity and Real Options," Working Paper #93-026, Harvard Business School.

Deneckere, R. J., and R. P. McAfee (1996). "Damaged Goods," *Journal of Economics and Management Strategy*, Blackwell Publishing, 5, 2, 149–174.

Dobson, G., and S. Kalish (1988), "Positioning and Pricing a Product Line," *Marketing Science*, 7, (Spring 1988), 107–125.

Fisher, M. L., K. Ramdas, and K. T. Ulrich (1999), "Component Sharing in the Management of Product Variety: A Study of Automotive Braking Systems," *Management Science,* 45, 3, 297–315.

Fonte, W. G. (1994), A De-Proliferation Methodology for the Automotive Industry, Master of Science Thesis, Massachusetts Institute of Technology, Leaders for Manufacturing Program.

Gerchak, Y., M. J. Magazine, and A. B. Gamble (1988), "Component Commonality with Service Level Requirements," *Management Science*, 34, 6, 753–760.

Goldberg, J., and J. Zhu (1989), "Module Design with Substitute Parts and Multiple Vendors," *European Journal of Operational Research*, 41, 3, 336–346.

Green, Paul E., and Abba M. Krieger (1989), "Recent Contributions to Optimal Product Positioning and Buyer Segmentation," *European Journal of Operational Research*, 41, 127–141.

Gupta, S., and V. Krishnan (1999), "Integrated Component and Supplier Selection for a Product Family," *Production and Operations Management*, 8, 2, 163–181.

Kekre, S., and K. Srinivasan (1990), "Broader Product Line: A Necessity To Achieve Success?" *Management Science*, 36, 1216–1231.

Kim, K., and D. Chhajed (2000), "Commonality in Product Design: Cost Saving, Valuation Change, and Cannibalization," *European Journal of Operational Research*, 107, 3, 614–624.

Kim, K., and D. Chhajed (2002), "Product design with multiple quality-type attributes," *Management Science*, 48, 11, 1502–1511.

Krishnan, V., R. Singh, and D. Tirupati (1999), "A Model-Based Approach for Planning and Developing a Family of Technology-Based Products," *Manufacturing & Service Operations Management*, 1, 2, 132–156.

Krishnan, V., and S. Gupta (2001), "Appropriateness and Impact of Platform-Based Product Development," *Management Science*, 47, 1, (January 2001), 52–68.

Krishnan, V., and K. Ulrich (2001), "Product Development Decisions: A Review of the Literature," *Management Science*, 47, 1, 1–21.

Krishnan, V. and W. Zhu (2006), "Designing a Family of Development-Intensive Products," *Management Science*, 52, 6, 813–825.

MacDuffie, John Paul, Kannan Sethuraman, and Marshall L. Fisher (1996), "Product Variety and Manufacturing Performance: Evidence from the International Automobile Industry," *Management Science*, 42, 3 (March 1996), 350–369.

Meyer, M. H., and A. P. Lehnerd (1997), *The Power of Product Platforms*, New York: The Free Press.

Moore, W. L., J. J. Louviere, and R. Verma (1999), "Using Conjoint Analysis to Help Design Product Platforms," *Journal of Product Innovation Management*, 16, 1 (January 1999), 27–39.

Moorthy, K. S. (1984), "Market Segmentation, Self-Selection, and Product Line Design," *Marketing Science*, 3, 288–307.

Moorthy, K. S., and I. Png (1992), "Market Segmentation, Cannibalization, and the Timing of Product Introductions," *Management Science*, 38, 345–359.

Mussa, M., and S. Rosen (1978), "Monopoly and Product Quality," *Journal of Economic Theory*, 18, 301–317.

Pahl, G., and W. Beitz (1988), *Engineering Design: A Systematic Approach*, New York: Springer Verlag.

Pigou, A. C. (1920), *The Economics of Welfare*, London: MacMillan,.

Quelch, John A., and David Kenny (1994), "The Logic of Product-line Extensions: When does Variety Become Redundancy?" *Harvard Business Review*, 72, 6 (Nov.–Dec. 1994), 53–59.

Robertson, D., and K. T. Ulrich (1998), "Planning for Product Platforms," *Sloan Management Review*, 39, (Summer 1998), 19–31.

Rutenberg, D.P. (1969) "Design Commonality to Reduce Multi-Item Inventory: Optimal Depth of a Product Line," *Operations Research*, 19, 2, 491–509.

Sanderson, S. W., and M. V. Uzumeri (1996), *Managing Product Families*, Irwin Publishing, Burr Ridge, IL.

Weber, T. A. (2002), Delayed multiattribute product differentiation. Working Paper, University of Pennsylvania.

Whitney, Daniel E. (1988), "Manufacturing by Design," *Harvard Business Review*, 66, 4 (July–August 1988), 83–92.

5 Creativity in new product development: An evolutionary integration

Lee Fleming and Santiago Mingo

We would like to thank John Elder for editing help and the Harvard Business School Department of Research for supporting this research. Errors and omissions remain ours.

1. Introduction

Very few firms can survive today without new products, for these provide revenue, increase market share, improve prestige (attracting future employees and external endorsements), and provide effective vehicles for organizational renewal and strategic change (Wheelwright and Clark, 1992). Breakthrough products offer explosive growth as well. Although the abundant research and literature on how to develop new products has helped firms improve their new product development processes, truly creative product development remains difficult. Breakthrough product development, in particular, remains elusive and seemingly random.

We focus in this chapter on the very beginning of the product development process, adopting an evolutionary perspective because it explains why firms tend to invent incrementally and why truly creative product development remains so difficult. Because the evolutionary perspective (Darwin, 1858; Campbell, 1960; Basalla, 1988; Simonton, 1999; Gierer, 2004) recognizes the differences between an idea's birth and its ultimate success, it helps firms recognize and manage the inherent tensions between creativity and execution (March, 1991; Christensen, 1997; Hansen, 1999; Repenning, 2002; Sutton, 2002; O'Reilly and Tushman, 2004). These tensions become especially difficult when a firm attempts to invent a breakthrough.

While it would be impossible to cover even a fraction of the research on creativity and product development, in this chapter, we organize some of the dominant themes of that research according to the three stages of evolution defined by Darwin – variation, selection, and retention. The variation stage covers the generative sources of creativity. We argue that this process can only occur within a single individual, although it can be improved (within the individual) by collaboration. The selection phase covers the initial sorting of the occasional good idea from the modal bad idea. The last stage, retention, covers the development of prototypes and products, experimentation, technology transfer, portfolio management, and marketing – in short, the classic elements of product development. Given that the other papers in this volume (and the new product development literatures as a whole) focus mainly on the selection and retention stages, we will do little justice to the selection stage and no justice to the retention stage. We conclude with a discussion of how managers can influence the early stages of creativity.

2. Definition of creativity

The consistency of definitions of creativity in the literature is surprising. Leonard and Swap (1999) and Runco (2004) define creativity as a process of developing and communicating novel ideas that are likely to be useful or influential. Similarly, Simonton (1999) considers an idea or product creative if it is original and adaptive in some sense. Creativity can be the use of old ideas in new ways, places, or combinations, as long as the result is potentially valuable to someone (Sutton, 2002). Amabile (1996) also agrees that a product or response will be judged as creative if it is both a novel and an appropriate response to the task. However, she adds another element to the definition: The task must be heuristic rather than algorithmic; i.e., the path to the solution cannot be completely straightforward.

We agree with the flavor of these definitions, but adopt a full evolutionary perspective to differentiate between the original creation of novelty and its subsequent use. This avoids the normative bias of 'creativity,' 'invention,' and 'innovation' by separating search from success. Most new ideas are bad and never get past their initial formulation, so it makes little sense to lump all new ideas into a single desirable bucket. Instead, we can define an invention or creative idea as a new combination or reconfiguration of components or ideas and seek to understand the recombinant search process (Schumpeter, 1939; Basalla, 1988; Henderson and Clark, 1990; Baldwin and Clark, 2000; Iansiti, 1997; Fleming, 2001). This definition keeps search and ultimate success separate, but also fits in well with the operations management perspective, which naturally envisions creativity as a search process over a multi-dimensional landscape. The surface of the landscape can reflect technological, strategic, or competitive search problems and can interact with search strategies (Gavetti and Levinthal, 2000; Rivkin, 2000; Fleming and Sorenson, 2004).

3. The variation stage: Generating new ideas

We argue that, while many external forces influence the creative process, the generation of variation ultimately takes place within single minds (Campbell,

1960; Simonton, 1999). New combinations (variation) do not arise in the 'ether' between individuals. Social influences are obviously strong; creative combinations arise within an individual, are expressed (though not necessarily understood correctly), and inspire colleagues in their further recombinant search. Simonton (1999: 29) quotes Einstein's description of the boundary between internal creativity and external expression: 'The combinatory play takes place, "before there is any connection with logical construction in words or other kinds which can be communicated to others."' Starting from this (admittedly) strong psychological perspective, the pertinent questions for managers of product development are: 'How do I identify creative individuals?' 'Which ones do I hire?' 'How do I make my product development professionals more creative?' In the following sections, we group answers to these questions by their various perspectives: psychological, social-psychological, group research on creativity and product development, and sociological.

4. Psychological perspectives

There is an excessively skewed distribution of creativity among any population. As Price (1965) first demonstrated, only a few individuals produce much of the creative and high-impact work (Simonton, 1999). Ernst et al. (2000) corroborated this argument in a corporate setting by demonstrating that the technological performance of a company usually relies on a very small fraction of its inventors (as measured by numbers and quality of patents).

Managers seeking creative product development must try to hire such individuals. Nevertheless, how? Raw intelligence provides a good first indication of creative potential. Many studies link IQ and individual creativity, though the main finding is that, beyond a reasonable threshold, the relation between creative behavior and intelligence becomes minimal (Simonton, 2000). Barron and Harrington (1981) demonstrate that creativity correlates with many characteristics of intelligence, such as divergent abilities to think, to make associations, to form numerous and unusual associations, to use analogies and metaphors, and to identify problems. Other personality characteristics also correlate strongly with creativity; examples include risk-seeking, high valuation of esthetic qualities in experience, broad interests, attraction to complexity, high energy, independence of judgment, autonomy, intuition, self-confidence, ability to resolve antinomies or to accommodate apparently opposite or conflicting traits in one's self-concept, and a firm sense of self as 'creative' (Barron and Harrington, 1981; King and Pope, 1999; Simonton, 2000). Historical, psychiatric, and psychometric studies lend support to the hypothesis that outstanding creativity bears some relationship to psychopathology (Simonton, 1999). Certain aspects of an individual's childhood have been found to favor the emergence of a creative personality; high birth order, early parental loss, marginality, and the availability of mentors and role models all correlate with creativity (Simonton, 1987). It should be noted that, while managers can look for clues to creativity in an individual's career history, they would also do well to test for creativity in a work sample interview.

Given the correlation between creativity and potentially dysfunctional behavior, managers should not swing to an extreme and staff their entire organizations with exceptionally creative people (Staw, 1995). Other observations support this argument. Many exceptionally creative individuals loathe to complete tasks and would prefer to move to new challenges; rather than testing and documenting a product through its release to manufacturing or customer acceptance, they would prefer to start new products. If their relative strength lies in the variation stage, managers would do well to respect their innate abilities. Foreshadowing our arguments below, successful product development requires a variety of skills and well-managed transitions. Product development teams function more effectively with a mix of eccentric creativity and more mundane discipline and skepticism. Hewlett Packard's thermal ink jet, e.g., was invented by a less-disciplined high-variance genius and a skeptical, disciplined engineer. Ironically, the genius never completed college, while the engineer had three degrees in physics and engineering from Worcester Polytechnic Institute and MIT (Fleming, 2001). Managing such contrary personalities and 'creative abrasion' remains a challenge; we refer the reader to Leonard and Swap (1999).

Once creative engineers have been hired, managers can implement a variety of techniques and strategies to increase their creativity. Providing a buffer from immediate pressures enables engineers to explore new possibilities (March, 1991). Managers can implement such buffering strategies as 3M's 10 per cent time for personally directed invention or by moving research from within line divisions to a central laboratory or skunk works. However, centralizing research entails trade-offs between exploration and exploitation. The resource allocation process remains complex and interdependent on technological trajectories, marketing, and current customer focus (Christensen, 1997).

5. Socio-psychological perspectives

Much socio-psychological research on creativity focuses on how people perceive their work environment. Amabile (1996) argues that creative people need to perceive encouragement for creativity, autonomy, availability of resources, freedom from pressure, and a lack of organizational impediments to creativity. Edmondson (1999) formulated the concept of psychological safety, a shared belief that well-intentioned action will not lead to punishment or rejection. Thus, a team or organization where psychological safety is present supports public risk-taking, which should lead to more creativity and idea generation. Consistent with these arguments, Ruppel and Harrington (2000) demonstrated with survey methods that openness in communication between employees and trust within the organization correlate with higher perceptions of innovation within the subunit. Glynn (1996) also argues that flexible environments with increased worker autonomy and good communication flows are more innovative. Amabile (1996) also documents how extrinsic motivation – things such as money, prestige, fame, or other inducements besides the work itself – will decrease creativity. Amabile's research implies that explicit and extrinsic motivators for creativity – e.g., large awards for achieving objectives or for patenting them – should be avoided.

6. Group research perspectives

Social interactions provide the tantalizing possibility to exploit individual potential so that the whole is greater than the sum of its parts. Research on groups and creativity can be differentiated from the more psychological perspectives by its focus on such interactions. The main assumption is that all individuals can contribute to the creative process. A group perspective also affords greater opportunities for managerial influence than psychological and socio-psychological perspectives do. After all, managers choose a group's composition, influence its norms of collaboration, and shape its creative process. Leonard and Swap (1999) break these managerial opportunities down into five steps: preparation, during which group members are selected to maximize creativity; innovation opportunity identification, during which members search for opportunities to apply their skills; generation of options, which maximizes divergent thinking; an incubation period in which to digest and evaluate the different possibilities; and convergence, during which the group must agree on one option.

The step of team selection – in particular, the question of whether diversity helps or hurts creativity – has generated much controversy in the group research literature. Many social-psychology researchers have argued and found that groups that are heterogeneous with respect to abilities, skills, and knowledge perform more creatively than homogeneous groups (Shaw, 1976). The explanation given is that the team members bring different backgrounds, functions, views, and skills to the group, which is beneficial for innovation and creativity (Kanter, 1988; Dougherty, 1992). Ely and Thomas (2001) showed that when managers are motivated to diversify because of the integration and learning work group performance improves, as measured by process and product innovation. Smith et al. (1994) found support for the hypothesis that heterogeneity in the years of education of top management team members is positively associated with firm performance. Bantel and Jackson's (1989) examination of top management teams and innovation in banking indicated that more innovative banks are managed by more educated and functionally diverse teams.

On the other hand, there is also evidence that diversity can interfere with group innovation because of its deleterious effects on social integration and group identification, especially in organizations that emphasize individualism and distinctiveness (Polzer et al., 2002; Chatman et al., 1998; Williams and O'Reilly, 1998). Pelled et al. (1999) suggested a complex link between work group diversity and group functioning. For example, work group diversity can augment *emotional* conflict between members, which is detrimental to any team performance measure, including innovation. However, they also proposed that *task* conflict could be good for improving team performance. One potential resolution to this controversy is that diversity leads to less creative outcomes on average but that the variability of creativity is greater (Fleming, 2001). Another is that diversity provides a marginal benefit in situations with closed collaborative structure (Fleming, Mingo, and Chen, forthcoming).

The option generation step, popularly known as brainstorming, has also received much attention, although there is less recent work on the topic. With effective communication and a supportive environment, collaboration and social interaction can provide the individual with very quick access and iteration across a range of unfamiliar disciplines, ideas, and potential combinations. Brainstorming techniques, e.g., have been formalized to support rapid recombinant search among collaborators (Osborn, 1957). Four rules are traditionally used in these sessions: do not criticize, quantity is more important than quality, combine and improve suggested ideas, and say all ideas that come to mind, no matter how wild. One designer offers this justification: 'The main reason I use brainstorming is to generate ideas that I know I wouldn't have on my own' (Sutton and Hargadon, 1996). Without sharing, an individual would find it very difficult to access so many new and disparate areas of knowledge. A diversity of collaborative perspectives facilitates fast exploration of tangents and asides, though the effectiveness of these sessions remains controversial (Sutton and Hargadon, 1996). Critical to the success of these sessions are the incentives used to encourage participants to focus their energy on ideas that are both new and relevant. Well-designed incentives can help in overcoming some common problems in brainstorming sessions, such as free riding, fear of evaluation, and production blocking (which occurs when participants are unable to express themselves simultaneously). Surprisingly, little formal research has paid attention to the influence of incentives on the creative output of individuals within groups dedicated to idea generation (for an exception, see Toubia, 2005).

7. Sociological perspectives

Whereas psychological approaches focus on innate abilities, socio-psychological approaches on perceptions, and group research on demographics and process, sociological approaches investigate how patterns of relationships influence creativity, both within and outside the immediate group. Networks of trusting – or manipulative – collaboration and information flow replace the view of the lone genius seen in strictly psychological research. The sociological perspective can be motivated by the realization that engineers (like all people) usually benefit from exposure to new ideas and approaches. Given that most people learn socially, rather than from written material (Katz and Lazarsfeld, 1955; Allen, 1977), there would seem to be a crucial role for network position and design.

The most directly relevant sociological underpinnings of creativity research come from Granovetter's strength of weak ties argument (Granovetter, 1973). This paper argues that individuals develop their strongest ties with others who are also connected to each other. As a result, strong and insular cliques develop and tend to recycle redundant information. This implies that non-redundant information tends to come from weak or bridging ties. In a creative context, weak ties are more likely to provide fresh information and new combinatorial opportunity, because they provide access to people with different interests and diverse perspectives. The access to different kinds of information and diverse social circles facilitates the creative process, because of the enhanced ability to generate different alternatives and the higher autonomy of the individual who is not strongly attached to a particular group. Empirical studies have found that weak ties enhance the search process but also make the transfer of complex knowledge and information more difficult (Hansen, 1999). Recent work (Perry-Smith and Shalley, 2003) proposes that weak ties are better than strong ties for creativity and that a peripheral position with many connections outside of the network is likely to be more creative. Ironically, however, successful individuals might then become more central and ultimately less creative.

Perhaps the most active topic in the sociology of creativity is the current controversy over the importance of cohesive networks, which facilitate trust, versus the importance of brokered networks, which enable privileged access to fresh information. Coleman (1988) argues that cohesion and closure in social networks – when an individual works with others who also work with each other, independent of the first person – encourage cooperation and trust. Trust is difficult to develop in open and brokered networks because an individual who defects can only be sanctioned by the immediate person he or she injures. In the creative context, cohesion and closure enable inventors to take risks, share resources, and communicate difficult information more effectively (Uzzi and Spiro, 2005). In contrast to the arguments for the benefits of cohesion, Burt highlights the importance of brokers, who span 'structural holes,' in providing non-redundant information. 'People who stand near the holes in a social structure are at higher risk of having good ideas' (Burt, 2004: 349).

People working in closed clusters have comparatively less opportunity to learn about new ideas and results.

Empirical work on the benefits of brokerage versus cohesion remains mixed. Ahuja (2000), in a study of firms and alliance structure in the international chemicals industry, found that brokerage had a negative impact on innovation. Obstfeld's (2005) survey evidence demonstrates that actors within cohesive networks are more likely to be involved with successful innovations. His arguments stress the importance of resource mobilization and motivation of colleagues in developing an idea. In contrast to these results that support closed, Burt (2004) analyzes the networks around managers in a large American electronics company and finds that brokers generate more innovative ideas.

Small world networks have been proposed recently as a means to incorporate the benefits of closed while avoiding its information homogeneity. Small world networks consist of dense local clusters of collaboration, tied together by occasional non-local ties to other dense clusters. Uzzi and Spiro (2005) focus on the clustering mechanism and demonstrate a non-monotonic and positive relationship between creativity in New York musicals and the average clustering of the entire network for a given year. The non-monotonicity results from the redundancy of information that circulates within clusters. Schilling and Phelps (forthcoming) demonstrate a positive interaction between clustering and path length for firms with strategic alliances and their patenting. Fleming, King and Juda (forthcoming) study patent co-authorship networks and their influence on subsequent patenting in a region. They argue that the effectiveness of clustering depends on local contingencies, which cannot be captured with an average and network-wide, clustering measure. They demonstrate a negative influence of clustering, a weak clustering and path-length interaction, and a much stronger effect of simple connection into the network's largest connected component. To resolve these conflicting empirical results will require further research, preferably at the individual and group levels in order to model local contingencies and avoid aggregation bias (Robinson, 1950). Furthermore, given the fact that inventors have become increasingly mobile, the most important implication for firms is that collaboration networks increasingly cross organizational boundaries (Schilling and Phelps forthcoming, Fleming et al. forthcoming). Rather than generating more ideas internally, firms can increasingly find them outside the firm. As a result, the pertinent managerial challenges are to retain and manage the most creative gatekeepers and compete on back-end development (Fleming and Marx, 2006).

In contrast to social brokerage of personal relationships, technological brokerage occurs when individuals or firms span technological communities or recombine previously disparate technologies (Hargadon and Sutton, 1997). Technological gatekeepers (also known as boundary spanners, see Allen, 1977; Tushman and Scanlan, 1981a; Tushman and Scanlan, 1981b) keep their organizational colleagues in touch with current developments by means of informal connections with the outside world:

> There will always be some people who, for various reasons, tend to become more acquainted with information sources outside their immediate community. They either read more extensively than most or develop personal contacts with outsiders. A large proportion of these people in turn attract colleagues from within the community who turn to them for information and advice (Allen, 1977: 150).

The gatekeeping role correlates with creativity but the causality remains unclear. Technological gatekeeping should improve creativity, yet demonstrated creativity could lead to the role. Technological brokerage can also occur at the firm level of analysis. Hargadon and Sutton (1997) performed an ethnography at IDEO, a US product design consulting firm. By working for clients in many different industries, IDEO enjoyed the position of a technological broker at the firm level. The access to experiences in multiple industries allowed the company to use knowledge acquired from one industry in designing new products for another industry.

A burgeoning literature has documented the creativity benefits of strategic research-and-development alliances (Stuart and Podolnly, 1996). Conferences provide another opportunity for information gathering, though peer-reviewed presentations, like written material, probably lie outside the comprehension of most engineers (Allen, 1977). Hence, managers must still rely on gatekeepers. Though no research we are aware of has mapped the cross-organizational networks that must result from strategic research-and-development relationships, we assume that gatekeepers perform a similar role for information transfer.

Finally, managers must remain realistic in their expectations for creativity. Expertise plays a significant role in a person's creative capacity. It usually takes a decade of systematic practice and training for a person to attain world-class skills and know-how in a particular field. 'Creative individuals do not produce new ideas de novo, but rather those ideas must arise from a large set of well-developed skills and a rich body of domain-relevant knowledge' (Simon, 1981; Simonton, 2000: 152). Fresh-out graduates, particularly from undergraduate programs, will be less capable on average of creative syntheses. Ideally, teams should have a mix of seasoned experts and inexperienced contributors. Guimerà et al. (2005) demonstrate the benefits of expertise on team outcomes with a century-long record of Broadway musicals.

8. The selection and retention stages: Sorting through and developing the best combinations

After an idea or new combination has been developed, the next step is evaluation. Most ideas prove wanting and are discarded almost immediately.

The first winnowing occurs with the individual's own thought trials. The inventor and scientist Faraday described the process (Simonton, 1999: 27): 'The world little knows how many thoughts and theories which have passed through the mind of a scientific investigator have been crushed in silence and secrecy by his own severe criticism and adverse examinations; that in the most successful instances not a tenth of the suggestions, the hopes, the wishes, the preliminary conclusions have been realized.'

In contrast to variation, however, selection also takes place outside of the individual. Although the roles are rarely defined so starkly, the poet Paul Valéry (Simonton, 1999: 27) proposes that 'it takes two to invent anything. One makes up combinations; the other chooses and recognizes what he wishes and what is important to him in the mass of things which the former has imparted to him.' Campbell concurs: 'Such considerations suggest complementary combinations of talent in creative teams, although the uninhibited idea-man and the compulsive edit-and-record type are notoriously incompatible office mates' (Campbell, 1960: 105). One huge advantage of social interaction is that combinations can be judged by a greater number of selection criteria. 'Much of creative thought is opportunistic in the sense of having a wide number of selective criteria available at all times, against which the thought trials are judged' (Campbell, 1960: 104).

From a managerial perspective, the challenge changes from generating new ideas to choosing the most promising ones for further development. Fortunately, it becomes easier (or at least more of a repeatable process) to manage the product development process as it progresses from idea creation to ultimate commercialization. A process, which relies initially on individual creativity – relatively unpredictable, possibly unbalanced, and seemingly 'blind' – begins to rely more heavily on social interaction and more 'manageable' processes. The research literature on the selection phase reflects this shift as well. Rather than coming from psychology and sociology research (as the literature on variation did), it comes from operations management, economics, and marketing and focuses on traditional product development issues such as prototyping, testing, and marketing. These literatures have begun to reach back into the creative stages and consider promising applications for technologically 'pushed' ideas (Dahan and Hauser, 2001).

Recent research has documented a tremendous improvement in product development tools for both the variation and the selection phases. Drug development provides a powerful archetype (Drews, 2000). Firms and universities now maintain libraries with hundreds of thousands of compounds for recombinant search. These library components are recombined and tested for efficacy against thousands of possible disease models. Ideally, such high-throughput screening constitutes an automatic variation generator and selector, which can run largely by itself. The process is not always effective, since model fidelity varies greatly, and even if a 'hit' occurs, the mechanism remains to be explained. Still, high-throughput screening remains an attractive model for the automation of creativity in the product development process.

Simulation provides another promising tool for selection and, to a lesser extent, variation (Thomke, 1998; see also Thomke's chapter in this volume). The combination of the inexorable advance of computing power and the improvement in digital representation of products and product systems has greatly increased the efficacy of modeling products before manufacturing them – even before prototyping them. The approach is particularly effective for complex systems with thousands of interacting parts. If the interactions between individual parts can be modeled accurately, the overall system dynamics will emerge accurately and without the need for hierarchical design and control. Engineers can test overall product hypotheses without delving into the details of component–by-component interactions. The tools also uncover unpredicted interactions. For example, BMW engineers discovered that overall vehicle safety was improved by weakening a particular frame support (Thomke et al., 1999). Ideally, these tools are integrated into a design methodology that fully explores the recombinant space through systematic generation of variation and experimentation against high-fidelity models (Thomke, 2003).

Firms are often faced with too many product development possibilities. While this may seem to be an enviable position, it is in fact a bad situation, especially from a production process perspective (Wheelwright and Clark, 1992). Given the inherent organizational and managerial difficulty of killing projects, firms tend to allow too many to continue in their development pipelines. In any production system, throughput time increases as the system approaches capacity, with the result that all projects become late and over-budget. When there is an overabundance of product development possibilities, rigorous selection processes become imperative for the firm's survival. Implementation of aggregate project planning processes (Wheelwright and Clark, 1992) that incorporate capacity, risk, and market analyses can help managers to avoid behavioral biases in project selection and to justify the painful process of project selection. However, recent simulation work has demonstrated how simple and reasonable green-light rules can also cause extreme variance in the arrival of finished products (Gino and Pisano, 2005).

We also draw attention to a new trend in technology development, the rise of open-innovation communities (von Hippel, 2005), because they provide a new model for an evolutionary view of product development. Open-innovation communities generate variance by the voluntary contributions of thousands of people. Motivated by a variety of reasons – including personal need, distrust of corporate goals, or community spirit – volunteers submit innovations with little guidance. The innovations are selected by community leaders (who are chosen for their technical and leadership abilities) and tested by the entire community. Open-innovation communities tackle problems ranging from software for operating systems to genetic research on agriculture (Broothaerts et al., 2005) to sporting equipment (Shah, 2005).

It is not yet clear whether open-innovation communities are mostly capable of refining modular systems or whether they are also capable of seminal breakthroughs. Community infrastructure, such as SourceForge, that enables any user to start a project may prove that open-innovation communities are indeed capable of very original and creative front-end ideation.

Probably the most valuable lesson for the classical literature on product development is the value of early product release to a dedicated, motivated, and diverse community of users. This subjects products to a huge variety of operating conditions and quickly identifies bugs. The process requires strong community leaders to outline modular architectures and to keep the voluntary associations from forking. A firm can benefit from such an open approach (MacCormack et al., 2001) but needs to manage its community's perception of the firm's proprietary motives.

9. Why is breakthrough product development so difficult? An evolutionary answer

The greatest benefit that an evolutionary perspective offers managers is to highlight the contradictions inherent in the different stages of product development. The variation stage requires diversity, free association, and acceptance of all potential. The selection stage requires discipline, rigorous criteria, and rejection of almost all potential. Retention calls for informing and motivating professionals who had nothing to do with the initial stages. The repertoire of skills required for successful product development remains large and inherently contradictory within a single organization (March, 1991; O'Reilly and Tushman, 2004). Long-term viability in an innovative industry relies on both separating and integrating the three different stages.

Varieties of scholars have highlighted this contradiction. March (1991) suggests that the key to the generation of successful product innovations is to maintain an appropriate balance between exploration and exploitation: 'Exploration includes things captured by terms such as search, variation, risk taking, experimentation, play, flexibility, discovery, and innovation. Exploitation includes such things as refinement, choice, production, efficiency, selection, implementation, and execution.' Benner and Tushman (2002) demonstrated that firms, which focus on the variance reduction inherent in quality control processes, suffer from a decrease in creativity. Repenning (2002) demonstrates analytically how promising variations can founder on the problems of motivation and transfer within an organization. Such inherent contradictions are good topics for future research in product development. O'Reilly and Tushman (2004) coined the term *ambidextrous organization* to capture the inherent tensions between exploration and exploitation.

10. Practical suggestions

We have a number of suggestions – although in many cases the ideas remain empirically untested – for managers who wish to increase the possibility of generating a breakthrough. Most of these suggestions aim to increase the variance of inventive draw (Fleming and Szigety, 2006); managers must therefore couple these ideas with more rigorous selection processes to avoid increasing the number of failed projects further down the development funnel. Uncombined technologies and multi-disciplinary teams have been shown to increase the variability of inventive outcomes, though at the expense of the average outcome (Fleming, 2001). Using science as a map in the process of search has been shown to decrease the variability of search, though its main benefit is in application to interdependent and coupled technologies (Fleming and Sorenson, 2004). More speculatively, managerial action to decrease risk aversion or to increase aspirations should increase the odds of a breakthrough. This might happen naturally because of particularly poor or successful recent performance. Collaboration probably decreases the variability of inventive outcomes (though not at the expense of the mean), so encouraging non-collaborative invention should increase the chance of a highly skewed outlier. Inventors who change fields can also be expected to generate outcomes that are more variable. Managerial pressure probably decreases the chances of a breakthrough, assuming that it decreases intrinsic motivation (Amabile, 1996). Slack resources, in contrast, will encourage play and goofing off (March, 1991). Personnel turnover through hiring and firing probably increases the possibility of inventing a breakthrough, though it surely makes the selection and retention processes more difficult.

An evolutionary perspective also points the way to resolution of conflicting results within the creativity and product development literature. For example, the aforementioned controversy over the benefits of closure and brokerage to creativity can be resolved with an evolutionary perspective. This resolution has remained obscure because researchers do not differentiate between the generation of variation and whether the variation is selected and retained for future use. Brokerage, as argued above, provides a superior position for creating new combinations, because the broker is the first to receive new information and access to creative opportunities. However, brokerage hampers the selection and retention of the broker's inventions for four reasons (Fleming, Mingo, and Chen, forthcoming). First, new combinations are less likely to be criticized thoroughly because they are conceived (and to some extent controlled) by a single individual. Second, the perception of mutual ownership will be less and other people, apart from the broker will be more concerned about for 'scooping' another's idea. Third, the new combination will not be as well understood by others, given the lack of distributed invention processes and socially visible iterations. Finally, the diffusion of the new combination will be hampered, for the same reasons that enhanced the broker's initial creativity – there will be fewer social relationships that are capable of acting as conduits for the diffusion of the new combination.

Similar arguments might help resolve the controversy over diversity and creativity. Teams that are more diverse probably make greater variation possible, while less diverse teams probably handle the selection and retention stages more effectively.

11. Conclusion

We organized the literature on product development under an evolutionary rubric, with a special focus on the creativity of the variation stage. We began with the classic definition of creativity as a new combination of technologies, components, or ideas. Such a definition lends itself to search analogies and differentiates between creating a new combination and whether or not the new combination is selected and ultimately retained as a successful innovation. We argued that, while new combinations only occur within the mind of a single person, social influences can greatly improve a person's creativity. The creativity literatures that pertain to the variation stage can be organized into four categories, namely psychological, social-psychological, research on groups and creativity, and purely structural perspectives from sociology. Moving on to the selection phase, we described how recent developments in simulation and high-throughput screening technologies have enabled greater creativity in the product development process. We concluded by identifying the inherent contradictions in trying to manage an evolutionary process and offered an evolutionary resolution to one set of conflicting results in the sociology and creativity literature. Figure 5.1 summarizes the main ideas and concepts we have discussed in this paper.

The literature on the front end of product development and creativity has become better elaborated of late. We know some of the basic correlations between individual and social characteristics and creativity and we have tools, which work reasonably well in transforming incremental invention into new

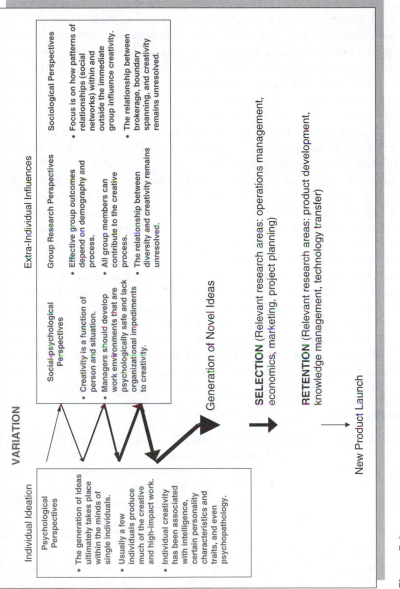

Figure 5.1
Creativity in new product development: An evolutionary integration.

products. However, many questions remain unanswered. Among them: What are the sources of breakthroughs? How can managers increase their chances of inventing an internal breakthrough or adopting and exploiting an external breakthrough?

The ill-defined sources of breakthroughs may also be changing. For example, some open-innovation communities are thought to be capable only of modular and incremental invention (such as Linux) while other open-innovation communities invented the protocols for both the Web and Internet (the scientific community and the Internet Engineering Task Force, respectively). Universities are also increasingly a source of breakthrough technology. A variety of actors in the university technology-transfer space would benefit from a better understanding of how to transfer the technology, including the firms that license technology, the venture capitalists who fund new firms, and the universities and inventors themselves.

Researchers will need to innovate methodologically to continue making progress on these questions. Research would greatly benefit from better tools for modeling creative search and from better measurements of creativity and success in product development. Simulation has become a very popular tool for modeling uncertain search (Rivkin, 2000), but closed-form models would also be welcome, if only to make the work more acceptable to formal modeling communities. Careful empirical work also remains to be done, since much managerial prescription is still based on anecdotal wisdom, or case studies, which are illustrative but not sampled representatively. This will be difficult, since product development data are longitudinal, very proprietary, and difficult to gather. The challenge is worth undertaking, however, since what comes out the developmental back end of the product development tunnel will only be as good as, what goes into the creative front end.

References

Ahuja, G. 2000. Collaboration Networks, Structural Holes, and Innovation: A Longitudinal Study. *Administrative Science Quarterly* 45: 425–455.

Allen, T. J. 1977. *Managing the Flow of Technology.* Cambridge, MA: MIT Press.

Amabile, T. M. 1996. Assessing the Work Environment for Creativity. *Academy of Management Journal* 39: 1154–1184.

Baldwin, C. and K. Clark 2000. *Design Rules – Vol. 1 The Power of Modularity.* Cambridge, MA: MIT Press.

Bantel, K. A., and S. E. Jackson. 1989. Top Management and Innovations in Banking: Does the Composition of the Top Team Make a Difference? *Strategic Management Journal* 10: 107–124.

Barron, F., and D. M. Harrington. 1981. Creativity, Intelligence, and Personality. *Annual Review of Psychology* 32: 439–476.

Basalla, G. 1988. *The Evolution of Technology.* Cambridge: Cambridge University Press.

Benner, M. and M. Tushman 2002. Process Management and Technological Innovation: A Longitudinal Study of the Photography and Paint Industries. *Administrative Science Quarterly* 47(4): 676–706.

Broothaerts, W., H. J. Mitchell, B. Weir, S. Kaines, L. M. A. Smith, W. Yang, J. E. Mayer, C. Roa-Rodriguez, and R. A. Jefferson. 2005. Gene Transfer to Plants by Diverse Species of Bacteria. *Nature* 433: 629–633.

Burt, R. S. 2004. Structural Holes and Good Ideas. *American Journal of Sociology* 110: 349–399.

Campbell, D. T. 1960. Blind Variation and Selective Retention in Creative Thought as in Other Knowledge Processes. *Psychological Review* 67: 380–400.

Chatman, J. A., J. T. Polzer, S. G. Barsade, and M. A. Neale. 1998. Being Different yet Feeling Similar: The Influence of Demographic Composition and Organizational Culture on Work Processes and Outcomes. *Administrative Science Quarterly* 43: 749–780.

Christensen, C. M. 1997. *The Innovator's Dilemma: When New Technologies Cause Great Firms to Fail.* Boston, MA: Harvard Business School Press.

Coleman, J. 1988. Social Capital in the Creation of Human Capital. *American Journal of Sociology* 94: S95–S120.

Dahan, E., and J. Hauser. 2001. Product Development – Managing a Dispersed Process. In: B. Weitz and R. Wensley (Eds.) *Handbook of Marketing.*

Darwin, C. 1858. *The Origin of the Species by Natural Selection.* Reprinted in 1979. New York: Random House Publishing.

Dougherty, D. 1992. Interpretive Barriers to Successful Product Innovation in Large Firms. *Organization Science* 3: 179–202.

Drews, J. 2000. Drug Discovery: A Historical Perspective. *Science* 287: 1960–1964.

Edmondson, A. 1999. Psychological Safety and Learning Behavior in Work Teams. *Administrative Science Quarterly* 44: 350–383.

Ely, R. J., and D. A. Thomas. 2001. Cultural Diversity at Work: The Effects of Diversity Perspectives on Work Group Processes and Outcomes. *Administrative Science Quarterly* 46: 229–273.

Ernst, H., C. Leptien, and J. Vitt. 2000. Inventors are Not Alike: The Distribution of Patenting Output among Industrial R&D Personnel. *IEEE Transactions on Engineering Management* 47: 184–199.

Fleming, L. 2001. Recombinant Uncertainty in Technological Search. *Management Science* 47: 117–132.

Fleming, L. 2002. Finding the Organizational Sources of Technological Breakthroughs: The Story of Hewlett-Packard's Thermal Ink-jet. *Industrial and Corporate Change* 11(5): 1059–1084.

Fleming, L., and O. Sorenson. 2004. Science as a Map in Technological Search. *Strategic Management Journal* 25: 909–928.

Fleming, L., C. King, and A. Juda. (Forthcoming) Small Worlds and Innovation. To appear in Organization Science.

Fleming, L., and M. Marx. 2006. Managing Creativity in a Small World. *California Management Review* 48(4).

Fleming, F., S. Mingo, and D. Chen. (forthcoming). Brokerage and Collaborative Creativity. *Under revision at Administration Science Quarterly*.

Fleming, L., and M. Szigety. 2006. Exploring the Tail of Creativity: An Evolutionary Model of Breakthrough Invention. *Advances in Strategic Management* pp. 339–364.

Gavetti, G., and D. Levinthal. 2000. Looking Forward and Looking Backward: Cognitive and Experiential Search. *Administrative Science Quarterly* 2000.

Gierer, A. 2004. Human Brain Evolution, Theories of Innovation, and Lessons from the History of Technology. *Journal of Biosciences* 29: 235–244.

Gino, F., and G. Pisano. 2005. Holding or Folding? R&D Portfolio Strategy Under Different Information Regimes. Harvard Business School Working Paper No. 05–072.

Guimerà, R., B. Uzzi, J. Spiro, and L. A. Nunes Amaral. 2005. Team Assembly Mechanisms Determine Collaboration Network Structure and Team Performance. *Science* 308: 697–702.

Glynn, M. A. 1996. Innovative Genius: A Framework for Relating Individual and Organizational Intelligences to Innovation. *Academy of Management Review* 21: 1081–1111.

Granovetter, M. 1973. The Strength of Weak Ties. *American Journal of Sociology* 78: 1360–1380.

Hansen, M. T. 1999. The Search-Transfer Problem: The Role of Weak Ties in Sharing Knowledge across Organization Subunits. *Administrative Science Quarterly* 44: 82–111.

Hargadon, A., and R. I. Sutton. 1997. Technology Brokering in a Product Development firm. *Administrative Science Quarterly* 42: 716–749.

Henderson, R. M., and K. B. Clark. 1990. Architectural Innovation: The Reconfiguration of Existing Product Technologies and the Failure of Established Firms. *Administrative Science Quarterly* 35: 9–30.

Iansiti, M. 1997. *Technology Integration.* Cambridge, MA: Harvard University Press.

Kanter, R. M. 1988. When a Thousand Flowers Bloom: Structural, Collective, and Social Conditions for Innovation in Organizations. In: B. M. Staw and L. L. Cummings (Eds.) *Research in Organizational Behavior.* 10: 97–102, Greenwich, CT: JAI Press.

Katz, E., and P. F. Lazarsfeld. 1955. *Personal Influence.* New York: Free Press.

King, B. J., and B. Pope. 1999. Creativity as a Factor in Psychological Assessment and Healthy Psychological Functioning. *Journal of Personality Assessment* 72: 200–207.

Leonard, D., and W. Swap. 1999. *When Sparks Fly: Igniting Creativity in Groups.* Boston, MA: Harvard Business School Press.

MacCormack, A. D., R. Verganti, and M. Iansiti. 2001. Developing Products on Internet Time: The Anatomy of a Flexible Development Process. *Management Science* 47: 133–150.

March, J. 1991. Exploration and Exploitation in Organizational Learning. *Organization Science* 2: 71–87.

Obstfeld, D. 2005. Social Networks, the Tertius Iungens Orientation, and Involvement in Innovation. *Administrative Science Quarterly* 50: 100–130.

O'Reilly, C., and M. Tushman. 2004. The Ambidextrous Organization. *Harvard Business Review* Apr. 82(4):74–81, 140.

Osborn, A. F. 1957. *Applied Imagination.* 2nd Edition. New York: Scribner.

Pelled, L. H., K. M. Eisenhardt, and K. R. Xin. 1999. Exploring the Black Box: An Analysis of Group Diversity, Conflict, and Performance. *Administrative Science Quarterly* 44: 1–28.

Perry-Smith, J. E., and C. E. Shalley. 2003. The social side of creativity: A static and dynamic social network perspective. *Academy of Management Review* 28: 89–106.

Polzer, J. T., L. P. Milton, and W. B. Swann. 2002. Capitalizing on Diversity: Interpersonal Congruence in Small Work Groups. *Administrative Science Quarterly* 47: 296–324.

Price, D. J. 1965. Networks of Scientific Papers. *Science* 149: 510–515.

Repenning, N. 2002. A Simulation-Based Approach to Understanding the Dynamics of Innovation Implementation. *Organization Science* 13: 109–127.

Rivkin, J. 2000. Imitation of Complex Strategies. *Management Science* 46(6): 824–844.

Robinson, W. 1950. Ecological Correlations and the Behavior of Individuals. *American Sociological Review* 15: 351–357.

Runco, M. A. 2004. Creativity. *Annual Review of Psychology* 55: 657–687.

Ruppel, C. P., and S. J. Harrington. 2000. The Relationship of Communication, Ethical Work Climate, and Trust to Commitment and Innovation. *Journal of Business Ethics* 25: 313–328.

Schilling, M. A., Phelps. C. (Forthcoming) Interfirm knowledge networks and knowledge creation: The impact of "small-world" connectivity. To appear at *Management Science*.

Schumpeter, J. 1939. *Business Cycles.* New York: McGraw-Hill Book Company, Inc.

Shah, S. K. 2005. Open Beyond Software. In: Danese Cooper, Chris DiBona and Mark Stone (Eds.) *Open Sources 2.* Sebastopol, CA: O'Reilly Media.

Shaw, M. E. 1976. Group Dynamics: *The Psychology of Small Group Behavior*. New York: McGraw-Hill.

Simon, H. A. 1981. *The Sciences of the Artificial*. 2nd Edition. Cambridge, MA: MIT Press.

Simonton, D. K. 1987. Developmental Antecedent of Achieved Eminence. *Annals of Child Development* 5: 131–169.

Simonton, D. K. 1999. *Origins of Genius: Darwinian Perspectives on Creativity*. New York: Oxford University Press.

Simonton, D. K. 2000. Creativity: Cognitive, Personal, Developmental, and Social Aspects. *American Psychologist* 55: 151–158.

Smith, K. G., K. A. Smith, J. D. Olian, H. P. Sims, D. P. O'Bannon, and J. A. Scully. 1994. Top Management Team Demography and Process: The Role of Social Integration and Communication. *Administrative Science Quarterly* 39: 412–438.

Staw, B. 1995. "Why No One Really Wants Creativity." Creative Action in Organizations. In: C. Ford and D. Gioia (Eds.) *Thousand Oaks*. Ca: Sage Publications, pp. 161–166.

Stuart, T., and J. Podolnly. 1996. Local Search and the Evolution of Technological Capabilities. *Strategic Management Review* 17: 21–38.

Sutton, R. I. 2002. *Weird Ideas that Work: 11 $\frac{1}{2}$ Practices for Promoting, Managing, and Sustaining Innovation*. New York: The Free Press.

Sutton, R. I., and A. Hargadon. 1996. Brainstorming Groups in Context: Effectiveness in a Product Design Firm. *Administrative Science Quarterly* 41: 685–718.

Thomke, S. 1998. Managing Experimentation in the Design of New Products. *Management Science* 44: 743–762.

Thomke, S. 2003. *Experimentation Matters: Unlocking the Potential of New Technologies for Innovation*. Boston, MA: Harvard Business School Press.

Thomke, S., M. Holzner, and T. Gholami. 1999. The Crash in the Machine. *Scientific American* 280(3): 92–97.

Toubia, O. 2005. Idea Generation, Creativity, and Incentives. Working Paper. Columbia Business School.

Tushman, M. L., and T. J. Scanlan. 1981a. Characteristics and External Orientations of Boundary Spanning Individuals. *Academy of Management Journal* 24: 83–98.

Tushman, M. L., and T. J. Scanlan. 1981b. Boundary Spanning Individuals: Their Role in Information Transfer and Their Antecedents. *Academy of Management Journal* 24: 289–305.

Uzzi, B., Spiro, J. 2005. Collaboration and Creativity: The Small World Problem. *American Journal of Sociology* 111(2) September 2005: 447–504.

Von Hippel, E. 2005. Democratizing Innovation, Cambridge, MA: MIT-Press 2005.

Wheelwright, S. C., and K. B. Clark. 1992. *Revolutionizing Product Development*. New York, NY: The Free Press.

Williams, K. Y., and C. A. O'Reilly. 1998. Forty Years of Diversity Research: A Review. In: B. M. Staw and L. L. Cummings (Eds.) *Research in Organizational Behavior*. Greenwich, CT: JAI Press, 20: 77–140.

6 Resource allocation and new product development portfolio management

Stylianos Kavadias and
Raul O. Chao

1. Introduction

Developing the 'right' new products is critical to the firm's success and is often cited as the key to a sustained competitive advantage. Managers often set ambitious goals for future revenue generated from new products. Statements such as '*innovate or die*' overflow the popular business press and confirm the importance of successful new product development (NPD).

Any company that engages in NPD faces the important problem of allocating resources between innovation initiatives in a portfolio. Companies that make poor choices with respect to their NPD portfolio run the risk of losing their competitive advantage. Examples abound in practice: DuPont experienced trouble because the company diverted the majority of its estimated $2 billion yearly R&D budget to improving established business lines (Barrett, 2003). Drug maker AstraZeneca revealed the decision to restructure its portfolio to include more incremental projects (Pilling, 2000). Kodak is investing resources in revolutionary new technologies to catch up in the digital photography market, despite the fact that the company was synonymous with photography for the better part of the twentieth century (Schoenberger, 2003). These cases underscore the reality that effective resource allocation and NPD portfolio management profoundly impact firm success. The NPD portfolio practically determines the firm's strategy for the medium and long-term future, and is the responsibility of the senior managers of the firm (Roussel et al., 1991; Cooper et al., 1997). When managers make resource allocation and NPD portfolio decisions they take an implementation step that links innovation strategy with reality. This step embodies a difficult choice: allocate resources to the development of fundamentally new technologies, products, and markets that are naturally more risky investments or improve existing technologies, extend product lines, and entrench existing market position without excessive risk. Of course, the problem is exacerbated by the fact that the former investments have the lure of potentially high-payoffs while the latter often result in smaller payoffs (Tushman and O'Reilly 1996).

From the dawn of Operations Research in the early 1950s, to the emergence of managerial frameworks (such as the BCG matrix) in the 1970s, through today, the problem of developing the 'right' new products has motivated academics and practitioners to propose a number of solutions. Several tools and theories have been developed by different constituencies, resulting in an interesting dichotomy: a collection of rigorous analytical efforts with minimal adoption and minimal practical impact (Loch et al., 2001; Shane and Ulrich, 2004), and a variety of managerial frameworks grounded in individual case studies with widespread impact but little theoretical foundation. In either case, managerial guidelines are limited to a generic notion of 'balance' among different value determinants due to the lack of understanding about fundamental problem drivers. Hence, senior managers, R&D managers, and project managers are forced to make resource allocation decisions based primarily on intuition or heuristic rules.

Recent data verify that the overall impact of NPD portfolio methods and research remains largely in doubt. A study conducted by the Product Development Management Association (PDMA) reveals an interesting result: between 1994 and 2004 development cycle times have significantly improved. A portion of this effect is a due to overall improvement in the management of the product development process. However, the percentage of resources allocated to minor product changes and small improvements also increased significantly during the same period of time. Hence, there is evidence that firms are increasingly focused on incremental NPD efforts. The bad news is that high performing firms emphasize diverse portfolios that include 'cutting edge,' 'new to the market,' or 'new to the world' initiatives in addition to incremental efforts (Adams and Boike 2004). Figure 6.1 illustrates these results.

Collectively these facts indicate that a deeper understanding of NPD portfolio management is necessary. The purpose of this chapter is to provide a theoretical framework that can be used to study resource allocation and NPD portfolio management. We begin in Section 2 with an important underlying premise: NPD portfolio management is a complex problem. This discussion sets the stage for Section 3 in which we provide a theoretical framework for resource allocation and NPD portfolio management. In Section 4, we associate our framework with existing literature that addresses different levels of decision making with respect to the NPD portfolio. We summarize the current state of knowledge and highlight some important open questions in Section 5.

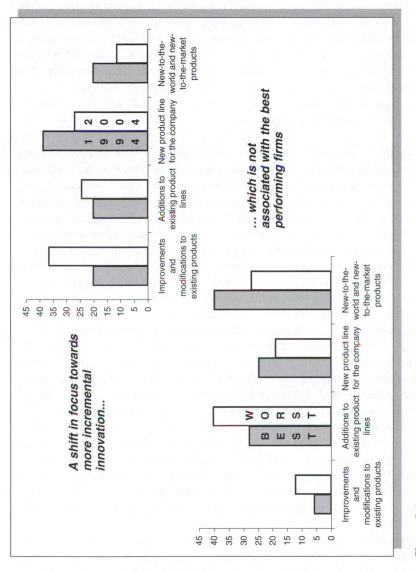

Figure 6.1
Product development institute report, 2004.

2. What makes NPD portfolio management so difficult?

NPD portfolio management is concerned with methods and tools that ensure effective resource allocation among an ensemble of innovation efforts. The NPD portfolio determines the minor improvements, new product introductions, or radical breakthrough developments associated with the product mix of a company. In doing so, the NPD portfolio influences the balance between market segments and the time to market profile for each innovation effort. The essential feature that defines the NPD portfolio problem is that projects should be viewed together rather than in isolation. The portfolio view necessarily gives rise to several considerations:

- *Strategic alignment.* The NPD portfolio allows a firm to operationalize and implement strategy over time. This point implies that the NPD portfolio problem entails a large component of ambiguity and complexity, since the determinants of firm success and their interactions are rarely known. Moreover, successful NPD portfolio management rests upon the ability to effectively communicate firm strategy and cascade it down to an implementable NPD program or project level (Loch and Tapper, 2002).
- *Resource scarcity.* Scarce resources often critically constrain the NPD portfolio problem. It is common practice to pursue many projects in parallel to achieve broader product lines (mass customization) and higher market share (e.g., Reinertsen, 1997; Ulrich and Eppinger, 2003; Cusumano and Nobeoka, 1998). In multi-project environments, scarce resources render the resource allocation decision a critical factor for success (Adler et al., 1995). Scarcity may involve the total R&D budget, testing equipment availability (analogous to bottleneck machines in production scheduling), or specialists with unique areas of expertise. In several contexts, project managers need to 'queue' for access to these specialized resources.
- *Project interactions.* Companies often develop multiple products and services in closely related market segments. Hence, the new products that are developed exhibit synergies or incompatibilities in their technical aspects. Similarly, on the market side, products may substitute or complement one another. Interactions between success determinants play a critical role in the resource allocation decision, since interactions proxy decision complexity.
- *Outcome uncertainty.* NPD projects are characterized by lack of precise knowledge regarding their outcomes. Hence, management faces uncertainty along the dimensions of the potential market value and technical output of any given project. NPD managers face risks related to the overall functionality of the product (technical risk) and to the adoption of the product from the end customers (market risk). Moreover, the type of

uncertainty determines the ability to 'optimize.' Pich et al. (2003) discuss such a typology within the context of project management.

- *Dynamic nature of the problem.* Decision makers must allocate resources over time and NPD programs evolve over time. Therefore, managers must take into account future values and risks when allocating resources to a promising idea. However, it is often difficult to quantify the potential of promising ideas or precisely measure the risks involved. Furthermore, the various innovation initiatives in a portfolio do not typically evolve at the same pace.

The five sources of decision complexity outlined above highlight the difficulties associated with NPD portfolio management. Moreover, they illustrate that resource allocation and NPD portfolio decisions, like several other NPD decisions, are not necessarily centralized decisions; rather, they span across different levels of management. As the locus of decision-making moves from strategic to tactical and operational, resource allocation decisions are driven by more tangible and specific project metrics. However, they are constrained by significantly less flexibility (Anderson and Joglekar, 2005). In this chapter, we will not delve into the issues of product line design and competitive product positioning, since there are other chapters in this book that focus on such decisions. Rather, we will consider a general framework for resource allocation and NPD portfolio management, and we will link decisions to different organizational levels.

3. A theoretical framework for NPD portfolio management

In this section, we present a general model of resource allocation and NPD portfolio management. We use the model as a foundation upon which we build, and we discuss how the drivers of the resource allocation decision change depending on the organizational level at which the decision takes place (from senior management, to the NPD program level, and finally the individual project level). Once the differences are presented we introduce the associated literature and we overview the findings.

Figure 6.2 depicts the resource allocation decision and illustrates the different elements of the decision. A number of NPD programs must be funded by a pool of resources (the budget) in every period. The NPD programs are targeted at different, but not necessarily independent products that serve customer markets. Each product delivers an uncertain payoff at each period in time. The possibility of technical synergies and/or incompatibilities between program outcomes complicates the decision further.

We begin by considering that the firm's product portfolio is comprised of n distinct products. Each product is defined as a configuration of technology and

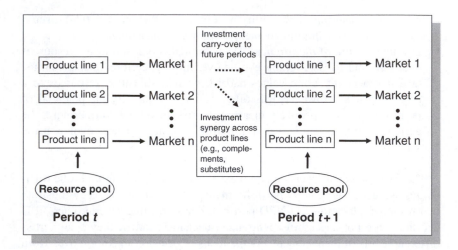

Figure 6.2
The dynamic portfolio selection decision(s).

market attributes. Management decides to develop and introduce products that employ specific technologies and target various customer needs. Therefore, managers must specify the product attributes such as core technology utilized and aesthetic design elements in addition to market-related variables such as price or distribution channel. Formally, each product is a vector

$$\vec{y}_i = (x_{i,1}, x_{i,2}, \ldots, x_{i,M(i)}) \tag{1}$$

where $i = 1, 2, \ldots, n$ is the number of products in the portfolio, $M(i)$ denotes the number of attributes that define product i, and $x_{i,j}$ is the j-th attribute that defines product i (e.g., whether a microchip has wireless capabilities or not). The firm operates in an environment where $M(i) \leq M$ and M defines the complete space of known and unknown product attributes. Thus, we allow for situations in which decision-makers are not aware of the existence of some product attributes that influence performance. Note at this point that a subset of the attributes are deliberate choices of management while others may not be (e.g., some technologies are used simply because of the absence of better alternatives or a particular distribution channel may be used because of prior experiences). The configuration of technology and market attributes determines product performance (sales or revenue) and the portfolio of products determines firm performance. We assume that each product i generates revenue $V_i(\vec{y}_i, \vec{y}_{-i})$ where $\vec{y}_{-i}$ represents all products in the firm's portfolio other than product i. Decision-makers may have precise knowledge of how the attributes contribute to the overall performance, or not. Therefore, the mapping from $\vec{y}_i$ to $V_i(\cdot)$ may be known precisely, or not. The reasons for

$V_i(\cdot)$ being unknown lie in the extent of decision maker's information processing capabilities and the interactions among the $x_{i,j}$ that define each product. Limited information processing capability leads to bounded rationality and a large number of interactions defines very complex $V_i(\cdot)$ functions.

On a periodic basis (e.g., quarterly or semi-annually), the firm conducts portfolio review meetings. The focus of the portfolio review meetings are the NPD programs that address the improvements or changes for each product or product line. We consider each NPD program to be a collection of projects that drive improvement and/or innovation in a single product line. In our formal representation, an NPD program drives a transition from configuration $\vec{y}_i$ to a new configuration $\vec{y}_i'$. Note that such a transition may not necessarily be the result of one individual project. It could rather be the outcome of several ongoing parallel efforts. In addition, note that NPD programs determine the innovation strategy of the firm. Innovation may be more or less incremental or radical depending on the number of attributes that are actually altered in a transition from $\vec{y}_i$ to $\vec{y}_i'$. Thus, innovation acquires a 'spatial' (Schumpeterian) quality, reflecting the notion of how different the innovation effort is compared to the existing configuration. Two distinct effects must be addressed here:

1. Depending on the magnitude of innovation pursued, as denoted by the number of attribute changes in the product configuration $\vec{\delta}_i = \vec{y}_i' - \vec{y}_i$ and its Euclidean distance $\Delta_i = |\vec{\delta}_i|$, the risk for obtaining a configuration that results in superior performance depends on the distance of search. For any set of configurations with the same distance Δ_i, the likelihood that configuration $\vec{y}_i + \vec{\delta}_i$ results in higher performance compared to $\vec{y}_i$ is a decreasing function of Δ_i. Formally, $\text{Prob}\{V_i(\vec{y}_i') \geq V_i(\vec{y}_i)\}$ is a decreasing function of Δ_i. This represents the fact that radical innovation is more risky than incremental innovation due to the distance of search.

2. The resources required to explore a transition from $\vec{y}_i$ to $\vec{y}_i'$ also depend on the distance of search. Formally, $C_i(\Delta_i)$ is an increasing function of Δ_i. This observation implies that for the same amount of resources allocated to an NPD program, either few very innovative or multiple incremental innovation configurations can be explored.

Finally, the portfolio decision involves the solution of a complicated dynamic problem:

$$J_t(\vec{y}_1, \vec{y}_2, \ldots, \vec{y}_n) =$$

$$max_{\vec{y}_j' \in \Omega, j=1,2,\ldots,n}(-\Sigma_i C_i(|\vec{y}_i' - \vec{y}_i|) + \Sigma_i V_i(\vec{y}_i') + J_{t+1}(\vec{y}_1', \vec{y}_2', \ldots, \vec{y}_n'))$$

$$(2)$$

subject to the budget constraint on a period basis: $\Sigma_i C_i(|\vec{y}_i' - \vec{y}_i|) \leq B_t$. The equation to be maximized consists of the total resource expenditure for changing each product, the immediate revenue generated by each new product configuration, and the value of the portfolio in period $t+1$ and beyond.

The general description above gives rise to several immediate questions regarding (i) the potential solution space and the degree of available knowledge regarding that space (i.e., *'what are the maximization levers available to management?'*), (ii) the level of knowledge regarding the performance functions $V_i(\cdot)$, as well as the interdependencies across the performance determinants $x_{i,j}$ (i.e., *'how do decisions change the performance value obtained?'*), and (iii) how strict is the resource constraint (i.e., *'does management have flexibility with respect to resource allocation or does management operate within the confines of a strict budget?'*).

In this chapter, we posit that a hierarchical perspective on the resource allocation and NPD portfolio management problem is appropriate. We argue that depending on the level of decision-making within the organization, and on the unit of analysis (be it a choice within single project versus the investment in an NPD program or even the composition of the entire NPD portfolio) the resource allocation decision faces distinct challenges. Our thesis here relates to an already growing body of research on NPD decisions across different levels in the organization – a 'hierarchical planning approach' – and the emerging knowledge gaps therein (see the chapters by Joglekar, Anderson, and Kulatilaka and Terwiesch and Loch in this book).

Figure 6.3 introduces the main decisions, variables, and challenges encountered at different organizational levels. Across different organizational levels the decisions relate to (i) the degree of knowledge regarding the solution space, (ii) the degree of knowledge regarding the underlying performance structure, and (iii) resource availability (and flexibility). The notion of 'degree of knowledge' captures full, partial, or lack of knowledge and maps directly into deterministic, foreseeable uncertainty, or ambiguous situations (Pich et al., 2003).

At the level of senior management the decision involves several dimensions that include target markets (e.g., industrial or consumer), basic technologies (e.g., process specifications), revolutionary technologies (e.g., hybrid engines), strategic considerations of the organization (e.g., generalists versus niche players), and external influences (e.g., regulations from antitrust committees) among others. Therefore, individual product performances are no longer seen as independent, rather they are highly coupled due to the interactions across different performance determinants. In addition, uncertainty, ambiguity (Pich et al., 2003), and bounded rationality (Simon, 1982) are confounded disallowing the use of standard risk assessment models. Although the decision is highly complex, an interesting consideration is that resource allocation is flexible at this level of decision-making, and the decision objective transforms

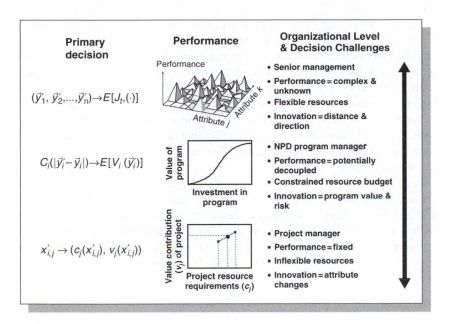

Figure 6.3
NPD portfolio selection in the organization.

from one of constrained optimization to a search for the best NPD portfolio. Given these observations, the maximization aspect introduced in our previous theoretical framework is overly limited and managers reside on methods and tools that aim to decipher potential trade-offs and shed some light on the decision process (e.g., market potential versus competitive position for each product line).

The NPD program level addresses a collection of focused innovation efforts (projects) aimed towards the improvement of a product or product line. At this level, several dimensions introduced previously become clearer without rendering the decision extremely easier. Given the innovation goal (e.g., 'need to radically change this product line' versus 'need to advance performance to the next stage'), the NPD program team performs within the boundaries of a specific search strategy. Therefore, the NPD manager faces a specific return on investment curve, where the magnitude of performance change is positively correlated with the degree of innovation, but so is the risk of the endeavor. Eventually, the NPD program manager must select how to invest a specific budget (thus resource availability becomes an issue) across projects with potentially different returns on investment and different risk profiles. However, as the focus becomes more specific (e.g., a specific product line), management has better understanding of the $V_i(\cdot)$ functions and can appropriately value the innovation outcome.

Finally, at the individual NPD project level, priorities are well established. In this case, different solutions that address specific product attributes (or a small subset of attributes) are designed and tested (e.g., the drop-down menu design team for a software company has to account for their strictly defined budget as well as the dictated performance goals). Performance determinants at this operational level are well understood and the residual risk lies in the exact resource requirements necessary to make a solution work. The flexibility associated with decisions at this level is limited but there is ample opportunity for optimization. Unfortunately, due to inflexible project characteristics and the combinatoric nature of the selection problem, optimization is not always guaranteed to work. Once again, managers must reside on heuristics that trade-off higher project performance with capacity utilization ('knapsack' problems).

Thus far we have established a hierarchical framework for resource allocation and NPD portfolio management. For the remainder of this chapter we attempt to highlight different insights obtained from the literature and how they relate to the framework presented in this chapter.

4. Existing literature

This section offers a literature review of the resource allocation and NPD portfolio management problem. We summarize the research undertaken, and we categorize it along two dimensions: the unit of analysis (firm portfolio, versus R&D program, versus individual projects) and the timing considerations of a static versus a dynamic analysis (Figure 6.4).

Figure 6.4 exhibits upfront an interesting finding. The inverse relationship between the amount of theoretical work performed and the level of analysis. Hence, at the strategic (firm) level of decision-making the amount of work is significantly less than the work in the 'tactical' level of project selection. The work at the latter level, as attested by our summarizing figure needs to be classified in sub areas. Even more interestingly, the tactical work has not managed to make a substantial impact to the upper levels of the managerial community reflecting the misalignment between the complex reality of the decision and the introduced simplifications of the modelling abstraction. The latter observation, has first been recorded by Souder (1973), and Schmidt and Freeland (1992); and iterated by Loch et al. (2001), Kavadias and Loch (2003), and very recently by Shane and Ulrich (2004) in their review paper for the fiftieth anniversary of technology management and product development research in *Management Science*.[1] Below, we discuss the main findings and

---

[1] '*A substantial body of research has focused on which innovation projects to pursue . . . surveys have shown that these models have found very little use in practice . . . If 50 years of research on an area has generated very little managerial impact, perhaps it is time for new approaches*' (Shane and Ulrich, 2004; p.136).

	Static	Dynamic
Firm level	• Roussel *et al.* (1991) • Wheelwright and Clark (1992a) • Ali *et al.* (1993) • Adler *et al.* (1995) • Cooper *et al.* (1997) • Comstock and Sjolseth (1999)	• Balasubramanian *et al.* (2004) • Girotra *et al.* (2005) • Gino and Pisano (2005) • Chao and Kavadias (2006)
R&D program level	• Analytical Hierarchy Process models, Liberatore (1987) • Jones (1999) • Fridgeirsdottir and Akella (2005)	• Chikte (1977) • Nobeoka and Cusumano (1997) • Loch and Kavadias (2002) • Ding and Eliashberg (2002) • Blanford (2004) • Setter and Tishler (2005) • Chao *et al.* (2006) • Bhattacharya and Kavadias (2007)
Project level	• Mathematical Programming Formulation Models, Fox, Baker and Bryant 1984, Loch *et al.* 2001 • Multi-criteria decision making tools, Brenner 1994 • Net Present Value (NPV) analysis, Hess (1993), Sharpe and Kellin (1998) • Break-Even Times (BET), House and Price (1991)	• Multi-Armed Bandit (MAB) models, Gittins and Jones 1972, Whittle 1980, Asawa and Teneketzis1996 • Dynamic Scheduling Models, Smith 1956, Harrison 1975, Wein1992, Van Mieghem 2000, Kavadias and Loch 2003 • Optimal admission models, Stidham 1985, Kleywegt and Papastavrou 1998, Lewis *et al.* 1999 • Economic models, Weitzmann 1979, Fox and Baker 1985, Vishwanath 1992

Figure 6.4
Overview of portfolio selection literature.

limitations of the previous work in the different groups. Our focus is to link them back to the overall framework we have established.

4.1. NPD portfolio management at the strategic level

The NPD portfolio problem has attracted strategy and management research interest, reflecting its importance for senior management. Because of the complexity of the decision at this level of decision making, as we argued in our general framework, the literature has mainly grown to a set of 'best practices' recorded through case studies. Yet recently, several theoretical studies have tried to open the 'black box' of the $V(\vec{y}_i)$ product performance functions. We start off by presenting the former group, which has shaped managerial decision making in a significant way. We then proceed to discuss further the recent studies.

Roussel et al. (1991) popularized the importance of portfolio selection for top management in organizations. Cooper et al. (1997) and Liberatore and Titus (1983) carried out a large survey of top management decision making concerning their NPD portfolios. Also, Wheelwright and Clark (1992a) recognized the importance of portfolio selection for strategic decision making. Most of these studies confirm a general trend: top management tend to complement their routine financial project evaluations with ad hoc tools, in particular resource allocation balances over 'strategic buckets,' and the comparison across market competition and newness and/or technological risk Wheelwright and Clark 1992a, Cooper, et al., 1997). We depict some representative, and often used,[2] managerial tools in Figure 6.5.

In *scoring models* (upper left of Figure 6.5), various projects are ranked with respect to a weighted average of their performance on multiple criteria as the latter ones are defined by management. The n best projects, according to their overall score, 'make it' to the portfolio. The upper right classification tool, a *risk-return 'bubble diagram'* categorizes the different R&D programs or projects along their technology risk and their potential return (as indicated by the net present value). The objective for top management is to achieve **balance** between the overall risk and the return of the portfolio. An efficient frontier could characterize the best returns that are being obtained at given risk levels. This tool is widely used in practice (see, e.g., Cooper et al., 1997). Finally, the division of resources into different 'strategic buckets' as illustrated in the bottom of Figure 6.5 aims to **balance** resource allocation across efforts of different innovation levels given that long term programs with very risky outcomes would always be undermined when compared financially

---

[2] See, e.g., Taggart and Blaxter (1992), Braunstein and Salsamendi (1994), Foster (1996), Groenveld (1997), Stillman (1997), Comstock and Sjolseth (1999), and Tritle et al. (2000)

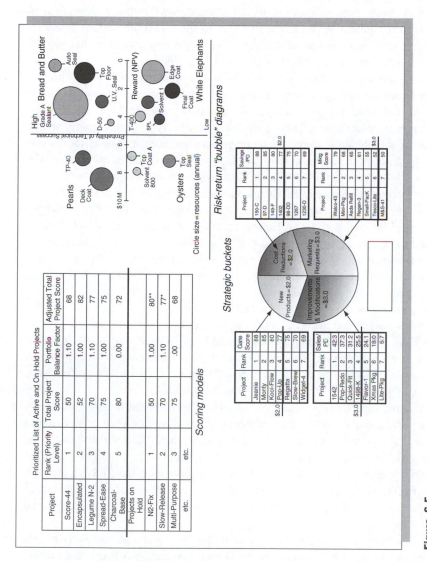

Figure 6.5

Qualitative portfolio selection tools. © Adapted from Cooper *et al.* (1997).

with short term, 'quick cash' initiatives. Different case studies have argued for the determinants of the bucket sizes (Cooper et al., 1997), but the only one that has managed to achieve an abstract approach to this issue has been Wheelwright and Clark (1992a). They identify the (manufacturing or sales) process change versus the extent of product change as the classification factors. Their idea is that a large change in either of these two dimensions increases risk, which must be *balanced* to achieve better 'planning, staffing, and guiding of individual projects' (Wheelwright and Clark 1992a).

The main insight of these studies is the notion of *balance* across the different dimensions/factors that determine the product performance and subsequently the overall portfolio performance. At the same time, the very same issue becomes their limitation. These tools have the ability to generate only ad hoc rules of thumb: thus, they help management to 'think through' the factors that help out in the decision, but they lack additional theoretical or empirical basis for further recommendations. Still, we need to recognize the fact that these methods have been heavily used in practice, because they facilitate useful discussions in managerial meetings (Loch 1996, describes the challenges that arise in such a setting). Hence, this line of work, albeit descriptive or based on a few examples, has aimed at addressing the central challenge of the top management decision: its complexity. All the previously cited tools, encompass efforts for understanding the implications of multi-period effects, of market variables, technology factors, and 'external' performance determinants, as well as their interactions. Due to the lack of a theoretical focus, these methods are obliged to stay at a very aggregate level, without really assessing the exact balance that management should keep in the portfolio. However, their result is essential, since they illustrate that further work should be performed in analyzing in detail the trade-offs between the various performance determinants, the $x_{i,j}$ attributes of our general model.

As a response to the difficulty of assessing all potential factors a relatively new approach has promoted the idea that generic criteria, such as risk, return or any type of score, are not sufficient. Rather, the NPD activities should be explicitly linked to the goals of the business strategy (e.g., Kaplan and Norton (1996), Wheelwright and Clark (1992b), and Comstock and Sjolseth (1999)). The R&D strategy must be 'cascaded' down to the individual activities instead of allocating a given budget according to (generic or customized) scores (Loch and Tapper, 2002).

A few normative studies have tried to uncover potential trade-offs at that level. Ali et al. (1993) model an R&D race between two firms that choose among two different products. They show the effect that competition has on project choice, given heterogenous firm capabilities to innovate (i.e., time and resource effectiveness). Although, their approach is static, they highlight the importance of the 'external' factors and identify the fact that for different conditions different strategies are suggested, a notion closer to the performance 'landscape' advocated by our framework.

Two studies (Adler et al., 1995; Gino and Pisano, 2005) emphasize the capacity choices on portfolio success. They both view the R&D department of a firm as a manufacturing shop floor where different 'servers' process each project before it is completed. Issues of internal delays due to congestion arise, revealing the latent technical interactions across innovation efforts that shall be considered when defining the portfolio. Gino and Pisano (2005) also argue for the behavioral component in the decision of which projects should be admitted in each stage. In a pioneering empirical effort, Girotra et al. (2005) try to draw a systematic link between the portfolio choices and the overall value of the firm. They conduct an event study in the pharmaceutical industry, and they show that project failure without the appropriate build-up of 'back-up' alternative compounds may result in high company value loss. We believe that such studies are of crucial importance to really uncover the performance drivers and apply optimization techniques to product portfolio management. Along similar premises Balasubramanian et al. (2004) analyze the changes in the product portfolio breadth over time within several high-tech industries, as a response to environmental factors like market opportunities and uncertainty. Although their work focuses on R&D program choices we classify it here due to the firm level data and the effort to once more quantify the trade-offs between performance determinants.

Chao and Kavadias (2006) introduce a theoretical framework that relies upon similar premises as the general model presented in this chapter. They explore factors that shift the proposed balance in the NPD portfolio, and they attempt to offer a theoretical basis for the strategic buckets tool presented above. Their findings show that the amount of interactions among the performance drivers is a major determinant of the portfolio balance. Thus, highly coupled marketing and technology performance attributes prompt for the existence of buckets, i.e. the 'protection' of resources aimed at risky and radical innovation efforts. They also show the pro-incrementalism effect of environmental turbulence (likelihood that structural features of $V(\cdot)$ may change) and competition (likelihood of survival in the future).

4.2. Resource allocation and NPD programs

The decision of how to allocate resources among NPD programs necessarily operates under a set of constraints: (i) the type of innovation balance as defined at the strategic level, and (ii) the limited available resources, which can be flexibly assigned. Hence, studies at that level of analysis entail the flexibility of varying investment because different individual projects may be started or stopped within the program. At the same time, due to the focus on one product line the complexity is reduced and due to the proximity to the specialists (the R&D program manager and his/her project managers) there is finer understanding of the underlying performance structure. Thus, as we have argued, the value can be better estimated given a specific configuration $\vec{y}_i'$ and the issue is the investment in different projects that could gradually – over time – capture the potential value.

The need for a hierarchical analysis, investment-wise, has been advocated by Liberatore and Titus (1983). It allows the break down of the difficulty associated with the combinatoric nature of the problem at the single-project level. At the same time, it encompasses the same notion as the strategic buckets. Resources are divided based on a hierarchy of criteria. Hence first a division based upon the upper level criteria is done and then each subset of resources is allocated across individual projects.

Some empirical studies suggest the formation of 'within a product line' development strategies (Nobeoka and Cusumano, 1997; Jones, 1999). They highlight the importance of product line management for firm performance, and they focus on the value of platforms.[3] These studies offer empirical evidence from the automotive and the telecommunications industries. Along similar lines Setter and Tishler (2005) try to estimate the technology investment curves with the defense industry context, and Blanford and Weyant (2005) analyze the technology investments in climate change prevention initiatives.

There have not been many studies in a dynamic context, where the presence of uncertainty lead to allocation changes in the optimal allocation over time. Chikte 1977, models parallel development activities and corresponding resource allocation strategies. He assumes that investment in an innovation effort impacts its likelihood of success. He analyzes general structural properties without any attempt to outline some managerial decision rules.

In the same category, there is extensive literature on the dynamic financial portfolio investments (e.g., Merton, 1969; Constantinides and Malliaris, 1995; Samuelson, 1969). These financial models generally assume linear returns (e.g., number of stocks multiplied by stochastically changing prices). Instead, the returns from NPD investments are non-linear in the amount of resources (e.g., Arthur, 1994; Brooks, 1975).

Loch and Kavadias (2002) have developed a dynamic allocation model that addresses part of the previous challenges. Hence, they focus on R&D program investments, and account for the carry over feature of the investment, that is the fact that investments within the product line may build up gradually over time. They assume knowledge of the potential value and of the interactions across product lines rendering the applicability of the model limited in cases of radical innovation efforts were both the value and the potential interactions are

---

[3] We should note here that the notion of a platform and its derivative products, aligns very well with the definition of an R&D program. The key concept here is the fact that all these efforts revolve around a specific configuration $\vec{y}_i$ or its close 'neighbors.'

unknown. They show that the investment should follow a 'marginal benefit' logic where management should try to invest the next dollar to the program with the highest *overall* marginal benefit (i.e., the benefit in the current and the subsequent periods). Along similar lines, Ding and Eliashberg (2002) analyze the number of parallel efforts in each different stage within an R&D program (they assume that all efforts aim at obtaining the same goal), to ensure success. Their main insight prompts for overinvestment in each stage due to the individual project potential failures. Fridgeirsdottir and Akella (2005) explore the capacity optimization decisions given the congestion effects that may arise within an NPD program.[4] Their insight links idea arrival rates to a capacity *ex-ante* division, a notion that approximates the hierarchical suggestions by Liberatore and Titus (1983). Recently, Blanford (2004) analyzes the resource allocation dynamically between two innovation endeavors, an incremental one and a radical risky one. Chao et al. (2006) build along the same notion, and they consider the problem of dynamic investment in NPD programs under the assumptions that the overall budget depends on how cash is generated over time, and that resource availability may be constrained at different points in time as the programs evolve. Under this situation, they analyze how the investment in incremental or revolutionary NPD programs depends on the level of autonomy given to decision-makers. Also, Bhattacharya and Kavadias (2007) explore how the R&D resources can be allocated over time on different product development efforts given that these rely upon different underlying technologies. They look at the efforts of learning that some technologies may exhibit in conjunction to their time of 'arrival,' on the optimal allocation of resources.

4.3. NPD project selection at the tactical level

At the tactical level of decision-making, a fixed budget must be allocated among multiple ongoing projects, both statically (one-time) and dynamically (repeatedly, once per review period, or whenever a new project idea emerges). The fact that the single project may focus on a smaller subset of performance drivers (i.e., $x_{i,j}$) as dictated by the NPD program decisions, implies that the associated complexity is significantly reduced, resulting in more accurate value estimates and resource requirements. However, at the same time the rigidity of the resource requirements and the fixed outcome (value) lend a combinatoric nature to the problem and do not allow standardized solution processes. Thus, the majority of the proposed solutions reside on heuristic methods.

From a practice-oriented standpoint, such approaches encompass findings from the financial literature like net present value (NPV) analysis (Hess, 1993; Sharpe and Kellin, 1998) and break-even time (BET) (House and Price, 1991)

---

[4] They assume that all undertaken projects are of the same 'type,' i.e. same processing rate with different categories of payoffs.

applied at the operational level of a single project. Each project is assigned an index (its financial value), and these indices are ranked to determine the n best candidates. Observe, however, that the resulting portfolio is not necessarily optimal.[5] Decision theorists have also proposed project ranking via a composite average score on multiple 'qualitatively' assessed dimensions, choosing the n best candidates for the portfolio (Brenner, 1994; Loch, 2000). Similarly, the analytical hierarchy process (AHP, see Liberatore (1987), Saaty (1994), Hammondsetal et al. (1998), and Henriksen and Traynor (1999)) is a structured process of multi-criteria decision-making. However, apart from the previously mentioned combinatoric nature due to capacity, the multi-dimensional decision-making methods lack a significant determinant of project choice, namely interactions among projects, both on the technical and on the market side.

The majority of the normative literature has treated the problem at hand through two different sets of lenses: either as a 'knapsack problem'[6] or as a dynamic allocation of a critical resource across projects (dynamic scheduling literature).

Along the first category, there have been many attempts to model the selection problem with different mathematical programming formulations. Hence, formulations such as knapsack have been examined in depth in Operations Research (OR) and they have utilized many variants of mixed-integer programming heuristics for their solutions. Several of these efforts were applied in specific companies (Beged-Dov, 1965; Souder, 1973; Fox et al., 1984; Czajkowski and Jones, 1986; Schmidt and Freeland, 1992; Benson et al., 1993; Belhe and Kusiak, 1997; Loch et al., 2001; Dickinson et al., 2001).

Although mathematical programming is a sound methodology for optimization problems, and it has been successfully applied in several specific cases, it has not found widespread acceptance by practitioners (Cabral-Cardoso and Payne, 1996; Gupta and Mandakovic, 1992; Loch et al., 2001). This gap stems partly from the complexity and sophistication of the methods, which are difficult to understand and to adopt for people who are not trained in OR, and partly from the lack of transparency and from the sensitivity of the results to changes of the problem parameters (an example is demonstrated for a mixed-integer programming application in Loch et al., 2001). In addition, mathematical programming formulations to retain some level of analytical

---

[5] The simpler counterexample is the following: consider two projects with requirements c_1, c_2, respectively. $c_1 + c_2 > B$, where B is the budget, $c_1 < c_2$, and $\frac{R_1}{c_1} >> \frac{R_2}{c_2}$, where R_i are the respective project revenues. Although from an ROI perspective project 1 is better eventually project 2 is chosen. Similar arguments can be built for all such ranking methods.

[6] The *knapsack problem*, proposed by Operations Research theorists, considers a set of projects with specific resource requirements and value propositions and a fixed total budget (i.e., the knapsack). The objective is to maximize the value 'put' into the knapsack.

tractability they rarely account for dynamic decision making, such as the option to abandon some of the projects during development, or the fact that different projects start and end at different points in time. Recently, Beaujon et al. (2001) made the observation that project funding is not a 'zero or one' decision, but that it can be continuously adjusted. Kavadias et al. (2005) rely upon the observation of Beaujon et al. (2001) but consider upper and lower limits of funding. They propose a heuristic method that relies upon a marginal benefit ranking. Still, the main message from this literature is the extreme difficulty to obtain wide diffusion due to the lack of managerial 'buy-in.'

With respect to the second stream of literature, several authors have explored the dynamic portfolio selection decision emphasizing optimal policies rather than algorithmic solutions. Reflecting the uncertainty in projects, this work mostly considers stochastic settings. This literature comprises four groups.

The largest group is the multi-armed bandit (MAB) problem literature, which has strongly influenced the scheduling literature in Operations Research (OR). It was first solved by Gittins and Jones (1972), and since then, many variants have been proposed and solved by other researchers. The general formulation concerns K projects proceeding in parallel, and a critical resource that should be devoted to only one project at a time. Gittins and Jones formulated the well-known *Gittins index*, a number that can be assigned to each project at each time t, and that characterizes the optimal policy. At any time t, it is optimal to work on the project with the highest Gittins index, which depends only on each individual project's state (Bertsimas and Niño-Mora, 1996; Whittle, 1980; Whittle, 1988; Ross, 1982) and corresponds to the reward that would make the decision-maker indifferent as to whether to continue the project or exchange it for that reward.

The MAB policy rests upon a number of assumptions, which makes extensions to more realistic settings extremely hard to obtain reverting us back to algorithmic approximations. Gittins (1989) shows that, for differing general discount functions, there is no general index (pp. 27–29). Banks and Sundaram (1994), prove that the existence of switching costs across projects leads to the absence of a general index solution. The characteristics of NPD projects, challenge as well the basic premises of MAB, payoffs are earned only after the project outcomes are launched onto the market. Moreover, projects tend to be interdependent due to prioritization. The latter causes penalties due to delayed market launch.[7] Kavadias and Loch (2003) expand existing results to incorporate these characteristics of NPD, and provide a useful discussion on the limitations for policy extensions.

The second group of models approaches the project prioritization problem as a multi-class queueing system, where different classes of jobs (i.e., types

---

[7] Which violates the basic MAB assumption that a project's value function remains unchanged while it is not worked on.

of projects) share a common server. Each job class requires a stochastic time on the server and incurs a linear delay cost. The main result is the '$c\mu$ rule' (Smith, 1956; Harrison, 1975): give priority to the job with the highest delay cost divided by the expected processing time (marginal cost c, over time $\tau = \frac{1}{\mu}$). The rule is optimal for linear delay cost structures in various applications (Wein, 1992; Ha, 1997; Van Mieghem, 2000).[8] For non-linear delay costs, the 'generalized $c\mu$ rule' (G-$c\mu$) has been shown to be asymptotically optimal in heavy traffic (Van Mieghem, 1995).

The third group outlines optimal admission rules when a budget has to be allocated over time to several project ideas.[9] Kavadias and Loch (2004) present such an NPD setting (chapter 5; for an overview of the general problem, see Stidham (1985) and Miller (1969)). The NPD reality differs from manufacturing settings in two aspects: (i) The project attractiveness measure is continuous (there are uncountably many customer classes). (ii) The NPD system has a waiting buffer of size 1, from which the waiting project disappears when a new project idea arrives. In other words, the new idea is not turned away, but the old idea is superseded. This assumption represents project obsolescence, which is more important in NPD than in manufacturing. These model features lead to results that are consistent with recent literature (more available capacity lowers the threshold for acceptance, see, e.g., Stidham (1985) and Lewis et al. (1999)).

Finally, the stochastic and dynamic version of the knapsack model. Kleywegt and Papastavrou (1998) show that if all items are of the same size, a threshold policy is optimal, the value function is concave in the remaining amount of resource, and the threshold increases as the resource is depleted. Kleywegt and Papastavrou (2001) show that the results generalize to the case of stochastic resource requirements of the items, but only if the resource requirement distribution fulfills certain conditions (concavity), and the terminal value function is concave non-decreasing. Still, the NPD reality imposes additional constraints on the problem, such as the fact that the investment in a given project may not be a one shot decision but it progresses through milestones, where additional action may be taken.

5. Conclusions and open research questions

Management researchers and practitioners have proposed many methodologies for tackling the complexity of the portfolio selection problem. The literature

[8] The $c\mu$ rule is a 'continuous time' approximation of the Gittins index. Van Oyen et al. (1992) among others have pointed out the similarity between bandit policies and the $c\mu$ rule.
[9] The third and second groups of work share methodological foundations, but differ in the main research question: prioritization versus admission.

review suggests that quantitative research efforts have been restrained at the tactical level of analysis and they have not been widely adopted in practice because of the complexity associated with the decision.

This chapter introduces a theoretical framework that outlines the main project decisions at the different organizational levels, and the challenges that accompany them. In that light we emphasize that as we move down the organizational hierarchy, resource allocation to different innovation efforts acquires a finer and better defined success measure (the effort output is easier to estimate or approximate) with a much tighter budget constraints and a finer search strategy for the solution(s). Within this context, we offer a comprehensive literature review, highlighting several of the previous research findings, and some of the lessons drawn for for researchers and practitioners. In this final section, we draw some general conclusions that we believe to be relevant for managers responsible for portfolio management and we identify a few open questions for the NPD portfolio selection problem.

Insights

- At the highest level, the context of making funding decisions is unstructured and messy; it depends on an uncertain future, actions by competitors, and a complexity of the overall 'business problem' that defies orderly problem solving. This is the realm of strategy. Strategy should provide a structured business proposition within which the organization can perform targeted problem solving. Strategy should align the actions of the various players, and outline 'categories' of different types of NPD and R&D activities, each of which is homogenous enough to be managed consistently.

- It is within these categories (i.e., the different R&D programs that have a 'next generation' scope, or 'a product line technical support' objective) where we can hope to perform quantitative project selection. So the R&D program investment will depend on the potential return (e.g., ROI) as defined from the various project ideas, given the program objectives and goals.

- These 'return' functions associated with each NPD program stem from three conceptually distinct activities within each program, where projects are managed as an *ensemble*, and not individually: *idea screening, quantitative selection for funding*, and *ongoing prioritization*. Basic theoretical structures have been proposed for the distinct tasks, but unfortunately, there has been little work that approaches the various distinct stages as a unified coherent process (Ding and Eliashberg (2002) and Chan et al. (2002) are steps towards this direction).

In conclusion, our framework serves to accomplish two things: (a) characterize the portfolio problem through the *structure* of the optimization problem that the organization faces at its different levels of decision making, and (b) to establish some solid foundation, which can add value by outlining the problem intuition to practicing managers.

Open research questions

The last point allows us to make the transition to the set of open ended research questions associated with NPD portfolio management decision. We summarize them in the following figure.

Figure 6.6 illustrates that the research community should try to acquire a holistic view of the portfolio decision-making process, where the fact that different parameters are defined at different levels of organization hierarchy is recognized. In addition:

1. We need to target finer methods that can shed light into the structure and measure of the cross interactions among profit determinants at a strategic level. A few models have tried to isolate specific influence factors, but we feel that research here is at an embryonic stage.
2. The research methodologies proposed need to identify the notion of organizational hierarchy and its impact on the decisions; the infamous quote that '*resources are allocated to the project manager that screams the*

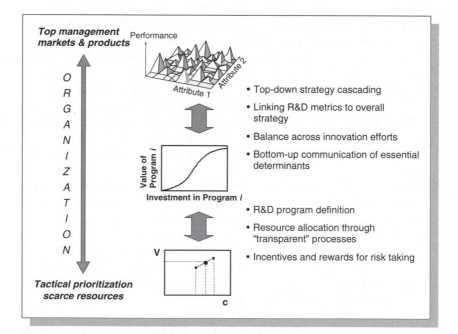

Figure 6.6
Management challenges in NPD portfolio decisions.

loudest' signifies that project managers associate their career paths with specific activities of the portfolio and that they may 'game' the system. Thus, we need to build additional intuition as to the incentive and motivation structures associated with R&D portfolio decisions. Moreover, Sosa (2005), in an insightful case study, highlights an additional dimension of importance: the organizational design. Its impact on portfolio decisions stems from the ability to exploit or explore. Thus, management needs to decide whether to invest on integrating or specialization capabilities.

3. The theoretical structures that look at isolated decisions of the R&D 'funnel' (Wheelwright and Clark, 1992a) should be extended to allow for a *holistic* process view. In addition, we should note that since the overall portfolio value emerges from single project outputs, we ought to look for new methods that aggregate the individual project information into a total value.

4. Finally, additional empirical effort should assess the importance of different NPD portfolio strategies. R&D portfolio decisions are of vital importance to firm competitiveness, therefore, portfolio data are extremely sensitive and often confidential. However, event studies (such as Girotra et al., 2005) offer a reasonable methodology for assessing the impact of portfolio decisions.

We believe that the NPD portfolio selection problem remains largely an open problem especially at its top management decision-making. We also echo previous observations (Shane and Ulrich, 2004) that call for new approaches and methods. Since the NPD project portfolio determines the medium to long-term company future, it is essential that we further understand the various steps for operationalizing such a complex decision.

References

Adams M. and Boike D. 2004. "The PDMA Foundation 2004 Comparative Performance Assessment Study". *Visions* 28 (3), 26–29.

Adler P. S., Mandelbaum A., Nguyen V. and Schwerer E. 1995. "From Project to Process Management: An Empirically-Developed Framework for Analyzing Product Development Time". *Management Science* 41 (3), 458–484.

Ali A., Kalwani M. U. and Kovenock D. 1993. "Selecting Product Development Projects: Pioneering versus Incremental Innovation Strategies". *Management Science* 39 (3), 255–274.

Anderson E. G. and Joglekar N. R. 2005. "A Hierarchical Product Development Planning Framework". *Production and Operations Management* 14 (3), 344–362.

Arthur W. B. 1994. *Increasing Returns and Path Dependence in the Economy*. University of Michigan Press, Ann Arbor.

Asawa M. and Teneketzis D. 1996. "Multi-Armed Bandits with Switching Penalties". *IEEE Transactions on Automatic Control* 41 (3), 328–348.

Balasubramanian K., Randall T. and Ulrich K. T. 2004. "Product Variety and the Industry Lifecycle". *Wharton School Working Paper*.

Banks J. S. and Sundaram R. K. 1994. "Switching Costs and the Gittins Index". *Econometrica* 62 (3), 687–694.

Barrett A. 2003. "DuPont Tries to Unclog a Pipeline". *Business Week*, 27, January 2003, 103–104.

Beaujon G. J., Marin S. P. and McDonald G. C. 2001. "Balancing and Optimizing a Portfolio of R&D Projects". *Naval Logistics Quarterly* 48 (1), 18–40.

Beged-Dov A. G. 1965. "Optimal Assignment of R&D Projects in a Large Company Using an Integer Programming Model". *IEEE Transactions on Engineering Management* EM-12, 138–142.

Belhe U. and Kusiak A. 1997. "Dynamic Scheduling of Design Activities with Resource Constraints". *IEEE Transactions on Systems, Man, and Cybernetics* 27 (1), 105–111.

Benson B., Sage A. S. and Cook G. 1993. "Emerging Technology Evaluation Methodology: With Application to Micro-Electromechanical Systems". *IEEE Transactions on Engineering Management* 40 (2), 114–123.

Bertsimas D. and Niño-Mora J. 1996. "Conservation Laws, Extended Polymatroids and Multi-Armed Bandit Problems: A Polyhedral Approach to Indexable Systems". *Mathematics of Operations Research* 21 (2), 257–306.

Bhattacharya S. and Kavadias S. 2007. "Defining Products by Sequential Investment in R&D with Learning Across Projects". INSEAD Working Paper.

Blanford G. J. 2004. "Dynamic Allocation of R&D Investments Between Uncertainty Resolution and Technology Development". *Stanford MS&EE Working Paper*.

Blanford G. J. and Weyant J. P. 2005. "A Global Portfolio Strategy for Climate Change Technology Development". *Stanford MS&EE Working Paper*.

Braunstein D. M. and Salsamendi M. C. 1994. "R&D Planning at ARCO Chemical". *Research Technology Management*, September–October, 33–47.

Brenner M. S. 1994. "Practical R&D Project Prioritization". *Research Technology Management*, September–October, 38–42.

Brooks F. P. 1975. *The Mythical Man Month*. Addison Wesley, Reading.

Cabral-Cardoso C. and Payne R. L. 1996. "Instrumental and Supportive use of Formal Selection Methods in R&D Project Selection". *IEEE Transactions on Engineering Management* 43 (4), 402–410.

Chan T., Nickerson J. A. and Owan H. 2002. "A Dynamic Theory of Why Firms Differ in Their R&D Project Selection Rules". *Working Paper Olin School of Business*, Wahsington University, Saint-Louis.

Chao R. O. and Kavadias S. 2006. "A Theoretical FRamework for Managing the NPD Portfolio: When and How to Use the Strategic Buckets". *Georgia Institute of Technology Working Paper*.

Chao R. O., Kavadias S. and Gaimon C. 2006. "Budget Creation and Control for Effective NPD Portfolio Management". *Georgia Institute of Technology Working Paper*.

Chikte S. 1977. *Markov Decision Models for Optimal Stochastic Resource Allocation Problems*. Unpublished Ph.D. Dissertation. Polytechnic Institute of New York.

Comstock G. L. and Sjolseth D. E. 1999. "Aligning and Prioritizing Corporate R&D". *Research Technology Management*, May–June, 19–25.

Constantinides G. M. and Malliaris A. G. 1995. "Portfolio Theory". R. A. Jarrow, V. Maksimovic and W. T. Zemba (Eds.) *Handbook in Operations Research and Management Science*. Elsevier Press, Amsterdam, Holland.

Cooper R. G., Edgett S. J. and Kleinschmidt E. J. 1997. *Portfolio Management for New Products*. Perseus Books, New York, NY.

Czajkowski A. F. and Jones S. 1986. "Selecting Interrelated R&D Projects in Space Technology Planning". *IEEE Transactions on Engineering Management* 33 (1), 624–640.

Cusumano M. A. and Nobeoka K. 1998. *Thinking Beyond Lean: How Multi-Project Management is Transforming Product Development at Toyota and Others*. The Free Press, New York, NY.

Ding M. and Eliashberg J. 2002. "Structuring the Product Development Pipeline". *Management Science* 48 (3), 343–363.

Dickinson M. W., Thornton A. C. and Graves S. 2001. "Technology Portfolio Management: Optimizing Interdependent Projects Over Multiple Time Periods". *IEEE Transactions on Engineering Management* 48 (4), 518–527.

Foster T. M. 1996. "Making R&D More Effective at Westinghouse". *Research Technology Management*, January–February, 31–37.

Fox, G. E., Baker N. R. and Bryant J. L. 1984. "Economic Models for R and D Project Selection in the Presence of Project Interactions". *Management Science* 30 (7), 890–904.

Fox G. E. and Baker N. R. 1985. "Project Selection Decision Making Linked to a Dynamic Environment". *Management Science* 31 (10), 1272–1285.

Fridgeirsdottir K. and Akella R. 2005. "Product Portfolio and Capacity Management". *London Business School Working Paper*.

Gino F. and Pisano G. 2005. "Holding or Folding? R&D Portfolio Strategy Under Different Information Regimes". *Harvard Business School Working Paper*, No. 05–072.

Girotra K., Terwiesch C. and Ulrich K. T. 2005. "Managing the Risk of Development Failures: A Study of Late-stage Failures in the Pharmaceutical Industry". *Wharton School Working Paper.*

Gittins J. C. 1989. *Multi-armed Bandit Allocation Indices.* John Wiley, New York.

Gittins J. C. and Jones D. M. 1972. "A Dynamic Allocation Index for the Sequential Design of Experiments". *Progress In Statistics: European Meeting of Statisticians.* Budapest: 1972.

Groenveld P. 1997. "Roadmapping Integrates Business and Technology". *Research Technology Management*, September–October 1997, 48–55.

Gupta D. K. and Mandakovic T. 1992. "Contemporary Approaches to R&D Project Selection, a Literature Survey". D. F. Kocaogly, (Ed.) *Management of R&D and Engineering.* Elsevier Publishers, 67–86.

Ha A. Y. 1997. "Optimal Dynamic Scheduling Policy for a Make to Stock Production System". *Operations Research* 45 (1), 42–53.

Hammonds J. S., Keeney R. L. and Raiffa H. 1998. "Even Swaps: A Rational Method for Making Trade-offs". *Harvard Business Review*, March–April, 137–149.

Harrison J. M. 1975. "Dynamic Scheduling of a Multi-class Queue: Discount Optimality". *Operations Research* 23 (2), 270–282.

Henriksen A. D. and Traynor A. J. 1999. "A Practical R&D Project-Selection Scoring Tool". *IEEE Transactions on Engineering Management* 46 (2), 158–170.

Hess S. W. 1993. "Swinging on the Branch of a Tree: Project Selection Applications". *Interfaces* 23 (6), 5–12.

House C. H. and Price R. L. 1991. "The Return Map: Tracking Product Teams". *Harvard Business Review* 69 (1), 92–100.

Jones N. 1999. "Competing After Radical Change: The Significance of Product Line Management Strategy". *Strategic Management Journal* 24 (12), 1265–1287.

Kaplan R. S. and Norton D. P. 1996. *The Balanced Scorecard.* Harvard Business School Press, Boston.

Kavadias S. and Loch C. H. 2003. "Dynamic Prioritization of Projects at a Scarce Resource." *Production and Operations Management* 12 (4), 433–444.

Kavadias S. and Loch C. H. 2004. *Project Selection Under Uncertainty: Dynamically Allocating Resources to Maximize Value.* Kluwer Academic Publishers, Boston, MA.

Kavadias S., Loch C. H. and Tapper U. A. S. 2005. "Allocating the R&D Budget at GemStone". INSEAD Working Paper.

Kleywegt A. J. and Papastavrou J. D. 1998. "The Dynamic and Stochastic Knapsack Problem". *Operations Research* 46 (1), 17–35.

Kleywegt A. J. and Papastavrou J. D. 2001. "The Dynamic and Stochastic Knapsack Problem with Random Sized Items". *Operations Research* 49 (1), 26–41.

Lewis, M. E., Ayhan H. and Foley R. D. 1999. "Bias Optimality in a Queue With Admission Control". *Probability in the Engineering and Informational Sciences* 13, 309–327.

Liberatore M. J. 1987. "An Extension of the Analytical Hierarchy Process for Industrial R&D Project Selection". *IEEE Transactions on Engineering Management* 34 (1), 12–18.

Liberatore M. J. and Titus G. J. 1983. "The Practice of Management Science in R&D Project Management". *Management Science* 29 (8), 962–974.

Loch C. H. 1996. "American Switching Systems". INSEAD Case Study.

Loch C. H. 2000. "Tailoring Product Development to Strategy: The Case of a European Technology Manufacturer". *European Management Journal* 18 (3), 246–258.

Loch C. H. and Kavadias S. 2002. "Dynamic Portfolio Selection of NPD Programs Using Marginal Returns". *Management Science* 48 (10), 1227–1241.

Loch C. H., Pich M. T., Urbschat M. and Terwiesch C. 2001. "Selecting R&D Projects at BMW: A Case Study of Adopting Mathematical Programming Models". *IEEE Transactions on Engineering Management* 48 (1), 70–80.

Loch C. H. and Tapper S. 2002. "Implementing a Strategy-Driven Performance Measurement System for an Applied Research Group". *Journal of Product Innovation Management* 19 (3), 185–198.

Merton R. C. 1969. "Lifetime portfolio selection under uncertainty: the continuous-time case". *Review of Economics and Statistics* 51 (8), 247–257.

Miller B. L. 1969. "A Queueing Reward System With Several Customer Classes". *Management Science* 16 (3), 234–245.

Nobeoka K. and Cusumano M. A. 1997. "Multiproject Strategy and Sales Growth: The Benefits of Rapid Design Transfer in New Product Development". *Strategic Management Journal* 18 (3), 169–186.

Pich M. T., Loch C. H. and DeMeyer A. 2003. "On Uncertainty, Ambiguity and Complexity in Project Management". *Management Science* 48 (8), 1008–1024.

Pilling D. 2000. "Success Gives AstraZeneca Indigestion". *Financial Times* 17, October 2000.

Reinertsen D. 1997. *Managing the Design Factory*. The Free Press, New York.

Ross S. M. 1982. *Introduction to Stochastic Dynamic Programming*. John Wiley Press, New York, NY.

Roussel P. A., Saad K. M. and Erickson T. J. 1991. *3rd Generation R&D*. Harvard Business School Press, Boston, MA.

Saaty T. L. 1994. "The Analytic Hierarchy Process". *Interfaces* 24 (6), 19–43.

Samuelson P. A. 1969. "Lifetime Portfolio Selection by Dynamic Stochastic Programming". *Review of Economics and Statistics* 51 (1), 215–227.

Schmidt R. L. and Freeland J. R. 1992. "Recent Progress in Modeling R&D Project-Selection Processes". *IEEE Transactions on Engineering Management* 39 (2), 189–199.

Schoenberger C. 2003. "Can Kodak Make Up For Lost Moments?". *Forbes* 6, October 2003.

Setter O. and Tishler A. 2005. "Investment Policies in Advanced R&D Programs". *Tel Aviv University Working Paper*.

Shane S. A. and Ulrich K. T. 2004. "Technological Innovation, Product Development, and Enterpreneurship in *Management Science*". *Management Science* 50 (2), 133–144.

Sharpe P. and Kellin T. 1998. "How Smith Kline Beecham Makes Better Resource-Allocation Decisions". *Harvard Business Review* March–April, 45–57.

Simon H. 1982. *Models of Bounded Rationality. MIT Press*, Cambridge, MA.

Smith W. E. 1956. "Various Optimizers for Single-Stage Production". *Naval Research Logistics*. 3, 59–66.

Sosa M. 2005. "R&D Management at the Universal Luxury Group". INSEAD case study.

Souder W. E. 1973. "Analytical Effectiveness of Mathematical Models for R&D Project Selection". *Management Science* 19, 907–923.

Stidham S. 1985. "Optimal Control of Admission to a Queueing System". *IEEE Transactions on Automatic Control* AC-30 (8), 705–713.

Stillman H. M. 1997. "How ABB Decides on the Right Technology Investments". *Research Technology Management*, November–December, 14–22.

Taggart J. H. and Blaxter T. J. 1992. "Strategy in Pharmaceutical R&D: A Portfolio Risk Matrix". *R&D Management* 22 (3), 241–254.

Tritle G. L., Seriven E. F. V. and Fusfeld A. R. 2000. "Resolving Uncertainty in R&D Portfolios". *Research Technology Management*, November–December, 47–55.

Tushman M. and O"Reilly C. 1996. "Ambidextrous Organizations Managing Evolutionary and Revolutionary Change". *California Management Review* 98 (4), 8–30.

Ulrich K. and Eppinger S. D. 2003. *Product Design and Development*. 3rd Edition. Irwin-McGraw Hill, New York, NY.

Van Mieghem J. 1995. "Dynamic Scheduling with Convex Delay Costs: The Generalized $c\mu$ Rule". *The Annals of Applied Probability* 5 (3), 808–833.

Van Mieghem J. 2000. "Price and Service Discrimination in Queueing Systems: Incentive-Compatible G-$c\mu$ Rules". *Management Science* 46 (9), 1249–1267.

Van Oyen M. P., Pandelis D. G. and Teneketzis D. 1992. "Optimality of Index Policies for Stochastic Scheduling With Switching Penalties". *Journal of Applied Probability* 29, 957–966.

Vishwanath T. 1992. "Optimal Orderings for Parallel Project Selection". *International Economic Review* 33 (1), 79–89.

Wein L. 1992. "Dynamic Scheduling of a Multiclass Make-to-Stock Queue". *Operations Research* 40 (4), 724–735.

Weitzman M. L. 1979. "Optimal Search for the Best Alternative". *Econometrica* 47 (3), 641–654.

Wheelwright S. C. and Clark K. B. 1992a. *Revolutionizing New Product Development*. The Free Press, New York, NY.

Wheelwright S. C. and Clark K. B. 1992b. "Creating ProjectPlans to Focus Product Development". *Harvard Business Review*, March–April, 70–82.

Whittle P. 1980. "Multi-Armed Bandits and the Gittins" Index". *Journal of Royal Statistical Society* 42 (2), 143–149.

Whittle P. 1988. "Restless Bandits: Activity Allocation in A Changing World". *Journal of Applied Probability* 25A, 287–298.

7 Organization design for new product development

Manuel E. Sosa and Jürgen Mihm

1. Introduction

Developing a new product is a complex process that typically involves contributions of many disciplines. The more complex the product, the larger the number and arguably the heterogeneity of the people involved in the development effort. At the peak of the design effort, Airbus involved several thousand individual contributors into the development of its new A380. Automobile manufactures typically involve several hundreds of people in the core development plus additional hundreds that indirectly contribute through the network of suppliers. In the computing industry, firms typically involve several dozens of people in the development of new products such as printers, copy machines, and other electronic products. Unless the product is very simple, no single person carries out a new product development (NPD) effort on his or her own. Considering that many people from different disciplines need to be involved in the development effort, one fundamental question arises: How are they and how should they be organized to maximize the chances of successful product development? In this chapter, we aim to compile current knowledge to answer this question.

Organizations developing new products face two fundamental challenges: decomposition and integration. The overall design effort needs to be broken into individual tasks and more importantly work on these tasks needs to be integrated into an overall design. Central to the question of organizing NPD is how the development actors are linked into groups. In general, organization is the result of the establishment of formal links and the emergence of informal ones among individuals so that, acting as a group, they fulfill a specific purpose such as developing a new product. Putting a formal organizational structure together implies assigning individuals to groups and creating the boundaries and scope of work for these groups. Informal organizational structures are determined by the actual communication ties that emerge between individual actors within and across groups during the development effort. As will become apparent in this chapter these two views of the organization are both important and dependent on each other.

The two main sections of the chapter are devoted to formal and informal organization structure, respectively. In the language of Eisenhardt and Brown (1995), our discussion dedicated to formal organizational structure centers on the structures and mechanisms to enable 'disciplined problem solving' while the section on the informal organizational structure focuses on the 'communication web' associated with product development. Both sections examine determines the emergence of links between individual contributors (or the lack thereof) as well as their effectiveness. While early research on the organization of NPD has contributed to both streams (Allen, 1977), the focus in subsequent years has been on the formal organization before turning back to the informal one. In that sense, this chapter progresses from a well established set of research streams on R&D organizations to newer research findings in NPD settings. We conclude the chapter with summarizing remarks and four directions for future research in organizing NPD.

2. The formal organizational structure

As noted in the introduction the nature of many development projects requires the collaboration of many individual contributors. Consequently, the overall effort of developing a new product or service is divided into many different tasks. These tasks have different requirements as to the knowledge and the skills of the organizational entity responsible, be it an organizational subunit or an individual. In most organizations, organizational entities repeatedly work on similar tasks so that they become specialized. Development organizations need to engage in *specialization*. Specialization is the rationale to institute functions such as manufacturing, R&D or marketing. In NPD, specialization also occurs within functions, along the lines of different components of the product or service to be designed. Yet, for a complete product or service to be conceived, there needs to be a mechanism for integrating such a specialized knowledge into an overall solution. Development organizations need to provide for *integration*. Combining the knowledge of different product or service components and determining how they will eventually be delivered is the challenge of integration. Determining the level of specialization, organizing the specialized subunits and providing for integration mechanisms is the task of the formal part of organization design for NPD.

There are many conceptualizations of the NPD process. Each one has its merits and disadvantages. A certain perspective necessarily focuses attention on some features while pushing others to the background. In general, the most widely assumed conceptualization of organizing for NPD draws on the contingency and the information processing views (Tushman and Nadler, 1978).

Since Burns and Stalker (1961) it has generally been assumed that the appropriateness of how specialization and how integration are conceived may depend on environmental factors and strategic goals. Not all product development efforts should be organized the same way. Applying the contingency approach to organizational design (Woodward, 1965; Thompson, 1967; Lawrence and Lorsch, 1967) implies that we need to understand what factors drive successful NPD organization and that we find ways of trading off opposing requirements. In that sense, it is generally agreed that NPD means taking a set of uncertain inputs on the market side as well as a set of uncertain inputs on the technical side and gradually transforming them into an integrated product. Thus, it is natural to assume that market uncertainties, technological uncertainties and the complexity of the product to be designed will be major drivers of the organizational design.

From its earliest time, the information processing view of the organization (Galbraith, 1973) has dominated the way organizational design was conceptualized in a NPD setting. Taking informational inputs and transforming them into informational outputs is intimately related to communication. The study of organizational structures in innovation settings starts with the research stream focused on understanding communication in R&D organizations. From that research stream, we learned that intensive communication between scientists and engineers was an important determinant of R&D performance (Allen, 1977; Eisenhardt and Brown, 1995).

Thus, we view the task of formally organizing NPD as separating the overall design task in appropriately selected pieces and assigning them to organizational subunits and then ensuring their collaboration such that uncertain information about markets and technology on the input side is translated into certain outputs on the product side. We expect the appropriateness of the formal organization structure to depend on the nature of the uncertainties involved. (The elements of the formal structure need to not only include reporting relations but also coordinating and control mechanism such as decision rights, problem-solving approaches, and incentive relations outside the reporting relations).

The flow of information depends on the structure assigned to the organization. All organizational entities create internal focus by defining primary goals, by building group identities, languages, and thus cultures, by organizing reward and incentive systems (Walker and Lorsch, 1968; Sethi, 2000). Thus, formal organization structure establishes boundaries within the organization which in turn the informal organizational structure. For example, Allen (1977) found that organizational bonds increase the probability of two team members engaging in technical communication.

Since organizational boundaries emphasize within group communications and hinder across-groups communications, establishing groups becomes one of the most fundamental tasks of organization design. How to formally group individuals for effective product development, and how to facilitate communication across groups are important questions whose answers depend on the trade-off that managers face when developing new products. Two prototypical answers to these questions have been put forward: the functional organization and the project organization.

2.1. Functional organization

In the functional organization, individuals, working on one or a limited number of tasks each, are grouped according to their technical expertise (see Fig. 7.1). Thus, individuals with similar technical background form the basic building blocks of the formal reporting lines. The depth of the specialization depends on the level of expertise that the individual contributor needs to achieve.

The main mechanism for achieving integration is the process – the definition of who has to contribute what information at what time. Typically, the functional organization coincides with a staged process by which the NPD progresses with function after function adding their input to the design.

It is clear that functional organizations allow for very good exploitation of critical technical knowledge since they concentrate technical skills in one spot. In that sense, they allow for deeper specialization in technical aspects (Allen, 1977). Individuals strongly identify with their functional agenda, their values, and their language. Dougherty (1990, 1992) finds that functions are 'thought worlds,' with their own knowledge base. Technical knowledge is appreciated and generates status. Career paths emphasize technical competence. Inter-entity communication mainly happens about technical topics. As a result, organizations can easily assimilate new technological developments from the outside by creating strong technological links with the outside (Cockburn

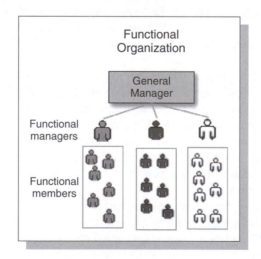

Figure 7.1
A functional organizational structure.

and Henderson, 1998). Alternatively, they are good sources for technological advances themselves. Allen (1986), therefore, calls the functional organization the input-focused organization.

In addition, central coordination among several different products is facilitated by a functional setup (see Walker and Lorsch, 1968). This way any form of knowledge transfer between products (e.g., the creation of a set of platform parts to be reused in many products) is made quite possible.

The prototypical functional organization is the university. Its goal is to create deep functional expertise. Pharma companies or high tech companies in the semiconductor equipment industry may also lean towards a functional organization. Being able to assimilate the latest advances in science, maybe even creating the advances themselves these companies focus on incorporating the latest technology into their products.

Functional cohesiveness, the form's major strength is also its biggest weakness. The functional focus makes integration with other functions a tedious task. Because people are motivated by the need to deepen their knowledge base in certain area, these groups face tremendous difficulties when attempt to integrate their findings into a specific product to address a specific market need. Communication within a project combining the effort of several functions tends to be formal and infrequent. Compared with other integration methods, members of different functions engage in little face to face communication (Walker and Lorsch, 1968). Communication about technical decisions happens late, since functional units do not want to appear incompetent in the eyes of other functions. Thus, functional organizations lack product focus. The organization may easily neglect the view of the customer. As a result, functional organizations tend to show low external integration. Furthermore, functional organizations pose the question of business responsibility. In its purest form, the only person responsible for the success of any product is the CEO. Functional organizations do not excel at integration.

To address the drawbacks of a functional organization a project-based organizational structure emerged.

2.2. Project organization

In the project organization, individuals of different technical/functional expertise are grouped into an organizational subunit responsible for one product or service (or potentially a limited set of closely related products/services). All members report to a team leader (see Fig. 7.2).

Although from different technical/functional backgrounds the group builds a group identity (Sethi, 2000). Their focus is to create a product (Allen, 1986). The team leader takes the customer's perspective and focuses the team on defining and creating a cohesive product or service. High congruence

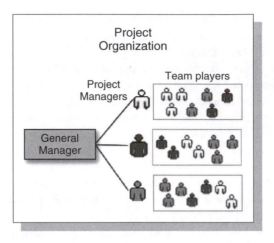

Figure 7.2
A project-based organizational structure.

of goals between the team members leads to fast decision-making. Intra-entity communication mainly concentrates on the product. The communication between functions is rich, frequent, and not overly formal. The team leader tends to be responsible for the economic viability of the project and thus balances firm and customer interests. Thus, a high external integration with the market, a rich focus on the timeline and the overall profitability of the project are the strength of the project organization.

Start-ups with just one product in the making are a prime example of project organizations. Consulting firms or those IT providers focusing on custom solutions for individual customers tend to also organize in this way.

Three major drawbacks limit the effectiveness of this organizational setup. First, since communication is strongly encouraged among team members and since organizational barriers limit the communication outside the organizational bounds (Allen, 1977), the interaction with other individuals of similar technical background is sparse. As a result, it is difficult for the overall organization to build technical excellence. Integration with outside technical communities is a persistent problem. Second, for the same reason coordination among projects becomes a challenge. All projects fiercely take the position of their customers and fiercely defend their own economic viability. Therefore, reaping synergies from inter-project coordination such as product and service component sharing is notoriously difficult. Third, the homogeneity of teams may lead to psychological phenomena such as groupthink and an escalation of commitment. Therefore, management oversight is crucial.

In a sense, project organization is the exact mirror of functional organization. It focuses on the result, the product itself while neglecting building technological excellence in the long term. Functional organizations, in contrast, focus on building technological excellence, while neglecting the cohesion of the product.

2.3. Project matrix organization

The consequent application of the information processing view of the organization to NPD (Clark and Fujimoto, 1991) has fostered the insight, that the two alternatives of functional and project organization are only polar ends of a continuum of different ways of organizing NPD. The information processing view of organizations (Galbraith, 1973; Tushman and Nadler, 1978; Clark and Fujimoto, 1991) shifts the focus away from formal reporting lines as major design element of organizational structures and suggests further solutions. Galbraith emphasized the role of what he termed lateral relationships (Galbraith, 1972) such as liaison roles, task forces, teams, integration personnel and integrating departments. Integration can also take place through establishing a secondary structure, overlaying the primary functional structure with a project organization creating a project matrix organization (see Ulrich and Eppinger, 2004 for terminology). In NPD cross-functional teams have become the major vehicle of that secondary structure (Clark and Fujimoto, 1991).

Cross-functional teams convene members from functional entities such that all technical and functional expertise necessary is represented in the team. While members keep their affiliation with their functional homes, they are also responsible for commonly achieving project success. This way a second reporting line is established. The usefulness of cross-functional teams in many diverse settings has been verified (e.g., Dougherty, 1992; Pinto et al., 1993; Ittner and Larcker, 1997; Kahn, 2001; Leenders and Wierenga, 2002) thus ensuring that interdepartmental collaboration is more important than just mere exchange. Therefore, cross-functional teams, which share values and create a common 'thought world' produce better results in NPD than a formal system of pre-scheduled meetings and paperwork. Several antecedents of success have been discussed. For example, Pinto et al. (1993) stress the importance of overriding themes and goals as well as operating procedures while Kahn (2001) stresses market orientation as a major management factors.

The intensity of contributions of different functional entities at different points in the development process may have different effects (Song et al., 1998). Marketing input is most necessary at the very beginning (and very end) of the development process. Especially during the earliest phases of development, during market opportunity development, involvement of manufacturing may sometimes even prove to be counterproductive (presumably, because it is deflating in an expansive phase). In later stages, R&D – manufacturing integration is most required. It seems that integration in the first half of the

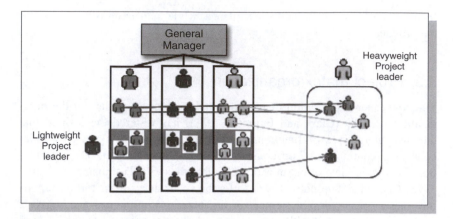

Figure 7.3
Two forms of matrix organizational structures.

project is more unambiguously related to project success than at later stages (Olson et al., 2001).

Beyond the mere installation of cross-functional teams, several organizational building blocks need to be aligned to make these teams work appropriately. What role does the team leader play and what his decision rights are, are the most important questions Fig. 7.3 illustrates the two structures that have emerged to address such questions, which we describe next.

Light weight team structure

A project manager, typically a junior person, with limited status and influence coordinates activities. He tracks progression of the project and raises issues to the attention of functional managers as needed. Technical decisions are taken by functional managers. The lightweight manager has no reporting lines with the team members. He typically cannot address them directly. In the lightweight team structure, team member's major affiliation remains with the function. They typically physically reside with their technical peers (Wheelwright and Clark, 1992; Clark and Wheelwright, 1993).

This structure can be viewed as a modification of the functional structure. While adding some project focus, and thus mitigating some of the disadvantages of the functional organization, it still exhibits strong technical expertise and a lack of project responsibility and development speed.

Heavy weight team structure

In a heavy weight team structure (Clark and Fujimoto, 1991; Clark and Fujimoto, 1995), the team leader can directly address all members working for his team. He may even take decisions about the development project and development content directly. If not he is supported by strong liaison managers to influence functional decision-making. The team leader takes the position of the customer and thus focuses the organization strongly towards the integrity of the product. He is a senior and seasoned manager who is well respected. While team member's long-term affiliation rests with the function, they work a substantial amount of time in the team context. Sometimes there is even collocation of the team members.

The heavyweight team structure is a mix of functional organization and project organization. As such, it tries to combine the major advantages of the project organization such as speed, high level of product integration and accountability while still allowing for reasonable technical expertise.

2.4. Contingency of organizational forms

The appropriateness of organizational structures depends on environmental factors and task characteristics (Burns and Stalker, 1961; Woodward, 1965; Thompson, 1967; Lawrence and Lorsch, 1967; Tushman and Nadler, 1978). Thus, organizational structures are good to the extent that they 'fit' the task requirements of the groups they form. Maximizing the 'fit' is important to minimize the unnecessary interactions that consume organizational resources during product development.

We saw that grouping individuals by common disciplines fosters interactions of the same type and deepens knowledge of the same discipline whereas grouping individuals from different disciplines to complete specific projects facilitates coordination when developing specific products. Cross-functional integration in its different forms allows for intermediate choices. The designer of the formal organization thus has a continuum of choices at hand, spanning the functional and the project organization.

While many factors may influence the details of the structure to be created (Allen, 1986), we see two variables mainly determining the structure: technological uncertainty and market uncertainty (see Fig. 7.4). If the rate of change in basic technologies is high and market needs can be easily formulated, functional organizations and their kindred are appropriate. In that case, technical expertise is the best predictor of product success and the organization needs to reflect that. As the rate of change in technologies declines and the rate of market change increases, more project-like organizations become preferable. In the extreme case where the technology is well established and there is not much change, project organizations provide for the market integration that companies in such an environment typically compete in.

For example, in the R&D center of the cosmetics division of a luxury goods conglomerate we have studied (Sosa and Balmes, 2006) we found how their formulation labs faced this trade-off in different ways. The skin care formulation lab, which develops products with active ingredients for

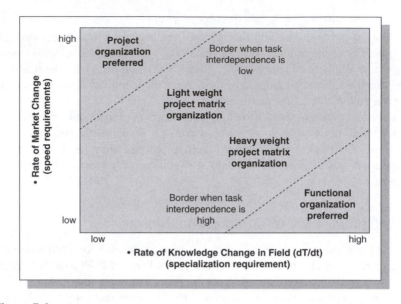

Figure 7.4
A framework to evaluate organizational forms for NPD (based on Allen 1986).

anti-aging, skin hydration, and skin whitening, had the need to deepen their knowledge on these different technological demanding areas even though they also need to develop complete skin-care product lines. On the other hand, the make-up formulation lab stresses fast and flexible development. The lab creates a large variety of products that integrate technologically simple textures with many different color shades. Given the organizational priorities of this organization and an imminent reorganization at hand, their skin care lab leaned towards an organizational form that emphasized their functional priorities whereas the make-up lab was considering merging their texture and color labs into one to emphasize more cross-discipline integration.

2.5. Beyond function versus Project: Modular organization design

So far our exposition of formal organization design for NPD has covered a stream of research that is by now well established and agreed. However, recent research focus is shifting. With the rise of the complex systems view of organizations, the importance of interacting microstructures has been recognized. Complex systems are characterized as 'made up of a large number of parts that interact in non-simple ways, . . . [such that] given the properties of the parts and the laws of their interactions, it is not a trivial matter to infer the properties of the whole' (Simon, 1969: 195). Hence, the minutiae of detail design may affect organizational behavior at the macro level. One of the first studies to uncover the organizational impact of changes in the architecture of the product was carried out by Henderson and Clark (1990). Based on the premise that 'architectural knowledge tends to become embedded in the structure and information-processing procedures of established organizations' (p. 9), they suggest that established firms fail to design novel product architectures because their organizational routines and communication patterns are anchored on the architecture of their previous products. By studying several architectural changes in the photolithography equipment industry, they found that subtle shifts in the optimal product architecture, which were not reflected in the organization structure of the respective market leader, could be exploited by new entrants to turn the industry structure around. Such a seminal finding suggested that a strong relationship between the product structure and the formal and informal organizational structure exist.

The most comprehensive conceptualization of product architecture was first introduced by Ulrich (1995), who defines it as the scheme by which the functional components of the product map into its physical components. Such a mapping defines the way product components share interfaces. Within the concept of product architecture, the notion of *modularity* is crucial. Modular product architectures are those in which the functions of the product map (almost) entirely to one or few product components. This implies that modular products are formed by modules, which are independent of each other while integral products are formed by highly coupled sets of components (Ulrich and Eppinger, 2004). Because the notion of modularity implies decoupling of components (or sets of components) that form a complex system (Simon, 1969), modularity has been considered as a mechanism to obtain flexibility to manage complexity and uncertainty (Ethiraj and Levinthal, 2004). In the product domain, modularity has been associated with flexibility to adapt and generate product variety (Ulrich, 1995). Bringing product and organization design together, Sanchez and Mahoney (1996) discuss the value of using modular designs both in the product and organizational domain as a way to gain flexibility and handle complexity. They use the term modularity to refer to products and organizations that use standardized interfaces between their physical components and organizational groups, respectively. They suggest that both product and organizational structures need to be considered simultaneously for the organizational form to take advantage of the coordination mechanisms embedded in the product architecture. Moving the unit of analysis one-step up to the industry level, product, and organizational modularity have been credited with the evolution of platforms used by an entire industry and thus industry structures, which allow teams in different organizations to work independently on loosely coupled problems (Baldwin and Clark, 2000;

Schilling, 2000). Indeed, Schilling and Steensma (2001) show after analyzing data from 330 US manufacturing firms, that industries with greater pressures for flexibility due to the heterogeneous inputs and demands tend to adopt more modular organizational forms as opposed to integrated hierarchical. Baldwin and Clark (2000) use the personal computer industry to show, how an entire industry can innovate and grow at significantly higher than expected rates by taking advantage of the modularity embedded in PC architectures. They argue that by following established 'design rules' in the industry developers of product components could innovate at higher than normal rates without generating design rework to other components of the product. Complementing this line of research, Langlois (2002) discusses the implications of modular organizational forms and the way property rights are partitioned in technology organizations.

These findings emphasize the need to deepen our understanding of how the product and organizational structures map into each other. To this end, Sosa et al. (2004) study how the architecture of complex products map to the formal and informal organizational structure of the organization that designs it. To do this they capture (a) the architecture of a large commercial aircraft engine by documenting how its engine components share technical interfaces, and (b) the actual technical communication patterns of the teams responsible for the design of each engine component. They found that the actual communication patterns highly correlate to the interfaces identified in the product architecture. More interestingly, they also found a significant number of cases in which there was a mismatch of technical interfaces and team interactions. Understanding the sources of these mismatches was critical because many of them were associated with costly design rework and project delays. The occurrences of these mismatches were systematically associated with product and organizational factors. In particular, they found that interdependences across organizational boundaries exhibit a higher risk of being missed by team interactions and such a risk is even higher between components that belong to different modular systems. Because complex systems are 'nearly decomposable' instead of perfectly modular (Simon, 1969) some interfaces occur across system and organizational boundaries and those interfaces are the ones that are harder to identify and attend during the development of complex products (Ethiraj and Levinthal, 2004).

This interaction of organizational design and product design has an additional dimension. Structuring organizations is one way to handle the inherent complexity of the design process. It has been shown that reduction of design complexity is necessary to avoid problems with excessive design conversion times and even to avoid design instability (overall project failure) (Yassine et al., 2003; Mihm et al., 2003). In that context, Mihm et al. (2006) show that under certain circumstances it may be beneficial to deliberately use organizational boundaries to weaken interdependencies and channel communication.

Considering too many component interdependencies may lead to system instability and information overload on the team members. Using organizational boundaries to reduce the information flow stabilizes the development process, sacrificing performance for the sake of speed and predictability.

In this section, we sketched the current state of the discussion about formal organization in NPD. We argued that organization in NPD centers around a trade-off between specialization and integration. NPD organizations need to create strong technical expertise on the one hand and show high market integration on the other hand. Functional organization forms and project organization forms represent the polar points of potential organization implementations. Heavy and light-weight project matrix organizations form the middle ground.

In our discussion, we deliberately neglected that integration can be achieved through many mechanisms other than primary reporting relations or secondary cross-functional team structures. Lateral relations Galbraith's (1972) such as liaison mangers, task forces, integration personnel and integrating departments are classic. Consistent goal setting as well as a shared culture, rules, and a leadership style play a subtle role in the integration effort. Moreover, the design of the process (Ulrich and Eppinger, 2004) may turn out to be a powerful method.

3. The informal organizational structure

In this section, we examine development organizations as a network of individuals or teams, which informally establish social relationships amongst each other to develop new products and services. That is, instead of looking at the formal organizational structures and mechanisms that managers use to steer the organization to create new products and services, here we examine how design decisions are actually taken by team members. More formally, we keep on using an information-processing perspective of product development organizations in which its members use their social interactions to exchange knowledge and resources. We not only examine what determines the establishments of such communication links but also how these communication patterns impact the outcome of these organizations.

The notion of considering R&D organizations as a communication network starts with the pioneering work of Allen dedicated to investigate how effective internal and external communications stimulate the performance of R&D organizations (1977). The basic premise in this line of research is that communication is an important determinant of project performance in product development contexts. This premise generated two streams of research focused around the two questions: (1) What factors determine technical communication in R&D development organizations? (2) How do technical communication patterns impact product development performance? In this section, we examine how these questions have been addressed by past research and then integrate such lessons with findings in the area of social network analysis.

3.1. Determinants of technical communication

Under the information processing perspective product development organizations transform a set of inputs (e.g., customer needs, product strategy, and manufacturing constraints) into a set of outputs (e.g., product design and production plans), which requires that members of a product development team communicate with others, either within or outside the development team, to accomplish their development activities. Thus, communication becomes an important factor of R&D performance.

One of the most extensively studied factors that influence communication in R&D organizations is distance separation between their members. Arguably, the best known of studies in this context is Allen's (1977) research on communication processes in R&D organizations, describing how increasing distance between team members reduced the chances of two team members communicating for technical matters. Allen summarizes his findings about how individual location influences technical communication in the 'communication-distance' curve for face-to-face communication in collocated R&D organizations (1977: 239). Allen found that the probability of two engineers engaging in technical communication rapidly decays with distance. It is important to note that Allen's results imply that distance is a non-linear determinant of communication, which rapidly fades after a few meters of separation. As Allen (1977) emphasizes, 'one would expect probability of communication to decrease with distance. One might even expect it to decay at a more than a linear rate. It is the actual rate of decay that is surprising. Probability of weekly communication reaches a low asymptotic level within the first twenty-five or thirty meters' (p. 236). Allen's work uses distance as a proxy for a wider issue of the influence of physical architecture on communication. The implications of these results for designing the layout of R&D centers have been extensively used in practice (Allen, 1977).

One could argue, however, that the effect of distance on communication is just due to high correlation of distance with other important variables that are determinants of communication. One of such factors is the membership of a certain organizational group. People sharing organizational bonds are probably located closer to each other in their R&D facilities and, therefore, have higher chances of engaging in technical communication. Allen tested for such a possibility and found that people sharing organizational bounds indeed have a higher likelihood of communicating, yet the rapid decay due to distance separation was still evident for people sharing organizational bonds as shown in Fig. 7.5.

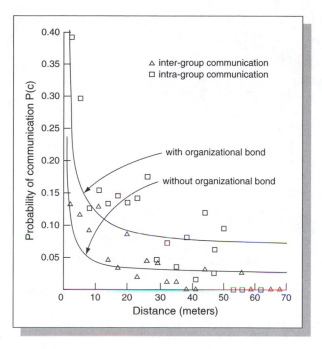

Figure 7.5
Allen's communication-distance curve (Allen, 1977: 241).

Although other empirical studies have supported Allen's results (e.g., Keller and Holland, 1983; Keller, 1986), more recent studies in product development organizations show that other important factors moderate the negative effect of distance. In addition to organizational bonds already mentioned, these factors include the choice of communication media and the nature of the work. As for the effect of media choice, Sosa et al. (2002) conducted an empirical study in global product development organizations in the telecommunications industry and found that the effect of distance is significantly moderated by the medium used to communicate. Interestingly, they found that the use of telephone and email substitute face-to-face communication as distance increases. As shown in Fig. 7.6, the use of telephone increases with distance and then decays when the effects of time zone difference become apparent while the use of email increases exponentially with geographic and cultural distance (including language difference). Although their empirical evidence supports the detrimental impact that distance has on technical communication, there is also evidence that organizations have found ways to mitigate such hindering effects. Having a portfolio of communication media that allows managers to substitute rich face-to-face medium for combinations of other less rich but

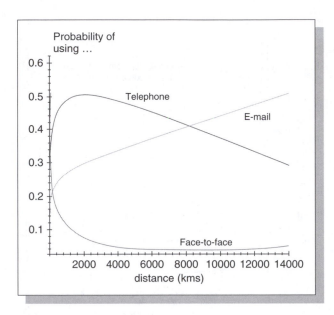

Figure 7.6
Communication media choice as a function of distance (Sosa et al., 2002, p. 53 © 2007 IEEE).

more flexible communication media has certainly allow for the formation of global product development networks (e.g., McDonough III et al., 1999).

How the type of communication moderates the effect of distance, separation has also been investigated. For example, Van den Bulte and Moenaert (1998) found that collocation of R&D team members did enhance communication amongst them. However, they also discovered that the communication frequency between R&D and marketing was not affected by the resulting increase in physical distance. That is, marketing and R&D kept the same asymptotically low level of communication needed to address their basic interdependencies even after increasing their physical distance separation. Task interdependence matters: it is an important determinant of communication. Indeed, Morelli et al. (1995) used the task structure of the development process in a firm in the telecommunications industry to predict technical communication. They found that by examining the task structure of the project, managers could obtain better technical communications predictions than by using distance-separation probability models based on Allen's curve. These empirical results confirm previous theoretical arguments about how organizations use technical communication to address task interdependencies and resolve task uncertainty during the product development (Thompson, 1967; Galbraith, 1973; Daft and Lengel, 1986). Examining the sources of task interdependencies and task uncertainty is therefore crucial to understand the determinants of technical communication patterns in product development organizations.

As discussed in the previous section, an important source of interdependencies between members of a product development organization is the architecture of the product they design. As shown by Henderson and Clark (1990), organizations tend to anchor their formal and informal communication channels on the architecture of the product they have successfully designed. As a result, established firms have difficulties designing novel architectures. To address such a challenge, managers need to start by understanding how their current design efforts map to the products they design. To do so, Sosa et al. (2004) proposes a structured approach to overlay a design structure matrix representation of the product and sociomatrix representation of the organization that designs it so that managers can evaluate whether or not people are communicating when they are supposed to (see Fig. 7.7).

Finally, other researchers have focused on how communication links evolve over time to resolve uncertainty during the development process (Adler, 1995). On this topic, Terwiesch et al. (2002) used an ethnography approach to study the content of information exchanges in an automobile manufacturer. They studied how design teams exchanged preliminary information in product development scenarios. Based on field data they categorize the information exchanged based on the precision and stability of its content (as seen by the communication source) as well as its impact (on the receiver). Such a categorization allowed them to develop a framework to enable managers to choose between different strategies to handle task interdependencies and reduce uncertainty.

In sum, we have argued that distance is a key factor that can hinder technical communication in R&D organizations. That alone has had important implications not only on the physical layout of R&D centers (Allen, 1977), but also has started a research stream focused on studying the key determinants of technical communication. Recent findings suggest that the hindering effects of distance can be overcome not only by enabling communication technologies but also by managers' intervention on empowering team members to attend the interdependences that matter for the process and product under development. Hence, learning 'where interdependencies come from' is perhaps the most significant challenge to handle to predict and shape technical communication in development organizations. Ultimately, only by aligning process, product, and informal organizational structures managers would be able to avoid unnecessary design rework due to lack of communication about critical interdependencies (Sosa, 2007).

Although this stream of literature assumes that the existence of communication links positively impacts product development performance, we still need to understand how and why such links determine performance. We turn to that point next.

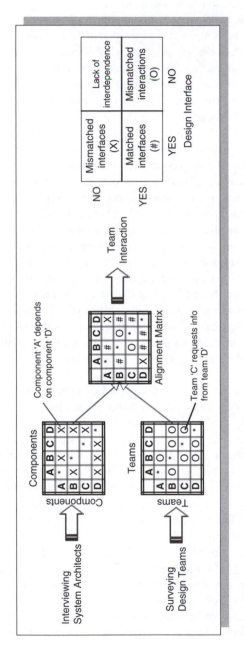

Figure 7.7
Aligning Product and Organizational Structures (adapted from Sosa et al., 2004).

3.2. Communication and team performance

Here, we discuss how communication patterns impact project performance. Work in this area has focused on the value of communication both with team members and outsiders (Eisenhardt and Brown, 1995). Next, we discuss the effects of both internal and external communication.

The effects of internal communication

Intense internal communication enhances collaboration and team cohesiveness, which in turn favor problem solving and cross-functional integration resulting in better project and product performance. For example, Keller (1986), in a study of 32 group projects in a large R&D organization, found that group cohesiveness was the most important and consistent predictor of group performance even after controlling for the type of R&D project and the source of performance ratings (both by group members and management). The role of project managers is also critical in promoting internal communication in their teams. Katz and Allen (1985) found, in a study of 86 teams in nine technology-based organizations using a 'matrix' formal structure, that higher team performance is achieved when *project* managers were influential on organizational and administrative matters while *functional* managers were influential on technical issues of the group tasks.

As mentioned in Section 2 of this chapter, a key role of internal communication is to overcome cross-functional integration issues within the team. To investigate this issue, Dougherty (1992) completed an inductive study over 18 NPD projects in five different firms. Her research shows that it is not the amount of cross-functional integration issues faced but the way they are overcome what determines the likelihood of having a successful product that meets or exceeds expectations after introduction. She observed that those teams that used a highly interactive and iterative approach to overcome cross-functional barriers instead of 'over-the-wall' approaches were the ones that ended up with a successful product. Central to these observations is the notion that successful teams tend to violate established routines and divisions of tasks to work and collaborate on the tasks that were highly iterative (Dougherty and Heller, 1994). Having adaptive teams that rely on intense experimental and iterative interactions appears to be even more important on fast changing industries such as the computer industry (Eisenhardt and Tabrizi, 1995).

Although empirical findings support the notion that intense internal communication positively influences performance because it fosters collaboration and cross-functional integration, a word of caution needs to be raised if internal communication comes at the expense of external communication. Being too internally focused while neglecting what happens outside team boundaries raises the chances being affected by the 'not invented here NHI' syndrome

(Katz and Allen, 1982). Hence, finding a blend of intense internal communication with external communication is crucial for project performance (Katz, 1982).

The effects of external communication

Communication of team members with outsiders does impact product development performance. Yet, it is not the frequency, but the way of communicating and the content, which determine its impact on project performance. Key findings in this stream of research include the role of gatekeepers, the value of information diversity and external support, and the gathering of inputs from innovative users.

Allen (1971) uncovered 'technological gatekeepers' by combining both internal and external communication patterns. He found that the individuals, to whom others frequently turned for information, differed from other colleagues to the extent in which they exposed themselves to sources of technical information outside their organization. These highly performing individuals are the 'technological gatekeepers' of the organization (Tushman, 1977). Tushman and Katz (1980) investigated the role of gatekeepers by studying 61 R&D projects (with and without gatekeepers) in a large corporation. They found that because these gatekeepers provided an efficient mechanism for the team to both gather external information useful for the team and translate it into meaningful information for internal team members, teams working on product development activities with active gatekeepers tend to exhibit better project performance than those without gatekeepers. However, the presence of gatekeeper was detrimental to project performance when the activities of the team were focused on 'universal tasks' such as 'scientific research' rather than a task associated with product development activities. For the cases of groups involved in 'scientific research,' team members did not need the translation offered by gatekeepers and were better off accessing external information directly by themselves.

Another important theme related with external communication focuses on the portfolio of communications with outsiders. Ancona and Caldwell (1992) studied a sample of 45 NPD teams and examined how their external communication patterns would relate with their performance (as rated by both the team and the management). They found that high performing teams used a balance portfolio of external communications that combines 'political' interactions to gain resources and support from top level management and 'task coordination' interactions related with technical or design aspects of the project. Furthermore, it has been shown that the value of external communication is associated not only with the support and resources, brought to the team from top level management, but also with the diversity of external knowledge the team exposes itself which in turn offers novel views for problem solving, learning, and innovation (Cummings, 2004).

External communication is also critical to gather information about the market for which products are developed. The marketing literature has extensively investigated the importance of communicating with target customers to gather and understand customer needs (Griffin and Hauser, 1993). Recognizing that some users innovate all by themselves when they face emerging needs that are at the leading edge of what the market offers, von Hippel (1986, 2005) suggests to identify and establish rich communication with these *lead users* to maximize the chances of developing breakthrough products.

Summarizing, past research has shown that both internal and external communication are 'good' for project performance for distinct reasons. Internal communication is beneficial because it favors collaboration and cross-functional integration while external communication is advantageous because it increases information diversity and provides access to resources and support from top management levels. Next, we compare these findings with relevant results, which have emerged from social network analysis in collaboration and innovation contexts.

3.3. Lessons from social network studies

Social network analysis studies the social relations among a set of actors and argues that the way an individual actor behaves depends in large part on how that actor is tied into the larger web of social connections (e.g., Wasserman and Faust, 1994; Freeman, 2004; Burt, 2005). Beginning in the 1930s, a systematic approach to theory and research, began to emerge when Moreno (1934) introduced the ideas and tools of sociometry. In the 1940s, Bavelas noted that the arrangement of ties linking team members had consequences for their productivity and morale and started studying basic structural properties of team members (Bavelas, 1948). Since then, social network analysis has extended into many different areas of organizational research (Borgatti and Foster, 2003). Here, we do not attempt to make a comprehensive review of the social networks field, but instead focus on two areas where social network research has produced results that directly relate to product development organizations. We look at: (1) the role of network structure on collaboration and innovation; and (2) the role of tie strength on searching and transferring knowledge.

The structure of social networks in product development: Cohesion versus Sparseness

The emphasis on the role of communication networks – and network structure in particular – on team performance has gained increasing attention from scholars using social network analysis to study how the structure of a team's communication network can affect its performance. There are two competing organizational theories about how the social network structures may impact social outcomes. One stream of research highlights the benefits

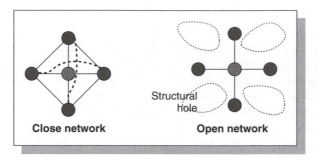

Figure 7.8
Basic social network structures.

offered by being connected with a cohesive tightly connected network of actors (Coleman, 1990) while another line of research shows the advantages of being connected to disconnected groups of actors separated by 'structural holes' between them (Burt, 1992). These two types of network structures are shown in Fig. 7.8.

In both networks, the focal actor at the center has four communication partners, yet their network structures differ significantly. The 'closed' network presents a highly cohesive structure because all the communication partners of the focal actor communicate with each other. On the other hand, the 'open' network presents a focal actor with a sparse network structure full of 'structural holes' between her four disconnected communication partners.

In product development contexts, organizational research suggests that the communication network of an individual (or team) can have two distinct effects on its ability to perform product development activities. On the one hand, the communication network can make it easier for the team to obtain the *collaboration* of other teams involved in the design of the product. On the other hand, a team's communication network can facilitate access to non-redundant information on the activities carried out by other teams, which can help with the generation of novel and useful ideas (*innovation*). These two outcomes (collaboration and innovation) are likely to be related to different network structures. More specifically, the ability to elicit the collaboration of other actors is normally related with dense and closely knit networks, whereas access to non-redundant information necessary for innovation is typically associated with open and sparse networks.

The appropriateness of the network structure depends on the outcome of interest and context at hand. Indeed, Ahuja (2000) tested these two competing theories in a longitudinal empirical study in the chemicals industry spanning over 10 years. He studied how the collaboration network structure of a firm would influence its innovation output. He found that firms with a denser network of collaborative partners (i.e., other firms with which the focal firm has a joint venture or a research or technology-sharing agreement) have higher innovation output (i.e., larger number of patent counts). Ahuja (2000) concludes that during development closed and dense networks offer collaborative advantages and therefore are likely to be more beneficial than sparse networks rich in structural holes. This is consistent with Obstfeld (2005), who found that dense social networks and a willingness to 'close' structural holes were significant predictors of individual innovation involvement in the automobile industry. Moreover, using a social network analytical approach, Sosa et al. (2007) found that when Pratt &Whitney developed their PW4098 engine, design teams with a more dense communication networks were more likely to attend a larger fraction of their critical technical interdependencies than teams with less cohesive network structures. Yet such benefits were less salient for teams designing more modular components (i.e., components with fewer and weaker connections with other components in the engine). Interpreting these findings, we conclude that, when strong collaboration among product development participants is a key requirement to succeed, having a dense network increases organizational performance.

However, when the critical outcome is the generation of novel and useful ideas, sparse social networks appear to be more beneficial than dense networks because they provide diverse and non-redundant information to the focal actor. Consistent with this argument Hargadon and Sutton (1997) proposed a technology-brokering model of innovation based on an ethnography study at the product design firm IDEO. They argue that a firm like IDEO is able to routinely generate innovative design solutions because they have access to diverse and separated pools of 'technologies' associated with different industries and are able to act as 'technology brokers' by recombining existing solutions from one industry into novel solutions for another industry. At the individual level of analysis and using a social network approach, Burt (2004) found support to the hypothesis that an actor that is connected to a number of other actors not connected to one another (i.e., in between 'structural holes') has better access to non-redundant information which in turn enables her to generate better ideas than her peers in the organization. In another network study, Rodan and Gallunic (2004) found marginal support for the direct effect between network sparseness and innovation, yet in the presence of knowledge heterogeneity having a sparse social network would increase innovative outcomes.

In sum, theoretical arguments and empirical evidence suggest that while dense communication networks enforce trust and reciprocity, which are key elements to establishing a collaborative environment, sparse networks favor information diversity and open brokering opportunities, which are ideal conditions for learning and creativity. Aiming to achieve the benefits of both structures takes us back to our previous section in which we discuss the benefits of internal and external communication. From the previous section, one could conclude that to achieve higher project performance teams must use internal communication to increase team cohesiveness and use sparse external communication to maximize access to diverse sources of information. Reagans and Zuckerman (2001) found support for such a proposition. They show, in a study of 224 corporate R&D teams (in which they also control for demographic diversity of the team) that more productive teams were the ones with a dense internal network among team members (which foster coordination and collective action) and an external communication network that bridges across global divisions (which favors learning, creativity, and effective action). These results are consistent with other results in social networks, which explore how organizations can take advantage of both internal density and external sparseness (Reagans and McEvily, 2003; Reagans et al., 2004; Burt, 2005).

Tie strength and knowledge sharing in product development

Although the structure of social networks has an impact on the way people search for knowledge and information for the products they are developing (Borgatti and Cross, 2003), other researchers have examined the characteristics of the tie (between product developers) to study how they impact organizational performance (Argote et al., 2003). An attribute that has received particular attention is the strength of the social relationship (also called *tie strength*). Tie strength is defined as a combination of communication frequency and emotional closeness between the source and the recipient (Marsden and Campbell, 1984). Although the role of tie strength has been investigated in various social contexts, we are interested here in its impact on product development activities. Early research on R&D management suggests that the more communication the better (Eisenhardt and Brown, 1995), hence stronger ties should lead to higher product development performance. Research in social networks show that such an assumption is not entirely correct. Weak ties offer important benefits associated with information access while strong ties can be costly to maintain.

Early work in social networks by Granovetter (1973) suggests that weak ties (infrequent and distant relationships) can be helpful because they can provide efficient access to diverse and distant groups of people. Weak ties are easy to maintain because they occur infrequently with people with whom there is no strong obligation to reciprocate any social interaction. Uzzi's (1997) ethnography study, however, reveals that strong ties are associated with relational mechanisms that facilitate knowledge transfer.

The tension between these observations is particularly important to consider in product development where two fundamental process take place during the development of new products: (1) *Searching* for new knowledge, and (2) *transferring* new knowledge from the source to the recipient. Hansen (1999, 2002) shows, based on an empirical study on 120 NPD projects, that those projects that use weak ties to *search* for new non-codifiable knowledge and use strong ties to *transfer* well-codifiable knowledge finish their projects faster than other project teams that do not align their tie strength with the search-transfer requirements. Although some factors such as 'trust' and 'knowledge codifiability' moderate the relationship between tie strength and knowledge sharing the empirical evidence supports the basic proposition that weak ties favor 'search' while strong ties facilitate 'transfer' (1999) (Argote et al., 2003; Reagans and McEvily, 2003; Levin and Cross, 2004).

To summarize, in this section we started with the premise that communication would positively influence product development performance and therefore it was important to understand the factors that drive and hinder technical communication in product development. Then, we discussed how communication impacts product development performance by examining internal and external communication patterns. Finally, we complement this view with the findings from social network studies focused on product development organizations.

4. Conclusions and future directions

How should NPD be organized? We have compiled and structured key findings on research about formal and informal organizations. Concluding, we argue that managers need to look at both the formal structures and mechanisms to design and plan development efforts and the informal communication networks of the people involved in such efforts. By balancing these formal and informal structures, managers can overcome the challenges of ever changing conditions associated with product development. This is consistent with an adaptive view of product development organizations which suggests that high performing organizations are always discontent with their current form and constantly look for better ways to address the trade-offs they face (Eisenhardt and Brown, 1997). As one successful R&D manager in the pharmaceutical industry indicated, 'We've tried organizing by therapeutic class. We've tried organizing by scientific discipline. We've tried using project teams. Nothing works as well as being continually aware of the need to be both at the leading edge of the science and in total command of the important developments in other areas.' (Henderson, 1994: 105).

The topic is vast. Many more important aspects of organizing NPD could be raised. Questions about team management, about embedding the organization into external networks or questions about building and advancing core capabilities and many others impact the organization of NPD. We could not possibly address all of these questions in the article. Therefore, we stuck to our core topic of linking people.

Although research related with organizing for effective NPD has come along way since the early studies of Allen, still many avenues need to be explored.

We outline several areas of future research (without trying to be exhaustive) which we think will provide fruitful findings for managers of innovation.

Incentives. Generally, the information processing view of the design effort has implicitly fostered a belief that management's main task is to provide for the flow of necessary information at the required stage in the design process and organizations will make the right choices. While there is evidence that information was the bottleneck factor in the past and may still be for many organizations, we also come to understand that the premise of the information processing view may not be ubiquitously applicable. There is evidence that incentivation of participants in the design game may be a factor worth analysis (e.g., Mihm, 2007).

Organizing for global NPD. There is a growing trend to increase the share of NPD done outside the home country (Zedtwitz and Gassman, 2002, Eppinger and Chitkara, 2006). Market penetration and support of production and marketing through local R&D are often cited as a rationale, but in addition, there is also absorption of foreign technologies. However, that raises 'the challenge is to coordinate the dispersed R&D, how should the units be linked' (De Meyer 1993; De Meyer and Mizushima 1989). Some segmentations and descriptive classification with some normative advice of what to use when have been defined (e.g., Kümmerle, 1997; Chiesa, 2000). Chiesa (2000), e.g., identifies major categories of global R&D setups describing how international NPD can be organized. His unit of analysis is the national center. He gives qualitative reasoning as to advantages and disadvantages of different setups. Although some hypotheses have been put forward, generally the contingent determinants of what defines good or bad international setups have not been sufficiently identified. We do not know whether macro factors of general setup or micro factors of individual project setup should drive design. In addition, the extension of informal networks in international organizations also offers additional research avenues worth exploring (Doz et al., 2005).

Managing radical change. Preparing organizations for radical change is notoriously difficult. (e.g., Leifer et al., 2001) More generally, there are massive problems introducing innovations, which require radically different environmental factors (Zollo and Winter, 2002). Corporate venturing has been advocated by several writers as a solution. However, corporate venturing is only one solution of many (e.g., Colarelli and DeMartino, 2006). Moreover, how is the interplay with existing organizational entities? How do we formally institute an organization which provides the stability and efficiency of a well-established stream alongside radical change agents still using knowledge and operational synergies?

The dynamics of organizations. Product development is a dynamic process that goes through very distinct phases. Yet, research has paid very little attention to the dynamics of organizations within NPD projects. How do formal and informal organizations differ (or should differ) across project phases? As projects progress and the informal organization evolves, should the formal organization adapt?

Organizing for user innovation. The research on user innovation has shown significant evidence that users do innovate, and *lead users* typically innovate before the manufactures do. Moreover, communities of users are getting self organized to innovate themselves (von Hippel, 2005). How could manufactures organize to integrate user innovation into their innovation process?

Alternative communication network structures. Recent studies have suggested that actors who have social networks which exhibit 'small-world' properties have the benefit of being locally clustered as well as the access to distant and diverse sources of information by the existent of random connections in the network (Uzzi and Spiro, 2005; Phelps and Schilling, 2007; Fleming et al., 2007). These results suggest the possibilities to use alternative social network structures to gain the benefits of both collaboration and information diversity. What other alternatives do managers have to address the cohesion-diversity trade-off faced when both collaboration and creativity are needed? What other organizational trade-offs are NPD organizations facing and how informal communication network structures help (or hinder) the way to address them?

Finally, we have seen that research on organizing NPD has always benefited from the interaction with other research streams, be it the original organization literature or the literature on network structures. Therefore, we call for reaching out even further into other areas tangential to NPD to enrich our knowledge on how NPD organizations work.

References

Adler, P. S. 1995. Interdepartmental interdependence and coordination: The case of the design-manufacturing interface. *Organization Science* 6 (2): 147–167.

Ahuja, G. 2000. Collaboration networks, structural holes, and innovation: A longitudinal study. *Administrative Science Quarterly* 45: 425–455.

Allen, T. J. 1971. Communications, technology transfer, and the role of technical gatekeeper. *R&D Management* 1: 14–21.

Allen, T. J. 1977. *Managing the Flow of Technology*, Boston, MA: MIT Press.

Allen, T. J. 1986. Organizational structure, information technology and R&D productivity. *IEEE Transactions on Engineering Management*, EM-33, 4: 212–217.

Ancona, D., and D. Caldwell. 1992. Bridging the boundary: External activity and performance in organizational teams. *Administrative Science Quarterly* 37: 634–665.

Argote, L., B. McEvily, R. Reagans. 2003. Managing knowledge in organizations: An integrative framework and review of emerging themes. *Management Science* 49 (4): 571–582.

Baldwin, C., and K. B. Clark. 2000. *Design Rules, Vol. 1: The Power of Modularit,* Cambridge, Mass: MIT Press.

Bavelas A. 1948. A mathematical model for small group structures. *Human Organization* 7: 16–30.

Borgatti, S., and R. Cross. 2003. A relational view of information seeking and learning in social networks. *Management Science* 49 (4): 432–445.

Borgatti, S., and P. C. Foster. 2003. The network paradigm in organizational research: A review and typology. *Journal of Management* 29: 991–1013.

Brown, S. L., and K. M. Eisenhardt. 1997. The art of continuous change: Linking complexity theory and time-paced evolution in relentlessly shifting organizations. *Administrative Science Quarterly* 42: 1–34.

Burns, S., and G. M. Stalker. 1961. *The Management of Innovation*, London: Tavistock Publications.

Burt, R. S. 1992. *Structural Holes, The Social Structure of Competition*, Cambridge, Mass: Harvard University Press.

Burt, R. S. 2004. Structural holes and new ideas. *American Journal of Sociology* 110: 349–399.

Burt, R. S. 2005. Brokerage and closure. *An Introduction to Social Capital*, Oxford University Press.

Clark, K. B., and T. Fujimoto. 1991. *Product Development Performance,* Boston, MA: Harvard Business School Press.

Clark, K. B., and T. Fujimoto. 1995. The power of product integrity. In: K. B. Clark and S. C. Wheelwright (Eds.) *The product development challenge,* Boston, MA: Harvard Business School Publishing.

Clark, K. B., and S. C. Wheelwright. 1993. *Managing new product and process development*, New York: The Free Press.

Chiesa, V. 2000. Global R&D project management and organization: A taxonomy. *Journal of Product and Innovation Management* 17 (5): 341–359.

Cockburn, I. M., R. M. Henderson. 1998. Absorptive capacity, coauthoring behavior, and the organization of research in drug discovery. *The Journal of Industrial Economics* 46 (2): 157–182.

Colarelli O'Connor, G., and R. DeMartino. 2006. Organizing for radical innovation: An exploratory study of the structural aspects of RI management systems in large established firms. *Journal of Product Innovation Management* 23 (6): 475–497.

Coleman, J. S. 1990. *Foundations of social theory*, Cambridge, Mass: Belknap Press.

Cummings, J. 2004. Work groups, structural diversity, and knowledge sharing in a global organization. *Management Science* 50 (3): 352–364.

Daft, R. L., and R. H. Lengel. 1986. Organizational information requirements, media richness and structural design. *Management Science* 32 (5): 554–571.

De Meyer, A. 1993. Internationalizing R&D improves a firm's technical learning. *Research Technology Management Journal* 36 (4): 42–49.

De Meyer, A., and A. Mizushima. 1989. Global R&D management. *R&D Management* 19: 135–146.

Dougherty, D. 1990. Understanding new markets for new products. *Strategic Management Journal* 11 (Special Issue: Corporate Entrepreneurship): 59–78.

Dougherty, D. 1992. Interpretive barriers to successful product innovation in large firms. *Organization Science* 3 (2): 179–202.

Dougherty, D., and T. Heller. 1994. The illegitimacy of successful product innovation in established firms. *Organization Science* 5 (2): 200–218.

Doz, Y., K. Wilson and P. Williamson. 2007. *Managing Global Innovations*, forthcoming 2007.

Eisenhardt, K. M., and B. N. Tabrizi. 1995. Accelerating adaptive processes: Product innovation in the global computer industry. *Administrative Science Quarterly* 40: 84–110.

Eisenhardt, K. M., and S. L. Brown. 1995. Product development: Past research, present findings, and future directions. *Academy of Management Review* 20 (2): 343–378.

Eppinger, S. D., and A. Chitkara. 2006. The new practice of global product development. *MIT Sloan Management Review* 47 (4): 22–30.

Ethiraj, S. K., and D. Levinthal. 2004. Modularity and innovation in complex systems. *Management Science* 50 (2): 159–173.

Fleming, Lee, C. King, and A. Juda. 2007. Small worlds and regional innovation. *Organization Science*.

Freeman, L. C. 2004. *The Development of Social Network Analysis: A Study in the Sociology of Science*. BookSurge Publishing, North Charleston, South Carolina.

Galbraith, J. 1972. Organization design: An information processing view in organization planning: Cases and concepts. In: J. Lorsch and P. Lawrence (Eds.) *Studies in Organization Design*, Homewood, Il: Richard D. Irwin, Inc.

Galbraith, J. 1973. *Designing Complex Organizations*, Cambridge, MA: Addison Wesley.

Granovetter, M. 1973. The strength of weak ties. *American Journal of Sociology* 6 (6): 1360–1380.

Griffin, A., and J. R. Hauser. 1993. The Voice of the Customer. *Marketing Science* 12 (1): 1–27.

Hansen, M. 1999. The search-transfer problem: The role of weak ties in sharing knowledge across organization subunits. *Administrative Science Quarterly* 44 (1): 82–111.

Hansen, M. 2002. Knowledge networks: Explaining effective knowledge sharing in multiunit companies. *Org.Sci.* 13 (3): 232–248.

Hargadon, A., and R. Sutton. 1997. Technology brokering and innovation in a product development firm. *Administrative Science Quarterly* 42: 716–749.

Henderson, R., K. Clark. 1990. Architectural innovation: The reconfiguration of existing product technologies and the failure of established firms. *Administrative Science Quarterly* 35(1): 9–30.

Henderson, R. 1994. Managing innovation in the information age. *Harvard Business Review* 99–105.

Ittner, C. D., D. F. Larcker. 1997. The performance effects of process management techniques. *Management Science* 43: 522–534.

Kahn, K. B. 2001. Market orientation, interdepartmental integration, and product development performance. *The Journal of Product Innovation Management* 18: 314–323.

Katz, R. 1982. The effects of group longevity on project communication and performance. *Administrative Science Quarterly* 25: 67–87.

Katz, R., and T. J. Allen. 1982. Investigating the not Invented Here (NIH) Syndrome: A look at the performance, tenure and communication patterns of 50 R&D projects groups. *R&D Management* 12 (1): 7–19.

Katz, R., and T. J. Allen. 1985. Project performance and the locus of influence in the R&D matrix. *Academy of Management Journal* 29: 715–726.

Keller, R. T. 1986. Predictors of the performance of project groups in R&D organizations. *Academy of Management Journal* 29: 715–726.

Keller, R. T., and W. E. Holland. 1983. Communications and innovations in research and development organizations. *Academy of Management Journal* 29: 715–726.

Kümmerle, W. 1997. Building effective R&D capabilities abroad. *Harvard business review* 75 (2): 61–72.

Langlois. R. N. 2002. Modularity in technology and organization. *Journal of Economic Behavior and Organization* 49: 19–37.

Lawrence, P., J. Lorsch. 1967. *Organizations and Environment*, Boston, MA: Harvard Business School Press.

Leenders, Mark A. A. M., and Berend Wierenga. 2002. The effectiveness of different mechanisms for integration marketing and R&D. *Journal of Product Innovation Management* 19 (4): 305–317.

Leifer, R. G., C. o'Connor, M. Rice. 2001. Implementing radical innovation in mature firms: The role of hubs. *Academy of Management Executive* 15 (3): 102–113.

Levin, D., and R. Cross. 2004. The strength of weak ties you can trust: The mediating role of trust in effective knowledge transfer. *Management Science* 50 (11): 1477–1490.

Marsden, P. V., and K. E. Campbell. 1984. Measuring tie strength. *Social Forces* 63: 482–501.

McDonough III, E. F., K. B. Kahn and A. Griffin. 1999. Managing communication in global product development teams. *IEEE Transactions on Engineering Management* 46 (4): 375–386.

Mihm, J., C. H. Loch, A. Huchzermeier. 2003. Problem solving oscillations in complex engineering projects. *Management Science* 49 (6): 733–750.

Mihm, J., C. H. Loch, D. Wiklinson, B. Huberman. 2006. Hierarchies and problem solving oscillations in complex organizations. *INSEAD working paper*.

Mihm, J. 2007. The Effect of Incentives on new product development outcomes and timing. *INSEAD working paper*.

Morelli, M. D., S. D. Eppinger, R. K. Gulati. 1995. Predicting technical communication in product development organizations. *IEEE Transactions on Engineering Management* 42 (3): 215–222.

Moreno, J. 1934. *Who Shall Survive?: Fundations of Sociometry, Group Psychotherapy, and Sociodrama,* Second edition in 1953 and third edition in 1978. Washington, DC: Nervous and Mental Disease Publishing Co.

Obstfeld, D. 2005. Social networks, the *Tertius iungens* orientation, and involvement in innovation. *Administrative Science Quarterly* 50: 100–130.

Olson, E. M., O. C. Walker Jr., R. W. Rueckert, J. M. Bonner. 2001. Patterns of cooperation during new product development among marketing, operations and R&D: Implications for project performance. *Journal of Product Innovation Management* 18: 258–271.

Phelps C., and M. Schilling. 2007. Interfirm Collaboration Networks and Knowledge Creation: The Impact of Large Scale Network Structure on Firm Innovation. *Management Science* (Special Issue on *Complexity across Disciplines*).

Pinto, M. B., J. K. Pinto, J. E. Prescott. 1993. Antecedents and consequences of project team cross-functional coorperation. *Management Science* 39: 1281–1297.

Reagans, R., E. Zuckerman. 2001. Networks, diversity, and productivity: The social capital of corporate R & D teams. *Organization Science* 12: 502–517.

Reagans, R., and B. McEvily. 2003. Network structure and knowledge transfer: The effects of cohesion and range. *Administrative Science Quarterly* 48: 240–267.

Reagans, R., E. Zuckerman and B. McEvily. 2004. How to make the team: Social networks vs. Demography as criteria for designing effective criteria. *Administrative Science Quarterly* 49: 101–133.

Rodan, S., and C. Gallunic. 2004. More than network structure: How knowledge heterogeneity influences managerial performance and innovativeness. *Strategic Management Journal* 25: 541–562.

Sanchez, R., and J. T. Mahoney. 1996. Modularity, flexibility, and knowledge management in product and organization design. *Strategic Management Journal* 17: 63–76.

Schilling, M. 2000. Toward a general modular systems theory and its application to interfirm product modularity. *Academy of Management Review* 25 (2): 312–334.

Schilling, M., and H. K. Steensma. 2001. The use of modular organizational forms: An industry-level analysis. *The Academy Management Journal* 44 (6): 1149–1168.

Sethi, R. 2000. Superorinate identity in cross-functional product development teams: Its entecedents and effects on new product performance. *Journal of the Academy of Marketing Science* 28 (3): 330–344.

Simon, H. A. 1969. *The Sciences of the Artificial,* Cambridge, MA: MIT Press (2nd edition).

Song, X. M., J. Thieme, J. Xie. 1998. The impact of cross-funcitonal joint involvement across product development stages: An exploratory study. *Journal of Product Innovation Management* 15: 289–303.

Sosa, M. E., S. D. Eppinger, M. Pich, D. McKendrick, S. Stout. 2002. Factors that influence technical communication in distributed product development: An empirical study in the telecommunications industry. *IEEE Transactions on Engineering Management* 49 (1): 45–58.

Sosa, M. E., S. D. Eppinger and C. M. Rowles. 2004. The misalignment of product architecture and organizational structure in complex product development. *Management Science* 50 (12): 1674–1689.

Sosa, M. E., and C. Balmes. 2006. R&D management at universal luxury group – perfumes and cosmetics division. *INSEAD* Case 07/2006-5260.

Sosa, M. E. 2007. Aligning process, product, and organizational architectures in software development. *INSEAD working paper*.

Sosa, M. E., M. Gargiulo and C. M. Rowles. 2007. Component modularity, team network structure, and the attention to technical interdependencies in complex product development. *INSEAD Working Paper*.

Terwiesch, C., C. H. Loch, and A. De Meyer. 2002. Exchanging preliminary information in concurrent engineering: Alternative coordination strategies. *Organization Science* 13 (4): 402–419.

Thompson, J. D. 1967. *Organizations in Action*, New York: McGraw Hill.

Tushman, M. 1977. Special boundary roles in the innovation process. *Administrative Science Quarterly* 22: 587–605.

Tushman, M., and R. Katz. 1980. External communication and project performance: An investigation into the role of gatekeeper. *Management Science* 26(11): 1071–1085.

Tushman, M., and D. Nadler. 1978. Information processing as an integrating concept in organizational design. *Academy of Management Review* 3(3): 613–624.

Uzzi, B. 1997. Social structure and competition in the interfirm networks: The paradox of embededdness. *Administrative Science Quarterly* 42: 35–67.

Uzzi, B., and J. Spiro. 2005. Collaboration and creativity: The small world problem. *American Journal of Sociology* 111: 447–504.

Ulrich, K. 1995. The role of product architecture in the manufacturing firm. *Research Policy* 24: 419–440.

Ulrich, K., and S. D. Eppinger. 2004. *Product Design and Development*. New York: McGraw Hill (3rd edition).

Van den Bulte, C., R. K. Moenaert. 1998. The effects of R&D team co-location on communication patterns among R&D, marketing, and manufacturing. *Management Science* 44: S1–S19.

von Hippel, E. 1986. Lead Users: A Source of Novel Product Concepts. *Management Science* 32(7): 791–805.

Von Hippel, E. 2005. *Democratizing Innovation*. MIT Press Cambridge, Massachusetts.

Walker, A. H., J. W. Lorsch. 1968. Organizational choice: Product versus function. *Harvard Business Review* 46 (6): 129–138.

Wasserman, S., K. Faust. 1994. *Social Network Analysis*, New York: Cambridge University Press.

Wheelwright, S. C., and K. B. Clark. 1992. Revolutionizing product development. *Quantum Leaps in Speed, Efficiency, and Quality*, New York: Free Press.

Woodward, J. 1965. *Industrial Organization: Theory and Practice*. Oxford: Oxford University Press.

Yassine, A., N. Joglekar, D. Braha, S. Eppinger, D. Whitney. 2003. Information Hiding in Product Development: The Design Churn Effect, *Research in Engineering Design* 14 (3): 145–161.

Zedtwitz, M. V., and O. Gassman. 2002. Market versus technology drive in R&D internationalization: Four different patterns of managing research and development. *Research Policy* 31 (4): 569–588.

Zollo, Maurizio, and Sidney G. Winter. 2002. Deliberate learning and the evolution ofd dynamic capabilities. *Organization Science* 13 (3): 339–351.

8 Product development performance measurement

Mohan V. Tatikonda

1. Introduction

'Faster, better, cheaper, pick any two' is conventional wisdom among professionals working diligently to complete a product development project. However, is it true that aggressive targets must be limited to two of the three dimensions? To answer that, we first need to *measure* the *performance* dimensions of 'faster,' 'better,' and 'cheaper' before we can evaluate potential trade-offs and other management options. That is crux of it. Without performance measurement, we cannot answer even the most fundamental managerial questions of 'how well are we doing,' 'what have we learned,' and 'what should we do in the future.'

This chapter addresses NPD performance measurement. NPD performance measurement is a surprisingly expansive and elusive subject. This is due to the multiplicity of meanings associated with performance measurement; the varied, but simultaneous, roles that performance measurement plays; and the numerous, distinct customers of performance measurement. NPD performance measurement is further complicated by the inherent intangibility, non-routineness, uncertainty, and multi-functionality that make up contemporary new product development efforts. There is also confusion over what can be, versus what should be, measured and why. A performance measure appropriate for one project may be inappropriate for another. In addition, NPD is not monolithic – no single measure is ever fully appropriate because it cannot tell the full story. Different decision-makers and organizations need different arrays of measures. Finally, even the phrase 'performance measurement' is ambiguous since it means so many different things to different players in different contexts at different times.

So then, what exactly is 'performance measurement?' It has three meanings, listed here in order of increasing sophistication. First, it can imply a specific *performance measure* (i.e., an actual, definable metric). Second, it can mean the *process of measurement* (i.e., the systems and organizational processes for going about measuring performance). Third, it can indicate an essential aspect of a *comprehensive strategic planning process* (i.e., the management process of setting appropriate performance targets and evaluating their achievement to validate or revise the organization's strategy). The richest consideration of performance measurement must include all three of these definitions.

Given all this, NPD performance measurement in practice is a significant and almost daunting challenge. However, it is a challenge that must be overcome to achieve higher levels of organizational effectiveness. Scholarly research has provided some important insights on NPD performance measurement. However, as a whole, this research stream is still largely nascent. There is so much to learn yet. In that spirit, the aim of this chapter is to provide a framework for considering NPD performance measurement. This chapter aims to clarify the numerous aspects of NPD performance measurement and to guide future academic and industry inquiry into NPD performance measurement philosophy and practice.

2. The roles, customers, and challenges of NPD performance measurement

2.1. Roles

A performance measure plays three simultaneous roles (see Fig. 8.1). One role is that of an *objective* (a goal or a target). This represents the disaggregation or statement of a strategy or a plan. For example, one objective is to 'complete the development project within 180 days.' The second role is as a *metric* (an actual measurement tool or instrument). This represents a defined and agreed upon way to measure the managerial construct of interest. For example, one

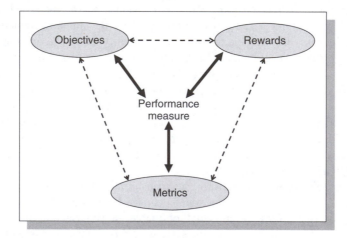

Figure 8.1
The three roles of a performance measure.

metric to capture project duration is 'the number of days elapsed between formal project approval and first customer shipment of completed product.'[1] The third role is as a *reward* mechanism (a means for apportioning benefits and advancement to individuals or groups). For example, a group-based salary bonus could be made contingent on successful timely completion of the project (i.e., within the 180-day target).

The three roles of a performance measure are distinct but highly inter-related. The statement of an objective publicly presents a goal, a direction to work towards, and a constructive challenge to organizational personnel. The reward role is inherently incenting (or punishing) and indicates account-ability of development personnel (individual, group, or unit level). As such, the 'objective' and 'reward' roles serve important motivating and behavioral functions. The 'metric' role reflects the desire and ability to collect infor-mation to monitor development progress and outcomes. This also allows data-supported business planning and execution, rather than seat-of-the-pants, ad hoc decision-making. Importantly, the metrics role makes individual and organizational learning and improvement possible, and supports fair awarding of rewards.

The organization that does not recognize the three roles of a performance measure will also neglect the essential inter-relationships among the three roles. For example, consider how rewards interact with objectives and metrics. Rewards can be given more fairly when objectives are clear and metrics are in place to assess achievement of those objectives. However, if rewards are given separate of or in competition with the stated objectives, then the orga-nization is not truly working towards achieving those objectives. In addition, if metrics are not in place, or are deemed irrelevant or unreliable, then again the motivating effect of rewards is lost. An organization that does not rec-ognize the linkages is likely to have disconnected or incongruent objectives, metrics, and rewards where each is developed and stated in isolation. This is dysfunctional – its causes organizational actions that are at cross-purposes. The organization does not ultimately state, motivate, or measure the desired targets and actions.

Each of the three roles has a second face as well. Regarding objectives, have we selected the right objective? Have we put in place the most appropriate goals? This reflects the quality of the strategic planning process. Regarding metrics, are we measuring the right things and in the appropriate manner? It is often said, 'you get what you measure.' Individuals and organizations can 'game' a measure or work towards high achievement of a measure to the

---

[1] It is further helpful to distinguish between a 'metric' itself and the 'value' of a given metric. Here, the *metric* is the measurement tool defined as 'number of days elapsed.' The *value* of the metric is the actual number of days elapsed for the project at hand (e.g., 120 days). The metric can be applied to many projects, resulting in unique values of the metric for each project.

detriment of other (perhaps unmeasured or unrewarded, but critical) organizational objectives. Regarding rewards, have we put in place the right rewards? Are our rewards congruent with the objectives? In addition, are the rewards perceived as sufficiently material and unbiased to motivate the appropriate behaviors? In sum, the organization benefits most from understanding the existence, purpose, and interactions of the three roles, and from putting in place the appropriate manifestations of each role.

2.2. Customers

There are many customers or users of performance measurement, each having unique needs, and relying on different sets of performance measures to aid their decision-making. For example, at the top of an organization, executives typically rely on a small number of performance measures that are summary in nature, often predictive and necessarily broader and strategic. At lower levels in the organization, managers typically need a greater array of measures on many dimensions of a narrow and tactical nature. As such, performance measurement has many strata, and can take on different forms. The measures might be strategic or tactical, quantitative or qualitative, financial or not, retrospective or current or predictive, and may range from a summary few to a highly granular many, all depending on the level in the organization and specific managerial purpose brought to bear by the performance measurement effort.

A comprehensive, integrated performance measurement system – still a holy grail to many companies – effectively meets the needs of decision-makers at all organizational levels (and even across different organizations). It does this in large part by linking and aligning the sets of metrics employed by one customer with the sets of metrics used by other customers.

2.3. Challenges

Conducting performance measurement poses notable challenges regardless of industry type or application context, be it public or private sector, manufacturing or services. This is evidenced by all the efforts in recent years to develop activity-based costing, balanced scorecards, strategic figures of merit and customer service indexes in diverse industries. Unfortunately, performance measurement is even more difficult and nuanced in NPD than in many other managerial contexts. NPD activity is intrinsically intangible, non-routine, uncertain, and organizationally complex. These special characteristics combine to make NPD performance measurement especially challenging.

First, much NPD work is not viewable. Most NPD work is knowledge work, involving the collection and transformation of information and the development of knowledge and organizational learning. This *intangibility* makes it much harder to capture and measure NPD phenomena and performance (than, e.g., the transformation of materials, which is far more tangible).

Second, repetitive, transactional and routine tasks and processes are easier to measure than the unique and *non-routine* tasks and processes that make up a significant portion of any NPD effort. As such, some aspects of NPD are easier to measure than others (e.g., task times, part costs, and items relating to product features and project budgets). These types of elements are more finite, tangible and definable, and are more likely to be captured in project databases and corporate accounting and ERP systems. New product development by definition involves 'newness,' i.e., something that is different from before. This newness can manifest in non-standardized work and departures from extant routines. Established measures may be irrelevant when the work is novel since they may not address the substance of the new work approach. Again, the information and knowledge aspects – the information collection, creation, codification, transfer, and application, which can be quite unique to each project – are much harder to capture.

Third, NPD activity exhibits *uncertainty* in many dimensions (including markets, technology, the internal organization, and external organizational networks). Uncertainty makes performance measurement more difficult because it is harder to select appropriate measures and to evaluate the actual outcomes achieved. Under conditions of uncertainty, unanticipated, uncontrollable, and even unmeasurable factors may exert significant influence on the outcomes achieved.

Fourth, NPD work is rarely localized. It is commonly recognized that NPD tasks and projects are cross-functional and multi-level, involving disparate disciplines as well as numerous worker, supervisory, management, and executive levels within the organization. In addition, today's NPD efforts are often significantly cross-organizational as well, spanning highly differentiated suppliers, co-developers, distributors and customers. This *organizational complexity* adds further difficulty to NPD performance measurement because of misaligned objectives, differing metrics and incongruent information and reward systems amongst the functions, levels, and organizations.

3. Framing NPD metrics: Purpose, object, form, and linkage

This section aims to state and organize characteristics of NPD metrics. There is much confusion (both in practice and in the scholarly literature) over the many characteristics of metrics. Below we explain that a given metric is characterized by its: (1) managerial purpose (i.e., what managerial question does the measure help answer?); (2) its object (i.e, the 'thing' that is measured, also called the unit of observation or unit of analysis); (3) its forms (i.e., how it measures, such as quantitative versus qualitative, historical versus predictive); and (4) its linkages (i.e., what other measures it is connected to, informs or influences). The aim of this section, by stating and organizing these characteristics and their sub-dimensions, is to provide a formative framework for considering types of metrics and a firmer basis for discussion, comparison and criticism of metrics.

3.1. A metric's managerial purpose

An organization utilizes a performance measure to gain insights and answer important managerial and technical questions. These questions motivate why a metric is required, and so state the managerial *purpose* of the metric. Different questions necessarily require focus on different NPD aspects and phenomena. Typical questions or purposes include:

- To provide decision-support, to aid in NPD planning, goal-setting, and execution
- To assess or review performance of a task or project that is in-progress or has been completed
- To compare and contrast across tasks, projects, and organizations
- To track and assess the direction or achievement of strategic and tactical objectives
- To allocate or reallocate resources
- To determine valuation, net benefits, and financial returns
- To design incentives and parcel rewards
- To aid in individual and organizational learning.

3.2. The metric's object of interest

Now we identify the different NPD phenomena that can be measured. The phenomenon that is measured is the metric's *object* of interest. This is also known as the 'unit of observation' or the 'unit of analysis.' A rampant flaw in NPD practice and research is the use of the wrong unit of observation. Clearly, performance measures must be designed to measure the object that they are intended to measure, or else we have irrelevant and misleading information. A similar problem is the negligent commingling of objects. This leads to comparison of 'apples and oranges' rather than 'apples and apples.' Projects should be compared to projects and portfolios to portfolios, not projects to portfolios. Without careful definition of the object of interest, we do not really know what we are measuring, and cannot reliably interpret the measurement results, all leading to inadvertent managerial prescription.

What are the relevant units of observation? Here, we do not try to be exhaustive in delineating all possible units of observation in NPD. Rather, we aim to identify two key dimensional spectra and identify salient points along these spectra.

The unit of observation is defined along two dimensions. The first and primary dimension of the object of interest is its *organizational depth*. This is a vertical perspective, and is analogous to organizational levels or strata. The elements on this dimension, from lowest to highest, are:

- Individual,
- Task,
- Function (discipline),
- Project,
- Portfolio,
- Pipeline, and
- Strategic business unit (SBU).

The second dimension is the *organizational breadth* of the unit of observation. This is a horizontal perspective. At its narrowest, the breadth is limited to a unitary organization. This broadens to the dyad, where two distinct organizations (e.g., the developer and one of its suppliers) work together on the development effort. This broadens further to triads (e.g., three development organizations, each independently owned and operated, and each having unique development competencies, working together in a co-development effort). At its broadest, we have the network organization, which is a complex set of distributed organizations with differing linkages among particular organizations in that set. This represents the highest degree of inter-organizational complexity.

3.3. Forms of metrics

Metrics take on different *forms*. Below we list some key forms of metrics:

1. Quantitative versus qualitative metrics. Quantitative metrics are stated in strict numerical terms, and are often described and perceived as more 'objective,' while qualitative metrics are stated verbally, and are often described and perceived as 'subjective.'
2. Processing versus outputs metrics. Output metrics assess actual outcomes of a completed work effort, while processing metrics (this includes 'Inputs') characterize aspects of a work effort that is underway. Processing metrics can be intermediate outcomes or lower-level outcomes relative to a stated output metric. Examples of processing metrics include: number of creative ideas entered into Phase 0; number of projects underway; percentage of engineering staff dedicated to a given NPD project; and number of prototype designs waiting in queue at the prototype lab.

In general, output measures are more tangible and easily defined, and organizations seem to emphasize output metrics over process metrics. However, as we noted in Section 2, one of NPD's performance measurement challenges is uncertainty. In cases of high uncertainty, there is less of a direct or specified relationship between inputs and outputs, and as such excessive focus on outputs alone is not managerially instructive. However, management can influence the process, and so should capture process metrics.

3. Historical versus current versus predictive metrics. A predictive measure uses trend projections or formulae to forecast future states and outcomes ('looking out the front window of the car, viewing what is coming'). Historical metrics have a non-trivial lag between the occurrence of the phenomena in question and the reporting of results ('looking at the rearview mirror, seeing what has already passed by'). A current metric is one where the lag is trivial, and so the information presented is practically instantaneous ('the speedometer on my car'). A general characteristic and criticism of many NPD performance measures is that they are lagged. They provide a time-delayed, retrospective look on performance, rather than an instantaneous evaluation or notable predictive insight.

The following metrics types elaborate on and combine characteristics described above:

4. Financial (monetary-based) versus Non-Financial metrics.
5. Planning versus Execution metrics. Planning metrics tend to be less routine, more difficult to measure, and broader than Execution metrics, which are typically more routine, easier to measure, and more focused.
6. Tactical (short-term oriented) versus Strategic (longer time orientation). Tactical metrics tend to be more focused, quantitative and numerous in number, while strategic metrics are broader, can be quantitative or qualitative, and tend to be few in number.

3.4. Linking and aligning metrics

Metrics can be *linked* and aligned to other metrics. The linkages are an important characteristic of a given metric. A simple example of such linkages involves 'time to market.' Executives are often concerned with reducing time to market to achieve greater competitive success. Project-level managers share that concern, but are more operational in that they must manage NPD projects in a day-to-day manner to achieve lead time reductions. Moreover, engineering section managers, who report to project managers in a dotted-line fashion, also share the concerns but only have control over work directly assigned to their sub-unit (see Table 8.1).

Table 8.1
Linked metrics

Organizational Level	Representative Measure(s) of Interest
SBU Level (e.g., CEO)	• Reduce time to market
Project Level (e.g., project manager)	• Project duration (time from formal project approval to first customer shipment) • Project lateness (actual first customer shipment date versus target date)
Task or Function Level (e.g., engineering section manager)	• Slippage on achieving target date for Gate 2 • Downtime on prototyping equipment • Number of design engineering drawings redrawn

In this example, each metric is linked to metrics at higher and lower levels. Cohesively linked metrics are 'aligned' and are supportive. The network of linkages shows a duality, where objectives and guidelines cascade top-down, while more granular information content (in the form of measures and data) aggregates bottom-up ('rolls-up').

At different organizational levels, the players have access to different information about processes and outcomes, and need different metrics to guide decisions under their purview. At an executive level, information is much more uncertain and evaluation happens with respect to the broad competitive and operating environment of the firm. Yet, for project and engineering managers, performance is measured with respect to more 'objective' measures (e.g., achievement of product specifications, project timing, and cost targets).

A critical contemporary NPD management challenge is in creating systems where metrics are linked and aligned purposefully rather than by accident or not at all. This systematically supports the business strategy, increases management decision-making ability at all levels, aids in construction of meaningful metrics 'dashboards,' and provides greater richness to the organization's ability to learn. In sum, an essential characteristic of a metric is its linkages, or pointers, to other metrics. Still, not all metrics must have links – some metrics are localized but still have notable value in achieving their managerial purpose.

4. The state of NPD performance measurement

Broadly speaking, there is relatively little academic research on the development of NPD performance measurement systems. Selected research does focus on particular metrics in some detail (especially 'time'). Many studies, empirical and analytical, employ diverse NPD performance measures as intermediate and outcome variables. Moreover, there is now a decade of research literature presenting surveys of management practices in NPD performance measurement.

The previous section explained that a given performance measure is characterized by the combination of four aspects: its managerial purpose, object of interest, measurement forms, and linkages with other metrics. The dimensions and elements of these four characteristics make up a formative framework defining the space of conceivable NPD metrics. This framework helps identify the current NPD performance measurement state of knowledge. The framework also exposes the gaps, helping identify the performance measurement questions and issues that remain unanswered and merit both practical and scholarly inquiry.

4.1. Established metrics areas and relevant gaps

Two areas in the framework have received the most attention in the literature at large and are quite well developed. They are:

1. Project-level tactical outcomes, such as project duration, project budget achievement, achievement of product specification targets, product sales volume, and customer satisfaction.
2. SBU-level financial and market outcomes, such as return-on-investment, revenue from new products, revenue growth, overall sales, and market share.

A number of important areas in the framework are far less developed. These include:

1. Objects at the intermediate organizational level: portfolios and pipelines. In contrast, on one end, the objects of individuals, tasks, functions and projects, and at the other end, SBUs, have many well-defined outcomes metrics that are utilized in practice. However, measurement for the intermediate levels, which cut across projects and functions and often have shared responsibility across managers, is understudied (with small exceptions) and merits more research attention.
2. Linkages between metrics: This is a relatively undeveloped area *within firms* – linking and aligning metrics across the different organizational levels. Such linkages help in strategy deployment and enhanced decision-making. An even less developed but especially pressing area is that of linking and aligning metrics *across firms*. This is necessary for effective collaborative innovation.

3. Development of metrics sets: Realizing the non-monolithic nature of measures, organizations need to devise appropriate arrays of measures that can be considered as a set without undue emphasis on any unitary measure.
4. Predictive measures (versus historical measures). This allows the most proactive guidance of organizations, and could contribute to organizational agility and competitiveness. Predictive measures may rely on processing measures, established historical patterns and a more sophisticated understanding of cause and effect in NPD phenomena.
5. Processing (versus outputs) metrics: Given the uncertainty inherent in NPD and the preponderance of lagged information, focusing on output measures alone is frustrating and provides an incomplete view of the NPD activities. It provides insufficient managerial guidance regarding what exactly to act on. Instead, intermediate or in-process metrics capturing operating aspects of the NPD activity underway are needed. Temporally these metrics are predecessors to output metrics. This involves a shift from the measurement of (completed) transactions to the measurement of transformation activity in progress.

5. An illustrative example: Project execution success

How should an organization assess the performance of a recently completed project? Let us consider the case of project-level outcomes. This helps illustrate metrics arrays, trade-offs among metrics and the necessarily non-monolithic nature of NPD performance measures (see Table 8.2).

The first row captures 'internal' measures, items that are largely observed or realized within the organization. The second row captures 'external' measures,

Table 8.2
Arraying NPD project outcome measures

	Short-term (Tactical)	**Long-term (Strategic)**
Internal	Time Cost Performance	New technology development New personnel skills
External	Customer satisfaction Sales Return on investment	New market entry and development Company survival

items that relate to the company's interface with the marketplace. The first column captures 'short-term' measures. These tactical measures relate to outcomes realized directly at the conclusion of the project and shortly afterward. The second column captures 'long-term' measures. In general these long-term (strategic) measures reflect capabilities or benefits obtained now that have value beyond the immediate product and its introduction.

The 'internal/short-term' cell captures the three classic tactical project management outcomes (note that 'Performance' may be alternatively referred to as 'features' or 'quality'). These outcomes reflect the quality of the execution of the project management aspects of the NPD effort. The 'external/short-term' cell captures the classic near-term market- and finance-based results attributed to a new product introduction. The 'internal/long-term' cell captures new internal capabilities to the organization, gained during or because of the project, that may have value later. The development project might have involved first-time use of a new technology, and this technological learning could be leveraged for future, more enhanced products. Similarly, new skills might have been developed by personnel within the firm, or new relationships developed with suppliers or distributors, all of which could be leveraged for benefits in the future without incurring significant costs. This cell is all about organizational learning. The 'external/long-term' cell captures company marketplace and environmental elements that are strategic and often qualitative. The new product introduction might open up a new market to the firm, and so might help garner significant sales of future new products.

The array in the table shows that no NPD project is ever truly just a 'success' or a 'failure.' A project that fails in the marketplace (due to low sales) might well help the firm in the long run because new technology was tested as part of that development effort. The multi-dimensionality of project success becomes clear in the table.

Each product development project has different emphases on different cells. This is due to competitive context. Some firms work on a development project quite leisurely and without a constraining focus on cost, because they have little competition in a given market and are simply trying to prove new technology in their new product. Here, the firm's emphasis is on internal/long-term over anything short-term (internal or external).

Moreover, each product development project has different emphases on elements within a cell. Much NPD research looks at the time, cost, and performance outcomes of projects. A subset of this research actually weights the importance of each target or outcome. Again, due to competitive context, some firms rush to bring a product to market, and accept the possibility of higher cost. Here, due to the competitive market window, they aim to hit the window early or in time, and then follow-up with cost-reductions implemented via engineering changes or future new products. Other development projects prioritize technical performance above all else, accepting a trade-off with time and/or cost. What is clear is that a universal view of the measures and their priorities simply does not exist. It would be wrong to assume that one measure alone would be sufficient and that all measures in the array should have equal weighting.

In a similar vein, a purely functional perspective on NPD project performance leads to limited focus. For example, a traditional marketer might look only at metrics in the short-term external cell. A purely operational view leads to sole consideration of the traditional generic project management outcomes of time, cost, and performance (here the tactical, internal outcomes). A strategist who is today looking five years ahead might only consider the strategic measures capturing leveragable investments and growth opportunities in the long-term. She might completely ignore the short-term measures. Finally, a corporate finance person, if unschooled in marketing and operational issues, might only look at short- and long-term financial outcomes. In all, this approach defines functional myopia, and clearly does not provide a complete picture of all the relevant elements of project execution success.

Finally, we note that each metric is a double-edged sword. For example, to reduce NPD time to market, an organization might excessively cut product scope or maximize reuse of part designs from previous products, resulting in a less innovative, 'me-too' product that lacks marketplace differentiation and captures limited customer attention, satisfaction and sales. Here, the unitary focus on 'time' means sales comes at a trade-off to timeliness. There is no way around this! Any conceivable metric has this double-edged sword quality.

Hence, organizations benefit from use of a balanced scorecard or dashboard approach that contains an array of relevant metrics and reduces excessive focus on one metric. In this example, such an array would consider product performance (features) and potential sales in addition to time targets. An even more complete array would consider all elements of the four cells in the project outcomes table.

6. Conclusions: Emerging issues in NPD performance measurement

NPD performance measurement is an exciting topic for further exploration. Practitioners now realize that coherent performance measurement is central to informed management, and researchers are starting to recognize the criticality of effective performance measurement systems to overall product development effectiveness. Research on NPD performance measurement systems is in its infancy compared to research on many other aspects of product development. This is at least in part due to the difficulty of studying NPD performance measurement systems.

To aid practice, five metrics areas (identified in Section 4) merit further study: development of metrics for intermediate organizational levels (such as portfolios and pipelines); establishing effective linkages between metrics; developing metrics sets or arrays (in contrast to a monolithic performance measure); developing more sophisticated predictive measures; and further development of measures capturing NPD activity-in-process rather than at its conclusion. In addition, there are three emerging concerns in practice that also call for future research.

First, companies these days are engaging in more collaborative innovation than ever. This comes in the forms of co-development, outsourcing, joint ventures, alliances, and open innovation networks. Distributed and collaborative innovation call on the organization to put in place new and different skills in technology scouting, partner selection, contract development, protecting intellectual property, relationship management and coordination of schedules and plans across organizations and cultures. Accordingly, firms need to devise, test, and implement *co-development metrics*. A greater understanding of goal congruence and metrics alignment across organizations would be helpful. Finally, working towards a standardized set of metrics for co-development instances reduces the transaction costs of collaborative innovation.

Second, determining the *universality of measures* would be helpful. This is in contrast to measures that are contingent and useful to limited instances. The aim is to identify when a metric employed in one place has the same interpretation when employed in another place. This is the challenge of 'apples to apples' comparison across organizational functions and units. Organizations would benefit from determining when and where a given metric can be successfully applied in different functions, divisions, or even companies in a network. Identifying potential universality of metrics aids in the cascading-down of objectives, rolling-up of data, aggregation of data, and comparing across organizational units in a meaningful way. Not all metrics need be universal. It needs to be determined which ones can be universal, and which ones must be localized, customized, or contingent on a specific NPD phenomenon or location to extract the best managerial guidance.

Third, performance measures and measurement systems do not just happen. The development and refinement of metrics, the design of linked metrics, the collection and analysis of data, and the monitoring of external partners, all call for organizational resources dedicated to the management of *performance measurement and metrics programs*. This may involve a trained, centralized staff or distributed resources utilizing standardized protocols. It certainly involves information systems tools and can be part of an ERP system. This also aids in knowledge management and organizational learning. The ability to effectively manage a performance measurement program is a distinctive organizational competence. It is appropriate to view such a program or system as a critical dynamic capability of the organization. Future research should address the development and value of a dedicated performance measurement program office or system.

Given its practical nature, performance measurement can easily be seen as an atheoretical topic. However, it is not. Several promising theoretical avenues for future research exist. *Organizational Learning* theory can be applied to investigate the linkage and alignment of metrics; selection and design of metrics; knowledge management systems; continuous improvement of metrics; and the evolution and dynamism of performance measurement programs. *Principal–Agent* theory can be applied to evaluate cross-functional, cross-organizational, and collaborative innovation contracting, coordination, operationalized metrics, and reward mechanisms. In addition, the theories of *Lean Operations* may be applied to develop new process-oriented metrics for NPD.

NPD performance measurement should be seen as a dynamic capability in organizations. There will never be an ideal set of metrics or a perfect performance measurement system. Some important NPD aspects may even prove unmeasurable. Nonetheless, organizations can strive towards a meaningful and informative metrics program, one that evolves and innovates along with the organization. Performance measurement systems and metrics are living entities changing and adapting as the organization's environment, strategies and NPD actions evolve. As such, the organization need not aim to create the 'perfect' metrics program, because even if it could, it would not remain perfect for long in today's dynamic, competitive environments.

For further reading

Recent overviews of organizational learning theories

Argote, L., B. McEvily and R. Reagans (2003). "Managing Knowledge in Organizations An Integrative Framework and Review of Emerging Themes," *Management Science*, 49(4): 571–582.

Easterby-Smith, M. and M. A. Lyles (2003). "Introduction: Watersheds of Organizational Learning and Knowledge Management," Chapter 1 in *The Blackwell Handbook of Organizational Learning and Knowledge Management*, Oxford UK: Blackwell Publishing.

A fine review of research on agency theory (principal and agent interactions)

Gibbons, R. (2005). "Incentives Between Firms (and Within)," *Management Science*, 51(1): 2–17.

Excellent work on lean operations

Liker, J. (2004). *The Toyota Way*, New York: McGraw-Hill.

Shah, R. and P. T. Ward (2003). "Lean Manufacturing: Context, Practice Bundles, and Performance," *Journal of Operations Management*, 21(2): 129–149.

Other fine work on metrics and performance measurement systems

Adams, M. and D. Boike (2004). "PDMA Foundation's Comparative Performance Assessment Study," *Visions Magazine*, July.

Bayus, B. (1997). "Speed to Market and New Product Performance Trade-Offs," *Journal of Product Innovation Management*, 14(6): 485–497.

Griffin, A. (1997). "PDMA Research on New Product Development Practices," *Journal of Product Innovation Management*, 14: 429–458.

Griffin, A. and A. L. Page (1996). "The PDMA Success Measurement Project: Recommended Measures for Product Development Success and Failure," *Journal of Product Innovation Management*, 13: 478–496.

Hauser, J. R. (1998). "Research, Development and Engineering Metrics," *Management Science*, 44(12): 1670–1689.

Hauser, J., G. J. Tellis and A. Griffin (2006). "Research on Innovation: A Review and Agenda for Marketing Science," *Marketing Science*, 25(6): 687–717.

Kaplan, R. S. and D. P. Norton (1996). *The Balanced Scorecard*, Boston, MA: Harvard Business School Press.

Lehmann, D. R. and D. J. Reibstein (2006). *Marketing Metrics and Financial Performance*, Marketing Science Institute.

Loch, C. H., L. Stein and C. Terwiesch (1996). "Measuring Development Performance in the Electronics Industry," *Journal of Product Innovation Management*, 13:3–20.

Loch, C. H. and U.A. Tapper (2002). "Implementing a Strategy-Driven Performance Measurement System for an Applied Research Group," *Journal of Product Innovation Management*, 19:185–198.

Menor, L. J., M. V. Tatikonda and S. E. Sampson (2002). "New Service Development: Areas for Exploitation and Exploration," *Journal of Operations Management*, 20(2): 135–157.

Meyer, M. H., J. Tertzakian and P. Utterback (1997). "Metrics for Managing Product Development Within a Product Family Context," *Management Science*, 43(1): 88–111.

Montoya-Weiss, M. and R. Calantone (1994). "Determinants of New Product Performance: A Review and Meta-Analysis," *Journal of Product Innovation Management*, 11(5): 397–417.t

Rosenthal, S. R. and M. V. Tatikonda (1993). "Time Management in New Product Development: Case-Study Findings," *IEEE Engineering Management Review*, 1993, 21(3): 13–20.

Swink, M., S. Talluri and T. Pandejpong (2006). "Faster, Better, Cheaper: A Study of NPD Project Efficiency and Performance Tradeoffs," *Journal of Operations Management*, 24(5): 542–562.

Tatikonda, M. V. and M. M. Montoya-Weiss (2001). "Integrating Operations and Marketing Perspectives of Product Innovation: The Influence of Organizational Process Factors and Capabilities on Development Performance," *Management Science*, 47(1): 151–172.

Tatikonda, M. V. and S. R. Rosenthal (2000). "Technology Novelty, Project Complexity and Product Development Project Execution Success: A Deeper Look at Task Uncertainty in Product Innovation," *IEEE Transactions on Engineering Management*, 47(1): 74–87.

Terwiesch, C. and C. H. Loch (1999). "Measuring the Effectiveness of Overlapping Development Activities," *Management Science,* 45(4): 455–465.

9 Modularity and supplier involvement in product development

Young Ro, Sebastian K. Fixson, and Jeffrey K. Liker

1. Introduction

Many industries have long been characterized by large hierarchical organization forms. The aerospace, petroleum, automotive, and telecommunication industries are just a few examples of industries where in the past several decades, the dominant companies were characterized by large vertically integrated firms. These organizations have traditionally been built around stable product architectures, which, in turn, define key functional relationships, information processing capabilities, and communication channels within and among organizations (Brusoni and Prencipe, 1999). Product architecture has been defined as, 'the scheme by which the function of a product is allocated to its constituent components' (Ulrich, 1995). Once a dominant product design is accepted by an industry, the design and the processes by which to create the product are encoded, and thus become implicit within organizations (Henderson and Clark, 1990).

Over the past two decades, many different products have been undergoing changes in their product architecture. The growing popularity of product platforms and modules has caused many products to migrate from an integral product architecture to a more modular architecture. An *integral* product architecture is characterized by parts that perform many functions, are in close proximity or close spatial relationship, and are tightly synchronized (Fine, 1998). A *modular* product architecture is characterized by parts that are interchangeable, individually upgradable, and have standardized interfaces (Fine, 1998).

Over the past two decades, many industries are moving to more loosely interconnected organizational forms such as strategic alliances and outsourcing (Snow et al., 1992; Schilling and Steensma, 2001), coinciding with changes in the product architecture seen within many of the same industries. This change in organization architecture has occurred in the US automotive industry since the 1990s (Fixson et al. 2005). In addition, since then, the industry has been undergoing changes in both product and firm architectures, affecting product development practices and firm relationships.

Accompanying this move towards more loosely interconnected organizational forms is a growing movement towards a less integral, or modular, vehicle architecture. With the introduction of modules to the US auto industry in the late 1990s, product development practices are beginning to change and even the structure of firm relations in the auto industry is no longer static. Since modularization of products calls for integrated organizational setups and integrated systemic knowledge (Brusoni and Prencipe, 1999), there is a movement in the US auto industry towards this integration at the firm level. However, many of the product and organizational design implications of incorporating modules into vehicles still need to be addressed. Not much is known when firms in an industry characterized by products with an integral architecture make the move to produce products with a non-integral, or modular, architecture. What impacts, if any, are there on the way products are made and the way the firms operate? How are these processes and practices affected? What valuable lessons can be gained from observing an industry undergo this change?

The automotive industry is a relevant context in which to study this issue since it is experiencing the transition from integral to modular at both the product and firm levels. By investigating the state of the automotive industry as it moves toward a more modular product and firm architecture, the changes over time can be observed. This chapter explores an ongoing understanding of the implications of increasingly modular (or less integral) product and architectural forms.

2. Background

In today's competitive automobile industry, companies that can rapidly design and produce vehicles with the latest features customers desire have a competitive advantage. Automakers all over the world are trying to gain a lead in product development. They bring different capabilities to the market and use different approaches, but they are all seeking to reduce development lead time and hit the market with the right product at the right time. This is particularly important as customers expect more and more products made to order for them.

Long seen as slow-moving and stable, the automotive industry is becoming a leaner, agile, and more competitive fast-paced industry. For example, advances in information technology such as e-business initiatives and use of the internet have brought greater speed of communication and data exchange to the auto industry. In addition, the growing popularity of lean manufacturing and six sigma programs are resulting in higher quality products, provided at shorter lead times, and produced at lower cost. Since the 1980s (a decade where there was a large emphasis on improving the quality of American-made cars), US automakers have reached a point where the initial quality of its automobiles rivals that of its foreign competitors (Liker, 1997).

Now, companies in the United States and elsewhere are seeking ways to develop products more quickly and efficiently by considering the efficiency and effectiveness of the total value stream. As companies think in value stream terms they are identifying their core competencies and outsourcing everything else, including design and development responsibility for major vehicle subsystems. This means completely recasting their relationships with the supply base (Kamath and Liker, 1994). The best models for supply-chain management, from a performance point of view, still remain those based on the Japanese *keiretsu* relationships, characterized by the close ties exhibited between the automaker – Original Equipment Manufacturers (OEM) – and its direct suppliers (Dyer, 1996c; Liker et al., 1999). In many studies, Japanese automaker plants continue to outperform US plants from a productivity and quality perspective; two measures of performance that have been used to delineate plant performance (Liker et al., 1999; Krafcik, 1988). In terms of both final product quality and supplier product quality, US plants generally perform worse than their Japanese counterparts, although the performance gap has narrowed in recent years (MacDuffie and Pil, 1999).

2.1. Involving suppliers in product development

Following the quality craze of the 1980s that occurred in the US auto industry, attention quickly turned upstream to product development. It took until the early 1990s before product development and supplier relationship issues among Japanese automakers began to be studied (Clark and Fujimoto, 1991; Kamath and Liker, 1994; Dyer, 1994). Clark and Fujimoto, in their book, *Product Development Performance: Strategy, Organization, and Management in the World Auto Industry*, stated that one of the key features of Japanese supplier management was the substantial involvement of suppliers in product development. That the early involvement of suppliers in product development was instrumental in reducing lead time and avoiding production problems downstream that could prove costly (Clark and Fujimoto, 1989). They also reported 'the average Japanese firm had almost double the development productivity, and could develop a comparable product a year faster than the average US firm.'

If OEMs need to rely more and more on the technical capabilities of their suppliers, then it would only seem reasonable that the OEMs would try and court suppliers with the best product development and design skills for their business. However, having the best suppliers may help, but is not enough to ensure the best overall performance. Moreover, in an industry such as the automotive industry, where only a few OEMs are courting many of the same top-tier suppliers, much of the same resources will be available to more than one OEM. Therefore, how these supply base resources are managed in an OEM/Supplier relationship can make the difference between high- and low-performance (Liker et al., 1999). As the General Manager of Engineering Design at one of the automakers voiced in answer to what it must be like for suppliers to work with different OEMs described the differences across divisions supporting different customers, 'Everything in our product development process – people, systems, integration, that make (us who we are) are different (across customers). The differences are subtle but they add up to huge differences overall. Suppliers are square pegs trying to fit into different holes. It takes a while to figure out how to fit in and get the edges off.'

As recently as the early 1990s, there were suggestions of movement by US auto companies toward the Japanese supplier management model (Helper, 1991; Cusumano and Takeishi, 1991), but information on how far the US has come in this regard has been quite sketchy (Liker et al., 1996). Instead, the new emerging models in the US of supplier management in product development are taking such concepts as modularity and systems integration (explained later in the paper) to a new level, and adding onto the fundamental Japanese concept. At the same time, some of the foundations for partnership and trust so prominent in the Japanese model were never developed and have deteriorated over time.

2.2. History of supplier management in the US and Japan

The auto industry is perhaps leading the way in the US in attempting to apply Japanese design and manufacturing methods (Liker et al., 1996; Liker et al., 1999). The role of suppliers in product development is no exception. The Japanese approach to supplier management has been frequently studied and benchmarked in the past (Dyer, 1994; Kamath and Liker, 1994; Dyer, 1996c; Clark and Fujimoto, 1989; Cusumano and Takeishi, 1991; Sobek et al., 1998). It forms the basis for supplier management policies in automotive companies throughout the world. Thus, it is important to accurately understand the Japanese approach to supplier management, and to know what aspects US companies are attempting to emulate and how these are being modified to fit the US context.

The picture that emerges from the past literature about supplier management models is one of cooperative partnerships in product development in Japan, predominately among assemblers and first-tier suppliers, and adversarial relationships in the United States, with suppliers brought on board after most product development is complete (Clark and Fujimoto, 1989). However, with the new supplier management trends occurring in the auto industry in the 1980s and 1990s, a far more complex picture is emerging.

During the middle of the twentieth century, Edward Deming, the famous quality expert came to Japan and helped fuel a quality revolution that brought the Japanese economy to world prominence. He introduced to Japanese managers the concepts of statistical quality control and it was accepted in Japan with much enthusiasm. During the 1950s, Japanese automakers were vertically integrated, much like their US counterparts (Smitka, 1991; Nishiguchi, 1994). However, due to a more organized labor force, lack of capital, and a lack of financing for new capacity, the Japanese automakers began to adopt a subcontracting strategy. By the mid-1960s, 11 Japanese firms had each developed a network of 200–300 direct close suppliers. Over time, they institutionalized a supply management practice whereby relationships were governed neither by market nor by hierarchy but by trust (Bensaou and Anderson, 1999), strongly bolstered by equity holdings and the tremendous purchasing power of automakers. A practice of dual sourcing for a type of component, while awarding business for a particular vehicle, served to create intense competition within the keiretsu. Eventually, the Japanese automakers got to the point where they gave their suppliers responsibility for the quality of the parts and components that were being produced. In the late 1980s, American automakers took note of the Japanese success and decided they needed to better utilize the design capabilities of the US supply base.

2.3. Buyer–supplier relations in the US auto industry

When the US automakers studied the supplier management practices of their Japanese counterparts, they began to mimic some of the practices utilized by the Japanese. In the 1990s, some OEMs developed concepts such as 'full-system suppliers' (e.g., Ford Motor Company), and even certification methods to formalize the capabilities required of these top-tier suppliers. There was much talk among executives within the auto industry of having top-tier suppliers as long-term partners.

In 1992, Jose Lopez was named GM's vice-president of worldwide purchasing and quickly gained a reputation as a relentless cost-cutter. Lopez gained a reputation for streamlining GM's purchasing operations and made an immediate impact by forcing GM suppliers to dramatically cut prices, a major component in GM's financial turnaround. Suppliers often complained of his aggressive tactics, saying he tore up contracts and shared confidential material with their competitors (The Detroit News, 5/23/00). Under Lopez, GM would identify cost saving opportunities in the supplier plants and reduce payment to the suppliers accordingly, thus forcing suppliers to make cost reductions to retain GM business. Lopez clamped down on inefficiency at GM by rapidly reorganizing GM's massive parts purchasing activities and aggressively promoting the use of Purchased Input Concept Optimization with Suppliers (PICOS) workshops by its suppliers. The PICOS sessions were one-shot, several day workshops in which cost reductions were identified. Suppliers were then tasked with continuing the process, to lower costs throughout GM's supply chain. Lopez used PICOS workshops to pressure suppliers to lower prices across the board. The workshops were vehicles for cost-cutting activities resulting in reductions in investment costs, floor space, direct labor, and setup time. In short, Lopez promoted PICOS to make GM's suppliers 'leaner,' thus lowering GM's costs. Very quickly, this cost-cutting/cost-reduction emphasis at GM became nicknamed the 'Lopez model,' and soon, other OEMs in the industry (outside Japan) wanted the same low prices.

In contrast to the Lopez model, another member of the Big 3, the Chrysler Corporation, under the leadership of Thomas Stallkamp, began to emerge strongly with the partnership model in dealing with their suppliers. Chrysler started the 'Extended Enterprise' that emphasized long-term contractual relationships with their top-tier suppliers. Chrysler also had the SCORE (Supplier Cost Reduction Effort) program, which was a cost reduction program to help Chrysler's top suppliers achieve cost savings as well as help Chrysler maintain a supply base of closely knit full-service suppliers (Dyer, 1996b). The basic premise of the program was for Chrysler and its lead suppliers to reduce system-wide costs without negatively affecting supplier profits. There was a variety of ways to achieve SCORE credits, including cost avoidance. It also involved Chrysler splitting cost savings with its suppliers, which created an incentive for suppliers to strive to make their processes more efficient. Over a seven-year period, the SCORE program was responsible for over $1 billion in savings and helped build partnership business relations with several suppliers (Corbett and Associates, 2002). In the words of then President, Thomas Stallkamp, the SCORE program was successful because it was a 'communications program, not just a cost-cutting program.' By improving communications, Chrysler and its suppliers had developed a system to learn to help each other.

Due to the success of the Extended Enterprise and the SCORE program at cost reduction plus positive relationships, other OEMs like Ford Motor Company started to take steps in adopting a more partnership relationship style with their top suppliers. Moreover, among the Big 3, Chrsyler had created a name for itself as having the most partner-like approach in dealing with their suppliers. As Chrysler grew with the partnership model of supplier management, there was talk and publicity in the industry regarding the mutual benefits of partnership OEM–Supplier relationships (Sheridan, 1990). In fact, in the early 1990s, there was a general trend away from short-term contracting with numerous suppliers and so-called arm's length relationships (Sako, 1992) and a move towards greater commitment with sole-sourcing and with long-term contracts in the context of partnerships and alliances with a much more compact supply base (Helper and Sako, 1995). Yet, evidence of adversarial hardball negotiation tactics continued through their period of 'partnership.'

The coexistence of the adversarial and partnership relationship styles coinciding with the merging of the Traditional US and Japanese keiretsu supplier management models in an American context sets the backdrop for the issues discussed in this chapter.

2.4. The modularity movement

Modularity is a trend occurring in many industries, including the computer, book publishing, and furniture industries, to name a few (Baldwin and Clark, 1997; Schilling, 2000). It is a growing characteristic of the products of other industrial sectors such as the aeronautical and chemical industries as well (Brusoni and Prencipe, 1999). Modularity is a general concept that describes the 'degree to which a system's components can be separated and recombined, and it refers both to the tightness of the coupling between components' and the 'degree to which ... the system architecture enables or prohibits the mixing and matching of components' (Schilling, 2000).

However, modularity is not limited just to products. Even organizations can be characterized by various degrees of modular form. Some researchers have studied the separation of many large, vertically integrated, hierarchical organizations into more modular, loosely coupled production arrangements, such as contract manufacturing, alternative work arrangements, and strategic alliances (Schilling, 2000; Schilling and Steensma, 2001). In many cases, rapidly changing environments will drive firms to use more modular organizational forms (Nadler and Tushman, 1999; Baldwin and Clark, 1997; Snow et al., 1992).

The American auto industry began to move towards the idea of modularity in the mid-1990s, its proponents claiming modularity offered strategic benefits such as cost and lead time reductions and the ability to customize product lines in mass quantities. These benefits were realized in the computer industry in the 1980s, which made modularity seem that much more attractive to the American auto companies. 'Modularity, systems integration, how much responsibility to outsource, and how to manage it, is THE question in the industry,' is a statement coming from a Senior Systems Manager at a leading Tier 1 automotive supplier. This was his declaration during an interview regarding the emerging impact of modularity upon the automotive industry.

Late in the 1990s through the turn of beginning of the twenty-first century, the US automotive industry – OEMs and suppliers – has been characterized by corporate mergers, acquisitions, takeovers, management reshuffling, and general upheaval. The products themselves have seen an increase in the number of niche vehicles with innovative and trendy designs. Companies that position themselves to be leaders in the area of product development, and rapidly design and produce these vehicles with the latest amenities that an increasingly particular customer base demands, have a distinct competitive advantage. In an industry as competitive as the automotive industry, where cost reductions and slim profit margins are the way of life, a strategic advantage in product development and design is the key to survival.

Cost reduction is a major focus in manufacturing and supplied parts are one of the easiest targets. Suppliers are pressured with 'target prices' set by OEMs that go down each year and are expected to make a profit through relentless cost reduction. At the same time, OEMs want a broader range of services such as building entire modules and delivering them in sequence right to the assembly line with near perfect quality. While pushing manufacturing costs onto suppliers by outsourcing the building of modules is an easy cost reduction target, the real benefits of modularity will come from the integration of product development, process design, and supply chain coordination (Fine, 1998).

It seems as if most of the global auto companies have at least seriously experimented with modularity, albeit to various extents. The popular press has reported on several examples of modularity being used extensively by various vehicle makers and automotive suppliers on various programs. For example, one automotive supplier that has realized great gains in the use of modularity is the Dana Corporation. In the very late 1990s, Dana reorganized itself to take advantage of the growing interest in modular systems. The move to system modularization caused the corporation to adopt a growing responsibility for supply chain management, both with its customers and its own supply base. With these new responsibilities, Dana was able to produce the 'rolling chassis' module, manufactured in Brazil, seen in the 1999 Dodge Dakota. The chassis module is complete enough to be rolled right into the assembly plant, where the rest of the vehicle can then be assembled and put into place. Also reported in the popular press are advertisements promoting the capabilities of various companies to deliver on modular parts and production as a competitive strategy, promising product solutions that 'enhance your vehicle brand and support your assembly requirements' (*The Automotive News*, 2001). Some of the promises offered by module suppliers to OEM customers include 'cost reductions, weight reductions, warranty reductions, feature enhancement, improved quality, integrated design, and increased throughput' (*The Automotive news, 2001*).

3. Investigation

3.1. Problem clarification

Regarding OEM/supplier relationships among automotive companies in the late 1990s, there seemed to be a change in the nature of firm relations in the US auto industry from what was seen in the United States in the early 1990s. The acquisition of Chrysler by Daimler-Benz, the spin-offs of the parts divisions for GM and Ford, and mergers and acquisitions among suppliers, such as the purchase of Lucas-Varity by TRW, were just a few examples of these changes. As a result, larger independent suppliers began emerging in the supply base. Also in the late 1990s, changes began to take place in how automobiles were being designed and manufactured. Talk of modules began to spread among the US auto companies and they began to study how the concept of modules could be incorporated into the automotive industry. Automakers and suppliers were interested in the benefits modularity could provide in their design and assembly processes.

Researchers began to study product development and supplier relationship issues among Japanese automakers in the 1980s (Clark and Fujimoto, 1991; Kamath and Liker, 1994; Dyer, 1994). It was at this point that there were suggestions of movement by US auto companies toward the Japanese supplier management model (Helper, 1991; Cusumano and Takeishi, 1991). However, since then, there has been 'very little data' on how far the US auto industry has come regarding supplier involvement in product development (Liker et al., 1996). Traditionally, the picture that exists in the past literature is one of cooperative partnerships in product development in Japan, predominately among assemblers and first-tier suppliers, and adversarial relationships in the United States, with suppliers brought on board after most product development is complete (Clark and Fujimoto, 1989).

However, with the supplier management trends occurring in the auto industry in the 1990s, a far more complex picture than what was originally observed in the literature is emerging. Companies in the United States and elsewhere are seeking ways to develop products more quickly and efficiently by considering the efficiency and effectiveness of the total value stream. As companies think in value stream terms they are identifying their core competencies and outsourcing everything else, including design and development responsibility for major vehicle subsystems. This means completely recasting their relationships with the supply base (Kamath and Liker, 1994). Indicators of mergers and acquisitions in the automotive supply base as well as among automakers in the late 1990s seem to indicate that the nature of OEM/supplier relationships in the US is changing. And with the introduction of modules into the vehicle design and assembly process, the newly emerging issue of modularity is bringing about changes in US automotive product development that are not evident in the Japanese context. As a result, the primary impetus for this chapter is to discuss *how changes in product architecture affect buyer–supplier relationships in product development,* using US auto as an illustrative context.

3.2. 'Evolving models of supplier involvement in design: The deterioration of the Japanese model in US auto'

The Japanese approach to supplier management and product development has been frequently studied and benchmarked in the past (Dyer, 1994; Kamath and Liker, 1994; Dyer, 1996c; Clark and Fujimoto, 1989; Cusumano and

Takeishi, 1991; Sako and Helper, 1998; Sobek et al., 1998). It forms the basis for supplier management and product development policies in automotive companies throughout the world today. Thus, it is important to accurately understand the Japanese approach to supplier management, and to know what aspects US companies are attempting to emulate and how these are being modified to fit the US context. The best models for supply chain management, from a performance point of view, remain those based on the Japanese *keiretsu* relationships, characterized by the close ties exhibited between the OEM and its direct suppliers (Dyer, 1996c; Liker et al., 1999). With US OEMs attempting to learn from the Japanese model in auto, a look at how the process is unfolding is warranted.

The purpose of this section is to describe the evolving models for supplier involvement in design in US auto as US companies are adapting the Japanese model and to provide multiple frameworks that explain the current OEM/Supplier relationship trends seen in the US auto industry today. The evolution of supplier involvement in design in the United States involves more than technology transfer encompassing fundamental changes in design approaches, commercial relationships, and even institutional arrangements. Such fundamental relationship and institutional changes cannot merely be picked up from Japan and set down in the United States. The transfer of practices, especially social processes, is much more an adaptation of automakers' interpretation of the Japanese model and often, because of re-contextualization of these processes in a new environment (Brannen and Wilson III, 1996), the result is very different from the starting point in Japan (Liker et al., 1999). To make sense of all this, the research method used included semi-structured, qualitative interviews with a broad range of managers and directors in automakers and suppliers. This allowed for an in-depth picture of the dynamics of buyer–supplier relationships, albeit at a slice of time (1998–2001) within this transformation process.

4. Methods summary

Semi-structured interviews were conducted at various OEMs and first-tier suppliers between the years 1998–2001. A pre-set list of questions was used to help guide the topics of discussion in the interviews, but the interviews were left open-ended so that conversation could flow freely and allow for interesting topics that arose to be pursued. The suppliers interviewed in this study included suppliers responsible for subsystems within both the interior and chassis systems. Door panels, seating, brakes, climate control, fuel systems, steering, and exhaust systems were components and sub-systems produced by suppliers involved in our study. Engineers, managers, and directors involved with product development were targeted for their knowledge of various aspects of OEM/supplier relationships during the product development phase. In total,

66 different people in 28 different companies were interviewed. The conceptual models and frameworks generated from this data collection are presented below.

5. Findings and observations

5.1. Definition of terms

Many of the important trends surfacing in the suppliers' role in automotive product development deal with how OEMs and Suppliers address the issue of modules and systems in the vehicle. It is important to delineate the differences between a *component, module,* and *system* in the automotive context. Based on the interviews conducted, the working definition of these terms is summarized in Table 9.1.

For several decades, automobiles were designed and assembled around the use of components, with the components being produced either in-house

Table 9.1
Working definitions of modules and systems

Concept	Description	Popular Examples
Component	An individual physical part that can be attached to, or separated from, a larger composite entity, such as a sub-assembly or even the vehicle itself.	Door handle Steering Wheel
Module	A physical standardized, self-contained assembly of automotive components designed for easy installment into the vehicle as a unit, performing tasks in conjunction with other components and modules to support the major functions of the vehicle.	Door module Cockpit module
System	An entity defined by the function it performs and is part of an organized, coherent, and interacting set of functions constituting the overall functioning of the vehicle as a complex whole. In some cases, it can be determined by the physical architecture of the vehicle.	Electronic system (not determined by physical architecture) Exhaust system (determined by physical architecture)

or outsourced to various suppliers. Many of the systems in an automobile have also been in place for several decades. However, all that began to change in the mid to late 1990s; the concept of modules began taking prominence in the US automotive industry. What used to be accomplished by the interaction of components was starting to be accomplished by the use, and interaction, of modules. Since that time, the dominant architectural paradigm in the design and development of automobiles was to have the systems and functions of the vehicle being performed by an interacting combination of components/sub-assemblies and modules.

5.2. Shifting responsibility

Over the last decade and a half, there has been a shifting of production and design responsibilities from automakers to the Tier 1 suppliers. OEMs began requiring top-tier suppliers to adopt more and more of what Kamath and Liker (1994) call a *mature* role in not only performing the technical work but also taking substantial responsibility for development and, testing components, and even managing other suppliers making components of their subsystems. As one Vice-President of a supplier company stated, 'There has been a significant shift of having the supply base taking leadership roles in benchmarking, marketing vehicle strategy, setting the vehicle package and styling to reach the targeted consumer base.' There was also a growing understanding that so-called 'full service' suppliers were expected to manage their own costs in research and development of new technologies and not to expect reimbursement for these costs except for the price per piece of goods shipped long after the R&D was done.

As of the turn of the twenty-first century, OEMs were mostly purchasing components and subassemblies for their vehicles. The number of suppliers at this level was as many as 300 for any of the Big 3 American auto suppliers. Only about 50–60 suppliers were considered modular or system-level suppliers supplying larger chunks of the car. OEMs have expressed a desire for their suppliers to move towards a greater level of responsibility, including system and vehicle-level testing of their modules and systems. Although a future hope, the diagram in Fig. 9.1 depicts the direction in which many of the OEMs are purposely consolidating their supply bases to create a pool of high-level module and system suppliers. The diagram also conveys the increasing amount of design, production, and testing responsibility the OEMs are expecting the supply base to absorb.

The desired 'full service' supply base that the OEMs are hoping for would involve only a few lead Tier 1 suppliers that would be responsible for large chunks of the car and for systems-level and vehicle-level testing of their products and then in turn manage lower tier suppliers. With much of the production and testing being increasingly spun off to the supply base, the

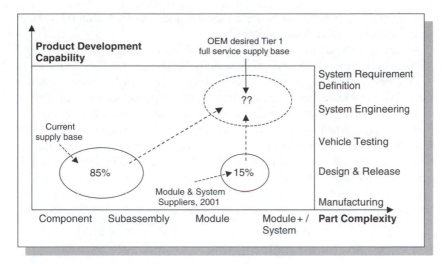

Figure 9.1
Product development capability of supply base.

OEMs will be able to focus more on the design, assembly, and coordination of overall vehicles.

5.3. New trends in automotive product development

Two new points of note concerning buyer–supplier relationships in automotive product development deal with *modularity* and *systems integration*. First seen in successful widespread use in the computer industry, OEMs and suppliers alike have been working to incorporate the concept of modules into the auto industry. This more recent modularity trend in the auto industry aims to design and produce vehicles and their components with standardized units and dimensions to facilitate easier vehicle assembly, design flexibility, and arrangement of use. Since the mid-1990s, there has been an embracing of modularity (at the system, sub-system, and component levels) on both the supplier and OEM sides of the relationship. From an assembly, cost, and logistics standpoint, practitioners in the US auto industry seem to have a favorable opinion of modularity. The idea of systems integration, or the capability of a large Tier 1 supplier to manage and coordinate the design, production, and logistical issues involved in providing large vehicle systems to the OEM, was also prevalent throughout the study. (It is important to mention that the reader should not confuse an automotive *system* with *systems integration*. As explained earlier, an automotive *system* is defined by a performed function in the vehicle. However, the concept of *systems integration* deals with managing the design and assembly activities of large-scale modules and systems within the vehicle across a number of various suppliers.).

A variety of relationship styles, ranging from adversarial to partner-like relationships, currently exist between various OEMs and suppliers. In the early to mid-1990s, there occurred noticeable shifts in relationship styles between these OEMs and suppliers, from adversarial to the partnership model. This is evident in much of the literature that came out during that time concerning buyer–supplier relationships (Dyer and Ouchi, 1993; Helper and Sako, 1995; Kamath and Liker, 1994). However, toward the late 1990s, there appeared to be a trend towards a hybrid between the adversarial and partnership styles, with characteristics of the adversarial relationship style being dominant. This cyclical relational trend occurring between automotive buyers and suppliers in the United States will be analyzed in more depth later in the chapter.

5.4. Supplier integration models

The Traditional US Supplier Model existed for many decades and operates primarily as a functional organization (see Fig. 9.2).

There is a parent department, such as the Chassis department. This parent department is then further divided into more specialized functional departments, such as steering, suspension, and braking. Each of these functions is assigned an OEM Release Engineer who interacts with the steering, suspension, and braking divisions of first-tier suppliers. The OEMs kept considerable control over individual components, in some cases designing the component and sending the design out for bid to suppliers. They also acted as program managers and systems integrators, with departments with titles like 'systems engineering.' In this capacity, the OEM directly coordinates the design and

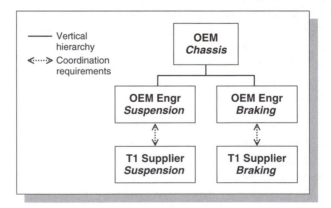

Figure 9.2
Traditional US supplier model.

logistics efforts of their suppliers. As shown in Fig. 9.2, the functions that are deemed to be part of the OEM's vertical hierarchy are designated with solid lines, while the dotted lines symbolize the coordination requirements needed between the OEM and the Tier 1 suppliers.

Unlike the US supplier management model, the Japanese model of supplier development gives substantial responsibility for design to the suppliers. However, in the Japanese model, the organizational relationship between the OEM and its suppliers tends also to be functional, as it is in the US supplier model. Figure 9.3 displays the Japanese model.

Since the OEM generally has equity ownership in the supplier that is given design responsibility, the Japanese supplier model is also termed the *keiretsu* model. As shown in the figure, the dotted lines (as in the case of the Traditional US Supplier Management Model) designate the OEM's vertical hierarchy, whereas the dual dotted lines signify the stronger intimate and inter-locking nature of the keiretsu relationships found in the Japanese model of supplier management.

Two new emerging US supplier models are the *module supplier model* and the *systems integrator model*. Based on anecdotal evidence, it appears that the module supplier model is a transitional form, with the systems integrator model apparently being the desired future evolutionary form of the US supplier integration model.

Although gaining mainstream popularity, the modular notion in the automotive industry was still in its infancy in North America near the turn of the century. OEMs were going through a phase where they are trying to discover the best type of organization to adopt, both within themselves and their

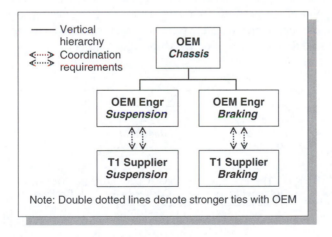

Figure 9.3
Japanese Keiretsu supplier model.

supply base, to maximize the benefits of modularity. The Business Development Director of Modules and Systems of a leading chassis supplier pointed out that, 'At this point, there are still some differences across OEMs. Some try to add modularity over their existing organization, and it does not work well yet. In large part this is due to the fact that all the major OEMs in North America have buyers in the purchasing departments organized by component commodity groups, and modules can cut across those groups (e.g., braking, electrical, and chassis).' The move to modularity is causing corporations to adopt a growing responsibility for supply chain management, developing relationships with both their customers and their own supply bases.

It is this relationship building with other suppliers that causes the evolving US supplier management model to be so different from its predecessors. The organizational interactions that occur when assembling and designing modules are what make the module supplier model different from the traditional US and Japanese keiretsu models. Figure 9.4 is a depiction of the module supplier model.

This module supplier model shows an important difference from the Traditional US supplier model. The presence of a Module Supplier (i.e., in the picture below, the Module Supplier is providing the corner module of a vehicle, which typically consists of the headlight, braking, suspension, and other components) requires coordination between the chassis OEM, and the first-tier suppliers. Other first-tier suppliers provide their parts to the Module Supplier, who may very well be another first-tier supplier. This Module Supplier then assembles a module that is to be sent to the OEM. Door panels and corners of a vehicle are common products that would fall into the module category.

In the module supplier model, we see that the module supplier serves as the primary point of contact with the OEM. Thus, the coordination requirements and flow of communication between the customer OEM and the module supplier is vitally important. The OEM may pass along design specifications

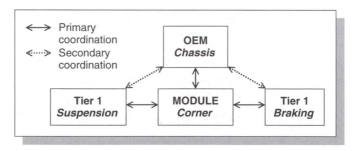

Figure 9.4
Module supplier model.

and requirements across the coordination and communication channel. Gone are the functional chimneys prevalent in the traditional US supplier model where the OEM is required to talk directly with every single major supplier involved in a project through a release engineer. In the module supplier model, it is not necessary for the OEM to have frequent direct contact with the other Tier 1 suppliers, although it may occur from time to time. Instead, the module supplier works closely with the other suppliers and provides the coordination responsibility necessary to communicate with the other Tier 1 suppliers involved in the project.

In many cases, the module may be a significant part of the whole car. Therefore, by the time the OEM approaches the module supplier, they may have already done some styling and packaging studies, and may even have done some preliminary layouts of the module design. There needs to be a lot of information presented up-front to the module supplier by the OEM if modularity is to work.

Practitioners seem to regard modularity as an inevitable trend sweeping the automotive industry. 'None of the OEMs want to be behind on the modularity bandwagon,' asserts one Product Director. Moreover, the Executive Director of Business Development at a leading Tier 1 supplier explained, 'Modularity is basically the way of life now. If you do not have the capability of supplying modules, then you *will* be relegated to a Tier 2 supplier level.'

Since the turn of the century, the term '*systems integration*' has become prevalent in the American automotive industry, particularly in the area of product development. In the past American OEMs viewed themselves as the systems integrator purchasing components and sometimes component designs. In traditional product development, the basic problem in planning coordination is that parts are interdependent and developed by specialized engineering departments. Thus, inter-component coordination within a project involves negotiations among several engineering groups. So a change in one component tends to trigger countermeasures elsewhere, and the chain reaction of mutual adjustment makes coordination across the total vehicle time-consuming (Clark and Fujimoto, 1991). As modularity is evolving even systems integration is being pushed down the top-tier supplier level. According to the words of the Product Director of Modules at a leading braking systems supplier:

'A module in and of itself, is a combination of a lot of components. But we don't want to just assemble a bunch of pieces. We want these things to be value-added to a system. Many of these systems are going to talk to each other soon. The systems will be more interrelated. You need to handle synergy of design, synergy of performance. The module strategy is to develop module capability as a systems integrator. (The systems integrator) takes modules to another level compared to (other) people in the industry.'

The newest type of supplier integration model is that which takes the role of managing systems integration, namely, the Integrator Supplier Model. For all practical purposes, a systems integrator is an Integrator Supplier. Since systems integrators are capable of managing large-scale programs for their OEM customers, the Integrator Supplier Model can also be called the Supplier Program Management Model. This is a recent concept that has emerged in the United States within the last decade, and has been called by such names as Tier 0.5.

It appears the Integrator Supplier Model may be the next evolutionary form of the US Supplier Model. Similar to the Module Supplier Model, it highlights the role of the lead Tier 1 supplier (a.k.a. the systems integrator) as the coordinating entity of much of the design activity occurring in an OEM's supply base. Unlike for individual parts, sub-systems, or modules, a systems integrator is concerned about maintaining design and manufacturing responsibility of a whole system through methods of program management among a number of component suppliers, in some cases competitors.

Due to the reciprocal task interdependence that occurs when several suppliers work together on the design and assembly of large-scale modules, it is necessary for the Integrator Supplier model to address the coordination concerns that arise from such complex responsibility. In this particular model, the OEM creates self-contained tasks and a reduction of environmental complexity, much like in Galbraith's information processing model (Galbraith, 1977) by relinquishing much of the program management responsibility to the systems integrator. The systems integrator then becomes the primary point of contact with the OEM. Since the OEM only has to worry about communicating with a few systems integrators for any given vehicle program, the information processing requirements and communication channels are easier for the OEM to manage and oversee than a broad base of several dozen Tier 1 suppliers. The systems integrator, in turn, acts to reduce its own information processing and communication difficulties by creating stronger communication channels with the suppliers it has to work with through the use of more intimate lateral organizational relations such as direct contact and cooperative teams with the other suppliers involved in the project. The systems integrator thus manages the interdependence of all these tasks and communicates directly with the OEM throughout the development project. The Integrator Supplier Model gives great authority to the System Integrator while allowing OEMs to maintain direct control over the System Integrator. This is depicted in Fig. 9.5.

The suppliers that are leading the systems efforts are often expected to house other suppliers in their R&D facilities, even competitors in some cases depending on the size of the module or sub-system being designed, and on whether the suppliers' and OEM's facilities are within close proximity

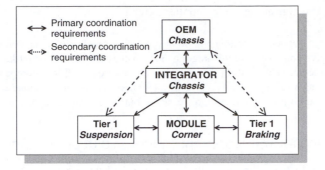

Figure 9.5
Integrator supplier model.

geographically. From the engineering design side of systems integration, there is a need for common facilities, common equipment, and tools. Moreover, in some cases, the systems integrator supplier can rent out the computers and the space. With simpler systems and close distances, it may not be necessary to co-locate. 'For component suppliers, these firms may be located anywhere in the world. For less complex parts, you can communicate with one another electronically. They may meet in person weekly if the part is more complex in nature, and then go back home to do the design. However, the core team for the module supplier needs to be on-site daily with the customer.' The key, however, seems to be the complexity of the technical interface between the commodity and the vehicle. The more that the component defines the character of the vehicle, as opposed to just being a commodity, the more communication and interaction between engineers in suppliers and OEMs is necessary.

Security and confidentiality issues also arise among suppliers when they act as system integrators, particularly when housing competitors. As an engineering Director of a systems supplier described, 'you build fire walls to protect core technologies but for the betterment of the (OEM) customer, (all the suppliers) work together. For non-competing sub-suppliers, it is not an issue.'

Why would any supplier want to be a systems integrator, since they do not get specially paid for this role? One of the Directors at a Tier 1 interior systems supplier answered the question this way.

'Being a systems integrator is more responsibility, but in the end it's a better position to be in. It's not a profit motive, but you get notoriety and a reputation. It does open up doors for you. (We) would opt to be the systems integrator if given a choice because we then call the shots and run the show.'

Another Director at the same supplier agreed.

'(Being a systems integrator) will not necessarily provide additional content, but it will give you control of the program. Your name may become better known for that particular vehicle. It raises our customers' awareness of (our company). We do not make money for being system integrators... We make money making parts. You do not do it to get more content, but to raise awareness.'

5.5. Supplier management model evolution timeline

The appearance of the four different supplier management models in the United States mentioned in this report are roughly plotted on a time line in Fig. 9.6.

For several decades in the middle of the twentieth century, the Traditional Supplier management model was the dominant paradigm in the auto industry. Then in the 1980s, with the Japanese transplants in the United States, the Americans were introduced to the Japanese keiretsu model, which had formed in Japan over several decades. Moreover, extreme interest turned towards the Japanese method of supplier management since it was credited as being a more successful model. Then in the mid-1990s, the auto industry began to see the emerging of Module Suppliers responsible for more and more real estate in the automobile as OEMs began outsourcing more and more vehicle content to the supply base. Then in the late 1990s and into the twenty-first century, the Integrator Supplier emerged among the lead Tier 1 suppliers and began forming a 'new' level of supplier, the Program Manager or System Integrator Supplier.

5.6. Buyer–supplier relationship styles: Exit and voice

Some US and European companies, adopting the Japanese tier structure, seemed to believe they should treat all their suppliers as partners. However,

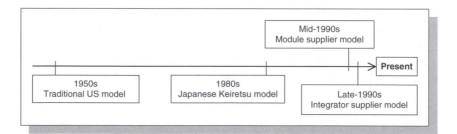

Figure 9.6
Supplier management model timeline.

in some cases, suppliers that make simple, routine products do not always need to be treated as partners since the OEM customers can manage their suppliers in various ways (Kamath and Liker, 1994). For example, in the case of producing a commodity or standard part (such as a spark plug), the relationship between the OEM and supplier would most likely be a contractual relationship where the supplier simply manufactures the parts specified by the OEM customer. The OEM would provide detailed blueprints or orders from a catalog, and the supplier would simply be seen as an extension of the customer's manufacturing capability, responsible for building the part. For a simple assembly part, the OEM/supplier relationship would probably be characterized by the OEM establishing most of the design specifications for the assembly and making demands on the supplier, with the supplier responding to meet the demands (Kamath and Liker, 1994).

From observations in the late 1990s, there appeared to be two basic types of buyer–supplier relationships among the OEMs and Tier 1 suppliers in the US auto industry. The first type of relationship, and the least intimate in regards to frequent communication and supervising, tended to be very adversarial in nature. This type of buyer–supplier relationship was often characterized by market control in which the lowest-bidder-takes-all. The free market, then, is the mechanism that decides the choice of supplier for the OEM and provides the system of control (Williamson, 1981). Such a relationship has been termed an 'exit relationship' in the literature (Hirschman, 1970; Helper and Sako, 1995) and in an exit relationship, an OEM that has a problem with a supplier simply finds a new supplier to do business. This type of adversarial exit relationship was characteristic of the relationship between OEMs and Suppliers in the US prior to the 1980s.

The second type of relationship tended to be very partnership. The partner buyer–supplier relationship was more Japanese in its origin, but had made significant headway into companies such as Chrysler (Dyer, 1996b), before the Daimler-Benz acquisition. The use of relational contracting (Ouchi, 1980; Dore, 1986; Nishiguchi, 1994) is common in this type of relationship, and incumbent suppliers are generally in a position where the customer's business is theirs to lose. OEMs and suppliers in this type of relationship tend to look at one another as long-term partners. This partnership form of relationship has been described as a 'voice relationship' in the academic literature (Hirschman, 1970; Helper and Sako, 1995) and is characterized by the customer and original supplier working together to resolve problems. In such a relationship, the OEM makes a commitment to the supplier that it will continue to buy the supplier's product for an extended period. Moreover, this assurance comes from mechanisms that make it difficult for the customer to exit from the relationship, such as acquiring the supplier and the use of long-term contracts (Helper and Sako, 1995). Table 9.2 shows a listing of some of the differences between the Exit and Voice types of relationships seen in the auto industry.

Table 9.2
Differences in exit and voice relationships

Relationship Framework	EXIT	VOICE
Relationship type	Adversarial	Partnerial
Contract lengths	Short-term	Long-term
Sourcing	Multiple parallel	Single dedicated
Attitude toward incumbent	No favors granted to incumbent	Commitment to helping incumbent
Communication with supplier	Infrequent	Frequent

Figure 9.7 shows (qualitatively) the state of US automotive buyer–supplier relationships as of 1998 (denoted as t_1) mapped onto the Hirschman Exit-Voice framework based on our interviews (Hirschman, 1970; Helper and Sako, 1995). The type of buyer–supplier relationship exhibited by the Big 3 at time t_2 will be described later in the paper.

Among the Big 3 in 1998, GM in the past was often cited as being the most adversarial in their relationship with suppliers. By aggressive cost-cutting, questionable record in keeping commitments, and awarding business to the lowest bidder, GM created a reputation of being a ruthless customer. A Vice President at an interior systems supplier stated in 1998, 'GM gets a bad reputation, and deservedly so. The auto industry is a ruthless industry, and people are competitive for survival. If GM reneges on commitments, their ability to do it the next time reduces their credibility with suppliers.' With regards to being an incumbent supplier for GM, there seemed to be no promised rewarding of future business, a characteristic distinctive of adversarial relationships dictated by market control. A Director at a Tier 1 brakes supplier supported this fact by stating, 'GM will give the incumbent a chance to match the lowest bidder price, but if (the incumbent supplier) can't, GM gives (the business) to the lowest bidder.' Due to the adversarial nature of the relationships, and the use of the free market to create control over suppliers, GM's relationship with their suppliers at the time could best be categorized as an 'exit relationship.'

As of the 1998–1999 time frame, Chrysler was still keeping its partnership model with its suppliers. After the merger with Daimler-Benz in 1998, the new Daimler-Chrysler was open to keeping the Extended Enterprise and SCORE program within the corporation. When asked what OEM/supplier relationships were like just a few months after the merger, the same Director at the

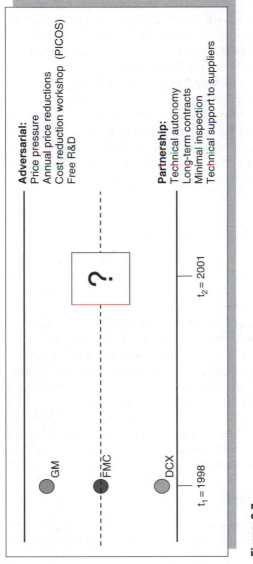

Adversarial:
Price pressure
Annual price reductions
Cost reduction workshop (PICOS)
Free R&D

Partnership:
Technical autonomy
Long-term contracts
Minimal inspection
Technical support to suppliers

GM

FMC

DCX

$t_1 = 1998$

$t_2 = 2001$

Figure 9.7
US Buyer–supplier relationship mapping on exit-voice framework.

previously mentioned brakes supplier stated that, 'In general, DaimlerChrysler is more partner-like than GM.' Another Director in the Truck Division of an interior systems supplier stated that, 'At DaimlerChrysler, the good relationships are still holding. There is still trust and loyalty – more than Ford or GM.' The fact that much of Chrysler's former partnership supplier management structure was still in place shortly after the merger, in addition to comments such as these, indicated that at least in the 1998–1999 time frame, Daimler-Chrysler still resembled more closely the "voice relationship" delineation than GM or Ford in the Exit-Voice framework.

Also during the same time frame, many engineers and executives in the US auto industry cited Ford Motor Company as a mix between the adversarial style of GM and the partnership style of Daimler-Chrysler. Though not having as extensive supplier development programs as Chrysler's Extended Enterprise and SCORE Program at the time, Ford was taking steps with its Ford Product Development System (FPDS) and Ford 2000 initiative to develop a consolidated full-service supply base with no more than four or five dozen lead suppliers.

5.7. Relationship convergence

As of the beginning of the twenty-first century, there appeared to be a shifting when it came to the relationship styles between US OEMs and their Suppliers. Characteristics of the adversarial style slowly became apparent as the more frequently used relationship style in the OEMs' dealings even with their 'partner' suppliers. In a few of the later interviews of Directors and Managers in Tier 1 suppliers occurring in the 2000–2001 time frame, there were complaints about how some OEMs that were less adversarial in their treatment of suppliers in the past were now becoming more antagonistic. In one of the interviews, the Director of Sales at a leading full service supplier explained his dealings with Ford in the following way.

> 'Some customers are partnerships. Other customers could be more like extortion. Ford swings in the middle-of-the-road. They talk partnerships, but play the GM game. They award new business based on the Chrysler philosophy of partnering-up, but negotiate costs similar to GM; very aggressive and can get in your face.'

With regards to the partnership style that Chrysler has been known for in the past, especially in the days of Stallkamp, the Director quotes,

> 'DaimlerChrysler is moving away from the partnership model somewhat. They are starting to entertain other suppliers, rather than their chosen suppliers. A lot of it has to do with their global capability. This is because DaimlerChrysler has some suppliers that are not capable of becoming global suppliers.'

When Daimler-Benz came into the picture and acquired Chrysler in 1998, a major transition in leadership occurred that caused Chrysler to rethink its supplier management model, which had been moving in the direction of 'voice.' Chrysler, which then became Daimler-Chrysler, reevaluated the whole Extended Enterprise program. When it was finally realized that GM and Ford were paying their suppliers less than what DaimlerChrysler was paying its suppliers, both the Extended Enterprise Program and the SCORE Program were terminated. Afterwards, DaimlerChrysler started to revert to the Lopez model of awarding business to the lowest competent bidder.

In the late 1990s, Ford Motor Company was still incorporating aspects of the partnership style in their supplier management model but was also investigating alternate forms of market bidding simultaneously. Carlos Mazzorin, who was Vice-President of Global Purchasing at the Ford Motor Company, was sharing savings with Ford's suppliers, and many of the lead suppliers created dedicated business units that would cater specifically to Ford's needs. While at the same time helping suppliers achieve savings, Ford began to investigate the use of the Internet for e-business and e-bidding. Then during the days of CEO Jacque Nasser, Ford learned of the cost targeting and annual cost reductions that the Japanese OEMs were requiring from their suppliers. Ford then adopted mandatory cost savings for its own supply base, requiring set annual cost reduction programs be implemented by their suppliers. Eventually, within recent years, both Ford and DaimlerChrysler made major strides toward e-bidding, where cost alone, between qualified suppliers, was the determining factor in gaining customer business.

Figure 9.8 is a conceptual representation of the buyer–supplier relationship style shift occurring in the US auto industry within the 1998–2001 time frame. The previous exit-voice framework is used again. The new hybrid form of relationship style dominant today is termed the 'modern adversarial' relationship style where some of the characteristics of the original adversarial style (use of price pressures, cost reductions, free R&D, etc.) exist in the formal arrangements (long-term contracts, dedicated business divisions, etc.) created from the partnership style.

In a sense, one could argue that the way OEMs interact with their suppliers has come nearly full circle. However, with lean manufacturing and Six Sigma initiatives gaining popularity in the auto industry, companies are trying to streamline their in-house and supply chain operations by cutting out wasteful costs, material, and time while at the same time fine-tuning their product quality, and improving their business and engineering processes. This creates an environment where the emphasis is no longer on cost alone (as business was often awarded many decades ago), but OEMs are going after the suppliers and insisting they meet the demands of the customer from not only a cost perspective, but with shorter lead times and near-perfect quality. The result? A leaner,

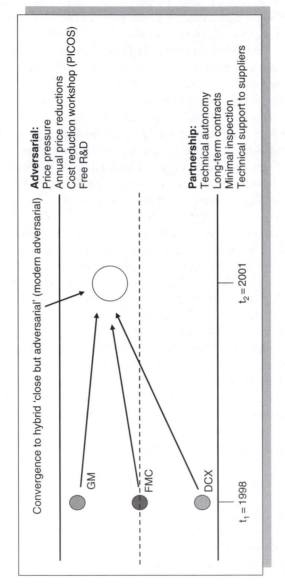

Figure 9.8
Relationship convergence of US auto.

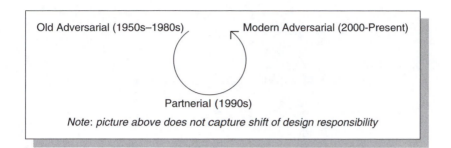

Figure 9.9
Cyclical nature of buyer-supplier relations in US auto.

but meaner modern adversarial form of buyer–supplier relationships seen among OEMs and Suppliers today. Figure 9.9 depicts this circular relationship.

It should be noted, however, that the circular diagram in Fig. 9.9 only captures the relationship style, and does not convey the shifting of design and engineering responsibility from the OEMs to the supply base that occurred over this same time period. In parallel with the outsourcing of design and engineering responsibility, there was also an increase in relationship specific assets acquired by OEMs and suppliers during this same time frame. If both the shift in design responsibility and asset specificity were to be pictured over time in conjunction with the changing buyer–supplier relationship style, it could be depicted on the same conceptual Exit-Voice framework described earlier. The last 50 years of US buyer-supplier relationship styles in the auto industry could then be mapped on this framework as follows in Fig. 9.10.

By coming nearly full-circle and traversing the adversarial and partnership continuum, the US auto industry has shown that by this point in time, it has learned certain aspects of the Japanese OEM/supplier relationship style. These aspects, characteristic of what is termed an *enabling bureaucracy* (Adler, 1999), create a partnership buyer–supplier relationship and encourage suppliers to develop problem-solving competencies, become trained in the tools and knowledge relevant to the OEM customer, share control with the OEM in the design and development phase, participate in the strategic formulation process, and engage in collaborative control and learning between OEM and Supplier. These characteristics of an enabling OEM/supplier bureaucracy include giving suppliers autonomy in the product design, encouragement of technical innovation, and ideas of continuous improvement, albeit in an American context.

However, the US only learned selected features of the Japanese OEM–supplier relationship style, and is missing other features that lead to organizational integration and aligned goals. Some features the US auto industry has not adopted include the use of cross-equity holdings between OEM and

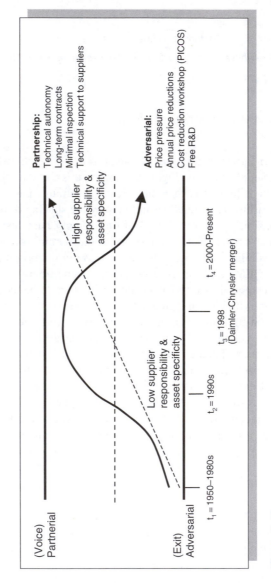

Figure 9.10
Relationship evolution over time (not to scale).

supplier, and the formal-legal control that this creates. American OEMs also tend to not extensively teach suppliers their product development systems and instead push increasing design responsibility down to the supply base. American OEMs do not develop suppliers or make the long-term commitments that engender trust and a sense of mutual destiny (Kamath and Liker, 1994). Yet, they have adopted mandatory annual cost reductions that put cost pressures on suppliers and have adopted characteristics of a *coercive bureaucracy* (Adler, 1999), which results in an adversarial buyer–supplier relationship style and is characterized by the OEM working with several suppliers possessing narrowly defined specialized skills, and the OEM exercising unilateral top-down control of these suppliers. The process of formulating product strategy and concept tends to be very autocratic on the OEM's part, and exertion of strict control over suppliers through underlying market pressures also describe a coercive OEM–Supplier bureaucracy. Such coercive OEM–supplier bureaucracies involve mandatory annual price reductions, expectations for the supplier to absorb R&D costs, invasive micro-management by the OEM into supplier design and production practices, and excessive cost-cutting pressures. Table 9.3 summarizes these two OEM/Supplier bureaucracies within the context of the model developed by Adler (1999).

5.8. Buyer–supplier network structure

Two types of buyer–supplier network structures were apparent in our study – suppliers that were *captive* to the OEM, and those that were *non-captive*. In a very broad sense, a *captive* supplier would traditionally be regarded as one where there exist formal ties, commitments, or mechanisms to the OEM buyer. More specifically, in the Japanese context, this would be represented in the Japanese keiretsu in which the OEM would have equity holding in its suppliers. Formal mechanisms may take place in the existence of interlocking directorates, where an executive in the Japanese OEM would actually sit on the board of directors of one of its keiretsu suppliers. That way the fate of the supplier is directly tied to the fate of the customer, and provides an incentive for both sides to engage in mutually beneficial activities. It also provides a disincentive for unilateral opportunism. More formal commitments would also exist where the Japanese OEM would also have resident engineers residing in the suppliers to facilitate an intimate working relationship, and the suppliers are often restricted from selling their business to other competing customers.

In the historical American automotive context, there were no such things as a captive supplier since American OEMs produced most everything in-house. Internal divisions that were 100 per cent-owned by the OEM were responsible for the production of components needed in the vehicle. Any parts that needed to be outsourced were given to outside companies. However, in

Table 9.3
Enabling versus coercive bureaucracy

Type of OEM/Supplier Bureaucracies	Enabling Bureaucracy	Coercive Bureaucracy
Description	• Partnerial OEM/Supplier relationship • Problem-solving competencies • Dedicated training of supplier • Intimate familiarity with tools/knowledge relevant to OEM • Shared control in product design & development • Participative product strategy & concept formulation • Collaborative learning between OEM & Supplier • Giving Supplier autonomy in product design • Encouragement of technical innovation • Continuous improvement	• Adversarial OEM/Supplier relationship • Narrow, specialized skillset • Contractually acquired expertise • Unilateral top-down control • Autocratic product strategy & concept formulation • Strict control through market pressures • Mandatory annual price reductions • Absorbtion of R&D costs • Invasive micro-management • Excessive cost-cutting pressures

the contemporary American automotive context, the outside system integrator suppliers (such as the ones interviewed in this study) are operating as captive suppliers. Every system integrator had specific divisions set up within the supplier company to specifically cater to the needs of each OEM customer that it had business with and protect its intellectual property. These divisions were often set up as long-term or permanent units dedicated to each customer. Although not as deeply interlocking as in the case of the Japanese keiretsu, these dedicated business units within the supplier are solely devoted to the customer and learn to work together with the customer. The mechanisms that bind this relationship can be transaction specific investments in the form of equipment and capital that is shared between the buyer and supplier. It can also include personnel working on-site for the other organization. Long-term contracts and supplier development are also common so that the supplier's processes can better serve the OEM customer. By design, these divisions cannot share customer-specific information with another business division within the same supplier organization. Due to the relatively resource intensive nature of having multiple business units, the captive supplier network structure is generally seen only among the largest lead Tier 1 suppliers.

Non-captive suppliers in the current environment are mostly lower tier. A table summarizing the differences between captive and non-captive suppliers is shown in Table 9.4.

When considering the captive buyer–supplier network form in the US, it may seem paradoxical that the largest lead suppliers given the highest degree of design and production responsibility are also the suppliers most often subordinate to the demands and control of the buyer, almost like the situation of a vertical hierarchy. The highest degrees of responsibility for complete systems, such as those seen in the Systems Integrator role, are actually not accompanied by more autonomy and independence. Rather, the relationship between OEM and Supplier becomes more subordinate, and even semi-hierarchical, sometimes to the chagrin of the subordinate supplier. The Director of Full-Sized

Table 9.4
Captive versus non-captive supplier network structures

Network Structure	Captive	Non-Captive
Japanese Keiretsu	• Equity holdings • Executives on Board of Directors • Guest engineers • Restrictions on sales to competitors	• Unaffiliated suppliers • No formal ties to any particular OEM
Past US OEMs	• Internal divisions (100 % owned)	• Outside companies
Contemporary US OEMs	• Dedicated business units in 1st tier mega-supplier • No equity ownership	• Smaller 1st tier and lower tier suppliers

Truck Programs for the systems supplier of one dedicated Ford business unit inside a Tier 1 supplier put it this way:

> 'In a sense when you are in a role like this you are giving up a certain amount of your autonomy. They are in here. You are opening up the door to let them "help" run your business. Being a full service supplier actually reduces your autonomy rather than increasing it. They have so many people who are constantly digging, digging, digging. It's a paradox. They call us a full service supplier and expect us to take more responsibility, yet they are trying to be more forceful and end up digging deep into the Tier 5 and Tier 6 level to get their way.'

The OEM will generally exercise this tight level of control over the supplier for the sake of accountability and monitoring of progress. The largest Tier 1 suppliers even have dedicated business units for each OEM in separate dedicated facilities (e.g., Lear, a leading interior supplier has a division for each big-3 customer). As a result of this type of business relationship, the OEM in a sense owns each division (or business unit). The business unit caters to the needs of its particular OEM, and is hierarchically controlled by that OEM.

5.9. Supplier management model framework (4-square model)

When considering the interdependence and complexity of the designed product, a 4-square model framework, such as the one depicted in Fig. 9.11, can be constructed. The four different types of supplier management models described earlier in this report can also be mapped onto this framework. This conceptual framework consists of axes representing both the level of product interdependence and level of product complexity displayed on a relative continuum.

A product which possesses a *high* level of part complexity and a *high* level of interdependence is most often produced by an Integrator Supplier. The Integrator Supplier would possess the amount of resources required to design and manufacture a product of high complexity and interdependence, which in most cases would be a large-scale module or vehicle system. The Integrator Supplier would be able to provide the broad technical competence needed to put together a complex product that interfaces with several different systems in the vehicle. Moreover, it would possess the resources to provide the program management responsibility needed to coordinate such an endeavor.

A product that has a *high* level of part complexity but a *low* level of interdependence would most likely be made by a Module Supplier. The Module Supplier would also have a broad level of technical expertise necessary to create a complex product such as a whole module, but would not necessarily handle the same extensive program management responsibility needed by the Integrator Supplier.

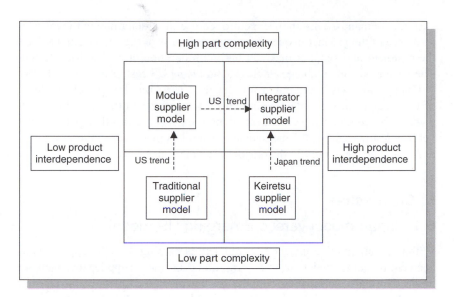

Figure 9.11
The 4-square model of supplier models.

Products characterized by *low* part complexity and *high* product interdependence are generally produced by the Japanese Keiretsu Supplier. For decades, most Japanese keiretsu suppliers did not produce large-scale modules or systems. They focused more on producing components and sub-assemblies for the vehicle. However, issues concerning the interfacing and interdependence of the product to other systems in the vehicle were, and still are, given very serious consideration. In one real life illustration (Liker et al., 1996), a Japanese exhaust system supplier received 'rather ambiguous requirements from its primary customer.' The supplier then proceeded to create a dozens of prototypes that might possibly satisfy the customer's requirements instead of picking out existing mufflers that could have been obtained through a vendor catalog. Most non-Japanese exhaust system suppliers would probably have factored in things such as cost, weight, and manufacturability of the muffler shape. However, in this particular example, the Japanese supplier went well beyond that. They ran tests on their prototype designs and accumulated a wealth of data regarding performance characteristics such as backpressure, noise dampening, and vibration frequency distribution. Then charts and tables compared the various trade-offs among design alternatives (e.g., backpressure versus noise reduction). The supplier communicated these trade-offs in explicit, technical terms to the OEM customer so that sound decisions regarding the vehicle's exhaust system could be made (Sobek et al., 1999). This exhaust system manufacturer, through designing, building, and testing prototypes, created a knowledge database of the possible designs to meet customer demands. This knowledge proved useful in determining the interdependence of the product in question with other parts of the vehicle, and helped the customer and supplier make an optimum decision on the muffler design. There were no comparable examples found in any US case (Liker et al., 1996).

Finally, products exhibiting a low level of part complexity and low level of interdependence are often commodity-like, and very little regard is given to how the commodity component or part interacts with other parts of the vehicle. Many traditional American auto suppliers, particularly those in lower tiers, can be categorized in this quadrant of the framework.

6. Discussion

6.1. Japan model versus Emerging US model

Within the automotive industry, modularity is causing the US supplier management model to deviate from the traditional Japanese supplier management model. Normally, in Japanese supplier management, the OEM retained design control of much of the vehicle, and would delegate the manufacture and assembly of various components and sub-systems to their captive keiretsu suppliers. However, with modularity, there is a move toward outsourcing the assembly, and in some rare cases even the design, of more and more real estate in the automobile to top-tier suppliers.

The emerging US model (which we have termed the Integrator Supplier Model), like the Japanese model it grew out of, gives a great deal of design responsibility to first-tier suppliers. Moreover, the similarities do not stop there. Both models incorporate the use of relationship-specific assets. In the Japanese keiretsu, this takes shape in the investments in brick-and-mortar dedicated to the OEM customer as well as the time and resource intensive training that the OEM gives its suppliers. In the US context, dedicated business units within the systems integrator devoted solely to the OEM customer and the use of resident engineers at the supplier facilities are examples of relationship specific investments.

Both models are also hybrids of hierarchy and market control structures. The US systems integrator is an evolution from the Traditional US model with a Japanese-inspired flavor. In the case of GM and Ford, for decades, these American auto companies created nearly all of the vehicles they produced in-house. The various components that were needed were produced by divisions internal within the GM and Ford themselves. Then in the 1999–2000 time frame, both GM and Ford sold off their parts supplier divisions, creating Delphi and Visteon. Both of these new companies had business units dedicated to their former OEMs as well as other divisions that were responsible for getting other outside business. These new business units within Delphi and Visteon, and the other large mega-suppliers, are US hybrids. There may not be equity ownership or an interlocking board of directorates as in the Japanese case, but the dedicated business units within the suppliers cater wholly to the needs of the OEM with investments in relationship specific assets being commonplace. At the same time, the OEM exerts cost pressures on the supplier, reminiscent of the adversarial (exit) style of buyer–supplier relationship.

However, not everything about these two models is similar. In addition to the above similarities, there are important differences. A comparison between the two is summarized in Table 9.5.

According to this comparison table, the bureaucratic mechanisms between the two models are quite different. As explained earlier in the paper, the Japanese OEM/Supplier bureaucratic structure can be viewed as an enabling bureaucracy. Here, the structures and systems established in the relationship serve to facilitate the work and processes needed to effectively carry out performance objectives. However, in the US systems integrator role, the OEM/Supplier bureaucratic structure resembles more of a coercive

Table 9.5
Japanese model versus new emerging US model

Japanese Model & New Emerging US Model		
Similarities	**Japanese keiretsu supplier**	**US Systems Integrator**
Asset investments:	Relationship specific	Relationship specific
Suply chain structure:	Hybrid (make/buy)	Hybrid (make/buy)
Differences	**Japanese Keiretsu Supplier**	**US Systems Integrator**
Bureaucratic mechanism:	Enabling	Coercive
Responsibility:	Vertical coordination	Horizontal coordination
Role:	Manage lower-tier suppliers	Manage competitors
Goal:	Meet target specifications (both cost & technical)	Meet OEM's consumer expectations
Link:	Keiretsu dependent	Independent with dedicated business unit

bureaucracy. In this type of bureaucracy, suppliers are guided into following protocol and the OEM's wishes by authority hierarchy, procedure manuals, and financial pressure. The excessive cost reductions seen in the US OEM/Supplier management model benefit the OEM financially, but run the danger of putting the supplier out of business. In addition, rarely is there deep loyalty to a supplier, resulting in an OEM–Supplier relationship where deep integration and sharing of resources and knowledge does not occur.

The responsibility for overseeing Japanese first-tier suppliers lies in the vertical coordination that the OEM maintains, whereas in the new US Integrator Role, much of this responsibility belongs to the supplier selected as the system integrator and is thus more horizontal in focus. The role of the first-tier supplier in the Japanese first-tier supplier model is to manage lower-tier suppliers. However, the new US system integrator must devote time and energy to managing other suppliers and even competitors to successfully fulfill the desires of the customer. Part of these suppliers are lower tier suppliers whom the first-tier supplier contracts with and thus has some formal control. However, in other cases they are competitors who have a similar level of design responsibility and who in some cases are designated by the OEMs and directly contracted by the OEMs. This directed sourcing causes the system integrator to have a certain degree of responsibility without formal authority.

There are also subtle but important differences in goals. The Japanese Supplier tries to meet target specifications (e.g., weight, cost, and functional) and satisfy the OEM on overall design quality. However, the Japanese OEM determines what the end customer wants and reflects these in specifications to the supplier. The US System Integrator has this as a major responsibility, but is also concerned about meeting consumer expectations – defining what the end consumer wants. This is crucial if the Integrator Supplier wishes to improve its standing with its OEM customer, and to increase its reputation for quality products and service.

When so much responsibility is given to outside suppliers, OEMs must retain considerable control over their design activities. As described earlier, the US version of the keiretsu structure is the use of dedicated divisions of its top tier suppliers. They are often staffed by former managers from the customers who provide inside information and have extensive networks within the OEM. This in a sense approximates the keiretsu ties in a decentralized way within the outside supplier.

6.2. Recontextualization barriers

When considering how the Japanese supplier management model is being transplanted here to the US, one must realize that recontextualization is likely to occur and that the transplanted model or concept may actually take on different form in a foreign environment (Liker et al., 1999). From our anecdotal evidence, there appear to be three basic relational barriers that create an environment non-conducive for a direct transference of the Japanese model here in the US, and thus caused the US auto industry to respond with new emerging models such as the Module Supplier model and the Integrator Supplier model.

The first barrier involves the practice of the awarding of projects based on *competitive bidding*, where business is awarded to the lowest bidder. This still tends to be a common form of supplier selection in the US extending to e-bidding. According to typical practice, an OEM will give the incumbent supplier a chance to match the lowest bidder price, but if the incumbent cannot match or beat it, the OEM will award the business to the lowest bidder. There is little advantage for the incumbent supplier to perform a proper job in meeting its targets, since the awarded business may easily go to someone else. In addition, the excessive cost reduction policies, like the ones seen at Ford Motor Company, which an OEM may place on a supplier to meet rigid cost targets puts additional pressure on an incumbent supplier to reduce their cost margins considerably to not lose their business to another supplier due to competitive bidding. This lack of loyalty caused by competitive bidding and cost reduction policies sacrifices the relationship with suppliers. It will continue to be a barrier to a more partner-like working relationship between OEMs and their suppliers.

The second major observed barrier was within the area of general *trust issues*. This can take form in many ways. First, the aforementioned competitive bidding policies causes a lack of trust between the supplier and the OEM and little desire to invest in customer-specific R&D, thereby hindering mutual cooperation which would benefit the OEM–supplier relationship in the long run. When the OEM micro-manages Tier-2 suppliers, it is again conveying a message of distrust to the first-tier suppliers. One Director in the Ford division of a lead Tier 1 interior supplier complained,

'There is a different climate in dealing with Ford. Years ago there was a better feeling or era of trust. Individuals within Ford were people of their word. You made an agreement, and people kept their word. Their word was good. Now, I do not do anything without having it in writing – I can't trust these people.'

In the Integrator Supplier Model, systems integrators are moving more and more upstream in the product development process, trust issues need to be taken seriously. Eventually, systems integrators may well deal directly with the end customer, so a way will have to be found to bridge these trust issues.

The third and final type of observed barrier preventing the direct transference of the Japanese keiretsu model here in the US is that of *poor coordination and communication* between OEM and suppliers. Based upon the information gathered in our interviews, there seems to be a lack of internal coordination inside the OEM regarding decisions concerning the supplier. There also seems to be a lack of communication regarding issues such as last-minute design changes, causing frustration on the supplier's part and confusion on the OEM's part. Moreover, there is no timely commitment for heavy investment (i.e., tooling). Often times, the OEM's commitment to the supplier and the design comes after the supplier is well into the design and even production phases of the project.

6.3. Dominant model?

Over decades, the Japanese OEMs and their keiretsu suppliers increased their information processing capabilities (Galbraith, 1977). American companies sought the cost benefits of efficient suppliers who take on engineering responsibility without the investment in an enabling infrastructure. However, there is an inherent misfit between coercive mechanisms and task interdependence and asset specificity in this model, creating a hodge-podge collection of selected features from the Japanese supplier management model intermingled with aspects of the old traditional US supplier model. The Japanese have evolved a hybrid of market and hierarchy, but the US companies are using a dysfunctional hybrid and are missing the control and enabling features that are apparent in the Japanese model. The Japanese OEMs are able to keep control by buying part of the supplier, but the American OEMs do not have the leverage provided by equity holdings in their suppliers. So instead, they turn to market and cost pressures to get the suppliers to do what they want. The Japanese have facilitated knowledge and resource transfer by partnering with their suppliers, which is consistent with some of the thinking found in knowledge-based theory. In fact, the result has been more than compliant suppliers. Japanese suppliers act as mutual learning partners continuously improving processes and operations (Ahmadjian and Lincoln, 2001). By not partnering with their suppliers, American OEMs have a more difficult task of developing compatible practices for mutual improvement.

What the US supplier management model does do well, however, is exert business control in a hierarchy. American OEMs are good at controlling suppliers through purchasing and market power and independent business units. They exert business control in a simulated hierarchy, so even though the suppliers are not owned by the OEM, the relationship is set up in a way such that the supplier is more strongly tied to the OEM than in the past traditional US supplier management configuration. However, unless the organization integration issues are addressed in the US supplier management model, the US's failing will be on the technical integration side. They will get good cost reductions, but at the expense of systems integration that leads to the highest quality automobiles. The result is also financially weakened suppliers that cannot invest in the R&D required by this new business model.

There is a danger that the Big 3 approach to supplier management will become the dominant organizational design in America. Old ways are hard to change, and paradigms have a constraining effect. The US supplier management model has broken technical and organizational systems that will not go away just by coercive market forces. The underlying systems problem is still there, and this underlying problem that is more difficult and challenging to fix.

7. Conclusion

7.1. Future direction and concluding remarks

Throughout this section, we have seen significant involvement of suppliers in design in the US. It seems that the number of suppliers getting involved in product design is growing at an increasing rate, and will only continue to do so in the near future. It should be noted that the Japanese supplier model served as a starting point, or benchmark, for the supplier models that have been witnessed emerging here in the United States; a combination of modular and system integrator roles. The US OEM purchasing strategy still appears to be in a state of transition and a hybrid of market control and relational contracting.

Future research on this topic is needed to investigate the ongoing evolution of supplier management models in the United States; and how modularity and systems integration will mature in the US automotive industry context. If Integrator Suppliers are truly the higher-evolutionary form, then we should see the lead Tier 1 Suppliers continuing to dominate this position with their program management capabilities and taking the lead or projects with coordination oversight over both module and component suppliers. A greater discrepancy in the amount of design responsibility should also continue to occur between the Integrator Suppliers and the rest of the supply base.

This then brings up another question of power relationships between the lead Tier 1 Integrator Suppliers and the OEMs themselves. As the outsourcing of product development and coordination responsibilities to the supply base increases, do the relationships between the OEMs and System Integrators become more antagonistic as early trends indicate? Since System Integrators are buying up competencies to handle the growing amount of responsibility they have over larger and larger pieces of vehicle real estate, is this also leading to an increase in power or leverage in relation to the OEMs? Will this be a threat to the brand recognition or OEMs' leverage over some suppliers? How much of the 'Intel Inside'® phenomenon will happen in the auto industry? Several years ago, Intel practically became a household name with their 'Intel Inside'® logo campaign. The logo was pasted on every PC that contained an Intel microchip as a stamp of technical and quality credibility. Consumers and businesses everywhere soon began buying PCs that had the logo stamped on the computer body. Soon, the brand recognition of Intel began to overshadow the brands of the PCs themselves. Will the same trend that we saw with Intel in the personal computer industry happen in the automotive industry? Then how would the OEMs differentiate themselves?

Recent mergers occurring among automotive suppliers are reducing the supply base, and are reducing the differentiation between OEMs. There is also a growing movement among OEMs to move more toward acting like marketing, assembly, and distribution systems, while relinquishing more of the manufacturing and production responsibilities onto first-tier suppliers. There have been substantial efforts on the part of American OEMs to try and optimize their customer–supplier relationships. Of course, the barriers that exist are challenges that will need to be overcome. But as time progresses, it is quite clear that although the US auto industry began at a point where it was copying the Japanese model of supplier management, the United States has come a long way in evolving the model. Moreover, in the cases of modularity and systems integration, they are deviating from the traditional Japanese model, into something much more distinctly American.

Bibliography

Adler, Paul S. 1999. "Building Better Bureaucracies," *Academy of Management Executive*, 13(4, Nov 1999): 36–47.

Ahmadjian, C.L. and J.R. Lincoln 2001. "Keiretsu, Governance, and Learning: Case Studies in Change from the Japanese Automotive Industry," *Organization Science*, 12(6, Nov–Dec): 681–701.

Automotive News, March 5, 2001 edition.

Baldwin, Carliss Y. and Kim B. Clark 1997. "Managing in the Age of Modularity," *Harvard Business Review,* 75(Sep–Oct): 84–93.

Bensaou, M. and E. Anderson 1999. "Buyer-Supplier Relations in Industrial Markets: When Do Buyers Risk Making Idiosyncratic Investments?" *Organization Science*, 10(4, July–Aug 1999): 460–481.

Brannen, M.Y. and J.M. Wilson III 1996. "Recontextualization and Internationalization: Lessons in Transcultural Materialism from the Walt Disney Company," *CEMS (Community of European Management Schools) Business Review*, 1st edition, Volume 1.

Brusoni, S and A. Prencipe 1999. "Modularity in complex product systems: Managing the knowledge dimension," Working paper, (Earlier version presented at workshop at University of Sussex, June 23–24, 1998).

Clark, K.B. and T. Fujimoto 1989. "Lead Time in Automobile Product Development Explaining the Japanese Advantage" *Journal of Engineering and Technology Management*, 6: 25–58.

Clark, K.B. and T. Fujimoto 1991. *Product Development Performance: Strategy, Organization, and Management in the World Auto Industry*. Boston, MA: Harvard Business School Press.

Corbett and Associates, 2002. (need reference).

Cusumano, M.A. and A. Takeishi 1991. "Supplier Relations and Management: A Survey of Japanese, Japanese-transplant, and U.S. auto plants," *Strategic Management Journal*, 12: 563–588.

Detroit News, May 23, 2000 edition.

Dore, R.P. 1986. *Flexible Rigidities: Industrial Policy and Structural Adjustment in the Japanese Economy*. 1970–1980, California: Stanford University Press.

Dyer, J.H. 1994. "Dedicated Assets: Japan's Manufacturing Edge," *Harvard Business Review*, (Nov–Dec): 4–8.

Dyer, J.H. 1996b. "How Chrysler Created an American keiretsu?" *Harvard Business Review*, (July–Aug): 42–56.

Dyer, J.H. 1996c. "Specialized Supplier Networks as a Source Of Competitive Advantage: Evidence from the Auto Industry," *Strategic Management Journal*, 17: 271–291.

Dyer, J.H. and W.G. Ouchi 1993. "Japanese-style Partnerships: Giving Companies a Competitive Edge," *Sloan Management Review*, 35: 51–63.

Fine, C. 1998. *Clockspeed: Winning Industry Control in the Age of Temporary Advantage*. Reading, MA: Perseus Books.

Fixson, S.K., Ro, Y., and J.K. Liker 2005. "Modularization and Outsourcing: Who drives whom? – A Study of Generational Sequences in the US Automotive Cockpit Industry," *International Journal of Automotive Technology and Management*, 5(2): 166–183.

Galbraith, J.R. 1977. *Organization Design*. Reading, MA: Addison-Wesley.

Helper, S. 1991. "How much has Really Changed Between U.S. Automakers and their Suppliers?" *Sloan Management Review*, 32: 15–28.

Helper, S.R. and M. Sako 1995. "Supplier Relations in Japan and the United States: Are they Converging?" *Sloan Management Review*, 36: 77–84.

Henderson R.M. and K.B. Clark 1990. "Architectural Innovation: The Reconfiguration of Existing Product Technologies and the Failure of Established Firms," *Administrative Science Quarterly*, 35: 9–30.

Hirschman, A. 1970. *Exit, Voice, and Loyalty*. Cambridge, MA: Harvard University Press.

Kamath, R.R. and J.K. Liker 1994. "A Second Look at Japanese Product Development," *Harvard Business Review*, 72: 154–170.

Krafcik, John F. 1988. "Comparative Analysis of Performance Indicators at World Auto Assembly Plants," M.S. thesis, Sloan School of Management, Massachusetts Institute of Technology, Cambridge.

Liker, J.K. Becoming Lean? Inside Stories of US Manufactures, 1997, Portland Oregon.

Liker, J.K., Fruin, M. and P.S. Adler 1999. *Remade in America: Transplanting and Transforming Japanese Management Systems*. New York: Oxford University Press.

Liker, J.K., Kamath, R.R., Wasti, S.N. and Nagamichi, M. 1996. "Supplier Involvement in Automotive Component Design: are there really large US Japan differences?" *Research Policy,* 25: 59–89.

MacDuffie, John Paul, and Frits K. Pil 1999. " 'High-Involvement' Work Systems and Manufacturing Performance: The Diffusion of Lean Production in the World Auto Industry," In: Liker, J.K., Fruin, M. and P.S. Adler (Eds.) *Remade in America: Transplanting and Transforming Japanese Management Systems.* New York: Oxford University Press.

Nadler, D. and M. Tushman 1999. "The organization of the Future: Strategic Imperatives and Core Competencies for the 21st Century," *Organizational Dynamics,* 28(1): 45–60.

Nishiguchi, T. 1994. *Strategic Industrial Sourcing: The Japanese Advantage.* New York: Oxford University Press.

Ouchi, W.G. 1980. "Markets, Bureaucracies, and Clans," *Administrative Science Quarterly,* 25: 124–141.

Sako, M. Price, Quality and Trust: Interfirm Relations in Britain and Japan, 1992 Cambridge University Press, Cambridge, UK.

Sako, M., and S. Helper 1998. "Determinants of trust in Supplier Relations: Evidence from the Automotive Industry in Japan and the US," *Journal of Economic Behaviour and Organization,* 34: 387–417.

Schilling, M.A. and H.K. Steensma 2001. "The Use of Modular Organizational Forms: An Industry-Level Analysis," *Academy of Management Journal* 44(6): 1149–1168.

Schilling, M.A. 2000. "Towards a General Modular Systems Theory & Its Application to Interfirm Product Modularity," *Academy of Management Review* 25(2): 312–334.

Sheridan, J.H. 1990. "Suppliers: Partners in Prosperity," *Industry Week,* March 19, 12–19.

Smitka, M.J. 1991. *Competitive Ties: Subcontracting in the Japanese Automotive Industry.* New York: Columbia University Press.

Snow, C., R. Miles and H. Coleman 1992. "Manging 21st Century Network Organizations," *Organizational Dynamics,* 20(3): 5–20.

Sobek, D., Liker, J.K. and Ward, A. 1998. "Another Look at how Toyota Integrates Product Development," *Harvard Business Review,* 76(4, July–Aug 1998): 36–50.

Sobek, D., Ward, A. and Liker, J. 1999. "Toyota's Principles of Set-Based Concurrent Engineering," *Sloan Management Review,* 40(2, Winter 1999): 67–83.

Ulrich, K.T. 1995. "The role of Product Architecture in the Manufacturing Firm," *Research Policy,* 24: 419–440.

Williamson, O.E. 1981. "The Economics of Organization: The Transaction Cost Approach," *American Journal of Sociology,* 87: 548–577.

10 The effects of outsourcing, offshoring, and distributed product development organizations on coordinating the NPD process

Edward G. Anderson Jr., Alison Davis-Blake, S. Sinan Erzurumlu, Nitin R. Joglekar, and Geoffrey G. Parker

1. Introduction

In recent years, the use of organizational arrangements involving multiple organizations that are separated by firm, geographical, or other organizational boundaries (e.g., outsourcing, offshoring, and alliances) to implement business processes has spread dramatically. In the past, such outsourcing arrangements were confined primarily to peripheral activities, such as payroll management, benefits administration, and janitorial services. Today, however, these arrangements are increasingly used to execute more core activities, such as new product development (NPD) (AMA, 1997; Eppinger and Chitkara, 2006). Some of these arrangements remain fairly centralized with a clear lead organization (or organizations) and subsidiary supplier organizations (Parker and Anderson, 2002a); other arrangements – known as open-source networks – are decentralized (von Hippel, 2005). Because the extensive use of any of these and other multi-organizational arrangements in new product development – which we shall collectively term 'distributed product development' (or DPD) – is a relatively new phenomenon, their impact upon a firm's NPD processes is still poorly understood. Our goal in this chapter is to create a framework that begins to address this knowledge gap. In particular, the chapter will identify a number of specific impacts of distributed product development upon the search, selection, transformation, and coordination processes involved in NPD. This framework is consistent with the terminology set up by Loch and

Kavadias on pp. 3–4. However, we extend and granularize their terminology in Sections 3–5 of this chapter based on their applicability within distributed development setting. (We exclude commercialization due to its necessary link with marketing concepts that are beyond the scope of this discussion, which focuses only on operations.) Additionally, for each effect of DPD identified, the chapter will also seek to identify the relevant literature or lack thereof.

This chapter, however, will not attempt to address the nature or evolution of the DPD relationship itself because – with certain exceptions[1] – answering these questions requires either (1) a much longer history of widespread distributed product development than typically exists or (2) a better process knowledge of the impact of DPD than is currently extant. Hence, we restrict the chapter's focus to solely the process issues previously identified, because not only we believe such knowledge is important in itself but also we believe this gap in process knowledge has precipitated many of the disputes over the more complex questions involved in DPD. For example, the explosively disputed question of whether outsourcing, portions of product development, is beneficial at the firm and national levels (Drezner, 2004; Smith, 1999).

In particular, we shall give special emphasis to the effect of distributed arrangements on the coordination and transformation processes. While much study has been given to the impact of good coordination upon firm success (Cyert, 1991; Siggelkow and Levinthal, 2003; Loch and Huberman, 1999), a theoretical analysis of which procedural elements actually constitute good coordination is generally lacking (Anderson et al., 2007). One of these elements that we will propose as essential for successful distributed product development is a robust capability for product integration – that is, the reweaving together of a new product's components that have been distributed across organizational boundaries back into a coherent end product.

The remainder of this chapter is organized as follows. Section 2 develops the terms used in this chapter such as 'distributed product development', 'outsourcing', and 'offshoring' as well as defines several terms necessary to establish a theoretical framework to examine DPD. Then, because of its importance, we examine the impacts of distributed product development upon the coordination process, followed by, an examination in Section 4 of DPD's impacts upon the transformation process. Section 5 discusses the impacts of DPD upon the search and selection processes in new product development.

---

[1] The well-known Japanese *Keiretsu* has a much longer history than most forms of DPD relationships. Hence, its nature, evolution, and benefits can be identified with much more confidence than is typical for other forms of DPD. For an examination of the *Keiretsu* environment and its evolution, please refer to the chapter in this handbook by Liker (Chapter 9). Similarly, alliances have been studied over many years. For an excellent example of this work, see Doz (1996), which addresses questions regarding the evolution of alliance relationships.

Finally, Section 6 concludes the chapter by highlighting the research opportunities detailed in the previous sections.

2. Distributed product development terminology

Much of the discussion revolving around distributed arrangements in product
development centers upon outsourcing and offshoring. Unfortunately, 'outsourcing,' as it is used by different authors, can mean sourcing a project across
a firm boundary, a geographical border, or both. Additionally, some authors
restrict the term 'outsourcing' to projects that were once done in house and
have since been transferred to other firms. Others use the term to include
projects that have never been done internally. Finally, in the authors' experience, personnel at some firms, such as IBM and General Electric, use the term
'outsourcing' to describe their relationships with other organizations *within
the same firm!* To clarify this ambiguity, we shall now explicitly define the
terms that are used in this chapter. First, we restrict the term 'outsourcing' to
relationships between organizations in different firms. However, we explicitly
include 'outsourcing' both projects that were once performed in-house and
those that never were. 'Offshoring' is restricted to projects that are distributed
across geographical boundaries, *whether or not the organizations involved
reside within the same firm or different firms.*

Interestingly, Eppinger and Chitkara (2006), Sosa et al. (2004) and Allen
(1977), among others, have identified many challenges in product development
conducted across organizational boundaries within the same firm that are
also present – though perhaps to a greater extent – in outsourced product
development projects conducted across firm boundaries (Parker and Anderson,
2002a; Gulati et al., 2005; Sinha and Van de Ven, 2005). A great deal of work
indicates that similar issues may also be present in open source networks (von
Hippel, 2005) and alliances (Gulati et al., 2005; Anderson et al., 2006). Hence,
it would be useful to define a term that embraces all of these arrangement and
any others that rely on cross-organizational cooperation in NPD, *whether any
or all of the involved organizations lie within the same firm or not.* For this
more inclusive term, we will use the phrase 'distributed product development'
or DPD, mentioned earlier. Hence, outsourcing product development can be
seen as an extreme form of DPD (and open source as even more extreme). DPD
also embraces other forms of multi-organizational product development such
as alliances, joint ventures, and hybrid open-source networks – a form that
mixes both corporate and open-source components to develop one product,
see Bonacorrsi and Rossi (2003) and Terwiesch and Xu (2006). Of course,
managing some forms of DPD will be more problematic than others, either
because of the number of organizations involved is greater or because the
boundaries between the organizations involved are particularly difficult to
bridge. We discuss this topic in more detail in Section 3.

We also need to differentiate among the organizations involved. Generally, in the absence of clear, fixed, and highly modular partitions within a project, one organization will emerge as a hub to hierarchically organize (through both explicit and implicit contracts and controls) the efforts of the other involved organizations. Typically, this is done by exercising architectural control over the product design, monitoring the other organizations' progress, and retaining other decision rights associated with the project (Iyer and Gottlieb, 2004). We refer to this hub as the 'lead organization.' Of course, a single lead organization may not emerge to meet the conditions above. If a small number of organizations, particularly from different firms, emerge together to share the organizational, control, and other decision powers described above, a joint venture or alliance will develop. If more than a small number of organizations share these powers, what will emerge will be either an open-source (or perhaps hybrid) network of organizations that contribute to the product (MacCormack and Iansiti, 1997; von Hippel, 2005).

Because the challenges of coordinating across organizational boundaries within the firm are often similar in kind, though not necessarily degree, to across firm boundaries, we shall refer to all organizations other than the lead organization as suppliers, *whether or not these other organizations reside in the same firm as the lead organization.* (In the authors' direct experience, this usage is consistent with practice in many firms such as IBM, General Electric, and General Motors, in which personnel often refer to other organizations within the same firm as 'suppliers.') We refer to the portion of the product provided by a given supplier organization as a component, but we use that term in the broad sense to indicate a physical component part, a distinct subsystem, a software module, a service, or any other delivered portion of the final product.

We denote the firm in which the lead organization resides as the lead firm. As stated earlier, a supplier may reside either within the lead firm (e.g., a different division) or outside of it. However, we shall only use the term 'outsourcing' when the supplier belongs to a different firm than the lead firm. Note that it is quite possible, even likely, in a distributed product development effort to source some portions of the project to supplier organizations within the lead firm and other portions to organizations located inside other firms. We will also make use of the concept of 'partial outsourcing' in which the lead organization (or organizations) executes some percentage of design projects for a class of components within the lead firm while outsourcing the remainder (Anderson and Parker, 2002). For example, at one time Ford Motor Company developed a number of its electronic engine control modules in house, but outsourced the development of the remainder to Motorola.

Using this terminology, we now examine the impact of DPD on NPD processes.

3. DPD and coordination

In this section, we create an initial framework to examine the impact of DPD upon the coordination process in NPD projects. The coordination process 'ensures information flows, cooperation, and collaboration across the multiple actors in the NPD process' (Loch and Kavadias, 2002; Chapter 1 in this book). As shown in a number of studies, coordination is often of decisive importance in NPD (e.g., Iansiti and Clark, 1994). However, to understand the role that coordination plays in NPD, it is helpful to begin with a discussion of what constitutes coordination in the NPD process.

3.1. Product integration

Because managing product development involves a greater degree of process, marketing, creative, and technical uncertainty than typically found in other settings such as production management – or even project management of 'simpler' activities such as ship building (Anderson and Joglekar, 2005) – predicting what situations will arise during any given project is difficult. Hence, designing norms, practices, or guiding principles that employees 'on the spot' can use to cope with each and every one of these situations is problematic. In all likelihood, many 'exceptions' to the standard operating procedures or principles will arise during any given product development project resulting in 'interruptions' to routine activity (Zellmer-Bruhn, 2003). In fact, according to the information-processing model in the organizational theory literature (Galbraith, 1973; Tushman and Nadler, 1978; Huber, 1990; Carley and Lin, 1997; Sinha and Van de Ven, 2005), most, if not all, of organizational coordination mechanisms – including hierarchies, contracts or incentive structures, lateral resources (e.g., boundary spanners such as Supply Chain Integrators, see Parker and Anderson, 2002a), information systems, and modularization of tasks – exist to manage these 'interruptions' (Galbraith, 1973). Because one would presume that the most dangerous threats to a product's development are the ones for which no contingency plans exist, successful interruption management is critical to product development success.

Interruptions in the execution of a product development project can either exist completely within the span of one organization's task during product development or involve two or more organizations' tasks. In the former case, any threat to the product development success is due to an inferior component – in the broad sense of being the task's deliverable, physical component, software module, or element of service – of the project as a whole. However, if the interruption lies at the interface of the two or more organizations' tasks inferior project performance can also result from undesirable interactions among the components. These interaction problems can also threaten the project's success. Iansiti and Clark (1994) and Iansiti (1995a,b, 1998) emphatically make this point:

> 'The functionality and cost of the new design concept [relative to initial vision or specifications] will not strictly be a function of the individual properties of the new components, but of the interaction of these properties with a multitude of other design elements that, together, make up the system.' (Iansiti, 1995a).

Iansiti's work as well as Henderson and Clark's (1990) confined their examination of coordination issues to the technical. Moreover, technical issues were, in fact, responsible for the initial development of the field of systems engineering. However, in recent years, the system's engineering definition of coordination or as it is generally referred to in product development, 'integration' has gone beyond this technical focus to also include cross-organizational problems. Below is a passage from a well-known systems engineering text describing the coordination issues involved in NPD.

> For the system [product] to perform correctly . . . the various elements [components] cannot be engineered independently of one another and then simply assembled to produce a working system. Rather, systems engineers must guide and coordinate the design of each individual element as necessary to assure the interactions and interfaces between system elements that are compatible and mutually supporting. *Such coordination is especially important when individual system elements are designed, tested, and supplied by different organizations* [emphasis in the original]. Successful systems integration of a project is concerned with setting its [the project's] objectives, guiding its execution, evaluating its results, and prescribing necessary corrective actions to keep it on course. (Kossiakoff and Sweet, 2003).

Hence, managing interruptions over the entire project – particularly the cross-organizational interruptions that one might see in DPD – requires the guidance and coordination of all of the product's technical work across component and organizational boundaries to create a final customer deliverable that meets the product's initial specification or vision (Blanchard and Fabrycky, 1998; Kossiakoff and Sweet, 2003). For the remainder of this paper, we use the term 'product integration' to embrace this broader definition of integration that includes systems engineering and organizational management theory concepts as well. Note that this definition of 'integration' is distinct from the economic concept of vertical integration.

3.2. How DPD complicates product integration: numbers, cultural dissimilarity, and geographical isolation

Iansiti and Clark (1994), Iansiti (1995b), and Henderson and Clark (1990) established that product integration often decisively influences a product's success by focusing the work of several organizations within a single firm. However, Parker and Anderson (2002a), in a case study at Hewlett-Packard, showed the importance of product integration in DPD as well. In fact, one would logically expect that product integration in a DPD setting would be even more critical than within a single firm for two reasons. One is that the number of organizational barriers requiring attention necessarily increases with the number of organizations involved in any given effort. Hence, ceteris paribus, one should expect product integration to increase with the number of involved organizations. Extreme examples of organizational numbers – in which the organization is often effectively one individual – can be found among open-source networks such as Apache Web Server Software – which has 60 per cent of the Web Server Market – or Wikipedia – the on-line encyclopedia (von Hippel, 2005). Perhaps the inherent difficulty involved in managing so many organizational boundaries helps to explain why so many successful cases of product development in the shared or open-source community have either:

1. A tiered structure in which: a small group of participants retain final approval authority to modify the product (in other words, a strong hierarchy); a somewhat larger number of individuals, but still a small minority of the total network, is involved in major development; and the vast majority confine themselves to bug detection and potentially small repair efforts to fix them (von Krogh and von Hippel, 2006); or
2. An architecture that is extremely modular, imitative, or both (Bonacorrsi and Rossi, 2003; von Krogh and von Hippel, 2006). We return to architecture in the section on selection.

The second reason DPD complicates product integration is more subtle. An organization's norms, practices or routines, and guiding principles are generally referred to collectively as its organizational culture (Beyer and Trice, 1993). Crossing any organizational boundary necessitates bridging two organization's cultures, which are likely to differ from each other (Beyer and Trice, 1993). For example, mismatches between cultures in the two organizations should create more interruptions in the standard operating procedures used by the employees coming from different organizations than if they all shared the same standard operating procedures, which they would if they belonged to the same organization. Some typical differences include the timing and number of stages of development in each firm's 'stage-gate' process (Griffin, 1997; Yassine et al., 2003). Another is that one or more organizations may use an alternative structure during product development process such as the massively parallel and frequent design-build-test development cycle of software features seen at Microsoft (Cusumano and Selby, 1998) or Netscape (MacCormack and Iansiti, 1997) rather than a more standard stage–gate process. Mating such divergent processes can create numerous coordination issues. Other aspects of organizational culture (Martin and Siel, 1983), such as jargon and organizational structure (e.g., heavy versus light-weight project managers, see Clark and Fujimoto, 1991) would also be likely to contribute to the interruption generation rate because each cultural difference increases the probability of misunderstandings between organizations. A nice illustration of these issues is a comment from a Vice President at a major aerospace firm. He stated that the biggest complication in working with other firms in developing products resulted from cultural differences and gave the following example.

> Boeing is an excellent aerospace company. Yet, when we work [on a product] with them, we find that we speak different languages. We have different words for the same thing. And we have different ways of doing the same thing such as qualifying parts. Most of our procedures don't even correspond cleanly to theirs. But we know that both our companies are good at what they do. Sorting this out is difficult (Anderson, 2005).

Interestingly, the differences described above are at least codifiable. However, much of the procedural knowledge about an organization's operational processes, which is critical to product development success, is tacit (Kusunoki et al., 1998). The difficulty of transferring tacit knowledge across organizational and firm boundaries has been shown in various studies (e.g., Kogut and Zander, 1992). Hence, coordinating the appropriate tacit information to ensure successful product integration is probably even more difficult than coordinating codifiable information. In short, the greater the cultural dissimilarity between any two organizations, the greater the likelihood for miscommunication, 'miscoordination,' or other 'interruptions' that require some manner of managerial resolution.

A list of the drivers that might contribute to the degree of cultural dissimilarity between any pair of organizations would likely include whether.

1. The two organizations are separated by a departmental, divisional, or firm boundary (i.e., the two cultures have likely evolved different organizational traditions, because they are isolated from one another (see Beyer and Trice, 1993)).
2. The two organizations are in dissimilar industries (Beyer and Trice, 1993; Gordon, 1991).

3. The two organizations are different in age, size, or both – because the organizational inertia associated with age and size leads to resistance to industry-induced changes (Gordon, 1991; Hannan and Freeman, 1984).
4. The two organizations have different national business cultures (Kogut and Zander, 1992; Hofstede, 1980). As a simple example, 'Yes' in many nation's cultures implies only 'I heard what you are saying' rather than 'I agree with you' as assumed by many Americans. (See also Thomke and Nimgade, 2001 for further examples.)

Hence for all these reasons, one would expect that DPD would in general complicate efforts of coordination in the NPD environment. However, a few words are required of two special distributed relationships:

Alliances and university relationships

Alliances in product development are essentially a form of DPD in which the rights of the lead organization are distributed between two organizations separated by a firm boundary. As such, all the issues of coordination created by the dilution of hierarchical power across the organizational interface are exacerbated because the final 'say' in the hierarchy must itself be coordinated across firm – and perhaps other – boundaries. Needless to say, this complicates coordination enormously. Yet, by definition, all DPD relationships dilute hierarchical power to some degree. Alliances, in this sense, merely present an extreme version of the coordination issues inherent in all distributed arrangements. For more details of the complications in coordinating decision rights inherent in alliances beyond the scope of this paper, see Gulati et al. (2005) and Anderson et al. (2006).

In contrast, industry–university relationships are an extreme example of cultural dissimilarity. The motives driving universities are inherently different from those of for-profit firms. Yet, universities still possess a hierarchy, incentives, standard operating procedures and all the other managerial trappings of organizations (Scott, 2003). Hence, in some sense, working with a university is conceptually an extreme case of crossing an industrial boundary, and we shall treat it as such. For a deeper look at the peculiarities of these particular relationships, see Shan et al. (1994) and Santoro and Chakrabarti (2002).

We next turn to the impact of coordination on the other processes involved in developing new products.

4. DPD and transformation

4.1. Communication failures in transformation

For the most part, the impact of DPD upon the transformation of a final product concept into the delivered product is primarily mediated by product integration. In fact, one would simply expect that a greater intensity of product integration activity is required in a DPD context relative to that required for a similar effort concentrated within one organization, to compensate for DPD's inherently higher interruption rate. However, greater integration effort is often is not the case in DPD efforts. For example, Sosa et al. (2004) documented that communication between engineers working to develop two components of the same product – without which product integration is not possible – was reduced if the two parties came from different divisions, even when that interface was important to the integration of the product (i.e., it was non-modular). Allen's (1977) work corroborates this result. Furthermore, one would naturally expect that such communication of technical and procedural matters, on average, would be attenuated even more by crossing firm boundaries rather than divisional boundaries within the same firm, which has indeed been supported by case evidence (Ancona and Caldwell, 1992; Parker and Anderson, 2002a).

Why is this? In part, most product-development communication still occurs largely through physical meetings, telephone calls, or electronic mail, because much of the promise of more complex information systems and video conferencing to substitute for these three media has not yet been realized (Anderson et al., 2004). Furthermore, of the three communication modes used, physical meetings have a greater 'media richness' – which is in essence the bandwidth at which information can be communicated *without error* (Daft and Lengel, 1986) – than do telephone calls, which have, in turn, a higher media richness than electronic mail. Hence, other forces that might attenuate communication would be those that encourage a substitution of physical meetings by telephone calls or telephone calls by e-mail. Such forces would include geographical distance (reducing the likelihood of physical meetings in favor of other communication modes), time zone differences (reducing the likelihood of telephone calls in favor of e-mails), and language differences (reducing the likelihood of other modes of communication in favor of e-mails). Moreover, indeed, Sosa et al. (2002) confirms that these substitutions do occur for technical projects. Interestingly, many of these factors are also contributors to cultural dissimilarity, creating a 'double-whammy' when offshoring product development by both increasing the interruption rate (inherent in distribution among culturally dissimilar organizations) and inhibiting the communication (from a shift in communications media) that is necessary to rectify the interruptions.

Managing product integration is further complicated in distributed product development by the fact that the primary means used by organizations to manage interruptions are hierarchies and incentives (Galbraith, 1973). Hierarchies will be much less immediate – and hence effective – as the level of the lowest-ranking manager with authority over participants in both organizations increases. In the extreme case of outsourcing, there will be no common management whatsoever, reducing the ability of the project manager to exert fine-grained coercive control over the project (Parker and Anderson, 2002a). Incentives may help, but designing their structure will be complicated by the fact that – at least with outsourcing – the ultimate owners, and hence objectives, of the two organizations will differ (Cyert and March, 1992). There is ample evidence for information hiding and gaming in DPD created by differing incentives for each organization such as the 'Liar's Club' (Yassine et al., 2003; Ford and Sterman, 1998).

4.2. The vicious cycle of interruptions

Another wrinkle in managing the transformation process is that unresolved interruptions can create a vicious cycle that interferes with the integration of various suppliers' components into a coherent final product. In particular, a large number of interruptions that remain unresolved by management action will *in and of itself* increase the rate of future interruptions (Ford and Sterman, 1998). Figure 10.1 illustrates that this arises from a structure that links the driving mechanisms into a reinforcing loop. In Fig. 10.1, the number of unresolved interruptions is a presented as a stock, which increases with the inflow of newly generated interruptions and decreases with the interruption resolution rate much like the level of water in a bathtub is increased by the inflow rate from the spigot and the outflow rate down the drain. The interruption generation rate will increase with the number of organizations involved in a DPD project as well as the average cultural dissimilarity between firms. However, if the interruption resolution rate or 'bandwidth' is less than the interruption generation rate, the number of unresolved interruptions will begin to accumulate. As the number of unresolved interruptions increases, product developers must design their components using more encompassing design assumptions and institute supplemental coordination mechanisms that usually remain in place even after the bulk of the interruptions is finally resolved. Except in an extremely modular environment, some of these changes will inevitably create incompatibilities with other suppliers' components in unpredictable ways, creating yet more interruptions requiring more management attention, resulting in the runaway growth of unresolved interruptions, which in turn hampers successful product integration ever more. Hence, it is critical that there is sufficient management bandwidth to prevent a build-up of unresolved interruptions in the first place. Otherwise, an 'out-of-control' project may well result.

4.3. Improving managerial coordination during transformation

How does one increase management's bandwidth to cope with the increased interruption rate resulting from DPD, particularly when the primary

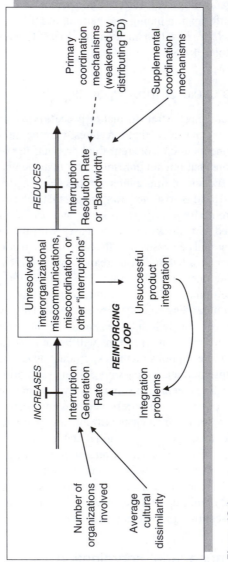

Figure 10.1

A structure for amplifying and attenuating interruptions.

coordination mechanisms (routines or procedures, hierarchies, and incentives) are necessarily vitiated by the DPD environment? Fortunately, managerial 'bandwidth' can be increased either through (1) improving management's coordination productivity, (2) redesigning incentives, or (3) by employing supplemental coordination mechanisms such as boundary spanners, information systems, and modular design.

Coordination productivity

In addition to deploying boundary spanning personnel, such as the supply chain integrators mentioned above, lead firms can enhance the aggregate productivity of their entire development team. Anderson and Parker (2002) have put forth a model-based argument for incorporating learning effects within the make/buy decisions. Indeed, the existence of learning curves has been documented for managing distributed development both for inter-organizational settings (Sobrero and Roberts, 2001) and in product development (Boone and Ganeshan, 2001). Sobrero and Roberts identify the trade-off of efficiency versus learning in terms of two critical dimensions: (1) the design scope and (2) the level of task interdependency. The design scope dimension characterizes the type of problem-solving activities outsourced by the manufacturer. The level of task interdependency dimension characterizes the influence of any given supplier–manufacturer interaction on other activities.

Joglekar and Rosenthal (2003) have looked into task level mechanisms that enable such learning during product integration. They describe a scenario where the lead firm and each of its design supply chain partners follow disparate stage–gate processes. The need for handling interruptions arises when these processes are synchronized, owing to the differing aspirations and routines underlying each organization's process. As mentioned in Section 2.2, the know-how for managing stage-gate reviews, like much else in product development, is often tacit. Repeated interactions amongst development partners allow the teams on both sides to understand better the gaps between disparate practices. Improved understanding decreases the need for coordination effort. In a related study, Gomes et al. (2005) unpack the development effort for each product integration task within a set of projects into coordination and technical problem solving efforts, respectively. They found significant learning effects, i.e., coordination effort reduces over successive executions comparable tasks. However, a comparable effect is not observed for technical problem solving. Field interviews suggest that learning about problem solving during distributed development may suffer from a 'technical know-how paradox.' That is, as the developer's understanding of technical problems improves, it is able to design better technical interfaces that allow it to outsource these problems, thereby reducing opportunities for developing problem-solving skills further in the future.

Incentives and supplier selection

Handfield et al. (1999) suggest that a number of factors should influence the selection of suppliers in product development. Predominant among them is the alignment of long- and short-term objectives between the lead organization and the supplier. If they are not initially aligned, certain contractual steps can be drawn to bring them closer together, such as – for moderately low anticipated demand – both parties committing in advance to price and quantity objectives (Gilbert and Csva, 2003). Another example of a mechanism to align objectives favored by firms in Japan and Korean – but illegal in many other countries including the United States – is a mutual ownership arrangement between a lead firm and its more important suppliers. Such arrangements also create the secondary benefit of promoting stabile relationships between the involved parties. Hence, in a learning curve-like effect, over time each organization becomes familiar with its counterparts and is less prone to misunderstandings and miscoordination based on cultural dissimilarity. Another possibility is joint buyer–supplier cost reduction sharing (McIvor and McHugh, 2000). Another factor cited by Handfield et al. (1999) that enables successful supplier selection is an extensive knowledge by the lead organization of the supplier's capabilities and future technological roadmap. Presumably, this knowledge would facilitate product integration (Fine and Whitney, 1999) as well as prevent lock-in to an inferior technology (Handfield et al., 1999).

Modularization

Partitioning is of critical import in outsourcing tasks, the goal of which typically is to design the bundle of tasks assigned to each firm to be as self-contained (modular) as possible without compromising other short or long-term lead-organization objectives (Sanchez and Mahoney, 1996). Baldwin and Clark (2000) have written the seminal study on the benefits and theory modularity. Some of the general factors driving an organization towards more or less modularization in its components include many of the same factors that drive DPD in the first place. For example, factors such as access to other organizations' technology or capabilities and market uncertainty or heterogeneity will not only drive DPD but also encourage modularity (Schilling and Steensma, 2001).

Actual tools to ensure proper partitioning of modules include design structure matrices (DSMs), which explicitly map interdependencies between functions in a project (Steward, 1981; Browning, 2001). To the extent that it can create self-contained tasks, the lead firm minimizes the communication necessary between different organizations, which necessarily reduce the number of miscommunications or other interruptions resulting from different organizational cultures (Parker and Anderson, 2002a). An additional benefit is that

Sosa et al. (2004) showed that organizational boundaries attenuate communications across critical design interfaces, which is exactly the wrong direction that one would expect for a successful project (Allen, 1977). Hence, one would suspect that partitioning projects into relatively self-contained components with a minimal number of critical cross-component interactions and then aligning those components with known supplier capabilities would facilitate product integration under DPD.

Other methodologies have been devised to aid communication between the organizations responsible for different modules, once they have been partitioned. One particularly well known one is Quality Function Deployment (QFD). Hauser and Clausing (1988) describe it as a conceptual map for interfunctional planning and communications that can facilitate disseminating the 'voice of the customer' throughout the product development process (Griffin and Hauser, 1993). Also known as the 'House of Quality,' a QFD, by explicitly mapping the interacting characteristics of a product, can also aid partitioning. Gomes and Joglekar (2005) analyze a set of software projects to propose several measures (e.g., task visibility and feedback dependence) that can be used to measure the modularity of partitions, each of which involve different managerial trade-offs between problem solving and coordination efficiency.

Interestingly, however, while DSMs have been used to design organizational structures (Lorsch and Lawrence, 1972), with the exception of Browning (1999) and Gulati and Eppinger (1996), it is unclear whether they, QFDs, or any other tool have ever been used to incorporate supplier capabilities when partitioning products so as to align organizational and component boundaries in an efficient manner.

Boundary spanners

Another possibility for improving communications and coordination between organizations in the DPD environment is the use of boundary spanners (Ancona and Caldwell, 1992), which provide additional 'bandwidth' across the system. Das and Narasimhan (2000) as well as Fine and Whitney (1999) called for the establishment of a 'purchasing competence' to span organizational boundaries during new product development. An interesting example of this was described in Parker and Anderson (2002a). By approximately 1998, Hewlett-Packard's notebook division had evolved into a 'network orchestrator' (Häcki and Lighton, 2001) or 'impannatore' (Jaikumar, 1986), in which the lead organization outsources most of its development work to suppliers in other firms (Parker and Anderson, 2002a). However, unlike many other orchestrators, Hewlett-Packard also retained a significant portion of the notebook's high-level design in house. Hence, it needed to create a new capability staffed with personnel whom Parker and Anderson (2002a) termed 'supply chain integrators.' Extending Clark and Fujimoto's (1991) terminology of heavy and lightweight project managers, these supply chain integrators are essentially ultra-lightweight project managers, who – instead of direct or dotted-line supervisory control over their reports – employ a mix of 'soft skills' to coordinate, translate, negotiate, and mediate across organizational interfaces to ensure successful product integration. To facilitate this, integrators typically possess hard skills such as product design or systems engineering, business skills such as project management, costing or business case evaluation, and perhaps miscellaneous skills such as process or information systems analysis. Jaikumar (1986) and Fung and Magretta (1998) describe personnel with analogous functions and capabilities within the textile industry as do Davis-Blake et al. (1999) in the plant design and construction industry.

Another aspect of boundary spanning is the adaptation of procedures to bridge organizational interfaces with suppliers. One such is the use of highly concurrent engineering. This can promote communication to balance the effects of rework (Loch and Terwiesch, 1998), which DPD might otherwise generate. Another possibility is to change one's capacity allocation strategies to account for product integration and other rework induced by distributed product development (Joglekar and Anderson, 2005). Early involvement of suppliers is also typically beneficial (Handfield et al., 1999), although this increases lead organizations' exposure to the hold-up problems discussed earlier. McIvor and McHugh (2000) discuss other beneficial organizational changes for working more effectively with suppliers.

Finally, investment in boundary spanning capability must be appropriately sized to the technical coupling between different organizations' components. At least initially, firms often tend to invest too little in boundary spanning to couple different components together organizationally (Anderson et al., 2004). However, over-investment in boundary spanning – relative to the technical coupling of any two components – can also be undesirable (Martin and Eisenhardt, 2003).

Information systems

Historically, enhancements to the technical dimensions of product development processes have been encapsulated within software environments such as mechanical CAD tools (Whitney, 1995). The advent of ubiquitous and easy to use web-based interfaces have ushered the trend towards IT-based collaboration (Hameri and Nihtila, 1997; McGrath and Inasiti, 1998). Such collaboration touches all facets of distributed development: problem solving effort at the system and component levels (Joglekar and Whitney, 1999), virtual customer interfaces (Nambisan, 2002), communication of development intent (Aoshima et al., 2004), synchronization of product life cycle management tools and exchange of bills of materials across organizational boundaries (Bardhan et al., 2005). In many industries, the use of information systems tools remains much more widespread for technical problem solving rather than the coordination of distributed efforts.

Argyres (1999) analyzes a case study of the B-2 'Stealth' bomber, an aircraft that was designed by four firms almost entirely by computer. The key information systems used in the project were: (1) a common-access database to manage part designs and (2) an advanced system to perform structural analysis. These systems played a crucial role in enabling the four firms to coordinate their design and development activities precisely enough to meet the demanding engineering requirements imposed by the aircraft's unique mission. Information systems aided coordination directly by making information processing less costly. Second, this enhanced information processing made the governance of the project more efficient. In particular, by establishing a 'technical grammar' for communication, the systems helped to create social conventions around which firms could coordinate their activities, thus limiting the need for a hierarchical authority to promote coordination.

Often, the diffusion of such technology is driven by the needs of the lead development firms. Sethi et al. (2003) have argued that organizations desiring to employ the web in their development processes can use it at varying levels of functionality and sophistication, ranging from a tool for automating manual tasks and exchanging data to a means of integrating various intra- and inter-organizational functions and processes. Each increasing level of integration brings with it higher costs – not only the direct costs of technology acquisition but also the costs of implementing a complicated system, which typically involve redesigning intra- and inter-organizational processes.

The use of automated collaboration tools results in a higher quality product (Joglekar and Whitney, 1999) in a manner analogous to the information system productivity paradox (Brynjolfsson and Hitt, 1998): productivity gains are offset by firm's tendency to deliver higher quality. Thomke (2006) argued that productivity improvements with new development tools are subject to pitfalls such as (1) utilizing them as mere substitutes for existing practices and (2) introducing additional interfaces into the NPD process. Mechanisms for handling DPD interruptions, in the presence of sophisticated development tools, remain an open arena for enquiry.

Implementation of complex application software, project management protocols, and the rise in the use of web-based information exchange mechanisms has increased the amount of information in each development project. It is not unusual for a large development project at an Aerospace lead firm, such as Boeing, to have data that cut across more than 5000 individuals. Similarly, some recent FDA filings for approval of drug development projects have involved more than a terabyte of data. Size and quality of data are particularly important concerns due to the trend toward DPD. Joglekar and Anderson (2005) have illustrated that errors in progress status data can shift optimal task sharing strategies dramatically. The potential for the gaming of progress status information constitutes another important, but scantily studied concern in this context (Ford and Sterman, 2003).

4.4. Summary

Managing the transformation process of NPD in a distributed environment will most likely involve the creation or augmentation of supplementary coordination mechanisms to ensure successful product integration. Otherwise, transformation is likely to result in unsuccessful product integration and an inferior delivered product. Needless to say, such mechanisms are expensive, nor, like most capabilities (Wernerfelt, 1984), can they be developed overnight. Hence, the challenge is to determine when DPD is worthwhile and then, once that path is chosen, to manage it as efficiently as possible.

5. DPD and search and selection

In contrast to coordination and transformation, search is the process that identifies potential combinations of suppliers, technologies, and market opportunities that could potentially benefit the lead organization (or organizations). Selection chooses among these new combinations for projects that will be invested in. We combine them together because many of the impacts of DPD upon these processes simultaneously span both processes. This deep tie between search and selection is reflected in much of the search literature (see e.g., Siggelkow and Levinthal, 2003 or March, 1991).

5.1. Benefits of DPD to search and selection

To manage an organization's search and selection processes effectively requires an integrated vision incorporating the mission, culture, and strategy for the organization's business as well as a clear understanding of the market environment as a whole, including customer wants, technological possibilities, potential partners, and the firm's own capabilities (Nellore and Balachandra, 2001). Numerous reasons exist for embracing a DPD structure to achieve this vision rather than developing the product completely within one organization or firm. It should be noted that the sourcing of a component's manufacturing or delivery often influences or even determines the sourcing of its development because design and delivery are often tightly bundled, particularly if development costs are small relative to delivery costs. However, this need not always is the case. For example, many firms provide engineering services without corresponding manufacturing or delivery capabilities (Hargadon, 2002). With this caveat, some of the more common reasons to distribute product development outside the lead organization include:

- **Access to Technology**. The core competency of a lead organization comprises those difficult-to-imitate capabilities that create 'an area of specialized expertise that is the result of harmonizing complex streams of technology and work activity' (Prahalad and Hamel, 1990). Depending on market conditions, keeping in-house technological capabilities outside an organization's core competence is often undesirable (Fine, 1998). Dell Computer, e.g., does not make its own motherboards. Outsourcing component technology is especially beneficial to the search process when there is a great deal of environmental uncertainty regarding which non-core component technologies may become important, or even viable, over time (Fisher, 1997; Ramdas, 2003; Ramdas et al., 2003; Thomke et al., 1998). Embracing such a flexible strategy may require leveraging product architecture to enable inexpensive switching between components from different suppliers (Thomke and Reinertsen, 1998).
- **Cost and Quality**. A supplier may provide superior cost or quality than can be found in house either because of economies of scale, scope (Hayes and Wheelwright, 1984), market competition (Baldwin and Clark, 2000), or simply geography. However, Novak and Eppinger (2001) showed in their study of the automotive industry that cost benefits tend to lessen as the complexity of the final product increases. This is probably related to loss of component development expertise affecting product integration capability as described in the next section on DPD risks in search and selection.
- **Surge Capacity**. The search process may reveal that a lead organization may theoretically have the technological capability to design a component but not enough technical resources (e.g. engineers, programmers, etc.) to execute it in a timely manner (Anderson and Joglekar, 2005). Similarly, a lead organization may lack enough capacity in house to produce or otherwise deliver a component. In this case, if development is tightly bundled with delivery, it may be impractical to retain development in-house and outsource delivery to a supplier (Clark, 1985; Clark and Fujimoto, 1991). If development and delivery are thus tied, there exist several other reasons for outsourcing delivery and hence development. Another reason for engaging a supplier to provide surge capacity is to protect the lead organization in case demand for the outsourced component does not materialize (Hayes and Wheelwright, 1984). Other variations on this argument include outsourcing some a component of the final product to customize the product near the point or time of delivery (Lee and Billington, 1992) or to align incentives in some manner (Xu, 2005). Under any of these scenarios, the ultimate effect of DPD is to allow potential projects to avoid being discarded during the selection process because of inadequate in-house capabilities.

- **Leveraging Knowledge Brokers**. Sometimes the range of technologies and capabilities visible to the lead organization during the search process is felt to be insufficient, particularly if the firm is in an industry that is too 'inward-looking.' In these cases, involving a firm such as IDEO or other 'technological brokers' that arbitrage technological breakthroughs from one industry to another can increase the number of potential projects for consideration during the selection phase (Thomke and Nimgade, 2000; Hargadon, 2002).
- **Resolving Market Uncertainty**. MacCormack and Iansiti (1997) and MacCormack et al. (2001) describe an interesting form of distributed product development in which internet software is released early to the market to gather data on product performance (including bug detection), which is then used to further refine the product.[2] Von Hippel (1994) described this phenomenon extensively in his study of using lead users as sources of product innovation, which he has now extended into a broader study of the open source community (von Hippel, 2005). Hence, under open source networks, the criticality of selecting precisely the right concept initially is somewhat less, because the product can be modified based upon market response.

Hence, DPD can often have desirable effects upon search and selection. Of course, if this were not the case, it is questionable whether many organizations would ever bear the extra coordination and transformation effort associated with DPD.

5.2. Risks of DPD to search and selection

However, DPD also can impact the search and selection processes in a negative manner as well, as shown by the following list of issues.

- **Hold-up Costs**. One inevitable side-effect of distributing control over portions of the new product development process among multiple organizations is the potential for conflicts between the organizations involved (Anderson and Joglekar, 2007). Some of these conflicts will be caused by incentive incompatibilities similar to the well-known risk of hold-up costs (Alchian and Demsetz, 1972). Briefly, hold-up costs occur when a supplier extracts extra rents from a lead organization because the supplier's contribution to the final product cannot be easily replaced (Williamson,

---

[2] Hierarchical decomposition is a related mechanism for managing uncertainty in complex development processes. Such decomposition accounts for the presence of suppliers and distributed decision rights. A detailed discussion of the risks and the opportunities associated with hierarchical searches is offered in a chapter by Joglekar et al. (pp. 291–313) in this handbook.

1975; Klein et al., 1978). Sourcing to two or more suppliers can ameliorate this problem – although that solution exacerbates other coordination issues that will be discussed later in the paper. For these reasons, the potential for hold-up costs must be accounted for when choosing a final product concept during the selection process.

Interestingly, Handfield et al. (1999) note that hold-up costs may manifest themselves as a supplier's lack of innovation, once the threat of competition has been removed. In the long term, this can eventually result in technological lock-in by the lead organization into an inferior component technology if preventive steps are not taken (Gilbert and Cvsa, 2003). In this form, distributed product development can potentially lead to a restricted search process and, ultimately, an inferior product.

- **Information leakage**. Another risk of DPD is that information concerning key differentiating technologies (or perhaps some other vital information such as market projections) may leak, perhaps inadvertently, through a supplier to another one of its customers, perhaps one of the lead organization's competitors. In other words, leakage may improve the options available to the lead organization's competitors during their search processes. To some extent, information leakage can be ameliorated with appropriate contracts. An extreme form of leakage risk occurs when so much of the intellectual property behind a product is placed into the hands of competitors that it becomes relatively simple for a third party to buy those suppliers' components and re-integrate them into a competitive product (Anderson and Anderson, 2000). The story of the emergence of Compaq and the other PC clone companies using IBM's own suppliers to challenge IBM and eventually push it out of the PC industry it created is perhaps the best-known example of this phenomenon (Carroll, 1993). A related possibility is that the supplier itself will even take on this role as did the Japanese consumer electronics manufacturers in the 1960s and 1970s (Dertouzos et al., 1989).
- **Loss of Component Expertise**. Another risk that must be accounted for in the selection phase is that once a component is sourced outside an organization, that organization's capability to understand even the technology at a fundamental level may deteriorate. The effects of this are far-reaching, influencing future search, selection, and transformation processes. First, the ability of the lead organization to monitor the supplier becomes compromised, often leading to an increased component price to the lead organization (Parker and Anderson, 2002b). The other effect is that the reduced component expertise interferes with proper integration of the component into the product as a whole (Nellore and Balachandra,

2001; Anderson and Parker, 2002). For example, much of an automotive passenger's ride experience with respect to vibration, handling, and road feel is mediated by the seating system, which over the last decade most automotive firms have outsourced to suppliers like Leer and Johnson Controls to reduce costs (Bowens and Sedgwick, 2005). Because most of these automotive firms 'sold off' their employees who had expertise in seating systems to these suppliers, their capability to make informed cost-functionality judgments concerning seating systems has been impaired. For example, one could easily imagine an automotive firm purchasing a seating system for a vehicle that duplicates in its reduction of road vibration the functionality already present in its suspension system – with all the costs that might entail. One solution to both the costing and integration problems is partial outsourcing, that is producing some small portion of critical components in house while outsourcing the remainder to capture the bulk of component cost or other benefits associated with outsourcing. Toyota makes extensive use of this policy with respect to transmissions and other critical technologies (Fine and Whitney, 1999).

Developing the expertise to enable a partial outsourcing capability for a component once the expertise has dissipated from the lead organization can be extremely expensive (Anderson and Parker, 2002, 2005). However, this very expense creates a third potential benefit from partial outsourcing, because it creates a real option to pull the remainder of a critical component's design and production back in-house at some future date. Because of this threat, suppliers will presumably be more cooperative with the lead firm by, e.g., forgoing the exploitation of potential hold-up costs.

- **Architectural Risk.** Some risks related to product and organizational architecture from outsourcing can have implications for search. For example, while modularity can enable outsourcing that results in sourcing flexibility, Ethiraj and Levinthal (2004) point out that too much modularity can create its own problems. In particular, they show that excessive modularity can create a product architecture that inhibits discontinuous, radical innovation by limiting the potential combinations of new technology that may be examined in the future. We speculate here that architectural lock-in to a highly modular or well-developed, extant standard, such as UNIX, may partly explain why open-source networks seem to thrive best in highly modular or derivative architectures.

Hence, while lead organizations can derive many benefits in the search and selection processes from distributed product development, they also incur numerous risks, which need continual monitoring. For example, Toyota outsourced its automotive electronics capabilities to Denso (or Nippondenso as it was known then) in the 1950s, when electronics were confined to modular systems such as sound, lighting, and the starter. However, by the 1990s, automotive architecture had shifted from relying on mechanical and hydraulic controls and actuators to employing a critical – and ever-increasing – number of electronic substitutes. In short, electronics became integral to controlling the automotive system. Hence, Toyota hence began to employ partial outsourcing during the mid-1990s to rectify the product integration issues discussed resulting from loss of component expertise discussed earlier (Anderson and Parker, 2002, 2005).

6. Conclusion

In this chapter, we have developed a framework for understanding when to distribute product development, the operational challenges involved, and the potential consequences that might eventually result. A leitmotif of this discussion has been the peculiar challenge to coordination created by DPD environments. Because this area has been relatively neglected, we have sought to build a theory to explain this challenge. However, the argument proposed is merely a first step in an area that requires far more study.

In general, the entire area of DPD – with a few exceptions such as alliance partnerships and certain aspects of the economics of modularization – requires more research. However, the exact organizational mechanics of how the various organizations involved should be coordinated, particularly when different firms are involved in developing an integral product, seems a particularly fertile area for new research. For example, why information systems seem to be underemployed by organizations engaged in DPD (Anderson et al., 2004) seems particularly puzzling, yet of great interest. Another fruitful area of inquiry is the use and nature of boundary spanning personnel and tools (such as stage-gate processes, Quality Function Deployment, and Design Structure Matrices) to coordinate development efforts across multiple organizational boundaries. A third potential area lies in the realm of empirical studies, most of which have been restricted to developmental projects with incremental innovation inside well-established firms. Product integration and other aspects of DPD should also be explored when developing products with radical innovations, both in established firms and in entrepreneurial settings. This work will become more important in the future if the responsibility for product development continues to evolve from the vertically integrated firms of yesteryear to the virtually integrated supply chains of today and to – perhaps – the open network of user–suppliers of tomorrow.

References

Alchian, A.A. and H. Demsetz (1972). Production, Information Costs, and Economic Organization. American Economic Review 62(5): 777–795.

Allen, T.J. (1977). Managing the Flow of Technology. Cambridge, MA: MIT Press.

AMA (1997). Outsourcing: The AMA Survey. AMA Research Report. New York: American Management Association.

Ancona, D.G. and D.F Caldwell (1992). Demography and Design: Predictors of New Product Team Performance. Organization Science 3(3): 321–341.

Anderson, E.G. (2005). Personal communication.

Anderson, E.G. and M.A. Anderson (2000). Are Your Decisions Today Creating Your Future Competitors? Avoiding the Outsourcing Trap. The System Thinker 11(3): 1–5.

Anderson, E.G., Alison Davis-Blake, and Geoffrey G. Parker (2004). Managing Outsourced Product Design: The Effectiveness of Alternative Integration Mechanisms. Presented at the 2004 New Orleans, Louisiana: Academy of Management Conference.

Anderson, E.G. Jr., A. Davis-Blake, G.G. Parker (2006). Organizational Mechanisms to Manage Outsourcing during Product and Process Development. University of Texas Working Paper.

Anderson, E.G., A. Davis-Blake, and G.G. Parker (2007). Hypotheses Concerning the Effectiveness of Alternative Integration Mechanisms to Manage Outsourcing. University of Texas McCombs School of Business Working Paper.

Anderson, E.G. and G.G. Parker (2002). The Effect of Learning on the Make/Buy decision. Production and Operations Management 11(3): 313–329.

Anderson, E.G and G.G. Parker (2005). Partial Outsourcing and Linked Learning Processes. University of Texas Working Paper.

Anderson, Edward G. and Nitin Joglekar (2005). A Hierarchical Modeling Framework for Product Development Planning. Production and Operations Management 14(3): 344–361.

Anderson, Edward G. and Nitin Joglekar (2007). Risk Management, Opportunism, and Management Bias in Distributed Product Development. University of Texas Working Paper.

Aoshima, Y., K. Nobeoka, and Y. Takeda (2004). The Impact of 3d-CAD on New Product Development. Journal of Korean Economic Development 10(2): 65–89.

Argyres, N. (1999). The Impact of Information Technology on Coordination: Evidence from the B-2 "Stealth" Bomber. Organization Science 10: 162–180.

Baldwin, C.Y. and K.B. Clark (2000). Design Rules, Volume 1: The Power of Modularity. Cambridge, MA: MIT Press.

Bardhan, I., V. Krishnan, and S. Lin (2005). A Model to Measure the Business Value of Information Technology: The Case of Project and Information Work. University of Texas Working Paper, March 2005.

Beyer, J. and H.M. Trice (1993). The Cultures of Work Organizations. Englewood Cliffs, NJ: Prentice-Hall.

Blanchard, B.S. and W.S. Fabrycky (1998). Systems Engineering and Analysis (Third Edition). Prentice Hall, 1998: Eaglewood Cliffs, NJ.

Bonacorrsi, A. and C. Rossi (2003). Why Open-source Software Can Succeed. Research Policy 32: 1243–1258.

Boone, T. and R.Ganeshan (2001). The Impact of Information Technology on Learning in Professional Service Organizations. Journal of Operations Management 19(4): 485–495.

Bowens, G. and D. Sedgwick (2005). GM Takes Interior Work In-house. Automotive News 79(6155): 1, 26.

Browning, T.R. (1999). Designing System Development Projects for Organizational Integration. Systems Engineering 2(4): 217–225.

Browning, T.R. (2001). Applying the Design Structure Matrix to System Decomposition and Integration Problems: A Review and New Directions. IEEE Transactions on Engineering Management 48(3): 292–306.

Brynjolfsson, E. and L. Hitt (1998). Beyond the Productivity Paradox. Communications of the ACM 41(8): 49–55.

Carley, K.M. and Z. Lin (1997). A Theoretical Study of Organizational Performance under Information Distortion. Management Science 43(7): 976–977.

Carrol, G.R. (1993). A Sociological View on Why Firms Differ. Strategic Management Journal 14(4): 237–249.

Clark, K.B. (1985). The Interaction of Design Hierarchies and Market Concepts in Technological Evolution. Research Policy 14: 235–251.

Clark, K.B. and T. Fujimoto (1991). Product Development Performance: Strategy, Organization, and Management in the World Auto Industry. Boston, MA: Harvard Business School Press.

Cusumano, M.A. and R.W. Selby (1998). Microsoft Secrets: How the World's Most Powerful Software Company Creates Technology, Shapes Markets, and Manages People. New York: Simon & Schuster.

Cyert, R.M. (1991). Knowledge and Economic Development. Operations Research 39(1): 5–8.

Cyert, R. and J.G. March (1992). A Behavioral Theory of the Firm. 2nd Edition. New York: Blackwell.

Daft, R.L. and R.H. Lengel (1986). Organizational Information Requirements, Media Richness and Structural Design. Management Science 32(5): 554–571.

Davis-Blake, A., K.E. Dickson, J.P. Broschak, E.E. Gibson, F.J. Rodriquez, and T.A. Graham (1999). Owner/Contractor Organizational Changes: Phase II Report. Center for Construction Industry Studies, Report Number 2.

Das, A. and R. Narasimhan (2000). Purchasing Competence and Its Relationship with Manufacturing Performance. The Journal of Supply Chain Management (Spring 2000): 17–28.

Doz, Y (1996). The Evolution of Cooperation in Strategic Alliances. Strategic Management Journal 17(Summer): 55–83.

Dertouzos, M.L, R.K. Lester, and R.M. Solow (1989). Made in America: Regaining the Productive Edge. Cambridge, MA: MIT Press.

Drezner, D.W. (2004). The Outsourcing Bogeyman. Foreign Affairs 83(3): 22–34.

Ethiraj, S. and D.A. Levinthal (2004). Modularity and Innovation in Complex Systems. Management Science 50(2): 159–173.

Eppinger, S.D. and A.R.Chitkara (2006). The New Practice of Global Product Development. Sloan Management Review 47(4): 22–30.

Fine, C.H. and D. Whitney (1999). Is the Make-Buy Decision a Core Competence? In: Logistics in the Information Age, Moreno Muffatto and Kulwant Pawar (Eds.) Padova, Italy: Servizi Grafici Editoriali.

Fine, C.H. (1998). Clockspeed: Winning Industry Control in the Age of Temporary Advantage. New York: Perseus Books.

Fisher, M.L. (1997). What is the Right Supply Chain for Your Product? Harvard Business Review 75(March–April): 105–117.

Ford, D. and J. Sterman (1998). Dynamic Modeling of Product Development Processes. System Dynamics Review 14(1): 31–68.

Ford, D. and J. Sterman (2003). The Liar's Club: Concealing Rework in Concurrent Development. Concurrent Engineering: Research and Applications 11(3): 211–220.

Fung, V. and J. Magretta (1998). Fast, Global, and Entrepreneurial: Supply Chain Management Hong Kong Style: An Interview with Victor Fung. Harvard Business Review 76(5): 102–114.

Galbraith, J.R. (1973). Designing Complex Organizations. Boston, MA: Addison-Wesley.

Gilbert, S.M. and Viswanath Cvsa (2003). Strategic Commitment to Price to Stimulate Downstream Innovation in a Supply Chain. European Journal of Operational Research 150(3): 617–639.

Gomes, P. and N. Joglekar (2005). Linking Modularity with Problem Solving and Coordination Efforts. Boston University Working Paper.

Gomes, P., N. Joglekar, and S. Rosenthal (2005). Learning while Sourcing: Evidence of Productivity Gains in Coordinating Software Development. Academy of Management Annual Meeting Honolulu, HI.

Gordon, G.G. (1991). Industry Determinants of Organizational Culture. Academy of Management Review 16(2): 396–415.

Griffin, A. (1997). PDMA research on new product development practices: Updating trends and benchmarking best practices. Journal of Product Innovation Management 14(6): 429–458.

Griffin, A. and J.R. Hauser (1993). The Voice of the Customer. Marketing Science 12(1): 1–27.

Gulati, R.K. and S.D. Eppinger (1996). The coupling of Product Architecture and Organizational Structure Decisions. Working Paper No. 151, MIT International Center for Research on the Management of Technology, Cambridge, MA, May 1996.

Gulati, R., P.R. Lawrence, and P. Puranam (2005). Adaptation in Vertical Relationships: Beyond Incentive Conflict. Strategic Management Journal 26: 415–440.

Häcki, R. and J. Lighton (2001). The Future of the Networked Company. The McKinsey Quarterly (Fall 2001): 26–39.

Hameri, A.-P. and J. Nihtila (1997). Distributed New Product Development Project based on Internet and World-wide web: A Case Study. Journal of Product Innovation Management 14: 77–87.

Handfield, R.B., G.L. Ragatz, K.J. Petersen, and R.M. Monczka (1999). Involving Suppliers in New Product Development. California Management Review 42(1): 59–82.

Hannan, M.T. and J. Freeman (1984). Structural Inertia and Organizational Change. American Sociological Review 49(2): 149–164.

Hargadon, A.B (2002). Brokering Knowledge: Linking Learning and Innovation. Research in Organizational Behavior 24(1): 41–85.

Hauser, J. and D. Clausing (1988). The House of Quality. Harvard Business Review 66(3): 63–73.

Hayes, R.H. and S.C. Wheelwright (1984). Regaining Our Competitive Edge: Competing through Manufacturing. Hoboken, NJ: Wiley.

Henderson, R.M. and K.B. Clark (1990). Architectural Innovation: The Reconfiguration of Existing Product Technologies and the Failure of Established Firms. Administrative Science Quarterly 35: 9–30.

Hofstede, G. (1980). Culture's Consequences: International Difference in Work-Related Values. Beverly Hills, CA: Sage.

Huber, G.P. (1990). A Theory of the Effects of Advanced Information Technologies on Organizational Design, Intelligence, and Decision Making. Academy of Management Review 15(1): 47–71.

Iansiti, M. (1995a). Technology integration: Managing technological evolution in a complex environment. Research Policy 24(4): 521–542.

Iansiti, M. (1995b). Technology development and integration: An empirical study of the interaction between applied science and product development. IEEE Transactions on Engineering Management 42(3): 259–269.

Iansiti, M. (1998). Technology integration: Making critical choices in a dynamic world. Boston, MA: Harvard Business School Press.

Iansiti, M. and K.B. Clark (1994). Integration and Dynamic Capability: Evidence from Product Development in Automobiles and Mainframe Computers. Industrial and Corporate Change 3(3).

Iyer, B. and R.M. Gottlieb (2004). The Four-Domain Architecture: An Approach to Support Enterprise Architecture Design. IBM Systems Journal 43: 587–597.

Jaikumar, R. (1986). Massimo Menichetti. Harvard Business School Case, Case number 9-686-135.

Joglekar, N.R. and E.G. Anderson (2005). Distributed Innovation with Imperfect Progress Status Information. University of Texas Working Paper.

Joglekar, N. and S. Rosenthal (2003). Coordination of Design Supply Chains for Bundling Physical and Software Products. Journal of Product Innovation Management 20(5): 374–390.

Joglekar, N. and D. Whitney (1999). Automation Usage Pattern during Complex Electro Mechanical Product Development. CTPID Report, MIT, available at: esd.mit.edu/esd_books/whitney/whitney_online.html.

Klein, B., R.G. Crawford, and A.A. Alchian (1978). Vertical Integration, Appropriable Rents, and the Competitive Contracting Process. Journal of Law and Economics 21(2): 297–326.

Kogut, B. and U. Zander (1992). Knowledge of the Firm, Combinative capabilities, and the Replication of Technology. Organization Science 3(3): 383–397.

Kossiakoff, A. and W.N. Sweet (2003). Systems Engineering: Principles and Practice. Hoboken, NJ: Wiley.

Kusunoki, K., I. Nonaka, and A. Nagata (1998). Oraganizational Capabilities in Product Development of Japanese Firms: A Conceptual Framework and Empirical Findings. Organization Science 9(6): 699–718.

Lee, H.L. and C. Billington (1992). Managing Supply Chain Inventory: Pitfalls and Opportunities. Sloan Management Review 33(3): 65–73.

Loch, C. and B. Huberman (1999). A Punctuated-Equilibrium Model of Technology Diffusion. Management Science 45(2): 160–177.

Loch, C. and S. Kavadias (2002). Dynamic Portfolio Selection of NPD Programs Using Marginal Returns. Management Science 48(10): 1227–1241.

Loch, C. and C. Terwiesch (1998). Communication and Uncertainty in Concurrent Engineering. Management Science 44(8): 1032–1048.

Lorsch, J.W. and P.R. Lawrence (1972). Managing Group and Intergroup Relations. Homewood, IL: Richard D. Irwin.

MacCormack, A.D. and M. Iansiti (1997). Developing Products on Internet Time. Harvard Business Review 75(5): 108–117.

MacCormack, A., R. Verganti, and M. Iansiti (2001). Developing Products on "Internet Time": The Anatomy of a Flexible Development Process. Management Science 47(1): 133–150.

March, J.G. (1991). Exploration and Exploitation in Organizational Learning. Organization Science 2(1): 71–87.

Martin, J.A. and K.M. Eisenhardt (2003). Cross-business Synergy: Recombination, Modularity and the Multi-business Team. Academy of Management 2003 Best Paper Proceedings.

Martin, J. and C. Siehl (1983). Organizational Culture and Counterculture: An Uneasy Symbiosis. Organizational Dynamics 12(2): 52–64.

McGrath, M. and M. Iansiti (1998). Envisioning IT-enabled Innovation. PRTM: Insight Magazine (Fall/Winter 1998).

McIvor, R. and M. McHugh (2000). Partnership Sourcing: An Organization Change Management Perspective. Journal of Supply Chain Management 36(3): 12–20.

Nambisan, S. (2002). Designing Virtual Customer Environments for New Product Development: Toward a Theory. Academy of Management Review 27(3): 392–413.

Nellore, R. and R. Balachandra (2001). Factors Influencing Success in Integrated Product Development (IPD) Projects. IEEE Transactions On Engineering Management 48(2): 164–174.

Novak, S. and S.D. Eppinger (2001). Sourcing by Design: Product Complexity and the Supply Chain. Management Science 47(1): 189–204.

Parker, G.G. and E.G. Anderson (2002a). From Buyer to Integrator: The Transformation of The Supply Chain Manager in the Vertically Disintegrating Firm. Production and Operations Management 11(1): 75–91.

Parker, G.G. and E.G. Anderson (2002b). Supply Chain Integration: Putting Humpty-Dumpty Back Together Again. In: Future Directions in Supply Chain and Technology Management, Tonya Boone and Ram Ganeshan (Eds.) pp. 352–376. Amacom Press.

Prahalad, C.K. and G. Hamel (1990). The Core Competence of the Corporation. Harvard Business Review 68(3): 79–91.

Ramdas, K. (2003). Managing Product Variety: An Integrative Review and Research Directions. Production and Operations Management 12(1): 79–101.

Ramdas, K., M. Fisher, and K. Ulrich (2003). Managing Variety for Assembled Products: Modeling Component Systems Sharing. Manufacturing & Service Operations Management 5(2): 142–156.

Sanchez, R. and J.T. Mahoney (1996). Modularity, Flexibility, and Knowledge Management in Product and Organization Design. Strategic Management Journal 17(Winter Special Issue): 63–76.

Santoro, M.D. and A.K. Chakrabarti (2002). Firm Size and Technology Centrality in Industry–University Interactions. Research Policy 31(7): 1163–1180.

Schilling, M.A. and H.K. Steensma (2001). The Use of Modular Organizational Forms: An Industry-level Analysis. Academy of Management Journal 44(6): 1149–1168.

Scott, W. Richard (2003). Organizations. 5th edition. New York: Prentice-Hall.

Sethi, R., S. Pant, and A. Sethi (2003). Web-Based Product Development Systems Integration and New Product Outcomes: A Conceptual Framework. Journal of Product Innovation Management 20(1): 37–56.

Shan, W., G. Walker, and B. Kogut (1994). Interfirm Cooperation and Startup Innovation in the Biotechnology Industry. Strategic Management Journal 15(5): 387–394.

Siggelkow, N.A. and D.A. Levinthal (2003). Temporarily Divide to Conquer: Centralized, Decentralized, and Reintegrated Organizational Approaches to Exploration and Adaptation. Organization Science 14(6): 650–669.

Sinha, K.K. and A.H. Van de Ven (2005). Designing Work Within and Between Organizations. Organization Science 16(4): 389–408.

Smith, P. (1999). Preston Smith on the Pros and Cons of Outsourced Product Development. Product Development Best Practices Report. http://www.roundtable.com/PDBPR/Preston_outsourcing.html. Waltham, MA: The Management Roundtable.

Sobrero M. and E.B. Roberts (2001). The Trade-off between Efficiency and Learning in Interorganizational Relationships for Product Development. Management Science 47(4): 493–511.

Sosa, M.E., S. Eppinger, M. Pich, D.G. McKendrick, and S.K. Stout (2002). Factors that Influence Technical Communication in Distributed Product Development: An Empirical Study in the Telecommunications Industry. IEEE Transactions on Engineering Management 49(1): 45–58.

Sosa, M.E and S.D. Eppinger, C.M Rowles (2004). The Misalignment of Product Architecture and Organizational Structure in Complex Product Development. Management Science 50(12): 1674–1689.

Steward, D.V. (1981). The Design Structure System: A method for Managing the Design of Complex Systems. IEEE Transactions on Engineering Management 28: 71–74.

Terwiesch, C. and Y. Xu (2006). Economic Models for Open Innovation Systems and Multi-agent Problem Solving. Wharton School working paper.

Thomke, S. (2006). Capturing the Real Value of Innovation Tools. Sloan Management Review 47(4): 25–32.

Thomke, S., V. Krishnan, and A. Nimgade (1998). Product Development at Dell Computer Corporation. Harvard Business School Case number 9-699-010.

Thomke, S. and A. Nimgade (2000). IDEO Product Development. Harvard Business School Case, Case number 9-600-143.

Thomke, S. and A. Nimgade (2001). Siemens AG: Global Development Strategies (A). Harvard Business School Case No. 602062.

Thomke, S. and D. Reinertsen (1998). Agile Product Development: Managing Development Flexibility in Uncertain Environments. California Management Review 41(1): 8–31.

Tushman, M.L. and D.A. Nadler (1978). Information Processing as an Integrating Concept in Organizational Design. Academy of management Review 3(3): 613–624.

Von Hippel, E. (1994). The Sources of Innovation. Oxford: Oxford University Press.

Von Hippel, E. (2005). Democratizing Innovation. Cambridge, MA: MIT Press.

Von Krogh, G. and E. von Hippel (2006). The High Promise of Research on Open Source Software. Forthcoming in Management Science.

Wernerfelt, B. (1984). A Resource-Based View of the Firm. Strategic Management Journal 5(2): 171–180.

Whitney, D.E. (1995). State of the Art in the United States of CAD Methodologies for Product Development. CTPID Report, MIT (esd.mit.edu/esd_books/whitney/whitney_online.html).

Williamson, O.E. (1975). Markets and Hierarchies: Analysis and Antitrust Implications. New York: Free Press.

Xu, Xiaohui (2005). Managing Vertical and Horizontal Supply Chain Relationships in the Absence of Formal Contracts. Ph.D. Dissertation. University of Texas Department of Management.

Yassine, A., N. Joglekar, D. Braha, S. Eppinger, D. Whitney (2003). Information Hiding in Product Development: The Design Churn Effect. Research in Engineering Design 14(3): 145–161.

Zellmer-Bruhn, M.E. (2003). Interruptive Events and Team Knowledge Acquisition. Management Science 49 (4): 514–528.

11 Hierarchical planning under uncertainty: Real options and heuristics

Nitin R. Joglekar, Nalin Kulatilaka, and Edward G. Anderson Jr.

Abstract

Many development organizations set up a hierarchy of planning levels for making and revising complex product development decisions: strategic, tactical, and operational. This hierarchy enables modular exploitation of capital, labor, and product markets, which can improve decision making by reducing the organizational and cognitive complexities faced by managers. Modularity also creates real options for exploiting these three markets. Initially, some of these options may only be revealed at lower levels of the hierarchy. However, to properly recognize and exploit these options, all levels must be able to conduct experimentation and make decisions regarding them. The actual decision-making process differs across levels not only in its sources of uncertainty but also in its frequency, objectives, and information available. We argue that hierarchical options and the use of heuristics allow effective implementation of product development planning processes because these options *speed up value propagation, extend search spaces*, and *enhance learning opportunities*. We also identify several limitations of hierarchical product development planning, primarily due to the modular exploitation of new product development processes: competency traps, incentive incompatibility, information loss, and increased organizational inertia within and across levels of decision making. We end this chapter by suggesting avenues for further empirical and analytical research in this area.

1. Introduction

Complex and uncertain product development processes are often modularized into multiple levels of decision making. This is done to exploit a vast variety of innovation capabilities distributed hierarchically within a firm and across its network of suppliers and partners. A 'hierarchy' refers to a system that is composed of interrelated subsystems, in which decisions in certain subsystems are subordinated to decisions in other parts of the system. 'Modularization' in this context refers to the decomposition of organizational and technical decisions into smaller blocks and at different levels, such that the dependencies between these blocks are reduced (Simon, 1969; Galbraith, 1974; Williamson, 1975; Thompson et al., 1991; Eppinger et al., 1994; Sanchez and Mahoney, 1996; Baldwin and Clark, 2000). Often, a reduction in organizational and cognitive complexity results in more effective, e.g., speedy and profitable, decision making at each level. The three levels of decision making generally encountered by most product development organizations are strategic, tactical, and operational. Managers at each level work on different objectives, face different types of uncertainties and constraints, and manipulate different decision variables at different intervals of time. Decisions across levels are coordinated through a multi-level process that we term as 'hierarchical product development planning' (HPDP) process.

The benefit from retaining flexibility for putting an alternative course of action into play, at any one level of decision making, is termed an option. In this chapter, we argue that multi-level decision processes create 'hierarchical options' for generating and realizing value. We define hierarchical options as flexible decisions that are nested through path dependency (i.e., options that create options). In the hierarchical setting, options associated with higher level decisions are of valuable only if intermediate/lower level decision makers are able to observe and act on uncertainty, independent of the higher level decision-making process, and then communicate their actions in an efficient manner to other (higher/lower) levels of decision making.

These efficiencies play a central role in the development of three insights offered by our argument: hierarchical options in R&D processes can *enlarge search spaces, speed up value propagation*, and set up opportunities for active learning through deliberate *'macro-micro' information exchanges*. However, such a hierarchical decision structure does not lend itself to global optimization while computing these options. Hence, the best available methodologies for addressing the options embedded in this decision structure, as well as for understanding the organizational choices that lie beneath it, require suitable approximations for the decisions made at multiple levels. Managers typically resort to heuristics to cope with these issues.

The goals for this chapter are to introduce the notion of hierarchical options and allied heuristics, to point to potential insights uniquely associated with this view of new product development (NPD) planning, and then to delineate the organizational and analytical research opportunities that are a consequence of this view.

Our chapter is organized as follows. In Section 2, we provide a stylized example. We draw upon this example throughout our subsequent discussion to illustrate key issues and insights associated with hierarchical planning.

In Section 3, we summarize relevant new product development (NPD) literature on the benefits and limitations of hierarchical planning. In Section 4, we outline a framework that allows global coordination of local options. In Section 5, we draw upon Kogut and Kulatilaka's (2001) stylized model for assessing options at a single level of planning. This model links switching costs with technological and organizational learning and shows that options are effective in accounting for the inertial effects associated with underlying organizational decisions. In Section 6, we extend Kogut and Kulatilaka's idea to multiple levels within our framework by introducing the concept of hierarchical options. Search and value appropriation issues and opportunities associated with hierarchical options are outlined in Section 7. We end this chapter by summarizing research and application opportunities.

2. Stylized example

Imagine an in-line skates manufacturer who produces a portfolio of skating products specialized for different markets, which are differentiated by consumer size, skill levels, skating surfaces, and activities (e.g., hockey versus skiing or recreational use). Senior managers of this firm meet every few months (or annually) to assess the portfolio mix and make strategic choices about platform architectures, budget allocations, and 'go, no-go' decisions for each development project within this portfolio. Their objective is to maximize firm value by looking at the portfolio in terms of profits and anticipated shareholder value. Major sources of uncertainty for this strategic process are the demand in each market, the readiness of various technologies, and the aggregate amount of resources – budgets and personnel with various skill sets, such as mechanical designers or sales specialists – needed by each project. The firm, of course, has only a finite set of resources to allocate. Hence senior managers need to make choices such as, develop in-line skates either for high-end consumers (who may interested, e.g., in new technologies such as shock absorbing liner pads) or for the mass market (which wants basic functionality at a minimal cost). Alternately, as a stretch move, they may wish to develop and sell wheels for toy scooters (which, though made of similar materials, are larger in diameter than those for in-line skates) with an ultimate aim of producing the entire scooter. Alternatively, they might attempt to change the architecture of an in-line skate wheel to permit integral disk braking at each wheel or some other integral brake-on-wheel system rather than the entirely distinct and separate heel-braking system in use today.

Middle managers meet every month (or every quarter) and create value by making tactical decisions about accessing the labor market for skilled developers. They then try to match aggregate in house and outside development resources with individual project needs. Their objectives involve maximizing resource utilization and nurturing needed capabilities (such as polymer design for wheels, boot design capabilities, brake system design, wheel chassis design, and shock absorbing liner design). These capability decisions are subject to uncertainties resulting from variations in aggregate productivity and changes in the labor market. Aggregate productivity can fluctuate based on whether an outsourced labor pool is being accessed and whether generalists or specialists are conducting these tasks.

At the operational level, individual project managers try to create value by maximizing the desired technical performance of each product while minimizing either cost or lead-time, or some combination of both. Project managers can create, crash, delete, or schedule tasks. For example, if they develop the new integral disk braking concept to improve ease and effectiveness of braking, they will need to devise new tests to determine what level of novice can use them most effectively, whether they hamper experienced in-line skaters, and whether the wheel speed-handling tradeoff for any given wheel hardness is affected in the face of performance and resource uncertainty.

Decisions at each level take the overall planning process into various path-dependent scenarios: for instance, if the in-line skates firm decides to follow the integral brake-on-wheel route, they then could introduce electronic sensors to improve braking action using an anti-locking brake (ABS) system. However, that implies that they must also hire electronics engineers to implement the controls. Hence, in the short term, introducing the electronics into the skates and changing the mechanics of the braking system will likely drive up the cost and hence the price for a specific product offering, which may lead to a loss of market share. However, over the longer term, the electronic design effort might create skill sets and open up other options. Examples of lower level options in this case are the use of harder plastics for the wheels. Hierarchical options (i.e., decisions at one level creating path dependent multi-level choices) associated with this scenario include:

1. The development of integral brake-on-wheel technology combined with electronics controls may create a decisive performance advantage that could enhance entry prospects at the high end into the related markets of skateboards and scooters.
2. The ability to outsource (through aggregate planning) electronic aspects of wheel development for each existing product might reduce costs and provide access to new markets, such as video games based on electronic skates or special skates for handicapped children, which will change the strategic planning of the portfolio dramatically.

This example illustrates path dependencies that link disparate types of information structures and uncertainties across levels of decision making. Such path dependences characterize many NPD scenarios because goals, task structures, and boundaries not only *evolve* during NPD planning processes;

the NPD processes in fact *create* additional goals, structures, and boundaries that govern the subsequent decision processes.

3. Literature[1]

Hierarchical planning processes reflect the organizational realities in many industries. Hierarchical structures reduce planning complexity through modular management of a network of NPD decisions (Wheelwright and Clark, 1992; Ulrich and Eppinger, 2000; Thomke, 2003a). Detailed examples of multiple levels of planning hierarchies are available in a diverse set of firms, e.g., General Motors (Clark and Fujimoto, 1991), Hewlett-Packard (Parker and Anderson, 2002), Ericsson (Miranda, 2003), and Frito-Lay (Anderson, 2004). It is a common practice in these scenarios to hide information such that managers at each level are presented with a parsimonious view of the planning problem that is as relevant as possible to their immediate objectives. This decomposition allows for effective search at each level of planning. Hierarchy also enables modular and efficient, e.g., speedy, exploitation of design-related uncertainties in the capital, product, and labor markets (Baldwin and Clark, 2000) and creates real options similar to those outlined in the in-line skates example. Further, some NPD organizations build in the ability to conduct experimentation (Thomke, 2003b) and decision making at each level of planning. The hierarchical, real-option view of the planning problem comes with certain shortcomings.

Figure 11.1 highlights perhaps the most important – coordination of local and system wide decisions.[2] The left-hand side depicts reinforcing actions

[1] There is a large body of relevant engineering design literature, grounded in research on artificial intelligence, that explores the hierarchical tradeoffs associated with engineering design decisions (Sriram, 1997). This literature addresses a variety of decomposition and integration techniques, computational environments, and associated heuristics. Insights from this literature describe policies that can improve the technical performance of product under development. There is also a growing body of process modeling literature that addresses optimization of process performance, such as minimization of development time and risks (see Browning and Ramasesh 2007). However, their level of analysis, stakeholders and their objectives differ from the strategic, tactical, and operational planning processes described in this chapter. Both these bodies of literatures have been excluded from our discussions for ease of exposition.

[2] This problem is materially equivalent to the coordination problem outlined in two other chapters in this handbook: *Coordination and Information Exchange* by Loch and Terwiesch, and *The Impact of Outsourcing on Product Integration and Other Organizational Challenges in Distributed Product Development Environments* by Anderson et al. Loch and Terwiesch argue that decomposition and hierarchy are relevant choices for handling the coordination problem that is so complex that it cannot be 'analyzed' but a satisfying solution must be searched. Anderson et al. argue that the coordination burden enlarges and becomes more complex with the onset of distributed decision making, and a variety of path dependencies can be created in many types of R&D sourcing scenarios under uncertainty. A fuller treatment of path dependencies and nested R&D options analysis remains beyond the scope this chapter.

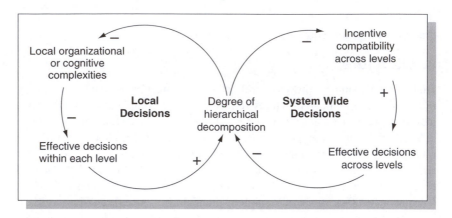

Figure 11.1
Tradeoff between local and system wide effectiveness.

within local decisions, i.e., increase in local effectiveness due to hierarchical decomposition raises the degree of hierarchical decomposition in NPD processes. The right-hand side of this figure depicts a balancing loop: hierarchical decomposition leads to incompatible incentive structures and reduces information exchange across levels. Local decision makers may not communicate appropriate information to other levels of decision making because of incentive incompatibly. Owing to goal incongruence, other managers may simply fail to understand the value of resulting real options even when appropriate information is communicated. Hence, managers must coordinate the local and system-wide effects of their actions. Hierarchical decisions, while locally (i.e., within one level) effective, probably will be sub-optimal for the overall process.

Typically, hierarchical decompositions of stochastic search problems are not amenable to closed-form solutions (Dempster et al., 1981). Solutions of these problems would require access to a variety of data that are usually not available. The absence of appropriate, detailed data, the existence of multi-level uncertainties, and path-dependence created by the interaction of uncertainties with various decisions may explain why many NPD portfolio managers apparently forego the advantages of quantitative models in favor of a set of integrated heuristics across levels. These practices typify situations in which systematic analysis and oversight of hierarchical coordination issues can improve the efficacy of NPD processes.

4. Coordination of hierarchical plans

Ruefli (1971) has argued that differing forecast horizons and levels of uncertainty can lead to a decomposition of product development problems into a hierarchy of rolling horizon decision-support models of linked sub-problems.

The term 'rolling horizon' refers to repeated, often periodic review of decisions. Indeed, hierarchical approaches have proven to be quite successful in reducing the complexity of production and inventory management problems through stage-wise decomposition of decisions and revelation of uncertainty (Graves, 1982). However, such a wide set of variables, planning horizons, and dimensions of environmental uncertainty among various planning levels makes global optimization extremely difficult, if not impossible. In addition, even if it were possible, such a global model, as Bitran and Tirupati (1993) suggest, would not be appropriate because it would not respond to management needs at each level and would indeed inhibit each management level's interaction with the model.

Hierarchical methodologies have been applied beyond production management problems into the realm of management of multiple projects (Herroelen and Leus, 2004; Hans et al., 2004). Conventional project management problems, witnessed in settings such as shipbuilding or in consulting firms, differ from the production problem in the sense that there is little opportunity to deploy inventory as buffers and the productive capacity is closely tied with labor productivity. Anderson and Joglekar (2005) showcase the existence of multiple uncertainties and offer a HPDP framework that accounts for these uncertainties and decisions. Models based on this framework would reflect the decision-making reality of many networked product development projects. This framework is reviewed next.

Anderson and Joglekar (2005) point out that NPD decisions in many organizations have been disaggregated into four different but linked levels – strategic, tactical, operational, and infrastructural planning. The frequency of reviews, choice of objectives, decisions variables, and skill sets of the decision makers at each level are different. The decisions at each level inform each other through feedback mechanisms shown by arrows in Fig. 11.2. The framework identifies typical constrains, decisions, feedbacks, objective functions, uncertainties and recourses at each level. Users can set up analytical models and linked spreadsheets based on this framework to explore the impact of local (i.e., within level) decisions on the overall NPD process performance.

Recall from the in-line skates example that during strategic planning, the senior (level 1) managers select and shape the project portfolio so that the profits can be maximized. Tactical managers (level 2) are concerned with labor markets, capacity acquisition, allocation, and utilization across all the projects. The operational (level 3) managers are charged with the fastest and high quality execution of individual projects. Consequently, the nature of uncertainty and frequency of planning are also quite different between the three levels. The quarterly (in some cases annual) strategic planning processes address uncertainly in the market (price and quantity to be sold), along with suitable choices of product and process technologies in aggregate. The monthly (or quarterly) tactical planning exercises are subject to fluctuations in

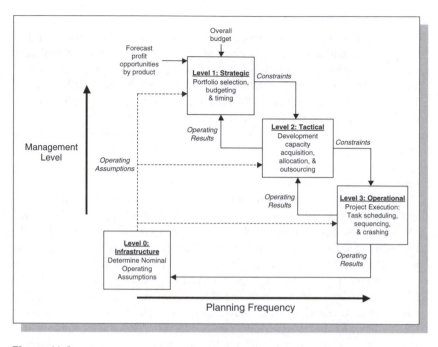

Figure 11.2
Hierarchical product development planning framework (Anderson and Joglekar, 2005).

the demand and availability of skilled labor. Individual projects are reviewed daily (or weekly) to deal with task execution uncertainty.

NPD literature recognizes the importance of taking a contingent view of development problems. Bhattacharya et al. (1998) and MacCormack et al. (2001) have proposed frameworks to manage contingencies at any one level from concept to execution. Loch and Kavadias (2002) have provided a framework for linking resource dependence into NPD portfolios. They have also explored recourse with respect to a single scarce resource (Kavadias and Loch, 2003). The introduction of hierarchical planning, with multiple uncertainties and decisions, opens up the possibility of path dependent evolution of decisions that are linked across levels. Since the decisions at any one level of planning feed into the uncertainty and shapes the options available to next level, the overall process creates nested options. Some of these options may evolve relatively quickly while others options may evolve only more gradually. For instance, in the in-line skates example, the decision to introduce electronics might affect pricing and the mix within the portfolio in a matter of months. On the other hand, hiring full time electronics engineers and building electronic design capability may be more gradual. In the next section, we review the literature on single level options and the evolution of organizational capability based on these options.

5. Search for value: A primer on flat options

Product development is a creative process in which development teams search for value by trying different alternatives (Baldwin and Clark, 2000). For instance engineers, at the in-line skates firm in our example, can modify the design of wheels by integrating brakes (a.k.a. an action) by using different types of electronic controls. Each one of these actions will lead to different follow-on actions, e.g., the choice for the hardness of the wheel material. The team is interested in comparing the values of alternative courses or sequences of actions.

In this section, we summarize the relation between options and organizational capability put forth by Kogut and Kulatilaka (2001). In doing so, we introduce key concepts associated with real options: dynamic objective functions, switching costs, and competency traps. For ease of exposition, we assume that managers are only faced with a single level of decision making, and in this instance, they are only charged with strategic (Level 1 in Fig. 11.2) planning. Because these concepts relate to a single level, we refer to them as flat options (FO). These concepts will be extended to multiple levels of planning in the next section.

The strategic view of value depends on three sets of variables: capability, switching costs, and uncertainty (c, δ, θ). The goal is to capture value in terms of maximizing the expected profit. The decision variable (c) is a multi-dimensional construct. It may consist of the schedule for launching products into the market place, product differentiation, technology availability, and the ambition levels. Uncertainty is captured by random disturbances to the input and the output (e.g., technology readiness, price, market demand, etc.). Switching costs or options in this case can be quantified for each recourse variable (e.g., extraordinary budgets needed, launch delays or cancellations, etc.). Uncertainty (θ) could reflect the variation in the technology or market price.

Figure 11.3 captures the decision tree in term switching costs and the elapsed time. The squares in Fig. 11.3 denote strategic (i.e., Level 1) decisions. Initial decisions open up options after the technology and market uncertainties are revealed. We also depict the value function on the right-hand side of the Fig. 11.3. Such a depiction assumes that the ordinates on the left-hand side for the figure (δ) can be suitably be transformed into a value function. We illustrate switching costs evolution by assuming that only the blade technology can change initially (e.g., move from one hardness to another) and only the organization (e.g., increasing engineering productivity by adjusting the plastic processing technology) changes later.

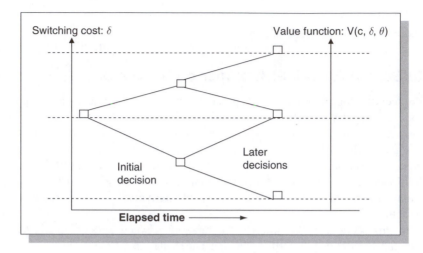

Figure 11.3
A decision tree for evolution of switching cost and value function.

Let the in-line skates firm have a choice of two portfolios of capabilities: L and H. Capability L refers to an existing portfolio with low variety and H represents an alternate portfolio with higher variety of in-line skates products. Figure 11.4 shows a stylized profit function that is associated with switching costs for this firm. Notice that δ is the switching cost associated with the price $\theta = \theta'$. A special case is $\theta = \theta^S$, when the switching cost is zero. If $\theta > \theta^S$, then the firm switches from L to H.

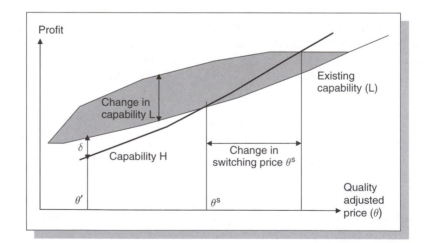

Figure 11.4
Switching with learning effects.

Switching is not a static decision. For example, in the in-line skates firm, managers can make to some investments in organizational learning to improve technology L. That is, the profit function can be enhanced by adjusting the profit curve for capability L, as shown in by top edge for the gray area in Fig. 11.4. The anticipation of improvements (either due to induced or autonomous learning effects) leads to the gray band of relations for existing capabilities, termed as inertial effect. This inertia increases the switching price θ^S as shown in the figure.

A dynamic analysis can take into account the impact of a current switching decision on all future switching decisions. By staying with current technology L, inertia can build up and the firm can become increasingly more competent in existing capabilities. The danger remains, of course, that the price θ can suddenly jump and cross a critical threshold in which the firm's competence is no longer profitable. In a sense, the accumulated learning in the old techniques is a 'competency trap,' that could be captured in terms of a 'explore or exploit' tradeoff (March, 1991). For example, in the in-line skates firm, enhancing the knowledge of technology from the current level (L) may increase switching costs to the next technology (H), such as brake-on-wheel or electronics. However, this would make the firm vulnerable to losses – even if the firm continues to improve its performance through learning processes – if the price suddenly increases beyond the critical value (θ^S) shown in figure.

To speed its transition to the new technology, the firm may decide proactively to allocate funding to exploration by experimenting with new techniques. This diversion of resources slows down its accumulation of learning with the current technology. At the same time, it increases the value of the option to switch to new capabilities by lowering the costs of switching. For instance, Ford and Sobek (2005) have used a real options framework to explain the organizational choices underlying the 'Second Toyota Paradox,' i.e., how delaying early decisions across various phases of NPD results in a robust and fast development process at the Toyota Motor Company.

6. Multi-level search: Hierarchical options

The presence of hierarchy, with multiple uncertainties and decision makers, leads to nested situations: options can create options. Some of these options are initiated at the lower level within the hierarchy. For instance, in the in-line skates example, the possibility of using electronic controls within skates can only be put into play by an operational team (Level 3) with hands on involvement of design engineers. Over the long haul, this action can create a product platform (e.g., use of the blade sensing features to develop safe transportation for handicapped children) that is aimed at a new market niche. Exercising this option might require that Level 1 planners explore this platform concept through market research.

In order to benefit from some course of action at an intermediate level, the upper decision-making level has to keep open the possibility of alternative courses of action. The high level options are of value, only if the intermediate or lower level decision makers face and resolve uncertainty independent of higher level planning processes, and then communicate the status efficiently upwards (or further downwards). This independence allows low-level decision makers and engineers to act quickly, when an opportunities is noticed, without waiting for a scheduled high-level review.

Hierarchical or nested options have been explored in the finance (Geske, 1977; Kulatilaka, 1994; Amram and Kulatilaka, 1999) and computer science (Russell and Norvig, 2002) literatures. However, these literatures have typically been restricted to situations where agents across hierarchies are working on identical objectives. We have argued in Section 4 that the objective functions and nature of available information for the three decision levels in HPDP differ due to the modular decomposition of decision-making process. In this section, we discuss the set up for a stylized hierarchical options problem and explain why nesting and incentive incompatibility might occur within this stylized set up. For ease of exposition, we restrict our attention to the interaction between Level 1 (strategic) and Level 2 (tactical) decisions.

One way to think about the timing of these two decision-making processes is as follows; let the tactical decisions be made at least once during the duration between two successive sets of strategic reviews. The objective during a strategic review is profit maximization. For example, the strategic review at the in-line skates firm will alter the product capabilities, while addressing capital market considerations (e.g., borrowing money). The objective for the tactical planning process is to maximize the utilization of internal resources (Holt et al., 1960; Gaimon and Thmpson, 1984; Anderson, 2001).

6.1. Nested evolution of options

In Section 4, we have pointed out that the uncertainties and switching costs associated with each level of the hierarchy differ substantially. For instance, in the in-line skates example, level capabilities are characterized in terms of aggregate development projects and technologies that can be presented into the product market for a price. The strategic planners are making decisions about completing (or canceling) a variety of these capabilities. The switching costs between low and high variety of product in this instance result from investments in aggregate technologies such as electronic versus mechanical controls, as well as the investments that will be needed for repositioning the brand. That is, options such as repositioning the brand or access to new types of markets are usually easier to recognize at this level, than at other levels of planning.

On the other hand, tactical planning managers are not expected to think about branding and product market pricing considerations. They are focused on managing labor market issues, such as switching between mechanical design and electronic design skills. Their switching costs will include considerations such as outsourcing, learning, and cannibalization of disaggregate technology know-how. Recognition of options such as repositioning of skill sets through training or multi-tasking usually takes place at this level of planning.

In certain settings, such as a start up firm developing its first product, the CEO and the board can and will look at all the options (e.g., brand repositioning, skill set, and detailed decisions on product architecture). However, in most development settings such an evaluation is not feasible. Managers at the higher level would simply lack the know-how needed to recognize even lower level options, unless these options are aggregated and translated into a language that they can understand. This translation takes place either through a formal specification or through existing mental models within the firm. These options are nested because there exists certain mapping between the decisions at the strategic level, e.g., c (process capability to develop a suite of electronic controls in a cost effective manner) and the decisions at the lower level, e.g., S (the engineering skills needed to run verilog electronic design tools correctly).

The strategic planners would be informed by the tactical planners about the aggregate ability of skilled engineers to deliver a particular mix of in-line skates controller designs over the next macro-planning horizon. Given time, the knowledge about the use of tools will evolve, and engineers can create new software libraries, whenever the tactical (i.e., micro) planners update their decisions. Since the micro planners will hold at least one review before the macro-planning meeting, these planners can shape the aggregate capability in terms the aggregate cost of a suite of electronic controls. The reverse is also true. At each review, the strategic planners can change the resource constraints, e.g., total amount of engineers who can be on the payroll. Thus, the options decisions of two levels of planning are nested.

6.2. Incentive compatibility

Two separate mechanisms can create incentive problems. As long as either the switching costs or the uncertainties across the levels are not equivalent, using optimal decisions based on any one set of options will yield suboptimal decisions for the other. Alternatively, we can assume that the mapping between the aggregate and disaggregate capabilities (c and S) are not unique. This is likely to be the case because typically, returns to scale are not fixed while conducting innovative tasks; and the relationship between the competencies and the skill set are based on mental models and aggregate assumptions.

Moreover, the budget constraints established by strategic planners are likely to be binding, where as the reverse may not be true. Thus, even if the effects of uncertainty in the two models were equivalent, the optimal choices made by one level of planning will not yield optimal results for the other level.

Such incompatibilities affect managerial behavior. Seasoned middle managers recognize that they need to look beyond their own incentives. For instance, lower level managers are subject to exogenous budget constraints. These constraints are established based on a zero-sum game for resource allocation at higher levels of planning. Hence, these managers expend considerable efforts trying to observe and even anticipate changes at the higher levels. In effect, these managers are playing *linked games* due to the hierarchical nature of the decision structure (Baldwin and Clark, 2003).

7. Discussion

We describe research issues associated with hierarchical options along two dimensions: analytical and heuristic search opportunities. This is followed by a discussion of empirical opportunities available for studying hierarchical NPD processes.

7.1. Analytical features

We now discuss the following features for hierarchical options:

- Size of search landscape
- Speed of value propagation
- Potential for reinforcement learning

To illustrate the search landscape, we have drawn Fig. 11.5 by superimposing Level 2 (i.e., tactical) options on the Level 1 (strategic) decisions tree developed in Fig. 11.3. Consistent with our notation, the Level 1 value function V is specified in terms of capability c, switching cost δ, and uncertainty θ. Level 2 value function J is specified in terms of skills S, and corresponding switching cost γ, and uncertainty w. For ease of depiction, we assume that Level 2 decisions, shown as diamonds, are made twice as frequently as the Level 1 decision. We also exclude Level 3 decisions from this figure. When Level 1 and Level 2 arches and nodes are aligned, we only show Level 1 decision structure. While the objective functions and the decision variables for the two levels are different (as shown by the ordinates on the left- and the right-hand sides), we assume that mappings between underlying variables can be established. For instance, S (i.e., skill set) is a Level-2 variable and competency (c) is a Level-1 variable.

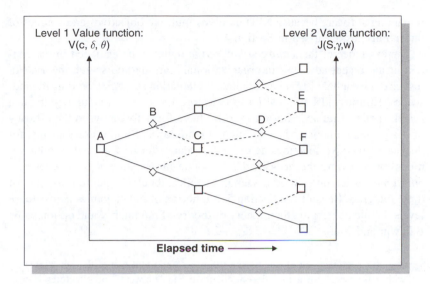

Level 1 Value function:
V(c, δ, θ)

Level 2 Value function:
J(S,γ,w)

Elapsed time ──────➤

Figure 11.5
Multi-level decision tree with hierarchical options.

During the planning process, managers at the in-line skates firm make projections, based on past performance, about how the available stock of skills (e.g., mechanical and electrical engineers) would contribute to product competence at the firm (e.g., the degree of technology readiness at next stage of planning), i.e., S maps into c, and hence it can be linked into the value function V. The availability of an enlarged value landscape at Level 1 is established by the inclusion of nodes C, D, as well as E: A_B_C_D_E as one course of action and A_B_C_D_F is an alternative course in Fig. 11.5. The mapping between the underlying constructs at the two search levels may be non-linear and each one of these options must be tested for feasibility.

Hierarchical searches have been an established part of the analysis and planning tool kits within the computer science literature (Russell and Norvig, 2002). For instance, many heuristics have been implemented in video gaming software for searching value landscapes over a coarse and a fine grid concurrently. Within the software search contexts, it has been shown that the value propagation, i.e., search for the maximum value for $V(c, \delta, \theta)$, speeds up with the introduction of hierarchical options (Barto and Mahadevan, 2003). This literature also illustrates heuristics that allow for active learning through reinforcement, i.e., swapping macro-micro information across the coarse and finely meshed search grids. We argue that similar acceleration in the propagation of value as well as the macro-micro learning opportunities will be available in the context drawn up in Fig. 11.5. However, assessment of options in NPD settings is more complex than reuse of algorithms deployed in gaming software because NPD involves multiple objectives and sources of uncertainty, as discussed in Section 4.

The existence of this *enlarged landscape* ought to be analyzed in the context of the recent advances in organizational learning and search theory. For instance, Levinthal (1997) has simulated adaptation strategies on rugged landscapes. Ethiraj and Levinthal (2004) explore the role of modularity in such search spaces. Erat and Kavadias (2004) have formally analyzed the efficacy of design search policies in such rugged landscapes. Similar assessments, for disparate objective functions across levels, can offer new analytical opportunities for assessing the *acceleration* in value propagation and for exploring *micro-macro* learning. It is essential to think about the gaming aspects of these searches. Recall from Section 5, the notion of linked games across these levels. While developing their theory of theory of modularity and option value Baldwin and Clark (2003) have argued that:

> 'Our task becomes that of identifying the most important games that are played "within the walls" of a modular architecture and "between" architectures. For each game, we need to explain how equilibrium gets constructed (or, in some cases, does not); what value is created; how it is captured and distributed; and what beliefs must be fostered and fulfilled.'

That is, it is not merely enough to endow the value creation landscape with additional layers of search space. We argue that it is crucial to admit multiple agents, with differing objectives and beliefs, within search heuristics that are implemented to explore this space.

7.2. Heuristics

Currently, heuristics are developed at a single level and then extended to multiple levels by trial and error. For instance, the in-line skates firm might allow its engineers to search for the electronic options, if the electronics can reduce the development time for all the products by at least 20% while increasing the firm's cost by no more than 10%. At a higher level of planning, the firm may be willing to take a larger ($\sim$20%) cost burden, if there is at least 50% chance that a new market segment, with $50MM annual revenues, can be developed. Such guidelines or heuristics may work well because they are easy to communicate. Decision making at all levels can be accelerated by these heuristics because managers are asked to focus on choices that are relevant to their sphere of influence.

Kogut and Kulatilaka (2001) argue that a good heuristic has four qualities: it is easy to use, easy to communicate, provides a better direction than those currently employed, and motivates people who have to implement the strategy. For instance, the Boston Consulting Group growth matrix (with stars, dogs, question mark, and the cash cow as the ideograph that indicate alternate strategies) is an effective heuristic. It requires only two inputs: market growth and relative positions. Moreover, these ideographs are comprehensible and memorable.

Examples of simple, easy to communicate, heuristics in NPD settings are: 3M's Level 1 mandate, '40% of its sales revenues from products launched within the past four years.' Corresponding Level 2 mandate indicates, 'Scientists are encouraged to spend 15% of their time pursuing their own ideas.' Unfortunately, these heuristics cannot be used in isolation to set up and compare options related to competencies, skills, or specific product features. A revised statement that can allow sensitivity analysis of resource allocation heuristics is:

- Initial Level 1 Planning: Allocate resources to projects at Level 1, by looking ahead in multiples of 'x' time steps, such that products that are less than four years old generate 40% of the revenues.
- Level 2 Planning: Use the resources made available by Level 1 planning to conduct tactical analysis by looking ahead, and assess the fraction of time 'y' that ought to be devoted to pursuing own ideas. Make and test assumptions about the fraction of time when own ideas can lead to new revenue streams. If this leads to infeasible solutions, make local adjustments by overriding Level 1 allocation.
- Subsequent Level 1 Planning: Use the adjusted information generated by Level 2 plans as the starting point for Level 1 allocation.

The HPDP framework could be used to set up simulations to test the choice of 'x' and 'y,' by looking at their impact on two separate value functions. The modular structure of these heuristics allows for the possibility that when an option results in high scores, management may decide for the course of change. Mixing and matching decisions across levels can improve in the overall process performance. However, the optimization of a given set of modular processes does not guarantee that this evolutionary process can ever arrive at a 'best' system.

How does a firm generate starting policies that can be tested within the multilevel framework? There are a number of studies in the NPD literature (discussed in other chapters of this book) that provide insights for single level of planning. These insights could be good starting points for coming up with test heuristics. Examples of such starting points are:

- Level 1: Recognize that the value of market price reflects the assessment on entry. Kulatilaka and Perotti (1998) follow this approach while evaluating the decision to launch a new technology in the context of different conjectures about market structure.

- Level 2: Limit annual hiring to a percentage of current year's demand growth over and above the long-run demand growth rate, while adjusting for attrition (Anderson, 2001).
- Level 3: Look at the stock of remaining work for a set of tasks, with adjustments for reworks, and assign the resources to various tasks in a proportional manner (Joglekar and Ford, 2005).

It might be difficult to quantify whether these heuristics serve the best interests of the firm taken as a whole. With ever-more finely disaggregated and outsourced product development sub-projects, system-wide business complexity may eventually exceed the unaided cognitive capacities of development managers and obviate some of the benefits of existing heuristic planning mechanisms. However, if heuristics are appropriately integrated and tested using the framework described in Section 4, then more effective algorithms for computing the value created by these hierarchical options can be devised, organizational choices can be compared and global pitfalls can be avoided. We argue that need for testing these heuristics by linking together appropriate stochastic decision models at all levels of NPD planning will increase as the underlying organizational complexity rises.

7.3. Empirical research

Following Simon's (1969) arguments, the information processing view has become an important lens for exploring the organizational arrangements within the NPD context (Clark, 1985; Clark and Fujimoto, 1991). Alternative organizational opportunities surface when the NPD organizations are set up in a hierarchical manner to take advantage of the component-system dichotomy (Joglekar et al., 2001; Mihm et al., 2003) or to take advantage of the gaps across labor, product, and capital markets (Baldwin and Clark, 2000). Empirical research opportunities for organization of HPDP could be grouped into three themes:

- Governance mechanisms for recognizing and communicating value
- Modes of exploration and exploitation of hierarchical landscapes
- Inertia and competency traps

The designs of governance mechanisms have to reconcile with the fact that managers at different levels may fail to recognize certain information in front of them because of organizational routines and filters (Henderson and Clark, 1990). Even with the best of intentions, managers may ignore, hide, or delay communications (Yassine et al., 2003) because of the modular organization of their objectives. Noise in the progress status data (Joglekar and Anderson, 2005), either due to intentional aggregation within the design structure or owing to gaming (Ford and Sterman, 2003; Zenios, 2004), is a major concern while designing governance mechanisms in these settings.

Mihm et al. (2003) created a fit function to explore the organizational goals at multiple levels and shown that a hierarchical structure will help dampen rework probabilities and create inertia. However, this analysis does not explore uncertainty in terms of real options. Kogut and Kulatilaka (2001) have argued that the use of discounted cash flow techniques may be appropriate for situations when firms are interested in exploiting a market place, whereas real options are more appropriate when the firm is after exploration of the landscape. Some NPD studies have developed alternative parallel testing and selection strategies for exploration of complex landscapes (Sommer and Loch, 2004). Exploration and exploitation choices during search (Katila and Ahuja, 2002; Ethiraj and Levinthal, 2004) or selection-based hierarchical organization of experimentation, and micro-macro learning described in Section 7, are open avenues for further analytical and empirical studies.

Recall from Section 5 that the presence of inertia can promote learning *and* result in competency traps. The effects of hierarchical decomposition on the evolution of organizational inertia have not been studied systematically in NPD settings. We hypothesize that the presence of hierarchy, and multiple objectives, will increase the ambiguity within the system and reinforce inertial effects. Empirical analysis of modular organizational choices, and unintended consequences, such as increased inertia, are other avenues open for further research.

8. Conclusion

Complex product development processes are often modularized into multiple levels of decision with different objectives, uncertainties, and constraints. Managers manipulate different decision variables at different intervals of time. Decisions across levels are coordinated through a multi-level process that we term as a hierarchical planning process. Such a planning process creates hierarchical (i.e., nested) options for generating and realizing value. In Section 7, we have argued that HPDP process can *expand search spaces, promote macro-micro learning, and speed up the propagation of value*.

While it may be easier to recognize some the options at lower levels of analysis than an aggregate process, one of the biggest concerns is the existence of incompatible incentives, such that managers may not communicate appropriate information to other levels of decision making. Worse yet, other managers may simply fail to understand the value of the options even when the appropriate information is communicated. Hence, hierarchical planning can add to organizational inertia and create competency traps. Such inertia limits the applicability of the HPDP framework to settings where product life-cycles are rather short, or where accrual of value at any one level of planning far exceeds the value gains at the other levels. For instance, a start up firm with an eye towards an IPO may largely focus on the response of the financial market and ignore the value accrued at other levels. Similarly, a skunk works team in a firm charged with the exploration of truly new product concepts may focus on new product market and down play the ability to build up skills because these skill sets cannot be valued in these markets directly. Even with these limitations, modular management of financial, labor, and capital market through hierarchies will remain in place in a large population of NPD organizations.

These hierarchical NPD arrangements offer unique opportunities for studying mechanisms for recognizing and communicating value. Perhaps the need for detailed data sets, the existence of multi-level uncertainties and path-dependence may be some reasons why managers forego the advantages of detailed and quantitative models in favor of heuristics across levels. The rampant use of heuristics offers an opportunity for understanding underlying decision making and for the development of analytical tool kits. Currently, heuristics are developed at a single level and then extended to multiple levels by trial and error. If such heuristics are appropriately integrated, they may be more effective in quantifying the value created by the hierarchical options. The need for testing these heuristics by linking together appropriate stochastic decision models with recourse will rise with rise in the organizational and market structure complexities.

References

Amram, M., N. Kulatilaka (1999). *Real Options: Managing Strategic Investment in an Uncertain World*, Boston, MA: Harvard Business School Press.

Anderson, E. (2001). "The Non-stationary Staff Planning Problem with Business Cycle and Learning Effects," *Management Science* 47: 817–832.

Anderson, E. (2004). Personal communication with James Clearly, Vice-President of Contract Manufacturing, Frito-Lay, Plano, TX.

Anderson, E., N. Joglekar (2005). "A Hierarchical Product Development Planning Framework," *Production and Operations Management* 14(3): 344–361.

Baldwin, C., K. Clark (2000). *Design Rules Volume 1: The Power of Modularity*, Cambridge, MA: The MIT Press.

Baldwin, C., K. Clark (2003). *Design Rules Volume 1: The Power of Modularity, Preface to the Japanese Edition*. www.people.hbs.edu/cbaldwin

Barto, A., S. Mahadevan (2003). "Recent Advances in Hierarchical Reinforcement Learning," *Discrete Event Dynamic Systems* 13(4): 41–77.

Bhattacharya, S., V. Krishnan, V. Mahajan (1998). "Managing New Product Definition in Highly Dynamic Environments," *Management Science* 44: 11.

Bitran, G., D. Tirupati (1993). "Hierarchical Production Planning," Chapter 10 In: *Handbooks in OR & MS*, Volume 4, S. C. Graves et al., (Eds.) Elsevier Science Publishers.

Browning, T. R., R. V. Ramasesh (2007). "A Survey of Activity Network-based Process Models for Managing Product Development Projects," *Production and Operations Management* 16, Forthcoming.

Clark, K. (1985). "The Interaction of Design Hierarchies and Market Concepts in Technological Evolution," *Research Policy* 14: 235–251.

Clark, K., T. Fujimoto (1991). *Product Development Performance: Strategy, Organization, and Management in the World Auto Industry*, Boston, MA: HBS Press.

Dempster, M., M. Fisher, L. Jansen, B. Lageweg, J. Lenstra, A. Rinnooy Kan (1981). "Analytical Evaluations of Hierarchical Planning Systems," *Operations Research* 29: 707–716.

Eppinger, S., D. Whitney, R. Smith, D. Gebala (1994). "A Model-Based Method for Organizing Tasks in Product Development," *Research in Engineering Design* 6(1): 1–13.

Erat, S., S. Kavadias (2004). "Dynamic Testing of Product Designs," Dupree College of Management, Georgia Institute of Technology working paper.

Ethiraj, S., D. Levinthal (2004). "Modularity and Innovation in Complex Systems," *Management Science* 50(2).

Ford, D., D. Sobek (2005). "Modeling Real Options to Switch among Alternatives in Product Development," *IEEE Transactions on Engineering Management* 52(2): 1–11.

Ford, D., J. Sterman (2003). "The Liar's Club: Impacts of Concealment in Concurrent Development Projects," *Concurrent Engineering Research and Applications* 111: 211–219.

Gaimon, C., G. Thompson (1984). "A Distributed Parameter Cohort Personnel Planning Model that uses Cross-sectional Data," *Management Science* 30(6): 750–764.

Galbraith, J. (1974). "Organization Design: An Information Processing Perspective," *Interfaces* 4: 28–36.

Geske, R. (1977). "The Valuation of Corporate Liabilities as Compound Options," *Journal of Financial and Quantitative Analysis* 11: 541–552.

Graves, S. (1982). "Using Lagrangian Techniques to Solve Hierarchical Production Planning Problems," *Management Science* 28: 260–275.

Hans, E., W. Herroelen, R. Leus, G. Wullink (2004). "A Hierarchical Approach to Multi-project Scheduling under Uncertainty," Forthcoming *OMEGA, International Journal Of Management Science*. Also available as: Research report/Department of Applied Economics, Katholieke Universiteit Leuven: 0346.

Henderson, R., K. Clark (1990). "Architectural Innovation: The Reconfiguration of Existing Product Technology and the Failure of Established Firms," *Administrative Science Quarterly* 35.

Herroelen, W., R. Leus (2004). "The Construction of Stable Project Baseline Schedules," *European Journal of Operational Research* 156: 550–565.

Holt, C., F. Modigliani, J. Muth, H. Simon (1960). *Planning Production, Inventories, and Work Force*, Englewood Cliffs, NJ: Prentice-Hall.

Joglekar, N., A. Yassine, S. Eppinger, D. Whitney (2001). "Performance of Coupled Product Development Activities with a Deadline," *Management Science* 47(12): 1605–1620.

Joglekar, N., D. Ford (2005). "Product Development Resource Allocation with Foresight," *European Journal of Operational Research* 160(1): 72–87.

Joglekar, N., E. Anderson (2005). "Distributed Innovation with Imperfect Progress Status Information," Boston University School of Management Working Paper.

Katila, R., G. Ahuja (2002). "Something Old, Something New: A Longitudinal Study of Search Behavior and New Product Introductions," *Academy of Management Journal* 45(6): 1183–1194.

Kavadias, S., C. Loch (2003). "Optimal Project Sequencing with Recourse at a Scarce Resource," *Production and Operations Management* 12(4): 433–444.

Kogut, B., N. Kulatilaka (2001). "Strategy, Heuristics, and Real Options," *The Oxford Handbook of Strategy*, Oxford: Oxford University Press.

Kulatilaka, N. (1994). "The Value of Flexibility: A General Model of Flexibility", In: *Real Options and Capital Investments: New Contributions*, L. Trigeorgis (Ed.) New York: Praeger.

Kulatilaka, N., E. Perotti (1998). "Strategic Growth Options," *Management Science* 44(8): 1021–1031.

Levinthal, D. (1997). "Adaptation on Rugged Landscapes," *Management Science* 43(7): 934–950.

Loch, C., S. Kavadias (2002). "Dynamic Portfolio Selection of NPD Programs Using Marginal Returns," *Management Science* 48(10): 1227–1241.

Maccormack, A., R. Verganti, M. Iansiti (2001). "Developing Products on Internet Time: The Anatomy of a Flexible Development Process," *Management Science* 47(1).

March J. G. (1991). "Exploration and Exploitation in Organizational Learning," *Organization Science* 2: 71–81.

Mihm, J., C. Loch, B. Huberman (2003). "Hierarchies and Problem Solving Oscillations in Complex Projects," Presentation at INFORMS Conference, Atlanta.

Miranda, E. (2003). "Strategic Resource Planning at Ericsson Research Canada," Presented to PMI Global Congress 2003 in the Hague, the Netherlands.

Parker, G. G., E. G. Anderson (2002). "From Buyer to Integrator: The Transformation of the Supply Chain Manager in the Vertically Disintegrating Firm," *Production and Operations Management* 11(1): 75–91.

Ruefli, T. (1971). "A Generalized Goal Decomposition Model," *Management Science* 17: 505–518.

Russell, S., P. Norvig (2002). *Artificial Intelligence: A Modern Approach*, Englewood Cliffs, NJ: Prentice Hall.

Sanchez, R., J. Mahoney (1996). "Modularity, Flexibility, and Knowledge Management in Product and Organization design," *Strategic Management Journal* 17: 63–76.

Simon, H. (1969). *The Sciences of the Artificial*, Cambridge, MA: MIT Press.

Sommer, S. C., C. H. Loch (2004). "Selectionism and Learning in Projects with Complexity and Unforseeable Uncertainty," *Management Science* 50(10): 1334–1347.

Sriram, R. (1997). *Intelligent Systems for Engineering*, Berlin: Springer-Verlag.

Thomke, S. (2003a). "Managing Development Networks," Harvard Business School Teaching Note 9-603-901.

Thomke, S. (2003b). *Experimentation Matters: Unlocking the Potential of New Technologies for Innovation*, Boston, MA: Harvard Business School Press.

Thompson, G., J. Frances, R. Levacic, J. Mitchell (Eds.) (1991). *Markets, Hierarchies, & Networks: The Coordination of Social Life*, London: Sage Publications.

Ulrich, K., S. Eppinger (2000). *Product Design and Development*, New York: McGraw-Hill/Irwin.

Wheelwright, S., K. Clark (1992). *Revolutionizing Product Development*, New York: Free Press.

Williamson, O. (1975). *Markets and Hierarchies: Analysis and Antitrust Implications*, New York: Free Press.

Yassine, A., N. Joglekar, D. Braha, S. Eppinger, D. Whitney (2003). "Information Hiding in Product Development: The Design Churn Effect," *Research in Engineering Design* 14: 145–161.

Zenios, S. A. (2004). "Decentralized Decision Making in Dynamic Technological Systems," In: *Handbook of Supply Chain Analysis in the E-Business era*, Simchi-Levi, Wu, and Shen (Eds.), Kluwer Academic Publishers, Boston.

12 Coordination and information exchange

Christoph H. Loch and Christian Terwiesch

1. Introduction

Coordination in product development has often been viewed through the lens of information processing (Clark and Fujimoto, 1991; Adler, 1995). For example, members of product development teams receive information about consumer preferences, they proactively acquire information about product reliability, and they transfer information to manufacturing. Ideally, one would like one single 'master-mind' to process the information: all required information would be fed into this mastermind, an analysis performed, and the optimal solution returned.

Unfortunately, most product development problems of practical relevance are not amenable to such treatment. They are too large and too complex to be solved by one processor, be it human or machine, and hence they require a cooperative problem-solving effort. With 'too large and too complex,' we mean that the problem exceeds the capacity of information processing or information storage of any resource. In other words, it would take too much time for the resource to collect and process all required information. In some cases, the processing and storage requirements could exceed the amount that could be handled by the resource by so much that even with unlimited time a solution would not be found.

Adding more resources and having them process information concurrently can reduce the time of development. Taking a somewhat naïve perspective, one might argue that doubling the resources of a project would cut its completion time in half, tripling the resources would cut it to a third, and so on. This naïve perspective might apply to the creation of a telephone book or a mailing list, but it misses the complexity aspect of product development.

Once multiple resources are involved in solving the problem an additional problem arises. Because of the complexity of the problem, the parallel efforts are not independent, but they interact. Therefore, in addition to processing the information concerning the problem itself, one also needs to process information related to the control of the information processing efforts. These efforts reflect the work associated with decomposing the problem into sub-problems that are allocated to the various resources and synthesizing these sub-problem solutions. These efforts constitute the *coordination problem* that is at the subject of this chapter.

Note that the above dilemma, consisting of problem size and time constraints, is by no means limited to product development. The 'Science of Coordination' has sparked research in various disciplines, including Economics, Computer Science, Engineering, and Operations Research. Coordination among development tasks has been a central research theme in product development, including Simon (1969) and Alexander (1964), and more recent work by Clark and Fujimoto (1991) and Smith and Eppinger (1997).

In this chapter, we connect the coordination problem to its underlying cause, distributed problem solving. Rather than starting with the product development tasks and their associated interdependencies, we begin with the underlying *design problem* and the *solution search process* to examine coordination. In this discussion, we consider literature streams on search and complexity, as well as on coordination and communication in NPD. The emerging framework highlights that:

- The uncertainty in a project is not only an external or environmental phenomenon, but is – at least partially – caused internally, by the interactions among distributed activities;
- Interdependencies among tasks, which have previously been seen as given by nature, sometimes are the outcomes of (conscious or unconscious) choices.

The chapter is organized as follows. In Section 2, we introduce the two determining ingredients to the coordination problem: first, a conceptual '*design performance function*' that cannot be solved as a whole, but only in a decomposed approximation, and second, a *search process* that specifies how and in what order the sub-problems are solved and then integrated back. Section 3 overviews literature streams on modularity, concurrent engineering, complexity, and organizational barriers to coordination, viewed through the common framework of Section 2. Section 4 discusses open areas for further research.

2. Complex problems, decomposition, and coordination

2.1. Conceptual description of a complex optimization function

Generically, a product development problem, or generally a design problem, can be represented as the optimization of a complex function (bold symbols stand for vectors):

$$\text{Max}_x F(x, a) \tag{1}$$

In this abstract formula, the vector x represents a set of decision variables. The structure of the function F includes the form of the causal effects of the variables, e.g., whether a variable increases or diminishes performance, their interactions, and parameters influencing the causal effects. The shape of F is characterized by a vector a of exogenous parameters that are not under the control of the product development team. Examples of parameters might be demographics of the target population, material characteristics, limitations of a technology that must be incorporated (think, e.g., of batteries that an electronics company incorporates in its products).

An example of a performance function is the classic Cobb-Douglas production function $F(x_1, x_2) = Ax_1^{a1} x_2^{a2}$. A is a parameter indicating the base cost (e.g. efficiency), and a_1 and a_2 indicate the relative productivity of factor inputs x_1 and x_2. The functional form of F indicates interactions. Here, this means that using more of one factor increases the marginal productivity of the other.

If the problem is complex, there may be many decision variables. For example, a high-end car has many thousand components, each of which must be designed by choosing several parameters. Thus, the vector $x = (x_1, \ldots, x_n)$ might consist of over 100 000 variables. Moreover, the complex design objective function of the car is determined by the decisions such that they 'interact in non-simple ways [such that] given the properties of the parts and the laws of their interactions, it is not a trivial matter to infer the properties of the whole' (Simon, 1969: 195). In terms of the function in Eq. (1), this means that the optimal value of one decision, x_i^*, depends on the values of the other decisions, x_j.

A consequence of this complexity is that the overall performance function will be *rugged*, that is, it has *many local maxima*. A local maximum is a point from which no small deviation in any single decision can offer an improvement. When the performance function F is rugged, local (incremental) search cannot identify the global optimum, the overall best solution.

Worse, for new product designs that are carried out in cooperation by many individuals or teams, no one understands the overall product performance function F well enough to be able to 'optimize.' Products teams search through the 'space' of decisions x until they find an acceptable or 'good' design, but finding the 'best' is usually elusive.

2.2. Decomposing the problem into parts (Special case: Tree structure)

Optimizing a design problem with so many – possibly interacting – decision variables is usually not feasible. Typically, design teams divide the overall problem into a small number of 'chunks' or 'modules,' which are then considered separately (at least as a first cut). For example, the car might be divided into the front end, engine, drive train, chassis, body, and interior. In our formal framework, the overall product performance depends on the performance of modules:

$$F(\mathbf{x}, \mathbf{a}) = F'(G_1, \ldots, G_K, \mathbf{a}) \tag{2}$$

Each module performance, in turn, is a function of further subdivided aggregate components: $G_k = G_k(G_{k1}, \ldots, G_{kJ})$. For example, the drive train performance G_k is a composite of cost, size, contribution to acceleration and fuel consumption, and noise/vibrations. This performance is driven by the performances of the aggregate components clutch, gear-box, shaft, and differential. Each aggregate component performance is again driven by lower level components, e.g., $G_{kj} = G_{kj}(G_{kj1}, \ldots, G_{kjL})$. And so on, until at the bottom of the hierarchy, we have $G_{kj\ldots l} = G_{kj\ldots l}(\mathbf{x}_{kj\ldots l})$. The lowest level component performance (perhaps a gear in the gearbox or a valve) is a function of a subset $\mathbf{x}_{kj\ldots l}$ of all decision variables.

The division of the overall design problem into pieces (corresponding to the modules) supposes that the modules, and the components, are at least partially decoupled. Suppose each low-level component performance was influenced by the entire set of decision variables – in other words, $\mathbf{x}_{kj\ldots l} = \mathbf{x}$. In this case, the division into sub-problems would be futile, offering no benefit. Now imagine the other extreme: the design problem is perfectly *decomposable* if the modules are independent, that is, if the sub-modules of any high-level do not overlap:

$$(G_{k1}, \ldots, G_{kl}) \cap (G_{j1}, \ldots, G_{jl}) = \Phi,$$

and so on for the lower-level modules and components, down to $\mathbf{x}_{kj\ldots l} \cap \mathbf{x}_{nm\ldots r} = \Phi$. In other words, each component has its distinct set of decisions, and no decision for one component has any effect on any other component. This is the special case of a tree structure of the problem – the design can be decomposed in ever-finer substructures, which have no impact on the substructures in other branches (Alexander, 1964: 82; Clark, 1985). An example of a three-level tree structure is shown in Fig. 12.1.

A full decomposition is usually not achievable. At least some interdependencies usually exist across components, and even across modules. For example, the appropriateness of the strength of the block component in the engine block might depend on the bore of the cylinder (and the forces generated there). Alternatively, within the cylinder module, the efficiency of the piston surface may depend on the geometry of the rest of the burn chamber.

While full decomposition is rarely possible, *some* decomposition is often achievable, meaning that there is *some* overlap between the decision variables of $\mathbf{x}_{kj\ldots l}$ and $\mathbf{x}_{nm\ldots r}$, but not very much. Thus, decomposition is

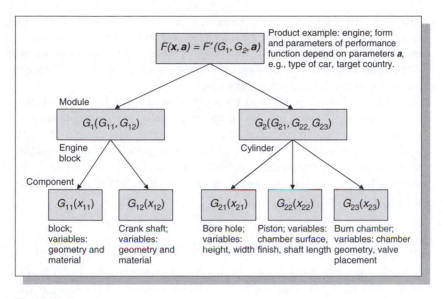

Figure 12.1
Tree structure of an engine design problem.

often very useful for the design team. In particular, the search through the space of possible decisions typically happens at the level of components – components are designed that are judged as high-performing, and then the development organization attempts to integrate those components into a functioning system. During the integration, interactions emerge and have to be reconciled.

The presence of interdependencies across components and modules makes it harder for the various component and module teams to work in parallel alongside one another. Because the decisions of one team affect (some of the) other teams, the teams must coordinate – they must communicate to one another the status of what they are doing, and they must adapt to decisions of other teams.

2.3. Interaction terms in the problem function

Since the overlap between the decision sub-vectors of $x_{kj...l}$ and $x_{nm...r}$ is the root cause of the coordination challenge, we believe it to be helpful to categorize these interactions into three types. First, an *additive* interaction means that the decision variable of one component does have an effect on the performance of another module, but it does not shift the optimal decision concerning the other decision variables in this other module (the optimal value x^* is the same whether I maximize $f(x)$ or $[f(x) + y]$). These are the most benign interactions – they do not force other teams to reconsider their decisions. With respect to the design problem, the two modules are independent. A communication and coordination need arises only to keep track of the overall performance achieved.

Second, a *substitute* interaction means that an increase in the interaction decision variable decided for one component causes a decrease in the best decision for the other component. Substitute interactions force trade-offs. Finally, a *complementary* interaction means that an increase of the interaction variable in one component enables a further increase for another module – the positive effects of the increase reinforce each other (as in the Cobb-Douglas example in Section 2.2).

2.4. Search process and types of interdependence

So far, we have focused on the problem structure $F(x, a)$. However, the problem structure alone does not determine coordination needs; they are also influenced by the *search strategy*. Realistic product development problems, for example, a 20 000 variable optimization problem, are not solved with a one-shot analytical exercise. Finding a good solution of F is not just a problem of computation, but also one of *search*. Search means that a series of solutions is tried; often starting from a design that one already has, varying decision variables in attempting to improve the performance or the characteristics of the design solution in desired directions.

Search is necessary because the design problem F is too large, complex and intractable to identify a good solution at one go. The structure of the 'solution landscape,' or the 'map' of local performance peaks and performance valleys over the myriad conceivable combinations of decision variables, is unknown and cannot be understood in sufficient detail by analysis alone. Search means that 'a development project can require literally thousands of experiments, all with the same objective: to learn whether the product or service concept holds promise for addressing a new need or problem, then incorporate the information in the next round of tests so that the best result can be achieved' (Thomke, 2003: 5). In other words, search means that points in the solution landscape F are tried out in a systematic way, learning about the structure of F on the way.

Call $\mathcal{S}(G_{i...i}, F, x, a)$ the search strategy of the module. The search specifies what decision variables are changed from one trial to the next, by how much and in what direction. Although an 'optimal' search is usually elusive, the actual search strategy often depends on the status of the module as well as on overall system performance (as far as it can be estimated), on the decision variables of other modules, and on the state of the environment.

It is important to re-emphasize that the evolution of the project is not determined by the problem structure F alone, but also by the search strategy S that is used. This has two implications. First, uncertainty in the project is both *externally* caused (by imperfect knowledge about parameters of F, as discussed in Section 2.3) as well as internally 'self-inflicted' by the search strategy. The choice of the search steps (which variables to change) influences which local optimum of F ultimately will be found, and usually, it is not known how the choice of search steps impacts the solution.

In addition, how interdependencies (overlapping variables across modules and components) are treated is a *choice* by the development team (whether this choice is conscious or not). For example, does a module team advancing to the next solution trial 'freeze' the overlapping variable for a while, or does it change the variable (at the risk that the other, interacting, team also changes it)? Of multiple interacting modules, which goes first in the search, and does this module 'create facts' (i.e., is frozen and not changed again afterward in response to what the other modules do)? When the interaction variable must be updated (say, after an integration test), which of the two module teams must search again and adapt to the changed interaction? These choices influence the 'path' toward a solution that the overall system will take over the search process, and they do so in ways that are not (fully) understood. Thus, they create uncertainty for the module teams.

The second implication of the importance of the search process is that *the nature of interdependencies among modules is decided, not exogenously given.* In particular, how would two interdependent module teams decide who gets to set the overlapping decision variable? Say two teams have an overlapping variable z (in addition to their module-specific variables x_i), so they face module performances $G_1(x_1, z)$ and $G_2(x_2, z)$. Team 1 would prefer the common variable to be z_1^* to optimize its module performance, and team 2 would prefer z_2^* to get its best performance. If the teams knew F, they could compare the impact of the decision on the system: If $F(G_1(x_1^*, z_1^*), G_2(x_2(z_1^*), z_1^*) > F(G_1(x_1(z_2^*), z_2^*), G_2(x_2(z_1^*), z_2^*)$, then optimizing module 1 at the cost of module 2 is better (and the opposite case is analogous). The result is a one-sided dependence of module 2 on module 1 – module 2 must adjust its design to the decision of module 1, and not vice versa. Sometimes, this can indeed be decided based on system performance – e.g., if in a sports car the engine requires a bit more space at the top to reach target torque, the shape of the hood must adjust (in an elegant sedan, the decision may not be so obvious!).

Often, however, the settlement of the overlapping variable cannot be accomplished based on system performance because it cannot be evaluated. In this case, heuristic rules often decide whether there is a one-sided dependence, or whether the two modules must reach a compromise, representing a two-sided dependence. If the decision is sufficiently ambiguous, social criteria also often play a rule – e.g., the status of the department or engineering specialty, or who is better able to articulate their logic.

The fact that interdependencies are decided not exogenously given has important implications for our discussions of the design structure matrix (Section 3.4) and the importance of culture (Section 3.5).

To see that the interdependence of tasks depends on the search process, consider an example with two decision variables, which we can graphically represent the performance function F, as shown in Fig. 12.2 (based on Loch et al., 2006: Chap. 7). The example is an engineering project in which one team each is responsible for one design parameter – setting the two parameters means adjusting the process recipe as well as fine-tuning the composition of the final product to suit emerging, currently unknown, process needs of the client. In a simple (non-complex) landscape, team 1 can first adjust the process recipe parameters, and when they work well, team 2 adjusts the final product composition. The second change does not invalidate the recipe choice, as the left-hand picture in Fig. 12.2. The two-parameter changes are independent – no matter in which order the process recipe and the product composition are varied, the same solution is found, and it happens to be the globally optimal solution.

Complexity of the solution function F means that the process recipe and the composition of the outcome product interact (right-hand side picture in Fig. 12.2). If the team first chooses the best recipe and then changes the product composition, the recipe now is no longer appropriate and must be changed again. Therefore, there are multiple performance peaks and valleys in the right-hand side picture of Fig. 12.2: the best choice of one parameter changes with the value of the other. Which solution the teams find will depend on the search, on how the team defines the interdependency between the two variables.[1]

1. *Independent.* The two teams search independently; each chooses its 'optimal' x_i along the search line from the starting point. The result is simply the combination of the two parameter values. As each team searched without taking into account what the other team decided (in contrast to the left-hand side of Fig. 12.2, this now matters because F is complex), the result might be really bad, as in Fig. 12.2.
2. *Sequentially dependent.* One team goes first and optimizes performance along its search direction, and then the other team searches for the best

---

[1] The search example in Fig. 12.2 is optimistic in the sense that each team searches 'globally' in one direction; that means that the team does not get stuck on the first peak in the direction (as it would be with an incremental, local, search, but the team is able to look further and identify the highest peak that lies on the search line along its entire length. The lesson remains unchanged if the parties search incrementally.

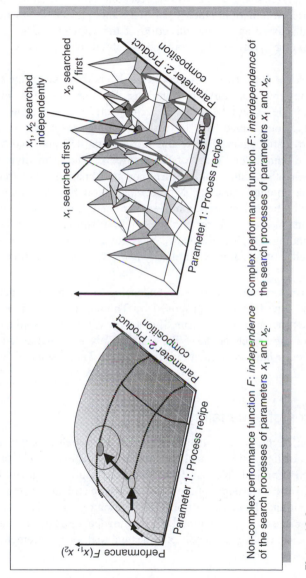

Figure 12.2
Search process in a simple and a complex solution landscape.

Non-complex performance function F: *independence* of the search processes of parameters x_1 and x_2.

Complex performance function F: *interdependence* of the search processes of parameters x_1 and x_2.

F value holding, the first variable fixed. As shown in Fig. 12.2, the two solutions found are different – the result found depends on the order of the search process. Moreover, it is often difficult, or impossible, to tell who should go first to find the overall best solution – who should preempt and constrain whom, or in other words, who should depend on whom? As we have discussed above, the direction of the sequential dependence is sometimes objectively set, but sometimes settled by experience or social criteria.

3. *Interdependent.* If the two teams recognize that both influence the solution quality, they may take turns in searching. For example, if in Fig. 12.2 (right-hand side), after the 'x_2 first' search, Team 2 could adapt its solution again, they would move back toward the starting point, and if Team 1 could then search again, they would move to the left and find the high peak in the bottom left corner of the landscape. The teams dynamically update each other, either taking turns, or coordinating more frequently during one another's search.[2] Mutual adaptation has the potential for finding much better solutions. On the other hand, it may also take a long time; the teams may circle around the solution landscape for a long time without finding a high performance peak (this problem of 'oscillations' is discussed in the section 'Complexity and preliminary information').

Thus, the classic taxonomy of interdependencies (independent, sequentially dependent, and interdependent) proposed by Thompson (1967) is not itself dictated by the problem at hand. Instead, it is a (possibly unconscious) choice by the rules of the search process. This has largely been neglected by the information processing theory paradigm that built on Thompson and Galbraith (1973).

2.5. Sources of uncertainty

Our discussion of the performance function F, the search strategy, and the resulting types of interactions, enables us to classify different types of *uncertainty* in the NPD project. We can distinguish four sources. Sources 1 and 2 refer to the intrinsic uncertainty of the design problem structure as imposed by the environment and the causal action-effect structure. Note that this uncertainty may be caused a by a genuine lack of knowledge, or by 'politics' (the inability of decision makers to settle on a design goal, or requirements).

---

[2] Note that static coordination, or the exchange of preferable parameter values for each team at the outset, is useful mostly when the solution landscape is well known, or not complex. In a complex landscape, by indicating a preferable value, the team assumes values of the other variables, and when the final values emerge, the preferred value may be entirely different.

1. *Uncertainty in a local parameter* refers to uncertainty in the causal structure of F as captured in the parameters a that define the shape of F. If the exogenous vector a changes, taking an action x_i has a different effect on performance. Similarly, a parameter may unexpectedly change over the course of the project. Consequently, the optimal system solution may change over time. The simplest case is if the parameter is additive and has an effect only on one variable, for example, $F(x_1, x_2) = a_1 x_1 + a_2 x_2$. The uncertainty about the effect of one decision does not influence the effect of the other decision.

2. *Uncertainty in an interaction.* A change in a parameter has a larger, and more difficult to respond to, effect if the parameter embodies an interaction between several modules or decision variables. For example, in the Cobb-Douglas production function $F(x_1, x_2) = A x_1^{a1} x_2^{a2}$, the parameters a_1 and a_2 embody complementary interactions between the decision variables. Thus, if one of these parameters is uncertain, a change in one decision has an uncertain effect on the optimal value for the other decision. It often happens that the interactions among multiple decisions are not fully understood.

    Uncertainty Sources 3 and 4 are related to the unforeseeable effects of the solution search strategy: when full optimization is not performed, the result of the search becomes stochastic ands erratic. There is a fundamental difference between uncertainty of type 1 or 2 and types 3 or 4: the latter can, in principle, be mitigated by investing more resources in more elaborate search. In practice, however, this is often not possible or not affordable.

3. *Uncertainty in final solution.* We have already pointed out in Section 2.1 that the performance function F is usually so 'rugged,' having many local optima, that 'the global system optimum' is usually elusive. That means that even if F was perfectly known, one of many local optima would be found over the course of the project, and it would still be unpredictable which one. Thus, uncertainty can (and often does) arise even if the performance function is deterministic and known, due to complexity.

4. *Uncertainty in other teams' decisions.* This source of uncertainty also has its root in the complexity of the performance function F, which cannot be fully analyzed and optimized. The design solution is not the result of a simultaneous setting of all variables (as in a computer simulation), but comes out of a decentralized *search process*, in which the various module teams vary their respective decisions over time, inching toward a good design. We will further examine the search process in Section 2.4, but we can already state now that over this search process, the values of many variables change. No one can keep track of all of these values over time – there might be a central database (which might even be

visualized for some aspects, such as geometry), but the decision makers simply do not have the bandwidth to keep in mind the status of all decisions. Therefore, module decision makers are often surprised by what other modules do – imperfect coordination means uncertainty for the participants in the process. Note that this can happen, again, even when F is, in principle, known and deterministic.

3. Past research streams

3.1. Modularity

The best way to manage coordination is to avoid it. To what extent this is possible depends on the structure of the problem. In the context of our model, this corresponds to a shape of F that is decomposable as in Fig. 12.1. Methods have been developed that allow an NPD team to change the structure of the problem (e.g., Ulrich, 1995) and often, teams sacrifice a certain amount of product performance to benefit from reduced coordination needs and other advantages of modularity.

Since the focus of this chapter is on coordination, we discuss three ways in which coordination is impacted by modularity: short-loop problem solving, parallel task execution, and the usage of prior knowledge about the behavior of other organizational units.

To understand the first two impacts of modularity on coordination, consider the task of opening a safe whose lock has eight dials, each with 10 possible settings, numbered from 0 to 9 (the example is an enriched version of Simon, 1969: 206). How long will it take to open the safe by using a trial-and-error search? Since there are 10^8 possible settings, the average number of trials needed to find the combination is 50 million.

For the sake of argument, imagine it takes 10 seconds to set one of the dials to a desired position (e.g., to set dial #3 to 7) and 5 seconds to attempt opening the safe once all dials are set. A single robber will need, on average, 50 million trials, which will occupy him for 50 million*(8 dials*10 seconds per setting + 5 seconds to attempt opening the safe) seconds. This equals 135 years!

Now, there is a hint of modularity in the problem, as there are eight dials and the value of one dial can be changed independently of the others. This allows eight robbers to work on the problem in parallel, which will speed up the search process to an expected 50 million*(10 seconds + 5 seconds) = 23.8 years. We see the first benefit of modularity: work can be carried out in parallel, and therefore, the overall time goes down. Note that although we have increased our resources by a factor of 8, we have only achieved a time reduction with a factor of $85/15 = 5.66$. This reflects the fact that we have to invest in system integration (the 5 seconds that we combine the work of all 10 robbers and test it); while search work can be carried out in parallel, the underlying problem structure is such that the overall system performance is still characterized by a strong interdependence.

To see the second benefit of modularity, suppose the safe lock is defective, so that a click can be heard when any one dial is turned to the correct setting. Now, each dial can be adjusted independently, and the search space has not 10^8, but only $10 * 8 = 80$ elements. Therefore, the expected number of trials is reduced to 8 dials $* 5 = 40$. The single robber will now be occupied for 8 dials $* 5$ settings $* 10$ seconds per setting $+ 5$ seconds $= 405$ seconds, or 6 minutes and 45 seconds. The team of 8 robbers will accomplish the task in 5 settings $* 10$ seconds per setting $+ 5$ seconds $= 55$ seconds.

We observe that increased modularity (the defective lock) has not only made the problem easier to solve (40 settings compared to 50 million settings), it has also reduced the need for system integration tests. With the intact lock, a setting could only be validated once all eight robbers have chosen the setting. In other words, learning in a non-modular system requires a coordination effort. Since learning typically is carried out in loops – also known as design-build-test cycles in NPD – each learning loop involves multiple parties. In a modular design, however, learning loops can be carried out locally, without system integration. Thus, in our example, adding 8 times the resources yields a 7.36-fold improvement in speed (405/55). Because of the reduced need for coordination, the eight robbers benefit proportionally from modularity, while the resource increase produces a strongly sub-proportional benefit in the original example without modularity.

The third way in which modularity facilitates coordination lies in the re-use of prior knowledge. With respect to a new product, such knowledge can take the form of standardized components, which are associated with higher scale economies and potentially higher performance (Ulrich, 1995). With respect to the development process for a new product, such knowledge might take the form of organizational routines that have proven successful in the past (Baldwin and Clark, 2000). From a coordination perspective, this re-use can be used as the basis for upfront coordination (we will define this as static coordination below): instead of relying on extensive information flows during the development effort (during the search), the NPD team simply considers the sub-system as a black box with interfaces that have been established in previous projects. Thus, the complex coordination need is reduced to one of occasionally coordinating a small set of parameters.

3.2. Concurrent engineering as overlapping of activities

While clever design can lead to modular products with reduced coordination needs, a perfect decomposition of the objective function is typically not feasible. In this section, we discuss the case of sequential dependence between two activities. The case of non-sequential relationships or interdependencies will be addressed in the following section.

In general, it is easiest to perform sequentially dependent tasks in their logical sequence. This results, however, in two disadvantages. First, the sequential process will be rather lengthy as there is no parallel execution of tasks. Second, it might well be that the sequentially dependent task requires certain pieces of information that the previous task is unaware of, which could lead to in-efficiencies once the dependent tasks starts its work.

Concurrent engineering attempts to overcome both of these disadvantages. Following the Webster dictionary, the English word 'concurrent' can have two meanings, which, interestingly enough, exactly match the two disadvantages described above:

- Two activities can be conducted concurrently, which means that they are carried out in parallel.
- Two parties can have concurrent views on a problem, which means that they agree.

We, therefore, break up the idea of concurrent engineering into a time aspect (parallel execution of tasks) and an information aspect (sharing of information).

The basic idea of time concurrency is to shorten the critical path of a project by 'softening' precedence relationships and conducting sequential activities in parallel. This is also referred to as 'task overlapping.' Eisenhardt and Tabrizi (1995) refer to this process as the compression approach to NPD. Overlap offers a fundamental time advantage, but also has drawbacks. In a fully sequential process, downstream starts with finalized information from upstream, whereas in an overlapping process, it has to rely on preliminary information. This approach can be risky if the outcome of the upstream activity is too uncertain to be accurately predicted. Under these conditions, overlapping activities creates uncertainty for the downstream activity, which would not exist in a sequential process. Thus, a trade-off arises between time gains from parallel execution and rework caused by uncertainty in the project. An optimal balance between parallelism and rework has been derived via analytical models and confirmed by several empirical studies showing that concurrence benefits decrease with increasing project uncertainty.

Several analytical models have been developed to address this trade-off. Krishnan et al. (1997) developed a framework for concurrence in case of sequentially dependent activities. They model preliminary information passed from an upstream to a downstream activity in the form of an interval. A parameter, e.g., the depth of a car door handle, is initially known only up to an interval, which narrows over time as the design becomes final. In this framework, two concepts determine the overlap trade-off. 'Evolution' is defined as the speed at which the interval converges to a final upstream solution. 'Downstream sensitivity' is defined as the duration of a downstream iteration to incorporate upstream changes associated with the narrowing of the interval. If upstream information is frozen before the interval has been reduced to a point value, a design quality loss occurs. The concept is illustrated for a door handle, a pager, and parts of a dashboard (Krishnan, 1996: Krishnan et al., 1997).

Loch and Terwiesch (1998) conceptualize uncertainty resolution as the distribution of engineering changes (ECs) over the course of the project: the more uncertain the upstream activity, the more ECs are likely to arise. ECs have the universal characteristic that they become more difficult to implement the later they occur. The authors investigate the trade-off between gaining time from overlapping and the downstream rework caused by implementing ECs. Sensitivity analysis on the optimal overlap level shows that gains from overlapping activities are larger if ECs can be avoided, if dependence among activities can be reduced, and if uncertainty (the rate of ECs) can be reduced early in the process.

The models of Krishnan et al. and Loch and Terwiesch were extended by Roemer and Ahmadi (2000, 2004). In addition to the overlap decision, the authors include the amount that an activity is crashed, i.e., shortened by adding resources.

Joglekar et al. (2001) look at the coupling of two sequentially dependent development activities, both of which contribute to the overall performance of the product by meeting a certain set of requirements. This is similar to our approach in Section 2. How much each activity contributes depends on the amount of work that is allocated to it. However, the tasks also cause rework to each other.

The above-cited models suggest that overlap in product development is not equally applicable in all situations. This is supported by several empirical studies. The most prominent study on this topic was carried out by Clark and Fujimoto (1991). The authors empirically find in the global automotive industry that teams that overlap product and process development more achieve shorter development times. In their study of the world computer industries, Eisenhardt and Tabrizi (1995) identify substantial differences across different market segments. For the stable and mature segments of mainframes and microcomputers, the authors find that overlapping development activities significantly reduces time-to-market. This has been refined further by Terwiesch and Loch (1999) who develop a measure for uncertainty resolution (a measure that describes how quickly a team is able to find the final design of the product). Using the uncertainty resolution variable as a moderating effect in the relationship between overlap and speed, they empirically show that teams with faster uncertainty resolution obtain more benefits from overlapping problem solving.

As far as information concurrency is concerned, it is helpful to separate between static coordination and dynamic coordination. In the context of sequential dependence, we define static coordination as information provided by members of the downstream task before the initiation of the upstream task. For example, in the context of automotive design, process engineers in charge of stamping tools could provide the product designers information about constraints or cost penalties that are associated with various body geometries. If this can be done completely before upstream begins its work, this form of coordination is relatively inexpensive and highly efficient (Adler, 1995).

For static coordination to be sufficient in meeting the coordination needs of a project, certain conditions concerning the performance function F exist. Static coordination corresponds to one party providing information to another party (or several parties) concerning how overall performance will change over a certain range of values before the other party initiates its own search. For a more rugged F, this becomes increasingly difficult.

If static coordination is not possible, information needs to be exchanged between upstream and downstream, not only before the initiation of the upstream task but also during the execution of the upstream task. In this case, we speak of dynamic coordination. In a context of dynamic coordination, upstream executes a piece of its overall workload and then presents an intermediate result to downstream. For example, an architect might create a schematic design of a new residential home and then ask a builder for a price estimate before continuing to the detailed design step. In this spirit, Ha and Porteus (1995) investigate a situation in which two development tasks are inherently coupled and must be carried out in parallel to avoid quality problems. They develop the 'how frequent to meet' problem as a dynamic program. If one design activity proceeds without incorporating information from the other, design flaws and corresponding rework result. Thus, parallel development together with design reviews save time and rework. Similar to a quality inspection problem in production, these gains have to be traded-off with the time spent on review meetings. The main question is how to coordinate, i.e., how often to communicate.

3.3. Complexity and the design structure matrix

The design structure matrix

The work on overlapping has concentrated on understanding how much to parallelize two sequentially dependent tasks, and how frequently to exchange information to coordinate the tasks. However, this problem is embedded in a larger question: which tasks, or components, interact and, therefore, need coordination?

In the terminology of our generic design problem in Section 2, *dynamic coordination* is required between any two modules whose performance functions $G_{ij} = G_{ij}(G_{ij1}, \ldots, G_{ijK})$ and $G_{lm} = G_{lm}(G_{lm1}, \ldots, G_{lmN})$ have common submodule function(s) G_{xyz} (appearing in both modules). Thus, the evolution of the common sub-modules must be shared in real time. If, in contrast, there are no common sub-modules, as in the perfect tree structure of Fig. 12.1, *static* coordination suffices – the definition of the 'territories' and interfaces as embodied in the common parent nodes of the tree coordinates the activities.

Alexander (1964) proposed to represent the design problem as a *graph* (a network of nodes and connecting arcs), in which nodes represent low-level modules or individual decisions, and arcs represent dependencies.[3] Steward (1981) formalized this idea to a formal tool, the design structure matrix (DSM), in which activities are listed in rows and columns, and entries represents interactions. Eppinger and his co-workers then developed the DSM further and developed methods of grouping activities such as to minimize interactions across groups (Eppinger et al., 1994; Smith and Eppinger, 1997). We now present a brief example of the application of this tool.

Based on the product architecture and component interfaces, the DSM describes inter-dependencies among development tasks (corresponding to components), capturing that tasks need input (physical or informational) from other tasks to be completed.

As is shown in Fig. 12.3, information-receiving tasks are listed along the columns, and information-supplying tasks along the rows. Crosses (X) mark information dependencies. Task B is sequentially dependent of task A, as the information flow goes only one way. Tasks B and C are independent. Tasks C and D require mutual information input and are coupled (interdependent).

	A	B	C	D	
Task A	A				A–B: sequential
Task B	x	B			B–C: independent
Task C			C	x	C–D: coupled
Task D	x		x	D	A–D: sequential

Figure 12.3
Design structure matrix (Ulrich and Eppinger, 2000: 262).

---

[3] In Alexander's proposal, the nodes represented 'performance gaps,' that is, unsolved problems. This can easily be generalized to decisions that must be taken (Alexander, 1964: 78–83).

The matrix suggests a plan for the order of the tasks: A, then B in parallel with C and D, the latter two being performed in a closely coordinated way.

Eppinger et al. (1994) included task completion times (marked on the diagonal) and strength levels of dependencies. By grouping the tasks with the strongest couplings together, the DSM can thus also be used to suggest design team formation, since a team is best able to perform coupled tasks in a coordinated manner. The application of the method is demonstrated in a semiconductor design project.

Smith and Eppinger (1997) extended the DSM to a Work Transformation Matrix (WTM) tool for planning project execution. If one assumes that all activities are performed in parallel, with rework arising stochastically when a task receives information input, then the eigenvalues of the WTM can be interpreted as the convergence rate of the project, analogously to a Markov chain. Thus, the completion times of the project can be estimated, and problematic iteration loops among closely coupled tasks can be identified in advance. The method is demonstrated on the example of brake system development in the automobile industry.

The DSM has become a widely used tool for understanding the interactions among the system modules and components. However, it is important to realize that the DSM treats the interactions as given – when the data are collected, engineers are typically asked, 'who depends on your input, and on whose input do you depend?' However, our model, and the discussion in Section 2.3, suggests that the direction of dependencies is partially *decided*. In other words, it is sometimes possible to ask, 'Is the fact that your component depends on component B truly required, or could component *B* not also adjust to design requirements of your component?' Often, the direction of dependence is settled by tradition, or just social power, in addition to basic engineering requirements. This implies that sometimes, an inconvenient dependence, which causes a loop in the cascading of changes, can be weakened or avoided by teams being willing to make small compromises. However, changing the social context of the definition of dependencies is difficult (we discuss this further in Section 3.4).

Complexity and preliminary information

The network representation of interacting components, and the associated DSM matrix, helps to explain an important phenomenon in large system development. When the system becomes bigger (number of components, or distributed actors), it quickly becomes complex and non-linear as it grows in size, even if all components and their interactions are very simple. This has three important implications. First, a rugged performance landscape easily arises in typical NPD situations, that means a performance function with many local peaks and valleys, which is very difficult to search. Second, the design problem becomes fundamentally more difficult to solve as it grows, even if resources (people) are scaled up with system size: the evolving design tends to 'oscillate' through numerous design solutions before converging to a solution. As the problem size grows, the probability of the design 'diverging' to something unreasonable (and thus having to be re-started) grows exponentially. Even if it converges, the time to conversion also grows exponentially.

This phenomenon has been explained analytically: the eigenvalues of the system DSM grow with system size, and they determine the convergence behavior of the search process (Mihm et al., 2003; Loch et al., 2003; Yassine et al., 2003). The associated oscillations and development time delays have been observed many times, in automotive design (Terwiesch and Loch, 1999b), software development (Iansiti, 1990; Cusumano and Selby, 1995), and aircraft development (Klein et al., 2003). In multiple industries, oscillations and rework can consume up to 50% of the engineering capacity and up to one third of the development budget (Clark and Fujimoto, 1991; Soderberg, 1989).

The only way to reduce problem-solving oscillations at their root is to eliminate complexity in itself, by limiting the system size or the number of interdependencies (modularity). Similarly, if the entire system, or at least large subsystems, can be optimized at one go, without decomposition, this has the same effect (with respect to problem solving oscillations) as a reduction of the system size. This is not always feasible, but there are less radical levers that engineering managers have at their disposal to at least mitigate oscillations (Mihm and Loch, 2006). These include, first, frequent communication of information across the board (to all affected parties). This is consistent with the findings of the influential information processing school, which showed in the 1970s that coordination in NPD requires high-bandwidth communication channels across different groups involved (Daft and Lengel, 1986).

However, rich information channels are not sufficient. The organization of work needs to be modified: sequential work reduces cycles of modifications, but at the cost of longer development time and the loss of integrated problem solving. Freezing of specs cut off modifications, but at the cost of a loss of flexibility (Bhattacharya et al., 1998). Satisficing means to forego the last few percent of performance optimization at the component level, which can save many cycles of modifications and greatly reduce development time. Finally, an important managerial lever of reducing problem solving cycles is to communicate *preliminary information*. This means overcoming the typical engineer's tendency to communicate a change to other parties only if the individual is sure the solution is complete and correct (Clark and Fujimoto, 1991; Hauptman and Hirji, 1996; Terwiesch et al., 2002).

Preliminary information exchange makes it explicit that the information is not final. The information may be *imprecise* (e.g., in the form of ranges) or *unstable* (that is, likely to change) (Terwiesch et al., 2002). Communicating the information in 'sets' (Krishnan, 1996; Sobek et al., 1999) helps affected component teams to leave themselves margins, or wait, depending on how hard it is for them to later modify their design decisions, while iterating with precise information is appropriate if modification costs are low or time pressure high. The explicit communication of preliminary information has two advantages: it allows the affected teams to be mentally prepared for future changes, overcoming problems of ambiguity and stress (see Section 3.4), and it enables better decisions about when to iterate, when to operate with flexibility margins (hedge), and when simply to wait. The decision of how to treat preliminary information depends on the relative costs of hedging or duplicating, of iterating, and of waiting, and this choice can be captured in decision models (Loch and Terwiesch, 2005).

Technical interactions and social interactions

The DSM represents technical interactions among system elements of the product developed. The product development *organization* must be able to recognize and manage these interactions. Sosa et al. (2004) empirically studied an aircraft engine development program and found that sub-project team interactions were overall well aligned with technical component interactions – in other words, teams that faced interactions of the subsystems that they were, respectively, responsible for, tended to exchange information. However, the failures to capture technical interactions that did occur happened largely across organizational departments – communication and collaboration somehow become more difficult across organizational boundaries. Moreover, system modularity, although reducing the number of technical interactions in the system, carries a cost: the few interactions across modular subsystems that do exist are significantly more likely to be overlooked buy the organization.

Thus, coordination and communication are driven not only by technical system requirements but also by *social interactions*. The social dimension of coordination has been examined by organizational theorists, as we discuss in Section 3.4 of this chapter.

3.4. Incentives, culture, and sense-making

Incentive schemes

Our discussion so far has implicitly assumed that all parties working on pieces of the problem of maximizing the performance function F share the same overall goal; there are no interest conflicts or disagreements other than those caused by possessing only partial information. However, this is not fulfilled in many real situations. The classic dilemma is well-known, in which the project manager wants to reduce project costs, subject to meeting a system performance hurdle, while the component engineers want to design 'cool' (high performance and typically high cost) components, independent of their contribution to system performance.

Not much work has addressed this incentive problem. Feltham and Xie (1994) have examined the difficulty of reconciling multiple performance measures in a situation of uncertainty. Mihm (2007) shows that component-level target costs are necessary to align system-level and component-level incentives.

The bulk of work on social interdependencies has been in organizational theory. We summarize some of this work in the next subsections.

Culture as problem solving routines

We have argued in Section 2 that large-scale design and development problems are too complex and uncertain to be understood by anyone person. The problem solving is distributed, with different actors holding different pieces of the overall puzzle. Section 3.2 has illustrated methods to achieve a 'rational' decomposition, one that 'optimizes' the interfaces and allows a re-integration of the pieces in the most efficient way. However, we have also discussed that the treatment of interactions in the search process is sometimes decided based on social criteria (when 'technical' criteria cannot be evaluated with sufficient clarity). Moreover, the problem decomposition itself is not always performed in planned and 'rational' way, but it evolves slowly, over multiple employee and product generations, by organizational trial-and-error, and by organizational learning that is then embodied in the organizational culture. This implies that the overall problem, and the solution methods collectively used, is not fully understood by anyone in the organization. The organization is running on 'autopilot.'

Culture can be defined as 'information capable of affecting individuals' behavior that they acquire from other members of their species through teaching, imitation, and other forms of social transmission' (Richerson and Boyd, 2005: 5). Successful cultural practices derive from 'a long tradition of incorporating good ideas and abandoning bad ones (. . .) they build in small steps. Individuals are smart, but most of the cultural artifacts that we use (. . .) are far too complex for even the most gifted innovators to create from scratch – human cultural institutions are very complex and rarely have been improved in large steps by individual innovators' (ibid, p. 54). Culture derives its power, especially in changing environments, by being cumulative: the 'imitators' (the people acquiring the cultural rules) can start their problem search closer to the best prevailing design than purely individual learners, and can invest the information production efforts efficiently in further improvements, which they can then transmit to more junior people (ibid., p. 115). Thus, culture is a human invention that allows groups to deal with problems that are bigger than any individual mind.

Organizational theorists have also emphasized the role of culture as an 'automated problem solving device.' For example, Nelson and Winter (1982) observe that organizational routines are repeated activity patterns through an entire organization, whose automation represents the organization's memory, and whose evolution is driven by trial-and-error and ex-post selection at least as much as through rational planning. Through evolution, the routines work successfully in the specific context of the surrounding routines, achieving static coordination through being co-designed. Similarly, Schein's (1992) classic definition of organizational culture emphasizes its problem solving role and its tacit and unconscious nature: 'culture is a pattern of shared basic assumptions that the group learned as it solved its problems of external adaptation and internal integration that worked well enough to be considered valid and, therefore, to be taught to new members as the correct way (. . .)' (p. 12).

To give another example, Hutchins (1995) shows, in his ethnographic study of navigation in the US and in Micronesia, that cognition (or problem solving) happens not only in the heads of individuals but also critically in the computational system of the surrounding artifacts (such as maps or devices), conventions (such as the definition of the vantage point – Western navigation holds the start or end point of the journey fixed and views the vessel as moving, while Micronesian navigation holds the vessel fixed and views the environment as moving), and routines (such as considering the positions of stars or using certain clues for estimating the vessel's speed). The individual can perform well by using the routines without fully understanding the entire computational system.

Group specific mental models block information exchange

We have seen that very complex problems are tackled via a problem decomposition and distributed problem solving (any individual deals with a small part of the problem) is a fundamental property of many human endeavors, and humans (have an in-built tendency to) use culture to define the individual pieces and to *statically* coordinate them. The power of this organizing principle is that groups are able to solve problems of staggering complexity, without any individual in the group understanding the entire problem (every individual understands a piece). The limit of this organizing principle is that the individuals view the world through the lens of their problem pieces, identify with those pieces, and have difficulties in *dynamically* coordinating and adjusting to one another as the problem evolves.

These limitations have abundantly been observed in innovation studies. For example, Lawrence and Lorsch (1967) showed that individuals in different functions have different goals, different time horizons, and different levels of formality. Dougherty (1992) interviewed participants in product innovation in 15 established organizations. The subjects came from engineering, sales, manufacturing, and planning (business analysis and market research). Dougherty found that the actors emphasized different knowledge bases depending on their background, emphasized different sources of uncertainty for the future (technology, user trends, manufacturing processes, business, and competition), and followed their own routines even when this caused friction with the other departments.

Similarly, von Meier (1999) interviewed operators and engineers in electric utilities and found that these two groups had different mental models of 'what is good for the organization' (p. 101). Their mental models were adapted to the task requirements of their respective responsibilities: engineers, responsible for designing systems, thought in abstract terms and viewed increased precision, speed, information, and control as desirable goals for innovation. Operators, in contrast, faced the daily challenge of keeping the system in equilibrium against myriad external disturbances, only some of which were identified and understood. This group viewed stability, transparency, veracity (of signals), and robustness as desirable innovation goals. As a result, coordination and information exchange suffered from conflicts and misunderstandings.

In the complex and uncertain endeavor of a product development project, explicit and analytical decision methods are insufficient, and people take decisions using at least a heavy dose of the basic assumptions that are embedded in the routines and organizational culture. The social psychologist, Karl Weick, calls this 'sense-making' (Weick, 1993). It can be very threatening and stressful for someone to feel that one's intuition is violated to a degree that one cannot interpret the situation, does not understand the causal connections, and does not know what the possible outcomes are. In particular, Weick has shown that the breakdown of sense-making, when the situation violates one's intuition and cannot be successfully interpreted, combined with the loss of social cohesion of the group, can have a traumatic and devastating effect, and even lead to the group's collapse.

Loss of sense-making can easily happen in a product development project when actions of individuals from different groups follow conflicting mental models, and the individuals know only their own routines, unaware of the logic of the other parties' actions. As a case in point, the development engineer for one component in an automotive development project had been constructing this component for over a year, based on design assumptions (such as the available space) that were formally written down and 'frozen' in previous information exchanges. Subsequently, he had to cope with 18 engineering change orders, many of them based on elements beyond his horizon, which thus had no obvious logic. As a result, his sense-making collapsed, leaving him in severe stress and prompting an extended sick leave (Terwiesch et al., 2002).

In addition to mental models of problem conceptualization, basic psychological mechanisms sometimes also stand in the way of coordination. Humans have a universal tendency of identifying with symbolically marked groups, following any 'seed' available. Attitudes to 'in-group' members tend to be positive and helpful, while attitudes are more hostile toward 'out-group' members (Tajfel and Turner, 1986; Kurzban et al., 2001). Marked status differences across the groups exacerbate the hostility and make them even more reluctant to exchange information. For example, people may identify with groups along the lines of race, organization, site, professional specialty, or department. These psychological mechanisms contribute to the 'Not Invented Here' syndrome (Allen, 1977), or the 'group think' phenomenon (Janis, 1971), and 'run-away teams' that act against the interests of the organization to which they belong (Levy, 2001). In all three cases, group identification has grown so strong that ideas from the outside are ignored, or even the goals of the surrounding organization rejected.

Possible remedies

The work on culture and interpretive barriers, carried out mainly by organizational theorists, complements work in Operations Management by an important aspect: the information exchange that allows dynamic coordination cannot be fully understood based only on considerations of channel bandwidth and efficiency. The fact that the various participants in the product development process specialize and understand only parts of the design problem fundamentally influences their mental models, their ability to communicate, and their social instincts. Devising efficient 'protocols' of information exchange is not enough – indeed, this metaphor that emphasizes a parallel situation of computers that must coordinate misses the important social aspect of communication.

Drawing the lessons from our discussion, successful coordination requires:

1. Setting an *organizational context* in which (a) the different participants have goals that are compatible, or at least not grossly conflicting (e.g., through target costing), and (b) in which an overarching social identity is emphasized, and status differences across groups are downplayed or diffused such that the groups are not highly reluctant to even engage with one another.

2. Creating a meaningful social identity of the development team, not only the core team but also the extended participants that may work on this project only part time and are also involved in other projects. The need for some initial identity-setting event is well-known in project management.

3. Equipping the individuals in the various groups to gain an at least rudimentary understanding of the responsibilities and working principles of other groups. Even if the individual does not understand exactly what other groups do, one may at least be informed enough to expect that some actions by other groups follow a different logic – an understanding of this fact, and reasons for it, can prevent a loss of sense-making even if a coordination breakdown unexpectedly occurs. Although this is a social process, tools such as the DSM, or the explicitly set-based or iterative strategies as discussed in Sections 3.3–3.4, can greatly help to articulate the coordination needs and barriers.

4. Establish a process of interaction and constructive engagement (with coaching if necessary). The social process of interaction itself positively influences the creation of a common identity. This can benefit the satisfaction of team members (Hauptman and Hirji, 1996) as well as the quality of the solutions provided (Sobek et al., 1999). Indeed, a definition of Concurrent Engineering that is broader than the narrow (overlapping-focused) definition that we use in Section 3.2. of this chapter, sees the social dimensions of collaboration and involvement of manufacturing and customer in the process as integral parts (Smith, 1997).

5. Using the different mental models as an asset rather than a liability – if the extended team understands that each party possesses some unique piece of information, the groups may be able to learn from one another and produce new, creative problem solutions as they go along and as the project progresses (von Meier, 1999).

4. Outlook: What we know, and where we must learn more

As we have discussed in this chapter, cumulative work over 40 years in the field of Operations Management and Organizational Behavior has produced a good understanding of the sources of coordination needs, of key challenges, and of some robust strategies for effective coordination and information exchange. However, significant knowledge gaps remain. Each one of them represents, in our view, a promising opportunity for relevant future research.

First, we need more models of what information is precisely exchanged when coordination takes place, and how the information changes in what the parties do. The original information-processing paradigm from the 1960s was too aggregate to allow a detailed understanding of coordination challenges. While we have made progress, as described in this chapter, more micro-models of types of problem solving, of information format, and of information use are needed.

Second, we have argued that the fundamental root of the need for coordination lies in the 'memory space' restrictions of the parties involved in the NPD effort – no one can hold in their minds, or systems, all the information of what the other parties are doing (this would be the case even if the system performance function was fully known). We do not have a complete explanation what causes the limit – is it human cognition, or an inability of our available NPD support systems to present the information is such a condensed way that the human project participants could consider it? For example, would it be possible to identify, from a DSM analysis, all the important links that a project component or party has, and communicate sufficiently along those links? Is it a time/progress trade-off, as the overlapping literature has assumed (by making an information transfer carry a 'communication time' τ), or is it a problem of limited capacity? None of the research to date has explored this fundamental question.

Third, while coordination problems exist in a wide range of academic areas, there exists almost no overlap between them and it appears that these areas are mutually unaware of each other. For example, Artificial Intelligence and computer science researchers have worked on problems of information exchange among computer subroutines and processors, in other words, on coordination needs. For example, Maes and Brooks (1990) discuss coordination needs between processors guiding the movements of a six-legged robot. It is unclear to what extent coordination research in NPD is 'ahead' or 'behind' the work in AI, but opportunities, for applications and transfers of knowledge, are likely to exist.

Fourth and finally, an important part of the coordination challenge lies in incentives, where much more work is needed, and in the social barriers discussed in Section 3.4 of this chapter. Much of the work has been descriptive, and we do not know whether mental communication barriers are inevitable, or whether it simply has not been sufficiently tried to overcome them. What type of incentives, training, or group building (motivation) would be required to eliminate the mental barriers problem? In addition, we have neither good empirical description nor models of how social barriers influence the information exchange – do they cause certain types of information (or information to certain parties) to be suppressed, or do they cause certain systematic information biases? Moreover, we have little knowledge of how the content of the information (e.g., uncertainty, domain, etc.) *interacts* with the social structure of the environment, in resulting in good coordination or poor coordination. Here, collaboration between the fields of OB and OM is called for (which is hard, exactly for reasons of social inequality and interpretive barriers).

References

Adler, P. S. 1995. Interdepartmental interdependence and coordination: The case of the design-manufacturing interface. *Organization Science* 6 (2), 147–167.

Alexander, C. 1964. *Notes on the Synthesis of Form.* Cambridge, MA: Harvard University Press.

Allen, T. 1977. *Managing the Flow of Technology.* Boston, MA: MIT Press.

Baldwin, C., and K. B. Clark. 2000. *Design Rules, Volume 1: The Power of Modularity.* Cambridge, MA: MIT Press.

Bhattacharya, S., V. Krishnan, and V. Mahajan. 1998. Managing new product development in highly dynamic environments. *Management Science* 44 (11) (Part 2), S50–S64.

Clark, K. B. 1985. The interaction of design hierarchies and market concepts in technological evolution. *Research Policy* 14, 235–251.

Clark, K. B., and T. Fujimoto. 1991. *Product Development Performance.* Boston, MA: Harvard Business School Press.

Cusumano, M. A., and R. W. Selby. 1995. *Microsoft Secrets.* NY: Free Press.

Daft, R. L., and R. H. Lengel. 1986. Organizational information requirements, media richness and structural design. *Management Science* 32 (5), 554–571.

Dougherty, D. 1992. Interpretive barriers to successful product innovation in large firms. *Organization Science* 3 (2), 179–202.

Eisenhardt, K. M., and B. N. Tabrizi. 1995. Accelerating adaptive processes: Product innovation in the global computer industry. *Administrative Science Quarterly* 40, 84–110.

Eppinger, S. D., D. E. Whitney, R. P. Smith, and D. A. Gebala. 1994. A model-based method for organizing tasks in product development. *Research in Engineering Design* 6, 1–13.

Feltham, G. A., and J. Xie. 1994. Performance measure congruity and diversity in multi-task principal agent relations. *The Accounting Review* 69(3), 429–453.

Galbraith, J. 1973. *Designing Complex Organizations.* Cambridge, MA: Addison Wesley.

Ha, A. Y., and E. L. Porteus. 1995. Optimal timing of reviews in concurrent design for manufacturability. *Management Science* 41, 1431–1447.

Hauptman, O., and K. K. Hirji. 1996. The influence of process concurrency on project outcomes in product development: An empirical study with cross-functional teams. *IEEE Transactions in Engineering Management* 43, 153–164.

Hutchins, E. 1995. *Cognition in the Wild.* Cambridge, MA: MIT Press.

Janis, I. L. 1971. *Victims of Groupthink.* Boston, MA: Houghton Mifflin.

Iansiti, M. 1990. Microsoft Corporation: Office Business Unit, HBS Case 9-691-033.

Joglekar, N. R., A. A. Yassine, S. D. Eppinger, and D. E. Whitney. 2001. Performance of coupled product development activities with a deadline. *Management Science* 47, 1605–1620.

Klein, M., D. Braha, H. Syama, and B. Y. Yaneer. 2003. Editorial: Special issue on a complex system perspective on concurrent engineering. *Concurrent Engineering Research and Applications* 11 (3), 163.

Krishnan, V. 1996. Managing the simultaneous execution of coupled phases in concurrent product development. *IEEE Transactions on Engineering Management* 43 (2), 210–217.

Krishnan, V., S. D. Eppinger, and D. E. Whitney. 1997. A model-based framework to overlap product development activities. *Management Science* 43, 437–451.

Kurzban, R., J. Tooby, and L. Cosmides. 2001. Can race be erased? Coalitional computation and social categorization. *Proceedings of the National Academy of Sciences* 98 (Dec 18), 15387–15392.

Lawrence, P., and J. Lorsch. 1967. *Organization and Environment.* Boston, MA: Harvard Business School Press.

Levy, P. F. 2001. The Nut Island effect: When good teams go wrong. *Harvard Business Review* 79 (3), 51–59.

Loch, C. H., and C. Terwiesch. 1998. Communication and Uncertainty in Concurrent Engineering. *Management Science* 44 (8), 1032–1048.

Loch, C. H., J. Mihm, and A. Huchzermeier. 2003. Concurrent engineering and design oscillations in complex engineering projects. *Concurrent Engineering Research and Applications* 11 (3), 187–200.

Loch, C. H., and C. Terwiesch. 2005. Rush and be wrong or wait and be late? Seven principles of when to commit to real-time information. *Production and Operations Management* 14 (3).

Loch, C. H., A. De Meyer, and M. T. Pich. 2006. *Managing the Unknown: A New Approach to Managing Novel Projects.* NY: Wiley.

Maes, P., and R. A. Brooks. 1990. *Learning to Coordinate Behaviors.* AAAI. Proceedings National Conference on Artificial Intelligence.

Mihm, J. 2007. The effect of incentives on new product development outcomes and timing. INSEAD Working Paper.

Mihm, J., C. H. Loch, and A. Huchzermeier. 2003. Problem Solving Oscillations in Complex Engineering Projects. *Management Science* 49 (6), 733–750.

Mihm, J., and C. H. Loch. 2006. Spiraling out of control: Problem-solving dynamics in complex distributed engineering projects. In: Braha, D., A. Minai, and Y. Bar-Yam (Eds.) *Complex Engineering Systems.* NY: Perseus Books.

Nelson, R. A., and S. G. Winter. 1982. *An Evolutionary Theory of Economic Change.* Cambridge, MA: Belknap.

Richerson, P. J., and R. Boyd. 2005. *Not by Genes Alone: How Culture Transformed Human Evolution.* Chicago: Chicago University Press.

Roemer, T. A., and R. Ahmadi. 2000. Time-cost trade-offs in overlapped product development. *Operations Research* 48 (6), 858–865.

Roemer, T. A., and R. Ahmadi. 2004. Concurrent crashing and overlapping in product development. *Operations Research* 52 (4), 606–622.

Schein, E. H. 1992. *Organizational Culture and Leadership.* San Francisco: Jossey Bass (2nd edition).

Simon, H.A. 1969. *The Sciences of the Artificial.* Cambridge, MA: MIT Press (2nd edition).

Smith, R. P. 1997. The historical roots of concurrent engineering fundamentals. *IEEE Transactions on Engineering Management* 44 (1), 67–78.

Smith, R. P., and S. D. Eppinger. 1997. Identifying controlling features of engineering design iteration. *Management Science* 43, 276–293.

Sobek, D. K., A. C. Ward, and J. K. Liker. 1999. Toyota's principles of set-based concurrent engineering. *Sloan Management Review* Winter 1999, 67–83.

Soderberg, L. G. 1989. Facing up to the engineering gap. *The McKinsey Quarterly* Spring 1989, 3–23.

Steward, D. V. 1981. *Systems Analysis and Management: Structure, Strategy and Design.* NY: Petrocelli Books.

Sobiezczanski-Sobieski, J., J. S. Agte, and R. R. Sandusky. 1998. Bi-level integrated system synthesis (BLISS). *7th AIAA Symposium of Multi-disciplinary Analytical Optimization Collected Technical Papers*, Part 3. (A98-39701 10-31), St. Louis, MO.

Sosa, M. E., S. D. Eppinger and C. M. Rowles. 2004. The Misalignment of Product Architecture and Organizational Structure in Complex Product Development. *Management Science* 50 (12), 1674–1689.

Tajfel, H., and J. C. Turner. 1986. The social identity theory of intergroup behaviour. In: Worchel, S., and W. Austin (Eds.) *Psychology of Intergroup Relations.* Chicago: Nelson Hall, 7–24.

Takeuchi, H., and I. Nonaka. 1986. The new product development game. *Harvard Business Review* 64 (1), 137–146.

Terwiesch, C., and C. H. Loch. 1999. Measuring the effectiveness of overlapping development activities. *Management Science* 45 (4), 455–465.

Terwiesch, C., and C. H. Loch. 1999b. Managing the process of engineering change orders. *Journal of Product Innovation Management* 16 (2), 160–172.

Terwiesch, C., C. H. Loch, and A. De Meyer. 2002. Exchanging preliminary information in concurrent engineering: Alternative coordination strategies. *Organization Science* 13 (4), 402–419.

Thomke, S. H. 1997. The role of flexibility in the development of new products. *Research Policy* 26, 105–119.

Thomke, S. 2003. *Experimentation Matters.* Boston: Harvard Business School Press.

Thompson, J. D. 1967. *Organizations in Action.* NY: McGraw Hill.

Ulrich, K. 1995. The role of product architecture in the manufacturing firm. *Research Policy* 24, 419–440.

Ulrich, K., and S. D. Eppinger. 2000. *Product Design and Development.* NY: McGraw Hill (2nd edition).

Von Meier, A. 1999. Occupational cultures as a challenge to technological innovation. *IEEE Transactions on Engineering Management* 46 (1), 101–114.

Van Zandt, T. 1999. Decentralized information processing in the theory of organizations, In: Sertel, M. (Ed.) *Contemporary Economic Issues.* Volume 4, London: MacMillan, 125–160.

Weick, K. E. 1993. The collapse of sensemaking in organizations: The Mann Gulch disaster. *Administrative Science Quarterly* 38 (4), 628–652.

Yassine, A., N. Joglekar, D. Braha, S. D. Eppinger, and D. Whitney. 2003. Information hiding in product development: The design-churn effect. *Research in Engineering Design* 14 (3), 131–144.

13 Who do I listen to? The role of the customer in product evolution

Kamalini Ramdas, Michael Meyer, and Taylor Randall

1. Introduction

Let us start by taking a quick look at the evolution of the laser printer industry from its inception in the early 1980s to its maturity in the late 1990s. We examine this evolution by plotting products offered to consumers over time, in attribute space. The primary performance attributes of a laser printer are printing speed and print clarity or resolution. Figures 13.1a through 13.1d are snapshots of the industry, taken at regular intervals in time. We observe rapid improvement in products along the dimension of printing speed followed by improvement in products along the dimension of resolution. Extant theories would offer several explanations for this evolution:

- Printers evolved in a predictable way along the key dimensions that core customers care the most about (incremental innovation, Bower and Christensen, 1995).
- Technological constraints and development expense may influence the path of evolution along performance dimensions (S-curve literature, e.g., Christensen, 1992A; Christensen, 1992B).
- In the early stages of the industry life cycle a number of attribute combinations are tried out, and over time firms migrate towards a few standard configurations (standards and dominant design literature, e.g., Christensen, Suárez and Utterback, 1998).

Much of what we know about the evolution of products is based on historical data like that found in Fig. 13.1. Our analysis and our resulting prescriptions have the benefit of hindsight. We know what worked and what did not. Retrospective studies have greatly increased our understanding of product evolution. Yet a big challenge in applying the insights from these studies is that things always seem clearer after the fact, while it is difficult to make

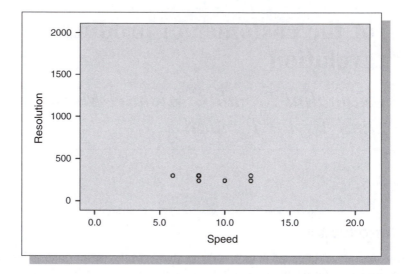

Figure 13.1a
Speed and resolution 1985.

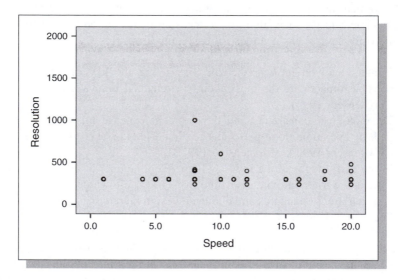

Figure 13.1b
Speed and resolution 1990.

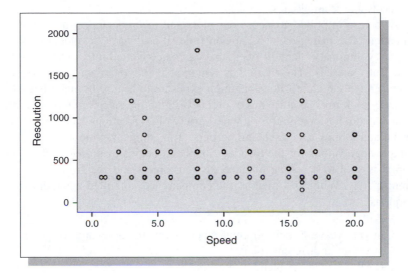

Figure 13.1c
Speed and resolution 1995.

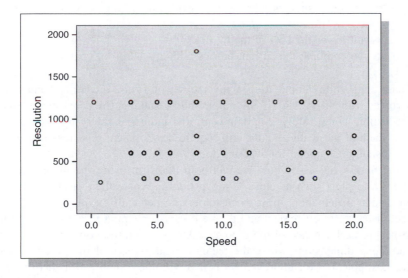

Figure 13.1d
Speed and resolution 1998.

sense of the chaos facing managers as they try to understand the evolution of products and technologies.

As a case in point, juxtapose our plots and theories against the following situation. The managers of Chapman Innovations[1] have developed a patent for a revolutionary blend of fibers that can be converted into a variety of fire resistant materials. The fabric has remarkable fire retardant properties and comparatively high tensile strength on exposure to heat, thus embodying two primary performance attributes of products in the fire retardant fabric market. The material has potential for a wide variety of applications including woven or knitted fabrics and insulating barriers. The company chooses a couple of simple applications for the blended fibers and begins to produce fabric. The fabric is sold to a couple of interested customers and the feedback begins immediately. Within six months, the company has compiled a laundry list of requests.

- Can you weave or knit different types of constructions and weights?
- Can we get a different color?
- Can you change the blend of the fibers?
- Can you increase the tensile strength of the fabric on exposure to heat?
- Can you improve the fire retardant properties of the fabrics?
- Can you give us a product with improved resistance to abrasion?
- We think you can use this yarn for products other than fabrics and insulating barriers, such as high-strength cables for lifting heavy objects. Can you help us?
- Can you lower the cost of the fabrics?
- Can you combine the current fabrics with a waterproof coating?

These suggestions come from a diverse set of firms, including companies involved with NASCAR, NASA, automobiles, banking, fire departments, steel production, home safety, entertainment, and industrial safety just to name a few. Each of these suggestions will require development resources and time. What should Chapman Innovations do?

Let us ask ourselves how we can help this firm using the theory developed from plots such as ours. A suggestion to evolve their product along a dimension that matters most to customers is met with the response 'I have been listening to customers and they all want something very different with respect to performance of the product.' A suggestion to evolve their product line along dimensions where the technological aspects of the product have the most potential for improvement is met with the response 'It is hard to tell which dimensions might have the most potential. Basic research might help

---

[1] Chapman Innovations is a startup firm in the fire retardant fabrics market.

determine this, but this research will take time to do, and it does not answer my short-term question. Who should I listen to?'

To whom should we listen? The remainder of this chapter seeks to provide guidance into this question and the critical role of customers in the evolution of products, and the determination of product platform strategy. By product evolution, we mean the way in which a product or product line evolves over the course of the product lifecycle. The product evolution pattern observed in a firm or an industry is a function of decisions that firms make at different points in time about product architecture, what products to introduce and what products to prune each year, and decisions that impact the evolution of the technologies embedded in the products. These decisions are in turn a function of macro-level market forces, revenue and cost structures associated with different alternatives, and, importantly, evolving customer needs. By product platform strategy, we mean architectural decisions for products, processes, and production and distribution networks, which impact resource sharing across products.

Many prescriptive models of the decisions that influence the evolution of product lines and product platform strategy use customer preferences as inputs. For example, the marketing literature in product line optimization treats products as bundles of attributes desired by consumers (e.g., Green and Krieger, 1985; Green and Krieger, 1989). However, attribute-based models of variety are often limited to examining product positioning within a single period. In recent years, there has been a spawning of economics-based models for product platform design and component sharing (e.g., Desai et al., 2001; Kim and Chhajed, 2002; Krishnan and Gupta, 2001), many of which are built on the classic Mussa and Rosen (1978) model of vertical differentiation. In this stream of research, products – or components – are differentiated along a single attribute, and consumers differ in their willingness to pay for quality. Some of these models are static and some are dynamic in nature, and they are mainly intended to increase intuition on issues such as what breadth of products to offer off a common platform. Ramdas (2003) provides a recent review the literature on product variety, which is one of the drivers of product evolution and product platform strategy.

While prescriptive models that build intuition have an important place in guiding managerial judgment, we believe that many of the decisions that influence product evolution and product platform strategy are made outside the current frameworks of analytical and prescriptive theory. Managers are operating with limited information and limited time. Most of the information they are using comes from the needs of current or potential customers. This information comes in an unorganized, ill-timed, and disjointed way. We believe that there is room for research and prescriptive policy that acknowledges this decision environment.

As a starting point, we present a conceptual model that might be used by a company like Chapman Innovations to organize the requests coming from customers. The model relies on two key questions:

- Does fulfilling the customer request involve making a compromise in product performance along a primary dimension of performance?
- Does the customer request focus on an established dimension of competition, or is the request for an attribute[2] that is not currently considered critical to the core market?

We consider each of these questions below.

1.1. Does the request require a compromise to a primary performance dimension of the product?

Analyzing this question requires some precise definitions. First, by *primary performance dimensions* we mean those technical dimensions[3] embodied in currently available products, which mainstream customers today care the most about. These dimensions are the basis of competition in the mainstream market now. In the evolution of laser printers, ever since their inception printing speed and print clarity have been primary performance dimensions. For the fabric in our Chapman example, the primary performance dimensions are the degree of fire retardance and tensile strength on exposure to heat.

At any point in time, aside from the primary dimensions, the firms in a market are actively pursuing other technical performance dimensions, because they know that their mainstream consumers care about them. We term such dimensions as *secondary performance dimensions*. The ability to print in color, and the quality of color printing, are examples of secondary dimensions in the laser printer market. Such dimensions may or may not be embodied in current products, but they are viewed as competitive dimensions by players in the mainstream market, albeit slightly less critical than the primary dimensions[4].

In addition, at any point in time, certain other technical dimensions may be embodied in products without being primary or even secondary performance dimensions. For example, footprint size is a technical attribute of a printer,

---

[2] We use the terms 'attribute' and 'dimension' interchangeably throughout.

[3] Technical dimensions are any dimensions that translate into product specifications. Even comfort is a technical dimension, as it is captured via particular product specifications.

[4] Rating dimensions as primary, secondary and tertiary based on their importance to the customer is widespread in design (e.g. Ulrich and Eppinger, 2004). Our definitions for primary, secondary, and dormant dimensions build on standard rating criteria by highlighting that these ratings are time specific, and also by underscoring that at any time, some dimensions may be a focus of competition without being offered on the market.

and ability to endure abrasion is a technical attribute of the fabrics produced by Chapman. However, these attributes are not currently the focus of competition. So long as they fall within reasonable limits, they are virtually ignored by competing firms, and current mainstream customers are not demanding improvements along these dimensions. We call these other technical attributes *dormant performance dimensions.*

We view attributes such as cost, customization or 'fit,' and delivery speed as conceptually different from the technical dimensions of a product's performance, and we term these attributes as *operational dimensions.* Unlike technical attributes, which are specific to a particular product – e.g., printer speed is not a relevant attribute of yarn – operational dimensions such as cost, degree of customization, or delivery speed can be defined for *any* product or service.

Over time, individual secondary attributes may become primary attributes, and individual dormant attributes may be elevated to primary or secondary attribute status. In addition, if performance improvement along primary and secondary attributes is no longer valued by customers, the locus of competition may shift to operational attributes such as cost, customization, or delivery speed.

One interpretation of what we have described above is that a consumer's utility from a product is a weighted sum of the utilities a consumer derives from its primary, secondary dormant, and operational attributes, and that these weights may change over time.

Finally, by a compromise in primary performance, we mean that fulfilling the customer request may result in a lowering of performance along one or more of the primary performance dimensions of the product. This occurs because of the design and engineering tradeoffs that are often made when creating a product. Thus, we use the term compromise in the same sense as Christensen (1997A).

1.2. Does the customer request performance along an established dimension of competition or along a latent dimension?

Often, a customer request focuses on improvement along a primary performance dimension of the product, i.e., one that is embodied in current products and is highly valued by mainstream customers. For example, in the printer market, a customer may request faster printing speed or better print resolution. Or else, the request may focus on a secondary performance dimension, which is one firms are competing over even though it may not yet be offered on the market. For example, in the laser printer market, firms knew much before color printers became available that this feature would be attractive to mainstream customers. Therefore, competition to achieve color printing ability was intense. In any market, customers may also request operational improvements such as greater customization and fit with respect to technical features, faster delivery, or simply lower cost. We term all of the above types of attributes as *established dimensions* of competition. Note that in referring to a dimension as established, we are really referring to its being established as a *competitive* dimension; such a dimension may or may not be embodied in current products.

What is unique about all of the above types of requests is that they are not too surprising. They come from two sources: (a) customers wanting more of the same – i.e., more along the primary or secondary performance dimensions, and (b) customers wanting greater customization, faster delivery, or lower cost, which are relatively obvious ways to compete in *any* industry.

On the other hand, some customer requests focus on a technical product dimension that is currently either not offered at all on the market, or is embodied in current products as a dormant dimension. In the case of Chapman Innovations, waterproofing is a dimension that is currently not offered at all. Somewhat differently, in the case of laser printers, a highly space-conscious customer might request a printer with a far smaller footprint than is currently offered. For dormant dimensions, such customer requests are often for an extreme level of the dimension, in that it is not within the currently offered range. We use the term *latent dimension* to describe dimensions that are altogether new, or that have so far been only dormant dimensions of competition.

Latent performance dimensions play a very important role in innovation. The focus of our work is on understanding how certain types of customers or users may bring a firm's attention to such latent performance dimension, and how dimensions impact product evolution and product platform strategy. In the next subsection, we discuss how firms can use customers as a guide to unearthing latent dimensions. Note that while a firm may also decide to compete on latent dimensions based on R&D driven technological breakthroughs that enable doing so, that is not the focus of our work.

1.3. Fringe users as a source of innovation

Ramdas and Meyer (2006) identify *fringe users* as an important resource for unearthing latent performance dimensions. Fringe users are defined as pockets of consumers who are in the market for the firm's products and who experience a heightened need along some product dimension. The needs of fringe users are underserved by current market offerings. These authors report that observing fringe users can highlight needs that are present, but much harder to discern, in the mainstream user. Once such latent needs are identified, a firm can design mainstream products, which cater to these needs. The OXO line of kitchen tools provides an excellent illustration of this point.

Sam Farber, retired founder of housewares company Copco, was inspired to create a line of hefty, soft-gripped tools for the mainstream market after watching the difficulty normal kitchen utensils posed for his wife, who was arthritic (Ramdas and Meyer, 2006). Rather than create a niche product line targeted towards the elderly or dexterity-impaired, Farber and his design and business team reasoned that tools inspired by this fringe group with heightened needs would be welcomed by mainstream users.

As another example, executives at Herman Miller told us that their very successful Aeron chair came out of the realization that insight gained from understanding the needs of elderly users could help develop a product that would be attractive to today's office workers. Both the elderly and office workers today spend a great deal of time in their primary chair. The unconventional fabric used in the Aeron chair addresses the need for heat dissipation and evenly distributed pressure points, which had been identified by observing elderly users.

Observing fringe users to inspire mainstream design is a powerful design concept, which although used by many leading designers, has received little attention in the literature on innovation (Ramdas and Meyer, 2006). One of the barriers to using this type of insight for product development may be that it is commonly perceived as leading only to niche products. Managers often make a 'gut call' that the information comes from an outlier representing an unattractively small market segment, or that it is simply an individual idiosyncrasy. However, as the OXO example shows, these insights from the fringes of a market can have the potential to resonate with the mainstream customer, and can move a product to dominate quickly mainstream markets. In this context, the critical task for managers is to distinguish latent needs that have the potential to resonate with the mainstream from those that are niche or idiosyncratic.

While requests for products that embody latent attributes often come from fringe users, mainstream customers may also request a product with unusual attributes. As an example, consider product evolution in Corning's optical glass business, as described to one of the authors by MacAvoy (2005). The optical glass division of Corning sold glass blanks, used in making eyeglasses, to industrial customers including the American Optical Company. In a meeting with Corning executives, the sales manager at American Optical who was handling the Corning account mentioned half-jokingly that it would be nice to have glasses that turned darker when exposed to sunlight, and lighter indoors. Corning's then head of R&D, William Armistead, who happened to be present at this meeting, thought back to the process that Corning used to make the glass backing for thermometers opaque. To make opaque glass, silver was added to the glass at a particular temperature during its formation, to create a colloidal dispersion. Armistead recalled that one of the glass samples they had used while refining this process had turned dark when exposed to sunlight. Putting this serendipitous observation together with the sales manager's request, Corning created photochromic glass.

Latent attributes can also be highlighted by non-users. For example, designing a TV remote for Toshiba, designers at Smart Design scoured New York City until they found a woman who had never used a remote. It turned out that the remote control, TV interface, and instruction manual were developed by entirely different groups within Toshiba. Watching a novice struggle to figure it out highlighted many opportunities to coordinate design across these groups and resulted in new design features such as an obvious power button.

Fringe users are not to be confused with lead users, identified by von Hippel and his colleagues (e.g., von Hippel, 1988; von Hippel, Thomke and Sonnack, 1999) as an important source of innovation. von Hippel characterizes lead users as those users who face an extreme need and, further, have innovated themselves to meet that need. Lead users sometimes *exapt* existing technologies, i.e., borrow them from other market applications and modify them for new uses[5]. A classic example of a product category first envisioned by lead users is mountain bikes – bike enthusiasts in Marin County, California, cut up car tires and mounted them onto the wheels of their bikes, to increase ruggedness for hill climbing. Similarly, sports bras and whiteout were first developed by users. Different lead users might use the same product or technology for very different applications. Consider diapers. Diapers are often used for floor mopping and window cleaning, even by some professional cleaning agencies, suggesting different market applications. In a less obvious application, we have found hospital nurses recommending the use of diapers to make homemade heating pads that can provide moist heat, which helps relieve some types of swelling.

Figure 13.2 summarizes the distinctions among fringe users, non-users, and lead users in unearthing new market opportunities. Fringe users and non-users are considered relative to their relevant core market space, and they can help a firm generate opportunities either for this market space, or for related market spaces. As the figure shows, lead users can generate opportunities relevant to a market space in which they are core users or fringe users. An example of core users as lead users is product work-arounds; where mainstream customers make modifications to products to enhance usability – e.g., many people color code the knobs and buttons on their home appliances. Importantly, lead users can also generate opportunities relevant to entirely different markets, based on re-applying a technology in a completely different market space.

Returning to our goal of making sense out of a jumble of customer requests, categorizing such requests as focusing on established performance dimensions

[5] The term 'exaptation' comes from evolutionary biology, where organisms sometimes modify existing bodily features for new uses (Gould and Vrba, 1982). Dew et al. (2003) document many examples of exaptation of technology.

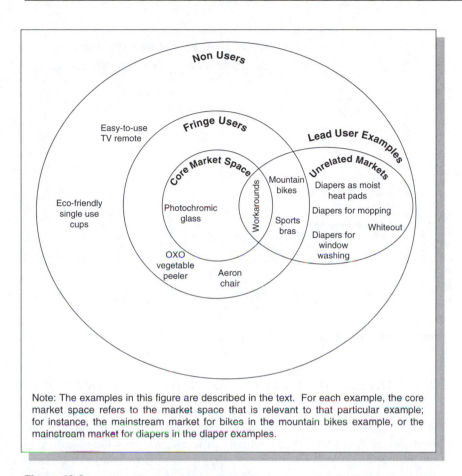

Note: The examples in this figure are described in the text. For each example, the core market space refers to the market space that is relevant to that particular example; for instance, the mainstream market for bikes in the mountain bikes example, or the mainstream market for diapers in the diaper examples.

Figure 13.2
Different types of users as a source of innovation.

on the one hand, and latent dimensions on the other, and considering whether fulfilling each request would result in compromised versus uncompromised primary performance help us establish a lens with which to scrutinize product requests. Using this lens, we consider product requests in each of the four quadrants of the resulting two-by-two matrix shown in Fig. 13.3. Each of these quadrants carries different managerial implications for how to deal with requests. Using this line of thinking helps categorize in a useful way the different types of disruptive innovation that Christensen and his colleagues have identified (e.g., Bower and Christensen, 1995; Christensen, 1997A; Christensen and Raynor, 2003), and it also helps identify other important types of innovation. Finally, this framework helps us to use the insight obtained from analyzing customer requests to provide input into product platform strategy.

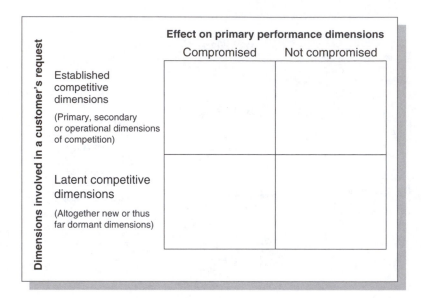

Figure 13.3
A framework to classify customer requests.

2. A conceptual framework for classifying customer requests

We discuss below how the customer requests that fall in each of the four quadrants of Fig. 13.3 are conceptually different, and how they need to be managed differently. We flesh out our framework using a variety of examples from different industries, to emphasize the general applicability of the ideas developed. These insights are summarized in Fig. 13.4. Then in the next section, we return to Chapman Innovations, the company introduced in Section 1, and examine how our framework can help them manage their diverse customer requests.

2.1. Requests for performance along established dimensions that do not compromise primary performance

Depending on the engineering tradeoffs in a product, in some cases requests for better performance along primary or secondary performance dimensions may not compromise performance along other primary dimensions. Sometimes technical performance dimensions happen to be independent, and in other cases, novel technologies can help eliminate tradeoffs amongst technical

Dimensions involved in a customer's request	Effect on primary performance dimensions: Compromised	Effect on primary performance dimensions: Not compromised
Established competitive dimensions (Primary, secondary or operational dimensions of competition)	***Sustaining innovation*** (e.g. faster *and* higher resolution printing) ***Low-end disruption*** (e.g. plastic eyeglass lenses) ***Modularization-based disruption*** (e.g. IBM's move to an open architecture in the 80's)	***Sustaining innovation*** (e.g. hands free dialing in cell phones) ***Operational improvement*** (e.g. cost reduction via better inventory management)
Latent competitive dimensions (Altogether new or thus far dormant dimensions)	***New market disruption*** (e.g. handheld computers) ***Non-obvious niche products***	***Resonant innovation*** (e.g. OXO vegetable peeler, Aeron chair, photochromic glass) ***Non-obvious niche products***

Figure 13.4
Conceptual differences among different types of customer requests.

performance dimensions, resulting in an ability to avoid compromise. For example, in analog cell phones, there was a direct tradeoff between signal-to-noise ratio and battery life: increasing signal-to-noise ratio required more power, which in turn reduced battery life. In contrast, digital cell phones use digital compression technology to transfer the signal in such a way that the clarity of the signal is unrelated to battery life.

Christensen and his colleagues use the term 'sustaining innovation' to describe improvements in performance along technical dimensions that core customers care for. To quote Christensen, Anthony and Roth (2004), page xvi, 'They (sustaining innovations) are improvements to existing products along dimensions historically valued by customers. Airplanes that fly farther, computers that process faster, cellular phone batteries that last longer, and televisions with incrementally or dramatically clearer images are all sustaining innovations.' Schmidt and Porteus (2000) and Schmidt and van Mieghem (2005) point out that sustaining innovations typically first attract share at the top of the market and trickle downward over time, displaying what they call 'high end encroachment.'

Meeting customer requests that focus on better performance along primary or secondary performance dimensions require sustaining innovation. This is true regardless of whether or not doing so would compromise any primary performance dimensions, i.e., it is true for both the upper left and upper right quadrants of Fig. 13.3. Although Christensen focuses on technical performance in describing sustaining innovation, a customer request for better performance along an operational dimension – e.g., lower cost – which a firm can meet without compromising primary performance, is conceptually very similar to sustaining innovation. The difference is that it is achieved via better operational effectiveness (*a la* Porter, 1996), not via improvement in product technology. Such innovations, which we term as 'operational improvements,' would also fall in the upper right quadrant of Fig. 13.3.

Mainstream customer segments may differ in terms of which primary performance dimensions they value the most, and conceivably some mainstream segments might even value secondary dimensions more highly[6], so a firm that serves multiple mainstream segments will need to continually improve along multiple primary and secondary performance dimensions. Firms that serve multiple mainstream segments must also decide what combinations of performance levels to offer, of the primary and secondary performance dimensions. If customer segments differ in their relative willingness to pay for different primary and secondary dimensions of performance, the firm can design multiple products targeted at these different customer segments. The techniques a firm can use for developing products that offer different combinations of levels of technical attributes at different price points are fairly well known in the context of classical marketing; needs can be prioritized using conjoint analysis, product lines structured as segmentation and positioning exercises, and resources allocated for R&D to support these goals. While tools such as conjoint analysis assume static conditions, firms typically deal with this limitation by periodically performing new conjoint analyses for established dimensions of performance, in each new product release cycle.

At some point in the product's life cycle, customers become increasingly less willing to pay for improvements in primary performance dimensions, as the performance offered along these dimensions starts to exceed their needs (Adner and Zemsky, 2005; Christensen and Raynor, 2003). At this point secondary dimensions start to play a bigger role in product evolution, and can move up to primary status.

In some cases, secondary dimensions may have been known to the firms in a market for a long time, but not offered because the technology was not ready, or was not cost effective. For example, again in the arena cell phones, hands-free dialing is a dimension that cell phone manufacturers know to be of importance to customers, and offering this feature does not entail major compromises on primary features such as the size of the phone, quality of the signal, etc., which would make the product unattractive to current core

---

[6] Recall that the difference between primary and secondary dimensions is partly a question of degree, and partly depends on whether or not the dimension is embodied in current products.

customers. Yet hands-free dialing is not offered on many phones because firms have not yet figured out how to do it right. In other cases, secondary dimensions may not have been offered because doing so would compromise performance along primary performance dimensions. This leads us to the upper left quadrant in Fig. 13.3.

2.2. Requests for performance along established dimensions that compromise primary performance

Often, customer requests for higher performance along a primary or secondary dimension require a compromise along other primary dimensions, due to the engineering constraints in a product's design (e.g., Krishnan and Zhu, 2006). Such requests would fall in the upper left quadrant of Fig. 13.3.

As in the upper right quadrant, sustaining innovation is needed to improve performance along primary and secondary dimensions. Further, since multiple primary dimensions may exist and pull in different directions, sustaining innovations in this quadrant would include breakthroughs that weaken or eliminate the *tradeoffs* among primary performance dimensions, which would cause a movement from the upper left to the upper right quadrant of our matrix.

As in the upper right quadrant, in the upper left quadrant of our matrix firms need to decide on what combinations of the multiple primary and secondary dimensions they will offer on the market, since mainstream segments will differ in their ordering of these dimensions. Tools such as conjoint analysis are relevant here as well.

As noted in Section 2.1, at some point, customers' willingness to pay for improved primary performance starts to drop off, and secondary performance dimensions start to become important. If enhancing such secondary dimensions will compromise performance along primary dimensions, it makes sense for a firm to introduce these secondary dimensions only after it has exceeded its customers' needs along primary dimensions, because at this point, some amount of performance along a primary dimension can be traded away to introduce a secondary technical dimension. For example, in the aircraft industry, early aircraft had only the most basic amenities because the primary performance dimensions –ability to be airborne at all, speed and maneuverability – were closely dependent on weight. In the first passenger air service, the passenger sat on a sack of mail. Over time, as technology evolution enabled heavier aircraft to be fast and maneuverable, creature comforts were added. Notice that within the market, customers with the greatest need for the primary performance requirements will be least willing to tradeoff primary performance for secondary performance – for example, a fighter plane pilot cares much more about speed and maneuverability than creature comforts, relative to a business traveler.

Operational performance dimensions such as customization, delivery speed, and cost, which are obvious dimensions to compete on in any market, can also compromise primary performance. Ulrich (1995) argues that moving from an integral to a modular product architecture can allow for greater customization and lower cost, but that this comes at the expense of reduced performance. In addition, while customers might request cheap, customized products that can be delivered right away, they will not buy these products unless they meet the basic primary performance requirements. So here as well, it makes sense for a firm to cater to requests for these operational dimensions of performance only after it has been able to exceed its customers' needs along the primary dimensions of performance.

Christensen and Raynor (2003) suggest that a firm should adopt an integral architecture for its product so long as the performance requirements of the market are not met. Beyond this point, the firm should consider moving to a more modular architecture to enhance customization and reduce cost. Since some compromise in primary performance dimensions is likely to occur due to modularization, modularized products will at first be more attractive to customers in the low end of the current market, who have the least stringent needs along the primary performance dimensions. Christensen and Raynor (2003) view a move to modularization as a type of disruptive innovation, as it fits their definition of disruption – i.e., innovations that compromise some performance dimensions that are of value to core customers while performing better on some dimensions that are not. They cite IBM's move to an open architecture in the 1980s as an example of modularization-based disruption in the computer industry.

For assembled products, moving to a modular architecture is often a way to increase customization and reduce cost. For other types of products, novel technologies can achieve the same end, albeit often initially at the expense of technical performance. For example, consider Corning Inc.'s optical glass business. When first faced with the option of making plastic lenses, Corning executives felt that while these would be cheaper than glass lenses, they would compromise lens quality (MacAvoy, 2005). In Christensen and Raynor's terminology, plastic lenses would be an example of 'low-end disruption.'

We view disruptions of the type discussed in this subsection, which fit in the upper left quadrant of our matrix, as qualitatively different from the other type of disruption – discussed in the next subsection – that fits in the lower left quadrant. The difference lies in the fact that all players in the industry are keenly aware of customer needs, and therefore product dimensions, that fall in the upper quadrants of our matrix. Therefore, disruptions that fit in the upper left quadrant are in a sense inevitable. It is only a matter of who will implement them first, and *how*. For example, while Corning and all its competitors in the glass business knew that customers value low cost, exactly how low cost would be achieved – e.g., via plastic lenses, modified manufacturing processes, outsourcing to cheaper but less qualified suppliers, etc. – was not known a priori.

2.3. Requests for performance along latent dimensions that compromise primary performance

Some customer requests involve attributes or dimensions that the firm's products do not currently compete on, and that are currently considered unimportant to the mainstream market. There are several reasons why a dimension might be considered unimportant by firms in the market. One reason this might happen is that these dimensions may not be initially perceived as important even by the customer. Customers' preferences could be lexicographic, with customers evaluating products first by one dimension, and then by another, until a choice is made (Fishburn, 1974; Nakamura, 2002). Because of lexicographic or more realistically, partially lexicographic preferences combined with limited cognitive processing and bounded rationality (Simon, 1982), a customer might focus in on the primary dimensions of performance, ignoring other dimensions that are in fact important to him or her. Another reason some dimensions might seem unimportant to the customer is that if there is little variation in the products offered in the marketplace along these dimensions of performance, consumers may not realize that these dimensions are important to them – i.e., it may be that they realize certain dimensions are important only when they see variation along these dimensions. In addition, some dimensions may become important due to macro level changes – e.g., eco-friendliness is likely become more important if world pollution increases.

Since latent performance dimensions are not recognized as important by all firms in a market, they can be a source of competitive advantage. It is in finding such latent dimensions that requests from users on the fringes of the market can come in handy, since fringe users face a heightened need along some dimensions of performance.

Borrowing from a utility theory framework, the weights placed on different dimensions of performance differ for mainstream users and fringe users, for a couple of reasons. First, users on the fringes of a market may have a different ordering of needs than users in the main market. For example, in Christensen's Kittyhawk disk drive example (Christensen, 1997B), HP's mainstream customers in the disk drive market were computer manufacturers, who cared more about having a high storage capacity disk drive than a small disk drive. In contrast, Nintendo was interested in very small size disk drives intended for hand-held games. Nintendo, whom we would call a fringe customer because of its heightened need for small size, had a much greater need for a small size drive than for a high capacity drive. Alternatively, fringe users may have the same ordering of needs as mainstream customers, but smaller gaps in the intensity of needs along different dimensions. For example in the case of laser printers, a highly space-conscious user might care most about printing speed and print resolution, just like any other user, but the need for small footprint comes close in intensity. What is common to both these scenarios of fringe user needs is that fringe users tend to highlight latent performance dimensions.

If meeting a customer request for performance along a latent dimension diminishes a product's performance along one or more primary dimensions that current core customers care about, we obtain, in effect, the classic scenario that defines the innovator's dilemma (Christensen, 1997B), which Christensen and Raynor (2003) reclassify as 'new market disruption.' In this situation, new products – often introduced by new entrant firms – rate lower along the primary dimensions of performance but offer performance advantages along some new technical performance dimensions that are not considered important by the core market. Such products are initially attractive only to a niche market, but as performance improves along the primary dimensions, they become attractive to mainstream customers.

A firm can always choose to develop a niche product that compromises primary performance to serve a fringe market. However, if the firm anticipates a steep trajectory of improvement in the product along primary performance dimensions, while maintaining or improving performance along the dimensions valued more by the niche market, there is a strong incentive to aim for a mainstream product. Notice that for such a firm, sufficiently rapid improvement along primary performance dimensions is necessary to achieve disruption. This is what separates a truly disruptive innovation from a *potentially* disruptive innovation. Adner and Zemsky (2006) develop an analytical model that shows how the threat of disruption depends on a number of factors including rate of technological advance of the disruptive technology, the number of mainstream and niche-focused firms, and the utilities that mainstream customers derive from existing products and niche customers derive from a niche product.

2.4. Requests for performance along latent dimensions that do not compromise primary performance

Customer requests that fall in this category have a special significance. If it turns out that the primary dimensions of performance are *not* compromised when latent dimensions are added on, and the latent dimensions resonate deeply with the mainstream market when products that incorporate those dimensions are presented, then the firm has the potential to develop a mass-market product with greater appeal to all consumers.

For example, consider the line of OXO kitchen tools. To develop a mass-market vegetable peeler that incorporated latent performance dimensions, which were unearthed by observing the fringes of the market, the OXO line offered a level of blade sharpness demanded by the mass market, as well as better ease-of-grip. Unlike in the case of a move to modularity, which is very likely to reduce performance along the primary dimensions, increased ease-of-grip would not necessarily imply reduced blade sharpness.[7] Note also that if the firm had decided to develop a niche market product rather than a mass market product, it might have even further enhanced the ease-of-grip, as the level at which an arthritic's willingness to pay for better performance along this dimension starts to drop off should exceed the corresponding level for a mainstream customer.

While requests for latent dimensions of performance often come from the fringes of the market, they can also come from mainstream customers, as we saw in the case of Corning's discovery of photochromic glass. Interestingly, Corning found that inducing a photochromic effect in glass did not in any way compromise the other key properties of its optical glass blanks, and it resulted in the creation of a product that was attractive to a number of Corning's mainstream customers.

We use the term 'resonant innovation' to describe the situation in which a mainstream product is inspired by the consideration of latent performance dimensions that do not compromise the product's primary performance dimensions. The addition of any latent performance dimension that does not compromise primary performance dimensions, results in a *potentially* resonant innovation. Only when the new dimension introduced is embraced by the mainstream market that a truly resonant innovation emerges.

Traditional market research – including quantitative methods such as conjoint analysis as well as qualitative methods such as focus groups – are well suited to testing products developed in response to requests that fall in the upper two quadrants of our matrix. We believe that a different type of testing is needed to separate potentially resonant innovations from truly resonant innovations. Since a latent dimension is being introduced, potential customers will find it hard to react to verbal or even pictorial depictions of the product. Intensive prototyping or even a small-scale launch may be needed so that consumers can actually try out the product and make the leap, to actually recognize the latent dimension as one that resonates with them.

2.5. Key insights from our framework

Our framework generates several insights useful to a company that is facing a multitude of customer requests and is struggling with the question of where to focus efforts to improve its competitive position. We discuss these insights below, and summarize them in Fig. 13.4.

---

[7] Of course, a firm may choose to offer a less sharp blade than is technically feasible if customers are no longer willing to pay for improved sharpness.

The benefits of distinguishing between established and latent dimensions of competition

It is now widely recognized that improving a product's performance along primary performance dimensions is an obvious path for any player in an industry, and therefore the competition in this arena will be intense. Since all players recognize the importance of primary performance dimensions, this type of improvement is likely to soon become an order qualifier, rather than an order winning criterion, forcing players further up market.

Once customers are no longer willing to pay for improvements along primary performance dimensions, it makes sense to start introducing other dimensions of performance, which customers *are* willing to pay for improvements in. Our framework helps focus attention on the *types* of requests customers are making, and to separate out requests based on whether they are for additional performance dimensions that are established, or are latent. Pursuing established performance dimensions that are the focus of all players in the industry is a necessary rat race. Pursuing latent dimensions can be a more subtle and less predictable way to compete.

We believe that deliberately separating out requests for established and latent dimensions is a useful exercise for managers, because there is a fundamental difference in how companies pursue the two types of requests. Successfully pursuing additional performance dimensions that are already established in the industry relies on the firm acquiring or developing technologies and manufacturing and distribution techniques that are better than their competitors'. In contrast, successfully pursuing latent dimensions requires that the firm have better insight into customer need than their competitors, and a better method for deciding which latent needs to pursue and how to do so, in addition to operational capabilities needed to deliver on latent dimensions.

It is important to note that neither a technology-based established dimensions approach nor an insight-driven latent dimensions approach is inherently better than the other. The best choice of approach depends heavily on a firm's capabilities and self-identity. We do not suggest that managers should always accept requests that highlight latent dimensions, nor that they should do so right away. Rather, once a dimension has been recognized as latent, a further decision is needed regarding whether or when to pursue it. The important thing is that having recognized the latent potential of a new dimension of competition reduces the chances of later being taken by surprise by a competitor.

Low-end disruption and modularization versus New market disruptions

Another useful feature of our framework is that it gives us a new way to think about the different types of disruptive innovation identified by Christensen and his colleagues. We find that both low-end disruption and modularization-based disruption (introduced in Christensen and Raynor, 2003) are conceptually different from what Christensen terms 'new market disruptions'. This can be seen by comparing the two quadrants in the left of the matrix in Fig. 13.4. A critical difference is that both low-end disruption and modularization-based disruption focus on improvement along operational dimensions – reduced cost and increased customization – which are relatively obvious, and hence established, ways to compete in *any* industry, while the types of disruption in the lower left quadrant introduce a new and non-obvious – i.e., latent – technical dimension of competition.

Disrupting an industry based on operational dimensions requires sufficient user insight to recognize that sustaining performance improvements are becoming less and less relevant, and in addition, it requires prowess and creativity in managing a firm's production and distribution network, and in configuring products differently to meet already established needs. In contrast, disrupting based on latent performance dimensions is a function of deep market insight that unearths these dimensions, combined with the operational capability to actually deliver on unearthed dimensions. Latent dimensions are only on the radar screen of those firms that seek them out and then actively pursue them. The user insight needed to unearth latent dimensions is unlikely to emerge from traditional market surveys and quantitative market research.

Resonant innovation

Importantly, our framework highlights the critical role that latent performance dimensions that *do not* compromise primary performance dimensions play in product evolution. By Christensen's definition, products that incorporate such innovations are *not* disruptive innovations. In fact, the resulting products, which fall in the lower right quadrant of our matrix, are completely different conceptually from both sustaining and disruptive innovations as defined by Christensen. Innovations in this quadrant are not sustaining innovations, because they introduce an altogether new or previously ignored performance dimension rather than improve along a performance dimension that mainstream customers already value. In addition, they are not disruptive innovations, as they do not compromise performance along primary performance dimensions. The products in this quadrant, which we call 'resonant innovations,' have significant potential in the mainstream market, as they do not compromise features that the mainstream market values, and they simultaneously incorporate new performance dimensions that no one had believed the mainstream market would value. Indeed, they have the potential to steal the entire mainstream market, or a sizeable portion of it, as reflected in the examples cited in Ramdas and Meyer (2006). Therefore, innovations in this quadrant need to be managed closely.

Since innovations in the lower right quadrant of Fig. 13.4 add new layers of performance without compromising existing performance dimensions, it is likely that such innovations will be costlier, at least initially. Unlike disruptive innovations, which often work from the bottom layers of the mainstream market towards the top, resonant innovations in the lower right quadrant of Fig. 13.4 are more likely to work from the top layers of the mainstream market towards the bottom. Consider as an example a new bio-degradable disposable cup that has been developed by International Paper, in collaboration with Green Mountain Coffee, a niche organic coffee roaster whose customers are highly environmentally conscious. This bio-degradable cup does not compromise any primary performance dimensions of a disposable cup, so it is in fact a potentially resonant innovation. However, for the cup to gain mainstream acceptance, its price will need to be reduced to a level that is acceptable to International Paper's mainstream customers, such as the major fast food chains.

A critical factor in uncovering and introducing resonant innovations is developing deep insight into user need, similar to that required for disruptive innovation, to surface latent needs that the company can satisfy. As we have discussed, fringe users, non-users and lead users can help unearth such latent needs. In addition, resonant innovations often involve operational upheaval. For example, making the OXO good grips line required a competence in rubber forming that was not needed for traditional kitchen tools. Similarly, International Paper needed new process competencies to make a bio-degradable disposable cup. Thus maintaining a nimble supply network can be crucial to resonant innovation. Resonant innovation can also require close coordination across previously independent entities, as highlighted by the example of the TV remote made by Toshiba, discussed in Section 1.3.

A subtle but important point with regard to resonant innovations is that while the latent needs that underlie the product requests in the lower right quadrant of Fig. 13.4 may often come from fringe segments, to have true mass-market appeal, the degree to which these needs are met should be in line with the needs of a mass-market user, not a fringe user. Ramdas and Meyer (2006) document many instances where the *inspiration*, but not the actual *specifications*, for mass-market products comes from designers observing fringe customers. Treating fringe users as a source of specifications for mainstream products is a costly mistake that results in narrowly appealing products.

Unlike disruptive innovations, which are typically introduced by new entrants, our research suggests that resonant innovations are typically introduced by established firms. In the race to protect themselves against disruption by new entrants, mainstream firms should not disregard this important source of breakthrough innovation. For example, Christensen and Raynor (2003), page 51, Table 2.1, highlight three approaches to creating new growth businesses: sustaining innovations, low-end disruptions, and new market disruptions. The type of innovation that we are calling resonant innovation does not belong in any of these categories. Yet it can result in tremendous growth.

Finally, the litmus test that separates potentially resonant innovation from truly resonant innovation differs from the type of traditional market research that is valuable in the upper two quadrants of our matrix. Because mainstream users often have difficulty imagining exactly what a new performance dimension is, much less how much they would want it, firms must develop capabilities to test high fidelity concepts in a meaningful way, to qualify them for launch.

Platform planning and product architecture

The framework we have developed also brings insights on product platform planning. Robertson and Ulrich (1998) define a platform as a set of common assets that is shared across products. By this definition, a platform may include shared components, shared production processes, or a shared distribution and after sales support network. These authors conceptually break down the process of mapping a platform onto a set of planned products into a differentiation plan, which determines what features make products unique, and a commonality plan, which determines what assets are shared. They suggest bundling the least differentiated features into common chunks, while keeping differentiating features in customized modules. Krishnan and Ulrich (2001) suggest that product architecture and platform planning are core elements of new product strategy, and require cross-functional thinking. Ramdas (2003) suggests that product architecture is linked to several key dimensions of variety management, such as the degree of customization, timing of new variants, and variety decoupling points in the production process, at which as-yet-undifferentiated work in process is converted into differentiated products.

One important insight from the framework that we have developed is that neither disruptive innovations nor resonant innovations are likely to share a platform with existing mainstream products in the market space at which they are targeted. Low cost disruptions often involve completely different processes, while modularization-based disruptions hinge on changing the product architecture and production and distribution network. Both new market disruptions and resonant innovations typically embody both new production processes and product architectures to enable performance along latent product dimensions. Thus, firms that seek to compete via disruptive or resonant innovation need to be prepared to invest significant amounts up front for the architectural changes involved in creating a new platform.

Another important insight pertains to how the cumulative information garnered from gathering and analyzing customer requests via our framework can be used for platform planning. Recall that requests in the lower two quadrants of Fig. 13.4, which involve totally new or thus far dormant technical dimensions, often come from users on the fringes of the market. However, even in the upper two quadrants, fringe users are likely to request the most extreme performance levels along established performance dimensions. Thus, overall, fringe users help define the boundaries to which established dimensions are likely to be stretched, while also identifying new dimensions of performance. This information is invaluable for platform planning, and it is arguably most useful early in the product life cycle. Ramdas and Meyer (2006) suggest that fringe users can be a valuable source of input into a company's platform strategy-definition process. By exploring the fringes of the market space upfront before designing any of the products in a product family, the firm will have a much better sense as to what directions it could later choose to expand into. For example, a firm might decide to develop niche products for some parts of the market, at different points in the future. Knowing the boundaries of the market space upfront will help with architectural decisions. If the firm plans to pursue some niches over time, a different architecture might be needed if it intends to build these niche products off the core platform.

Ramdas and Meyer (2006) warn that using fringe users as a way to identify product platforms requires a fundamental change in the role that designers play in a firm. In most firms, the responsibility for defining the scope of a product or service platform falls under marketing, and it is in fact a crucial element of marketing strategy. It is only after a platform has been designed and the products associated with it broadly envisioned, that designers and engineers are called in to flesh out the details of particular products. Academics can play a role in bringing about the culture change needed to bring designers into platform planning at an early stage, by providing rigorous evidence, based on empirical work, of the benefits from inviting designers into the platform formulation process.

3. Applying our framework to Chapman innovations

Let us now look back at the long list of customer requests faced by Chapman Innovations. How can we use the framework developed above to help this company decide what opportunities to pursue? Figure 13.5 provides a summary of our classification of Chapman's product requests.

For a start, we can try to classify the different types of requests using our matrix. For example, consider the request for color variation, and requests for different types of knits. Variety along these dimensions is known to be important to the core customers in the market, and many of Chapman's competitors compete on these dimensions. For Chapman, offering variety along these dimensions would in no way compromise the fire-retarding properties of its fabrics, or their tensile strength on exposure to fire. Thus, these dimensions of performance fall in the upper right quadrant.

Next, consider the requests for better tensile strength on exposure to heat. Increasing tensile strength compromises fire retardance – and vice versa – as

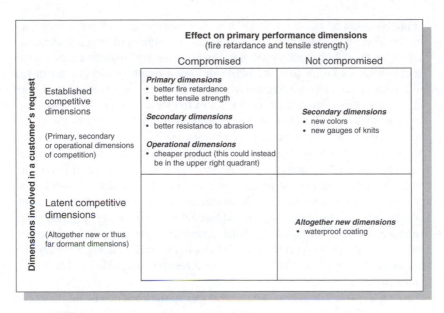

Figure 13.5
An application of our framework to Chapman innovations.

there is an engineering tradeoff between these two primary performance dimensions. Changing the tensile strength of the yarn requires a change in its chemical composition. In the current composition, fire-retarding carbon-based material accounts for 85% of weight, while strengthening agents account for only 15%. To increase tensile strength, the firm would need to increase the percentage of strengthening agents, resulting in a decrease in fire retardance. Similarly, increasing resistance to abrasion, an established albeit secondary technical performance dimension, also reduces performance along the primary dimensions due to engineering tradeoffs. Thus, these requests fall in the upper left quadrant of our matrix.

Next, consider the request, from some industrial customers, for high-strength ropes or cables made of Chapman's yarn, to be used for lifting heavy objects. From an engineering perspective, ropes or cables would need very high tensile strength, so this request also falls in the upper left quadrant.

Now consider the request for lower cost products. This request could fall in the upper right quadrant if the price reduction requested can be achieved via operational improvement without compromising technical performance. However, if the price reduction requested requires a major operational change that compromises technical performance, this request would fall in the upper left quadrant.

Finally, consider the request for a waterproof version of the firm's fabric. Developing a waterproof version would involve applying a waterproof coating to the fabric, and would *not* compromise fire retardance or tensile strength after exposure to heat. While the mainstream products sold in the fire-retardant products market today are not typically waterproof, and core customers in this market today do not seem to care about waterproofing, this is a performance dimension that core customers might be happy to have, particularly since no other important dimensions are compromised. Clearly, this request falls in the lower right quadrant of the matrix. If Chapman produces a mainstream product that offers some level of water proofing, this product would likely be more expensive than the standard fabric, and would likely first appeal to the higher echelons of the mainstream fire retardant fabric market. However, if the cost of offering this additional attribute can be whittled away over time, this type of product has the potential to gradually steal the entire market. As a thought experiment: would you not consider buying a waterproof sweatshirt if it looked and felt exactly like a regular sweatshirt, and cost only marginally more?

From the above discussion, we see that our framework can be applied both to a player that has been in a market for a while, and to a new entrant. Additionally, the framework can be applied to both new and mature markets. Chapman Innovations is a new entrant in a mature market. When applying the framework to a new entrant, it is possible that some of the secondary performance dimensions that are known by firms in the market to be attractive to core customers may already be offered by some of the firms, depending on their positioning and the tradeoffs they have made.

For Chapman, the upper right and left quadrants are less attractive in that Chapman finds very little advantage by competing with large competitors on established product dimensions. Interestingly, none of the requests fell in the lower left quadrant of potential new market disruptions. The request in the lower right quadrant has considerable appeal because it allows Chapman as a new entrant to differentiate its product resulting in a potentially resonant innovation. Since differentiating on a latent attribute often involves competence in processes new to the industry, imitation may be harder; but if the innovation turns out to be easily imitable, the advantage of differentiation could be short lived. A challenge with resonant innovations is to increase scale rapidly to move down the cost curve and establish a brand presence before other competitors step in and catch up.

4. Areas for future research

There are a number of ways in which academic researchers can help refine the ideas we have developed in this chapter. In the above discussion, we assumed that the firm receives requests for new products, from a variety of sources including fringe users or fringe segments. While this often happens, the firm may also actively seek out specific users from whom to glean useful information about needs. Given the high value of fringe users in identifying latent dimensions of performance, future research can help firms to better implement the process of identifying fringe users, learning from them, and translating the knowledge obtained into profitable new products. Several important questions arise around the concept of fringe users:

1. At what point in the product life cycle is it most valuable to pursue fringe users?
2. In what types of product markets is it most valuable to pursue fringe users?
3. How does one find fringe users? Is it better to find fringe users who face an extreme need along just one dimension of a product, or along multiple dimensions?
4. How should information gleaned from fringe users be used in a firm's product planning?
5. Having identified latent attributes, how can a firm ascertain which ones the mainstream market will embrace? In other words, how can it distinguish potentially resonant innovation from truly resonant innovation?

Regarding the question of when it is most valuable to pursue fringe users, in the section above named 'Platform planning and product architecture', we argued that it is useful to pursue fringe users early in the product life cycle, to use them as an input in platform planning. On the other hand, incorporating knowledge from fringe users later in the product life cycle allows the firm to first introduce a product, which embodies the most obvious and important performance dimensions and reap the value created by doing this. When the first generation of products is on the market, the firm has plenty of time to research the fringes of the market to discover latent dimensions that can be incorporated in later products. It should be possible to incorporate the costs and benefits of pursuing fringe users early versus late in quantitative modeling.

Next, consider the issue of the types of product markets in which is it most valuable to pursue fringe users. Clearly the value of information obtained from fringe users is lower in markets where user needs are quite transparent, in that needs are easily identifiable by the designer, rather than lying latent. Academic research can help firms develop ways to measure the degree of 'transparency' of user needs in a product market.

The value of information obtained from fringe users should also be lower in markets where there is little variation in the intensity of the need faced by different users for particular aspects of a product's functionality, or along particular product attributes. If this is the case, the market is very dense around the core and in effect, there is little difference in the preferences of mainstream users and those of fringe users.

How can a firm find fringe users? Ramdas and Meyer (2006) note that fringe users can be found based on physical extremes, cognitive extremes, and extremes in social values. Future research can identify other means, and evaluate the benefits of identifying users with extreme needs along multiple, versus a single attribute or dimension.

Our framework suggests that it is important for a firm to understand whether latent dimensions that it unearths will, or will not compromise performance along primary dimensions. We expect that the issue of whether or not introducing an additional performance dimension – latent or established – will result in some reduction in performance along the primary performance dimensions would depend on the particular product in question. Further research is needed to determine whether or not increasing the number of performance dimensions has systematic effects on the primary performance dimensions. It is possible that performance along some dimensions works synergistically, while there is a tradeoff in other cases. For example, if the sets of activities the firm needs to do to enhance performance along two different dimensions are 'complementary activities' as defined by Milgrom and Roberts (1990) – i.e., increasing the level of one activity increases the payoff from other activities – the performance relationship might be synergistic.

Next, consider the question of how the information garnered from fringe users can be used in a firm's product planning process at any point in time. If the latent dimensions of performance identified do not compromise primary performance, the alternatives available to the firm are: (a) to behave as it would have done in the absence of this information, (b) to introduce a niche product to serve the fringe market, (c) to exploit fringe users as a way to identify needs that may be latent in the main market and then develop a mainstream product resulting in a potentially resonant design, or (d) to implement a combination of (b) and (c), either on one common platform or on separate platforms. A potentially useful area for future research is to incorporate these alternatives into quantitative models, to obtain insights on which path to choose. A key input into such models would be the functions that reflect customers' willingness to pay for incremental improvements in performance along primary and latent dimensions, and how these functions vary for mainstream and fringe customers. Other inputs would include the costs associated with common versus separate platform strategies.

Finally, we expect that the type of testing required to separate potentially resonant innovation from truly resonant innovation differs from the traditional market research tools used to evaluate product opportunities in the upper two quadrants of our framework. Future research should develop and/or uncover good litmus tests for this question.

In our analysis, we have focused on customers as a source of new dimensions of product competition. Yet new dimensions may also be generated internally by a firm, via technology push. We believe that this type of internally driven identification of latent performance dimensions can also be viewed usefully using our framework, by considering whether the new dimension introduced is established or latent, and whether or not it compromises primary performance dimensions. However, these internally generated insights must be subjected to the same rigorous tests as insights gleaned from customer requests.

Acknowledgments

We are grateful to Tyler Thatcher, CEO of Chapman Innovations, for useful discussions about our framework. We are grateful to Sanjay Jain, Tom MacAvoy and the designers and executives at several companies for useful conversations.

References

Adner, R. and P. Zemsky, "A Demand-Based Perspective on Sustainable Competitive Advantage", Strategic Management Journal, 36(2), 229–254, Summer 2005.

Adner, R. and P. Zemsky, "Disruptive Technologies and the Emergence of Competition", RAND Journal of Economics, 27, 215–239, 2006.

Bower, J. L. and C. M. Christensen, "Disruptive Technologies: Catching the Wave", Harvard Business Review, Jan–Feb 1995.

Christensen, C. M., "The Innovator's Dilemma: When New Technologies Cause Great Firms to Fail", HBS Press, 1997A.

Christensen, C. M., "Hewlett-Packard: The Flight of the Kittyhawk", HBS Case No. 9-697-060, HBS Press, 1997B.

Christensen, C. M., S. D. Anthony and E. A. Roth, "Seeing What's Next", HBS Press, 2004.

Christensen, C. M., "Exploring the Limits of the Technology S-Curve, Part I: Component Technologies", Production and Operations Management, pages 334–357, 1992A.

Christensen, C. M., "Exploring the Limits of the Technology S-Curve, Part II: Architectural Technologies", Production and Operations Management, pages 358–366, 1992B.

Christensen, C. M., F. F. Suárez and J. M. Utterback, "Strategies for Survival in Fast-Changing Industries", Management Science, 44(12), 207–220, 1998.

Christensen, C. M. and M. E. Raynor, "The Innovator's Solution: Creating and Sustaining Successful Growth", HBS Press, 2003.

Desai, P., S. Kekre, S. Radhakrishanan and K. Srinivasan, "Product Differentiation and Commonality in Design: Balancing Revenue and Cost Drivers", Management Science, 47(1), 37–51, 2001.

Dew, N., S. D. Sarasvathy and S. Venkataraman, "The Economic Implications of Exaptation", Journal of Evolutionary Economics, 14(1), 69–84, 2003.

Fishburn, P.C., "Lexicographic Orders, Utilities and Decision Rules: A survey", Management Science, 20(11), 1442–1471, 1974.

Gould, S. J. and E. S. Vrba, "Exaptation – A Missing Term in the Science of Form", Paleobiology, 8, 4–15, 1982.

Green, P. E. and A. M. Krieger, "Models and Heuristics for Product Line Selection", Marketing Science, 4, Winter 1985.

Green, P. E. and A. M. Krieger, "Recent Contributions to Optimal Product Positioning and Buyer Segmentation", European Journal of Operational Research, 41(2), 127–141, 1989.

Kim, K. and D. Chhajed, "Product Design with Multiple Quality-Type Attributes", Management Science, 48(11), 1502–1511, 2002.

Krishnan, V. and S. Gupta, "Appropriateness and Impact of Platform-Based Product Development", Management Science, 47(1), 52–68, 2001.

Krishnan, V. and K. Ulrich, "Product Development Decisions: A Review of the Literature", Management Science, 47(1), 1–21, 2001.

Krishnan, V. and W. Zhu, "Designing a Family of Development-Intensive Products", Management Science, 52(6), 813–825, June 2006.

Porter, M. E., "What is Strategy?" Harvard Business Review, Nov–Dec 1996.

MacAvoy, T., retired President and Chairman of the Board of Corning, Inc., conversation with K. Ramdas, October 2005.

Milgrom, P. and J. Roberts, "The Economics of Modern Manufacturing: Technology, Strategy and Organisation", American Economic Review, 80(3), 511–28, June 1990.

Mussa, M. and S. Rosen, "Monopoly and Product Quality", Journal of Economic Theory, 8, 301–317, 1978.

Nakamura, Y., "Lexicographic Quasi-Linear Utility", Journal of Mathematical Economics, 37, 157–178, 2002.

Ramdas, K., "Managing Product Variety: An Integrative Review and Research Directions", Production and Operations Management, 12(1), 79–101, Spring 2003.

Ramdas, K. and M. Meyer, "Fringe Users as a Source of Innovation", manuscript, 2006.

Robertson, D. and K. T. Ulrich, "Planning for Product Platforms", Sloan Management Review, 39, 19–31, 1998.

Schmidt, G. M. and J. A. van Mieghem, "Seagate – Quantum: Encroachment Strategies", Case Article, Informs Transactions on Education, 5(2), January 2005.

Schmidt, G. M. and E. Porteus, "Sustaining Technology Leadership Can Require Both Cost Competence and Innovative Competence", Manufacturing & Service. Operations Management, 2(1), 1–18, Winter 2000.

Simon, H., "Theories of Bounded Rationality", In: Herbert Simon (Ed.) Models of Bounded Rationality, Behavioral Economics and Business Organization, Cambridge: MIT Press, volume 2, pages 408–423, 1982.

Ulrich, K., "The Role of Product Architecture in the Manufacturing Firm," Research Policy, Vol. 24, 419–440, 1995.

Ulrich, K. T. and S. D. Eppinger, Product Design and Development, 3rd edition, NY: Irwin, 2004.

von Hippel, E., The Sources of Innovation, NY: Oxford University Press, 1988.

von Hippel, E., S. Thomke and M. Sonnack, "Creating Breakthroughs at 3M", Harvard Business Review, September 1999.

14 Delivering the product: Defining specifications

Shantanu Bhattacharya

This chapter will deal with the part of the new product development (NPD) process during which the specifications of the product/products are finalized. The definition of the product (the phase where the underlying specifications that will deliver the functionality desired of the product are finalized) balances a combination of factors. In this phase, the marketing needs of the product need to be taken into account, i.e., the specifications of the product have to be matched as closely as possible to the needs of the market, market needs are elicited either through market research or from the understanding of the NPD team of market needs. The final definition of the product also has to be matched to the strategic goals of the firm. The firm may choose to design the product/products to fit with their existing portfolio, to generate savings in component cost from economies of scale and design costs, and to associate the new product with the reputation or brand strength of existing products. Finally, the definition of the product has to take into account the needs for manufacturing competitiveness: the product's specifications should be such that it can be manufactured at a low cost, in a short time, and if possible, using the manufacturing process and competencies of the firm.

The definition phase of the NPD process typically uses market preferences as an input for finalizing specifications. In practice, customer preferences are elicited using either quantitative market research techniques like conjoint analysis and Kano analysis (Lehmann, 1989) for products that are based on incremental innovation (customers can give meaningful feedback to the NPD team on features and functionality of products that they have seen before) or subjective market research techniques like one-on-one interviews or focus groups to provide the NPD team with a broad understanding of specifications and features that customers are looking for in the new product. There is an extensive literature on market research techniques that the reader can refer to (Lehmann, 1989; Smith and Fletcher, 2004), therefore in this chapter, we do not focus on market research techniques.

During the definition phase in the NPD process, input data, and information about customer preferences and competitive products are used to finalize key specifications of the product, such as its target customers, functionality, and features (Bacon et al., 1994). These specifications are used in the product realization and system integration phases (comprising of activities like prototyping, testing, and evaluation both internally and collaboratively with customers, these activities are analyzed in more detail in subsequent chapters of this book) to develop a producible and serviceable product. For example, in the development of portable computer systems at Dell, the product specifications constitute parameters such as the product dimensions, weight, battery life, etc. These specifications are finalized at Dell based on market studies, customer feedback, and analysis of competitive products, and are then used by the realization phase which involves the design of the boards and the housing and the integration phase which involves production tooling, pilot testing, and refinement of the product design to reduce the product's unit variable cost in production (Bhattacharya et al., 1998).

The definition phase in the NPD process does not have to be executed sequentially with the other activities, indeed, as represented in the schematic in Fig. 1.2 of Chapter 1 of this book, it can be executed in parallel with other activities like the generation and refinement of the concept of the product and design activities like prototyping and the testing and evaluation activities. This distinction of the definition phase from a solely sequential activity will be highlighted in the fourth section of this chapter.

The remainder of this chapter is organized by four sections. In the first section, we provide guidelines to answer the question: 'What is the input data to define the specifications and how is it represented?' Specifically, we describe how the information needed to finalize the specifications of the product (both the strategic inputs and the design inputs) are represented to all stakeholders in the NPD process. This section covers the use of commonly used design inputs like design libraries and commonly used strategic inputs like product innovation charters. The information in these input databases are refined as the NPD process evolves, and they give a guideline to the NPD team as to which set of specifications would meet with the marketing needs of the customer, the strategic direction of the firm, and could be produced at a low cost. The strategic direction of the firm can have non-conventional goals as well, which are described in this section.

In the second section, we provide guidelines to answer the question: 'How to define the specifications of the product based on the inputs?' First, we describe the Quality Function Deployment (QFD) approach to setting the technical specifications of a component of a new product. The QFD approach is widely in practice and encompasses the House of Quality (HOQ) framework. The QFD approach starts out by asking consumers subjective questions about the new component and then using a ranked response method, creates a set of weights for each customer attribute. Following this, the QFD framework describes the trade-offs associated with the engineering characteristics and helps the NPD team decide the value of the specifications of the key engineering characteristics. This process takes into account the responses of the participants in the consumer survey of competitive assessments as well. After that, we describe uncertainty and fuzzy set based approaches to enable the NPD team to define specifications. Tools like analytical target cascading to help decision-making on product specifications are also discussed.

The third section describes the management of the product definition process by analyzing the various trade-offs between the different forces such as addressing marketing needs better versus making the product easier to manufacture. In this section, we provide guidelines to answer questions like '*When the product specifications should be finalized?*' The key trade-offs analyzed are the balance between the attractiveness of the product to the market against a lower unit cost through better manufacturing process design, and assessing technology uncertainty through using new but risky technologies against old but proven technologies. Additionally, a tool using fuzzy logic to keep the specifications fuzzy until the point where the firm feels that they have understood customer preferences well is outlined. This section also provides rules of thumb to better manage trade-offs in the product definition process at the managerial level under different environments.

In the fourth section, the interaction of the product definition phase with other activities during the NPD process is outlined for better-integrated product development. We provide guidelines to answer questions like '*How does the definition phase interact with other parts of the NPD process?*' Coordination mechanisms between other activities and the definition phase are described, and the mechanisms are evaluated for appropriate use in different environments. This section also addresses the question of allocating different parts of the coordination activities to different parts of the organization, and which coordination activities that are resources more likely to be focused on during the NPD process. A summary of the flow of the chapter is presented in Fig. 14.1.

Based on the schematic, we now describe how the goals of the firm and the market needs and design knowledge are represented to enable the NPD team to define the specifications of the product.

1. Representation of input data

To define the specifications of the product, firms use a number of different tools to guide their design teams as to what aspects of NPD should be focused on in defining the product. Crawford (1980) was one of the first articles to define guiding policies for NPD at a firm. In this article, a set of organizational policies, objectives, guidelines, and restrictions are incorporated into a charter, which is called the firm's product innovation charter (PIC).

The PIC as envisaged by Crawford described three major areas as components, which were to be set by the senior management of the firm. (i) The first

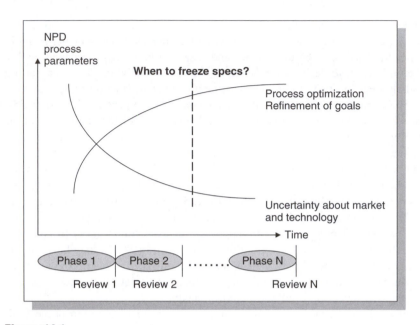

Figure 14.1
Schematic of chapter.

area was described as 'target business arenas,' this dimension described: (a) the product type to be focused on by the firm (e.g., if the firm Citra makes consumer goods based on packaged food, the product type by a firm positioning itself to be for health conscious markets would be 'low fat' or 'fat free'); (b) the technology to be used in products (listing technologies to be focused on, for Citra, examples would be to use baking instead of frying, or replacing whole milk with skim milk in milk-based products); and (c) intermediate or end-user markets (for Citra, intermediate markets would consist of firms that use their products based on a licensing agreement for integrating into their own products for customers, for instance firms that use low-fat yogurt developed by Citra for their ice-cream. End user markets would consist of health conscious working people in certain income segments who could afford their products on a regular basis). (ii) The second area was described as 'the goals of product innovation,' which included both quantitative and qualitative targets (e.g., Citra could choose to focus on a large market share for new products as one quantitative goal, this would mean products would be based on food materials that were popular, and that the products would not be too expensive, else price elasticity would reduce the market share. Qualitative targets would be exemplified by 'crispy' food items or 'fluffy' food items). (iii) The third major area identified by Crawford was 'the programme of activities selected to achieve the goals,' this encompassed items like resources available for developing the new products, the strengths of the firm that they could utilize, the weaknesses that had to be compensated for, etc. (e.g., Citra would identify in their PIC that their strengths are a certain packaging color that can be used for their products, and current distribution channels should be used as far as possible for their products).

The PIC is intended to convey the firm's strategic planning process results to the NPD teams, and serves as a formal communication tool of the strategic goals for innovation set by the senior management for the teams who are responsible for the innovation process. The PIC is conveyed to members of all functions in the firm, and serves as a complement to the firm's mission statement in that it translates the goals of the firm into goals for innovation.

It is interesting that the PIC can be used with non-traditional goals and objectives for the NPD program as well. For instance, Nissing (2005) proposes the goal of 'strategic inventing' as one possibility for a NPD program, whereby products are designed with an emphasis on securing revenue streams through patents, i.e., strategic positioning of intellectual property. In contrast to traditional product development in which a discovery or invention is first analyzed for fit with business objectives and then developed into a product with patent protection, strategic inventing takes a different route. The research conducted by the firm is focused on obtaining a valuable strategic position with patents, and this strategic position is considered more important than other concomitant, functional, or consumer benefits. Hence, strategic inventing involves defining a desirable IP position, and then defining a product that fits the position. In this aspect, it can be considered similar to products that are described as 'loss leaders.'

In the recent past, Bart (2002) explored how the use of the PIC and the content of PICs have changed since the original article by Crawford. He finds that some items get chosen largely in PICs than others, and PICs have a significant relationship with selected performance measures. Reinertsen and Smith (1991) also find that the time-to-market for new products launched by firms with a clear PIC is shorter. The cause of this effect is that since PICs have clearly defined the new product mission statement, new product ideas that do not match the PIC can be killed more quickly, enabling the efficient use of resources for new product ideas that are eventually chosen. Hence, by providing an effective screening mechanism, PICs add value by better selection of new product concepts, and consequently, a more effective use of resources for their development. A summary of the main PIC elements are shown in Fig. 14.2.

Bart (2002) finds that more than 75 per cent of the firms in their sample had some formal policies in place to guide their NPD teams, and 29 per cent of the respondents had a formal PIC. In addition, in the content of the PICs, some components like 'concern for customers,' 'new product purpose,' 'new product customers/markets,' 'general new product goals,' and 'new product type' were mentioned much more frequently (in more than 85 per cent of

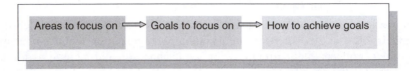

Figure 14.2
Main elements of PIC.

the cases). However, when a particular PIC item was mentioned, it was much more likely to be specified only 'somewhat' as opposed to 'clearly.' Bart conjectures that this could be due to two reasons: the reason working positively is that senior management would like to leave the PIC statement flexible so that NPD teams are not 'strait-jacketed' in their innovation effort. However, the ambiguity could also reflect that senior managers are unable to give more accurate guidelines as they themselves are not sure of what strategy elements should be reflected in new products, leading to a 'loss of focus.' In addition, he finds that if an item was specified in the PIC, it was significantly and positively correlated to performance, leading to the conclusion that stating goals in the PIC leads to better performance on that dimension.

There have been cases of firms having different PICs for different R&D divisions to articulate the fact that the goals, business arenas and programme of activities of product development for the different divisions are different. Crawford (1980) had highlighted that different product categories in the same firm could have different PICs. For instance, Microsoft's Advanced Technology Sector (ATC) based in Beijing in China has a different charter as it is responsible for technology transfer of products developed in China to the United States and vice versa (Buderi, 2005). Their mandate is to incorporate technologies or features in core Microsoft products for the local market, as well as change core products with new features developed by them for the purpose of global markets. In this case, having a separate PIC for the ATC makes clear to the ATC team that their mission is to encourage the technology transfer between the NPD teams in China and in the United States.

In our experience, we have seen that formal statements of the PIC are trying to balance different forces; hence, crafting the PIC carefully is an important element for the representation of input data. The main challenges of the PIC are:

- give sufficient guidance to the NPD teams
- leave enough room for flexibility for specific NPD projects
- play on and leverage existing strengths
- leave enough room for innovation and addition to core strengths

Balancing these forces is the key to enable NPD teams to develop the right specifications for new products. As mentioned earlier, PIC statements tend to be somewhat ambiguous, this ambiguity may be by design, or may be because it is difficult to craft more streamlined guidelines. In terms of best practices, we have seen successful firms playing to their strengths (more frequently if these strengths are sustainable strengths) in crafting rigorous guidelines. For example, if the brand image is a strength, we recommend that firms clearly articulate that the brand should be visible clearly on the product, and the advertising campaign should make use of the brand strength. If a firm is weak in a certain area, then the firm leaves more ambiguity in their PIC about that area, to give the NPD team more leverage in trying to find creative solutions to compensate for the weakness. Bart and Pujari (2007) provide an overview of the challenges faced by the firm in creating the right PIC statement to balance these forces.

The other main challenge for firms in writing the PIC as an input to defining specifications is to enable their NPD teams to maintain a mix of freshness/newness and diversification of products in addition to leveraging their strengths. This challenge often causes firms to confuse short-term advantages for long-term advantages, and introducing too many me-too products in the market, hence limiting the scope of radical innovation. In our experience, firms have managed this challenge by incorporating measures like profits or sales from radical new products should be a certain proportion of the total, e.g., 3M has made similar measures popular in practice. The recommendations for the PIC are summarized in Fig. 14.3.

In addition to the PIC, firms also create product design libraries to enable the rapid evolution of certain specifications. These product design libraries

	Seek additional strengths (increase diversification)	Play to strengths (low diversification)
Strengths/ Weaknesses known	Well defined PIC with goals for freshness	Well defined PIC with goals for ROI
Strengths/ Weaknesses unknown	Flexible PIC with goals for freshness	Flexible PIC with goals for ROI

Figure 14.3
Key recommendations for PIC.

showcase existing solutions that match the required functionality of certain components. Members of the NPD team can then use these solutions when needed either in 'shrink-wrapped' form where they are taken on an 'as is' basis of the shelf, or can be further modified. This database can also serve the dual purpose of integrating information for the purpose of innovation partners to enable them to get started early on their part of the development project by passing preliminary information about design specifications that were used in the past.

Underwood et al. (2000) describe the creation of one such design library using a technology for the Internet titled 'Product Data Technology (PDT)' that supports the definition and processing of information about a product. The technology developed provides an 'open data' paradigm that can be shared between project partners, and the paper describes the potential of the technology to be combined with Internet technology to support the direct specification of design elements from a product database website. The application enables the designer to retrieve and store their defined specifications (including technical information) in a standard format and upload this information to the project database to be accessed by other applications like CAD. There are a number of other examples of firms using shared libraries for the purpose of defining specifications and sharing them in real-time for other project partners.

We now describe some techniques and guidelines for defining specifications with the data available to the NPD team.

2. How to define specifications

In this section, we describe the House of Quality (HOQ) technique, which is a popular technique based on fuzzy modeling of product specifications, and a technique called analytical target cascading to define specifications given customer feedback and strategic inputs. The Quality Function Deployment (QFD) technique was first described in the literature by Hauser and Clausing (1988). The technique originated at Mitsubishi Motors Corporation Kobe shipyard site in 1972, and used extensively in a wide variety of applications since. The original intent of the House of Quality (HOQ) design tool that is the basic tool of the QFD technique was to translate the requirements of the upstream stage of the NPD process to the input parameters of the downstream stage, and enable the downstream stage to understand the trade-offs required by often conflicting requirements of the upstream stage. Hauser and Clausing (1988) suggested that the technique could be used as a tool from the start of the NPD process to the end of the NPD process for multiple activities, by using the House of Quality design tool to translate upstream requirements to downstream specifications at each stage. However, the most frequent use of the HOQ tool has been to translate the requirements specified by customers

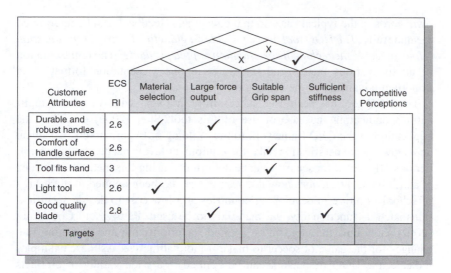

Customer Attributes	ECS RI	Material selection	Large force output	Suitable Grip span	Sufficient stiffness	Competitive Perceptions
Durable and robust handles	2.6	✓	✓			
Comfort of handle surface	2.6			✓		
Tool fits hand	3			✓		
Light tool	2.6	✓				
Good quality blade	2.8		✓		✓	
Targets						

Figure 14.4
The house of quality tool.

(also called customer attributes or CAs) to technical specifications of the component or the product (also called engineering characteristics or ECs). Figure 14.4 illustrates the HOQ framework being applied to the design of non-powered hand tools (Haapalainen et al., 1999/2000).

The process for using the HOQ tool starts out by eliciting from customers what the main attributes and features of the component or the product are in their judgement, and then ranking them on a quantitative scale, to enable the team members to know which attribute has the most importance, and should be accorded the highest priority in assessing trade-offs. These attributes elicited from consumers are called customer attributes (CAs) and the weights assigned to the CAs are called the relative importance (RIs), and they are represented on the vertical axis (Y-axis) of the HOQ.

The trade-offs between the various ECs and CAs are evaluated using the relative importance assigned to them by customers, the perceptions of the product with respect to the competitor's products, and the relative difficulty in changing one EC for another. These trade-offs are weighed against each other and the firm assigns a final set of specifications based on this trade-off resolution. The reader can get a detailed analysis of the HOQ framework in Hauser and Clausing (1988).

Hauser and Clausing suggest that for a typical application of the HOQ tool, one would work with between 30 and 100 CAs. Sometimes, the CAs are grouped together to represent an overall customer concern, and the NPD team groups CAs by consensus. CAs are generally reproduced in the consumer's own words in the typical case, so that consumers' feedback can be interpreted meaningfully. *The HOQ tool hence provides a guideline to answer the question 'How to decide the technical specifications of the product?'* The representation of all the various factors and trade-offs in one presentation format is an important advantage of the HOQ tool.

The HOQ tool has been used successfully in a very wide variety of applications, indicating the ease of use of this tool. Sher (2006) describes the application of the QFD framework to the building of hypermarkets in Taiwan and shows how specifications like the equipment levels needed and the number of staff needed for security can be determined using this method. Gonzalez et al. (2003–04) describes how this framework has been applied to the design of school furniture in developing countries at a low cost to decide specifications such as functionality and materials to be used. Partovi and Corredoira (2002) show how the tool can be applied for prioritizing and designing rule changes for the game of soccer to make it more attractive. As these examples indicate, the HOQ framework can be applied to a wide variety of products and services.

In our experience, the main advantages of the HOQ are: (i) it represents trade-offs with respect to customer attributes, engineering specifications, and competitive assessments parsimoniously; (ii) the tool is simple and easy to use; and (iii) it provides an easy representation to get consensus from various stakeholders from different functions and partnering organizations on the product specifications. As mentioned earlier, it is an effective tool for operationalizing the finalization of product specifications. However, it also requires that consumers have used the product before so that they can give meaningful feedback (although there are examples of applications of the HOQ framework where prototypes have been used to get effective feedback). If the product is complex (number of CAs and ECs is large), then as best practice, firms often collect related ECs and CAs by smaller independent groups and use the HOQ tool on these independent groups that have been delinked from the other groups as the links with the other groups are weaker.

There have been other tools developed to help the NPD team translate market requirements to technical specifications for the product. Deciu et al. (2005) propose a fuzzy logic-based configurable design model to translate customer requirements to product specifications. The configurable design model assumes that a family of products can be built around a common core and product variants can be designed by customizing some components for different customers. They call this set of product configurations as design for configuration and the deliverable of the model is a configuration of the product by defining the relationships between its components to satisfy a set of requirements and a set of constraints imposed on the product. The fuzzy product specification model lets each specification be part of a fuzzy set with known boundaries, which can be delivered by the main configuration of the core and the peripherals of the product design. As customer feedback is better understood, the boundaries of this fuzzy set are drawn closer to reflect the feedback received from the customer. This process is similar to the Bayesian updating process, where signals received from customers provide a refined posterior distribution (lower variance than the prior to the distribution). This method proposes a quantitative solution to finding the right specifications.

Similar to the above study, Michalek et al. (2005) suggest a tool called 'Analytical Target Cascading' to link marketing and engineering decisions during product design. They point out that in market research studies using conjoint analysis for instance, product specification levels are chosen to be conditional on engineering guidelines, and if the NPD team cannot engineer a specification level, consumers are not asked about it. Hence, the knowledge gained about consumer preferences are contingent on knowing in advance which targets are technically infeasible. Similarly, the engineering team would aim to maximize target levels of product specifications subject to constraints, conditional to knowing if customers would want to pay for them. The authors propose a multi-stage solution process, in which at each stage, the specifications are optimized in the marketing sub-problem based on given engineering design constraints and market demand information. Concurrently, at each stage, the engineering members of the NPD team minimize the deviation in the engineering sub-problem from the technical specifications that were the optimal solution to the marketing sub-problem, and propose their solution to the marketing members of the NPD team. This process is continued iteratively until the two teams converge. The recommendations to answer the question 'How to define products' are summarized in Fig. 14.5.

Figure 14.5 summarizes the approach to define products based on the trade-offs between market and technology uncertainty against the need for

	Engineering characteristics clear	Engineering characteristics unclear
Customers can give meaningful feedback	Use HOQ to define product	Use fuzzy ECs set to define product iteratively
Customers cannot give meaningful feedback	Use iterative customer feedback to define product	Define product based on internal feedback

Figure 14.5
Key recommendations for executing product definition.

process optimization and the refinement of goals with the passage of time. From Fig. 14.1, the HOQ framework is a tool for understanding the trade-offs between process parameters for optimization and market uncertainty. If the market uncertainty is high (customers cannot give meaningful feedback early), then the firm is advised to use the HOQ framework iteratively, until the engineering characteristics and customer preferences converge. When the engineering characteristics themselves cannot be expressed clearly (owing to technology uncertainty or lack of knowledge about process trade-offs), then a fuzzy set as outlined in the second part of this section can serve to reduce the uncertainty about ECs, as in Fig. 14.1.

We now describe how the marketing/manufacturing trade-offs affect the definition of specifications of the product and outline best practices to manage these trade-offs.

3. Managing different trade-offs in product definition

Defining product specifications during the NPD process in different environments is a complex managerial task. If market inputs are stable and customer preferences are static (as in mature markets like furniture where the dominant paradigm in product design seems to have stabilized) then defining products early enables the firm to focus on cost competence. This owes to the fact that once the technical specifications of the product are finalized, the firm can focus on making the manufacturing process efficient to reduce the unit variable cost of manufacturing the product.

Cooper (1993) concludes that having a sharp definition of the product early and prior to beginning the development work makes the NPD process more effective. The key benefit of early definition is the discipline it brings to the NPD process, as changes to the specifications of the product have to be incorporated in the subsequent manufacturing process design phase and this can be difficult and expensive to implement. In industries where the customer preferences are well-defined and understood at the beginning of the NPD process, early definition results in a stable NPD process and effective execution of the manufacturing process design.

The trade-offs associated with the timing of product definition are summarized in Fig. 14.6. Figure 14.6 illustrates the timing trade-off described in Fig. 14.1 with respect to the freezing of product specifications. In the figure, the definition phase of the NPD process illustrates the time spent by the firm before the freezing of specifications where the objective is to minimize the market and technology uncertainty. Whereas the testing and integration phase is the part of the NPD process where the objective of the firm is to minimize the unit variable cost of manufacturing the product. As the NPD process progresses, market uncertainty and technology choice uncertainty reduces, in that the firm has a better understanding of customer preferences, customer

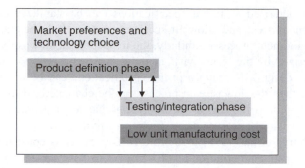

Figure 14.6
Trade-offs in product definition.

preferences have stabilized over time, and the feasibility of the technologies available to the firm has been better assessed. However, as the NPD process unfolds, if the firm delays freezing the specifications of the product, then the firm risks not having enough time to test, integrate and optimize the manufacturing process, leading to a higher unit variable cost, or having to switch to a proven technology for the product at a later stage. In the figure, the definition phase of the NPD process illustrates the time the firm spends before the freezing of specifications where the objective is to minimize the market and technology uncertainty, while the testing and integration phase is the part of the NPD process where the objective of the firm is to minimize the unit variable cost of manufacturing the product.

While early definition may be possible for defining successive generations of mature products, Bhattacharya et al. (1998) shows that early definition of products may not be possible or suitable in all environments. There are markets in which changes are so rapid and discontinuous that information collected in the beginning of the NPD cycle can become obsolete by the time of product launch (Bourgeois and Eisenhardt, 1988). For example, in the high technology industry, the advent of new architectures and technologies lead to high levels of uncertainty about customer preferences (Bacon et al., 1994; Iansiti, 1995), and customers find it difficult to articulate their preferences early in the design process. The definition of the product would depend on how rapidly customer preferences stabilize, and how much the manufacturing process is affected by changes in product specifications.

Krishnan et al. (1993) describes the impact of changing product specifications on the design of the manufacturing process in a generalized framework using the upstream and downstream process phases for the design of the specifications of the process and the design of the manufacturing process. They model the changing of the specifications over time of the product by the 'evolution' of the specifications. The 'evolution' of the specifications can be characterized as fast if specifications can be stabilized early in the development process and 'slow' if specifications can only be stabilized late in the development process. Similarly, the impact on the downstream process is characterized by the 'sensitivity' of the downstream process (manufacturing process design). If changes in the specifications can be incorporated at a low cost, then the downstream process can be characterized to have a low sensitivity, while if the cost of incorporating changed specifications is high, then the downstream process has a 'high' sensitivity.

Bhattacharya et al. (1998) model the NPD process as consisting of three phases: the upstream definition phase, the intermediate realization phase, and the downstream integration phase. In the definition phase, the NPD team sets the specifications of the product in conjunction with feedback from potential customers to enhance the attractiveness of the product. Incorporating feedback from customers increases the attractiveness of the product, and reduces the uncertainty about the product's attractiveness. During the realization phase, the NPD team implements virtual and real prototypes of the product, while in the integration phase, the team is primarily concerned with optimizing the process to develop the product at the lowest possible cost.

They find that a risk-neutral firm defines the product when the marginal benefit from taking more customer feedback is equal to the marginal increase in cost from a higher unit manufacturing cost. A risk-averse firm would define the product later than a risk-neutral firm. If the firm expects the unit manufacturing cost to decrease after launch due to learning, then the NPD team delays the definition compared to the case with no learning. In a competitive environment, if competition is based on performance, then the competing firms prefer to delay the product later, with the delay being lower for the first-mover firm. If competition is based on cost, then both firms prefer to define the product early, with the first-mover firm having the later definition point.

Kalyanaram and Krishnan (1997) investigate a similar subject in the definition of a new product, with the options of crashing the development project at a higher cost of development and with the possibility of concurrent engineering. They use a cost function to model the cost associated with delay in the introduction of a new product, and show that in the absence of the crashing option and concurrent engineering, the firm must define the product early to avoid being late to market. However, if the crashing and concurrent engineering options exist, then the firm can make use of those to delay the definition of the product to obtain a higher degree of flexibility in defining the product.

An additional question related to the definition of a product is the complexity of the product and the organizational structure used by the firm for the NPD process. Mihm et al. (2003) study complex design projects and show that as the complexity of the process increases, (complexity is measured by interdependencies between several different components), optimizing the performance of the product is a function of the complexity of the product and derive managerial implications for taking this complexity into account. This research stream raises some important hypotheses: for instance, for a complex project, defining the product early can result in fewer iterations or oscillations, however, the performance of the product can suffer, as better component and system designs could be available in the future. However, delaying the definition of the product when the product is complex could result in a lot of time for problem-solving iterations, which will have a negative impact on the time available for reducing the unit cost of manufacturing the product.

Similarly, the organizational structure used by the firm and the complexity of the product architecture play an important role in defining a product. Sosa et al. (2004) study the impact of communication patterns and the organizational structure of complex NPD projects on the ability of the firm to define the architecture of the product. For a complex project, the communication between sub-teams working on different components has an effect on the time of freezing specifications, as teams that communicate more often will influence the definition of the architecture towards combining their components into one module.

Similar to the above studies, Yazdani and Holmes (1999) classify product definition into four distinct types to incorporate the feedback of all functions within the firm: sequential, design centered, concurrent, and dynamic. Based on different concurrent engineering models, they use a case-based approach, to illustrate the suitability of these different models of product definition. The sequential model is an iterative model in which the specifications of the product are proposed by the design members of the NPD team, and then all other functions within the firm provide their input to refining the specifications, with the process being repeated until a satisfactory result is obtained from all functions. In the design-centered model, the different functions provide their feedback upfront to the design members of the NPD team, who take their considerations into account in their design. The iterations needed in the sequential model are minimized in this model, as most of the considerations are incorporated upfront. In the concurrent definition model, members of all functions provide early feedback and subsequently, provide the design team with feedback during the entire NPD process, i.e., they are active members in defining the specifications of the product in contrast to the design centered model. In the dynamic model of product definition, all functions are represented in the NPD cross-functional team, and the level of communications are more intensive, as all functions are active members in defining the specifications of the product in contrast to the concurrent definition model.

In addition to dealing with market uncertainty, product definition models have also been proposed to deal with technological uncertainty. Krishnan and Bhattacharya (2002) propose a model to define the specifications of a product when the NPD team is considering a new technology for a component in the product. The new technology potentially has a better performance compared to the existing technology, but it is still under development, and there exists an uncertainty if it can be developed successfully or not. They suggest a Bayesian model in which signals about the performance of the new technology are being provided to the firm, and the firm can choose to develop the product based on the proven technology or based on the new technology depending on the signals. They characterize the region of continuation in which the firm will not commit to either technology, as well as the regions where the firm commits early to one technology, i.e., defines the product specifications early. They also propose two flexible design options, the sufficient design approach, and the parallel path approach to give the firm more flexibility in defining the product. In the sufficient design approach, the firm over-designs the product so that both technologies can be used at the last minute. While in the parallel path approach, the firm develops two products based on both technologies. Conditions for the usage of both these approaches are also characterized.

For the definition of a family of products, Bhattacharya et al. (2003) develop a model based on sequential entry to determine what order of entry is best for product families that are based on better specifications over time. The NPD team can define and introduce a product based on existing technologies (low-end product) and introduce it in the market, or they can wait for improved technologies and refinements in the development process to introduce a better product first and then the low-end product later. Introducing the high-end product first and then the low-end product minimizes cannibalization, but revenue streams from the low-end product are delayed. The paper shows that when technologies improve rapidly and in competitive environments, the firm should prefer to introduce the low-end product as soon as it is available, even though cannibalization is higher. When technologies improve slowly and customers are more patient (have low discounting factors), the firm can delay the introduction of the low-end product and introduce it after the high-end product to minimize cannibalization.

We conclude this section by drawing on our observations of best practices in the industry on managing the trade-offs associated with the timing of product definition and the resources used. In almost all the firms performing well, we see a cross-functional NPD team deciding on the specifications, as this enables the gathering and incorporation of early feedback, avoiding expensive late design changes and the lack of consideration of design-for-manufacturability and other related issues in product design. We also see firms trying to delay the definition of the specifications of the product by using a flexible manufacturing process, so that late changes can be incorporated easily. In cases where discipline is of the utmost importance, i.e., in cases where late changes cannot be incorporated easily, we see firms adopting the traditional approach of an early definition, especially if marketing feedback stays stable over the NPD

	Risk-averse/ Uncertainty	Risk-neutral/ Deterministic
Competition based on price	Midpoint to late definition	Early to midpoint definition
Competition based on performance	Late definition	Midpoint to late definition

Figure 14.7
Key recommendations for managing the trade-offs in product definition.

cycle. When firms are introducing new technologies, our observations in the industry are that (i) firms have backup plans like over-designing the product if the new technology does not perform as envisaged, and (ii) they develop product lines rather than single products to have an option to develop products with existing technologies. Some of the key recommendations for managing the trade-offs in product definition are listed in Fig. 14.7.

We now describe the research and best practices of coordinating product definition with other activities in the NPD process.

4. Coordinating product definition in NPD

In this section, we describe the literature on how to integrate the product definition phase with the rest of the NPD process, with a special emphasis on considering the needs of downstream activities in deciding product specifications. A more detailed analysis of the impact of the need for coordination is described in the chapter 'Coordination and Information Exchange' in this handbook. The needs for coordination of product definition with the rest of the NPD process is summarized in Fig. 14.8.

Gerwin and Barrowman (2002) investigate the efficacy of integrated product development across all activities and find that integrated product development (IPD) has a positive symbiotic effect on deciding the specifications of the product. Specifically, IPD defines the product in a way that lowers task uncertainty by specifying the product requirements more clearly, thus reducing the need for coordination. This results in decisions by NPD teams to pursue incremental development more frequently than one leap for a new product, i.e., frequent smaller projects are preferred compared to a few large breakthroughs. Their research results are supported by Imai et al. (1985) and Kessler and Chakrabarti (1996), and they therefore conclude that the degree of incremental

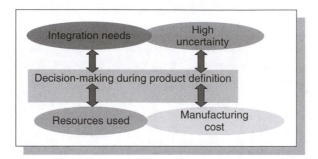

Figure 14.8
Needs for coordination in product definition.

development is a strategically selected characteristic of IPD that enables the firm to have clear technical specifications from smaller projects so that there is more discipline in the process.

Alonso-Rasgado et al. (2004) describe the development of functional or 'total care products,' where customers purchase a service to be used, and the firm maintains the hardware and software and provides service support for the product. Products falling in this category would include aircraft engines, which are leased from the manufacturer and the airline pays for their use per flying hour, or copier machines where customers pay for each page copied, and the firm maintains the copier machine. They describe two primary distinctions in the definition of such products from products that are sold to the customer: (i) total care products require a more iterative process between the concept generation phase and the product definition phase with a deeper involvement of the customer compared to other products; and (ii) defining total care products needs a more intimate knowledge of the architecture of the product (how different elements of the product and service interface with one another) than other products. Hence, coordinating the total development activities for defining total care products is crucial, and the firm often delays the definition of the product for that reason.

Bailetti et al. (1998) complements the above research by studying the coordination structure that highlights responsibility interdependencies among resources rather than the more widely studied task interdependencies. A more detailed description of the role of interdependencies in coordination is provided in the chapter on 'Coordination and Information Exchange' in this handbook.

A number of studies incorporate manufacturing concerns early in the definition of new products as well. For instance, at the meta-level, Ulrich et al. (1993) find that incorporating design-for-manufacturing requirements in the product definition phase reduces the unit cost of manufacturing the product, but increases the development time of the product. Govil and Magrab (2000) propose a methodology to incorporate production concerns early in the product definition process based on linear programming. They start out by estimating the time and cost of manufacturing a product based on the identification of critical resources, the capacity needed to manufacture the product, the production sequence and processing and setup times. Based on this data, they estimate the production rate of the new product at the desired launch time, and identify product component specifications and manufacturing resources that critically impact the production rate of the new product. Then, alternative design specifications for the product and the production system are proposed and analyzed to improve the production rate. The approach taken by them is to make the product as less expensive to manufacture as possible in as short a time as possible to reduce the unit manufacturing cost, with the price that the product can charge and the demand being determined externally.

Bramall et al. (2003) propose a similar methodology to reduce the unit cost of manufacturing a product, based on an aggregate planning methodology. Their planning system analytically explores the many alternative processing technologies and equipment choices available in conjunction with the design of components to satisfy a multi-criteria objective function encapsulating quality, cost, delivery, and knowledge criteria. The designer is thus presented with the opportunity to redefine the design elements or process specifications that would yield the greatest improvements in the unit manufacturing cost.

The main findings of the research on coordinating the definition phase with other activities in the NPD process are: (i) having a low uncertainty in product specifications makes a product easier to manage, and hence, a smooth NPD process. NPD teams in practice operationalize this principle by executing a series of incremental innovation projects rather than a few breakthrough projects to achieve the same target, as having a series of incremental projects provides the NPD team with clear product specifications at each stage. (ii) If products have higher integration needs, then the definition of the product needs to take a larger number of interactions into account, and hence, delaying the definition to encapsulate those interactions better in the product specifications is advisable. (iii) In practice, NPD teams focus on coordinating their various activities across functions until the definition of specifications as that largely determines the smooth execution of the rest of the NPD process. (iv) NPD teams should estimate the cost of manufacturing the design of the product based on the existing set of specifications, and try to reduce this cost if possible by changing the specification set; the section outlines some tools for this purpose. Figure 14.9 summarizes some of the key recommendations for coordinating product definition with the rest of the NPD process.

	High uncertainty	Low uncertainty
High integration needs	Series of incremental projects, late definition	One project, late definition
Low integration needs	Series of incremental projects, early definition	One project, early definition

Figure 14.9
Key recommendations for coordination product definition with the NPD process.

5. Conclusions

This chapter provides an overview to manage the product definition process, i.e., the process by which the NPD team defines the specifications of the product. The specifications of the product are tasked with balancing multiple requirements, and various tools and rules of thumb were provided to manage the product definition phase better. Various ways of presenting guidelines to NPD teams for defining products are provided, followed by techniques to execute the definition of specifications. The various trade-offs around defining products early and late are analyzed along with trade-offs between marketing and engineering and rules of thumb are provided to manage those trade-offs. Finally, the role of product definition in the NPD process is analyzed along with coordination requirements with other activities, and tools are provided to define products in conjunction with the needs of other functions like manufacturing and marketing. Our recommendation is that firms pay special attention to the product definition process as the research indicates, as the phase sets the stage for the entire NPD process' execution.

References

Alonso-Rasgado, T., G. Thompson and B.O. Elfstrom, "The Design of Functional (Total Care) Products", *Journal of Engineering Design*, Dec 2004, 15(6): 515–540.

Bacon, G., S. Beckman, D. Mowery and E. Wilson, "Managing Product Definition in High-Technology Industries: A Pilot Study", *California Management Review*, 1994, 36: 32–56.

Bailetti, A.J., J.R. Callahan and S. McCluskey, "Coordination at Different Stages of the Product Design Process", *R&D Management*, 1998, 28(4): 237–247.

Bart, C.K., "Product Innovation Charters: Mission Statements for New Products", *R&D Management*, 2002, 32(1): 23–34.

Bart, C.K. and A. Pujari, "The Performance Impact of Content and Process in Product Innovation Charters", *Journal of Product Innovation Management*, Jan 2007, 24(1): 3–19.

Bhattacharya, S., V. Krishnan and V. Mahajan, "Managing New Product Definition in Highly Dynamic Environments", *Management Science*, Nov 1998, 144(11): S50–S64.

Bhattacharya, S., V. Krishnan and V. Mahajan, "Operationalizing Technology Improvements in Product Development Decision-making", *European Journal of Operational Research*, 2003, 149: 102–130.

Bourgeois, L.J. and K. Eisenhardt, "Strategic Decision Processes in High Velocity Environments: Four Cases in the Microcomputer Industry", *Management Science*, 1988, 34: 816–835.

Bramall, D.G., K.R. McKay, B.C. Rogers, P. Chapman, W.M. Cheung and P.G. Maropoulos, "Manufacturability Analysis of Early Product Designs", *Journal of Computer Integrated Manufacturing*, 2003, 16(7–8): 501–508.

Buderi, R., "Microsoft: Getting from 'R' to 'D' ", *Technology Review*, March 2005, 28–30.

Cooper, R.G., *Winning at New Products*, Addison-Wesley Publishing Company, Reading, MA, 1993.

Crawford, C.M., "Defining the Charter for Product Innovation", *Sloan Management Review*, Fall 1980, 3–12.

Deciu, E.R., E. Ostrosi, M. Ferney and M. Gheorghe, "Configurable Product Design using Multiple Fuzzy Models", *Journal of Engineering Design*, April 2005, 16(2): 209–235.

Gerwin, D. and N.J. Barrowman, "An Evaluation of Research on Integrated Product Development", *Management Science*, July 2002, 48(7): 938–953.

Gonzalez, M.E., G. Quesada and A.T. Bahill, "Improving Product Design using Quality Function Deployment: The School Furniture Case in Developing Countries", *Quality Engineering*, 2003–2004, 16(1): 45–56.

Govil, M.K. and E.B. Magrab, "Incorporating Production Concerns in Conceptual Product Design", *International Journal of Production Research*, 2000, 38(16): 3823–3843.

Haapalainen, M., J. Kivisto-Rahnasto and M. Mattila, "Ergonomic design of non-powered hand tools: An application of Quality Function Deployment", *Occupational Ergonomics*, 1999/2000, 2(3): 179–189.

Hauser, J.R. and D. Clausing, "The House of Quality", *Harvard Business Review*, May–June 1988, 63–73.

Iansiti, M., "Shooting the Rapids: Managing Product Development in Turbulent Environments", *California Management Review*, 1995, 38: 37–58.

Imai, K., I. Nonaka and H. Takeuchi, "Managing the New Product Development Process: How the Japanese Companies Learn and Unlearn",

In: *The Uneasy Alliance*, K.B. Clark, R.H. Hayes, C. Lorenz, (Eds.) Harvard Business School Press, Boston, 337–381, 1985.

Kalyanaram, G. and V. Krishnan, "Deliberate Product Definition: Customizing the Product Definition Process", *Journal of Marketing Research*, May 1997, 34(2): 276–285.

Kessler, E. and A. Chakrabarti, "Innovation Speed: A Conceptual Model of Context, Antecedents, and Outcomes", *Academy of Management Review*, 1996, 21(4): 1143–1191.

Krishnan, V., S.D. Eppinger and D.E. Whitney, "A Model-based Framework to Overlap Product Development Activities", *Management Science*, 1993, 43: 437–451.

Krishnan, V. and S. Bhattacharya, "Technology Selection and Commitment in New Product Development: The Role of Uncertainty and Design Flexibility", *Management Science*, March 2002, 48(3): 313–327.

Lehmann, D.R., *Market Research and Analysis*, Irwin Publishers, 3rd Edition, 1989.

Michalek, J.J., F.M. Feinberg and P.Y. Papalambros, "Linking Marketing and Engineering Product Design Decisions via Analytical Target Cascading", *Journal of Product Innovation Management*, 2005, 22: 42–62.

Mihm, J., C. Loch and A. Huchzermeier, "Problem-Solving Oscillations in Complex Projects", *Management Science*, June 2003, 46(6): 733–750.

Nissing, N., "Strategic Inventing: In a War of Patents, Choose your own Battleground", *Research and Technology Management*, May–June 2005, 17–22.

Partovi, F.Y. and R.A. Corredoira, "Quality Function Deployment for the Good of Soccer", *European Journal of Operational Research*, March 2002, 137(3): 642–656.

Reinertsen, D.G. and P.C. Smith, "The Strategist's Role in Shortening Product Development", *Journal of Business Strategy*, July–August 1991, 12: 18–22.

Sher, S.S., "The Application of Quality Function Deployment (QFD) in Product Development – The Case Study of Taiwan Hypermarket Building", *The Journal of American Academy of Business, Cambridge*, March 2006, 8(2): 292–295.

Smith, D.V.L. and J.H. Fletcher, *The Art and Science of Interpreting Market Research Evidence*, Wiley Publishing, 2004.

Sosa, M., S.D. Eppinger and C.M. Rowles, "The Misalignment of Product Architecture and Organizational Structure in Complex Product Development", *Management Science*, Dec 2004, 50(12): 1674–1689.

Ulrich, K., D. Sartorius, S. Pearson and M. Jakiela, "Including the Value of Time in Design-for-Manufacturing Decision-making", *Management Science*, 1993, 39(4): 429–447.

Underwood, J., M.A. Alshawi, G. Aouad, T. Child and I.Z. Faraj, "Enhancing Building Product Libraries to Enable the Dynamic Definition of Design

Element Specifications", *Engineering, Construction and Architectural Management*, 2000, 7(4): 373–388.

Yazdani, B. and C. Holmes, "Four Models of Design Definition: Sequential, Design Centered, Concurrent and Dynamic", *Journal of Engineering Design*, 1999, 10(1): 25–37.

15 Learning by experimentation: Prototyping and testing[1]

Stefan Thomke

1. Introduction

When important development projects fail late in the game, the consequences can be devastating. In the pharmaceutical industry, e.g., more than 80 per cent of drug candidates are discontinued during the clinical development phases, where more than half of total project expenses can be incurred. The total investment lost to late-stage failure is very significant indeed. Results published by the Tufts Center for the Study of Drug Development show that the average cost of developing a new drug was about US$231 million in 1987 dollars. Results from the most recent study show that this amount has risen to $802 million in 2000 dollars, compared to $318 million if the previous $231 million had risen at the pace of inflation (Tufts, 2001). Moreover, spending increases in clinical trials exceeded pre-clinical (e.g., discovery) by a factor of five which means that late stage failures had become even more costly than before. Not surprisingly, there is much value in finding potential drug failures as early as possible through better testing strategies. Eliminating product candidates with little promise before they enter expensive downstream testing would also allow companies to focus and redeploy R&D resources on much stronger candidates. Unfortunately, companies in many industries often test too little and too late, as testing is often viewed as part of downstream *verification*, rather than opportunities for *learning* during early development.

2. Why testing strategies matter: the value of early information

Not only do companies often spend millions of dollars to correct problems in the later stages of product development, they generally underestimate the cost savings of early testing and prototyping that could result in information and team interactions, which in turn, would lower downstream expenses. Studies

---

[1] Some of the material in this chapter comes from Thomke (2003).

of product development have shown that late-stage problems can be more than 100 times as costly as early-stage ones (Boehm, 1981; Terwiesch, Loch and DeMeyer, 2002). For environments that involve large capital investments in production equipment, the increase in cost can be several orders of magnitude. In addition to financial costs, companies jeopardize their development schedules when those late-stage problems are on a project's critical path – as they often are. In pharmaceuticals, shaving six months off drug development means effectively extending patent protection when it hits the market. Similarly for electronics companies: shipping a product six months late can account for a very significant reduction of their life cycle profits. The result for R&D managers is that as development time passes and project commitment increases, the average cost and time of making changes rises exponentially. Millions of dollars need to be spent to solve a production problem that could have been prevented upstream at a small fraction of such cost. In addition, as the increase in cost gets steeper, the value of upstream testing gets higher.

Furthermore, managers can end up devoting an enormous amount of their time to dealing with late-stage problems – to meet launch dates, re-allocate resources, unsnarl schedules, and so on. Such 'fire-fighting' is taken for granted, moreover, because most product development processes are not set up, much less optimized, for early testing. In addition, opportunity costs in general are hard to assess; they are invisible in most management systems used today. How much more difficult it is to measure the 'opportunity' of *not* discovering a problem at an earlier stage in development or *not* testing with a more promising product design solution. In the absence of understanding the importance of these opportunities, then, the curious result is that managers have a de facto incentive to continue their last-minute 'heroics' – and not to create processes that can in fact leverage innovation. However, when the effort *is* made to create such a process, the difference is striking, as the following example from Microsoft reveals (Thomke, 2003).

2.1. Testing strategies at microsoft

Software development usually begins by creating specifications. In versions of Microsoft Office prior to its Office 95 software suite, Microsoft developers wrote such specifications but did not collect them across all groups or posted them in a central location. Not only were there few interfaces standardized across different Office groups (e.g., Word, Excel), there was no formal peer review process across these teams nor a process that could pinpoint problems at the earliest (specification writing) stage. As a result, erroneous assumptions about, for instance, a user interface control could lead to multiple difficulties later on, all of which would require extensive and expensive rework.

As part of the overhaul of its development strategy in the mid-1990s, Microsoft brought its testing group (a group traditionally involved relatively late in software design) into the very early stages of development: It created a formal process of specification inspection. Now under document management and revision control, each specification had to follow a prescribed template, undergo two formal review steps (initial review plus final inspection and sign-off), and had to be posted in a central location on a file share and then eventually to an internal web site. In contrast to a one-sided document prepared by program management without input from others, software specifications became a contract between program managers, developers, and testers. Once through final inspection and sign-off, every word, line, and concept in the new software specification was reviewed and agreed to by groups involved in up- and downstream development. Experienced testers were now able to provide their extensive experience on the relationships between specifications and software bugs when it mattered: as early as possible in the product lifecycle.

Grant George, Vice President of Testing and Operations for the Microsoft Office products, explained the new strategy of leveraging early information: 'The cheapest bug in any manufacturing process is always the one found earliest. Specification inspections, just like our formalization of structured and peer reviewed tests and build verification tests, are all about catching bugs as early as possible' (Thomke, 2003: 166). The results were significant. According to George, about 10–25 per cent of all late stage problems can be found (or avoided) by following this approach. Moreover, if the increasing cost of rework was included, the cost and timesaving were substantial.

3. Testing, experimentation, and uncertainty

In general, one can view testing as an activity that aims at resolving uncertainty in innovation in general and product development in particular. However, not all uncertainty is alike. *Technical uncertainty* arises from the exploration of solutions (e.g., materials) that have not been used before, or have not been combined in 'this' way before, or miniaturized in such a way before. As such, it often is related to product functionality and can be managed through rigorous prototype testing throughout development. *Production uncertainty* exists when we do not know if a technical solution that works well in prototypes can also be produced cost-effectively. What may work in small quantities may not be feasible when production ramps up. The entire manufacturing process itself may need to be revised. Beyond technical and production uncertainty, rapidly changing customer demands create *need uncertainty*. Customers are rarely able to fully specify all of their needs because they either face uncertainty themselves or cannot articulate their needs on products that do not yet exist. Finally, when innovations are novel, *market uncertainty* can be so significant that firms are reluctant to allocate sufficient resources to the development of products for those markets, as they cannot assess them. In such cases, the composition and needs of new markets evolve themselves, and are either difficult to assess or change so quickly that they can catch management by surprise.

Our understanding of *how* testing resolves uncertainty has benefited from different theories and perspectives. In this chapter, we will look at testing and prototyping through the lens of experimentation but the interested reader may find other work at least as informative. For example, Weitzman (1979) views testing as a sequential search for the best among a set of discrete choices and derives a cost-optimal method (Pandora's rule) through dynamic programming. Loch, Terwiesch, and Thomke (2001) build on Weitzman's approach but allow for parallel testing which introduces the aspect of lead time, in addition to cost. Other work regards design (and testing) as a search over a rugged solution landscape, which will be revisited later in this chapter (e.g., Alchian, 1950; Baldwin and Clark, 2000; Kaufman and Levin, 1987). The role of product testing with customers has also had a long tradition in marketing research and practice (for an overview, see Urban and Hauser, 1993). More recently, approaches to customer interactions have been proposed where customers could design and test their own products with the help of innovation toolkits (Thomke and von Hippel, 2002). While it is beyond the scope of this chapter to provide an exhaustive literature review, it should be noted that, in spite of different views and approaches, testing is widely regarded as a very important activity. To go deeper, we will discuss the *experimentation lens* in the remainder of the chapter.

3.1. Testing as learning from experimentation

When managers go beyond viewing testing simply as verification, they can integrate these activities more broadly as part of their company's *experimentation strategy*. Development teams that undertake the design of products and services rarely know in advance whether a particular concept will work exactly as intended. That means they have to find ways of rapidly discarding dysfunctional concepts while retaining others that show promise. At the same time, dysfunctional concepts themselves generate knowledge that guides additional rounds of experimentation via prototyping. Not surprisingly, research has shown that experimentation is an integral part of R&D: one classic study showed that project teams spent an average of 77 per cent of their time on experimentation and related analysis activities (Allen, 1977).

Structured experiments require a directed effort to manipulate or change variables of interest. In an ideal experiment, managers or engineers separate an independent (the 'cause') and dependent (the 'effect') variable and then manipulate the former to observe changes in the latter. The manipulation, followed by careful observation and analysis, then gives rise to learning about relationships between cause and effect, which, ideally, can be applied to or tested in other settings. In the real world, however, things are much more complex. Environments are constantly changing, linkages between variables are complex and poorly understood, and often the variables are uncertain or unknown themselves. Thus, testing and prototyping can be opportunities to learn from formal and informal experimentation found in development organizations.

When all relevant variables are known, formal statistical techniques and protocols allow for the most efficient design and analysis of experiments. These techniques are used widely in many fields of process and product optimization today and can be traced to the first half of the twentieth century when the statistician and geneticist Sir Ronald Aylmer Fisher first applied them to agricultural and biological science (Fisher, 1921, 1923). Today, these *structured* experiments are being used for both incremental process optimization as well as studies where large solution spaces are investigated to find an optimal response of a process (Box and Draper, 1969, 1987). In the more recent years, these techniques have also formed the basis for improving the robustness of production processes and new products (Clausing, 1993; Taguchi and Clausing, 1990).

However, when independent and dependent variables themselves are uncertain, unknown, or difficult to measure, learning from experimentation is much more informal or tentative. A manager may be interested in whether manipulating the incentives of an employee improves her productivity or a software designer wants to know if changing a line of code removes a software error. These *trial-and-error* type of experiments go on all the time and are so much an integral part of innovation processes that they become like breathing – we do them but are not fully aware of the fact that they are experiments. Moreover, good experimentation goes well beyond the individual or the experimental protocols but has implications for firms in the way they manage, organize, and structure innovation processes. It is not just about generating information by itself but about how firms can learn from trial-and-error and structured experimentation.

3.2. A framework for iterative testing and experimentation

Prototyping, testing, and experimentation often consist of iterating attempts to find the direction in which a solution might lie (Allen, 1966; Iansiti, 1997; Leonard-Barton, 1995; Marples, 1961; Thomke, 1998a; von Hippel and Tyre, 1995). The process typically begins by selecting or creating one or more possible solution concepts, which may or may not include the 'best possible' solutions – no one knows what these are in advance. Solution concepts are then tested against an array of requirements and constraints. These efforts (the 'trials') yield new information and learning, in particular, about aspects of the outcome the experimenter did not (or was not able to) know or foresee in advance: the 'errors.' Test outcomes are used to revise and refine the solutions under development, and progress is made in this way towards an acceptable result.

Specifically, such experimentation comprises four-step iterative cycles (Fig. 15.1):[2]

Step 1 – Design: During this step, individuals or teams define what they expect to learn from the experiment or which questions a test should address. Existing data, observations, and prior experiments are reviewed, new ideas

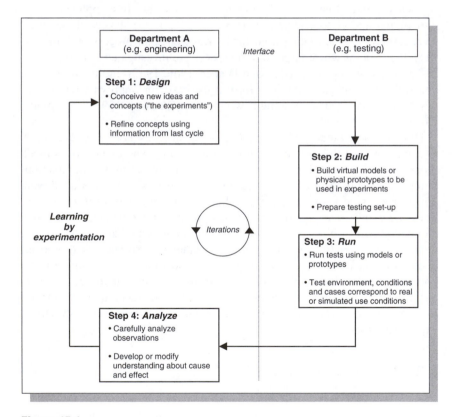

Figure 15.1
Experimentation as four-step iterative cycles.

[2] Similar building blocks to analyze the design and development process were used by other researchers. Simon (1969: chap. 5) examined design as series of 'generator-test cycles.' Clark and Fujimoto (1989) and Wheelwright and Clark (1992: chaps 9 & 10) used 'design-build-test' cycles as a framework for problem-solving in product development. I modified the blocks to include 'run' and 'analyze' as two explicit steps that conceptually separate the execution of an experiment and the learning that takes place during analysis (see also Thomke, 1998a).

are generated through brainstorming, and hypotheses are formulated based on prior knowledge. The team then selects a set of experiments to be carried out in parallel and analyzed.

Step 2 – Build: At this point, one builds (physical or virtual) prototypes and testing apparatus – models – that are needed to conduct an experiment.

Step 3 – Run: The test is then conducted in either laboratory conditions or a real-setting. The trade-off is that laboratory conditions are not real and a test apparatus is often designed for certain purposes. True 'errors' may go undetected or false 'errors' show up because of unique conditions under which the experiment is carried out. For example, the apparatus designed to measure the speed of an airbag deployment in the design of a car is unlikely to be able to detect unanticipated toxicity in the gas used to inflate the airbag, even though information regarding this 'error' would presumably be of great interest to a car company.

Step 4 – Analyze: The development team analyzes the result, compares it against the expected outcome, and adjusts its understanding of what is under investigation. It is during this step where most of the learning can happen and forms the basis of experiments in the next cycle. At a minimum, the team will be able to disqualify failed concepts from the potential solution space and continue the search by going to step 1 of another cycle. In many cases, however, an error or a failed experiment can help to adjust mental-, computer-, or physical prototype models to reflect what has been observed. The result will be a deeper understanding and less uncertainty about cause and effect.

If the results of a first experimental cycle (steps 1–4) are satisfactory or addresses the hypothesis in question, one stops. However if, as is usually the case, analysis shows that the results of the initial trial are not satisfactory, one may elect to modify one's experiment and 'iterate' – try again. Modifications may involve the experimental design, the testing conditions, or even the nature of the desired solution. For example, a researcher may design an experiment with the goal of identifying a new cardiovascular drug. However, test results obtained on a given compound might suggest a different therapeutic use, and cause researchers to change their view of an acceptable or desirable solution accordingly.

3.3. The challenge of managing interfaces

Iterations like those noted above are performed by individuals and teams that are often divided across different functional departments whose mis-aligned objectives, incentives, and resources can get in the way of effective testing. For example, some managers do not fully appreciate the trade-off between response time and resource utilization. Consider what happens when companies establish central departments to oversee computing resources for performing modeling and simulations. Clearly, testing ideas and concepts virtually can provide developers with the rapid feedback they need to shape new products. At the same time, computers are costly, so departments managing as cost centers are evaluated by how much those resources are being used. The busier a central computer is, however, the longer it takes for developers to get the feedback they need. The relationship between waiting time and utilization is not linear – queuing theory has shown that the waiting time typically increases gradually until a resource is utilized around 70 per cent, and then the length of the delays surge.[3]

An organization trying to shave costs may thus become a victim of its own myopic objective. That is, an annual saving of perhaps a few hundred thousand dollars achieved through increasing utilization from 70–90 per cent may lead to very long delays for dozens of development engineers waiting for critical feedback from their tests. A huge negative consequence is that the excessive delays not only affect development schedules but also discourage people from experimenting, thus squelching their ability to innovate. So in the long term, running additional computer equipment at a lower utilization level might well be worth the investment. An alternative solution is to move those resources away from cost centers and under the control of developers, who have strong incentives for fast feedback.

The problem of slowing down testing feedback through overutilized resources is by no means limited to computers – it is influenced by all activities in an experimentation cycle. How firms link experimentation and testing activities to major process phases, system stages, and development tasks, therefore, is an essential part of effective management practice. As projects progress and designs mature, cycles tend to include models of increasing fidelity, or representativeness, gradually moving towards functional prototypes and pilot vehicles. These models are used to test decisions affecting design appearance, function, structure, and manufacturability.

4. Managerial choices for testing and prototyping

An important objective of prototyping and testing is to learn. Information gleaned ultimately (ideally) leads to the development of new products, processes, and services that, in turn, will benefit the firm. The rate and effectiveness at which companies can learn will depend on many factors that require strategic and managerial commitment, and organizational flexibility.

---

[3] Research by Loch and Terwiesch (1999) explicitly addresses congestion effects that arise from scarce capacity and process variability when dealing with engineering change orders. Their proposed improvement strategies are aimed at reducing lead times: flexible capacity, balanced workloads, merged tasks, pooling, and reduced set-ups and batching.

While learning can be affected by multiple firm-specific conditions, we have found the following five managerial design choices to be an integral part of an effective testing and prototyping strategy. That is, these factors dictate, in general, how learning occurs (or does not occur). Please note that these choices cannot be managed in isolation; their interdependence requires mutual fine-tuning which makes the management of testing and prototyping particularly challenging.

4.1. Fidelity: what models and technologies should be used?

Experimentation is often carried out using simplified versions (models) of the eventually intended test object and/or test environment. For example, aircraft designers usually conduct experiments on possible aircraft designs by testing a scale model of that design in a 'wind tunnel' – an apparatus that creates high wind velocities that partially simulate the aircraft's intended operating environment. The value of using models is twofold: to reduce investment in aspects of the real that are irrelevant for the test, and to 'control out' some aspects of the real that would affect an experiment to simplify analysis of the results. Thus, models of aircraft being subjected to wind tunnel experiments generally include no internal design details such as the layout of the cabins – these are both costly to model and typically irrelevant to the outcome of wind tunnel tests, which are focused on the interaction between rapidly moving air and the model's exterior surface. Models used in experimentation can be physical in nature, as in the example just given, or they can be represented in other forms, e.g., by computer simulation. Sometimes designers will test a real object in a real context only after experimenting with several generations of models that isolate different aspects of 'reality' and/or that gradually encompass increasing amounts of model complexity.

Of course, while models and prototypes are necessary to run experiments they do not represent reality completely (if they did, they would be the reality they are to represent!). '*Fidelity*' is the term used to signify the extent to which a model does represent a product, process, or service in experimentation. Perfect models and prototypes, those with 100 per cent fidelity, are usually not constructed because an experimenter does not know or cannot economically capture all the attributes of the real situation, and so could not transfer them into a model even if doing so was desired. Lower fidelity models can be useful if they are inexpensive and can be produced rapidly for 'quick and dirty' feedback, which is often good enough in the early concept phase of product development, when experimentation itself is in 'early development.' As the development process itself unfolds, however, higher fidelity models become increasingly important, first, because the learning from prototypes is

Table 15.1
Possible outcomes from the use of incomplete models

Error Classes	Description	Example	Result
False negative (type I)	Experiment detects false problem	Crash test barrier is more rigid than actual obstacle	Over-design
False positive (type II)	Experiment fails to detect true problem	Crash does not test toxicity of airbag gas	Design Failure

increasingly vital to understanding how close to a solution the effort is; and second, because modeling errors can get 'carried along.'

Table 15.1 lists the two classes of unexpected errors that can result from incomplete models.

While type I errors can lead to wasted resources by 'overdesigning' a product (i.e., designing for failure modes that will not occur), it is errors of type II that can have dramatic consequences and are therefore of compelling interest to experimenters. The failure to detect the relationship between primary and secondary O-ring blow-by *and* low temperatures, in spite of extensive and documented testing, had catastrophic consequences for the Challenger Space Shuttle and the U.S. space program (Hauptman and Iwaki, 1991). One of the most dramatic – and highly publicized – Type II errors, this is a reminder that common to all 'good' experimentation is the development of increasingly accurate models as the process proceeds.

4.2. Feedback and noise: how fast can teams learn?

People learn most efficiently when their action is followed by immediate feedback (Garvin, 2000; Leonard-Barton, 1995; Sterman, 1989; Schön, 1983). Imagine that you were learning how to play the piano, but the sound of your 'keystrokes' took a day to be heard! How would you ever learn how to practice, much less learn how to 'produce' anything that could be performed? Yet, far too many developers must wait days, weeks, or months before their ideas can be turned into testable prototypes. Time passes, attention shifts to other problems, and when feedback finally arrives, momentum is lost and the link between cause and effect is severed. Moreover, time-to-market pressures do not allow people to wait around until results from a test become available. They usually continue with their work and more often than not, the delayed feedback is no longer relevant or used primarily for verification rather than learning.

Thus, the rate of team learning is influenced by the speed and frequency of feedback (and vice versa) which will be discussed later in the chapter.

This is precisely what still happens in some automotive development projects where prototype build times can be several months while overall lead times are being reduced, forcing managers to make project decisions faster than ever before. From the time that design data is made available for building physical prototypes until feedback is received, the project progresses and decisions (such as design freeze) have to be made. In some cases, the data even comes too late to contribute to planning the next round of tests. The result? Feedback contributes little to learning and improvement and is more or less used for verification that certain standards are met. Only when test results point towards major problems (such as not meeting minimal government safety standards in the case of crashworthiness) do they have a major impact.

When Thomas Edison planned his new West Orange (New Jersey) laboratory in 1887, he designed supply and apparatus rooms and the machine shop to be very close to the experimental rooms. The laboratory provided a larger space in which a system of experimentation could be put to work, where libraries and storehouses of common and not so common materials could be established. This 'workplace' design, in turn helped transform Edison's approach to invention. The result was the 'invention factory' – a physical arrangement that supported a more systematic and efficient definition, testing, refinement, and exploitation of his ideas. In fact, Edison firmly believed that all material, equipment, and information necessary to carry out experiments needed to be readily available since delays would slow down his people's work and creativity. When he or his people had an idea, it had to be immediately turned into a working model or prototype before the inspiration wore off. The West Orange library contained 100 000 volumes so information could be found quickly. Moreover, the facilities were designed such that experiments could flow quickly and machinists and experimenters could cooperate closely. The location of the precision machine shop next to the experimental rooms was built around the idea of speed – as ideas occurred, machinists could rapidly create models and devices that could be tested and provide feedback which, in turn, led to new ideas (Millard, 1990).

Another factor, one often overlooked, is how ambiguous or excessive feedback 'noise' can block learning. In a study of learning in semiconductor manufacturing, research found that production plants with low-noise levels could potentially learn much more effectively from their experiments than high-noise plants (Bohn, 1995). Using data collected at five plants, the study estimated that the probability of overlooking a three-percent yield improvement – a large number as first year improvements are usually between 0.5 per cent and 3 per cent – was about 20 per cent. The study concluded that brute-force statistical methods are ineffective or too expensive to deal with these high-noise levels.

This noise occurs either when certain variables cannot be controlled, or when too many variables are being manipulated – because the design of the experiment itself is poor or because the aim is to reduce the number of experiments overall (and too many variables are 'stuffed' into one or few tests). In either case, it is not possible to discern what is actually happening. What is interacting with what? The sad result is that rather than being cost-cutting maneuvers, experiments loaded with too many variables often need to be redesigned and re-run, making the whole endeavor more expensive than it would have been in a better-designed state. Alternatively, 'noise' can be a problem if the independent variable itself has too high a variability when observed. In this case, the experiment has limited value since the connection between cause (a variable change, procedure, or policy) cannot be linked to the observed effect (change in performance). Under such circumstances, effective learning cannot take place.

4.3. Capacity: what testing resources are needed?

The ability to provide rapid feedback to a developer is in part affected by an organization's capacity for testing. Not surprisingly, when the number of tests to be carried out exceeds our capacity, the waiting time will grow very rapidly and the link between action and feedback is severed. What often surprises people, however, is that the waiting time in many real-world queues increases substantially even when we are using not using our total capacity. In fact, the relationship between waiting time and utilization is not linear – queuing theory has shown that the waiting time typically increases gradually until a resource is utilized around 70 per cent, and then the length of the delays surge (Loch and Terwiesch, 1999; Reinertsen, 1997).

Moreover, when people expect long delays, they tend to overload queues, slowing down the system even further. More experiments are submitted in the hopes that one makes it through quickly but without any sense of how it may affect the overall innovation process. Alternatively, simply, firms often lack the right incentives and organization to remove queues and speed up testing feedback. Building sufficient experimentation, prototyping, and testing capacity is therefore not only important but also essential for effective learning.

Consider the changes in the world semiconductor industry. In the 1980s, US and European firms started to fall behind their Japanese and Korean competitors in the development of new process technologies. Having access to such technologies was especially important in the DRAM (Dynamic Random Access Memory) business where most profits were made immediately after a new technology generation was introduced. Companies such as Toshiba, NEC, and Hitachi were gaining control of the market while Motorola, Intel, and others exited the business. A six-to-twelve month lead at mastering new equipment, processes, and production yield provided firms with sizeable competitive advantage. Not surprisingly, the ability to learn from experimentation and improve technologies and processes rapidly was very important in gaining such a lead.

Research showed that by the early 1990s, US firms engineered a remarkable turnaround that erased the process technology lead of Japanese and Korean firms (Iansiti, 1997). The study attributed part of the success to changes in experimentation strategies; the way firms ran test batches of wafers in large process development facilities that were designed to simulate full-scale production plants. Data by TI, IBM, and Intel showed that these firms had made substantial investment into expanding their *capacity* to run millions of additional experiments, while reducing feedback time to speed-up learning. At the same time, they raised the *fidelity* of experiments and tests by increasing the proportion of standard manufacturing equipment in its process development facilities. This ensured that most learning could be applied to volume production.

4.4. Strategy: sequential or parallel protocols?

Most large-scale experimentation and testing involve more than one experiment or test, and, as we have seen, usually require multiple iterations within that effort. When the identification of a solution involves more than a single experiment, the information gained from previous trials may serve as an important input to the design of the next one. When learning from one cycle in a set of tests is incorporated into the next cycle, tests have been conducted sequentially. By contrast, when there is an established plan of experimental cycles that is *not* modified by the findings from previous experiments, the experiments have been performed in parallel. For example, you might first carry out a pre-planned array of design experiments and analyze the results of the entire array. You might then run one or more additional verification experiments, as is the case in the field of formal design of experiments (DOE) methods (Fisher, 1966; Montgomery, 1991). The cycles in the initial array are viewed as being carried out in parallel, while those in the second round have been carried out in series with respect to that initial array.

Parallel strategies can proceed more rapidly, but do not take advantage of the potential for learning between and among trials. As a result, when parallel experimentation is used, the number of trials needed is usually much greater – but it is usually possible to get 'there' faster. In comparison, getting 'there' takes longer with a sequential approach: the number of trials conducted depends very much on how much a firm expects to learn between each round of testing. For example, trying one hundred keys in a lock can be done one key at a time, or all keys at once, as long as enough identical locks are available. Since little can be learned between experiments, a sequential strategy would, on average, require fifty trials and thus cost only half as much – but also take fifty times longer (Loch, Terwiesch, and Thomke, 2001; Thomke, von Hippel, and Franke, 1998).

Typically, parallel and sequential approaches are combined, depending on the strategy chosen. In turn, that strategy depends on many factors: cost of trials, opportunity cost of time, the expected learning between experiments and how firms envision the 'value landscape' they plan to explore when seeking a solution for their problem (Baldwin and Clark, 2000). It is very helpful to imagine search strategies in terms of such 'space' developers are to search to *identify an acceptable solution to their problem and how to approach it.* In other words, what is the scope of the search that an experimentation strategy is to undertake to begin to solve a problem? This value landscape notion is not a guarantee of *a* solution but only specifies the parameters of the search for it and effective testing strategies – sequential and/or parallel – to employ.

Typically, a value landscape can be imagined as a flat plain with one or more 'hills' rising upon it. The total landscape represents the area developers plan to search for solutions, with the probability of finding *a* solution increasing as the 'hills' are ascended. Therefore, the developers' goal is to devise a series of experiments that will enable them to explore the hills efficiently. As they start out, developers may not have a lot of information about the landscape they are exploring or may hold very different prior theories on where to begin (Nelson and Winter, 1982). Indeed, one entire landscape may be jettisoned and another introduced as their work proceeds. Nonetheless, developers' expectations regarding the topography of the value landscape(s) they have chosen are central to their construction of efficient search strategies. Two extreme examples illustrate how this works.

First off, suppose that the problem for which tests are being conducted is to figure out how to open a combination lock. You, the developer, know that these locks typically have 10^6 or more possible combinations, only one of which will open the lock. You also know that the combinations themselves provide no indication of how close you may be to the solution – opening the lock – as you proceed through the experimental cycle defined earlier. In imagining the value landscape for this problem, then, you would envision an absolutely flat area with only a single steeply sided hill, which, when it was ascended, provided the right (and only) solution. You would like to employ a parallel approach to experimentation, therefore. The only information possible from any 'trial' is either 'error' or 'correct.' You get no further information about how to proceed in additional experiments if 'error' is the answer. The extreme example resembles the dilemma often faced by pharmaceutical firms in the search for new drugs. When only a few compounds ('the keys') fit a receptor ('the lock') that is hypothesized to cause a disease, a high degree of parallelism makes sense in early discovery, as long as the cost of an experiment can be kept relatively small.

Consider an alternative problem, one that is amenable to ongoing clues to its solution – much like a children's game in which each participant shouts 'warmer' as the one who is 'it' nears the right spot. There is again only one hill in this landscape, but its sides slope down, thereby covering more of the space then did the 'tower' in the example above. Developers seeking this 'hill,' therefore, would employ a sequential strategy, because they anticipate that each cycle will yield a 'warmer' result: information that would help them find the edges of the hill. The information gained from each step taken is so useful in guiding the direction of the next trial step that the correct solution is often found after only a few trials.

4.5. Frequency: how early and often should tests be carried out?

With the benefits of early prototyping and testing, there remains the question of how frequently or how many experiments should be carried out. As mentioned before, the problem for many companies is that they not only test too late but also too little. The quest for efficiency and cost-reductions often drives out testing until small problems become disasters or missed opportunities become competitive threats. Realistic prototype models can be very costly and money can be saved, so goes the logic, by delaying experimentation, and testing as long as possible and then conducting big 'killer' tests (Reinertsen, 1997). However, the opportunity cost of finding problems later or not experimenting on promising ideas is *not* fully factored into the cost accounting equation.

At the same time, some companies do test very frequently. For example, Microsoft runs automated tests continuously so problems are detected right away when developers check-in new software – which happens daily. They also 'rebuild' software systems and update test coverage frequently, ranging from 'daily prototype builds' to waiting weeks between builds. The frequency between builds depends in part on the particular needs and complexity of a project and the time required for a build. Complex software with many files and interdependencies such as Windows or Office have weekly or monthly build cycles, whereas single applications, such as Excel, have daily builds (Cusumano and Selby, 1995; Thomke, 2003). Microsoft commits a lot of its resources to testing and software testers receive not only solid training in its methodology but also face an attractive career path. In other words, the company takes its testing activities very seriously.

Unfortunately, not all companies take experimentation and testing as seriously as Microsoft, in spite of its fundamental role in R&D and innovation. In their book *Revolutionizing Product Development*, Wheelwright and Clark suggest that periodic prototyping as one way to manage testing effectively. They note that 'senior managers, functional heads, and project leaders who do not fully understand and fully utilize the power of prototyping unintentionally handicap their efforts to achieve rapid, effective, and productive development results' (Wheelwright and Clark, 1992: 255–256).

Thus, very frequent prototyping is most certainly desirable but probably not for all R&D environments. For example, one would not expect automotive firms to build and test full-scale prototypes on a daily basis, unless the cost and time of doing so is reduced a small fraction of what it has been for decades. This reality may come true fairly soon for some kinds of prototypes – for example, through modeling and simulation – where the building and testing happens inside a high-speed computer. Clearly, the number and fidelity of test is related to its cost and time. So when technologies drive down these costs, by how much should developers increase their testing? Building a simple spreadsheet model and explicitly recognizing the value of early information will already get managers halfway in the right direction – that is, to test more frequently than they currently do.

Finding the right frequency of testing can also be attempted analytically (Thomke and Bell, 2001). The set-up of such a mathematical model address the trade-off discussed earlier: its solution is 'optimal' when the cost of repeated testing equals the benefits of earlier information. While the cost of finding and solving problems increases with time, testing removes uncertainty each time it is carried out. Such a model would have to consider various drivers that matter even in a simple situation: how uncertainty evolves over the course of a project, the changing cost, and fidelity of a test, and the correlation between tests. For example, partially overlapping tests (i.e., only a fraction of problems identified earlier could be rediscovered) can take advantage of the bargain cost of low-fidelity tests whereas fully overlapping tests (i.e., problems identified in the second test include all those found in the first test) require each subsequent test to be of higher fidelity to benefit from them.

Such an analytical model was built showing how the solution is affected by these factors (the derivation is shown in Thomke and Bell, 2001). Even though the closed form solution can vary, we found a surprising yet robust result that is a good approximation for many cases and thus can be used as a 'rule of thumb.'

The rough estimate for the number of tests is the following simple ratio:

$$\text{Number of test rounds} = \sqrt{\frac{a}{t}}.$$

where: a = avoidable cost if continuous testing found problems without any delay.
t = cost of one round of tests.

For example, if a company spends $1 million on total redesign (engineering changes, new tooling, etc.) and would have only spent $50 000 if all problems had been identified and solved instantly as they occurred, the avoidable cost due to delayed testing is $950 000. Now, if running one round of tests costs on average $1000, then a rough approximation of the number of testing rounds is:

$$\text{Number of test rounds} = \sqrt{\frac{950\,000}{1000}} \approx 31.$$

Of course, the optimal number depends on many other factors but the simple expression above is a good starting point.

New technologies can slash the costs (both financial and time) of testing but to reap those benefits, though, organizations must prepare themselves for the full effects of such technologies. Computer simulations and rapid prototyping, e.g., increase not only a company's capacity to experiment frequently but also the wealth of information generated by those tests; ten times as many experiments will generate at least ten times more information that has to be processed, evaluated, understood, and used in the planning of a lot more experiments. That, however, can easily overload an organization if it lacks the capability and capacity to process and absorb information from each round of feedback quickly enough to be incorporated into the next round. Imagine that you are gathering bi-weekly feedback from your lead customers. In between, the information has to be prepared for presentation, analyzed, conclusions drawn, and the next round of interviews planned. Now imagine that feedback is suddenly arriving daily! Welcome to the testing swamp. In engineering, this effect has also been referred to as the hardware swamp (Clausing, 1993). Prototype iterations become so frequent and overlap in time that the team cannot keep up any more. They become swamped by problem debugging and hardware maintenance instead of learning from testing and prototyping and improving designs. In such cases, the result can be a waste, leading to confusion and frustration. In other words, without careful and thorough planning, a new technology might not only fail to deliver on its promise of lower cost, increased speed, and greater innovation, it could actually decrease the overall performance of an R&D organization, or at a minimum disrupt its operations. As a result, managers need to prepare their organizations for the full effects of more frequent experimentation so they can tap into its full potential. Rapid information transfers between groups, a focus on quick decision-making and the development of new tools (such as in bioinformatics for drug discovery) are all examples of lowering the risk of organizational overload.

References

Abernathy, W. and R. Rosenbloom (1968 March): "Parallel and sequential R&D strategies: application of a simple model," *IEEE Transactions on Engineering Management*, EM-15 (1).

Alchian, A. (1950): "Uncertainty, evolution and economic theory," *Journal of Political Economy*, 58 (3), pp. 211–221.

Alexander, C. (1964): *Notes on the Synthesis of Form.* Cambridge, MA: Harvard University Press.

Allen, T. J., (1966): "Studies of the problem-solving process in engineering design," IEEE Transactions on Engineering Management, EM-13, no. 2, 72–83.

Allen, T. (1977): *Managing the Flow of Technology*, MIT Press.

Baldwin, C. Y. and K. B. Clark (2000): *Design Rules: The Power of Modularity.* Cambridge, MA: MIT Press.

Boehm, B. (1981): *Software Engineering Economics.* Englewood Cliffs, NJ: Prentice Hall.

Bohn, R. (1995 January): "Noise and Learning in Semiconductor Manufacturing." *Management Science* 41, pp. 31–42.

Box, G. and N. Draper (1969): *Evolutionary Operations: A Statistical Method for Process Improvement.* New York: Wiley.

Box, G. and N. Draper (1987): *Empirical Model-Building and Response Surfaces.* New York: Wiley.

Clark, K. B. and T. Fujimoto (1989): "Lead time in automobile development: Explaining the Japanese advantage," *Journal of Technology and Engineering Management*, 6, 25–58.

Clark, K. and T. Fujimoto (1991): *Product Development Performance*, HBS Press.

Clausing, D. (1993): *Total Quality Development: A Step-by-Step Guide to World Class Concurrent Engineering.* New York: ASME Press.

Cusumano, M. and R. Selby (1995): *Microsoft Secrets.* New York: The Free Press.

DiMasi, J., R. Hansen, H. Grabowsky and L. Lasagna (1991):, "Cost of innovation in the pharmaceutical industry," *Journal of Health Economics* 10, pp. 107–142.

Fisher, R. (1921): "Studies in Crop Variation: I. An Examination of the Yield of Dressed Grain from Broadbalk," *Journal of Agricultural Science* 11, pp. 107–135.

Fisher, R. (1923): "Studies in Crop Variation: II. The Manurial Response of Different Potato Varieties," *Journal of Agricultural Science*, 13, 311–320.

Fisher, R. (1966): *The Design of Experiments*, 8th edition, Edinburgh: Oliver and Boyd.

Fleming, L. (2001): "Recombinant Uncertainty in Technological Search." *Management Science,* 47 (1).

Garvin, D. (2000): *Learning in Action*, Harvard Business School Press Boston, Massachusetts.

Hauptman, O. and G. Iwaki (1991): "The Final Voyage of the Challenger," *Harvard Business School Case,* pp. 691–037.

Iansiti, M. (1997): *Technology Integration: Making Critical Choices in a Turbulent World.* Harvard Business School Press.

Leonard-Barton, D. (1995): *Wellsprings of Knowledge.* Boston: Harvard Business School Press Boston, Massachusetts.

Loch, C. and C. Terwiesch (1999 March): "Accelerating the Process of Engineering Change Orders: Capacity and Congestion Effects," *Journal of Product Innovation Management,* 16, 145–159.

Loch, C., C. Terwiesch and S. Thomke (2001): "Parallel and Sequential Testing of Design Alternatives." *Management Science,* 47 (5).

Kaufman, S. and S. Levin (1987): "Towards a general theory of adaptive walks on rugged landscapes," *Journal of Theoretical Biology,* 128, pp. 11–45.

March, J. (1991): "Exploration and Exploitation in Organizational Learning." *Organization Science,* 2 (1), pp. 71–87.

Marples, D. (1961 June): The decisions of engineering design, *IEEE Transactions on Engineering Management,* pp. 55–71.

Millard, A. (1990): *Edison and the Business of Innovation,* John Hopkins University Maryland, Baltimore.

Montgomery, D. (1991): *Design and Analysis of Experiments,* John Wiley & Sons New York, New York.

Nelson, R. and S. Winter (1982): *An Evolutionary Theory of Economic Change,* Harvard University Press Cambridge, Massachusetts.

Pisano, G. (1997): *The Development Factory,* HBS Press.

Reinertsen, D. (1997): *Managing the Design Factory.* New York: The Free Press.

Schön, D. (1983): *The Reflective Practitioner: How Professionals Think in Action,* Basic Books.

Simon, H. (1969): *The Sciences of the Artifical,* MIT Press.

Sterman, J. (1989): "Modeling Managerial Behavior: Misperceptions of Feedback in a Dynamic Decision-Making Experiment," *Management Science,* 35, pp. 321–339.

Taguchi, G. and D. Clausing (1990 January-February): "Robust Quality," *Harvard Business Review,* pp. 65–75.

Terwiesch, C., C. H. Loch and A. De Meyer (2002): "Exchanging Preliminary Information in Concurrent Engineering: Alternative Coordination Strategies," *Organization Science,* 13 (4), pp. 402–419.

Thomke, S. (2003): *Experimentation Matters,* HBS Press.

Thomke, S. (1998a): "Managing experimentation in the design of new products," *Management Science,* 44 (6), pp. 743–762.

Thomke, S. and D. E. Bell (2001): "Sequential Testing in Product Development." *Management Science,* 47 (2).

Thomke, S. and T. Fujimoto (2000 March): "The Effect of 'Front-Loading' Problem-Solving on Product Development Performance," *Journal of Product Innovation Management.*

Thomke, S. and E. von Hippel (2002 April): "Customers As Innovators: A New Way to Create Value," *Harvard Business Review*.

Thomke, S., E. von Hippel and R. Franke (1998): "Modes of experimentation: an innovation process and competitive variable," *Research Policy*, 27, pp. 315–332.

Tufts Centre for the Study of Drug Development (2001): "Tufts centre for the study of drug development pegs cost of a new prescription medicine at $802 million," *Press Release*, November 30, 2001.

Ulrich, K. and S. Eppinger (1994): *Product Design and Development*. New York: McGraw-Hill.

Urban, G. and J. Hauser (1993): Design and Marketing of New Products, Prentice-Hall, Second Edition New York, New York.

Von Hippel, E. and M. J. Tyre (1995 January): "How 'learning by doing' is done: problem identification in novel process equipment," *Research Policy*, 24(1), 1–13.

Weitzman, M. (1979): "Optimal search for the best alternative," *Econometrica,* 47, pp. 641–654.

Wheelwright, S. and K. Clark (1992): *Revolutionizing Product Development*. New York: The Free Press.

16 Users, experts, and institutions in design

Karl T. Ulrich

Design is the creation of a plan for the production of an artifact that solves a problem. The first act of design was almost certainly *user design*, in that the plan was created by the user rather than by a third-party designer. Perhaps this first user designer contemplated frustration with a task tens of thousands of years ago, formed a plan to address the frustration, and then fashioned an artifact, possibly shaping a stick of wood into a digging implement. A clear distinction between expert designers and user designers emerged at some point possibly first in the domain of architecture. Certainly, by the time ancient Egyptians were creating pyramids, the roles of experts and users in design were separated. This separation was probably motivated by the comparative advantage of experts over users in designing enormous structures. The activity of design appears to have become increasingly professional and institutionalized over the next few thousand years. By the nineteenth century, as the industrial revolution developed in full, expert designers with specific technical training assumed distinct professional roles, both because of the comparative advantage of expertise and because institutions were formed to exploit the benefits of mass production.

Although a separation between users and designers has increased in many domains over the past several thousand years, the practice of design by users is emerging again in current society in specific domains. This chapter addresses the role of the user in design, with particular emphasis on design by users, and considers how experts and institutions interact with users to deliver artifacts in modern society. The approach is to first lay out a theory of design, based largely on the paradigm of design as *search*. Next, three modes of engagement by users, experts, and institutions that are exhibited in industrial practice are articulated. Then, the drivers of the selection of these modes are outlined. Finally, how emerging technologies and practices are enabling new modes in certain settings, and might enable additional modes in the future is discussed.

1. Design theory

An information processing view of design is adopted, largely consistent with that articulated by Simon (1996). Within this paradigm, design is part of a

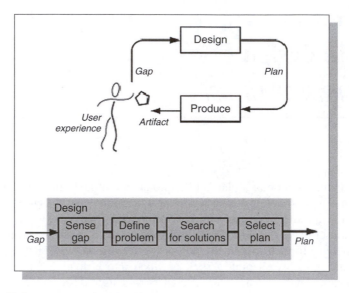

Figure 16.1
Exhibit MODEL - Model of design process.

problem-solving activity beginning with a perception of a gap in the user experience, leading to a plan for a new artifact, and resulting in the production of that artifact (Figure 16.1 - Exhibit MODEL).[1] '*Artifact*' is used in the broadest sense to describe any product of intentional creation, including physical goods, services, software, graphics, buildings, landscapes, and processes. Included in the model, along with the design process, is the production of the designed artifact, as this activity closes the loop between the original gap and the solution.

Exhibit MODEL further decomposes the design process into several elements. This is a codification of a process, which may be implicit for many designers, yet these elements can be discerned in some form in most design efforts:

- *Sense Gap*. Design begins with a perception of a gap in the user experience. Without a gap, there is no motive for design. The gap may be perceived by users themselves or by observers.
- *Define Problem*. In effect, problem definition is the creation of a causal model of why the user experiences a gap. This diagnosis can be thought of as an identification of user needs that are not being met in the current state and/or the recognition of criteria for a high-quality solution. Problem definition is implicit in many design efforts, particularly in user design efforts,

---

[1] Terwiesch (2005) provides a comprehensive discussion of product development as problem solving. Product development is a specific economic activity that includes design tasks.

but is generally an explicit part of professional design efforts, expressed in the form of a design brief, customer needs list, or other document.

- *Search for solutions*. Given a problem, designers search for *satisficing*[2] solutions. Search itself often includes some form of abstraction and representation. In only a very few domains are search spaces explicitly defined, and in even fewer cases are these spaces finite in scope. For example, the design of internet domain names is constrained to strings of finite length selected from 36 ASCII characters, an explicit search space of finite scope. However, the design of a custom-built home typically does not face explicit constraints on allowable geometry and may include arbitrary dimensions, and so this search space is infinite in scope. Furthermore, designers of houses rarely work within formal design languages, but rather work with mathematically imprecise representations such as architectural drawings.
- *Select plan*. Search typically exposes more than one solution alternative and so design requires some sort of evaluation and selection of plans. Some designers consider many alternatives simultaneously when selecting a plan. Others evaluate plans iteratively and select the first plan that satisfices. Sommer and Loch (2004) describe the parallel and iterative modes of problem solving.

Note that in the baseline model, design proceeds from experience to diagnosis to plan to artifact. In modern enterprises, the order is sometimes reversed. The designer begins with an artifact or a plan and searches for needs that the design might meet. This is typical of industries in which effective search methods are lacking, e.g., pharmaceuticals and basic materials. This sequence of problem-solving steps is sometimes called *technology push*.

This design process is typically executed multiple times, as the first artifact produced rarely results in a complete closing of the gap in the user experience. This iteration may occur on a continuum of time scales, ranging from high-frequency iterations by a single individual perhaps over minutes or hours to low-frequency iterations over multiple generations of artifacts within an entire society. For example, Rybczynski (2000) provides a detailed narrative of the evolution of the screw and screwdriver as many iterations of problem solving over hundreds of years.

1.1. Design quality

Design is difficult in that it absorbs substantial cognitive effort, typically requires multiple iterations, and rarely results in an optimal artifact, even in situations for which a formal notion of optimality is possible. The few

---

[2] 'Satisficing' is a term coined by Simon (1996) to refer to 'good enough' solutions created by agents with bounded rationality.

design domains that have been described by formal representations are, in the nomenclature of computational complexity, *NP-complete* search problems, meaning that the theoretically optimal solution cannot be reliably found.[3] Most design domains have not even been formalized, making the inherent complexity even greater and the prospect of optimality even more distant. However, users generally can still evaluate the quality of the outcome of the design process, and different artifacts designed to address the same gaps can certainly exhibit markedly different levels of quality.

At the most general level, design quality is derived from how well the artifact satisfies user needs, and thereby closes the perceptual gap between a goal state and the current state. The quality of an artifact is linked to at least these characteristics of the design process:

- How well did the designer diagnose the gap in the user experience? Is the problem as understood by the designer consistent with the causes of the gap experienced by the user? In simple terms, did the designer understand the problem?
- Has the search problem been defined in a way that the space of possibilities includes high-quality solutions? In the nomenclature of cognitive psychology, has the design problem been *framed* in a way that allows high-quality solutions to be found?
- Did the designer succeed in finding high-quality designs within the search space that has been defined? Often this result depends on the extent to which a causal model of the relationships between design attributes and user needs can be exploited in navigating the search space. The efficiency of search also depends on the ease and accuracy with which the designer can forecast the quality of a design without actually producing it and having the user experience it.

Although not specifically a risk associated with the design process per se, the fidelity of production of the plan is also a determinant of user satisfaction.

In sum, did the designer understand the problem, frame it in a way that search could potentially find a good solution, find such a solution within the search space, and deliver an artifact consistent with the design.

Another way of thinking about design quality is to identify *defects* that can arise in the design process. For each element of the process, there is at least one potential defect: The designer may fail to accurately diagnose the gap in user experience. The designer may frame the search problem in a way that excludes

---

[3] *NP* means that the time required for an agent to find a solution increases with the size of the problem according to a relationship that is *not polynomial* (e.g., exponential, factorial, etc.). In other words, the problem 'explodes' in magnitude in a way that finding a truly optimal solution is impossible in a reasonable amount of time, even with very fast computing.

many high-quality designs. The designer may only be able to explore a limited portion of the search space, finding only a few relatively lower-quality solutions. The artifact produced may not be an accurate embodiment of the plan.

2. Design modes

The design problem is described without characterizing the agents that perform the process steps other than referring to them as *designers*. For the purposes of this chapter, *users* are distinguished from *experts*. Users are the individuals experiencing the perceived gap between the current state and the goal state. They are essentially always a party to the design process.[4] Other terms for users include *customers*, *consumers*, and *stakeholders*, although these terms evoke a more specific commercial context than intended. Experts have acquired skills and capabilities that allow them to perform most design tasks more efficiently and at a higher level of quality than novices. In some cases, an expert may also be a user, but for most design domains, this is exceptional.

An additional distinction is made about the institutional context of design. Design may be performed for a specific individual or may be performed for a collection of users. When design is performed for a collection of individuals, some institution is required to coordinate the design and production of the artifact. These institutions are most typically firms, but may also comprise governments, clubs, religious organizations, universities, professional societies, user groups, or even neighborhood associations.

The modes of design are divided into three categories – *user design*, *custom design*, and *common design* – according to the roles played by users, experts, and institutions.

- *User design* comprises a single user designing for his or her own needs. Hence, the resulting plan is produced for a single individual, and therefore in low quantity, a flexible production process is required to deliver the artifact. Flexible processes need not be technologically intensive (e.g., *flexible manufacturing systems*), but rather need only exhibit relatively low-fixed costs for a unique artifact. In many cases, such flexible production processes are craft processes in which skilled people create artifacts with general-purpose tools, as is typically the case for unique furniture or unique buildings. An example of a flexible production process enabled by technology is digital printing.
- *Custom design* also comprises flexible production of a unique artifact. However, an expert creates a plan on behalf of a user. In most cases, the

---

[4] An exception is perhaps a *design study* done in isolation by a professional designer, but even in this case the designer typically contemplates a virtual user. Design without a user seems to be more 'my art' than true design.

user contracts with the expert for this service, as is the case when hiring an architect to design a unique house or engaging a machinery designer to design a unique piece of factory equipment.

- *Common design* differs from custom design and user design in that a single *common* artifact is delivered to a collection of users. Because this common artifact is produced in a relatively large quantity, it may be produced by mass production methods, processes, which typically incur substantial fixed costs for each variant of the product, but relatively low-marginal costs of producing additional units. Common design involves an institution of some kind; usually a firm, which assesses the gaps in a set of users, creates a common plan for addressing those gaps, and delivers a common artifact to those users.

This taxonomy focuses on the differences in the way design is performed and flexible production either by users or by experts is not distinguished. Mass production because of its very nature must be performed by an institution of some kind as it serves a collection of users with a common artifact.

These categories are intended to be exhaustive and mutually exclusive relative to the variables identified here. However, all three modes may exist to serve different individuals within the same community of users or market (Figure 16.2 - Exhibit MODES).

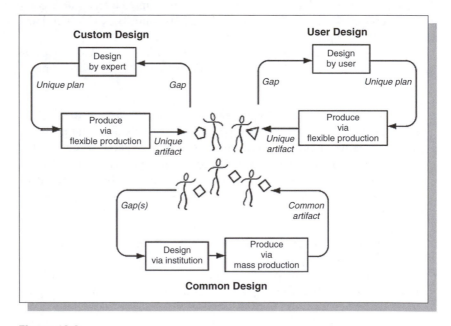

Figure 16.2
Exhibit MODES - Three modes of design, which may be exhibited within a community of users.

3. Drivers of mode choice

Assuming that historically the first design was user design, why did the other modes evolve and why do they exist? What are their relative advantages? What drives the choice of mode in a particular setting?

3.1. Economies of scale in production lead to institutional design

A very large fraction of the economic value in retail trade in current society is through just a few very large distribution channels (e.g., Wal-Mart, Target, Home Depot, and Carrefour). Most products in these channels are produced in high volume (e.g., 10k to 10M units/year) for a mass market. This is because for these products mass production offers a crushing advantage in satisfying user needs at low cost. This advantage arises because of economies of scale in design and production. Creating 10 000 pairs of identical shoes can be 100 times less expensive on a per-unit basis than creating only 1 pair of unique shoes. Very few consumers have distinct enough needs to be willing to pay a hundredfold premium for shoes made uniquely for them. In sum, the cost structure of most design and production processes provides a compelling motive for clustering similar groups of users and addressing their needs with a common design.

A common design requires an institution of some kind, because to achieve commonality, users must be grouped, the gaps in their experiences assessed, and a common artifact designed and produced for them. In sum, economies of scale lead to mass production; mass production requires a common design; a common design requires an institution. For this mode, user design is not generally possible. To the extent that design is performed by a single individual, or even by a team, the remaining individuals whose needs are addressed by the common artifact will not be designers. Instead, their experience will be assessed vicariously by others in the common design mode.

3.2. Advantage of expertise in design drives the selection of the custom design mode

Design is performed for a single user when that user's needs are unique enough, given likely economies of scale in design and production, that a unique artifact is preferred to a common artifact (Lancaster, 1990). This case arises frequently in architecture (custom homes, buildings, and landscapes), food, software, and graphics. This mode is also exhibited occasionally in furniture, apparel, sporting goods, and tools. It is exhibited rarely in home

427

appliances, automobiles, aircraft, medical devices, or computers, domains for which the economies of scale present nearly insurmountable barriers to unique artifacts, even for the very wealthy.[5] The design of a unique artifact in this context may be performed either by the user or by an expert on behalf of that user, leading to the two modes in the upper half of Figure 16.1 - Exhibit MODEL.

All other things equal, design professionals develop expertise that allows them to perform design tasks better than novices (Ericsson, 1996). Given that most users will be novices, experts will outperform novices in most design tasks. However, costs are incurred in engaging an expert, and so the expert design mode will only be selected when the advantages of expertise outweigh the costs of engaging the expert. These costs can be thought of as *direct costs* paid to the expert and as *transaction costs* associated with retaining the expert. Direct costs are straightforward. Most experts will be paid for their services. A 'do it yourself' (*DIY*) user values his or her required design effort at less than the cost of retaining the expert, accounting for possible differences in the resulting design quality.

Transaction costs are more subtle. Transaction costs are incurred in defining a design problem and in evaluating alternative solutions. On first reflection, a user would appear to have an advantage over an expert in diagnosing the gap in his or her own experience. It is believed that this is sometimes true but not necessarily so. Experts by definition have encountered similar design problems many times before and will likely have observed empirical regularities in user needs. Experts typically also deploy techniques for probing user needs, such as interviews and observational methods (Ulrich and Eppinger, 2004). In many cases, user needs are *latent*, and they cannot be spontaneously articulated by users, but if these needs were satisfied, the gap in the user experience would be addressed. Of course, a risk of expertise is that it frames the designer's diagnosis of the problem. An architect may define a gap in the communication patterns within an R&D organization as a problem relating to the built environment, whereas a management consultant may define the same gap as a problem of organizational structure.

Search almost never results in a single plan, but rather exposes several alternatives, which are promising enough for serious consideration. Evaluation of alternatives typically occurs 'on paper' before an artifact is produced. Once an artifact has been produced, there is usually an evaluation through testing by the user. Users are clearly best at assessing, through their own experience, whether an artifact actually closes the sensed gap in their experience. While experts may productively observe patterns in behavior, ultimately the user is

---

[5] Some artifacts can be decomposed into a platform and derivatives, with the platform a common artifact and the derivative a unique artifact. In a subsequent section, we discuss hybrid modes of design, which can arise in such cases.

the frame of reference for the gap in the first place, and is the only agent who can conclude that the gap has been addressed. However, users are typically ill equipped to forecast the extent to which a design alternative, represented abstractly, will meet their needs. Because they do not work daily with design representations, most users are not skilled at visualizing an artifact, at mental simulation of the artifact's function, and are not alert for common pitfalls for a category of artifacts.

Given these characteristics of transaction costs, users are actually likely to have an advantage over experts when design alternatives can be readily generated and when plans can be accurately evaluated quickly and at low cost, as when realistic prototypes can be produced readily. In such environments, the user can achieve high-quality design through rapid iteration and learning. Expert design in the same context can incur high-transaction costs because of the switching back and forth between search by the expert and evaluation by the user. In this situation, the more efficient search by an expert may be outweighed by the reduced transaction costs of user design.

An additional driver of user design is the utility (or disutility), which some users derive from solving their own problems. To the extent that there is a psychological benefit derived from the process of design ('I designed it myself!'). Then a user may be willing to accept a lower quality outcome even at the same cost of expert design.

For completeness, a comment on an additional form of transaction costs emphasized in *transaction cost economics (TCE)*. The TCE paradigm has been influential in thinking about industrial organization and so it should be mentioned here. Consistent with the view articulated in this chapter, TCE would predict a bias for user design in the face of high-transaction costs. However, the transaction costs contemplated in TCE are those associated with *asset specificity*. When a contracting relationship between a user and an expert requires a speculative investment in assets (e.g., knowledge and expertise), which are highly specific to a particular relationship between a user and an expert, both the user and the expert face a loss in bargaining power. This is because the asset that has been developed may only be used for the specific relationship. Under these conditions, TCE predicts that the user will prefer not to contract with another party, but will instead perform design for oneself. For a discussion of the theory of transaction cost economics and the related literature, see (Ulrich and Ellison, 2005). The problem with invoking TCE in this context is that most design is a 'one-off' effort, or at least highly episodic, and so when contracting with an expert, a user typically assumes that all transaction costs, including investments in specific assets, will be paid as part of the engagement. The expert rarely, if ever, would invest in specific assets without factoring those investments into the contract for design services. Terwiesch and Loch (2004) discuss some of these contracting and pricing issues in the context of customized artifacts.

3.3. Synergies among modes

All three modes of design can and typically do exist in the same community and for the same category of artifacts. Some people engage in user design. Some people engage in custom design. Everyone participates in common design, at least through their consumption and use of artifacts.

A commonly occurring pattern of innovation is for a new artifact to emerge through user design and then to be adopted, often with some refinement, as part of a common design effort. This process of appropriation and improvement may take place over many years and even generations. This pattern of innovation has been documented in detail by von Hippel (1988). However, the migration from a unique design to a common design need not originate in user design. An essentially similar pattern involves the migration from expert design of a unique artifact for a single user to common design by an institution for a collection of users. In either case, an individual user uncovers a set of user needs and a design that addresses those needs. This design is subsequently exploited by an institution to deliver a common artifact.

3.4. Hybrid modes

An artifact may be the result of more than one mode of design if it is comprised of more than one element. For example, a common component may be used in combination with a custom component. Alternatively, one or more attributes of a component may be customized, with the rest standardized. This approach is sometimes called a *platform strategy* and is closely related to the notion of *mass customization*. By adopting this strategy, a producer may be able to offer a user a unique design while exploiting the economies of scale associated with the standard elements of the product. Randall, Terwiesch, and Ulrich (2005) provide a detailed discussion of user design for customized products.

4. Enabling processes and technologies

Mode choice in design is strongly influenced by changes in design and production processes and technologies. New technologies and processes have emerged in the past few decades that are changing the way design modes are adopted in practice.

4.1. Templates

The problem of search is dramatically simplified if a *template* is adopted. A template is a fixed architecture for an artifact within which alternative elements may be placed (Ulrich, 1995). For example, iPrint is a web-based system by which users may design printed items such as business cards, stationery, and

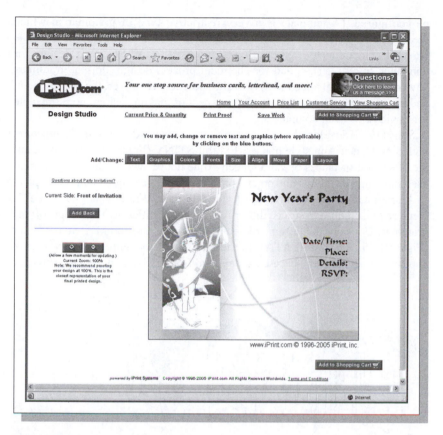

Figure 16.3

Exhibit IPRINT - Web-based interface for user design of a New Year's party invitation based on a template.

party invitations (Figure 16.3 - Exhibit IPRINT). Each of several types of items is represented with a standard template. Within that template, choices may be made of typeface, type size, colors, position of graphic elements, paper, and textual content. By constraining search to a selection of elements within a fixed template, the design problem is bounded sufficiently that many users find that they are able to find satisficing solutions without retaining an expert. Digital printing technology is sufficiently flexible that unique artifacts may be produced in relatively low volume (50–1000 units) at reasonable cost.

4.2. Design grammars

A design grammar is a set of rules defining 'valid' designs, including a definition of the elements of the design and the rules by which they may be configured. (A template is a very restrictive type of grammar in which the alternative selections of elements must always be configured in the same way.) Grammars have been developed and used for VLSI circuit design, for computer system design, and for chemical process design. Formal grammars have otherwise rarely been used in design practice. However, the development and use of such grammars offers the prospect of making search more tractable for novices, or even computers.[6]

Stiny (1978) developed a design grammar for several domains in architecture, including Queen Ann style houses. Exhibit STINY (Figure 16.4) is an example of several instances of valid Queen-Anne houses within Stiny's grammar, each showing a different valid porch configuration for a single main house plan.

A grammar defines a universe of valid designs. While it may enable efficient search, it also restricts the space of possibilities to the scope of the grammar. Consider the designs of Frank Gehry such as the MIT Stata Center (Figure 16.5 - Exhibit STATA). In the late twentieth Century, Gehry's work appeared fresh precisely because it deviated from existing grammars, possibly

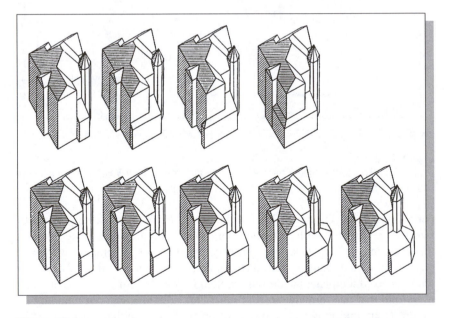

Figure 16.4
Exhibit STINY - A few instances of a 'Queen Anne' design composed within the Queen-Anne grammar. *Source*: Stiny (1978).

---

[6] Goldenberg and Mazursky (1999) make a compelling argument that what they call 'templates' (actually closer to a grammar in my nomenclature) can be used to characterize successful designs for advertisements and new product concepts.

Figure 16.5
Exhibit STATA - The Stata Center at MIT, designed by Frank Gehry. *Source*: http://yoda.zoy.org/copynotice.

the way the Queen Anne style appeared fresh in the late nineteenth Century. Interestingly, over his career Gehry has designed enough buildings that one can start to imagine a formal grammar defining a valid 'Gehry style.'

4.3. Search automation

If a design domain can be formalized through a design grammar, then the prospect of automating search emerges. A second requirement for automating search is that a formal evaluation function (or *objective function*, in the language of optimization) can be articulated. Without some way of automatically estimating the quality of a design, automating search is unlikely. For highly structured design problems, such as creating a customized personal computer to meet the needs of an individual, search automation is currently feasible (Randall, Terwiesch, and Ulrich, 2005). Additional problems are likely to be addressed by search automation in the future.

4.4. Rapid prototyping

Most design efforts require the designer to forecast the extent to which a contemplated alternative will satisfy the needs of the target user. A forecast is required when the cost of producing the artifact, even in prototype form, is relatively high. Rapid prototyping technologies, which might be called more appropriately *inexpensive* prototyping technologies, allow the designer to produce relatively more prototypes for actual testing and can therefore reduce the importance of accurate forecasting of design quality. In the hands of a novice designer, the act of testing many prototypes can substitute to some

Figure 16.6
Exhibit SLS - Chess pieces fabricated using the Selective Laser Sintering (SLS) process, a rapid prototyping technology. *Source*: http://www.kinzoku.co.jp/image/zoukei_p3_b.jpg.

extent for expertise in search and evaluation of designs and thereby enable user design where custom design or common design was previously the norm.

Exhibit SLS (Figure 16.6) shows several chess pieces made directly from computer models using the *selective laser sintering* (SLS) process. The cost and time required to produce physical models of complex geometric forms like these has fallen by at least a factor of ten relative to conventional prototyping technologies (in this case, carving by hand), enabling more frequent evaluation of physical prototypes as opposed to requiring the designer to completely refine the form of an object before committing to an expensive and time-consuming prototyping process.

4.5. Flexible production

Flexible production is a means of producing artifacts with relatively low-fixed costs per variant of the artifact. For example, laser printing of documents is quite flexible, allowing 10 different documents to be printed at about the same cost as 10 copies of the same document. Computer-controlled laser cutting machines allow arbitrary trajectories to be cut in plywood, sheet metal, and plastic sheet, with essentially no *set-up cost*. To the extent than an artifact can be produced by flexible production means, unique artifacts can be produced for individual users at reasonable cost. Flexible production technologies therefore enable custom design and user design. Exhibit CNC (Figure 16.7) shows a web-based design

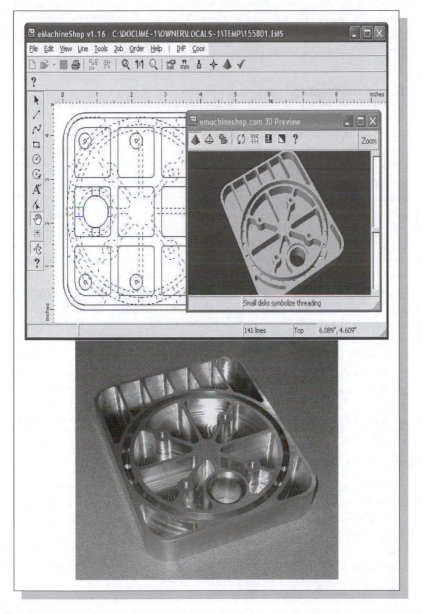

Figure 16.7
Exhibit CNC - Aluminum part flexibly produced by a CNC milling machine. A web-based design program can be used to create instructions for the milling machine. *Source*: emachineshop.com.

interface that creates instructions for a computer-controlled milling machine, which can be used to flexibly produce three-dimensional shapes as shown. CNC milling is a material removal process incurring only modest fixed costs per variant of the artifact and therefore enabling relatively low-volume production.

4.6. Tournaments

Tournaments in design have increased in popularity with the advent of mass media channels, but have probably been used by institutions for a long time. In a tournament, many individuals or teams submit plans or prototypes, which are typically evaluated by experts, sometimes with panels of users, and sometimes through testing. Some tournaments are intended to be primarily design mechanisms for a producer or user. Examples of these competitions are QVC's product road show, which visits 10 cities in the United States each year to screen new products, and the US government agency DARPA's *Grand Challenge* autonomous robotic vehicle competition. Other tournaments are intended primarily to deliver entertainment to an audience. An example of this type of competition is *Million Dollar Idea*, a televised competition in which a winner is granted $1 million to commercialize his or her invention. Tournaments exploit large numbers of parallel searches by individuals, sometimes collecting design alternatives from thousands of entrants. This strategy can be particularly powerful when seeking new ideas for products in that a raw plan, perhaps only partially developed, can be selected from the efforts of many individuals and then refined professionally in through common design by an institution. Tournaments may also exploit a tendency by entrants to overestimate the probability of success, possibly resulting in more design effort per unit of investment by the tournament sponsor than could be achieved by other means.

4.7. Open source

The practice of *open source* arose in the software engineering community and comprised, at a minimum, the free publication of the 'source code' for an artifact. For software, the source code is the program instructions in human-readable form, typically, as they were written by the designer. For documents, the source code is the text, in readable, editable form. For a physical good, the source code might include geometric information, materials specifications, control algorithms, and/or process specifications.

The rationale for open source is that some users will sense opportunities for improvement in an artifact and will themselves make those improvements (Terwiesch and Ulrich, 2007). Several open-source communities have developed and are active, with the most famous being the Linux computer operating system. Most of these communities have some mechanism for evaluating and ratifying potential improvements submitted by members of the user community. Remarkably, some open-source artifacts evolve with almost no managerial oversight. For example, the Wikipedia encyclopedia is open source, and can be modified by anyone in the world with access to an internet browser. Open source communities need not be firms, but they are nevertheless institutions that enable the common design mode.

4.8. Design kits

Design kits are tools to facilitate the design process, often provided at no charge by firms seeking to produce the unique artifacts of designers, or those who otherwise benefit from active design communities. Producers of specialized semiconductor devices will sometimes provide designers with 'breadboard' systems incorporating the devices to enable experimentation and trial, and in the hopes that these devices will be used in a new artifact. Design kits reduce the fixed costs of designing a unique artifact and so enable expert design and user design.

4.9. User groups

User groups are sets of users with communication mechanisms to facilitate the exchange of information relative to a class of artifacts. These mechanisms are increasingly electronic, typically implemented via the internet. User groups are often structured around issues or questions sometimes called discussion threads, although some user groups have formal administrative elements such as managers and committees. User groups enable user design by allowing plans from one user to be communicated to another with similar needs. User groups can also facilitate common design by allowing users to share information about gaps, coordinate plans, and even test prototypes.

An example of a user community is flashkit.com, a community of designers using the Macromedia Flash multimedia programming language. As of this writing there were about 500 000 members of this community. In this case, a primary beneficiary of the user group is the firm Macromedia.

5. Concluding remarks

This chapter articulates the modes of design adopted by users, experts, and institutions in creating new artifacts. User design is a tantalizing prospect by which users create unique artifacts to address their own needs. Yet, expert design and common design remain prevalent modes. The choice of a particular mode is driven by the comparative advantage of experts, by economies of scale in design and production, and by the transaction costs of engaging experts, features that remain the foundations of modern economic life. However, emergent processes and technologies such as rapid prototyping and design grammars can alter the economics of mode choice.

References

Ericsson, K.A., The Acquisition of Expert Performance: An Introduction to Some of the Issues. In K. A. Ericsson (ed.), *The Road to Excellence*, Lawrence Erlbaum, Mahwah, NJ, p. 1–50, 1996.

Goldenberg, J., D. Mazursky, and S. Solomon, "Creative Sparks," *Science*, Vol. 285, Issue 5433, September 1999, p. 1495–1496.

Lancaster, K., "The Economics of Product Variety: A Survey," *Marketing Science*, Vol. 9, No. 3, Summer 1990, p. 189–206.

Randall, T., C. Terwiesch, and K. Ulrich, "User Design of Customized Products," *Marketing Science*, forthcoming 2005.

Rybczynski, W., *One Good Turn: A Natural History of the Screwdriver and the Screw*, Scribner, New York, 2000.

Simon, H. A., *The Sciences of the Artificial*, Third Edition, MIT Press, Cambridge, MA, 1996.

Sommer, S.C. and C.H. Loch, "Selectionism and Learning in Projects with Complexity and Unforeseeable Uncertainty," *Management Science*, Vol. 50, No. 10, 2004, 1334–1347.

Stiny, G. and W.J. Mitchell, "The Palladian Grammar," *Environment and Planning B*, Vol. 5, p. 5–18, 1978.

Terwiesch, C. 2008, "Product Development as a Problem-solving Process," in S. Shane (editor), *Blackwell Handbook on Technology and Innovation Management*, forthcoming.

Terwiesch, C. and C.H. Loch, "Collaborative Prototyping and the Pricing of Custom Designed Products," *Management Science*, Vol. 50, No. 2, p. 145–158, 2004.

Terwiesch, C. and K.T. Ulrich, *Innovation: Managing the Value Creation Process*. Forthcoming. 2007.

Ulrich, K.T. and D.J. Ellison, "Beyond Make-Buy: Internalization and Integration of Design and Production," *Production and Operations Management*, Vol. 14, No. 3, Fall 2005, p. 315–330.

Ulrich, K.T. and S.D. Eppinger, *Product Design and Development*, Third Edition, McGraw-Hill, New York, 2004.

Ulrich, K., "The Role of Product Architecture in the Manufacturing Firm," *Research Policy*, Vol. 24, p. 419–440, 1995.

Von Hippel, E., *The Sources of Innovation*, Oxford University Press, New York, 1988.

17 Project risk management in new product development

Svenja C. Sommer, Christoph H. Loch, and Michael T. Pich

1. Introduction

We have known for a long time that product development can fruitfully be viewed as an 'information generating process': it starts with data about market opportunities and technical possibilities, and transforms them into information assets for production and delivery (Clark and Fujimoto, 1991: 20). In this process, highly uncertain and imprecise information is transformed into precise information (such as a production recipe, a market plan, production volumes, etc., see Loch and Terwiesch, 2005; Terwiesch et al., 2002). This implies that new product development (NPD) intrinsically faces uncertainty: the final 'recipe' is not known at the outset and emerges during the process, and therefore, decisions must be made with incomplete information. As the development of a product progresses, the uncertainty is gradually (although not necessarily monotonically) reduced.

As a result, any product development process bears various forms of risks, ranging from market related risks (demand, cash flow, and resource access) and completion risk (technical risk, operational risks) to institutional risks (regulatory risks, social-acceptability risk, and sovereign risk) (Miller and Lessard, 2000: 78–83). Across all categories, uncertainty tends to be high at the initial planning stage and to be reduced over the course of the project. 'Regulatory risks, for instance, diminish soon after permits are obtained, technical risk drop as engineering experiments are performed, elements of design are defined and construction is completed. Errors are identified and corrected as the system begins operation' (Miller and Lessard, 2000: 83).

Information created through experimentation, testing, analysis, and implementation reduces the uncertainty, and choosing when which information is created can be an important source of project value. As Browning et al. (2002: 444) point out, 'in many cases, lack of value stems less from doing unnecessary activities and more from doing necessary activities with the wrong information (and then having to redo them).' The quality of information available drives the value of flexibility: the less dispersion, or variance, is in the information about decision parameters, the less needed is flexibility (Huchzermeier and Loch, 2001). Indeed, the classic stage gate process of product development is originally a process of risk reduction: as long as little is known, feasibility studies and business cases attempt to make available as much information as possible, and as more information becomes available, progressively higher investments can be made. For example, initial prototypes are cheap CAD or non-functional models, and as the design space becomes constrained, more expensive but more informative prototypes can be used (Thomke, 1998; Thomke and Bell, 2001).

A variety of methods have been proposed to manage risk. This chapter provides an overview of current knowledge in project risk management, and proposes a contingency approach to it.

2. Concepts of uncertainty

Uncertainty is a fundamental concept that has a rich history of examination in economics and management, and we begin by reviewing its major characteristics.

The simplest form of uncertainty is 'risk,' or the possibility of several possible outcomes for a situation, each with a probability of occurrence that can be measured (e.g., from experience or experiments). For example, in roulette, black or red may come up, and although the outcome is not known in advance, the probability of 25/51 can be assigned to each (1/51 being the probability of a zero).

Knight (1921) pointed out that often the probabilities are not known. As Keynes (1937) put it later, 'there is no scientific basis on which to form any calculable probability whatever. We simply do not know.' This more challenging situation is referred to as 'Knightian uncertainty,' and sometimes as 'ambiguity' (the absence of a probability distribution).

Methods have been developed to deal with ambiguity. Savage (1954) introduced the concept of 'subjective probability' and showed that a mathematical treatment is still possible when people 'guess' their own probabilities. Second, ambiguity can be represented as a probability distribution over a multitude of possible probability distributions (e.g., Camerer and Weber, 1992), making possible the mathematical treatment of this extended concept of uncertainty. The discipline of project risk management has developed principles of risk identification, risk prioritization, and risk management (preventive, mitigating, and contingent action), and risk incentives (Amit et al., 1998) which can deal with ambiguity as long as all important factors (although not their values) and ranges of outcomes are known (e.g., Chapman and Ward, 1997; Smith and Merritt, 2002).

However, these concepts do not fully capture the uncertainty faced by a novel venture. They assume that the 'space' of relevant variables and influence factors, and their possible outcomes and causal connections, are known – only the probabilities are unknown. In a novel venture, management often knows much less; they face unforeseen uncertainty. An influential paper in Technology Management characterized it as 'the inability to recognize and articulate variables and their functional relationships' (Schrader et al., 1993).[1] The 'space' of parameters and outcomes is not known; there are things out there that are not on the horizon at all. Economists have called this difficult state of affairs 'unawareness' or 'unforeseen contingencies' (Kreps, 1992; Modica and Rustichini, 1994), scholars in public policy have referred to 'wicked problems' (as opposed to the 'tame problems' that we know how to analyze, see Rittel and Webber, 1973), and engineering and project management professionals have used the term 'unknown unknowns' (expanding the 'known unknowns' of Knightian uncertainty), or 'unk unks' (Wideman 1992).[2]

When an NPD project develops a new technology or tackles a new market, unknown unknowns are rampant. For example, Sun Microsystem's Java was conceived as a remote control with operating system for household devices, but it ended up being a programming language for the worldwide web (which had not existed when the project was started; see Bank, 1995). For a formal treatment of these different concepts of uncertainty, we refer the readers to Pich et al. (2002).

3. A model of managing uncertainty and complexity

Consider a model of decision-making in an NPD project with uncertainty (based on Pich et al., 2002 and Sommer and Loch, 2004). We conceptualize the project not as usual as a 'set of tasks' because the tasks may not yet be identifiable at the outset. Rather, we model the project as an *outcome*, represented by a payoff function $\Pi = \Pi(\omega, A)$. The project payoff depends on the state of the world $\omega \in \Omega$ and a *chosen* set of actions A (which represents what the management team does over the course of the venture).

Ω denotes the set of all possible 'states of the world' relevant to the outcome of the project, with $\omega = (w_1, \ldots, w_N)$ as a generic element. Each parameter w_i may take any value from its domain D_i. One ω represents one combination of realizations of all parameters. A state of the world may

---

[1] As a symptom of the disagreement in terminology across fields, consider that Schrader et al. actually called their concept 'ambiguity,' in contrast to the use of the term in economics and decision theory.

[2] The term is, in fact, 'folklore': it has been widely used in aerospace, electrical machinery, and nuclear power project management for decades.

include management team capabilities, resource costs, competitor moves, and market demographics, emergence of other technologies, technology difficulty, regulatory changes, and myriad additional influences. The actions A may influence the state of the world, such that $\omega_t = M(\omega_{t-1}, A_{t-1})$. M refers to the map of cause-effect relations.

It is the goal of the management team to choose a 'best' course of action A^*, which maximizes the expected payoff $E[\Pi(\omega, A)]$ (or some other risk-adjusted measure).[3] The more complex a project, the more parameters w_i interact and the less 'tractable' the payoff function Π and the transition matrix M become, where tractable refers to being able to find the optimal course of action A^* that optimizes the project payoff for the known influence factors $\omega: argmax_A \; \Pi[M(\omega, A), A]$. If the project is highly complex, optimization may be elusive because the causal map M is intractable for an evaluation of the consequences of actions. Thus, the team can only approximate a good course of actions or perform multiple parallel trials (Dahan and Mendelson, 2001).

Based on this conceptual model, we can now classify the most important risk management tools used. First, suppose that the influence parameters w_i are not known with certainty, but only as random variables. If there are too many influence variables and it is not practicable or too expensive to react to information on them, the project team may choose to simply take their variation as given and accept that the project payoff Π is also a random variable. If a certain deterministic payoff target Π_{target} must be guaranteed to external parties (e.g., senior management, or an investor, or a customer), the team may negotiate the target to be below the expectation, to have a desired probability of being able to meet the target. Then, $(E[\Pi(\omega, A)] - \Pi_{\text{target}})$ is a buffer. 'Service levels' (probability of meeting the target) and buffers are commonly used in project management.

Second, suppose there are certain identified major 'risks,' or influence variables w_j whose uncertainty has a large influence on the payoff. If the team has preliminary information about those risks (e.g., in the form of a 'prior' distribution $g(w_j)$), and if the state of the world resulting from the currently taken actions is another random variable, $M(\omega, A)$ the team can choose actions A^* to maximize $E[\Pi(M(\omega, A), A)]$. Thus, the team performs sequential decision-making, the decision in each round depending on the state of the world currently achieved (or an imperfect signal about that state). Mathematically,

---

[3] Theory in Decision Sciences is concerned with (possibly imperfectly observed) Markov processes and Bayesian updating (e.g., Marschak and Radner, 1972; Lovejoy, 1991). State of the world, conceptualizable events and probabilities can be mathematically represented with probability spaces. We do not describe the mathematical entities in full here, because we use the model to describe the concept of uncertainty and its effects on decision making but not to perform mathematical operations.

this corresponds to finding optimal dynamic (state-dependent) policies, which corresponds to Markov decision processes, in which optimal policies can be found by dynamic programming methods. In practice, situations with major identifiable risks (stochastic influence variables) are managed with 'contingency planning' or 'project risk management' methods, most of which are (quantitative or qualitative) applications of dynamic programming (Chapman and Ward, 1997; Loch et al., 2006).

Buffers and contingency plans (project risk management) are powerful tools when all important elements of the state vector ω have been identified and their ranges are known. In other words, all major influences on the project payoff can be identified, although the values of these influence factors may not be known beforehand. However, this assumption is often not fulfilled when the NPD project addresses a new and unknown market, or uses a new and unknown technology. In such situations of novelty, major influences often emerge that initially are not at all on the horizon of the project team. For example, unexpected side effects or constraints may emerge from a new technology, or unforeseen competitors, customer needs, or customer behaviors may emerge.

This third class of situations implies *unforeseeable uncertainty*: an entire set of influences is unidentified; the management team knows only of the existence of the first n influences $\omega_{known} = (w_1, \ldots, w_n)$. Thus, performance is also conceptualized in a smaller number of dimensions $\Pi_{known}(\omega_{known}, A_{known}) = \Pi(\omega_{known}, \overline{w}_{n+1}, \ldots, \overline{w}_N, A_{known})$, a function of fewer variables. The team is unaware of the $(N-n)$ unk unks, or unforeseen dimensions, and therefore not aware of additional actions that would be available if the team knew of the additional influence dimensions. For these unk unks, the team proceeds under implicit and possibly wrong 'default' assumptions, as if they were set to *fixed values* $(\overline{w}_{n+1}, \ldots, \overline{w}_N)$ (which, except by chance, will differ from the true values that the project will later encounter). Thus, the unforeseen dimensions are taken as parameters, as 'given,' without being recognized as such.

Note that this situation is worse than ambiguity (or the absence of probability distribution on the influence variables): in the case of ambiguity, dynamic programming methods can still be applied (by taking distributions over possible distributions, or applying techniques of partially observed Markov Decision Processes). When the influences are unknown and cannot be articulated, these methods can no longer be used. As we describe below, a combination of iteration (trial-and-error learning) and selectionism (parallel trials) is required.

The three fundamental cases of uncertainty identified in the qualitative model, variation and buffers, risks and contingency planning, and unforeseeable uncertainty, are further described in the next three sections, along with the approaches that have been identified in previous work.

4. Approaches to variation and buffers

All non-trivial NPD projects face uncertainty about task durations and costs. To manage these risks, firms commonly use **project buffers**, in form of schedule buffers, budget contingencies, or specification compromises. This has been a well-understood part of project risk management for a long time.

With the proposition of the critical chain methodology (Goldratt, 1997), **schedule buffers** have recently received a lot of attention, and have been incorporated as add-ons to commercial scheduling software packages such as Microsoft Project® (see an overview in Herroelen, 2005). The basic idea is to schedule all activities at their latest start times according to classic critical path calculations. (The critical path is the sequence of activities that have no 'slack' – that is, for which a delay of one day immediately translates into a project delay of one day). A safety buffer is added at the *end* of the project rather than during each activity. This buffer protects the promised (deterministic) completion time from variation in the tasks on the critical path. 'Feeding buffers' are placed whenever a non-critical activity feeds into the critical path, both to protect the critical path from disruptions caused by the feeding activities and to allow the critical chain activities to start early when things go well (see Fig. 17.1).

A critical step is moving the 'safeties' from the individual activities into the project buffer. Task completion time estimates should be at the median, implying that they are missed 50 per cent of the time. As activities evolve, management keeps track of how much the buffers are consumed. As long as there is some predetermined fraction of the buffers remaining, all is assumed well; otherwise, problems are flagged or corrective action is taken. Goldratt

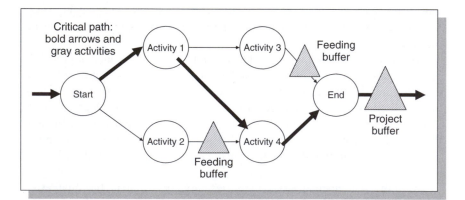

Figure 17.1
A project plan with project buffer (*Source*: Herroelen and Leus, 2001).

(1997: 157) recommends that the project buffer be 50 per cent of the sum of the safeties of the individual activities; Herroelen and Leus (2001) show that the project buffer may be even smaller, as little as 30 per cent, in large projects with a 'typical' structure of task distributions.

The key to the effectiveness of the schedule buffer is realizing that it is not mainly a calculation device, but a tool to change attitudes: Project workers no longer need to protect their own schedule (so they no longer need to 'low-ball' by giving over-conservative estimates), nor can they procrastinate because they impact the overall buffer that everyone looks at and depends on. The entire team 'sits in one boat.' This change in mutual commitment has made buffer management popular over the last five years.

In addition to time, *budget contingencies* can serve as project buffers. Schedule buffers add a reserve for estimation errors in time; similarly, contingency budgets serve as a buffer for errors in cost estimates. A 5 per cent or 10 per cent of the estimated cost are commonly added as a budget reserve (Meredith and Mantel, 1995: 303). Kezsbom et al. (1989: 63) propose a budget contingency of up to 20 per cent for the early project phases characterized by higher levels of uncertainty; if feasible they suggest obtaining better forecasts from analyzing past performances of similar R&D endeavors. Meredith and Mantel (1995: Ch. 8), on the other hand, recommend estimating the buffer based on the most likely and pessimistic estimates for the specific project. Budget contingencies can also serve as an alternative to schedule buffers. If a project completion time starts to slip, the team might revert to project crashing to shorten the duration of project activities. Typical ways to shorten project activity durations at a cost include working overtime, adding additional or utilizing more experienced staff, outsourcing activities, paying to expedite services, or upgrading equipment (Kendrick, 2003: 150; Roemer and Ahmadi, 2004). The time cost trade-off has been extensively studied (Berman, 1964; Kelly and Walker, 1959), more recently also considering the possibility to overlap activities as an alternative to crashing (Roemer and Ahmadi, 2004).

Finally, *specification compromises* can serve as buffers. Cusumano and Selby (1995, 1996) describe the use of features (in addition to time) as buffers in the development process at Microsoft. By assigning priorities to new or enhanced product features and by developing and testing feature by feature, Microsoft is able to relax some of the performance goals or cut or scale back features to stay relatively on time. A senior manager noted 'projects delete about 20–25 per cent of the features included in a product's initial specification' (Cusumano and Selby, 1995: 218). Cusumano and Selby conclude that by forcing developers to stick to a shipment date and settling for products that are 'good enough' (focusing on the most important features), Microsoft was able to enter and influence the direction of every major PC software mass market.

5. Approaches to project risk management and contingency planning

Project buffers assume that the uncertainty involves only minor variations around the plan. However, many projects face major events whose uncertain occurrence would have an important impact on the project. *Project risk management* has proposed a formal process to manage these identifiable risk factors. It is a systematic and analytical process, which identifies and responds to project risk throughout the life of a project to lower the probability or the magnitude of a loss. It typically consists of four phases: risk identification, risk assessment and prioritization, risk response planning (management), and documentation and learning (Fig. 17.2). In the following, we will discuss the first three in some detail.

Risk identification: The first step of risk management aims at identifying risks that can be a hurdle to the project's success. The identified risks are often summarized in risk lists, describing the nature and consequence of each possible risk. To ensure that no risks are overlooked, many firms use checklists of risk categories. Risk lists themselves can be summarized in 'generic' templates that group all the risks that have occurred in the past. Such templates are a powerful way of summarizing experience. Figure 17.3 shows a summary of a generic risk template from the pharmaceutical industry.

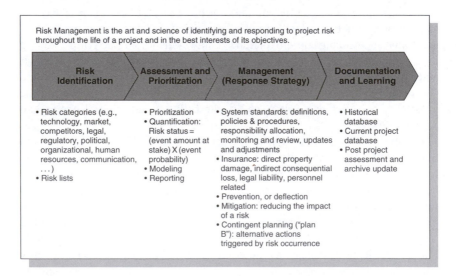

Figure 17.2
Project Risk Managment (*Source*: Wideman, 1992; Chapman and Ward, 1997; Loch et al., 2006).

Risk Category	Detailed Subcategories
Substance and Production	
Ingredients	Risk from suppliers (dependency, stability, transfer, contracts), cost of production, availability of drug substance, process (reproducibility, scale-up, impurities), stability (shelf life)
Final product	As above, plus dosage changes, formulation changes
Analytical methods	Specificity, transfer of license or to a different site
Regulatory issues	Ingredient status, toxicity documentation, mixtures, impurity limits
Preclinical	
Safety pharmacology	Findings in core battery studies, supplemental studies, toxicity in cell cultures
Primary pharmacology	Choice of endpoints and species, target selectivity, and specificity
Bioanalytics	Detection of parent compound and metabolites, toxicity or metabolism in test species different from humans, drug accumulation, oral bioactivity, *in vivo* tests, body penetration
Toxicology	Availability of test substance, pharmacodynamic side effects, high mortality rate in long-term studies, drug-specific side effects
Clinical	
Phase I	Pharmacokinetics (e.g., different in subpopulations, interactions with other compounds or foods), pharmacodynamics (e.g., subject tolerance different from patient tolerance)
Phase II	Appropriate dosage, exposure duration, relevance of placebo control
Phase III	Study delay (e.g., because of season), patient recruitment (e.g., tough criteria, special patient groups, dropout rates), negative outcome (not significant), new regulatory requirements
General regulatory risks	Status of comparator, toxants in environment, availability of guidelines, interaction with agencies (e.g., process time, contradictions among different agencies), requirement differences across countries
General risks	
Licenses	Dependence on licensing partners
Patents	Disclosure of new patents
Trademarks	Viability/acceptance of trademark at submission
Costs	Currencies, inflation, additional patients or studies needed
Market risks	New competitors, new therapies, patient acceptance, target profile, political risks (e.g., pricing, prevention versus therapy)

Figure 17.3
Generic risk list (template) of a pharmaceutical development project (*Source*: Loch et al., 2006).

The full template is 20 pages long; it embodies experience about risks in pharmaceutical development.

Risk assessment and prioritization: The next step is to assess or quantify each risk by determining the likelihood that the risk will occur as well as the potential financial impact of the event on the project. The risk status, defined as the (event amount at stake) * (event probability), is often used to prioritize the risks. While prioritizing risks based on risk status and concentrating on the most important risk factors is useful, it overlooks that risks typically do not occur in isolation. Therefore, many scholars propose to complement this risk assessment with *scenario planning*, possibly in combination with Monte Carlo simulations (e.g., Huss, 1988; Schoemaker, 1991). In scenario planning, several important risk factors are changed at the same time, grouped around different possible scenarios or narratives. This allows exploring the joint impact of various important risk factors. In addition, by thinking in terms of narratives, scenario planning might stimulate 'decision-makers to consider changes they would otherwise ignore' (Schoemaker, 1995: 27).

Risk response planning (management): The identified risks can be categorized into two groups: risks whose causes are at least partially under the control of the project team and uncontrollable risks, on which the project team has no influence. If the causes of a risk are controllable, project teams can attempt to prevent the occurrence of the risk. *Risk prevention* encompassed three strategies: (1) *Risk avoidance* refers to cases in which the project team is able to remove the cause of a risk completely by reconsidering some of the choices made in the project plan. For example, technology related risk might be avoided by choosing well-established technologies over novel, untried ones. (2) *Risk mitigation* refers to cases in which the team is able to reduce the probability or the impact of a risk, without eliminating the risk. For example, market risks can be reduced by communicating frequently with end customers and regularly testing prototypes with users. (3) Finally, *risk transfer* refers to cases in which the team is able transfer risks to outside parties. Insurance is certainly the most well-known example of risk transfer, where risks, such as property damage or legal liability, are transferred to outside financial institutions. By choosing appropriate incentive contracts, risk can also be transferred to outside contractors. For example, lump sum payments to contractors transfer the full financial risk of budget overruns to the contractor, while under cost-plus contracts the risk remains within the firm (von Branconi and Loch, 2004; for a detailed discussion on risk prevention see e.g., Kendrick, 2003, Ch. 8).

In many cases, the causes of a risk are not under the control of the project team and thus risk prevention is not possible. In this case, the team has to deal with the effects of the risks, if they occur. Project risk management suggests to identify an alternative course of action in the planning phase that will be triggered if and when the event occur (*contingency planning*). The idea is that a more effective action can be chosen up front, when there is sufficient time to analyze possible alternatives. These contingent actions then become part of the project plan, and must be considered in both the project schedule and the budget. Contingency planning can be done in various ways. Two methods for incorporating the identified risks into the project plan are most widely used: decision trees and extended risk lists.

The use of *decision trees* recognizes that decisions about project tasks and investments are made sequentially. Its analysis is an application of dynamic programming methodology – decision trees represent dynamic programs with a simple structure that can be graphically represented.

Figure 17.4 shows an example of a decision tree, corresponding to part of a drug research project for the development of a central nervous system drug (calcium channel receptor blocker for sleep disorder indication). Squares in the tree denote *decision nodes*, indicating decision points: Do/don't continue with the project at the stages of research, preclinical development, clinical development, and market introduction. Thus, each decision node has two branches, 'yes' and 'no.' Under the 'yes' branch, the time and cost of continuing are indicated.

The circles in the tree denote *chance nodes*, indicating major risks: in this case, the discovery of side effects that would prevent successful market introduction of the drug. The respective probabilities are indicated next to the branches (they are estimated based on historical statistics from similar drugs). The estimated market potential of the drug is indicated on the far right, amounting to $1.8 billion in profits (not revenues), cumulative over the life of the drug and discounted back to the time of market introduction (at an annual interest rate of 10 percent). This expected value has an estimation range of ± 60 per cent. The decision tree is analyzed backward: The value of 'yes' at the decision node 'market the drug?' is the expected value at the subsequent chance node, discounted by one year, minus the cost of continuing – that is, $1,466 = (.97)(1,787)/1.1 - 110$. This is higher than zero, the value of stopping, so the optimal decision is to continue. Based on the value at this decision node, the decision tree can be analyzed further backward, in the same way, up to the value of the initial decision at the root of the tree.

Accounting for the low overall success rate of 3.6 per cent and the discounting over 10 years (at 10 per cent p.a.), the expected net present value (NPV) at the time of the first decision, if the decision is 'yes,' is as little as $11 million. (If this value were negative, it would be preferable to not engage in the project in the first place according to NPV theory). This is typical for pharmaceutical drugs – 80 per cent of chemical entities entering clinical development fail, and pharmaceutical development takes a long time.

This example demonstrates several useful features of decision trees. First, the tree clearly identifies the *value of managerial flexibility*, or of contingent action in response to risk occurrence: If the company did not have the option of stopping after side effects occur in a given phase, all future investments would be wasted and the NPV of the project greatly reduced. This value of managerial flexibility is often referred to as real option value. The *real options* literature noted that having the right, but not the obligation to make further

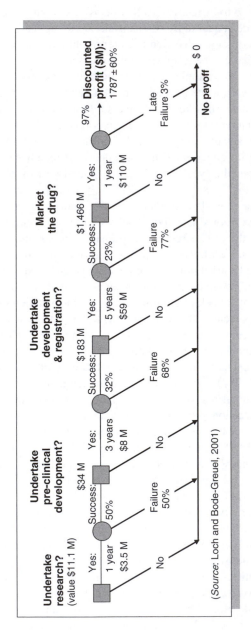

Undertake research?
(value $11.1 M)

Yes:
1 year
$3.5 M

No

Success:
50%

Failure
50%

Undertake pre-clinical development?
$34 M

Yes:
3 years
$8 M

No

Success:
32%

Failure
68%

Undertake development & registration?
$183 M

Yes:
5 years
$59 M

No

Success:
23%

Failure
77%

Market the drug?
$1,466 M

Yes:
1 year
$110 M

No

97% **Discounted profit ($M):**
1787 ± 60%

Late Failure 3%

No payoff

$ 0

(*Source:* Loch and Bode-Greuel, 2001)

Figure 17.4
Decision tree of a central nervous system drug.

investments in the course of the project is analogous to a financial call option (Dixit and Pindyck, 1994). Like a financial option it increases the project's value by limiting downside losses. However, since the method requires the replication of the project's risk with market traded assets – unavailable for many project specific risks – option pricing has been rarely applied in practice. Smith and McCardle (1999) suggest an integrated approach, using option valuation techniques to value market risk and a dynamic programming-based approach to value private risks.

Second, the tree can also help to identify the *value of preventive and mitigating* action; if, e.g., the failure probability after preclinical development (68 per cent) could be eliminated or reduced, the value of the drug (at the initial decision) would be increased. This increase would correspond to the value of the preventive/mitigating action and could be compared to the cost of that action. Similarly, the value of additional contingent actions can be calculated; e.g., in the case of a side effect, sell the drug patent for an industrial application. Third, the tree shows the *dependence among the risks*; for example, if the first one occurs, the future ones, as well as the contingent or preventive actions, become irrelevant. This dependence and ordering in time establishes a natural order of attention for the project manager.

Thus, a decision tree is a powerful tool that can be used in various stages of risk management; it not only identifies risks but also facilitates the subsequent PRM phases of risk prioritization and risk response planning. A decision tree offers a way of looking at project risks in a conceptually clear framework. However, decision trees have an important drawback: Their complexity explodes exponentially with the number of risks and decisions considered (for each decision and risk with n branches, the number of subsequent sub-trees is multiplied by a factor of n). Even when it might still be possible to 'crunch the numbers' of the tree on a powerful computer, the data-gathering effort quickly becomes unmanageable and the result of the tree analysis not transparent, and therefore much less useful, for the decision-making team or manager.

The exponential explosion renders decision trees unusable for projects with large numbers of risks. Therefore, decision trees are commonly used only to *focus* on a handful of the most important risks. Sophisticated project management companies – engineering service providers, for example – perform this focused analysis, ignoring other 'smaller' risks at the first cut and then incorporating them through risk lists. The pharmaceutical industry uses decision trees extensively in this way, which is facilitated by the fact that the *effect of major risks is simple*, i.e., decision and chance nodes have only two branches (*go/kill*), and thus a relatively large number of risks can be incorporated without losing transparency.

Another problem of contingency planning is that an organization cannot list or even anticipate all possible events. Weick and Sutcliffe (2001) call this danger of contingency planning 'double-blind': 'Contingent actions are doubly blind. They are blind because they restrict attention to what we expect, and they are blind because they limit our present view of our capabilities to those we now have. When we plan contingent actions, we tend not to imagine how we might recombine the actions in our current repertoire to deal with the unexpected. In other words, contingency plans reduce improvisation.' Adner and Levinthal (2004: 77) made a similar observation for the real options approach: 'Imposing rigid criteria for abandonment may result in the underutilization of discoveries made in the context of initiatives that are failures with respect to their initial agenda but that introduce promising possibilities not previously imagined.'

To address the issue of exponential explosion in case of a large number of risks, *risk lists* are often used also for risk response planning. In addition to the description of the nature and effect of each risk, the lists then contain the risk's probability, and preventive, mitigating, or contingent actions. Unlike decision trees, risk lists do not explode in complexity when the number of risks is large. If the risks do interact (that is, if a downstream risk looks different, as a result of what happened upstream), the simplification loses information compared to the decision tree. However, many project risks have a 'local' effect; they do not influence the actions downstream. In this case, a risk list is fully adequate, and a decision tree is not necessary at all.

An alternative technique has been proposed in artificial intelligence. In artificial intelligence, planning techniques explicitly differentiate between conditional planning, where actions may have unexpected effects but these can be enumerated and described as part of the action plan, and execution monitoring. Here unexpected effects are too numerous to elaborate and therefore require artificial agents to switch between planning and execution, *dynamically replanning* their course of action either after execution failure (errors in execution) or after the occurrence of unexpected effects (Ambros-Ingerson and Steel, 1988; Weiss, 2000). The basic idea is that 'actions will be executed before the plan is fully elaborated and the outcome of its execution is used to decide the expansion to use' (Ambros-Ingerson and Steel, 1988: 739), or in the terminology of decision trees, which branch to elaborate on. However, as Ambros-Ingerson and Steel (1988) point out, the ability to re-plan is limited by its locality; the basic structure of the problem must be known.

6. Approaches to unforeseeable uncertainty

The standard risk management approach works well if all major risks can be identified at the outset. However, organizations must recognize that especially in novel projects no amount of planning and risk management will identify all the risks or all the combinations of foreseeable events that might happen. The project team is simply not aware of all influence factors, interactions, or even actions available. They are not within the team's horizon; they are outside its knowledge. Therefore, the team cannot plan for them and must be prepared to deal with them as they arise.

Unk unks are fundamental for novel projects. This has been acknowledged by a variety of experts. For example, Miller and Lessard (2000: 76) conclude that the challenge is 'ignorance of the true state of nature and the causal structures of decision issues.' Similarly, researchers of new venture startup projects have observed, 'What has made or broken the companies . . . is the ability or inability to recognize and react to the completely unpredictable' (Brokaw, 1991: 54).

A number of recent advances have been made to address 'severe' uncertainty that can accommodate for unforeseeable uncertainty, as long as the unk unks, or gaps in knowledge, are minor and the target state of the project is well defined, – that is, the project team has a pretty good idea what it wants to achieve and more or less how it wants to do so. In the following, we give an overview of three approaches: (1) increasing project flexibility, (2) discovery driven planning (McGrath and MacMillan, 1995, 2000), and (3) information gap decision theory (Ben-Haim, 2001; Regev et al., 2006).

Thomke (1997: 105) defines *flexibility* as 'the incremental cost and time of modifying a design as a response to changes exogenous or endogenous to the design process.' Thomke and Reinertsen (1998) advocate the use of technologies and processes that accommodate multiple possible outcomes of risk. This includes using technologies such as computer aided design, choosing a modular architecture and minimizing interdependences between modules, deferring commitments to design requirement or committing only certain features allowing others to change, or keeping back-up alternatives for certain components.

The increase in flexibility by deferring commitment to a final product configuration and conducting rapid design iterations received particular attention (Bhattacharya et al., 1998; Eisenhardt and Tabrizi, 1995; Iansiti and MacCormack, 1997; MacCormack et al., 2001). By overlapping the development phase and the implementation phase and testing first versions of the product in the market, companies obtain quick feedback about customer requirements, while other features are still being developed (see Iansiti and MacCormack, 1997 for the product development process at Netscape). Consider the development process of the business magazine 'Capital' in the early 1990s. After developing a concept based on focus group discussions of existing magazines, the magazine went through several testing cycles. A first prototype of just 50 pages was mainly aimed at testing the layout and how far one could go in direction of entertainment by deliberately choosing sensational articles. Based on the feedback of two customer focus groups, a second prototype of 100 pages was created with more representative articles, testing the editorial style and diversity of topics demanded. Again the feedback of two customer focus groups (e.g., asking for more 'service' topics such as management techniques, career and salary or personal finance) was used to create the third prototype ('zero' issue). The 'zero' issue was identical to the real magazine in presentation and editorial content to test the readers response to real product as well as production process, while still keeping the launch data, distribution strategy and communication strategy open (see Fig. 17.5).

The second approach, *discovery driven planning*, proposes to explicitly acknowledge that unknown unknowns exist and to uncover them with four analyses (McGrath and MacMillan, 1995, 2000). (a) A reverse income statement calculates what market share and revenues must be achieved to reach a given return target. (b) A pro forma operations specification shows the key steps for producing the desired output and asks whether these steps can be performed with 'normal' process capabilities (or whether heroic feats are required for successful execution). (c) An assumptions checklist compares the plan with experiences in similar situations or with expert advice (e.g., 'we assume the average selling price to be around $1.60 – is that justified?' See McGrath and MacMillan, 1995: 51) (d) milestone planning anticipates the points at which risks can be eliminated so that the next investment round is justified (explicitly learning about and eliminating risks as a condition for continuation).

This approach is consistent with a body of work that explains how testing hypotheses and examining unexplainable outcomes that contradict initial assumptions can build knowledge and *reduce unforeseeable uncertainty* over the course of a venture (e.g., Thomke, 2003).

The third approach, *information gap decision theory*, proposes to address 'severe uncertainty' when no probability distributions, or even ranges, for certain important influence variables are known (e.g., the number of clients, or future market prices, see Ben-Haim (2001) and Regev et al. (2006)). Information gap theory develops a mathematical method of dealing with the situation where the variation of the parameter u around its believed value $\tilde{u}$ is unbounded.

Rather than choosing actions that maximize an expected outcome (which by definition is not possible for unknown distributions), information gap theory proposes to maximize the robustness or immunity to failure. The robustness of an action is defined as the greatest value of variation for which the reward function is no less than a certain critical value (robust satisficing). By choosing an action that maximizes robustness, the decision maker maximizes the immunity of the project to the unbounded uncertainty.

The approaches of flexibility, discovery driven planning, and information gap theory work well if unk unks are minor, in other words, if the project goal and fundamental project approach remain unchanged. However, unk unks may be so fundamental that the project goal and path are themselves, fundamentally unknown. In that case, flexibility in individual project parts and local design iterations are insufficient. Further, the lack of knowledge

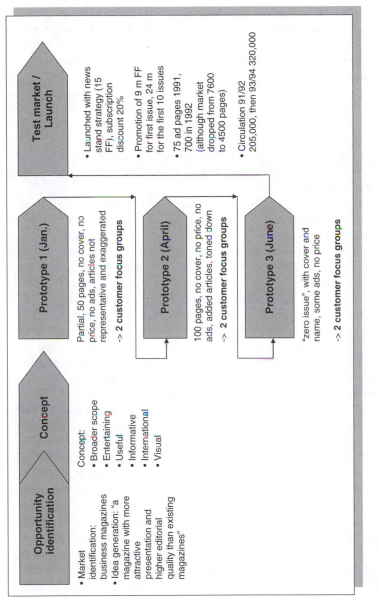

Figure 17.5

The 'fast feedback' process at Capital (*Source:* Angelmar, 1994).

may be so severe that management can neither 'calculate backward' from the desired end result nor check consistency of assumptions. (For example, suppose the desired return cannot be translated into a market share goal, not to mention operational milestones, because the market is too new and emerging.) Similarly, information gap theory cannot be applied unless the major relevant variables and possible actions can be determined.[4]

If a project faces important unk unks affecting the determination of the project goal, there is really no project plan. Any project plan will run into major surprises (many of them negative), and the plan will miss major actions that arise as attractive ex post but were not identified ex ante. While planning is always necessary to have a base line, adherence to a plan (even with contingencies) must not become an end in itself. Unk unks (whether they come from unknown influence factors or from complexity and ill-understood interactions) require the readiness to abandon assumptions and look for solutions in non-anticipated places.

If a project team knows little about the universe of possible project outcomes (and how to get there), it may not insist on choosing a target outcome at the outset. Two approaches have been identified for this level of unforeseeable uncertainty: Trial-and-error learning and selectionism (Leonard-Barton, 1995; Pich et al., 2002). Under *trial-and-error learning*, the team starts moving toward one outcome (the best it can identify), but is prepared to repeatedly and fundamentally change both the outcome and the course of action as it proceed, and as new information becomes available. The most important problem solving is distributed at the outset and throughout the duration of the project. Loch et al (2007) describe a systematic approach for diagnosing unforeseeable uncertainty at the outset of a project. Exploratory experiments, aimed at gaining information without contributing any progress to the current version of the plan, are an important part of this approach. Schoemaker and Gunther (2006: 11) advocate including experiments that up front are likely to fail and might traditionally be considered mistakes: 'If such a mistake unexpectedly succeeds, then it has undermined at least one current assumption (and, often, more).' Such early experiments, generating early failures, rather than analysis, are critical for learning. It is important the organization accepts failure as a source of learning. A failure is no mistake; a mistake is a failure that produces no new information. It is therefore important to track the learning and reduction in knowledge gaps rather than tracking only the progress towards a target. This is consistent with the venture capital literature, which advocates making small investments and determine project continuation when 'milestones' are met that eliminate important ambiguities or knowledge gaps (e.g., Bell, 2000; Sahlman, 1990).

---

[4] Information gap theory can handle minor unk unks, as long as they are not decision variables. For example, it is not necessary to know all external factors influencing market size, since one can check for robustness with respect to market size itself.

This approach has been given different names by project management scholars. For example, Chew et al. (1991) examined unk unks in the context of introducing new manufacturing technologies in plants and concluded that iteration, learning, original new problem solving, and adjustment are required. In the context of NPD, Leonard-Barton (1995) called the iterate-and-learn approach 'product morphing' (meaning repeated changes of a product concept over time), and Lynn et al. (1996) called it 'probe-and-learn,' referring to repeatedly pushing a project all the way into the market and then iterating *after* market introduction, an approach also advocated by Mullins and Sutherland (1998). In general, iteration and experimentation are a fundamental feature of problem solving in innovation and engineering projects (see e.g., Van de Ven et al., 1999; Chap. 2, De Meyer et al., 2002; Thomke, 2003) as well as venture startup projects (see e.g., Drucker, 1985; Pitt and Kannemeyer, 2000; or Chesbrough and Rosenbloom, 2002).

Alternatively, the team might choose to 'hedge' and opt for *selectionism*, or pursuing multiple approaches in parallel, observing what works and what does not (without necessarily having a full explanation why) and choosing the best approach ex post. This approach has been suggested by a variety of authors to address complex or highly uncertain problems. Ding and Eliashberg (2002: 343) suggest that multiple parallel approaches are necessary 'in case where no dominant approach can be identified a priori,' which is true for any project facing unforeseeable uncertainty. In operations research and engineering, this approach is called 'parallel trials,' and in management, Leonard-Barton (1995) has called it 'Darwinian selection,' and McGrath (2001) has called it 'creating requisite variety.' The term 'selectionism' emphasizes the fact that one out of many trials is selected ex post (whether the trials are executed in parallel or one after the other is secondary).

Examples of this approach abound. For example, pharmaceutical companies use this approach when investing in 'backup molecules' for the same target indication to provide insurance if the lead molecule fails. Similarly, Microsoft pursued several operating systems in parallel during the 1980s (DOS, Windows, OS/2 and UNIX), because it was still unclear which operating system would win (Beinhocker, 1999). Toyota builds many prototypes of a car, broadly considering sets of possible solutions to a design challenge, and gradually narrowing the set of possibilities to converge on a final solution (Sobek et al., 1999 have called this approach 'set-based engineering'). Some companies go all the way to market introduction to be able to select the best alternative. For example in the first half of the 1990s Japanese consumer electronics companies developed and launched multiple products to see which would succeed in the consumer market – a strategy known at 'product churning' (Stalk and Webber, 1993).

The uncertainty and complexity of a project can be, to some extent, determined by the initial project definition (Schrader et al., 1993). For example, major unk unks stemming from a new, unproven technology can be avoided by switching to a proven technology, and complexity may be reduced by reducing the project scope (Pich et al., 2002). However, by avoiding unk unks or high-complexity firms might also forgo major opportunities and might hence choose not do so.[5] For firms undertaking projects characterized by major unk unks, the question arises, when selectionism or trial-and-error learning offer the higher advantage.

Of course, the *costs* of selectionism and trial-and-error learning influence the relative attractiveness of the two approaches. This aspect is well-understood (Loch et al., 2001). Selectionism carries the sheer cost of running several solution search efforts in parallel, of which only one will be chosen in the end.[6] Trial-and-error learning results not only in direct costs of activities aiming to identify unknown influence factors (e.g., experimentation or hiring of experts), but also causes a time delay that may be unacceptable in the market, or politically in the organization. If the cost difference is large, looking at the relative costs might be sufficient (Fig. 17.6).

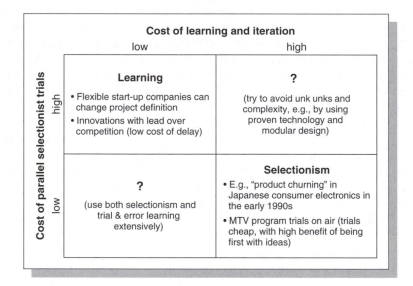

Figure 17.6
Cost comparison of trial-and-error learning and selectionism (*Source*: Sommer and Loch, 2004).

---

[5] See Miller and Lessard (2000).

[6] Selectionism is often applied not to the entire project, but to subproblems of it, which costs less. For example, parallel trials are run for the choice of a novel system component, or for the pursuit of a customer segment, or the choice of a partner.

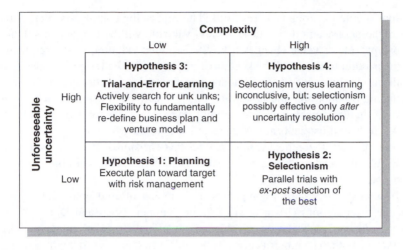

Figure 17.7
Benefit comparison of trial-and-error learning and selectionism (*Source*: Sommer, Loch and Dong, 2006).

Often, however, the costs are not known, or their difference dominated by differences in value creation. This situation requires a benefit comparison rather than a cost comparison. Figure 17.7 summarizes the benefit comparison based on theoretical work (Pich et al., 2002; Sommer and Loch, 2004) and an empirical test (Loch et al., 2006b; Sommer et al., 2006).

If neither unforeseeable uncertainty nor complexity is high, the standard risk management methods described in the section 'Approaches to project risk management and contingency planning' are sufficient. High complexity increases the benefit of selectionism: If the problem is becoming intractable, i.e., the optimal course of action A* cannot be determined, pursuing several approaches in parallel and at some point settling on the most promising one is the best course of action, a result well known in the search literature (e.g., Fox, 1993; Loch et al., 2001).

On the other hand, if major unforeseeable uncertainty is present, but complexity is not very high, trial-and-error learning offers the largest benefit. By adjusting the course of action to account for the value of the previously unknown influence variables (unconsciously fixed at some default $(\overline{w}_{n+1}, \ldots, \overline{w}_N)$, the team can determine the optimal course of action A*, that maximizes the performance with respect to the full state space.

The most difficult situation arises when unforeseeable uncertainty and complexity combine. Due to the intractability of the performance function Π or the causality mapping M, learning can no longer find the optimal course of action even after all unk unks are revealed. Selectionism, on the other hand, is of little help, if the 'best' parallel trial must be chosen before the unforeseeable uncertainty is resolved: The higher the complexity, that is the more the parameters w_i interact, the less valuable will be the picked solution if one parameter value changes from the assumed value $\bar{\omega}_j$ to its true value. If the parallel trials can all be kept alive until they can be tested in under fully realistic circumstances (e.g. by market testing fully functioning prototypes, including product mix and promotion mix), selectionism can do much better. Even if the unk unks themselves are not revealed or it is too late or costly to make further adjustments at this stage, at least the truly best of the trials can be chosen. In fact, theoretical results predict that for similar costs, selectionism with full market tests performs as well as trial-and-error learning (Sommer and Loch, 2004).

A survey of 65 startup companies in Shanghai offered empirical support for these predictions (Loch et al., 2006b; Sommer, Loch and Dong, 2006). In the survey, each startup involved a novel development in technology, market, or both. The empirical results provide a first answer to the question of whether selectionism with realistic tests or trial-and-error learning fares better under a combination of high-complexity and high-unforeseeable uncertainty. Selectionism with full market feedback significantly improves the success of the startups, while learning does not seem to do so, providing initial evidence that the benefits of selectionism might outweigh those of learning if market feedback on the final product is available.

7. Future directions

We expect project risk management to remain an important research area with important applications; in particular, risk management under high uncertainty is still an open area requiring much more work; the results reported above have only begun to explore the key issues. For example, how formalized and 'heavy' should a risk management system be; when is a minimal approach sufficient? How can coordination risks, which stem not from novelty but from the interactions among multiple parties, be included in risk management (this is related to Chapter 12 of this book)?

In addition to exploring process issues of risk management, a link to psychology and *behavior* under risk is needed. For example, it is known from decision theory that people commonly underestimate large and overestimate small probabilities, 'over'-discount the future, and respond strongly to the salience of risks (Russo and Schoemaker, 1990). This is clearly relevant for risk management. For example, the latter point may contribute to neglecting unk unks, which are not immediate and need effort to be imagined. In addition, people exhibit loss aversion, showing a willingness to take large risks in response to a perceived loss position. This may, e.g., lead traders suffering a loss to take dangerously large bets in the hope of recovering — remember the failure of Barings Bank? Analogous risk taking is relevant in high-stake R&D projects.

The question is, what are the circumstances under which technical personnel or management in R&D tend to be 'too cautious' or 'too adventurous'? Knowing these circumstances would help companies to put systems in place that help their staff to 'correct' for their biases and make better and more robust decisions. These research opportunities are but a few examples of a large set of interesting questions that need to be addressed in future work.

References

Adner, R., D.A. Levinthal. 2004. Real options and real tradeoffs. *Academy of Management Review*, 29(1) 120–126.

Ambros-Ingerson, J., S. Steel. 1988. Integrating planning, execution and monitoring. *Proc. Seventh National Conf. Artificial Intelligence*, **AAAI-88** 735–740.

Amit, R., J. Brander, C. Zott. 1998. Why do venture capital firms exist? Theory and Canadian evidence. *Journal of Business Venturing*, 13, 441–466.

Angelmar, R., A. Capital 1994. *INSEAD Case Study*. 05/94–4310.

Bank, D. 1995. The Java saga. *Wired* (December) 166–169, 238–246.

Beinhocker, E.D. 1999. Robust adaptive strategies. *Sloan Management Rev*, 40(3) 95–106.

Bell, J. 2000. Beauty is in the eye of the beholder: Establishing a fair and equitable value for embryonic high-tech enterprises. *VCJ* December, 33–34.

Ben-Haim, Y. 2001. *Information Gap Decision Theory: Decisions Under Severe Uncertainty*. London: Academic Press.

Berman, E.B. 1964. Resource allocation in a PERT network under continuous activity time-cost functions. *Management Science*, 10(4) 734–145.

Bhattacharya, S., V. Krishnan, V. Mahajan. 1998. Managing new product definition in highly dynamic environments. *Management Sci*, 44, S50–S64.

Brokaw, L. 1991. The truth about start-ups. *Inc* April, 52–67.

Browning, T.R., J.J. Deyst, S.D. Eppinger, D.E. Whitney. 2002. Adding value in product development by creating information and reducing risk. *IEEE Transactions On Engineering Management*, 49(4) 443–458.

Camerer, C., M. Weber. 1992. Recent developments in modeling preferences: uncertainty and ambiguity. *Journal of Risk and Uncertainty*, 5, 325–370.

Chapman, C., S. Ward. 1997. *Project Risk Management: Processes, Techniques and Insights*. Chichester, UK: John Wiley \& Sons.

Chew, W.B., D. Leonard-Barton, R. E. Bohn. 1991. Beating Murphy's Law. *Sloan Management Review* Spring. 5 – 16.

Chesbrough, H., R.S. Rosenbloom. 2002. The role of the business model in capturing value from innovation: evidence from Xerox corporation's technology spinoff companies. *Industrial and Corporate Change* 11(3) 529–555.

Clark, W.B., T. Fujimoto. 1991. *Product Development Performance*. Boston: HBS Press.

Cusumano, M.A., R.W. Selby. 1995. *Microsoft Secrets: How the World's Most Powerful Software Company Creates Technology, Shapes Markets, and Manages People*. New York : Free Press.

Cusumano, M.A., R.W. Selby. 1996. How Microsoft competes. *Research Technology Management*, 39(1) 26–30.

Dahan, E., H. Mendelson. 2001. An extreme value model of concept testing. *Management Science*, 47(1) 102–116.

De Meyer, A., C. H. Loch, M. T. Pich. 2002. Managing project uncertainty: From variation to chaos, *Sloan Management Review*, 43(2) 60–67.

Ding, M., J. Eliashberg. 2002. Structuring the new product development pipeline. *Management Science*, 48(2) 343–363.

Dixit, A.K., R.S. Pindyck. 1994. *Investment under Uncertainty*. Princeton, NJ: Princeton Press.

Drucker, P. 1985. *Innovation and Entrepreneurship: Practice and Principles*. New York: Harper & Row.

Eisenhardt, K.M., B.N. Tabrizi. 1995. Accelerating adaptive processes: Product innovation in the global computer industry. *Admin. Sci. Quart*, 40, 84–110.

Fox, B.L. 1993. Random restarting versus simulated annealing. *Comput. Math. Appl*, 27, 33–35.

Goldratt, E.M. 1997. *Critical Chain*. Great Barrington: North River Press.

Herroelen, W. 2005. Project scheduling: theory and practice. *Production and Operations Management*, 14(4) 413–432.

Herroelen, W., R. Leus. 2001. On the merits and pitfalls of critical chain scheduling. *Journal of Operations Management*, 19, 559–577.

Huchzermeier, A., C. H. Loch. 2001. Project management under risk: Using the real options approach to evaluate flexibility in R&D. *Management Science*, 47(1) 85–101.

Huss, W.R. 1988. A move towards scenarios. *International Journal of Forecasting*, 4, 377–388.

Iansiti, M., A. MacCormack. 1997. Developing products on internet time. *Harvard Business Review*, September – October, 108–117.

Kelly, J.E., M.R. Walker. 1959. Critical-path planning and scheduling. *Proc. Eastern Joint Comput. Conf.*, 160–173.

Kendrick, T. 2003. *Identifying and Managing Project Risk*. New York: American Management Association.

Keynes, J.M. 1937. The General Theory of Employment. *Quarterly Journal of Economics*, 51, 209–223.

Kezsbom, D.S., D.L. Schilling, K.A. Edward. 1989. *Dynamic Project Management: A Practical Guide for Managers and Engineers*. New York: John Wiley & Sons.

Knight, F. H. 1921. *Risk, Uncertainty and Profit*. Boston: Houghton Mifflin.

Kreps, D. 1992. Static Choice and Unforeseen Contingencies. In: Dasgupta, P., D. Gale, O. Hart, E. Maskin (Eds.): *Economic Analysis of Markets and Games: Essays in Honor of Frank Hahn*. 259–281. Cambridge: MIT Press.

Leonard-Barton, D. 1995. *Wellsprings of Knowledge*. Boston: HBS Press.

Lynn, G.S., J.G. Morone, A.S. Paulson. 1996. Marketing and discontinuous innovation: the probe and learn process. *California Management Review*, 38(3) 8–37.

Loch, C.H., K. Bode-Greuel. 2001. Evaluating growth options as sources of value for pharmaceutical research projects. *R&D Management*, 31(2) 231–248.

Loch, C.H., C. Terwiesch, S. Thomke. 2001. Parallel and sequential testing of design alternatives. *Management Science*, 47(5) 663–678.

Loch, C.H., C. Terwiesch. 2005. Rush and be wrong or wait and be late? Seven principles of when to commit to real time information. *Production and Operations Management*, 14(3) 331–343.

Loch, C.H., A. De Meyer, M.T. Pich. 2006. *Managing the Unknown*. Hoboken: Wiley.

Loch, C.H., S. C. Sommer, J. Dong, and M. T. Pich. 2006b. Step Into the Unknown. *Financial Times* Mastering Risk, March 24, 4–5.

Loch, C. H., M. E. Solt, and E. Bailey. 2007. Diagnosing unforeseeable uncertainty in a new venture. Forthcoming, *Journal of Product Innovation Management*.

Lovejoy, W. S. 1991. A survey of algorithmic methods for partially observed markov decision processes. *Annals of Operations Research*, 28(1–4) 47–66.

Marschak, J and R. Radner 1972. *Economic Theory of Teams*. New Haven: Yale University Press.

MacCormack, A., R. Verganti, M. Iansiti. 2001. Developing products on "Internet time": The anatomy of a flexible development process. *Management Science*, 47(1) 133–150.

McGrath, R.G. 2001. Exploratory learning, innovative capacity, and managerial oversight. *Academy of Management Journal*, 44(1) 118–131.

McGrath, R.G., I.C. MacMillan. 1995. Discovery driven planning. *Harvard Business Review* July-August. 44–54.

McGrath, R.G., I.C. MacMillan. 2000. *The Entrepreneurial Mindset*. Boston: Harvard Business School Press.

Meredith, J.R., S.J. Mantel, Jr. 1995. *Project Management: A Managerial Approach*. New York: John Wiley & Sons.

Miller, R., D. R. Lessard. 2000. *The Strategic Management of Large Scale Engineering Projects*. Cambridge: MIT.

Modica, S., A. Rustichini. 1994. Awareness and partial information structure. *Theory and Decision*, 37, 107–124.

Mullins, J.W., D.J. Sutherland. 1998. New product development in rapidly changing markets. *Journal of Product Innovation Management* 15, 224–236.

Pich, M. T., C. H. Loch, A. De Meyer. 2002. On uncertainty, ambiguity and complexity in project management. *Management Science*, 48(8) 1008–1023.

Pitt, L.F., R. Kannemeyer. 2000. The role of adaptation in microenterprise development: a marketing perspective. *Journal of Developmental Entrepreneurship*, 5(2) 137–155.

Regev, S. A. Shtub, Y. Ben-Haim. 2006. Managing project risks as knowledge gaps. *Project Management Journal. forthcoming*.

Rittel, H.W.J., M.M. Webber. 1973. Dilemmas in a general theory of planning. *Policy Sciences*, 4, 155–169.

Roemer, T.A., R. Ahmadi. 2004. Concurrent crashing and overlapping in product development. *Operations Research*, 52(4) 606–622.

Russo, E., P. J. H. Schoemaker. 1990. *Decision Traps*. Simon & Schuster, New York.

Sahlman, W.A. 1990. The structure and governance of venture-capital organizations. *Journal of Financial Economics*, 27 473–521.

Savage, L.J. 1954. *The Foundations of Statistics*. New York: Wiley and Sons.

Schrader, S., W.M. Riggs, R.P. Smith. 1993. Choice over uncertainty and ambiguity in technical problem solving. *Journal of Engineering and Technology Management*, 10 73–99.

Schoemaker, P.J.H. 1991. When and how to use scenario planning: A heuristic approach with illustrations. *Journal of Forecasting*, 10, 449–564.

Schoemaker, P.J.H. 1995. Scenario planning: A tool for strategic thinking. *Sloan Management Review*, 36(2) 25–40.

Schoemaker, P.J.H., R.E. Gunther. 2006. The wisdom of deliberate mistakes. *Harvard Business Review* June 109–115.

Smith, J.E., K.F. McCardle. 1999. Options in the real world: lessons learned in evaluating oil and gas investments. *Operations Research*, 47(1) 1–15.

Smith, P. G., G. M. Merritt. 2002. *Proactive Risk Management*. New York: Productivity Press.

Sobek, D.K. II, A.C. Ward, J.K. Liker. 1999. Toyota's principles of set-based concurrent engineering. *Sloan Management Review* 40 67–83.

Sommer, S. C., C. H. Loch. 2004. Selectionism and learning in projects with complexity and unforeseeable uncertainty. *Management Science*, 50(10) 1334–1347.

Sommer, S.C., C.H. Loch, J. Dong. 2006. Mastering unforeseeable uncertainty in startup companies: an empirical study. INSEAD Working Paper, July.

Stalk, G.Jr., A.M. Webber. 1993. Japan's dark side of time. *Harvard Business Review*, 71(4) 93–102.

Terwiesch, C., C. H. Loch, A. De Meyer. 2002. Exchanging preliminary information in concurrent engineering: alternative coordination strategies. *Organization Science*, 13(4) 402–419.

Thomke, S.H. 1997. The role of flexibility in the development of new products: An empirical study. *Research Policy*, 26 105–119.

Thomke, S.H. 1998. Managing experimentation in the design of new products. *Management Science*, 44(6) 743–762.

Thomke, S.H. 2003. *Experimentation Matters*. Cambridge, Mass.: Harvard Business School Press.

Thomke, S.h., D.E. Bell. 2001. Sequential testing in product development. *Management Science*, 47(2) 308–323.

Thomke, S.H., D. Reinertsen. 1998. Agile product development. *California Management Review*, 41 (1) 8–30.

Van de Ven, A.H., D.E. Polley, R. Garud, S. Venkataraman. 1999. *The Innovation Journey*. Oxford: Oxford University Press.

Von Branconi, C., C.H. Loch. 2004. Contracting for major projects: Eight business levers for top management. *International Journal of Project Management* 22(2) 119–130.

Weick, K.E, K.M. Sutcliffe. 2001. *Managing the Unexpected*. San Francisco: Jossey Bass.

Weiss, G. 2000. Planning and learning together. *Proc. Internat. Conf. Autonomous Agents*, Barcelona, Spain, 102–103.

Wideman, R.M. 1992. *Project & Program Risk Management*. Newton Square, PA: Project Management Institute.

18 Evaluating the product use cycle: 'Design for service and support'

Keith Goffin

1. Introduction

In striving to be more successful at new product development (NPD), companies normally focus on product features. Although competitive features are obviously important, effective NPD must deliver more; it must ensure that the product design also meets after-sales needs. *After-sales service* is the name given to all of the events that take place during the *product use cycle* – the time from the purchase to the time when a product is taken out of service by the customer. Typically, customers require assistance from manufacturers, such as maintenance and repair, to gain maximum value from their products during the use cycle. One of the most common examples of the importance of after-sales is the automobile, where maintenance, repair, and emissions testing are typical services that are essential to car owners. Designing for the whole of the product use cycle – known as *Design for Service* or *Support* (DFS) – has a positive impact on customer satisfaction and can enhance revenues. Surprisingly, many organizations overlook service and it is an area where there has been sparse academic research. DFS is an exciting area of product development where leading companies are the vanguard and where there are vast untapped opportunities for interesting research.

The aim of this chapter is to demonstrate the importance of evaluating after-sales service issues during NPD and discuss the current level of knowledge on this area. In covering these points, it will not only give readers an overview of the relevant literature but also present examples of leading edge companies that have made significant gains through DFS. Specifically, this chapter will:

- Discuss the nature and importance of after-sales service;
- Explain where DFS fits with the current theory on NPD;
- Describe in detail what is known from the practitioner and research literatures about how to implement DFS;
- Present the implications for practitioners, discuss where new research is needed and suggest suitable approaches.

2. The nature of after-sales service

End-users of many types of product, ranging from computer systems to domestic appliances, require after-sales service at some time. Typical forms of service include installation, documentation, maintenance, and repair, without which users can quickly become dissatisfied, as they are unable to make full use of products. Anyone who has ever been frustrated with a product that is hard to understand, or a repair taking too long, has experienced the symptoms of a product that has not been designed with after-sales service in mind. Many of the decisions taken at the product design stage affect all aspects of after-sales service.

After-sales service is referred to variously as *product support, customer support, technical support,* or simply *service*. Generally, the term *'service'* is perceived as being related to product maintenance and repair, whereas *'support'* includes broader aspects, such as user training and documentation (Fig. 18.1). In this chapter, we will use the dual term *'service and support,'* to stress that we are taking a broad view of all of the events in the use cycle. Today's customers are discerning. They demand easy to use, reliable, and environment-friendly products. This means that DFS will grow in importance for many types of products.

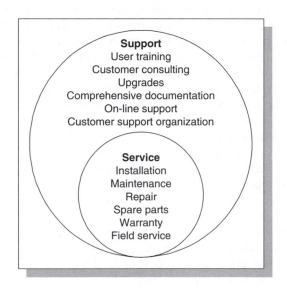

Figure 18.1
The key elements of service and support (*Source*: Goffin, 2000).

2.1. The importance of service and support

There are good business reasons why companies should treat service and support issues as being of strategic importance. In the literature, it has been recognized that service and support:

- Are essential for achieving customer satisfaction and good long-term relationships (Armistead and Clark, 1992; Athaide et al., 1996; Cespedes, 1995; Lele and Sheth, 1987; Teresko, 1994). Customers become quickly dissatisfied if maintenance or repairs are too costly;
- Can provide a competitive advantage (Armistead and Clark, 1992; Goffin, 1998; Hull and Cox, 1994). This is true in most high-tech industries (Goffin, 1994; Lawless and Fisher, 1990; Meldrum, 1995) but also in some low-tech sectors (Moriarty and Kosnik, 1989). As product differentiation becomes harder in many markets, companies are increasingly looking to service and support as a source of competitive advantage (Loomba, 1998);
- Play a role in increasing the success rate of new products (Cooper and Kleinschmidt, 1993);
- Are a major source of revenue and profits for manufacturers (Berg and Loeb, 1990; Bundshuh and Dezvane, 2003; Hull and Cox, 1994). Over the working lifetime of a product, the support revenues and margins from a customer may be far higher than the initial product revenue;
- Need to be fully evaluated during NPD, as good product design can make customer support more efficient and cost-effective (Armistead and Clark, 1992; Berg and Loeb, 1990; Cespedes, 1995; Goffin, 1998).

Despite the importance of service and support, most organizations have not yet recognized the need to put it 'at the top of the management agenda' (Bundshuh and Dezvane, 2003). Perhaps because of this lack of management attention, the topic has failed to attract the attention of management researchers (Hull and Cox, 1994).

2.2. Products where after-sales is key

A number of factors appear to determine whether service and support are pertinent for a particular type of product. Table 18.1 lists examples of products from both consumer and business-to-business markets, for some of which service and support is key, and for others it is less important.

Low-product reliability increases the need for support during the use cycle. More complex equipment, particularly if it includes mechanical components, is normally more prone to wear and failure and therefore requires more maintenance and repair. Examples from consumer markets include washing machines, cars, and printers. Manufacturing equipment is an example of a

Table 18.1
Examples of products where after-sales is key

Market	Service and Support Key	Service and Support Less Important
Consumer (B2C)	Cars, personal computers, domestic equipment, heating systems, medical products, and watches	Food, clothing, furniture, furnishings, disposable products (e.g., pens and batteries), and digital watches
Business (B2B)	Manufacturing equipment, computer networks, software systems, plant equipment (e.g., earth movers), safety equipment, aircraft, transport systems, and military equipment	Office supplies and some office equipment

business-to-business product that needs regular maintenance. For products with high-failure rates (i.e., low reliability) manufacturers need to provide fast response to their customers, often through organizations of *field service engineers,* who can repair equipment.

If the failure of a product raises serious financial or safety issues for the user, then support becomes crucial. Examples include medical equipment where failure can impact patient well-being and banking systems, where failure can be costly. Similarly, the failure of transport systems can cause inconvenience and loss or revenues.

Electronic products are normally more reliable than mechanical equipment and in either case customers may require *on-line support*; telephone advice on how to use equipment. Software products do not have mechanical components but are still support intensive; the complexity of operation or interaction with other software packages necessitates that manufacturers provide good documentation and help-desks. Therefore, many types of complex products are support intensive.

Although after-sales can be very important, it should be noted that is not equally important for all types of products. Short use cycles (e.g., fast consumption) normally imply that service and support are not important. Consequently, items such as manufactured food normally only require companies to provide help-lines for dietary and similar advice. Disposable products require little or no service and support (Lele, 1986) and some companies deliberately choose to only offer replacement products rather than repairs (e.g., most digital watches are disposable in contrast to higher priced watches that can be repaired).

The earth-moving equipment market and the US manufacturer Caterpillar demonstrate how after-sales service can play a key role (Fites, 1996; Mercer, 1999). The company's products are normally rented out by their owners to building projects (i.e., plant hire) at an hourly charge and so any breakdown – *downtime* – leads to a loss of revenue. To minimize the impact of failures, Caterpillar has offered for many years guaranteed 24-hour delivery of parts worldwide but increasingly it has focused on better-designed products. It now designs products to eradicate failure and to offer customers what the company terms 'negative downtime.' This has four main aspects. First, the components that are likely to fail are duplicated (so called *redundancy* in design, which is also very important for banking systems), so that a single component failure will not stop a machine working. Second, advanced diagnostics programs constantly monitor a product's performance. Third, earthmovers are connected via advanced telecommunications networks to Caterpillar and when a component fails (and the duplicate component takes over) this is automatically notified. Finally, service engineers will replace the failed component at a time that does not inconvenience the owner. In this way, the downtime is 'negative' because the first time the owner hears about a failure is when it already has been solved. The Caterpillar Company designs *serviceability* into all of its products (serviceability is the ease with which a product can be serviced) and strongly promotes the advantages this brings to customers in its advertising.

3. Links to NPD theory

The development of our understanding of DFS has been slow. Although Lele and Karmarkar stressed its importance in an article in Harvard Business Review in 1983, since that time publications on the subject have been sporadic. Therefore, it is important that DFS should now become recognized as an essential element of NPD, which is closely linked with the theory of NPD and how products should be manufactured.

3.1. Link to NPD framework

In Chapter 1 of this book, Loch and Kavadias introduced an evolutionary framework for the execution of NPD projects (Fig. 1.6). This covered concept generation, through development and testing, to product launch. Their framework included DFS and Fig. 18.2 shows how this can be expanded to cover all aspects of the product use cycle.

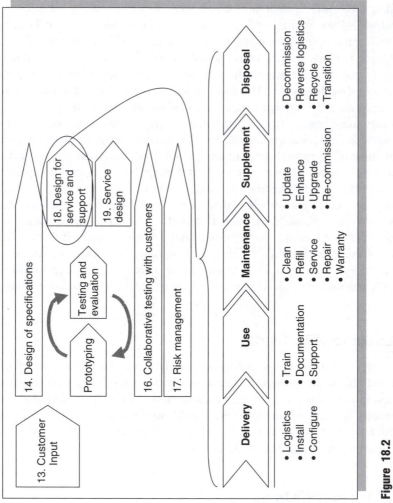

Figure 18.2
The NPD framework and design for service and support (based partly on Kim and Mauborgne, 2000).

There are five main elements to the generic use cycle: delivery, use, maintenance, supplement, and disposal (Kim and Mauborgne, 2000). The DFS needs to consider each of the following elements at the design stage:

1. *Delivery*. How will the product be delivered and installed for use? Obviously, this is dependent on the type of product being considered but the logistics of delivery and installation can be made easier if a product is suitably designed. For example, the 'flat pack' approach to furniture has significantly reduced shipment costs but needs suitable assembly instructions to be provided. Hi-tech companies also do everything possible to reduce the cost of logistics and, e.g., Hewlett-Packard carefully design their product packaging to minimize shipping volume (shipment costs are more dependent on volume than on weight). More complex products, or where safety issues are involved, may require personnel from the manufacturing company, or their representatives, to perform installation, and configuration of equipment to match the customer's needs. Computer mainframes, networks, and heating systems are all examples of products that normally require expert installation. In contrast, most domestic equipment is designed for the user to unpack and install themselves.

2. *Use*. To use a product, the customer or user may need some instruction. This can be provided as written or on-line documentation, or a company representative may give instruction. Learning how to use a product efficiently can be associated with significant costs. Some of these are highly visible (e.g., the costs associated with an expert providing training); whereas others may be less immediately obvious (e.g., the time wasted as a user tries to understand a complex product).

3. *Maintenance*. This includes a range of items from cleaning, refilling with consumables (e.g., printing ink), preventive maintenance, and repair. Cleaning may sound unimportant but for some products, such as hospital equipment, a poor product design can waste time and reduce equipment availability. On-line support is important in many industries today. Failure of products is nearly always a source of frustration, as the user can no longer utilize the device. The repair of a product may be at the customer site (performed by field service engineers), or if the product is relatively small it may be returned to a *service factory* (Alexander et al., 2002).

4. *Supplement*. Many products are used for a number of years and advances in product technology are often offered to existing customers in the form of *upgrades*. These are particularly important in the computer industry (both software and hardware upgrades) but, as other products such as cars include more electronics and software, upgrades will become commonplace.

5. *Disposal*. This is already a key issue in many industries. For example, regulations in the European Union and other trade groupings are giving manufacturers increasing responsibility for the collection and suitable

disposal of old and disused products. This covers how a product can be safely taken out of use (called *decommissioning* on major products and installations), returned (*reverse logistics*), and its components *recycled* (Parker, 1993; Pnueli and Zussman, 1997).

The characteristics of a product and its market determine which of the elements of the use cycle are most important. Over the last 20 years, there has been a change in the relative importance of different elements of the use cycle. In the past, when many products had high-failure rates, the most important aspect of support was maintenance and particularly fast and reliable repair (Lele and Karmarkar, 1983). New technologies have now typically led to more reliable products in many sectors. However, increased product functionality (which is often software-based) means that the importance of configuration, user training, and on-line support has increased (Goffin, 1998), as have all of the topics surrounding disposal.

3.2. Cost-of-ownership

As mentioned earlier, service and support revenues can be a significant source of income for manufacturers. In contrast, customers can view the cost of using and maintaining equipment over its use cycle – referred to as *cost-of-ownership* (Taylor, 1995), or *whole life costs* (Bradley and Dawson, 1999) – as prohibitive. For example, car cost-of-ownership has been estimated at five times product cost (Wise and Baumgartner, 1999), which includes fuel, tires, maintenance, and repair. Due to the high cost-of-ownership in many sectors, customers are demanding more cost-effective support (Loomba, 1996).

Medical equipment used in the demanding environment of hospitals needs to be durable, reliable, and when necessary, quick repairs are essential for obvious reasons – equipment is often used in critical care situations (Goffin, 1998). Hospitals demand effective support from manufacturers; they expect good user training, low-maintenance costs, and cost-effective upgrades. The medical market is increasingly cost-conscious, as governments throughout the world try to reduce healthcare costs. Consequently, hospitals look critically at the cost-of-ownership of medical equipment. It is important to note that some of the costs are transparent, while others may be *bundled* into (i.e., included in) the purchase price. Discerning hospital administrators know how to determine the full cost-of-ownership, as the time that highly qualified personnel are being trained and involved with other aspects of support can represent high-opportunity costs.

The five elements of the use cycle allow the identification of the cost-of-ownership of any product to be determined, by looking at the frequency of occurrence of every 'event' over the use cycle and the associated costs (Fig. 18.3). Continuing with the discussion of medical products, an intensive care monitoring device will be used to illustrate this.

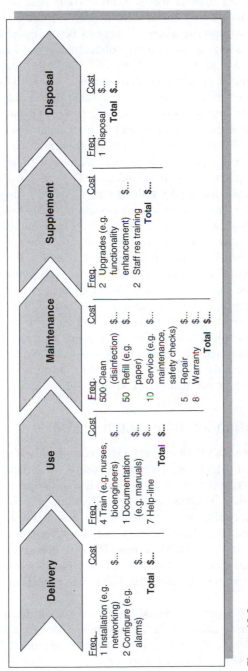

Figure 18.3
Estimating cost-of-ownership for medical equipment from the use cycle.

The typical working lifetime for monitoring equipment is 10 years. The installation of the monitoring device may require it to be connected to the hospital network and specific alarm settings to be configured. The manufacturing company's engineers normally conduct these tasks and the cost is often included in the purchase price. Figure 18.3 indicates that typically the networking is conducted once but the alarm settings may need to be set twice. Associated costs need to be estimated, as indicated by the diagram. Directly after installation, the four shifts of users (e.g., nurses and bioengineers) are trained by the manufacturer's personnel and the equipment is put into use. During use, hospitals will sometimes need to use help-lines to obtain answers to questions on product operation. Maintenance can have high-associated costs. Over 10 years the equipment may be disinfected 500 times (an average of once a week) and it this requires highly trained staff to spend a long time on this procedure, then there are high-associated but often hidden costs. Therefore, well-designed equipment that is efficient to clean is essential. Maintenance is usually on an annual basis (i.e., 10 times over the use cycle), combined with safety testing, which is a legal requirement for medical devices. The next aspect of support could be equipment repair (the frequency of which is determined by the failure rate). After repair, the equipment is used until further maintenance is required. During the equipment's lifetime, it will probably be upgraded to the latest software revision twice and staff will need re-training.

As indicted by the annotation on Fig. 18.3, every aspect of the use cycle, its frequency, and associated costs need to be estimated to determine the true cost-of-ownership of a device. The need to reduce cost-of-ownership is one of the factors that drives companies to consider DFS.

3.3. Link to design for manufacture (DFM)

The use cycle commences with delivery but preceding this is manufacture in the production plant, which has a strong influence on service and support. *Design for Manufacture* (DFM) is a widely applied technique used in product development to reduce manufacturing costs (Kumpe and Bolwijn, 1988). It evaluates manufacturing requirements at the design stage, enabling the development of products, which are easy and cost-effective to produce and there is a wide literature on DFM. It has also long been recognized in the practitioner literature that a similar approach to DFM is needed to evaluate service and support requirements during NPD (Berg and Loeb, 1990; Juran and Gryna, 1988).

There are various approaches to DFM but a common thread is that they evaluate manufacturing needs at the design stage and set quantitative goals for *manufacturability* (how easy it is to manufacture a product). For example, techniques can be used to check whether a product will be easy to assemble, and stimulate simplification of the design. This can result in a reduction of the number of components, thus reducing both material costs and assembly times. One leading technique uses quantitative scores based on the number and type of parts used (Boothroyd and Dewhurst, 1988). Taking DFM as an analogy, there is a need to fully evaluate service and support requirements at the design stage and set goals for the *serviceability* and *supportability* of a product.

It is not only an analogy that can be drawn between DFS and DFM; the relationship is closer. Historically, companies that have implemented DFM have often found that service and support issues must also be considered, as there may be trade-offs. For example, Rank-Xerox found that it was necessary to have a clear management process for deciding where design priorities lie, as manufacturing may have objectives, which can directly oppose those of service and support (Livingston, 1988). Manufacturing's objective is to reduce factory assembly costs, which may lead to a product, that is easy to manufacture but hard to disassemble and re-assemble at the customer site. Figure 18.4 illustrates the close linkage between DFM and DFS. The way a product is designed for manufacture will influence the logistics of how it can be delivered and configured, how it can be disassembled for repair, how it can be enhanced, and how it can be disassembled for disposal. The complex interactions between DFM and DFS are not well understood.

4. The literature on DFS

The majority of what has been written about service, support and NPD has been published for practitioners. Examples are articles in journals, such as AFSM International – The Professional Journal, (the journal of an association for customer support managers), and books (e.g., Wellemin, 1984; Patton, 1984; Laub and Khandphur, 1996). The practitioner literature strongly argues the need for service and support issues to be considered during NPD but, as we will see, the empirical data on this topic is sparse.

4.1. Service, support, and NPD

A number of authors have recognized the importance of support requirements being considered at the design stage (e.g., Cespedes, 1995; Armistead and Clark, 1992; Berg and Loeb, 1990; Goffin, 1998). Product design influences both the amount of support necessary and the means by which it can be delivered (Lele, 1986; Sleeter, 1991). For example, a modular approach to product design can reduce repair costs (Hedge and Kubat, 1989), as can good diagnostics (Armistead and Clark, 1992; Karmarkar and Kubat, 1987). However, beyond repair and maintenance, product design also influences the amount of user training, which is necessary and the ease of upgrading products. Appropriate product design can significantly reduce cost-of-ownership

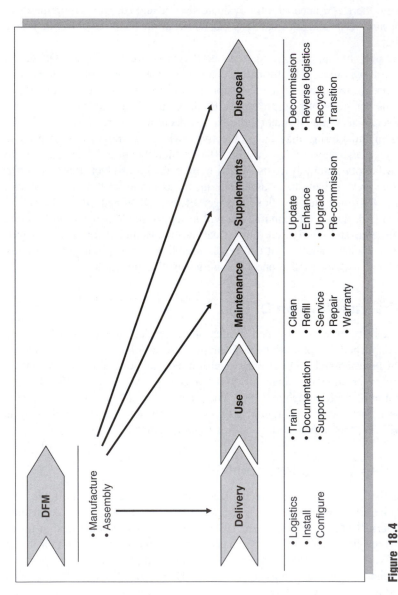

Figure 18.4
The Relationship between DFM and DFS.

(Blanchard, 1991) and therefore increase customer satisfaction. For example, Microsoft's *Windows 95* product was 'specifically designed to reduce total cost of ownership through increased ease of use, functionality, and support' (Taylor, 1995). Products that have been consciously designed for easy support can be differentiated in the market (Swink et al., 1996).

It is important not only to consider customer support requirements early in NPD but also to make a comprehensive evaluation. To achieve this, it has been recognized that engineers with experience of customer support should be involved in product development (Hull and Cox, 1994), as 'by participating in the development stage, the after-sales group can add substantial value by making the equipment more "maintenance-friendly"' (Knecht et al., 1993). However, surveys have shown that customer support personnel were seldom involved in NPD (Page, 1993), and many companies do not consider service and support until relatively late in the development cycle (Goffin, 1998). Low involvement of customer support personnel in NPD can lead to products that are difficult to repair and that have excessive warranty and service costs (Anthoney and McKay, 1992).

4.2. Empirical investigations

Although the need to evaluate support requirements is recognized, information on how this should be done is sparse – only nine articles discuss this aspect of NPD in detail (see Table 18.2).

Livingston described how Rank-Xerox recognized that low cost-of-ownership is important to customers and that it can be achieved by reducing costs throughout the use cycle (Livingston, 1988). This led to the adoption of a range of design goals covering ease-of-use, ease-of-cleaning, easier maintenance procedures, and ease-of-repair. Rank-Xerox found that it was necessary to have a clear process for setting design priorities, as different functional departments may have opposing objectives. The limitations of Livingston's article are that specific examples of the DFS goals are not given, only one company's approach is discussed, and the analysis is purely descriptive.

Hull and Cox (1994) conducted case study research at six leading electronics manufacturers. They focused mainly on these companies' customer support organizations but also identified the importance of DFS. For example at National Cash Register (NCR), 'maintainability and serviceability of products are a prime consideration in the design and manufacturing processes.' Similar approaches were found at International Business Machines (IBM); Hewlett-Packard; General Electric (GE); and Amdahl (data processing systems). At American Telephone and Telegraph (AT&T) 'products are designed for serviceability and [good] after-sales support is acknowledged as a prerequisite for product sales.' Although they clearly identified that leading

Table 18.2

Previous publications on evaluating service and support during NPD

	Article	Type of Article/ Methodology	Industry(s)	Sample	Key Points
1	Livingston, 1988	Practitioner conference presentation on design for service.	Photo-copiers	Rank-Xerox	• Rank-Xerox perform a detailed evaluation of support requirements at the design stage including cost-of-ownership • Clear design goals are set for all aspects of support.
2	Hull and Cox, 1994	Journal paper with in-depth case studies. Purposive sample of six companies. Main focus on field support but mentions DFS issues.	Electronics and computing	Amdahl, AT&T, Hewlett-Packard, GE, IBM, and NCR	• 'Leading' companies consider support during NPD. • For example, at IBM 'field service personnel . . . perform an important role as serviceability advocates' and at NCR 'maintainability and serviceability of products are a prime consideration in the design'
3	Teresko, 1994	Trade journal description of software for service design developed with a consortium of companies.	Electronics, automobiles and plant equipment	Caterpillar, Chrysler, Ford, and Hewlett-Packard	• DFM, DFS, and recycling of products are inter-related • All aspects need to be considered at the design stage • A software package for this purpose was developed with a consortium of five companies.

4	Galloway, 1996	Journal article with a description of the procedures for military procurement and the need for appropriately designed products.	Defence	US/UK defence	• Defence equipment has particularly strong service and support requirements • Defence DFS needs to cover maintenance, repair, documentation, training of personnel, etc.
5	Goffin, 1998	Journal paper with a survey of design for supportability at high-tech companies/Single case study.	Electronics/ medical electronics	Trade association/ Hewlett-Packard	• At many companies support is not considered until well into NPD • Importance of understanding cost-of-ownership • Key role of support-related design goals.
6	Knezevic, 1999	Journal article with a single descriptive case study.	Aerospace	Boeing	• Detailed insights into DFS at Boeing • Organization changes made at Boeing to promote DFS
7	Goffin and New, 2001	Journal paper with five (disguised) case studies based on multiple interviews, documentation, inspection of products and triangulation of data.	Telecommu- nications, automobiles, vending machines, aerospace, domestic appliances	'Leading companies' in various sectors	• The evaluation at the design stage must consider all elements of the use cycle. Different elements are more important for certain products. • Quantitative DFS design goals appear to lead to better products (from the service and support perspective). • There are different stages in the successful adoption of DFS ideas.

(Continued)

Table 18.2
(Continued)

Article	Type of Article/ Methodology	Industry(s)	Sample	Key Points
8 Ivory et al., 2003	Journal paper with two case studies with 'extensive and detailed interviews' but no mention of any analysis of company documentation.	Transport and materials handling	Alstrom transport; Clarke Chapman handling systems	• Capital projects have major requirements for maintainability, which go beyond those of the individual products involved • Achieving high maintainability requires timely cooperation between all of the organizations involved in the project
9 Markeset and Kumar, 2003	Journal paper with a single case with an element of action research. Very few details of methodology given.	Automated production systems	Unknown	• Cross-functional communication difficulties were found to hinder DFS • Employees need to be trained on the importance of the reliability, availability, maintainability and supportability of equipment.

electronics companies consider support at the design stage by involving service engineers, Hull and Cox gave no further information on how support is evaluated during NPD.

Teresko (1994) considered serviceability and its contribution to competitiveness. The article discusses a software package that calculates field disassembly and re-assembly times and identifies service costs (Parker, 1993; Teresko, 1994). This package was based on earlier software used to ensure that products are easy to manufacture (DFM). The apparent limitation of the approach is that it focuses on maintenance and repair and ignores the other elements of customer support, such as user training, documentation, etc. The article is also purely descriptive.

The cost-of-ownership of military equipment, such as helicopters, can be very high and so Design for Support is particularly important. Galloway (1996) describes the different issues that governments need to consider before they purchase new military hardware and emphasizes the need for defence equipment manufacturers to integrate DFS into NPD. A wide range of issues is important for the support of military hardware, including the training of personnel, technical documentation, the availability of parts and components, and many of these are influenced by product design. Unfortunately, Galloway's article only describes the procedures for military procurement and not how manufacturers should integrate requirements into product design. However, it is obvious that military equipment has particularly strong service and support needs, due to the long and demanding use cycles.

Goffin (1998) used a survey of a professional association to look at how companies plan DFS. It found that support requirements are typically not considered early enough during NPD and few companies use quantitative goals for DFS. The second part of the paper was a case study of a medical product. This found that support might have to 'compete' for resources with issues such as product features during NPD and so a clear understanding of the cost-of-ownership is required. Additionally, it demonstrated the importance of quantitative design goals, related to each of the support requirements. The main limitations of this research are the low-response rate to the survey and that a detailed investigation was made of only a single company.

Knezevic (1999) described how Boeing designed the 777 airliner to maximize the schedule reliability of airlines. Although this is a purely descriptive single case, with associated limitations, it indicates the importance of quantitative design goals being used for service and support issues. Comprehensive details of the goals set and the results achieved in the project give us further insights, as does the discussion of the importance of top management attention, if DFS is to be successfully adopted by an organization (the Boeing approach will be described in more detail later).

Five case studies give insights into how DFS is conducted in practice (Goffin and New, 2001). A range of industries was covered and there were several key findings. First, different elements of the use cycle are more important for certain products. Second, the level of evaluation of service and support at the design stage varied widely between the case companies and the use of quantitative goals at the design stage appeared to lead to better products, in terms of their *supportability*. Third, the cross-case analysis showed that strong management commitment helps drive the consideration of service and support requirements at the design stage. Finally, there appear to be a number of stages to the adoption and successful use of DFS approaches. The limitation of Goffin and New's paper is that it took a cross-sectional approach and did not longitudinally investigate how the different design decisions affect supportability.

Ivory et al., (2003) presented two case studies of capital projects – a railway system and a materials handling system. Both projects were found to have significant maintainability requirements, which go beyond those of the individual products involved. Therefore, to ensure a good complete system, timely and effective cooperation between all of the organizations involved in the project is necessary. The limitation of this study is that it appears to have focused only on interview data, with no triangulation.

The last empirical study to date is another single case study (Markeset and Kumar, 2003). This looked at the introduction of DFS ideas into a manufacturing company and showed that cross-functional communication problems hindered DFS and employees needed to be trained on the importance of the reliability, availability, maintainability, and supportability of equipment. The limitations of this study are that the trail of evidence is sparse and the researchers did not take the opportunity to build on the case study methodology of previous research.

Unfortunately, the methodology used by the several researchers does not appear to be systematic and has not built on the approaches taken in other investigations. Consequently, the empirically based literature provides us with adequate (but by no means exhaustive) case study evidence to make some recommendations for how companies can best implement DFS.

4.3. Implementing DFS

Detailed recommendations can be made for how companies can best implement DFS. (Van Bennekom and Goffin, 2002). Figure 18.5 shows how service and support requirements should be evaluated. Current product performance – in supportability terms – needs to be estimated. Questions need to be asked, such as, how easy are current products to install. Where possible, the answers to these questions should be objective and quantitative. The challenge is to quantify as many DFS goals as possible into cost terms. This makes cost aggregation and comparison simpler. However, the qualitative factors should also be included in comparisons.

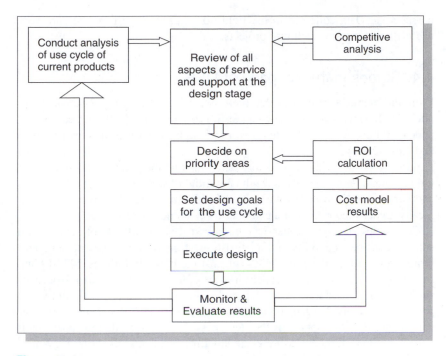

Figure 18.5
The DFS Process (based on Van Bennekom and Goffin, 2002).

A key part of the review of service and support at the design stage should be a comparison against competitors' products. It is best if competitors' products are actually obtained so that a real 'supportability benchmark' is available.

Development resources are limited and so conflicts with other aspects of product design – particularly product features – can arise. Therefore, the priority areas need to be identified, using a cost model. The cost model should summarize the frequency and cost of every event of the use cycle. Reviewing cost-of-ownership should give insights into how investments in designing products with better supportability will bring returns over the use cycle. Some of these returns will be in increased customer satisfaction and some will be in terms of revenue generation (e.g., a product designed for easy upgrades allow create more revenue opportunities). Appropriate priority areas can then be set and suitable quantitative goals set for the design team. A catalogue of potential measures for all aspects of design has been collated by Van Bennekom and Goffin (2002). It is important that the performances of products that are introduced to the market be monitored from a supportability perspective. Data collected in the field about product performance are very useful 'benchmarks' for future projects.

4.4. Stages in the adoption of DFS

From the literature, it is clear that there is a need for a *comprehensive* evaluation of all aspects of the use cycle at the design stage. Different companies appear to have reached different levels of sophistication in this area (Goffin and New, 2001).

Initially, customer support requirements may not be perceived as important. Often companies do not recognize the potential of service and support business and consequently do not evaluate it at the design stage. Poor product design means higher repair costs and can lead to customer dissatisfaction.

Companies that have recently recognized the importance of service and support consider reliability and repair times at the design stage and set quantitative goals for product reliability (mean-time between failures, MTBF) and ease-of-repair (mean-time to repair, MTTR). However, the broader aspects of support such as user training and upgrades are often neglected. As companies progress, they involve panels of service engineers in NPD reviews to evaluate all aspects of support at the design stage, i.e., installation times, fault diagnosis times, field access times, repair times/costs and user training times, upgrade times, etc. Integrating such approaches into the NPD process may be difficult and so it may take companies a long time to reach this stage. Advanced companies set quantitative goals at the design stage for all relevant aspects of support and use cost-of-ownership models. Goals are used to push development engineers to develop designs that are easier and cheaper to support than previous products.

The Boeing aircraft company has an advanced approach to DFS. The Boeing 777 was designed for a use cycle of more than 20 years and cost-of-ownership was one of the key factors for customers – the world's airlines. In the 777 project, Boeing concentrated on doing everything to reduce the number of times flights are delayed for aircraft-related technical reasons (Knezevic, 1999).

Many of the 777 design goals were based around *schedule reliability*, as this was perceived as the single factor that would best demonstrate improvements in maintainability.The goal was set at 98.8 per cent and related goals were set to achieve this. For example, reliability was measured by *mean time between failures* (MTBF). In setting the specific value for the chosen goals, Boeing made extensive use of their 'lessons learned' database, which records customer feedback on the performance of existing aircraft. BITE (industry jargon for *built in test equipment*) also received significant attention. During the typical 45-minute turnarounds between flights, engineers are under time pressure to locate faults. This can lead to them swapping components quickly, to see if this clears a fault. Consequently, the 777 has sophisticated test and troubleshooting capabilities to improve diagnosis of problems. Product design reviews were organized to include airline engineers from prospective customers. For example, representatives British Airways and United Airlines participated.

Boeing felt it was necessary to make some organizational changes to drive DFS within the organization. Top management showed their commitment by clearly stating the need for the 777 to have the best reliability in the industry. Following on this, a new position was created for a 'chief mechanic,' with responsibility to check that the 777 was reliable, had appropriate redundancy (or 'fault tolerance'), and components were easy to exchange if they failed. Every Boeing project has always had a 'chief pilot,' who takes a leading role in looking critically at the flying characteristics. Therefore, it was an important step to put a similar focus on maintainability. It was found that one of the most important parts of the chief mechanic's role was in educating design engineers, who are normally inexperienced in the maintenance side of the business and the regulations that apply. Overall, the Boeing 777 has set new industry standards for schedule reliability.

5. Discussion and conclusions

Service and support issues are very important for manufacturers of many types of products, since they can lead to both higher levels of customer satisfaction and increased profits. Therefore, it is important for practitioners to be aware of the implications for NPD, and for the researchers to take the opportunity to drive forward our knowledge.

5.1. Implications for practitioners

Several recent articles in widely read management journals have pointed out the increasing importance of after-sales service for manufacturing companies (Bundshuh and Dezvane, 2003; Kim and Mauborgne, 2000; MacMillan and McGrath, 1997; Wise and Baumgartner, 1999; Womack and Jones, 2005). Service and support can bring a competitive advantage, they are essential to achieving customer satisfaction, and furthermore can be the source of significant revenues at higher margins than product sales themselves. Therefore, managers have an ideal opportunity to capitalize on the potential of service and support and follow the example of leading companies.

The evidence from case studies, conducted by various researchers at about 20 companies, indicates that DFS can reduce cost-of-ownership. Cross-case comparisons show that DFS can best be approached by an analysis of every element of the use cycle, with the resulting use of quantitative design goals. To be successful at DFS, practitioners need to utilize cost-of-ownership models and have top management communicate the importance of service and support issues throughout their organizations.

5.2. Opportunities for researchers

As has been demonstrated (see Table 18.2), the relationship between service and support and NPD has not received enough attention from researchers, systematically conducted studies are rare, and so there are a number of exciting areas for study:

1. Case studies have been the most common type of previous research. However, the reliability of several of these studies is questionable. Therefore, there is a need to consolidate the learning to date and develop a robust design for further case study research.
2. After the various case study-based investigations conducted previously, it is time for a survey of how DFS is approached across a number of industry segments. The only survey on DFS to date (Goffin, 1998) looked largely at electronics, had a low-response rate, and is now dated.
3. Products that have been developed after a comprehensive evaluation of customer support requirements has been made at the design stage should be easier and more cost-effective to support. There is a real opportunity for a longitudinal or an action research-based investigation of how DFS leads to advantages and influences the work of field service organizations.
4. The interaction between DFM and DFS requirements at the design stage is not well understood and case studies of how these decisions are made would bring real insights.
5. The similarities and differences between DFS issues in business-to-business and business-to-consumer markets need to be understood. Here interviewing field service engineers in different markets could provide valuable data.
6. Leading companies strongly promote the supportability of their products and lower cost-of-ownership. The link between DFS and successful marketing of certain types of products needs to be studied. For example, conjoint analysis could be used to understand the trade-offs customers are willing to make between product features and cost-of-ownership.
7. It has been recognized by some authors (e.g., Van Bennekom and Goffin, 2002; Ivory et al., 2003) that achieving a focus on service and support requirements at the design stage is not easy and cross-functional teams will not automatically deal with such issues objectively. Similarly, top

management needs to focus on service and support if DFS implementation is to be successful. Therefore, there is ample opportunity to investigate the impact of organizational issues on DFS. This research could build on the work a decade ago, that looked at the functional 'wall' between R&D and manufacturing.

The above list should be taken as indicative of the opportunities available, rather than as exhaustive. No doubt, others will be able to identify further gaps in our knowledge. Overall, DFS is an area of management research where not only does much remain to be done but it is also one where insights can lead to higher profits because 'smart manufacturers are creating new business models to capture profits at the customer's end of the value chain' (Wise and Baumgartner, 1999).

5.3. The need for development of theory

Just as previous studies of after-sales service leave many issues unanswered, so it is with the development of theory. The case study investigations in the past have provided some insight but do not shed enough light into the factors, which determine whether service and support are pertinent for particular markets.

Examples in the literature indicates that product safety (e.g., medical products), data assurance (e.g., banking systems), loss of earnings (e.g., plant equipment, transport systems), cost-of-ownership (e.g., aircraft), and increasing product complexity all tend to impact customers and consequently force manufacturers to concentrate on service and support issues. However, the interaction between these factors and, e.g., the maturity of markets, or product life cycles is not understood. Similarly, the relative important of product features versus DFS (and DFM) is unclear.

There is a dual challenge facing researchers – they must not only conduct wider empirical research on service and support but they must go further than the largely descriptive approaches that have been adopted to date. A clearer conceptual understanding of service and support could help improve product design.

6. Summary

Service and support issues need to be fully evaluated at the design stage of NPD, as this can increase customer satisfaction throughout the use cycle. DFS has implications for all managers involved with NPD and, in particular top management who can exercise the greatest influence. Certain best practices can be identified:

- Closely involving customer support experts in NPD;
- Performing a comprehensive evaluation of support needs at the design stage and setting suitable design goals;
- Having top management that recognizes and communicates the importance of customer support;
- Using customer support to gain competitive advantage.

It has clearly been shown that customer support must be given a high enough priority during NPD. If they are not already doing so, manufacturing companies need to focus enough time and resources on this area. Overall, the evaluation of customer support needs to be recognized as an essential element of NPD.

References

Alexander, W.L., Dayal, S., Dempsey, J.J. and Vander Ark, J.D. (2002). The Secret Life of Factory Service Centers. *The McKinsey Quarterly* 3, 106–115.

Anthoney, M.T. and McKay, J. (1992). Balancing the Product Development Process: Achieving Product and Cycle-Time Excellence in High-Technology Industries. *Journal of Product Innovation Management* 9(2), 140–147.

Armistead, C.G. and Clark, G. (1992). *Customer Service and Support,* Pitman, London.

Athaide, G.A., Meyers, P.W. and Wilemon, D.L. (1996). Seller-Buyer Interactions During the Commercialization of Technological Process Innovations. *Journal of Product Innovation Management* 13(5), 406–421.

Berg, J. and Loeb, J. (1990). The Role of Field Service in New Product Development and Introduction. *AFSM International – The Professional Journal* 14(9), 25–30.

Blanchard, B.S. (1991). The Impact of Integrated Logistic Support on the Total Cost-Effectiveness of a System. *International Journal of Physical Distribution & Logistics Management* 21(5), 23–26.

Boothroyd, G. and Dewhurst, P. (1988). Product Design for Manufacture and Assembly. *Manufacturing Engineering* 100(4), 42–46 (April).

Bradley, M. and Dawson, R. (1999). Whole Life Costs: The Future Trend in Software Development. *Software Quality Journal* 8, 121–131.

Bundshuh, R.G. and Dezvane, T.M. (2003). How to Make After-Sales Services Pay Off. *The McKinsey Quarterly* 4, 116–127.

Cespedes, F.V. (1995). *Concurrent Marketing,* Harvard Business School Press, Boston, 243–266.

Cooper, R.G. and Kleinschmidt, E.J. (1993). Major New Products: What Distinguishes the Winners in the Chemical Industry. *Journal of Product Innovation Management* 10(2), 90–111.

Fites, D.V. (1996). Make Your Dealers Your Partners. *Harvard Business Review* 74(3), 40–51 (March–April).

Galloway, I. (1996). Design for Support and Support the Design: Integrated Logistic Support – The Business Case. *Logistics Information Management* 9(1), 24–31.

Goffin, K. (1994). Gaining a Competitive Advantage from Support: Five Case Studies. *European Services Industry* 1(4), 1, 5–7.

Goffin, K. (1998). Customer Support and New Product Development – An Exploratory Study. *Journal of Product Innovation Management* 15(1), 42–56.

Goffin, K. (2000). Design for Supportability: Essential Component of New Product Development. *Research-Technology Management* 43(2), 40–47 (March–April).

Goffin, K. and New, C. (2001). Customer Support and New Product Development – An Exploratory Study. *International Journal of Operations & Production Management* 21(3), 275–301.

Hedge, G.G. and Kubat, P. (1989). Diagnostics design: A Product Support Strategy. *European Journal of Operational Research* 38, 35–43.

Hull, D.L. and Cox, J.F. (1994). The Field Service Function in the Electronics Industry: Providing a Link between Customers and Production/Marketing. *International Journal of Production Economics* 37(1), 115–126.

Ivory, C.J., Thwaites, A.T. and Vaughan, R. (2003). Shifting the Goal Posts for Design Management in Capital Goods Projects: "Design for Maintainability". *R&D Management* 33(5), 527–538.

Juran, J.M. and Gryna, F.M. (1988). *Juran's Quality Control Handbook,* McGraw-Hill, New York, 1988.

Karmarkar, U.S. and Kubat, P. (1987). Modular Product Design and Product Support. *European Journal of Operational Research* 29(1), 74–82.

Kim, C. and Mauborgne, R. (2000). Knowing a Winning Business Idea When You See One. *Harvard Business Review* 78(5), 129–138 (September–October).

Knecht, T., Lezinski, R. and Weber, F.A. (1993). Making Profits After the Sale. *The McKinsey Quarterly* 4, 79–86.

Knezevic, J. (1999). Chief Mechanic: The New Approach to Aircraft Maintenance by Boeing. *Journal of Quality in Maintenance* 5(4), 314–324.

Kumpe, T. and Bolwijn, P.T. (1988). Manufacturing: The New Case for Vertical Integration. *Harvard Business Review* 66(2), 75–81 (March–April).

Laub, L. and Khandphur, K. (1996). *Delivering World-Class Technical Support,* Wiley, Chichester UK.

Lawless, M.W. and Fisher, R.J. (1990). Sources of Durable Competitive Advantage in New Products. *Journal of Product Innovation Management* 7(1), 35–44.

Lele, M.M. (1986). How Service Needs Influence Product Strategy. *Sloan Management Review* 28(1), 63–70.

Lele, M.M. and Karmarkar, U.S. (1983). Good Product Support is Smart Marketing. *Harvard Business Review* 61(6), 124–132 (November–December).

Lele, M.M. and Sheth, J.N. (1987). *The Customer is Key,* Wiley, New York.

Livingston, I. (1988). Design for Service. *Proceedings of the First International Conference on After-Sales Success*, London 29–30th November 1988, 45–71, ISBN 1-85423-0289.

Loomba, A.P.S. (1996). Linkages between Product Distribution and Service Support Functions. *International Journal of Physical Distribution & Logistics Management* 26(4), 4–22.

Loomba, A.P.S. (1998). Product Distribution and Service Support Strategy Linkages: An Empirical Investigation. *International Journal of Physical Distribution & Logistics Management* 28(2), 143–161.

MacMillan, I.C. and McGrath, R.G. (1997). Discovering New Points of Differentiation. *Harvard Business Review* 75(4), 133–145 (July–August).

Markeset, T. and Kumar, U. (2003). Integration of RAMS and Risk Analysis in Product Design and Development Work Processes: A Case Study. *Journal of Quality in Maintenance Engineering* 9(4), 393–410.

Meldrum, M.J. (1995). Marketing High-Tech Products: The Emerging Themes. *European Journal of Marketing* 29(10), 45–58.

Mercer, M. (1999). Let the Games Begin! *Diesel Progress* 65(3), 22.

Moriarty, R.T. and Kosnik, T.J. (1989). High-tech Marketing: Concepts, Continuity, and Change. *Sloan Management Review* 30(4), 7–17.

Page, A.L. (1993). Assessing New Product development Practices and Performance: Establishing Crucial Norms. *Journal of Product Innovation Management* 10(4), 273–290.

Parker, K. (1993). Being Green Doesn't Have to Hurt. *Manufacturing Systems* 11(10), 31–36.

Patton, J.D. (1984). *Service Parts Management* Instrument Society of America.

Pnueli, Y. and Zussman, E. (1997). Evaluating the End-of-Life Value of a Product and Improving by Redesign. *International Journal of Production Research* 35(4), 921–942.

Sleeter, M. (1991). How Product Usability Impacts the Service Organization. *AFSM International – The Professional Journal* 16(2), 59–61.

Swink, M.L., Sandvig, J.C. and Mabert, V.A. (1996). Customizing Concurrent Engineering Processes: Five Case Studies. *Journal of Product Innovation Management* 13(3), 229–244.

Taylor, P. (1995). New Moves to Reduce Cost of Ownership. *Financial Times Review*, pp.1–2 (Wednesday June 7).

Teresko, J. (1994). Service Now a Design Element. *Industry Week* 243(3), 51–52.

Van Bennekom, F. and Goffin, K. (2002). Best Practices in Design for Supportability: Gaining Competitive Advantage from Customer Support. *AFSMI*, Fort Meyers, USA.

Wellemin, J.H. (1984). *Professional Service Management,* Studentlitteratur, Lund Sweden.

Wise, R. and Baumgartner, P. (1999). Go Downstream: The New Imperative in Manufacturing. *Harvard Business Review* 77(5), 133–140 (September–October).

Womack, J.P. and Jones, D.T. (2005). Lean Consumption. *Harvard Business Review* 83(3), 58–68 (March).

19 New service development

Weiyu Tsai, Rohit Verma, and Glen Schmidt

1. Introduction

> There is no such thing as a service industry. There are only industries whose
> service components are greater or less than those of other industries. Everybody
> is in service.
>
> (Levitt, 1972).

There is ample evidence that a well-designed and developed service system
is a representation of 'quality of life' in societies. Furthermore, in most of the
modern economies, the service sector now not only accounts for close to three-
fourths of total employment and value-added, but also accounts for the largest
employment growth (e.g., Pilat, 2000). Even traditional manufacturers are
turning to services for growth (e.g., Sawhney et al., 2004). For example, General Motors boosted its production by offering its OnStar service in more than
50 car and truck models (Carty, 2004). Eastman Kodak bought Ofoto to expand
its on-line digital printing services (Bandler, 2001). IBM, which has historically been predominantly product-oriented, has in more recent years generated
over half of its total revenue from services. Yet until very recently, only
15 per cent of IBM's research and development budget was being allocated to
services (Fitzgerald, 2005). Realizing this discrepancy, IBM realigned its strategy and business plan emphasizing service-based innovations. The new strategy has been a resounding success and has added over 300 million dollars to
the firm's revenue (Fitzgerald, 2005). IBM therefore has 'reinvented' itself by
divesting of its personal computing business altogether (selling it to Lenovo)
and now mainly focuses on providing services in technology, and transformation solutions (IBM Press Releases, 2004). In fact, 'Service Science'
along with its management and engineering, has become the core component
of IBM's business (http://www.research.ibm.com/ssme/index.shtml). Some
researches even argue that several nations have become so service-oriented
that they can be described as 'experience economies.' Therefore, effective systems that creating satisfying customer experiences will increasingly become

order winners (e.g., Pine and Gilmore, 1998). Indeed, Levitt's 1972 statement (above) has never been more pertinent!

In goods-based industries, new product development has been widely studied (e.g., Wind and Mahajan, 1997). Given the inherent differences between the production of goods and services, application of NPD models to services might not suffice in adequately describing how new services are optimally developed (Bitran and Pedrosa, 1998). While Griffin (1997) reported that successful firms operating within the service sector expect 53.5 per cent of their sales and 56 per cent of their profits to come from new services in the next five years, it is shocking to read that nearly 60 per cent of the service firms in Griffin's (1997) study used ad-hoc approaches for their new service development (NSD). (In this chapter, we distinguish NSD from 'new goods development' (NGD) and infer that the term 'product' (and NPD) could apply to either a good or a service or some good–service hybrid.)

Johnson, Menor, and Roth (2000) define a new service as 'an offering not previously available to customers that results from the addition of offerings, radical changes in the service delivery process, or incremental changes to existing service packages that customers perceive as being new.' According to Johnson et al. (2000) the NSD research undertaken so far is largely descriptive rather than prescriptive. However, we believe that because of rapid developments in information technology, globalization, evolving customer needs/preferences, and because of changes in relative wealth of the developed and newly developing economies, effective design and development of services and associated goods will continue to become even more important during the coming years. In this chapter, we take a closer look at the topic of NSD.

The chapter is organized in the following manner. First, we present a brief introduction to services; second, we describe the similarities and differences in new product development practices for services and goods; third, we describe some of the key concepts in NSD research; and finally, we end the chapter by outlining emerging opportunities for further research on NSD and related topics.

2. Understanding services

In economics, a 'service' is generally considered the non-material counterpart of a 'good.' In practice, however, services are often defined as an economic *act* involving both provider and customer to create value (Sampson and Froehle, 2006). While the advancement in technology has made it possible to deliver services to customers located far from the provider (e.g., a telephone call center), still it requires interaction with the customer to complete production. The service provider and customer (or clients) coordinate their work (co-production), and in the process, both create and capture value (transformation).

The diversity of the service sector makes it difficult to make generalizations concerning all services organizations. Some of the commonly accepted characteristics of services (compared to manufactured goods) are listed below (Fitzsimmons and Fitzsimmons, 2005) as a brief review for the readers. These characteristics have direct or indirect impact on design and development of new services as descried below.

2.1. Customers as co-producers

- Perhaps the most distinctive feature of a service is the *involvement of the customer in the production process*. While most goods can be produced in factories far away from the customers, services require participation of the customer in the production process. The design of *Low Contact Services* (e.g., call center, check processing center, and e-retailing service) are typically driven by operational efficiency considerations. On the other hand, the design of *High Contact Services* (e.g., Doctor's Office, Full-Service Restaurant) is driven by marketing and customer preferences-related considerations. Similarly, *site selection* and *design of facilities* for low- and high-contact services are directed by proximity to customers or efficiency/cost considerations. We would, however, like to note that technological innovations are removing many of the barriers to service facility design constraints.
- Since many services tend to be consumed at the point of 'production' they *lack transportability* (e.g., the experience of staying in an 'Ice Hotel' in Norway means the customer has to visit the facility in Norway). Again, because of technological advances, one could argue that portability of many services is becoming similar to manufactured goods (e.g., video conferencing might allow a surgeon to participate and advise during a surgery while physically not being present in the hospital).

2.2. Intangibility and heterogeneity

- A service may include tangible products as its components (e.g., food in a restaurant; seat in an airplane ride; medical equipment in a physician's office), but is *primarily intangible* (e.g., dining experience; medical advice from the physician). From the customer's point of view, intangibility makes it difficult to evaluate or compare services prior to experiencing the service. Therefore, intangibility adds to subjective considerations in the design and development of new services.
- Because of intangibility and subjectivity, no two customers can be expected to evaluate a service in the same manner. At the same time since customers are part of the production process, the *degree of variability* in the quality of

services provided is considerably *higher than manufactured goods*. Therefore mass production and customization of many services and evaluation of quality is relatively difficult and subjective.

2.3. Simultaneity and perishability

- Since services cannot be delivered without customer involvement, they are *produced and consumed at the same time* (a dining experience is *produced* while customers in the restaurant *consume* the service at the same time). Therefore, it is almost *impossible to inventory services* similar to the way one can store finished goods (e.g., a psychological counseling session cannot be inventoried in advance).
- Furthermore, *production capacity is also perishable* in many services (e.g., an airline seat has no value after the airplane takes-off). Since services cannot be inventoried, the issue of perishability in services is even more crucial than in goods. Hence, the simultaneous production and consumption, and perishable nature of a service means the strong link between features of the service observed by the customer (e.g., waiting time) and operational processes (e.g., labor schedules and capacity) must be considered carefully in service development efforts.

2.4. Customer experience

- Recent papers argue that customer experience is also an important component of many services. There is no agreement yet if experiences are (or should be) part of all services or only for a selected few. The customers consume or re-live the experience again and again, as they remember the time when the service was first delivered (e.g., a visit to LEGOLAND or a fine dining establishment). Therefore designing experiences, which include temporal features in addition to being intangible, adds another layer of complexity to the NSD processes.

2.5. Operational considerations

- Services in general are *more labor intensive* than the production of goods. However, for certain services (e.g., customer service call and e-mail centers), technological advances are reducing the percent capital spent on labor in favor of technology and automation.
- Customers evaluate services on both tangible and intangible features and therefore it is relatively *difficult to measure productivity* in service processes.

From an operational viewpoint, according to Chase, Aquilano, and Jacobs (1998), the three dominant approaches to service design are: the *Production Line Approach* (e.g., McDonalds); *Self Service Approach* (e.g., ATM machines); or *Personal Attention Approach* (e.g., Nordstrom).

While many differences between manufactured goods and services remain, during the recent years, the distinct boundary between the two product categories is blurring. Most businesses see a continuum with pure service on one end and pure commodity goods on the other end. Most new products fall between these two extremes. Therefore many product offerings include services (in addition to manufactured goods) as part of their offering to customers and thus in their product development processes the firm needs to consider the essential characteristics of services as described above.

3. Comparison between NSD and NGD processes

In this section, we take a closer look at how and why NSD is different from development of new manufactured goods (NGD). We first show that on the surface, the stages (i.e., the structure) of successful NSD and NGD processes are very similar. However, we then discuss how, beneath the surface, there are some key differences in how each of these stages is carried out in NSD versus NGD (i.e., there are differences in the execution of the activities involved in NSD versus NGD). In discussing these differences, we review empirical work that suggests there are significant differences in the way firms approach NPD and the results they achieve.

3.1. The stages of NSD and NGD do not seem to differ significantly

We synthesize previous research regarding the structure of NSD activities by introducing a five-stage framework that describes the activities of NSD as 'Discover/Define/Design/Deliver/Debug.' We call this the 5-D NSD framework, and below we briefly compare it to other NSD frameworks. Later, in the subsequent section on 'Key Concepts in NSD Research,' we discuss each stage in more detail and relate the key finding of NSD research relative to that stage.

Our 5-D NSD framework synthesizes elements of the following previous frameworks in NSD. Ramaswamy (1996) offers an eight-stage framework involving the activities of (1) Defining service design attributes; (2) Specifying performance standards; (3) Generating and evaluating design concepts; (4) Developing design details; (5) Implementing the design; (6) Measuring performance; (7) Assessing customer satisfaction; and (8) Improving performance. Bowers (1987, 1989) described a NSD process with eight sequential stages in developing new services for banking, insurance, and health-care industries. The model is adapted from the BAH models in NGD. Scheuing and Johnson (1989) constructed 15 sequential stages in their NSD model designed for financial services. This model highlights the interactions and iterations between adjacent steps involved in NSD. However, the model does not address the important issues of cross-functional teams and project cycle-time reduction in NSD. Alam and Perry (2002) described a partial concurrent processing model with ten stages for financial business-to-business services. To emphasize the importance of cross-functional team in NSD, the model explicitly includes a stage of formulation of cross-functional team in the NSD process. We depict these NSD models in Fig. 19.1.

The above NSD models do not seem to differ significantly from those given in the rich stream of research devoted to NGD. These models include (1) NASA's PPP (phased project planning) model that strictly applied to the physical design and development of the product in the 1960s, (2) the seminal BAH models (Booz, Allen, and Hamilton 1968, 1982) that first delineated seven sequential NGD stages, (3) the stage-gate systems (Cooper, 1990; Cooper, Edgett, and Kleinschmidt, 2002a) that recognizes the importance of cross-functional teams, parallel processing in activities, and up-front pre-development activities in the NGD process, (4) the third-generation model (Cooper, 1994) that proposes the principle of parallel processing between stages to reduce project development time, (5) the fifth generation (5G) innovation process (Rothwell, 1994) that integrates the dimension of internal and external networking into the development model, (6) the 'block approach' model (Saren, 1994) that acknowledges the importance of external organizations' involvement in the process, and (7) the multiple convergent processing model (Hart and Baker, 1994) that focuses on information sharing among internal and external entities through the convergent points during the new product development process. We selectively depict several NGD models in Fig. 19.2.

Viewed in aggregate, Figs 19.1 and 19.2 show structural similarity between NSD and NGD processes. Despite the fact that NSD models show more stages (8–15 stages) than do NGD models (4–8 stages), these models all follow a common temporal sequence of steps from the moment that an idea about a new product/service is generated up to its launching into the market.

Empirical support from Avlonitis et al. (2001) further corroborates this observation. The authors empirically identified 29 activities that are adapted to the specific characteristics of the service industries and categorized each of the 29 NSD activities in five specific NSD stages. The scale of internal consistency of each stage is very high with Cronbach's Alphas between 0.80 and 0.90. These five NSD stages contain (1) Idea generation and screening activities, (2) Business analysis and marketing strategy activities, (3) Technical development activities, (4) Testing activities, and (5) Launching activities. Apparently, we can conclude that these five stages are no different from those in the seminal BAH and other NGD models.

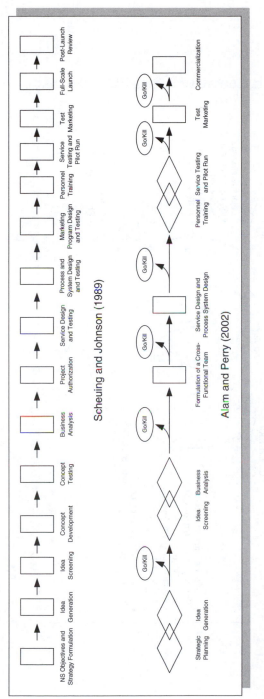

Figure 19.1
Selected NSD models.

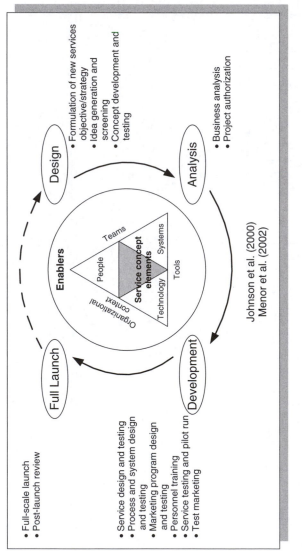

- Formulation of new services objective/strategy
- Idea generation and screening
- Concept development and testing

Design

Analysis

- Business analysis
- Project authorization

Enablers

Teams

People

Systems

Organizational context

Technology

Tools

Service concept elements

Johnson et al. (2000)
Menor et al. (2002)

Full Launch

Development

- Full-scale launch
- Post-launch review

- Service design and testing
- Process and system design and testing
- Marketing program design and testing
- Personnel training
- Service testing and pilot run
- Test marketing

Figure 19.1
(Continued)

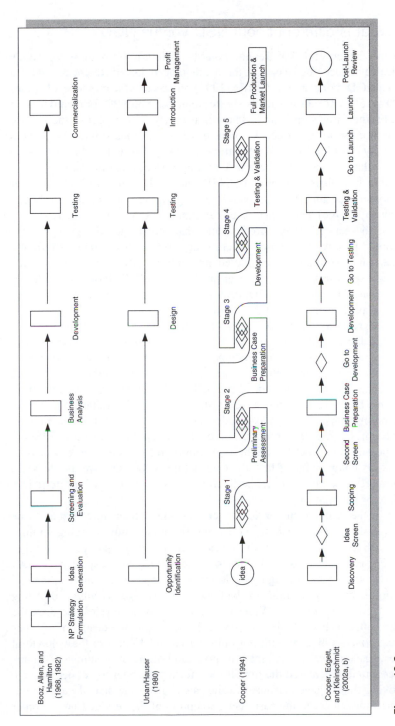

Figure 19.2
Selected NPD models.

3.2. What is different about NSD versus NGD?

While the stages of NSD are not notably different from those of NGD, empirical evidence suggests that there are indeed key differences between NSD and NGD. For example, Griffin (1997) reports that the project cycle times of NSD are 50 per cent statistically shorter than those of NPD for manufactured goods. Further, it is surprising to know that nearly 60 per cent of the service firms do not use a formal development process, let alone follow the process consistently (Griffin, 1997). We highlight four key distinctions between NSD and NGD that contribute to these different approaches and outcomes.

The first key distinction between NSD and NGD is that in NSD the user (or customer) remains at 'center stage' throughout the development process. Ramaswamy (1996) states that customer inputs should be considered in all stages of the service design process and that the service design specifications should be developed based on customer preferences in mind. Certainly, customer inputs should be considered not only in NSD but also in NGD, and design specifications for physical products should be based on customer specifications. However, in NGD, customers are not integral to design of the production process in the way that they are in NSD.

With physical products, the *use* of the product is separate from the *production* of that product. This means that the actual production process steps are of no real concern to the customer – the customer is only concerned with the physical product attributes that result from those process steps. For example, the car buyer does not care whether the seats were installed before the engine, but only concerns herself with the result: the vehicle's acceleration, handling, appearance, and so forth. In contrast, with services, the process itself becomes part of the product. The bank loan applicant incurs a different experience if he fills out the credit application on-line before he proceeds to the bank, as compared to if he fills it out while at the bank waiting to see a loan officer, as compared to if the loan officer fills it out for him during an interview of the applicant.

Thus in the delivery of services, there are many behavioral issues to be considered. For example, Chase and Dasu (2001) relate how seemingly minor factors such as the sequence of the service delivery process impact the experience. For example, it is preferable to position the 'bad' experiences early in the process; to finish strong by positioning the 'best' experiences at the end of the process; and to position all 'bad' experiences together while spreading out the 'good' experiences. While in the design of a physical product the designer concerns herself with the physical sciences, in the design of services one must concern himself with not only the physical but also the behavioral sciences. Larson (1988) highlights this point and offers the example of an airline that actually increased the time it took for a passenger to get her luggage (by moving the luggage carrousel further away from the arrival gate) but at the same time enhanced the customer perception of the service (the customer did not recognize the increased delay because most of her time was occupied walking from the gate to the carrousel).

This distinction between services and goods has significant implications on the product development process. It makes the design process more complex and integrated: the design of the product *and* the process (not just of the product) must be done considering customer needs and wants. One implication is that when designing goods, a mock-up or even a fully functional prototype can be generated using a process that is not fully representative of the eventual production process. If this were similarly done with services, it would dramatically change the product's attributes, because the process impacts the customer's experience, which is itself a key product attribute. (This is not to say that NGD does not benefit from the use of production-representative processes in prototyping (Whitney, 1988), but NGD benefits for subtly different reasons and the dependence is not as strong in all stages.)

Thus NSD processes may require even more concurrent and/or overlapped activities and stages than NGD. However, the more these activities/stages overlap, the more control is required in the process. Therefore, the NSD process is non-linear, highly iterative, and recursive. This reflects the cyclic essence of the 'NSD process cycle' framework proposed by Menor et al. (2002). The NSD process cycle, also shown in Fig. 19.1, is a conceptual framework proposed by Johnson et al. (2000) and adapted by Menor et al. (2002). Through the NSD process cycle, the authors emphasize the highly iterative and non-linear nature of the NSD process. Additionally, the NSD process cycle recognizes that the NSD stages revolve around the elements of service concept (i.e., people, systems, and technology) that are further supported by enabling functions (i.e., teams, tools, and organizational context).

A second key difference between NSD and NGD is that of greater heterogeneity in the way the product is produced and the way it is viewed. In NGD there may be many variants of a product but for any given variant the goal is to make all units identical (e.g., through SPC). In services, it is virtually impossible to make every unit of output identical (and it is questionable whether you even want to do so) because the customer is a co-producer, and every customer is different. Therefore, NSD processes must account for heterogeneity in the customers' 'co-production abilities' as well as heterogeneity of customer preferences. To insure output quality (which generally cannot be easily assessed prior to the actual purchase and production of the service), NSD activities require constant emphasis on training of those staff that work with customers in the co-production of the service.

The fact that customers are co-producers and introduce heterogeneity in the process also has a significant impact on the process of experimentation, which is a vital, key activity in NPD. Thomke (1998) suggests that once the design requirements are established, the design activities can be described as design-build-run-analyze. With a physical good, this design-build-run-analyze cycle is relatively straightforward: if the product is an engine, one can design an engine, build a prototype, run it in the lab under precise conditions, and analyze its performance against precise design requirements such as a 10 000-hour mean-time-between-failure. With a service, this design-build-test-analyze cycle becomes more nebulous as one cannot readily describe the design requirements (the requirement is that the customer have a 'good experience,' which may be hard to articulate), duplicate a set of test conditions, and measure the output of one product as compared to the design specifications (or as compared to another service offering). Considering the example of the bank loan application, it becomes more difficult to run tightly controlled experiments under customer–representative conditions and analyze results against design specifications. In short, the information regarding design requirements and with regard to how a particular service offering performs relative to those requirements is 'sticky' (von Hippel, 1994) – that is, it is hard to acquire and to transfer.

Because of these difficulties in experimentation, the market itself may become an alternative place to experiment and fine-tune the product – depending on how sensitive customers are to a 'beta' release. Testing in a laboratory setting may be costly and time consuming, and yield results that are not as informative as they are with physical product testing. Thus, it may become desirable to actually launch the product earlier than might be the case with physical products, possibly with the early launch targeted toward specific users who can provide 'accelerated' testing. This might help explain the empirical evidence suggesting that cycle times are shorter and NPD process are followed less rigorously in NSD as compared to NGD.

The customer-centric focus of services and the heterogeneity in customer inputs and demands suggest a market environment that is less predictable, and one that can change over time as customer perceptions change and as new customers are acquired. Iansiti and MacCormack (1997) suggest such an environment calls for a flexible product development process. They too stress the necessity of overlapped activities, continual feedback and early launch; offering the examples of how Netscape and Yahoo! handled beta testing.

This is not to say that the stage-gate processes discussed earlier should not be followed in NSD. Empirical studies support that using a formal development process is an important factor that determines the success of the new service. In addition, de Brentani (2001) concludes that installing a formal stage-gate NSD process is one of the most important factors that govern the success of new service ventures. These differences simply point out that while the stages of the processes in NSD are similar to those in NGD, the actual implementation of those stages may need to be adapted to the subtleties of services.

In our view it is because of these differences between services and goods that the experimentation cycle of design-build-test-analyze may best be applied to the whole of the NSD process rather than or addition to its individual stages as is feasible in NGD. We interpret Menor et al. (2002) to concur with this assessment.

A third difference between NSD and NGD is that the innovative service is not patentable due to its intangibility. Therefore, if any first-mover advantage exists, it cannot come from pricing power during the duration of the patent, but it may come from its (1) cost advantage in providing services and marketing, (2) research on future innovation or (3) larger market share by entering earlier (Tufano, 1989). Hence, the activities in service marketing design, service recovery design, and service personnel training are used to account for service intangibility. For the same reason that new services are mostly intangible in nature, potential customers are unable to articulate their need for the new service. In addition, the fact that services are not patentable could lead to lower overall imitation costs and may help explain why services are pushed to market (Avlonitis et al., 2001; Johne and Storey, 1998; Tufano, 1989).

At the same time, the intangibility aspect has implications that could make imitation of a successful service innovation difficult. Physical products can often be reverse-engineered and the physical parts reconstructed by a competitor. A service offering, whose attributes may be evaluated more on customer perception, may be difficult to reverse-engineer given that creating a 'favorable customer experience' is dependent on a complex interaction of factors that may be hard to articulate. Again using the language of von Hippel (1994), the key service process information may be 'sticky' and hard to acquire. Further, the perceived quality of the service may be based as much on reputation as on the actual quality itself. With physical products, customers can stack up two products side by side and compare. However, with services, unless a customer actually buys and experiences two competing products, she can only infer how the two would compare. Thus, customers may resort to making inferences through reputation effects. This may help explain why Cooper and de Brentani (2001) found that launch execution was one of the key success factors in NSD (we infer that launch execution helps build an early reputation). However, this also creates a tension between the desire to launch early (as discussed earlier) and the need to execute the launch 'correctly.'

An interesting finding regarding the impact of NSD and NGD is the relationship shown in Fig. 19.3. Kleinschmidt and Cooper (1991) found a U-shaped relationship between product innovativeness and commercial success for physical goods. That is, both high and low innovativeness products are more likely to be more successful financially than those in-between. However, Avlonitis et al. (2001) showed an inverted U-shaped relationship between the degree of innovativeness of a new financial service and financial performance. The broad existence of, and explanation for this reversal requires more

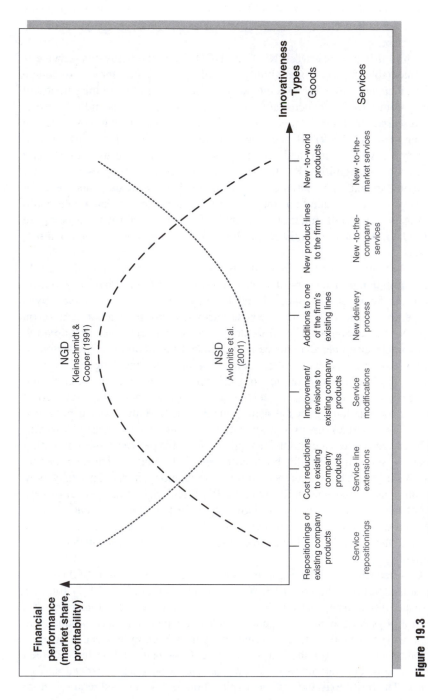

Figure 19.3
Financial performance versus NSD/NPD innovativeness.

study before definitive conclusions can be drawn. However, the following hypotheses are offered, based on the three key differences between NSD and NGD as noted above. For tangible products, highly innovative products do well because of strong product advantage; and non-innovative products do well because of high project synergies and being close-to-home. On the other hand, for services, highly innovative services seldom obtain a sustainable product advantage because of experimentation difficulties and lack of patentability. That is, it is hard to design and 'perfect' a highly innovative product before its introduction, especially in light of customer co-production, and thus it is hard to achieve a sustainable competitive advantage before imitation eats away at that advantage. At the other spectrum, even if a service is only incrementally innovative it still has an impact on co-production and may create unrecognized and unintended consequences on customer perception and thus on profitability. In other words, the 'stickiness' of service process information (von Hippel, 1994) creates a barrier to readily making incremental changes; changes that were intended to be positive may end up yielding little in the form of net positive profits.

Finally, the activities of service operations design are used to account for service perishability since service products are almost impossible to inventory and since service capacity is time sensitive. This again adds complexity to NSD, as the design of the process must take into account the fact that the resources used in fulfilling the service process can only be used to serve current demand, and not future demand. For example, Verma, Thompson, Louviere, and Moore (2001) demonstrate that customer choices and demand patterns not only effect the profitably of pizza (the product), its delivery service, but also the process configuration, operational costs, and efforts. In another example, Goodale, Verma, and Pullman (2003) illustrate how customers' relative preference for certain type of services (e.g., Deli versus a hot dog shop at an airport terminal) result in increased waiting time which in turn effects capacity and labor scheduling. Both these papers demonstrate that customers' impact on actual production of services is of critical importance in NSD.

In summary, while the stages of NSD and NGD are similar, the manner in which the activities are executed may be somewhat different. These differences arise mainly due to the characteristics of services as described in the previous section.

4. Key concepts in NSD research

This section summarizes the extant literature in NSD and further articulates our 5-D NSD framework of 'Discover/Define/Design/Deliver/Debug.' For each of these five stages we identify key concepts and findings in NSD research.

4.1. Discover new services

The main activity in this stage is to discover and generate new service ideas for future development. In this section, we address two important research topics related to new services discovery, namely, classifications of new services and techniques used to identify new services.

New services taxonomy

Developing a precise classification scheme of new services is one of the research challenges posed by Menor et al. (2002). While there is general agreement in the literature that new services differ in their types and newness, there is little agreement on how to categorize these differences (Heany, 1983; Johnson et al., 2000; Lovelock, 1984; Menor et al., 2002; Scheuing and Johnson, 1989; Tax and Stuart, 1997). For example, Tax and Stuart (1997) categorized new services based on the extent of change as compared to the existing service, from a service system perspective. Alternatively, Johnson et al. (2000) defined new services in terms of service offering. Their defined spectrum of new service offerings ranges from incremental innovations to radical innovations. Menor et al. (2002) distinguished new services on the basis of external newness and internal newness. External newness measures the degree of novelty that customers perceive in the new service; and internal newness measures the degree of change required for firms to offer the new service.

As pointed out by Garcia and Calantone (2002), to unify the findings in the NGD literature, it is important to identify the types of innovations from both a marketing and technological perspective and a macro-level and micro-level perspective. Following their innovation typology and consulting the extant NSD literature, we define a company's new service as a new business practice or offering that differs from any existing alternatives provided by the same company; and the innovativeness of the new service is defined as the degree of novelty perceived by its prospective customers (Alam and Perry, 2002; Avlonitis et al., 2001; Gadrey et al., 1995). Thus, we propose two-dimensional new services taxonomy based on company capability and customer perception in Fig. 19.4 and we further distinguish customer perceptions between the existing and prospective customers in the new services taxonomy.

Alternatively, readers can think of the new taxonomy in terms of supply and demand. The supply side (company capability) impacts NSD costs and the demand side (customer perception) impacts customer willingness to pay for the new service. In Fig. 19.4, we show radical innovation as being of high newness from the supply side (company capability) and of either low- or high-innovativeness from the demand (customer perception) side. In part, this is because in services it is relatively difficult to do something only incrementally different and yet have customers perceive it as being highly innovative.

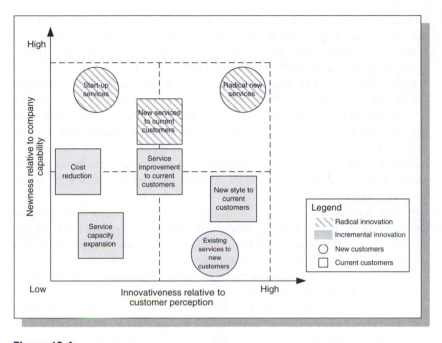

Figure 19.4
New services taxonomy.

The metrics used in the new service taxonomy to measure the newness relative to company capability (supply side) may include the extent of adjustment in information technology infrastructure, in non-IT physical infrastructure, in service delivery personnel training and development, and in facilitating goods (Menor et al., 2002). The metrics used to measure the innovativeness of customer perceptions (demand side) may include the level of novelty of administrative activities, customization, interior/exterior facilities, and service core. Apparently, the dimension of company capability (supply side) is important when considering operational issues such as technical feasibility and resources allocations. The dimension on customer perception (demand side) is important when considering marketing issues such as market uncertainty, and marketing position. Therefore, the degrees of newness and innovativeness will affect the implementation of the NSD process and the success factors in NSD project (see further discussion in Success Factors subsection).

Techniques used to discover new services

Besides the so-called 'traditional' market research techniques (Christensen et al., 2004), many other techniques in identifying new service ideas are reported in the recent literature. For example, Cooper et al. (2002a) described several proactive actions for idea generation used by leading companies. These actions include establishing an idea capture-and-handling system, conducting 'voice of customer' research, evaluating alternative scenarios of the future, and sponsoring major revenue generator (MRG) events.

In addition, the methodology of customer case research (CCR) has been used to find out the real reasons behind a customer purchase and therefore to generate new ideas/services (Berstell and Nitterhouse, 2005). The CCR approach tracks down the whole story behind a single purchase and reveals the real goals that the customer wants to accomplish. Many organizations, including home mortgage and life insurance, have successfully conducted studies using CCR to redesign their existing products/services and initiate new offerings.

Finally, Sawhney et al. (2004) advocated to focus on the 'customer-activity chain' when designing new product/service bundles. The customer-activity chain is the set of activities that customers engage to achieve certain desired outcomes. The customer-activity oriented approach re-defines markets in terms of customer outcomes and customer activities instead of products and services. The authors developed two matrices, the service opportunity matrix and the service risk mitigation matrix, to systemically explore the opportunities and associated risks for new services. Using several successful examples such as Kodak's on-line printing service and GM's OnStar service, they further demonstrate the benefits of the customer-activity chain approach.

4.2. Define new services

The key activities at the second stage include developing and testing the service concept as well as carrying out various pre-development business analyses.

The service concept

The service concept is the service 'in the minds' of customers, employees, and managers. It describes (1) the service outcomes and benefits offered to the customers, (2) the way that the service is delivered by the employees, and (3) the strategic alignment in services conceived by the managers (Clark et al., 2000; Edvardsson and Olsson, 1996; Goldstein et al., 2002; Roth and Menor, 2003). Developing a service concept requires translating a service idea into the statement of a service concept. A typical concept statement includes a description of problems or needs that a prospect might experience, the reasons why the new service is to be offered, and the outline of its features and benefits, and the rationale for its purchase (Cowell, 1988; Scheuing and Johnson, 1989). In the process of developing a service concept, the technique of concept testing is often used to examine buyers' and front-line personnel's responses to the service concept. A concept test of a new service is designed to evaluate whether a prospective user feels the new service answers unmet needs and whether front-line personnel understand the idea of the proposed new service. This technique eliminates ideas that find little buyer interest and at the same time shapes up the features of attractive concepts (Scheuing and Johnson, 1989).

Pre-development business analysis

Business analysis involves a comprehensive evaluation of the likely chances of success of the new service offering. This step encompasses a complete assessment including market analysis, financial analysis, competitive analysis, technical feasibility appraisal, and potential legality investigation. Along with these analyses, a project proposal including definition, budget, and timeline is prepared to management for further development consideration.

4.3. Design new services

This stage involves laying out the detailed specifications of service design. Service design consists of three interwoven activities: service features design, delivery process design, and delivery system design. The design of delivery process includes service operations design, service-marketing design, and service encounter/recovery design. The design of delivery system includes service facility (virtual or real) design and information system design.

Service features design refers to the design and prioritization of service attributes to fulfill the service concepts. *Service operations design* refers to the conversion of the new service concept into an operational entity, i.e., the development of the operational details of the service itself. *Service facility design* refers to the design of the physical layout of the facility (including virtual facility) where the service is delivered. *Service marketing design* involves formulating and testing the introductory marketing program with prospective users. *Service encounter design* pertains to the interactions process between the service provider and the customer. *Service recovery* is designed to help do it right the second time since it is impossible to prevent every possible service failure in all service encounters due to the heterogeneity and simultaneity nature of services.

Operations management literature has a lot to offer at this design stage. The focus of this operations-oriented research is on the tools used in designing activities. Techniques used to analyze and prescribe the service design include structured analysis and design (Congram and Epelman, 1995), function analysis (Berkley, 1996), discrete choice modeling and conjoint analysis (Verma et al., 2001, 2002, 2003, 2004), quality function deployment with information requirements (Berkley and Gupta, 1995; Wathen and Anderson, 1995), and mathematical modeling in capacity scheduling and waiting lines (Goodale et al., 2003).

Furthermore, *behavioral sciences* also have potential to contribute to the area of service design since human interaction is a particularly important issue in service encounter/recovery design (Cook et al., 2002). Because service encounter/recovery involves prospective customers, contact personnel, and service organizations, Cook et al. (2002) suggested focusing the research on establishing and measuring the links among the customer, the contact personnel, and the service organization. The focus requires more efforts in applying the basic behavioral science principles underlying human interactions into service design.

Interestingly, some researchers focus on a different approach in design services. Levitt (1972) advocated that 'discretion is the enemy of order, standardization, and quality' and suggested to 'systematically substitute hard technology (equipment) for people, and carefully plan on using soft technology to avoid inconsistency and human error.' Chase and Stewart (1995) disseminated the principle of *'failsafing'* in design for implementation (DFI). DFI emphasizes designing a service delivery process which is easy to implement and error proof because greater ease of service delivery can lead to lower contact personnel skill requirement, less facilitating goods and resource requirements, shorter service transaction times, and higher service quality and customer satisfaction in general.

4.4. Deliver new services

This stage includes the activities of field test/pilot run, test marketing, and new service launch. *Field testing* is used to determine potential customers' acceptance of the new service; and a pilot run is used to ensure smooth operations of the new service. These activities should build on the insights gained during the concept testing step earlier in the define stage. Service firms use the findings in these activities to fine-tune the new service offerings. *Testing marketing* is used in a few branches of the firm to examine the sale-ability of the new service. In addition to testing further the marketing reaction to a service, test marketing allows management to evaluate alternative marketing mix options as well as informs the key agents about the details of the new services.

As far as the ways that new services are delivered, due to the progress in information and communication technology, e-services have dramatically changed the way that service is delivered. E-services are defined as 'comprised of all interactive services that are delivered on the Internet using advanced telecommunications, information, and multimedia technologies' (Boyer et al., 2002). It seems that 'click and brick' has become the dominant business strategy for many service firms. Therefore, one of the important challenges for service firms is to decide how to balance the 'brick' and the 'click.' Boyer et al. (2002) proposed to use the e-operations profiling approach to design and evaluate e-service offerings. The *e-profiling technique* identifies nine operational decision areas where e-services can offer improvements: facility cost, self-sourcing, job specialization, scheduling, inventory, information intensity, shipping/handling, accountability/legality, communication barriers. The authors further used the case of Sothebys.com as example to demonstrate the e-profiling technique.

4.5. Debug new services

Even after all aspects of the new service and its marketing mix are carefully tested, the dynamic market conditions may require further modifications on the new service once it launches. This stage aims at determining whether the service objectives are being achieved or service adjustments should be called for. Correspondingly, two main research topics in the stage are identifying NSD success factors and implementing service recovery plans.

Success factors

Clearly, it is important for managers to know the key factors that characterize new service success since it addresses what should be done in a NSD process. Research on identifying NSD success factors has been very fruitful (Cooper and de Brentani, 1991; Cooper et al., 1994; de Brentani, 1989, 1995, 2001; Edgett and Parkinson, 1994; Froehle et al., 2000; Thwaites, 1992; van Riel et al., 2004; for a prior review see Johnson et al., 2000). Johnson et al. (2000) summarized the pre-1998 literature on NSD success factors using a five-category scheme. These five categories are nature of service, product–market characteristics, project synergy, NSD process, and service innovation culture. We update their review by adding the recent findings to their categorization scheme in Table 19.1. For the comparison purpose, we also include the key success factors for NGD (Cooper and de Brentani, 1991; Montoya-Weiss and Calantone, 1994) in the last two columns.

In Table 19.1, de Brentani (2001) related success factors to both innovative and incremental NSD projects. The factors of client/need fit, front-line expertise and a well-designed launch program are important to both types of service projects. However, project synergy, a formal stage-gate system, and cost-driven simple offerings are distinct factors to incremental service projects. In contrast, market potential, innovative culture, and senior management involvement play important roles in innovative service projects.

Table 19.1 also indicates similar success factors for NSD and NGD except those unique to services such as quality of service delivery, tangible evidence,

Table 19.1

Success factors in new service development

		Froehle et al. (2000)	de Brentani (2001)[1]	van Riel et al. (2004)	Cooper and de Brentani (1991)		Montoya-Weiss and Calantone (1994)
Study characteristics	Type	NSD	NSD	NSD	NSD	NGD	NPD
	Study level	Firm level	Firm level	Project level	Project level	Meta study	Meta study
	Surveyed industry	Multiple service industries	Multiple service industries	High-technology service industry	Financial services industry	Manufacturing industries	Most manufacturing industries
	Performance measurement	NSD speed and effectiveness	Sales/revenue, profitability, market expansion	Short-term and long-term success	Degree of success/failure and meeting sales and profit objectives	Varied	Varied
Success factor	Nature of service	Service quality	Both: front-line expertise Incremental: simple and cost driven		Unique/superior product Service expertise Service delivery Tangible evidence	Unique/superior product	Product advantage, Protocol

			Market orientation	Product/market fit Market attractiveness	Market attractiveness	Market competitiveness, Market potential
Product-market characteristics	Both: customer/need fit Innovative: market potential					
Project synergy	Incremental: project synergy			Business synergy	Technological synergy, Marketing synergy	Technological synergy, Marketing synergy
NSD process	Both: launch program Incremental: formal NSD process	Development speed, Process design, Use of IT		Launch execution Marketing execution Technology execution Pre-development activities	Marketing execution Technology execution Pre-development activities	Proficient technical, marketing, and pre-development activities, Speed to market
Service innovation culture	Innovative: entrepreneurship, creativity, senior managers' involvement	Team-based organizational structure	Information sharing organizational climate			Organizational factors

[1] The success factors are categorized according to the incremental and innovative new business services in de Brentani (2001) study.

and service expertise. However, as not shown in Table 19.1, Cooper and de Brentani (1991) indicate that the rank order of importance to the success of NSD and NGD is different. For example, 'unique/superior product' is the number one success factor for NGD, but it is number four for NSD. The number one factor for NSD is 'business synergy' including both technological synergy and marketing synergy.

Service recovery

The goal of service recovery is to provide a service firm with a second chance to get things right. Stewart and Chase (1999) found that a high percentage of service failure is a result of human error in the delivery process. Therefore, it is important for firms to know how to implement service recovery plans to retain customers who have had a service failure, and to learn from service failures to better design error-proofing services.

4.5. Research on the entire process

Besides focusing on a particular NSD stage, NSD research also studies the topics that have impact on the entire NSD process. These topics include customer involvement, cross-functional team, and service platform.

Apparently, it is very important to have customers involved in the NSD process. It is, however, not obvious for service firms to know how to effectively obtain and utilize customer inputs. In this regards, Alam (2002) identified four key elements of user involvement in NSD project, namely, objectives, stages, intensity, and modes of involvement. Alam and Perry (2002) studied how to obtain customer inputs and recognized the relative importance of different types of customer inputs in various NSD stages.

Sethi et al. (2001) studied the impact of the characteristics of cross-functional teams on the product innovativeness. The authors found that the factors of a strong superordinate identity in the team, encouragement to take risk, customers' influence, and active monitoring by senior management positively influence the innovativeness of the product; social cohesion among team members has a negative impact on innovativeness; and functional diversity donot affect innovativeness.

Platform concepts have been successfully used in developing physical products. Meyer and DeTore (2001) applied a platform-centric organization design to a service context to investigate the innovation process of a large international reinsurer. They found clear analogies in platform innovation between service and product development.

5. Direction for future research

In this section, we outline emerging research opportunities in each stage of the NSD process.

5.1. Discover stage

- *Customer-Activity Chain*: The concept of a customer-activity chain provides product manufacturers a systematic way to evaluate the opportunities and risks of entering the service world. We must ask whether service firms can use the same concept to enter the production world or should they? Should service firms focus on providing alternative service offerings within its boundary or cross the line to offer innovative product-service bundles as well?

5.2. Define stage

- *Serviced Concept*: Being the missing link in service design research (Goldstein et al., 2002), the service concept represents many research opportunities. Goldstein et al. (2002) and Roth and Menor (2003) raised several research questions related to how to apply the service concept as the driver in service recovery design and service operations design. For example, how can the service concept be used to align the strategic intent with customer needs, and to align service capability with service design and recovery?
- *Nature of Relationship with Customers*: Some services involve a formal relationship, in which each customer is known to the organization and all transactions are individually recorded and attributed (e.g., banking and financial services, frequent flyer in an airline). However, in other services, unidentified customers purchase one or more service from the organization and then disappear (e.g., fast-food). Therefore, the type of relationship should have an effect on the NSD process.

5.3. Design stage

- We believe that the behavioral sciences approach and the DFI approach complement each other. Obviously, it is not possible to completely substitute technology for contact personnel any time soon. Thus, it makes understanding human interactions in services the first step in designing error-proof services. Therefore, we need more research in both areas to find applicable theories and tools that can help designers conceptualize and test service design in the NSD process.

- *Customization*: An important product development decision is whether all customers should receive the same service or whether service features/processes should be customized or adapted to meet individual requirements. The level of service customization might also depend on a specific service industry.

- *Type of Service Processes*: Because customers are involved in the production and delivery of services, product developers need to understand the nature of processes to which their customers might be exposed. Unlike manufactured goods, many steps in the production process in services are observed by customers and therefore need to be considered carefully in service development.

- *Nature of Demand and Supply*: Some services face steady and predictable demand for their services whereas others encounter significant fluctuations. Similarly, in some services it is possible to alter capacity at the short notice whereas in other cases marketing mechanisms (e.g., pricing) must be used to deal with the unpredictable nature of demand. Again, since customers participate in the production process, demand fluctuations, and its resulting impact (e.g., increased waiting time) must be carefully considered in the service development process. However, there is a psychological side to waiting as well. For example, pre-process waits are often perceived to be longer than in-process wait. Furthermore, perceived waiting times are often not linearly related to actual waiting times. It has also been suggested that service waits are impacted by environmental factors (e.g., music) or culture.

5.4. Deliver stage

- Due to the advancement in information technology, the combined e-tailor/retailer business model seems dominant in current business settings. There is a need to test the e-profiling techniques for service firms to leverage and balance new services in the setting of 'brick' and 'click.'

- *Recipient of Service Process*: Some services such as air transportation are directed towards customers themselves whereas other services are directed towards things (e.g., cargo or package delivery services). The design and development of services focused on customers are very different from those services focused on things (e.g., airline passenger terminals versus cargo terminal).

- *Mode of Service Delivery*: When designing delivery systems, product developers need to decide if the customers will visit the service organization or whether the service should come to the customer. If the customer is to visit the delivery facility then the service development task must also include facilities design.

5.5. Debug stage

- It is interesting to observe the opposite impact that innovativeness has on financial performance for goods versus service industries (Fig. 19.3). Clearly, it requires further investigation to determine whether the causal U-shape versus inverted U-shape result is due to the inconsistencies in labeling innovation types. If innovativeness does financially affect NSD and NGD in different ways, what are the driving forces behind them? In addition, what are the implications for designing a product/service bundle?
- *Service Recovery and Error Proofing*: Service recovery is a firm's response to failures in its delivery system. Even the best-in-class services fail sometimes because service delivery systems are characterized by the simultaneous production and consumption, and because of inclusion of customers in the production process. Good service recovery systems provide a firm with a second opportunity to 'get things right' and win-back market share. Recently, Stewart and Chase (1999) found that substantial portions of service failures are a result of human error in the delivery process. Therefore, service recovery and error-proofing strategies and policies should be part of the service development processes.

5.6. Entire process

- Our review shows that the empirical studies on service innovation are sparse and the findings are mainly for the financial industry, more specifically for banking. Since service sectors include many other industries such as entertainment, food services, healthcare, financial services, transportation and distribution services, education, and professional services, it is clear that we need more empirical research efforts to test the current NSD findings in various industries.
- Most research to date focuses on the single NSD project. In other words, the topic of a NSD project portfolio is almost neglected. Since Meyer and DeTore (2001) reported that the platform principles in NPD are successfully applied to a re-insurer company, can these principles be applied more generally in service project selection? Furthermore, can the 5-D NSD representation be used in a project portfolio setting to select and monitor the various types of service innovation projects?
- *Growth of Experience Economy*: As the service economy continues to evolve, the traditional concept of service is changing from a transaction to an *experience*. Experiences create added value by engaging with the customer in a personal and memorable way. Depending on the level of customer participation in the service delivery process, the use of environmental factors, and social interaction between customers/service providers, different types of experiences can be created/staged and charged for by the service provider (Gupta and Vajac, 2000).

References

Alam, I. 2002. An exploratory investigation of user involvement in new service development. *Academy of Marketing Science*, **30**(3), 250–261.

Alam, I. and C. Perry. 2002. A customer-oriented new services development process. *Journal of Services Marketing*, **16**(6), 515–534.

Avlonitis, G. J., P. G. Papastathopoulou and S. P. Gounaris. 2001. An empirically-based typology of product innovativeness for new financial services: Success and failure scenarios. *Journal of Product Innovation Management*, **18**(5), 324–342.

Bandler, J. 2001. Kodak will acquire Ofoto in a move to expand services. *Wall Street Journal*, May 1, B8.

Berkley, B. J. and A. Gupta. 1995. Identifying the information requirements to deliver quality service. *International Journal of Service Industry Management*, **6**(5), 16–35.

Berkley, B. J. 1996. Designing services with function analysis. *Hospitality Research Journal*, 20(1), 73–100.

Berstell, G. and D. Nitterhouse. 2005. Let the customer make the case. *Strategy & Innovation* (http://innovaiton.harvardbusinessonline.org), March-April, 3–6.

Bitran, G. and L. Pedrosa. 1998. A structured product development perspective for service operations. *European Management Journal*, **16**(2), 169–189.

Booz, A. and Hamilton. 1968. *Management of New Products*. New York: Booz, A. and Hamilton.

Booz, A. and Hamilton. 1982. *New Products Management for the 1980s*. New York: Booz, A. and Hamilton.

Bowers, M. R. 1987. Developing new services for hospitals: A suggested model. *Journal of Health Care Marketing*, **7**(2), 5–44.

Bowers, M. R. 1989. Developing new services: Improving the process making it better. *Journal of Services Marketing*, **3**(1), 15–20.

Boyer K. K., R. Hallowell and A. V. Roth. 2002. E-service: operating strategy – a case study and a method for analyzing operational benefits. *Journal of Operations Management*, **20**(2), 175–188.

Carty, S. S. 2004. GM boosts production of cars equipped with OnStar service. *Wall Street Journal*, September 22, D6.

Chase, R. B., N.J. Aquilano and F. R. Jacobs. 1998. *Operations Management for Competitive Advantage*. 8th edition. New York, NY: McGraw-Hil/Irwin.

Chase, R. B. and D. M. Stewart. 1995. *Mistake–Proofing: Designing Errors Out*. Portland, OR: Productivity Press.

Chase, R. B. and S. Dasu. 2001. Want to perfect your company's service? Use behavioral science. *Harvard Business Review*, June 2001 78–84.

Christensen, C. M., S. D. Anthony and E. Roth. 2004. *Seeing What's Next: Using the Theories of Innovation to Predict Industry Change*, Boston, MA: Harvard Business School Press.

Clark, G., Johnston, R., Shulver, M. 2000. Exploiting the service concept for service design and development. In: Fitzsimmons, J. A. and Fitzsimmons, M. J. (Eds.), *New Service Development – Creating Memorable Experience*. Thousand Oaks, CA: Sage Publications, 71–91.

Congram, C. and M. Epelman. 1995. How to describe your service: An invitation to the structured analysis and design technique. *International Journal of Service Industry Management*, **6**(2), 6–23.

Cook, L. S., D. E. Bowen, R. B. Chase, and S. Dasu. 2002. Human issues in service design. *Journal of Operations Management*, **20**(2), 159–174.

Cooper, R. G. 1990. Stage-gate system: A new tool for managing new products. *Business Horizons*, **33**(3), 44–54.

Cooper, R. G. 1994. Third-generation new product process. *Journal of Product Innovation Management*, **11**(1), 3–14.

Cooper, R. G. and U. de Brentani. 1991. New industrial financial services: What distinguishes the winners. *Journal of Product Innovation Management*, **8**(2), 75–90.

Cooper, R. G., C. J. Easingwood, S. Edgett, E. J. Kleinschmidt and C. Storey. 1994. What distinguishes the top performing new products in financial services. *Journal of Product Innovation Management*, **11**(4), 281–299.

Cooper, R. G., S. J. Edgett and E. J. Kleinschmidt. 2002a. Optimizing the stage–gate process: What best–practice companies do – II. *Research Technology Management*, **45**(5), 21–27.

Cowell, D. W. 1988. New Service Development. *Journal of Marketing Management*, **3**(3), 296–312.

de Brentani, U. 1989. Success and failure in new industrial services. *Journal of Product Innovation Management*, **6**(4), 239–258.

de Brentani, U. 1995. New industrial service development: Scenarios for success and failure. *Journal of Business Research*, **32**(2), 93–103.

de Brentani, U. 2001. Innovative versus incremental new business services: Different keys for achieving success. *Journal of Product Innovation Management*, **18**(3), 169–187.

Edgett, S. and S. Parkinson. 1994. The development of new financial services: Identifying determinants of success and failure. *International Journal of Service Industry Management*, **5**(4), 24–38.

Edvardsson, B. and J. Olsson. 1996. Key concepts for new service development. *The Service Industries Journal*, **16**(2), 140–164.

Fitzgerald. 2005. Research in Development: IBM builds services-based R&D. http://www.TechnologyReview.Com, May 7.

Fitzsimmons, J. A. and M. J. Fitzsimmons. 2005. *Service Management: Operations, Strategy, and Information Technology*, 4th edition, New York: McGraw–Hill.

Froehle, C. M., A. V. Roth, R. B. Chase, and C. A. Voss. 2000. Antecedents of new service development effectiveness: An exploratory examination of strategic operations choices. *Journal of Service Research*, **3**(1), 3–17.

Gadrey, J., F. Gallouj and O. Weinstein. 1995. New modes of innovation: How services benefit industry. *International Journal of Service Industry Management*, **6**(3), 4–16.

Garcia, R. and R. Calantone. 2002. A critical look at technological innovation typology and innovativeness terminology: A literature review. *Journal of Product Innovation Management*, **19**(2), 110–132.

Goldstein, S. M., R. Johnston, J. Duffy and J. Rao. 2002. The service concept: The missing link in service design research? *Journal of Operations Management*, **20**(2), 121–134.

Goodale, J. C., R. Verma and M. E. Pullman. 2003. A market utility-based model for capacity scheduling in mass services. *Production and Operations Management*, 12(2), 165–185.

Griffin. A., 1997. PDMA research on new product development practices: Updating trends and benchmarking best practices. *Journal of Product Innovation Management*, **14**(6), 429–458.

Gupta, S. and M. Vajic. 2000. The contextual and dialectical nature of experiences. In: Fitzsimmons, J. A. and Fitzsimmons, M. J. (Eds.), *New Service Development – Creating Memorable Experience*. Thousand Oaks, CA: Sage Publications, 33–51.

Hart, S. J. and M. J. Baker. 1994. The multiple convergent processing model of new product development. *International Marketing Review*, **11**(1), 77–92.

Heany, D. F. 1983. Degrees of product innovation. *Journal of Business Strategy*, **3**(4), 3–14.

Iansiti, M. and A. MacCormack. 1997. Developing products on internet time. *Harvard Business Review*. Sep-Oct 1997 108–117.

IBM Press Releases. 2004. Lenovo to acquire IBM personal computing division (12/07/2004). Web address: http://www-1.ibm.com/press/PressServletForm.wss.

Johne, A. and C. Storey. 1998. New service development: A review of the literature and annotated bibliography. *European Journal of Marketing*, **32**(3/4), 184–251.

Johnson, S. P., L. J. Menor, A. V. Roth, and R. B. Chase. 2000. A critical evaluation of the new service development process: integrating service innovation and service design. In: Fitzsimmons, J. A. and Fitzsimmons, M. J. (Eds.), *New Service Development – Creating Memorable Experience*. Thousand Oaks, CA: Sage Publications, 1–32.

Kleinschmidt, E. J. and R. G. Cooper. 1991. The impact of product innovativeness on performance. *Journal of Product Innovation Management*, **8**(4), 240–251.

Larson, R. C. 1988. There's more to a line than its wait. *Technology Review*. July, 1988 60–67.

Levitt, T. 1972. Production-line approach to service. *Harvard Business Review*, **50**(4), 41–52.

Lovelock, C. H. 1984. Developing and implementing new services. In: George, W. R. and Marshall, C. E. (Eds.), *Developing New Services*. Chicago: American Marketing Association, 44–64.

Menor, L. J., M. V. Tatikonda and S. E. Sampson. 2002. New service development: areas for exploitation and exploration. *Journal of Operations Management*, **20**(2), 135–157.

Meyer, M. H. and A. DeTore. 2001. "Creating a Platform-Based Approach for Developing New Services." Journal of Product Innovation Management **18**(3), 188–204.

Montoya-Weiss, M. and R. Calantone. 1994. Determinants of new product performance: A review and meta-analysis. *Journal of Product Innovation Management*, **11**(5), 397–407.

Pilat, D. 2000. No longer services as usual. *The OECD Observer*, **22**(3), 52–54.

Pine, II, B. J., J. H. Gilmore. 1998. Welcome to the Experience Economy. *Harvard Business Review*, **76**(4), 97–105.

Ramaswamy, R. 1996. Design and Management of Service Processes: Keeping Customers for Life. Reading, MA: Addison-Wesley Publishing Co.

Roth, A. V., L. J. Menor. 2003. Insights Into Service Operations Management: A Research Agenda. *Production & Operations Management*, **12**(2), 145–164.

Rothwell, R. 1994. Towards the fifth-generation innovation process. *International Marketing Review*, **11**(1), 7–31.

Sampson, S. E. and C. M. Froehle. 2006. Foundations and Implications of a Proposed Unified Services Theory. *Production and Operations Management*. **15**(2) 329–343.

Saren, M. 1994. Reframing the process of new product development: From "stages" models to a "blocks" framework. *Journal of Marketing Management*, **10**(7), 633–643.

Sawhney, M., S. Balasubramanian and V. V. Krishnan. 2004. Creating growth with services. *MIT Sloan Management Review*, **45**(2), 34–43.

Scheuing, E. E. and E. M. Johnson. 1989. A proposed model for new service development. *Journal of Services Marketing*, **3**(2), 25–35.

Sethi, R., D. C. Smith and W. Park. 2001. Cross-functional product development teams, creativity, and the innovativeness of new consumer products. *Journal of Marketing Research*, **38**(1), 73–89.

Stewart, D. M. and R. B. Chase. 1999. The impact of human error on delivering service quality. *Production and Operations Management*, 8(3), 1999.

Tax, S. S. and F. I. Stuart. 1997. Designing and implementing new services: The challenges of integrating service systems. *Journal of Retailing*, 73(1), 105–134.

Thwaites, D. 1992. Organizational influences on the new product development process in financial services. *Journal of Product Innovation Management*, **9**(4), 303–313.

Tufano, P. 1989. Financial innovation and first-mover advantage. *Journal of Financial Economics*, **25**(2), 213–240.

Thomke, S. H. 1998. Managing experimentation in the design of new products. *Management Science*, **44**(6), 743–762.

Verma, R., G. M. Thompson, W. L. Moore and J. J. Louviere. 2001. Effective design of products/services: An approach based on integration of marketing and operations management decisions. *Decision Sciences*, **32**(1), 165–193.

Verma, R., Plaschka, G. and Louviere, J.J. 2002. Understanding Customer Choices: A Key to Successful Management of Hospitality Services. *Cornell Quarterly*, **43**(6).

Verma, R. and Plaschka, G. 2003. The Art and Science of Customer Choice Modeling: Reflections, Advances, and Managerial Implications, *Cornell Quarterly*, **44**(6).

Verma, R., Iqbal, Z. and Plaschka, G. 2004. Understanding Customer Choice in e-Financial Services, *California Management Review*, **46**(4).

van Riel, A. C. R., J. Lemmink and H. Ouwersloot. 2004. High-technology service innovation success: A decision-making perspective. *Journal of Product Innovation Management*, **21**(5), 348–359.

von Hippel, E. 1994. "Sticky information" and the locus of problem solving: Implications for innovation. *Management Science,* **40**(4), 429–439.

Wathen, S. and J. C. Anderson. 1995. Designing services: An information-processing approach. *International Journal of Service Industry Management*, **6**(1), 64–76.

Whitney, D. E. 1988. Manufacturing by design. *Harvard Business Review*. July-Aug 1988, 83–91.

Wind, J. and V. Mahajan. 1997. Issues and opportunities in new product development: An introduction to the special issue. *Journal of Marketing Research*, **34**(1), 1–12.

Index

3 5282 00643 5963